Elena Bashir and Thomas J. Conners
with Brook Hefright
A Descriptive Grammar of Hindko, Panjabi, and Saraiki

Mouton-CASL Grammar Series

Series editors
Anne Boyle David
Claudia M. Brugman
Thomas J. Conners
Amalia E. Gnanadesikan

Volume 4

Elena Bashir and Thomas J. Conners
with Brook Hefright

A Descriptive Grammar of Hindko, Panjabi, and Saraiki

Series editor responsible for this volume
Amalia E. Gnanadesikan

DE GRUYTER
MOUTON

This material is based upon work supported, in whole or in part, with funding from the United States Government. Any opinions, findings and conclusions or recommendations expressed in this material are those of the author(s) and do not necessarily reflect the views of the University of Maryland, College Park and/or any agency or entity of the United States Government. This material is being made available for personal or academic research use. If the intention is to use it for commercial reasons, please contact University of Maryland's Office of Technology Commercialization at otc@umd.edu or (301) 405-3947.

ISBN 978-1-5015-2660-2
e-ISBN (PDF) 978-1-61451-225-7

Library of Congress Control Number 2019945531

Bibliographic information published by the Deutsche Nationalbibliothek
The Deutsche Nationalbibliothek lists this publication in the Deutsche Nationalbibliografie; detailed bibliographic data are available on the Internet at http://dnb.dnb.de.

This volume is text- and page-identical with the hardback published in 2019.
Cover photo: A Panjabi phulkari dupatta, or floral embroidered scarf. Photo by Gitanjali Gnanadesikan.
Printing and binding: CPI books GmbH, Leck

www.degruyter.com

Elena Bashir dedicates her work on this book to the memory of her late husband, Muhammad Bashir, who was a proud and eloquent speaker of his mother tongue, Panjabi, and the inspiration for her enduring interest in this language and the other languages of Pakistan.

Thomas Conners and Brook Hefright dedicate their work on this book to their colleagues at CASL, past and present, whose commitment to scholarship—often in the face of unique challenges—has been inspirational.

Foreword

It is remarkable that, in this age of unprecedented global communication and interaction, the majority of the world's languages are as yet not adequately described. Without basic grammars and dictionaries, these languages and their communities of speakers are in a real sense inaccessible to the rest of the world. This state of affairs is antithetical to today's interconnected global mindset.

This series, undertaken as a critical part of the mission of the University of Maryland Center for Advanced Study of Language (CASL), is directed at remedying this problem. One goal of CASL's research is to provide detailed, coherent descriptions of languages that are little studied or for which descriptions are not available in English. Even where grammars for these languages do exist, in many instances they are decades out of date or limited in scope or detail.

While the criticality of linguistic descriptions is indisputable, the painstaking work of producing grammars for neglected and under-resourced languages is often insufficiently appreciated by scholars and graduate students more enamored of the latest theoretical advances and debates. Yet, without the foundation of accurate descriptions of real languages, theoretical work would have no meaning. Moreover, without professionally produced linguistic descriptions, technologically sophisticated tools such as those for automated translation and speech-to-text conversion are impossible. Such research requires time-consuming labor, meticulous description, and rigorous analysis.

It is hoped that this series will contribute, however modestly, to the ultimate goal of making every language of the world available to scholars, students, and language lovers of all kinds. I would like to take this opportunity to salute the linguists at CASL and around the world who subscribe to this vision as their life's work. It is truly a noble endeavor.

Richard D. Brecht
Founding Executive Director
University of Maryland Center for Advanced Study of Language

Series Editors' Preface

This series arose out of research conducted on several under-described languages at the University of Maryland Center for Advanced Study of Language. In commencing our work, we were surprised at how many of the world's major languages lack accessible descriptive resources such as reference grammars and bilingual dictionaries. Among the ongoing projects at the Center is the development of such resources for various under-described languages. This series of grammars presents some of the linguistic description we have undertaken to fill such gaps.

The languages covered by the series represent a broad range of language families and typological phenomena. They are spoken in areas of international significance, some in regions associated with political, social, or environmental instability. Providing resources for these languages is therefore of particular importance.

However, these circumstances often make it difficult to conduct intensive, in-country fieldwork. In cases where such fieldwork was impractical, the authors of that grammar have relied on close working relationships with native speakers, and, where possible, corpora of naturalistic speech and text. The conditions for data-gathering—and hence our approach to it—vary with the particular situation.

We found the descriptive state of each language in the series to be different from that of the others: in some cases, much work had been done, but had never been collected into a single overview; in other cases, virtually no materials in English existed. Similarly, the availability of source material in the target language varies widely: in some cases, literacy and media are very sparse, while for other communities plentiful written texts exist. The authors have worked with the available resources to provide descriptions as comprehensive as these materials, the native speaker consultants, and their own corpora allow.

One of our goals is for these grammars to reach a broad audience. For that reason the authors have worked to make the volumes accessible by providing extensive exemplification and theoretically neutral descriptions oriented to language learners as well as to linguists. All grammars in the series, furthermore, include the native orthography, accompanied where relevant by Romanization. While they are not intended as pedagogical grammars, we realize that in many cases they will supply that role as well.

Each of the grammars is presented as a springboard to further research, which for every language continues to be warranted. We hope that our empirical work will provide a base for theoretical, comparative, computational, and pedagogical developments in the future. We look forward to the publication of many such works.

Claudia M. Brugman
Thomas J. Conners
Anne Boyle David
Amalia E. Gnanadesikan

Contents

Foreword — vii
Series Editors' Preface — ix

1	**About this Grammar — 1**
1.1	Introduction — **1**
1.2	Scope of the present work — **1**
1.3	Past work and references consulted — **2**
1.4	Sources — **2**
1.5	Acknowledgements — **3**
1.6	Chapter organization — **3**
1.7	Examples — **3**
1.8	Glossing and formatting conventions — **4**
1.9	List of abbreviations and symbols — **4**
2	**Linguistic Context — 9**
2.1	Introduction — **9**
2.2	The language names — **10**
2.3	The languages and their speakers — **11**
2.3.1	Hindko — **13**
2.3.2	Panjabi — **14**
2.3.3	Saraiki — **14**
2.3.4	Other related languages — **15**
2.3.4.1	Pothwari — **15**
2.3.4.2	Dogri — **15**
2.4	Historical background — **15**
2.5	Writing systems — **18**
3	**Phonology and Orthography — 19**
3.1	Introduction — **19**
3.2	Transcription: Definitions and conventions — **19**
3.3	Segments — **20**
3.3.1	Consonants — **21**
3.3.1.1	Hindko consonants — **26**
3.3.1.2	Sound correspondences between Hindko and Panjabi — **26**
3.3.1.3	Saraiki consonants — **28**

3.3.2 Vowels — 33
3.3.2.1 Hindko vowels — 33
3.3.2.2 Panjabi vowels — 35
3.3.2.3 Saraiki vowels — 36
3.3.3 Diphthongs — 38
3.3.3.1 Hindko diphthongs — 39
3.3.3.2 Panjabi diphthongs — 39
3.3.3.3 Saraiki diphthongs — 41
3.4 Suprasegmentals — 43
3.4.1 Suprasegmentals affecting vocalic segments and syllables — 43
3.4.1.1 Nasalization — 43
3.4.1.1.1 Nasalization in Hindko — 44
3.4.1.1.2 Nasalization in Panjabi — 45
3.4.1.1.3 Nasalization in Saraiki — 46
3.4.1.2 Tone — 46
3.4.1.2.1 Tone in Hindko — 47
3.4.1.2.2 Tone in Panjabi — 48
3.4.1.2.3 Tone in Saraiki — 49
3.4.1.3 Stress — 49
3.4.1.3.1 Stress in Hindko — 49
3.4.1.3.2 Stress in Panjabi — 50
3.4.1.3.3 Stress in Saraiki — 52
3.4.2 Suprasegmental features affecting consonants: Gemination — 53
3.4.2.1 Gemination in Hindko — 53
3.4.2.2 Gemination in Panjabi — 53
3.4.2.3 Gemination in Saraiki — 55
3.5 Phonotactics — 55
3.5.1 Hindko phonotactics — 56
3.5.1.1 Hindko syllable types — 56
3.5.1.2 Hindko consonant clusters — 56
3.5.2 Panjabi phonotactics — 56
3.5.2.1 Panjabi syllable types — 56
3.5.2.2 Panjabi consonant clusters — 58
3.5.3 Saraiki phonotactics — 59
3.5.3.1 Saraiki syllable types — 59
3.5.3.2 Saraiki consonant clusters — 60
3.6 Orthography — 60
3.6.1 Segments in orthography — 64
3.6.1.1 Consonants in orthography — 64
3.6.1.2 Vowels in orthography — 67
3.6.2 Suprasegmentals in orthography — 71
3.6.2.1 Gemination in orthography — 71

3.6.2.2 Nasalization in orthography — **71**
3.6.2.3 Stress and tone in orthography — **72**
3.6.3 Additional diacritics and spelling conventions — **74**
3.6.4 Hindko orthography — **76**
3.6.5 Saraiki orthography — **77**

4 Nouns — 79
4.1 The lexicon — **79**
4.1.1 Persian loans — **80**
4.1.2 Words incorporating Arabic definite articles — **80**
4.2 Derivational morphology — **80**
4.2.1 Suffixal elements — **81**
4.2.1.1 Agent noun-forming suffixes (Indo-Aryan) — **81**
4.2.1.2 Abstract noun-forming suffixes (Indo-Aryan) — **82**
4.2.1.3 Abstract noun-forming suffixes (Perso-Arabic) — **85**
4.2.1.4 Diminutives — **86**
4.2.2 Persian compounding elements — **86**
4.2.2.1 Agent-noun forming — **87**
4.2.2.2 Locative-noun forming — **87**
4.2.3 Persian and Arabic conjunctive elements — **88**
4.2.3.1 و /-o-/ ‘and’ — **89**
4.2.3.2 The enclitic /e/ ‘izāfat’ — **89**
4.3 Nominal categories — **90**
4.3.1 Number — **90**
4.3.1.1 Persian and Arabic plural suffixes — **91**
4.3.1.1.1 ـَن /-æn/ Arabic dual ending — **91**
4.3.1.1.2 ـِن /-īn/Arabic plural — **91**
4.3.1.1.3 ات /-āt/ Arabic plural — **91**
4.3.1.2 Arabic broken plurals — **92**
4.3.2 Gender — **92**
4.3.2.1 Semantic criteria — **93**
4.3.2.2 Morphological criteria — **94**
4.3.3 Case — **96**
4.3.3.1 Direct — **97**
4.3.3.2 Oblique — **97**
4.3.3.3 Vocative — **97**
4.3.3.3.1 Hindko vocative case endings — **97**
4.3.3.3.2 Panjabi vocative case endings — **98**
4.3.3.3.3 Saraiki vocative case endings — **99**
4.3.3.4 Vocative particles — **102**
4.3.3.4.1 Hindko vocative particles — **102**
4.3.3.4.2 Panjabi vocative particles — **102**

4.3.3.4.3 Saraiki vocative particles — **102**
4.3.3.5 Ablative — **103**
4.3.3.6 Locative — **104** .
4.4 Declension classes and paradigms — **106**
4.4.1 Hindko — **108**
4.4.1.1 Hindko declension classes — **108**
4.4.1.2 Hindko noun paradigms — **108**
4.4.1.2.1 Masculine nouns (Classes I and II) — **108**
4.4.1.2.2 Feminine nouns (Classes III, IV, V, and VI) — **110**
4.4.1.2.3 Class VI Hindko nouns (masculine and feminine) — **112**
4.4.2 Panjabi — **113**
4.4.2.1 Panjabi declension classes — **113**
4.4.2.1.1 Marked masculine (Class I) — **113**
4.4.2.1.2 Unmarked masculine (Class II) — **114**
4.4.2.1.3 Feminine (Classes III and IV) — **115**
4.4.2.2 Panjabi noun paradigms — **115**
4.4.2.2.1 Marked masculine nouns (Class I) — **115**
4.4.2.2.2 Unmarked masculine nouns (Class II) — **116**
4.4.2.2.3 Feminine nouns (Classes III and IV) — **117**
4.4.2.2.4 Panjabi Inflectional paradigms — **119**
4.4.2.2.5 Some morphophonemic changes — **120**
4.4.3 Saraiki — **121**
4.4.3.1 Saraiki declension classes — **121**
4.4.3.2 Saraiki noun paradigms — **122**
4.4.3.2.1 Masculine nouns (Classes I, II, VIII) — **123**
4.4.3.2.2 Saraiki masculine noun paradigms — **123**
4.4.3.2.3 Saraiki feminine noun paradigms — **126**
4.4.3.2.4 Class VII (feminine) noun paradigm — **127**
4.4.3.2.5 Class VIII (masculine) noun paradigm — **128**

5 Adjectival and adverbial modification — 129
5.1 Adjectives and adjectival expressions — **129**
5.1.1 The adjectival lexicon: sources and derivation of adjectives — **129**
5.1.1.1 Indo-Aryan suffixal element: والا /-vāḷā/~ /-vālā/; آلا /āḷā/ ~ /ālā/ — **129**
5.1.1.2 Suffixal elements: Persian — **131**
5.1.1.2.1 ی /-ī-/ — **131**
5.1.1.2.2 آنہ /ānā/ — **131**
5.1.1.2.3 ناک /-nāk/ and گین /-gīn/ — **132**
5.1.1.2.4 دار /-dār/; آوار /-āvār/, وار /-vār/, ور /-var/; and مند /-mand / ~ وند /-vand/ Sr — **132**

5.1.1.2.5 The exclamation/exhortation باد /-bād/ ‘let it be, so be it’ — **133**
5.1.1.3 Prefixal elements – Indo-Aryan اݨ ~ ان ~ ا /a/ ~ /aṇ/ ‘not’ — **133**
5.1.1.4 Prefixal elements – Perso-Arabic — **134**
5.1.1.5 Persian past participles — **135**
5.1.1.6 Classes of adjectives — **135**
5.1.1.6.1 Marked (“black”) adjectives — **136**
5.1.1.6.2 Unmarked (“red”) adjectives — **138**
5.1.1.6.3 Saraiki stem-vowel alternating (“unfast”) adjectives — **139**
5.1.2 Adjectives in construction with nouns — **139**
5.1.2.1 Hindko example — **139**
5.1.2.2 Panjabi example — **140**
5.1.2.3 Saraiki examples — **141**
5.1.3 Comparative and superlative constructions — **142**
5.1.3.1 Morphological comparison — **142**
5.1.3.2 Syntactic comparison — **143**
5.1.3.3 Demonstrative, relative, and interrogative elements — **147**
5.1.3.3.1 Demonstrative adjectives — **147**
5.1.3.3.2 Relative adjectives — **148**
5.1.3.3.3 Interrogative adjectives — **149**
5.1.3.3.4 Adjectival-adverbial, declarative, interrogative, and relative sets — **151**
5.1.3.4 Quantifiers — **155**
5.1.3.4.1 Hindko quantifiers — **155**
5.1.3.4.2 Panjabi quantifiers — **155**
5.1.3.4.3 Saraiki quantifiers — **156**
5.1.3.5 Indefinite adjectival expressions — **156**
5.1.3.5.1 Indefinite adjectives – Hindko — **158**
5.1.3.5.2 Indefinite adjectives – Panjabi — **159**
5.1.3.5.3 Indefinite adjectives – Saraiki — **160**
5.1.3.6 Reflexive adjectives — **160**
5.1.3.6.1 Reflexive adjective – Hindko — **161**
5.1.3.6.2 Reflexive adjective – Panjabi — **161**
5.1.3.6.3 Reflexive adjective – Saraiki — **162**
5.1.4 Numbers — **162**
5.1.4.1 Common features — **162**
5.1.4.1.1 Large numbers — **163**
5.1.4.1.2 Fractional numbers — **164**
5.1.4.2 Cardinal numbers — **166**
5.1.4.2.1 Hindko cardinal numbers — **166**
5.1.4.2.2 Panjabi cardinal numbers — **167**
5.1.4.2.3 Saraiki cardinal numbers — **169**
5.1.4.3 Ordinal numbers — **172**

5.1.4.3.1 Hindko ordinal numbers — 173
5.1.4.3.2 Panjabi ordinal numbers — 174
5.1.4.3.3 Saraiki ordinal numbers — 174
5.1.4.4 Indefinite numerical expressions — 176
5.1.4.5 Totalizing (aggregating) suffixes — 176
5.2 Adverbs and adverbial expressions — 178
5.2.1 Hindko adverbs and adverbial expressions — 179
5.2.1.1 Simple adverbs – Hindko — 179
5.2.1.1.1 Quantity — 179
5.2.1.1.2 Time — 179
5.2.1.1.3 Place — 179
5.2.1.1.4 Reason — 180
5.2.1.1.5 Manner — 180
5.2.1.2 Oblique noun phrases – Hindko — 180
5.2.1.3 Indefinite adverbials – Hindko — 180
5.2.2 Panjabi adverbs and adverbial expressions — 181
5.2.2.1 Simple adverbs – Panjabi — 181
5.2.2.1.1 Quantity — 181
5.2.2.1.2 Time — 181
5.2.2.1.3 Place — 182
5.2.2.1.4 Reason — 183
5.2.2.1.5 Manner — 183
5.2.2.2 Indefinite adverbials – Panjabi — 183
5.2.3 Saraiki adverbs and adverbial expressions — 185
5.2.3.1 Simple adverbs – Saraiki — 185
5.2.3.1.1 Quantity — 185
5.2.3.1.2 Time — 186
5.2.3.1.3 Place — 186
5.2.3.1.4 Reason — 186
5.2.3.1.5 Manner — 187
5.2.3.2 Indefinite adverbials – Saraiki — 187

6 Pronouns — 189
6.1 Introduction — 189
6.1.1 Person and number — 189
6.1.2 Case — 190
6.2 Personal pronouns — 191
6.2.1 Hindko personal and third person pronouns — 191
6.2.2 Panjabi personal and third person pronouns — 193
6.2.3 Saraiki personal and third person pronouns — 197
6.3 Reflexive pronouns — 199
6.3.1 Hindko reflexive pronoun — 200

6.3.2 Panjabi reflexive pronouns — **201**
6.3.3 Saraiki reflexive pronouns — **202**
6.4 Reciprocals — **203**
6.4.1 Hindko reciprocal pronouns — **203**
6.4.2 Panjabi reciprocal pronouns — **204**
6.4.3 Saraiki reciprocal pronouns — **206**
6.5 Interrogative pronouns — **207**
6.5.1 Hindko interrogative pronouns — **207**
6.5.2 Panjabi interrogative pronouns — **209**
6.5.3 Saraiki interrogative pronouns — **211**
6.6 Indefinite pronouns — **212**
6.6.1 Hindko indefinite pronouns — **213**
6.6.2 Panjabi indefinite pronouns — **214**
6.6.3 Saraiki indefinite pronouns — **216**
6.7 Relative pronouns — **217**
6.8 Pronominal suffixes — **218**
6.8.1 Pronominal suffixes in Saraiki — **219**
6.8.2 Pronominal suffixes in Panjabi — **226**
6.8.3 Pronominal suffixes in Hindko — **237**
6.8.4 Comparison of functions of pronominal suffixes — **240**

7 Postpositions — 243
7.1 Layer II postpositions — **243**
7.1.1 Grammatical postpositions — **243**
7.1.1.1 Hindko grammatical postpositions — **244**
7.1.1.2 Panjabi grammatical postpositions — **245**
7.1.1.3 Saraiki grammatical postpositions — **246**
7.1.2 Adjectival postpositions — **248**
7.1.2.1 The genitive postposition — **248**
7.1.2.2 والا~آلا /-ālā ~ -vālā ~ -vāḷā ~ -āḷā/ — **249**
7.1.2.3 جوگا /jogā/ Hk, Pj ; جوڳا /joɠā/ Sr ‘capable of, worthy of’ — **250**
7.1.2.4 جیہا/jiā̃/; جیہاں ~ جھیاں/jehā̃ ~ jheā̃/ ‘like, similar to’ — **251**
7.1.2.5 ورگا /vargā/ ‘like’ Pj — **252**
7.1.2.6 Other adjectival postpositions — **253**
7.2 Layer III and complex postpositions — **253**
7.2.1 Sources of derived postpositions — **253**
7.2.2 Locative relations – spatial and temporal — **254**
7.2.2.1 Locative postpositions – Hindko — **254**
7.2.2.2 Locative postpositions – Panjabi — **256**
7.2.2.3 Locative postpositions – Saraiki — **257**
7.2.3 GOAL and direction of motion — **259**
7.2.3.1 Goal and direction of motion – Hindko — **259**

7.2.3.2 Goal and direction of motion – Panjabi — **261**
7.2.3.3 Goal and direction of motion – Saraiki — **261**
7.2.4 SOURCE (Ablative) — **263**
7.2.4.1 Ablative relations – Hindko — **263**
7.2.4.2 Ablative relations – Panjabi — **265**
7.2.4.3 Ablative relations – Saraiki — **267**
7.2.5 Spatial/temporal postpositions – Comparison — **268**
7.2.6 Accompaniment, instrument, cause, manner — **269**
7.2.6.1 Accompaniment, instrument, cause, manner – Hindko — **269**
7.2.6.2 Accompaniment, instrument, cause, manner – Panjabi — **270**
7.2.6.3 Accompaniment, instrument, cause, manner – Saraiki — **271**
7.2.7 Purpose, reason, and cause — **273**
7.2.7.1 Purpose, reason, and cause – Hindko — **273**
7.2.7.2 Purpose, reason, and cause – Panjabi — **273**
7.2.7.3 Purpose, reason, and cause – Saraiki — **274**
7.2.8 Similarity — **275**
7.2.8.1 وانگ ~ وانگوں /vāng ~ vāngũ̃/ Pj / وانگوں /vāngõ/ Sr ونگڑ /vangaṛ/ Hk 'like' — **276**
7.2.8.2 Genitive or oblique + طرح /tara/ 'like, similar to' — **277**

8 Verbs — 279
8.1 Verbal categories and terminology — **279**
8.2 The four basic non-finite verb forms — **281**
8.3 Hindko verbs — **281**
8.3.1 Overview — **281**
8.3.1.1 Stem formation — **284**
8.3.1.1.1 Simple stem — **284**
8.3.1.1.2 First causative stem — **284**
8.3.1.1.3 Double causative stem — **284**
8.3.1.1.4 Passive stem — **284**
8.3.1.2 Non-finite forms — **285**
8.3.1.2.1 Infinitive — **285**
8.3.1.2.2 Conjunctive participle — **285**
8.3.1.2.3 Imperfective participle — **285**
8.3.1.2.4 Perfective participle — **286**
8.3.1.2.5 Stative perfective participle — **286**
8.3.1.3 Finite forms of ہونڑا /hoṛ̃ā/ 'to be' — **287**
8.3.1.3.1 Present forms of ہونڑا /hoṛ̃ā/ 'to be' — **287**
8.3.1.3.2 Negative present forms of ہونڑا /hoṛ̃ā/ 'to be' — **288**
8.3.1.3.3 Future forms of ہونڑا /hoṛ̃ā/ 'to be' — **289**
8.3.1.3.4 Simple perfect forms of ہونڑا /hoṛ̃ā/ 'to be' — **290**

8.3.1.3.5 Past forms of ہوڑا /hoŗ̣ā/ 'to be' — **290**
8.3.1.3.6 Negative past forms of ہوڑا /hoŗ̣ā/ 'to be' — **291**
8.3.1.3.7 Subjunctive forms of ہوڑا /hoŗ̣ā/ 'to be' — **292**
8.3.1.4 The verb تھی /thī-/ 'become' — **293**
8.3.1.5 Forms constructed on the stem — **293**
8.3.1.5.1 Imperatives — **294**
8.3.1.5.2 Subjunctive — **295**
8.3.1.5.3 Perfect irrealis I — **296**
8.3.1.5.4 Future — **296**
8.3.1.5.5 Continuous tenses II — **298**
8.3.1.6 Forms constructed on the imperfective participle — **299**
8.3.1.6.1 Present imperfect — **300**
8.3.1.6.2 Present imperfect-habitual — **303**
8.3.1.6.3 Past imperfect — **303**
8.3.1.6.4 Past imperfect-habitual — **304**
8.3.1.6.5 Imperfect subjunctive — **305**
8.3.1.6.6 Future imperfect — **306**
8.3.1.6.7 Present continuous I formation — **307**
8.3.1.6.8 Past continuous I — **308**
8.3.1.7 Verb forms constructed on the perfective participle — **309**
8.3.1.7.1 Simple perfect — **309**
8.3.1.7.2 Present perfect — **310**
8.3.1.7.3 Present perfect-stative — **312**
8.3.1.7.4 Past perfect — **313**
8.3.1.7.5 Perfect irrealis II — **315**
8.3.1.7.6 Future perfect — **316**
8.4 Panjabi verbs — **318**
8.4.1 Overview — **318**
8.4.2 Non-finite forms — **321**
8.4.2.1 Stem — **321**
8.4.2.2 Infinitive — **322**
8.4.2.3 Conjunctive participle — **322**
8.4.2.4 Imperfective participle — **323**
8.4.2.5 Perfective participle — **324**
8.4.3 The verb ہونا /hoṇā/ 'to be' — **327**
8.4.3.1 Present tense of ہونا /hoṇā/ 'to be' — **327**
8.4.3.2 Past tense of ہونا /hoṇā/ 'to be' — **328**
8.4.3.3 Subjunctive of ہونا /hoṇā/ 'to be' — **329**
8.4.3.4 Future of ہونا /hoṇā/ 'to be' — **329**
8.4.4 Verb forms constructed on the stem — **331**
8.4.4.1 Imperative — **331**
8.4.4.1.1 Informal imperative — **331**

8.4.4.1.2 Polite/formal imperative — **332**
8.4.4.2 Subjunctive — **332**
8.4.4.3 Future — **335**
8.4.4.4 Continuous tenses — **335**
8.4.4.4.1 Present continuous II — **336**
8.4.4.4.2 Past continuous II — **337**
8.4.4.4.3 Past continuous II – habitual — **338**
8.4.4.4.4 Continuous II – subjunctive — **339**
8.4.4.4.5 Future continuous II — **340**
8.4.4.4.6 Continuous II – irrealis — **341**
8.4.5 Verb forms constructed on the imperfective participle — **342**
8.4.5.1 Bare imperfective participle — **342**
8.4.5.1.1 Irrealis II — **342**
8.4.5.1.2 Imperfective participle as attributive adjective — **343**
8.4.5.2 Imperfective tenses — **343**
8.4.5.2.1 Present imperfect — **343**
8.4.5.2.2 Present continuous I — **344**
8.4.5.2.3 Present imperfect – habitual — **344**
8.4.5.2.4 Past imperfect — **345**
8.4.5.2.5 Past imperfect – habitual — **346**
8.4.5.2.6 Imperfect subjunctive — **347**
8.4.5.2.7 Future imperfect — **348**
8.4.5.2.8 Imperfect irrealis — **349**
8.4.6 Verb forms constructed on the perfective participle — **350**
8.4.6.1 Bare perfective participle — **350**
8.4.6.1.1 Simple perfect — **350**
8.4.6.1.2 Perfective participle used adjectivally — **351**
8.4.6.2 Present perfect — **352**
8.4.6.3 Present perfect-stative — **353**
8.4.6.4 Past perfect — **354**
8.4.6.5 Past perfect-stative — **355**
8.4.6.6 Perfect subjunctive — **355**
8.4.6.7 Future perfect — **356**
8.4.6.8 Perfect irrealis — **357**
8.4.7 Form constructed on the oblique infinitive: Continuous III — **358**
8.5 Saraiki verbs — **360**
8.5.1 Saraiki stem types — **364**
8.5.1.1 Simple stem — **364**
8.5.1.2 Basic intransitive and transitive pairs — **364**
8.5.1.3 First causative/derived transitive stem — **364**
8.5.1.4 Second/double causative stem — **364**
8.5.1.5 Passive stem — **365**

8.5.1.6 Present-future stem — **365**
8.5.2 Other non-finite forms — **366**
8.5.2.1 Infinitive — **366**
8.5.2.2 Gerundive — **366**
8.5.2.3 Imperfective participle — **367**
8.5.2.4 Perfective participle — **367**
8.5.2.5 Stative perfective participle — **368**
8.5.2.6 Linking participles — **368**
8.5.2.6.1 Catenative participle — **369**
8.5.2.6.2 Conjunctive participle ("absolutive," "converb") — **369**
8.5.2.6.3 Connective participle — **369**
8.5.3 Finite forms — **369**
8.5.3.1 The verb ہووݨ /hovaṇ/ 'to be' — **369**
8.5.3.1.1 Present tense of ہووݨ /hovaṇ/ 'to be' — **370**
8.5.3.1.2 Past tense of ہووݨ /hovaṇ/ 'to be' — **372**
8.5.3.1.3 Past negative tense of ہووݨ /hovaṇ/ 'to be' — **373**
8.5.3.1.4 Future forms of ہووݨ /hovaṇ/ 'to be' — **375**
8.5.3.1.5 Subjunctive forms of ہووݨ /hovaṇ/ 'to be' — **375**
8.5.3.2 The verb تھیوݨ /thīvaṇ/ 'to become' — **376**
8.5.4 Verb forms built on the stem — **377**
8.5.4.1 Imperative — **377**
8.5.4.2 Future — **378**
8.5.4.3 Subjunctive — **379**
8.5.4.4 Irrealis I — **380**
8.5.5 Morphological passive forms — **381**
8.5.6 Verb forms built on the imperfective participle — **386**
8.5.6.1 Bare participial forms: Irrealis II — **386**
8.5.6.2 Imperfect tenses — **386**
8.5.6.2.1 Present imperfect — **386**
8.5.6.2.2 Present imperfect-habitual — **387**
8.5.6.2.3 Past imperfect — **388**
8.5.6.2.4 Past imperfect-habitual — **389**
8.5.6.2.5 Future imperfect — **390**
8.5.6.2.6 Imperfect subjunctive — **391**
8.5.6.2.7 Imperfect irrealis I — **392**
8.5.6.3 Continuous tenses — **393**
8.5.6.3.1 Present continuous I — **394**
8.5.6.3.2 Past continuous I — **395**
8.5.6.3.3 Future continuous I — **396**
8.5.6.3.4 Continuous I subjunctive — **397**
8.5.7 Verb forms built on the perfective participle — **398**
8.5.7.1 Simple perfect — **398**

8.5.7.2 Present perfect — 399
8.5.7.3 Present perfect-stative — 402
8.5.7.4 Present perfect-habitual — 405
8.5.7.5 Past perfect — 406
8.5.7.6 Past perfect-stative — 408
8.5.7.7 Past perfect-habitual — 409
8.5.7.8 Future perfect — 411
8.5.7.9 Future perfect-stative — 412
8.5.7.10 Perfect subjunctive — 414
8.5.7.11 Perfect-stative subjunctive — 415
8.5.7.12 Perfect irrealis I — 418
8.5.7.13 Perfect-stative irrealis I — 419

9 Sentential syntax — 421
9.1 Simple sentences — 421
9.1.1 Word order — 421
9.1.1.1 Default word order in simple sentences — 421
9.1.1.1.1 Scrambling — 424
9.1.1.1.2 Cleft constructions — 425
9.1.1.2 Word order in the noun phrase — 425
9.1.1.3 Status of the existential verb and copula — 427
9.1.1.4 Omission of subject and object pronouns — 428
9.1.1.4.1 Subject marked on verb — 428
9.1.1.4.2 Omission of repeated identical subjects, objects, or verbs — 430
9.1.2 Agreement — 431
9.1.2.1 Adjective agreement — 431
9.1.2.2 Verb agreement: split ergativity — 431
9.1.2.3 Verb agreement with coordinated nouns — 435
9.1.2.3.1 Verb agreement with compound subjects — 436
9.1.2.3.2 Verb agreement with compound objects — 439
9.1.3 Subject and agent marking — 441
9.1.3.1 The split-ergative system — 441
9.1.3.2 Grammatical and semantic subjects: "dative subjects" — 445
9.1.3.2.1 Dative subject – Hindko — 446
9.1.3.2.2 Dative subject – Panjabi — 447
9.1.3.2.3 Dative subject – Saraiki — 449
9.1.4 Object marking — 450
9.1.5 Negation — 453
9.1.5.1 Hindko negation — 455
9.1.5.2 Panjabi negation — 456
9.1.5.3 Saraiki negation — 459
9.1.6 Questions — 460

9.1.6.1 Yes-no questions — **460**
9.1.6.2 Constituent questions: Wh-phrases — **463**
9.2 Compound (coordinate) sentences — **466**
9.2.1 Compound (coordinate) sentences – Hindko — **466**
9.2.2 Compound (coordinate) sentences – Panjabi — **466**
9.2.3 Compound (coordinate) sentences – Saraiki — **467**
9.3 Complex sentences — **468**
9.3.1 Finite subordinate clauses — **468**
9.3.1.1 Nominal clauses — **468**
9.3.1.1.1 Finite nominal clauses – Hindko — **469**
9.3.1.1.2 Finite nominal clauses – Panjabi — **469**
9.3.1.1.3 Finite nominal clauses – Saraiki — **471**
9.3.1.2 Relative clauses — **471**
9.3.1.2.1 Adjectival relative clauses — **472**
9.3.1.2.2 Adverbial relative clauses — **475**
9.3.1.3 Conditional clauses — **479**
9.3.1.3.1 Realis conditionals — **479**
9.3.1.3.2 Irrealis conditionals — **482**
9.3.2 Non-finite subordinate clauses — **488**
9.3.2.1 Infinitive clauses — **488**
9.3.2.1.1 Infinitive clause as subject — **488**
9.3.2.1.2 Infinitive clause as (direct) object — **489**
9.3.2.2 Oblique infinitive + والا، آلا /vāḷā, āḷā/ — **496**
9.3.2.3 Conjunctive participial clauses in Hindko and Panjabi — **500**
9.3.2.4 Saraiki catenative, conjunctive, and connective participles — **501**
9.3.2.5 Imperfective participial phrases — **504**
9.3.2.6 Perfective participial phrases — **505**

10 Morphosemantics — 507
10.1 Complex predicates — **507**
10.1.1 Conjunct verbs, or N/ADJ - V, light verb constructions — **507**
10.1.2 Compound verbs, or V-V light verb constructions — **509**
10.1.2.1 Compound verbs – Hindko — **509**
10.1.2.1.1 Vector جل /jul-/ ‘go’ — **509**
10.1.2.1.2 Vector پے /pæ-/ ‘fall, lie’ — **510**
10.1.2.1.3 Vector چھوڑ /choṛ-/ ‘leave, let go’ — **511**
10.1.2.1.4 Vector کہن /kìn-/ ‘take’ — **512**
10.1.2.1.5 Vector رکھ /rakh-/ ‘put/keep’ — **513**
10.1.2.1.6 Vector سٹ /saṭ-/ ‘throw’ — **513**
10.1.2.2 Compound verbs – Panjabi — **514**
10.1.2.2.1 Vector جا /jā-/ ‘go’ — **514**

10.1.2.2.2 Vector او ~ آ /au- ~ ā-/ 'come' — 515
10.1.2.2.3 Vector بہ /bǽ-/ 'sit' — 516
10.1.2.2.4 Vector پے /pæ-/ 'fall, lie' — 517
10.1.2.2.5 Vector دے /de-/ 'give' — 517
10.1.2.2.6 Vector لے /læ-/ 'take' — 518
10.1.2.2.7 Vector سٹ /suṭṭ- ~ saṭṭ/ 'throw' — 518
10.1.2.2.8 Vector رکھ /rakh-/ 'keep, put' — 519
10.1.2.2.9 Vector مار /mār-/ 'beat, kill' — 519
10.1.2.2.10 Vector چھڈ /chaḍḍ-/ 'leave, let go' — 519
10.1.2.3 Compound verbs – Saraiki — 520
10.1.2.3.1 Vector ونج /vãʄ-/ 'go' — 520
10.1.2.3.2 Vector آ /ā-/ 'come' — 520
10.1.2.3.3 Vector پو /po-/ 'fall, lie' — 521
10.1.2.3.4 Vector بہہ /bah-/ 'sit' — 522
10.1.2.3.5 Vector گھن /ghin-/ 'take' — 522
10.1.2.3.6 Vector ڋے /ɗe-/ 'give' — 523
10.1.2.3.7 Vector رکھ /rakh-/ 'put, keep' — 523
10.1.2.3.8 Vector چھوڑ /choṛ-/ 'leave' — 524
10.1.2.3.9 Vector گھت /ghat-/ 'throw, cast' — 524
10.1.2.3.10 Vector سٹ /saṭ-/ 'throw' — 524
10.1.3 The invariant form چا /cā/ 'lift, raise' — 525
10.1.3.1 Hindko چا /cā-/ 'lift, raise' — 525
10.1.3.2 Saraiki چا /cā-/ 'lift, raise' — 527
10.2 Complex durative verbal constructions — 529
10.2.1 Forms using the imperfective participle — 529
10.2.1.1 Imperfective participle + 'remain' — 529
10.2.1.2 Imperfective participle + 'go' or 'come' — 530
10.2.1.3 Imperfective participle + both 'remain' and 'go' — 532
10.2.2 Forms using the perfective participle: Perfective participle + کرنا /karnā/ 'to do' — 532
10.2.3 Stem + /-ī/ + 'go', 'remain', or 'keep' — 534
10.2.4 Main verb + 'do' in the same TAM form — 535
10.3 Causativization and intransitivization: transitivity sets — 536
10.4 Passive constructions — 539
10.4.1 Passive construction – Hindko — 540
10.4.2 Passive constructions – Panjabi — 541
10.4.3 Passive constructions – Saraiki — 542
10.4.3.1 Saraiki morphological passive — 543
10.4.3.2 Saraiki periphrastic passive — 544
10.5 Deontic and epistemic modality — 545

10.5.1 Ability — **545**
10.5.1.1 The verb ‘to be able’ — **545**
10.5.1.2 Other intransitive abilitative constructions — **546**
10.5.1.3 Ability to perform learned skills: the verb ‘to come’ — **549**
10.5.2 Desirability or advisability — **549**
10.5.2.1 Vestigial morphological passive — **549**
10.5.2.2 The verb ‘to be wanted’ — **550**
10.5.3 Prospective meanings: Weak obligation, need, desire, intended or expected activity — **552**
10.5.3.1 Weak obligation, etc.– Hindko — **553**
10.5.3.2 Weak obligation, etc.– Panjabi — **554**
10.5.3.3 Weak obligation, etc.– Saraiki — **556**
10.5.4 Presumption (epistemic modality) — **558**
10.5.5 Strong obligation or compulsion — **559**
10.5.5.1 Strong obligation or compulsion – Hindko — **560**
10.5.5.2 Strong obligation or compulsion – Panjabi — **560**
10.5.5.3 Strong obligation or compulsion – Saraiki — **561**
10.5.6 Infinitive/gerundive as distanced (softened) imperative — **562**
10.5.6.1 Hindko and Panjabi infinitive/gerundive as distanced (softened) imperative — **562**
10.5.6.2 Saraiki gerundive as imperative — **563**
10.6 Referentiality: Definiteness, indefiniteness, genericity — **564**
10.7 Evidentiality and mirativity — **566**
10.8 Expression of “possession” — **568**
10.8.1 Inalienable possession — **568**
10.8.2 Alienable possession — **569**
10.8.3 Abstract “possession” — **570**
10.9 Causal relations — **571**
10.9.1 Expressions of reason/cause (SOURCE) — **571**
10.9.2 Expressions of purpose (GOAL) — **573**
10.10 Reduplicative processes — **577**
10.10.1 Full reduplication — **577**
10.10.1.1 Reduplication of nouns — **577**
10.10.1.2 Reduplication of adjectives — **580**
10.10.1.3 Reduplication of adverbs and postpositions — **582**
10.10.1.4 -o- reiteration — **584**
10.10.1.5 Reduplication of participial forms — **585**
10.10.2 Partial reduplication — **587**
10.10.2.1 Echo formations — **587**
10.10.2.2 Stem-vowel alternation — **588**
10.10.2.3 Alliterative partial reduplicates — **588**
10.10.2.4 Rhyming partial reduplicates — **589**

10.10.3 Semantic reduplication —— **591**
10.10.3.1 Same or similar meanings —— **591**
10.10.3.2 Intransitive-causative participial doublets —— **593**
10.10.3.3 Different or opposite meanings —— **594**
10.11 Discourse particles —— **595**
10.11.1 Emphatic or exclusive particle —— **595**
10.11.2 Inclusive particle —— **596**
10.11.3 Topic marker —— **597**

References Cited or Consulted —— 599
Index —— 605

List of Figures

1.1 In-line text example — 4
1.2 Interlinear example — 4

2.1 Map of Pakistan and environs with political boundaries — 11
2.2 Language varieties of the Punjab region — 13

List of Tables

3.1 Consonants of Hindko (IPA representation) — 22
3.2 Consonants of Panjabi (IPA representation) — 23
3.3 IPA representation and transcription of consonant sounds — 25
3.4 Correspondences between /v/ and /b/ in Panjabi and Hindko — 26
3.5 Correspondences between /kh/ and /x/ in Panjabi and Hindko — 27
3.6 Correspondences between word-initial vowel or /s/, and /h/ in Panjabi and Hindko — 27
3.7 Consonants of Saraiki — 30
3.8 Vowels of Hindko, adapted from Varma (1936) — 33
3.9 Centralized and peripheral vowels — 34
3.10 Vowels of Hindko, adapted from Rashid and Akhtar (2012) — 34
3.11 Centralized and peripheral vowels — 35
3.12 Centralized and peripheral vowels of Panjabi (IPA representations) — 35
3.13 Vowels in transcription — 36
3.14 Saraiki vowels — 37
3.15 Diphthongs of Panjabi — 40
3.16 Tone comparison in Hindko, Panjabi, Saraiki, and Urdu — 47
3.17 Summary of Panjabi stress placement — 51
3.18 Letters of the Perso-Arabic script, as used for Hindko, Panjabi, and Saraiki — 62
3.19 Consonant sounds in orthography — 64
3.20 Centralized vowel diacritics — 67
3.21 Representation of peripheral (long) vowels using diacritics — 68
3.22 Symbol-sound correspondences in writing without vowel diacritics — 71
3.23 Representation of Panjabi tones: historic voiced aspirated plosives — 73
3.24 Representation of Panjabi tones: the segment /h/ — 74

4.1 Hindko vocative case endings — 98

4.2 Panjabi vocative case endings — 99
4.3 Saraiki common noun vocative case endings — 100
4.4 Saraiki proper name vocative case endings — 101
4.5 Locative endings in Hindko, Panjabi, and Saraiki — 104
4.6 Comparison of Hindko, Panjabi, and Saraiki declension classes — 107
4.7 Marked masculine, ا /-ā/ -final (Class I) noun بُوہا /bū̃ā/ 'door' — 109
4.8 Unmarked, vowel-final masculine noun آلُو /ālū/ 'potato' (Class II) — 109
4.9 Unmarked, consonant-final masculine noun پُتّر /puttar/ 'son' (Class II) — 110
4.10 Unmarked, consonant-final (Class II) masculine noun کہار /kȁr/ 'house, home' (~کہر /kàr/) — 110
4.11 Marked feminine, unstressed /-ī/-final noun کُڑی /kuṛī/ 'girl' (Class III) — 111
4.12 Consonant-final feminine noun اگ /agg/ 'fire' (Class V) — 111
4.13 Kinship noun ماں /mā̃/ 'mother' (Class VI) — 112
4.14 Kinship noun تہی /tȉ/ 'daughter' (Class VI) — 112
4.15 Panjabi marked masculine noun مُنڈا /mũḍā/ 'boy' (Class I) — 116
4.16 Paradigm for پانی /pāṇī/ 'water' (Class II) — 116
4.17 Paradigm for دن /din/ 'day' (Class II) — 117
4.18 Paradigm for کُڑی /kuṛī/ 'girl ' (Class III) — 117
4.19 Paradigm for دھپ /tùpp/ 'sunshine' (Class IV) — 118
4.20 Paradigm for ہوا /havā/ 'wind' (Class IV) — 118
4.21 Inflectional endings for marked masculine nouns (Class I) — 119
4.22 Inflectional endings for unmarked masculine nouns (Class II) — 119
4.23 Inflectional endings for Panjabi feminine nouns (Class III and Class IV) — 120
4.24 Feminine nouns in /-ā̃/ /-ā́/ (Class IV) — 120
4.25 Saraiki masculine noun ending in -ā, چُوہا /cūhā/ 'rat' (Class I) — 124
4.26 Saraiki masculine noun ending in a non-/ā/ vowel, پیو /pyū/ 'father' (Class II) — 124
4.27 Saraiki consonant-final masculine noun گھر /ghar/ 'house, home' (Class II) — 125
4.28 Saraiki consonant-final masculine noun چھوہر /chuhar/ 'boy' (Class VIII) — 125
4.29 Saraiki /-ī/-final feminine noun, ٻلّی /ɓillī/ 'cat' (Class III) — 126
4.30 Saraiki /-ā/-final feminine noun, ما /mā/ 'mother' (Class IV) — 126
4.31 Saraiki consonant-final feminine noun چھت /chatt/ 'roof' (Class IV) — 127
4.32 Saraiki feminine noun بھیݨ /bheṇ/ 'sister' (Class VII) — 127
4.33 Saraiki feminine noun چھوہِر /chuhir/ 'girl' (Class VII) — 128

6.4 Genitive forms of pronouns, Panjabi — **197**
6.5 Saraiki personal pronouns — **198**
6.6 Hindko interrogative pronoun کونڑ /kɔṛ̃/ 'who' — **208**
6.7 Hindko interrogative pronoun کے /ke/ 'what' — **208**
6.8 Interrogative pronouns کون /kauṇ ~ kɔṇ/ 'who' and کیھ ~ کیہ /kī̃/ 'what' — **210**
6.9 Interrogative pronoun کون /kon (~kaon)/ 'who' — **211**
6.10 Interrogative pronoun کیا /kyā/ 'what' — **211**
6.11 Indefinite pronoun/adjective کُئی /kuī/ 'a, some, any' — **213**
6.12 Saraiki indefinite pronoun کوئی /kuī/ 'someone, anyone' — **216**
6.13 Relative pronoun جو /jo/ 'who, which' in Hindko, Panjabi, and Saraiki — **218**
6.14 Saraiki pronominal suffixes — **220**
6.15 Pronominal suffixes found in Lahore Panjabi — **226**
6.16 Pronominal suffixes found in Saraiki, Panjabi, and Hindko — **240**
6.17 Functions of pronominal suffixes in Saraiki, Panjabi, and Hindko — **241**

7.1 Dative-accusative and ergative postpositions in Hindko, Panjabi, and Saraiki — **247**
7.2 Complex Panjabi postpositions with -وں /-õ/ — **267**
7.3 Some basic spatial-temporal postpositions in Hindko, Panjabi, and Saraiki — **268**

8.1 Overview of Hindko verb forms — **282**
8.2 Irregular perfective participles: پینڑا /pæṛ̃ā/ 'to fall' and جلنڑا /julṛ̃ā/ 'to go' — **286**
8.3 Present tense forms of ہونڑا /hoṛ̃ā/ 'to be' — **288**
8.4 Negative present forms of ہونڑا /hoṛ̃ā/ 'to be' — **289**
8.5 Future forms of ہونڑا /hoṛ̃ā/ 'to be' — **289**
8.6 Simple perfect forms of ہونڑا /hoṛ̃ā/ 'to be' — **290**
8.7 Past tense of ہونڑا /hoṛ̃ā/ 'to be' — **291**
8.8 Negative past of ہونڑا /hoṛ̃ā/ 'to be' — **292**
8.9 Subjunctive forms of ہونڑا /hoṛ̃ā/ 'to be' — **293**
8.10 Imperatives of کرنا /karnā/ 'to do' — **294**
8.11 Personal endings of Hindko subjunctive — **295**
8.12 Subjunctive of آنڑا /āṛ̃ā/ 'to come' — **296**
8.13 Subjunctive of جُلنڑا /julṛ̃ā/ 'to go' — **296**
8.14 Future of آنڑا /āṛ̃ā/ 'to come' — **297**
8.15 Future of جُلنڑا /julṛ̃ā/ 'to go' — **297**
8.16 Present continuous II of کرنا /karnā/ 'to do' — **298**
8.17 Past continuous II of دوڑنا /dauṛnā/ 'to run' — **299**

8.18 Present imperfect of جلنڑا /julṛ̃ā/ ‘to go’ (actual forms) —— 301
8.19 Present imperfect of جلنڑا /julṛ̃ā/ ‘to go’ (hypothesized underlying forms) —— 302
8.20 Present imperfect-habitual of جلنڑا /julṛ̃ā/ ‘to go’ —— 303
8.21 Past imperfect of جُلنڑا /julṛ̃ā/ ‘to go’ —— 304
8.22 Past imperfect-habitual of جُلنڑا /julṛ̃ā/ ‘to go’ —— 305
8.23 Imperfect subjunctive of جلنڑا /julṛ̃ā/ ‘to go’ —— 306
8.24 Future imperfect of جلنڑا /julṛ̃ā/ ‘to go’ —— 307
8.25 Present continuous I of جلنڑا /julṛ̃ā/ ‘to go (actual forms)’ —— 308
8.26 Past continuous I of جلنڑا /julṛ̃ā/ ‘to go’ —— 309
8.27 Simple perfect of جلنڑا /julṛ̃ā/ ‘to go’ —— 310
8.28 Simple perfect of کرنا /karnā/ ‘to do’ —— 310
8.29 Present perfect of جلنڑا /julṛ̃ā/ ‘to go’ —— 311
8.30 Present perfect of کرنا /karnā/ ‘to do’ —— 312
8.31 Present perfect-stative of جُلنڑا /julṛ̃ā/ ‘to go’ —— 313
8.32 Past perfect of جُلنڑا /julṛ̃ā/ ‘to go’ —— 314
8.33 Past perfect of کرنا /karnā/ ‘to do’ —— 315
8.34 Perfect irrealis II of جُلنڑا /julṛ̃ā/ ‘to go’ —— 315
8.35 Perfect irrealis II of کرنا /karnā/ ‘to do’ —— 316
8.36 Future perfect of جُلنڑا /julṛ̃ā/ ‘to go’ —— 317
8.37 Future perfect of کرنا /karnā/ ‘to do’ —— 317
8.38 Overview of Panjabi verb forms —— 319
8.39 Verb stems—transitivity sets —— 321
8.40 Suffixes of the imperfective participle —— 324
8.41 Masculine singular perfective participles from regular and irregular perfective stems —— 324
8.42 Suffixes of the perfective participle —— 325
8.43 Present tense of ہونا /hoṇā/ ‘to be’ —— 328
8.44 Past tense of ہونا /hoṇā/ ‘to be’ —— 328
8.45 Subjunctive of ہونا /hoṇā/ ‘to be’ —— 329
8.46 Future of ہونا /hoṇā/ ‘to be’ —— 330
8.47 Panjabi imperative endings —— 332
8.48 Personal endings of the subjunctive —— 333
8.49 Subjunctive of بولنا /bolṇā/ ‘to speak’ —— 333
8.50 Subjunctive of جانا /jāṇā/ ‘to go’ —— 334
8.51 Subjunctive of لینا /læṇā/ ‘to take, get, buy’ —— 334
8.52 Future of بولنا /bolṇā/ ‘to speak’ —— 335
8.53 Present continuous II of کرنا /karnā/ ‘to do’ —— 337
8.54 Past continuous II of کرنا /karnā/ ‘to do’ —— 338
8.55 Past continuous II-habitual of کرنا /karnā/ ‘to do’ —— 339

8.56 Continuous II-subjunctive of کرنا /karnā/ 'to do' — **340**
8.57 Future continuous II of کرنا /karnā/ 'to do' — **341**
8.58 Continuous II-irrealis of کرنا /karnā/ 'to do' — **342**
8.59 Simple irrealis II of کرنا /karnā/ 'to do' — **343**
8.60 Present imperfect of کرنا /karnā/ 'to do' — **344**
8.61 Present imperfect-habitual of کرنا /karnā/ 'to do' — **345**
8.62 Past imperfect of کرنا /karnā/ 'to do' — **346**
8.63 Past imperfect-habitual of کرنا /karnā/ 'to do' — **347**
8.64 Imperfect subjunctive of کرنا /karnā/ 'to do' — **348**
8.65 Future imperfect of کرنا /karnā/ 'to do' — **349**
8.66 Imperfect irrealis of کرنا /karnā/ 'to do' — **350**
8.67 Simple perfect of جاݨا /jāṇā/ 'to go' — **351**
8.68 Simple perfect of کرنا /karnā/ — **351**
8.69 Present perfect of جاݨا /jāṇā/ 'to go' — **352**
8.70 Present perfect-stative of جاݨا /jāṇā/ 'to go' — **353**
8.71 Past perfect of جاݨا /jāṇā/ 'to go' — **354**
8.72 Past perfect-stative of جاݨا /jāṇā/ 'to go' — **355**
8.73 Perfect subjunctive of جاݨا /jāṇā/ 'to go' — **356**
8.74 Future perfect of جاݨا /jāṇā/ 'to go' — **357**
8.75 Perfect irrealis of جاݨا /jāṇā/ 'to go' — **358**
8.76 Present continuous III کرنا /karnā/ 'to do' — **359**
8.77 Overview of Saraiki verb forms — **361**
8.78 Present tense of ہووݨ /hovaṇ/ 'to be' — **371**
8.79 Syntactically negated present tense of ہووݨ /hovaṇ/ 'to be' — **371**
8.80 Morphological negative present of ہووݨ /hovaṇ/ 'to be' — **372**
8.81 Past tense of ہووݨ /hovaṇ/ 'to be' — **373**
8.82 Long form of negative past tense of ہووݨ /hovaṇ/ 'to be' — **374**
8.83 Fused negative past forms of ہووݨ /hovaṇ/ 'to be' — **374**
8.84 Future forms of ہووݨ /hovaṇ/ 'to be' — **375**
8.85 Subjunctive forms of ہووݨ /hovaṇ/ 'to be' — **376**
8.86 Imperative forms of ٹُرݨ /ṭuraṇ/ 'to walk, go' — **377**
8.87 Future of the verbs ونڄݨ/vãʄaṇ/ 'to go' (intransitive) and کرݨ /karaṇ/ 'to do' (transitive) — **379**
8.88 Subjunctive personal endings — **379**
8.89 Subjunctive of the verbs آوݨ /āvaṇ/ 'to come' (intransitive), ونڄݨ /vãʄaṇ/ 'to go' (intransitive), and کرݨ /karaṇ/ 'to do' (transitive) — **380**
8.90 Irrealis I of ونڄݨ /vãʄaṇ/ 'to go' — **381**

8.91 Comparison of simple, causative, and passive future forms of سُݨ /suṇ-/ 'hear' — 382
8.92 Present imperfect of مریج /marīj-/ 'be killed, beaten' — 383
8.93 Past imperfect of مریج /marīj-/ 'be killed, beaten' — 384
8.94 Future imperfect of مریج /marīj-/ 'be killed, beaten' — 384
8.95 Subjunctive of مریج /marīj-/ 'be killed, beaten' — 385
8.96 Irrealis I of مریج /marīj-/ 'be killed, beaten' — 385
8.97 Present imperfect of ونڄݨ /vãʄaṇ/ 'to go' — 387
8.98 Present imperfect-habitual of ونڄݨ /vãʄaṇ/ 'to go' — 388
8.99 Past imperfect of ونڄݨ /vãʄaṇ/ 'to go' — 389
8.100 Past imperfect-habitual of ونڄݨ /vãʄaṇ/ 'to go' — 390
8.101 Future imperfect of ونڄݨ /vãʄaṇ/ 'to go' — 391
8.102 Imperfect subjunctive of ونڄݨ /vãʄaṇ/ 'to go' — 392
8.103 Imperfect irrealis I of ونڄݨ /vãʄaṇ/ 'to go' — 393
8.104 Present continuous I of ونڄݨ /vãʄaṇ/ 'to go' — 395
8.105 Past continuous I of ونڄݨ /vãʄaṇ/ 'to go' — 396
8.106 Future continuous I of ونڄݨ /vãʄaṇ/ 'to go' — 397
8.107 Continuous I subjunctive of ونڄݨ /vãʄaṇ/ 'to go' — 398
8.108 Simple perfect of ونڄݨ /vãʄaṇ/ 'to go' — 399
8.109 Simple perfect of کرݨ /karaṇ/ 'to do' — 399
8.110 Present perfect of ونڄݨ /vãʄaṇ/ 'to go' — 400
8.111 Present perfect of کرݨ /karaṇ/ 'to do' — 401
8.112 Negative forms of present perfect of کرݨ /karaṇ/ 'to do' with oblique pronominal suffixes — 401
8.113 Present perfect of کرݨ /karaṇ/ 'to do' with oblique pronominal suffixes — 402
8.114 Present perfect-stative of ونڄݨ /vãʄaṇ/ 'to go' — 403
8.115 Present perfect-stative of کرݨ /karaṇ/ 'to do' — 404
8.116 Present perfect-habitual of ونڄݨ /vãʄaṇ/ 'to go' — 405
8.117 Present perfect-habitual of کرݨ /karaṇ/ 'to do' — 406
8.118 Past perfect of ونڄݨ /vãʄaṇ/ 'to go' — 407
8.119 Past perfect of کرݨ /karaṇ/ 'to do' — 407
8.120 Past perfect-stative of ونڄݨ /vãʄaṇ/ 'to go' — 408

8.121 Past perfect-stative of کرڻ /karaṇ/ ‘to do’ — **409**

8.122 Past perfect-habitual of وڃڻ /vãʄaṇ/ ‘to go’ — **410**

8.123 Past perfect-habitual of کرڻ /karaṇ/ ‘to do’ — **410**

8.124 Future perfect of وڃڻ /vãʄaṇ/ ‘to go’ — **411**

8.125 Future perfect of کرڻ /karaṇ/ ‘to do’ — **412**

8.126 Future perfect-stative of وڃڻ /vãʄaṇ/ ‘to go’ — **413**

8.127 Future perfect-stative of کرڻ /karaṇ/ ‘to do’ — **413**

8.128 Perfect subjunctive of وڃڻ /vãʄaṇ/ ‘to go’ — **414**

8.129 Perfect subjunctive of کرڻ /karaṇ/ ‘to do’ — **415**

8.130 Perfect-stative subjunctive of وڃڻ /vãʄaṇ/ ‘to go’ — **416**

8.131 Perfect-stative subjunctive of کرڻ /karaṇ/ ‘to do’ — **417**

8.132 Perfect irrealis I of وڃڻ /vãʄaṇ/ ‘to go’ — **418**

8.133 Perfect irrealis I of کرڻ /karaṇ/ ‘to do’ — **419**

8.134 Perfect-stative irrealis I of وڃڻ /vãʄaṇ/ ‘to go’ — **420**

8.135 Perfect-stative irrealis I of کرڻ /karaṇ/ ‘to do’ — **420**

10.1 ADJ - V conjunct verbs — **508**

10.2 N - V conjunct verbs — **508**

10.3 Derived intransitives — **538**

1 About this Grammar

1.1 Introduction

This book describes the grammar of Hindko, Panjabi, and Saraiki, three Indo-Aryan languages of Pakistan, treating their phonology, orthography, morphology, and syntax. The grammar is descriptive, not pedagogical or prescriptive. It is presented in a theory-neutral way to the greatest extent possible. The three languages described here represent closely related, geographically contiguous language varieties. In some cases, it may be hard to determine, for example, where one type of Panjabi ends and Hindko begins. As they share many common features, we have decided to present them together in a single work where general patterns that hold for all three can be described in detail and then language-specific patterns can be added to the general description. This kind of approach further recommends itself as many potential users of the current work with an interest in Hindko or Saraiki will already be familiar with Panjabi; so comparing this with the description of the other varieties will hopefully make them more accessible.

This grammar may be used in several ways:

- as a reference tool for understanding the major grammatical constructions in Hindko, Panjabi, and Saraiki;
- as a linguistic record of documentation of Hindko, Panjabi, and Saraiki;
- as a template for writing similar grammars of other languages;
- as a resource which is easily converted into computational tools.

While Panjabi is a major language as measured by number of speakers—having perhaps the world's twelfth-highest number of first-language speakers—published grammatical descriptions of it are surprisingly few, and those that do exist are often out of date. References for the related Hindko and Saraiki languages are even fewer. We hope that, with this grammar, we have made a contribution to the description of Hindko, Panjabi, and Saraiki. This is also the first major English-language grammar to provide exemplification of these languages in Perso-Arabic script.

1.2 Scope of the present work

This *Descriptive Grammar of Hindko, Panjabi, and Saraiki* focuses, where possible, on the variety of Hindko spoken in Abbottabad, the variety of Panjabi spoken in Lahore, and the variety of Saraiki spoken in Multan—all in Pakistan. It covers the orthography, phonology, morphology, and syntax of the languages. It is meant as a reference tool; however, the coverage of grammatical constructions is by no means exhaustive. As

https://doi.org/10.1515/9781614512257-001

noted in Chapter 2, there is significant variation from dialect to dialect and even from speaker to speaker within dialects. The current work does not attempt to describe the full range of variation, but rather presents a necessarily simplified "snapshot" of particular instantiations of each named variety.

Since Lahore is the largest urban center of Punjab, it has attracted people from all parts of Punjab and Khyber-Pakhtunkhwa, though relatively fewer from Sindh and Balochistan. Thus the Panjabi of Lahore, in addition to being subject to heavy Urdu and English influence, also contains elements of varieties from farther west or south, usually associated with Hindko or Saraiki. It is by no means a monolithic or "pure" variety.

1.3 Past work and references consulted

The current work has consulted several published studies of Panjabi, including reference materials such as Malik (1995), Gill and Gleason (1969), Bhatia (1993), and Cummings and Bailey (1912). For Hindko, the following sources were consulted: Hallberg and O'Leary (1992); Rensch, Hallberg, and O'Leary (1992); Shackle (1980); Shackle (1983); Varma (1936); Bahri (1962); and Bahri (1963). For Saraiki, the main published sources referenced are Shackle (1976) and Zahoor (2009).

Pedagogical materials have also been consulted, including Bhardwaj (1995), Ahmad (1992), Shackle (1972), and Kalra, Purewal, and Tyson-Ward (2004 [1999]).

Additionally, we have made use of the following dictionaries: Bashir and Kazmi (2012), Khan (2009), and Advanced Centre for Technical Development of Punjabi Language (2012). For Hindko, the Sakoon (2002) dictionary has been helpful; and for Saraiki, we have consulted Mughal (2010).

Linguistic work on the languages covered here is sparse. A few further publications are mentioned in the "References Cited or Consulted" section.

1.4 Sources

Each example is labeled with the language illustrated: Hk for Hindko, Pj for Panjabi, and Sr for Saraiki. The source of each example is indicated in parentheses following the example.

Each of the authors has made different contributions to the grammar. Thomas Conners and Brook Hefright wrote the draft chapters on Panjabi. These chapters were reviewed and edited by Elena Bashir. Elena Bashir wrote the sections on Hindko and Saraiki. These were reviewed and edited by Thomas Conners. Elena Bashir's collected field notes and knowledge represent a significant source that has been relied upon as a reference for the present work, including the source of some examples. Examples provided by her are marked with (EB).

Additionally, Elena Bashir conducted field work for four months in 2015 specifically working on data collection for the Hindko and Saraiki sections of the current work. During this time, she worked with two native speakers, Abdul Wajid Tabassum for Hindko and Umaima Kamran for Saraiki. Examples that are due to them are marked (AWT) and (UK), respectively. Additionally, the entire manuscript was reviewed by Nasir Abbas Syed. Without their significant contributions, the coverage of Hindko and Saraiki would not have been possible.

The authors take collective responsibility for all aspects of the grammar.

1.5 Acknowledgements

Elena Bashir would like to acknowledge the informal but extensive contributions of Nasir Abbas Syed and Ali Hussain Birahimani on Saraiki, and of Maqsood Saqib on Panjabi during the course of the writing of this book.

Thomas Conners and Brook Hefright have benefited from the insight of their coauthor, Elena Bashir, and the assistance provided by a number of colleagues at the University of Maryland Center for Advanced Study of Language. In particular, they would like to thank Mohini Madgavkar, with whom they studied and analyzed Panjabi and Urdu; Michael Maxwell, Aric Bills, Evelyn Browne, Shawna Rafalko, and Nathaniel Clair, who dedicated many hours preparing the manuscript; and Karen Fisher-Nguyen who played a large role in providing their original understanding of Panjabi—we thank them all.

The authors also thank Amalia Gnanadesikan for her dedication and attention to detail as the Series editor overseeing this volume.

1.6 Chapter organization

Each chapter of the current work covers in detail a specific aspect of the grammar of Hindko, Panjabi, and Saraiki, such as Phonology or Nouns. The initial section in each chapter discusses features common to Hindko, Panjabi, and Saraiki. After this, differences among the languages are discussed. In cases where we do not have sufficient information, a note is added.

1.7 Examples

In this grammar, we make use of both in-line text examples and interlinear text examples. In-line text examples are used when a single form is being referenced or explicated in the text. The format is as follows: the first section is in Perso-Arabic script, the second section renders it in phonemic transcription (between slashes), and the third section provides an English gloss (in single quotation marks). This is illustrated in Figure 1.1.

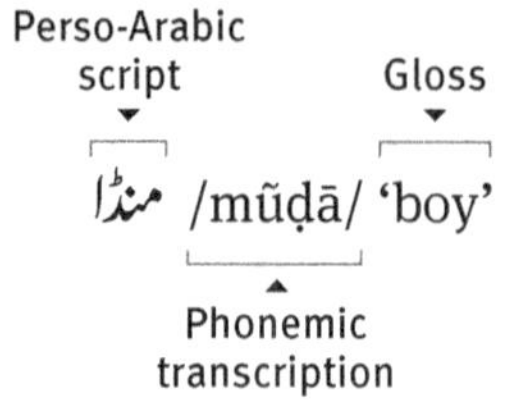

Figure 1.1: In-line text example

The format for an interlinear example is as follows: the first line is in Perso-Arabic script, the second line renders it in phonemic transcription, the third line provides a morpheme-by-morpheme gloss (including any grammatical category labels) and the fourth line gives a free translation into English.

Perso-Arabic script ▸	میں کتاب نوں ویکھیا اے				
Phonemic transcription ▸	*mæ̃*	*katāb*	*nū̃*	*vekh-iā*	*e*
Gloss ▸	I	book[F]	ACC	see-PP.SG.M	be.PRES.3SG
Free translation ▸	*‘I have seen the book.’*				

Figure 1.2: Interlinear example

1.8 Glossing and formatting conventions

Where possible, we have followed the Leipzig Glossing Conventions, which can be found at http://www.eva.mpg.de/lingua/resources/glossing-rules.php.

The following formatting conventions are used throughout the grammar:

Simple *italics* are used to indicate emphasis, often when contrasting two or more technical points.

Bold is used in the transcription and gloss lines to draw attention to the grammatical form being illustrated.

1.9 List of abbreviations and symbols

Commonly used abbreviations and symbols in this grammar include the following:

*	ungrammatical form
~	variation in forms
-	morpheme boundary in a transcription or gloss-line; indicates joining direction for Perso-Arabic character
.	a period indicates a mismatch between the number of Hindko/Panjabi/Saraiki elements and the number of elements in the English gloss
/ /	phonemic transcription
[ ]	phonetic transcription
< >	transliteration
()	marginal phoneme or morphological form
ˈ	stress on following syllable
´	high tone
`	low tone
1	first person
2	second person
3	third person
ABL	ablative
ACC	accusative
ALLIT	alliterative element
C	consonant
CAT	catenative participle
CONN	connective participle
CONT	continuous
CP	conjunctive participle
CS	causative
DAT	dative
DIR	direct

DIST	distal
ECHO	echo word
EMPH	emphatic
ERG	ergative
EZ	ezafat
F	feminine
FUT	future
GEN	genitive
GRDV	gerundive
HON	honorific
HORT	hortative
IMP	imperative
INF	infinitive
IP	imperfective participle
LOC	locative
M	masculine
NEG	negative
NMLZ	nominalizer
OBL	oblique
ONOM	onomatopoetic
P	perfective
PASS	passive
PF	present-future stem
PL	plural

POL	polite
PP	perfective participle
PRES	present
PS	pronominal suffix
PST	past
REDUP	reduplication
REFL	reflexive
REL	relative marker
RHYM	rhyming
SBJV	subjunctive
SG	singular
STAT	stative particle
Tnnn	reference to entry in Turner (1962–1966)
TOP	topicalizer
TOT	totalizing (aggregating)
V	vowel

2 Linguistic Context

2.1 Introduction

The question of whether a particular speech form constitutes a "dialect" or a "language" is deeply fraught, not only in the context of South Asia or Pakistan. We follow Joseph (1982) in treating the terms "dialect" and "language" as social facts, rather than linguistic ones; where it is useful to distinguish characteristic linguistic regularities, we prefer the terms "language variety" or "variety". Important social facts about the terms "dialect" and "language" in the South Asian context are that "dialect" is often used negatively to describe unstandardized or non-standard varieties, while "language" is often used positively to describe standard varieties that are used or recognized by government authorities. Given the social fact that speakers of varieties of Hindko, Panjabi, and Saraiki are increasingly aware of and describe their speech varieties as languages, we think it is appropriate to do so in this work as well.

We feel that the current book addresses a real need. There are so far no comprehensive descriptive English-language grammars of contemporary (2018) Hazara Hindko, Lahore Panjabi, or Multan Saraiki. Important existing grammars of Majhi Panjabi are mostly based on the Ludhiana or Amritsar dialects as they were before 1947. Bhatia (1993), for instance, is "primarily based on the Majhi dialect spoken in Lahore (Pakistan) and Amritsar, and the Gurdaspur district of the state of Punjab, India, as it was before the partition of the Indian subcontinent in 1947" (p. xxxii). Bahl (1969) is based on the Majhi dialect of Amritsar (pre-partition). Malik (1995) is "based mainly on the Majhi dialect spoken in the districts of Amritsar, Lahore, and Gurdaspur which constituted the central districts of [...] unpartitioned Panjab" (p. viii). Interestingly, of major published works, Cummings and Bailey (1912), though based on Bailey (1904b), which is subtitled "A brief grammar of Panjābī as spoken in the Wazīrābād District", comes closer to describing contemporary Lahore Panjabi (minus the heavy Urdu influence) than the other works mentioned. Perhaps this is because Lahore Panjabi is now a considerably mixed variety, and Wazirabad Panjabi of 1904 fell into that class of varieties considered by Bahl (1970) as extensive transitional areas between Lahnda in the west and Panjabi.

Although Peshawar Hindko has a better-established written literary tradition, Hazara Hindko has been chosen for treatment here because the largest number of Hindko speakers speak this cluster of varieties. "Hindko is most widely used in Hazara Division. [...] Abbottabad district in particular is heavily weighted toward Hindko, with more than 176,000 (92.31 percent) households speaking it as a first language. Mansehra, the other district in Hazara Division, also has a large Hindko population, accounting for 73,500 (46.8 percent) households and representing the largest single linguistic group" (Addleton 1986: 38). Also, it is more different from Lahore Panjabi than is Peshawar Hindko, which, like Lahore Panjabi, shows some characteristics of "big

https://doi.org/10.1515/9781614512257-002

city" speech—that is, speech which draws its features from a variety of sources.[1] Also, while there are at least two English-language discussions of Peshawar Hindko available (Shackle 1980 and Toker 2014), there is as yet, to our knowledge, no such published description of Hazara Hindko.

The Saraiki of Multan belongs to Shackle's Central Saraiki classification. Central Saraiki varieties are spoken in Districts Multan and Muzaffargarh, and northern Dera Ghazi Khan and Bahawalpur (Shackle 1976: 6). It has been chosen for renewed attention here because it is the major vehicle of literary expression in Saraiki. Multan is also the home of important Saraiki literary and cultural organizations, like the Saraiki Adabi Board. Shackle's 1976 grammar is comprehensive and authoritative, but it does not include analyzed and glossed examples of Saraiki written in Perso-Arabic script.

2.2 The language names

In his *Linguistic Survey of India* (1919), Grierson used the term *Lahnda*, 'west', to refer to the languages spoken to the west of Panjabi, including those today referred to as (varieties of) Hindko and Saraiki, as well as some still referred to by their local names—for example, Riyasati for the speech of Bahawalpur. No speakers of these varieties referred to their own languages as *Lahnda*; rather, they used names referring to local communities—for example, *Awankari*, the language of the Awan tribe, *Shahpuri*, the language of the town of Shahpur (near Sargodha), or *Multani*, the language of Multan (today's *Saraiki*). Grierson (and others among his contemporaries) considered these language varieties as constituting a group called *Lahnda*, and considered it clearly different from Panjabi. Some of these are now simply classified as Panjabi. Even District Gujranwala in Grierson's day was considered a partially Lahnda-speaking area.

The name *Panjabi* (also *Punjabi*) derives from the name of the geographical area in which it has traditionally been spoken, the (Persian) *panj-āb* '[land of] five waters'—that is, the five tributaries of the Indus that flow through modern-day northwest India and eastern Pakistan.[2] *Hindko* contains the element *hind-*, cognate with *sind-* 'river', as in *Hindustan*. It is thought to have originally designated the languages of the Indus Valley, as opposed to Iranian languages like Pashto.

The preferred spelling for the name of the language of southern Punjab in Pakistani universities today is *Saraiki* (originally *Siraiki*, also *Seraiki*).[3] Two etymologies are proposed for this name. The first derives it from *siro* 'a name for Upper Sindh', and

1 "Big city speech" is discussed for German dialects in Leopold (1968).

2 In this book, the name of the language is consistently spelled *Panjabi*, while the spelling *Punjabi* refers to political or administrative units or to institutions related to such units; for example, Punjab Province or Punjab University.

3 Comparison of these three spellings using Google's Ngram viewer yields a picture of the historical trends in their use.

the second from the ancient city name *Sauvira*. It is possible that the first derivation is relevant for the variety of Siraiki spoken in northern Sindh, and the second for the Saraiki language of southern Punjab to which it is now applied. Grierson explained the ambiguity present in the word *Siraiki* as follows. "From 'Siro' is derived 'Siraiki', which thus means 'the language of the upstream country'. It is evident that this can have two meanings. Either it may mean 'the Sindhi spoken in Upper Sindh,' or it may mean 'the Lahnda spoken higher up the Indus than Sindh,' and, as a matter of fact, it is used in Sindh in both these senses (1894–1928: 9)". Raza (2016) advocates the second explanation, arguing for a derivation *sauvira* > *sauvira* + the language-name suffix *-ki* > *saraiki* (by simplification). Whatever the origin of the name, today in 2019, the current name, Saraiki, clearly designates the language of the middle Indus Valley or southern Punjab. It was adopted in the 1960s as a result of cultural activities initiated by Riaz Anwar, a lawyer from Muzaffargarh (Rahman 1995).

2.3 The languages and their speakers

Figure 2.1: Map of Pakistan and environs with political boundaries

The languages in the Hindko-Panjabi-Saraiki (H-P-S) language area share many linguistic features, and are mutually intelligible to a greater or lesser degree. In addition to contact phenomena involving these languages, they have also undergone intensive contact from superstratal languages for many centuries, particularly Persian and, more recently, Urdu and English. Given this degree of language convergence, it would be difficult to delineate clear dividing lines between varieties of Panjabi and other languages spoken in adjacent regions.

Shackle (1979) discusses the complexities of language classification in Punjab. The term *Hindko*, for example, is applied variously to the Indo-Aryan language spoken in parts of Khyber Pakhtunkhwa (the former North West Frontier Province), the Potohar Plateau, and Hazara District, as well as, occasionally, to what is now usually referred to as Saraiki (Grierson 1968[1916]). There are, in fact, many varieties of Hindko. Shackle (1980) describes differences between the Hindko spoken in non-urban areas in Khyber Pakhtunkhwa, especially Kohat city, and that of Peshawar. (See also Lothers and Lothers 2010 for detailed discussion of other varieties.)

Boundaries between the H-P-S area, however, and Dardic languages to the north, Pashto to the west, and Sindhi and Balochi to the south and southwest are relatively clear (Shackle 2003: 583). Its southeastern boundary is somewhat less clear, as H-P-S forms the northwestern part of a linguistic continuum which includes Urdu, the central Indic varieties from Bihar to Rajasthan collectively referred to as Hindi, and some of the closely related languages of northern India, such as Gujarati and Marathi.

Panjabi is spoken in both Pakistan and India (See Figure 2.1). Saraiki is spoken in the central Indus Valley, in southern Punjab; and Hindko is found to the north and west of Panjabi extending as far west as Peshawar (See Figure 2.2).[4]

4 In places, Panjabi, Hindko, and Pashto border on Gujari-speaking areas (Hallberg and O'Leary 1992: 90).

Figure 2.2: Language varieties of the Punjab region

2.3.1 Hindko

In this work, *Hindko* refers to the language varieties spoken mostly in the Mansehra, Abbottabad, Haripur, Peshawar, Kohat, and Dera Ismail Khan Districts of Khyber Pakhtunkhwa and in the Attock and Rawalpindi Districts of Punjab (Rensch, Hallberg, and O'Leary 1992: 7). The majority of Hindko-speakers live in Abbottabad and Mansehra Districts of Hazara; we therefore focus here on Hazara Hindko.

In the 1981 census Saraiki and Hindko were listed for the first time as separate categories; in previous censuses, both had been included together with Punjabi (Addleton

1986: 35). According to this census, 2.43 percent of Pakistani households listed Hindko as the primary language spoken. In the 1998 census, however, Hindko speakers were, once more, not counted separately (Pakistan, Government of 2001: 339). Lewis, Simons, and Fennig (2015) gives a 1993 estimate of about three million total Hindko speakers in Pakistan.

Currently, the Gandhara Hindko Board and Gandhara Hindko Academy, based in Peshawar (http://www.gandharahindko.com), are active in organizing cultural events and conferences promoting the recognition and use of the Hindko language.

2.3.2 Panjabi

In Pakistan, there are some 77 million speakers of Panjabi, where it is by far the most widely spoken first language. The varieties of Panjabi spoken in Pakistan are collectively referred to as Western or Pakistani Panjabi. According to 1998 census figures, 44.1 percent of Pakistanis speak Panjabi as their first language, making it the most widely spoken first language. In India, Panjabi is the official language of the state of Punjab, and also one of the national languages recognized in the Eighth Schedule of the Indian Constitution. Large numbers of Panjabi speakers also live in the neighboring states of Haryana and Himachal Pradesh, as well as the cities of Delhi and Chandigarh. In total, there are some 33 million Panjabi speakers in India. There are also large Panjabi-speaking expatriate and diasporic communities in the United Kingdom, Canada, and the United States, as well as throughout the Persian Gulf.

2.3.3 Saraiki

Saraiki is spoken mainly in and around the cities of Multan, Muzaffargarh, Mianwali, Rahimyar Khan, and Bahawalpur in the southern region of Pakistani Punjab, and in District Dera Ismail Khan in Khyber Pakhtunkhwa. Since Independence, Pakistan has held six official censuses—in 1951, 1961, 1972, 1981, 1998, and 2017. Saraiki was included with Panjabi in the 1951, 1961 and 1971 (held in 1972) counts, and only became an independent option in the 1981 census. According to the 1998 national census, it is spoken as a first language by around eleven million people, or 10.5 percent of respondents, in Pakistan as a whole, making it the fourth most widely spoken first language in Pakistan. The 1998 Punjab Population Census Report lists Saraiki as the first language of 17.4 percent of respondents in Punjab (Javaid 2004: 46). In the 2017 census, Saraiki is listed as mother tongue by 12.19% of the population on the national level and by 20.68% of the population in Punjab Province (https://defence.pk/pdf/threads/census-2017-language-data.560777/). Since the 1960s a Saraiki nationalist movement has been active in Pakistani politics (Rahman 1995: 4; Javaid 2004).

2.3.4 Other related languages

Although in this work we focus on Hazara Hindko, Lahore Panjabi, and Multan Saraiki, it is worth noting several other closely related varieties which, for reasons of space, time, and available data, we have not addressed in this work.

2.3.4.1 Pothwari

Pothwari (also spelled Pothohari)-Pahari refers to a complex continuum of varieties spoken from the Potohar Plateau in western Punjab to Jhelum District and north to the Rawalpindi and Murree Districts, as well as in Mirpur, in Pakistan-controlled Kashmir. This hyphenated term reflects the fact that it covers numerous varieties spread over a wide area; some people, especially those in the Murree hills, refer to their language as "Pahari" (پہاڑی /pahāṛī/ 'mountain language'), while varieties found in the Pothwar Plateau are often called "Pothwari" or other local names like "Ghebi". Estimates put the total number of Pothwari speakers at around 2.5 million in Pakistan, with an additional half million outside of Pakistan (Lothers and Lothers 2010: 9).

2.3.4.2 Dogri

In 2001 there were approximately 2.3 million speakers of Dogri in India (Census of India 2001).[5] In India, where Dogri enjoys a vibrant literary and cultural scene, it is the main language of Jammu Province. Like Panjabi, Dogri has phonemic tone. It is also spoken in some parts of northern Punjab in Pakistan, but the number of speakers is difficult to estimate, since there is no separate category for Dogri on the Pakistani census forms, and it would fall into the "others" category.

2.4 Historical background

These languages were much more different from each other in the past than they are today (2019). Several earlier writers have noted this. For instance, according to the Ain-i-Akbari, in the time of the Mughal emperor Akbar I ("Akbar the Great"), who ruled from 1556 to 1605, the languages of Delhi and Multan were not mutually intelligible (Bahawalpuri and Bashir 1981: 3). Jukes (1900: v) noted that "The Western Punjabi or Jatki language is quite a different language from that spoken in the Eastern Punjab." Grierson (1915: 226) said: "The whole Panjab is the meeting ground of two entirely distinct languages, viz., the Piśâcha parent of Lahndâ which expanded from the Indus Valley eastwards, and the old Midland language, the parent of the modern Western

5 http://www.censusindia.gov.in/Census_Data_2001/Census_Data_Online/Language/Statement5.aspx. Figures from the 2010–2011 Census are not yet available.

Hindî, which expanded from the Jamna Valley westwards. In the Panjâb they overlapped." Grierson grouped Lahnda and Sindhi together as Northwestern Indo-Aryan languages, in contrast to Panjabi, which he considered a Central Indo-Aryan language.

In 1979, Shackle found "a maximal contrast between Siraiki, which has the typical complexities of conservatism, and Panjabi (closely allied to Pothohari), which has many innovating simplifications, with Hindko occupying an intermediate position" (Shackle 1979: 203). Today these languages continue to converge, and there is considerable mutual intelligibility among them, the degree varying with the degree of education and exposure to other languages of the individual speakers involved. For example, most speakers of Multan Saraiki can understand most of Lahore Panjabi, and most speakers of Lahore Panjabi can understand some Multan Saraiki.

As long ago as 1962, Hardev Bahri foresaw the developments that are reflected in this book: "Although Sir George Grierson has rightly excluded a part of Montgomery and Gujranwala and whole of Lahore and Sialkot Districts from the Lahndi tract, the time is not far off when these areas will be totally affected by Lahndi dialects lying to their west. The migration of population since the partition of India and the formation of West Pakistan into a single unit are some of the factors which are bound to shift the eastern boundary of Lahndi to the political border. For centuries, it has been noted, eastern Punjabi has pushed Lahndi further to the west, but the events since 1947 have not only stopped that encroachment by eastern Punjabi, but given Lahndi a chance to retrieve its position in the eastern districts of West Pakistan which has now no communication with the Indian tracts where eastern Punjabi is vastly spoken" (Bahri 1962: x).

The linguistic situation in Lahore is particularly complex because of the massive migration which took place in 1947, when the partition of British India split the province of Punjab between India and Pakistan. Nearly 12.5 million people in and outside of Punjab were displaced as a result of the partition, with many Muslim Punjabis relocating from India to Pakistan and many Sikh and Hindu Punjabis moving from Pakistan to India.

Contemporary (2019) Lahore Panjabi has diverged considerably since 1947 from the Panjabi spoken in India, so that the speech of Lahore is now quite different from that of Amritsar and Gurdaspur, all three of which were formerly considered together as the Majhi variety (Malik 1995: viii). The varieties on the Indian side of the border have come under the heavy influence of Hindi and Sanskrit, while Lahore Panjabi and, to a somewhat lesser extent, Hindko and Saraiki, have been influenced by Urdu. Additionally, since Lahore is the major urban center of Punjab Province in Pakistan, features of varieties spoken farther west and south of Lahore have entered the language. Lahore Panjabi thus displays typical features of "big city speech".

Panjabi and Saraiki literary languages can be traced through a continuous literary tradition dating back to the twelfth century. There is a long and rich tradition of Muslim Sufi literature and poetry in Panjabi and Saraiki that extends to the present day. Beginning in the sixteenth century, Sikhism developed in the Punjab, and much of the

Sikh canon, including the Adi Granth, is written in an early form of a mixed language which includes elements of Panjabi, Khari Boli, and what has become today's Saraiki. Shackle (1983: ii) stresses the mixed character of the language, as the Adi Granth scriptures contain many archaic forms and draw on a number of local languages; these are discussed in detail in Shackle (1977) and Shackle (1978).

Today (2019) Panjabi has a robust literary life in India, but this has been less so in Pakistan. The first Panjabi-language newspaper, *Sajjan*, survived only from February 1989 to September 1990. Recently, some online Panjabi-language newspapers have appeared; these include *Bhulekha*, with a presence on Facebook and *Lokaai* (http://lokaai.com). At present, only *Khabran*, based in Lahore, appears to have a print edition.[6] The website apnaorg.com publishes a quarterly Panjabi magazine *Sānjh*, with identical content in Gurmukhi and Perso-Arabic versions. Saraiki, despite its smaller number of speakers, has a relatively large literary production and three regularly published newspapers: *Kook* (Karachi), *Jhok* (Multan, and with a Facebook presence) and *Al-Manzoor* (Taunsa Sharif). Peshawar Hindko is used in *The Hindkowan*, *The Gandhara Voice*, *Sarkhail*, and a children's magazine *Tarey*. Abbottabad Hindko so far has less published literature or journalism.

Prior to Partition, colonial policy in the Punjab promoted the use of Persian and, later, Urdu in official contexts (Mir 2010: passim). After Partition, Urdu became even more closely associated with Muslim identity, and specifically with South Asian Islam. Despite being the most widely spoken language in Pakistan, Panjabi has no official status there. Historically relegated to use in informal, personal contexts, Panjabi and other local languages began to gain support during the administration of Prime Minister Zulfiqar Ali Bhutto (1973–1977). Bhutto, who came from Sindh, promoted local vernaculars, including Panjabi. During this period, the state established regional literary boards including the Pakistan Punjabi Adabi Board, and the University of Punjab established a Department of Punjabi. However, this period came to an end following the coup that brought General Zia ul-Haq to power in 1977, and many Punjabi writers and film makers saw their works censored or banned. Since the mid-1980s, however, Panjabi literature and film and the valorization of Punjabi identity have begun to revive in Pakistan (Ayres 2009: passim).

Nevertheless, Panjabi itself continues to be absent from official discourse. Urdu is the only national language of Pakistan, as decreed in the Constitution, although both Urdu and English can be used for official purposes.[7] Urdu and English remain the prestige languages of the Pakistani elite (Ayres 2009: 73).

---

6 See http://www.dawn.com/news/632447/another-daily-in-punjabi for historical discussion of Panjabi-language journalism in Pakistan.

7 The Constitution of the Islamic Republic of Pakistan, 1973, Chapter 4, Section 251, Clause 1–2 stated that both Urdu and English could function as official languages, but that English was to be phased out within fifteen years. In response to complaints that English was still being predominantly used in official matters, a Supreme Court of Pakistan decision ruled on September

2.5 Writing systems

In India, Panjabi is written in Gurmukhi ('speech of the mouth of the Guru') script, which ultimately derives from the Brahmi script. Gurmukhi has been in use since possibly the eleventh century, but came to be standardized in the sixteenth century by the second Sikh guru, or teacher, Guru Angad Dev Ji. Sikhs consider learning Gurmukhi a religious duty, as it enables them to read the Sikh holy text, the Adi Granth (Rahman 2007: 28).

In Pakistan, Hindko, Panjabi, and Saraiki are all written in a modified Perso-Arabic script, preferably in the Nastaʿlīq calligraphic style, which is sometimes called "Shahmukhi" or 'speech of the mouth of the king', a name modeled on "Gurmukhi" 'mouth of the Guru'. Muslim writers of Panjabi have been using this script since the seventeenth century. In most respects, it is identical to the script used to write Urdu; some writers, however, have tried to introduce conventions to capture phonological contrasts not present in Urdu (see Malik 1995). Panjabi spelling in Perso-Arabic has not yet been entirely standardized (Shackle 2003: 598) (See Section 3.6 for more detailed discussion). Orthographic conventions for Saraiki are more firmly established than those of Hindko. While representation of most Saraiki consonant sounds is identical to that of Panjabi, Saraiki writers have adopted an additional five distinct, non-Urdu letters to represent the four implosive consonants and the retroflex nasal (see Section 3.6.5 on Saraiki orthography). Orthographic conventions for Hindko are less standardized; most Hindko writers use the same set of letters used in Urdu and Panjabi to represent their language, but there is considerable variation in spelling, especially of vowel sounds (see Section 3.6.4 on Hindko orthography).

8, 2015 that Section 251 should be implemented with all possible speed and English be replaced with Urdu for all official functions.

3 Phonology and Orthography

3.1 Introduction

This chapter introduces the *phonology*, or sound patterns, of Hindko, Panjabi, and Saraiki; defines the transcription, in letters familiar to readers of English in the Roman script that is used in this grammar; and relates the sounds and their transcription to the *orthography*, or writing system used to represent these languages. In Pakistan, all three languages are written in the Perso-Arabic script, originally used to represent Arabic, expanded with additional letters to accommodate the sounds of Persian, and then further modified to represent sounds and phonological contrasts present in Urdu. Writers of Panjabi have mostly continued to use the unmodified Urdu script, though there is concern in some circles that two of the salient sounds of Panjabi are not represented in Urdu script—that is, retroflex /ɳ/ and /ɭ/, which we represent in this grammar as /ṇ/ and /ḷ/. This is less of a concern for Hindko, whose writers do represent retroflex /ṇ/ as a nasalized retroflex /ṛ̃/, and not at all for Saraiki, since the Saraiki-speaking community has developed and adopted unique letters to represent the sounds of their language.

3.2 Transcription: Definitions and conventions

In this grammar, we provide all words and example sentences in both Perso-Arabic orthography (described in Section 3.6) and in a Roman transcription. Transcription is distinct from transliteration. *Transcription* is a way of representing the *sounds*[1] of a language using a single letter or pair of letters for each; we have chosen letters that are likely to guide readers familiar with English to an approximation of the pronunciation of these languages, with some additions from the International Phonetic Alphabet (IPA). *Transliteration*, by contrast, is a way of representing the *letters* of one language's writing system using the letters of another language's writing system. The goal of transliteration is to simplify the representation of written text of one language using the writing system of another language, preferably in a way that allows knowledgeable readers to recover the original written version. The goal of transcription, however, and the goal of this grammar, is to help the reader understand how words and sentences are pronounced, regardless of how they may be written. To assist the reader in this, we have normalized the romanization of examples taken from secondary sources to the system used in this grammar.

1 In this book, we use a *phonemic* transcription, which represents the sounds that distinguish meaning in these languages, rather than a more fine-grained, *phonetic* transcription, which captures objective differences between sounds that may not be used to distinguish meaning in them.

https://doi.org/10.1515/9781614512257-003

Two aspects of these languages make transcription preferable to transliteration. First, due to inheritance of letters from Arabic and Persian for sounds which are not part of the phonology of Indo-Aryan languages like Hindko, Panjabi, and Saraiki, in several cases there are multiple letters for one sound—four characters for the sound /z/, three for /s/, and two for /h/ and for /t/. Therefore, any transliteration system for these languages that would allow readers to recover the original text would also have to assign multiple Roman letters to the same sound. We feel that if the goal is to pronounce and understand the spoken language, such transliterations would not be helpful. Second, the orthography of these languages—like most orthographies based on the Perso-Arabic writing system—marks centralized, or "short," vowels only sporadically. By providing both Perso-Arabic orthography and a transcription for each word and example sentence, we can present the languages as they are normally written in Perso-Arabic script, without centralized vowel symbols, while fully representing centralized vowels in the transcription.

In this grammar, material transcribed from Hindko, Panjabi, and Saraiki is placed in slanting brackets, like this: /transcription/. In cases where it is necessary to emphasize a difference between our transcription and the orthography, we place a transliteration in angled brackets, like this: <transliteration>. In cases where it is necessary to emphasize a difference between our transcription and a word's pronunciation, the pronunciation is given in square brackets, like this: [pronunciation].

- رہیا 'live.PP.SG.M'

  Transcription: /ryā́/

  Transliteration: <rahiyā>

  Pronunciation: [ryā́][2]

3.3 Segments

In phonology, a *segment* is understood as a discrete unit that is clearly identifiable in a linear sequence of sounds and thus separable for purposes of analysis and discussion. We first discuss consonantal segments, and then vowels and diphthongs.

2 The transcription and the pronunciation in this example use the acute accent to mark high tone. See Section 3.4.1.2 on tone in Panjabi and Hindko and Section 3.6.2.3 on the historical spellings that indirectly indicate tone.

3.3.1 Consonants

Observations in this section are relevant for the consonant systems of all three languages, both individually and from a comparative perspective. The consonant systems of Panjabi and Hindko are quite similar, but that of Saraiki is significantly different.

The following tables present the consonant segments that are contrastive in Hindko and Panjabi—that is, sounds that distinguish one word from another. In traditional linguistic terminology, these are the *phonemes* of the language. Table 3.1 and Table 3.2 present the consonants in terms of *places* and *manners* of articulation for all three languages—that is, the parts of the mouth (and/or nose or throat) where the sounds are produced, and how they are produced—whether, for example, by stopping the airflow (as in a plosive) or by causing turbulence in the airflow (as in a fricative). For Saraiki consonants, see Table 3.7 below. In these three tables, the sounds are represented according to the International Phonetic Alphabet (IPA).

Symbols in parentheses represent sounds that are marginal in the Hindko, Panjabi, and Saraiki sound systems. In Panjabi and Saraiki, the *fricatives* /x/ and /ɣ/ and the voiceless uvular *plosive* /q/ occur only in words originating in Arabic and Persian, while the fricatives /f/, /ž/, and /z/ also occur, increasingly frequently, in English loans as well as in words of Perso-Arabic origin. Most urban language users have no problem in pronouncing /f/, which can also merge with or be pronounced as /pʰ/, or in pronouncing /z/, which can also merge with /ʤ/. For those Panjabi and Saraiki speakers unfamiliar with Urdu, however, /x/ tends to be pronounced as /kʰ/ and /ɣ/ as /g/. For practically all speakers of these languages, original /q/ is pronounced as /k/ (Shackle 2003: 589; Bhatia 1993: 331). In this grammar, each of these sounds is represented according to the normal educated pronunciation—i.e., we retain /x/ and /ɣ/ in transcriptions of Perso-Arabic خ and غ if if they are really pronounced in that way, but use <kh> or <g> if the words are pronounced with these sounds. On the other hand, we represent orthographic /ق/ as /k/, as it is always pronounced. This reflects the historical origin of the lexical items in which they appear, their representation in present-day orthography, and their actual pronunciation.

		Bilabial	Labiodental	Dental	Retroflex	Palatal	Velar	Uvular	Glottal
Plosive	**voiceless unaspirated**	p		t̪	ʈ		k	q	
	voiceless aspirated	pʰ		t̪ʰ	ʈʰ		kʰ		
	voiced	b		d̪	ɖ		g		
Nasal		m		n̪	ɽ̃				
Tap or Flap				ɾ	ɽ				
Fricative	**voiceless**		f	s		ʃ	x		
	voiced			z		(ʒ)	ɣ		ɦ
Affricate	**voiceless unaspirated**					ʧ			
	voiceless aspirated					ʧʱ			
	voiced					ʤ			
Approximant			ʋ			j			
Lateral approximant				l					

Table 3.1: Consonants of Hindko (IPA representation)

		Bilabial	Labiodental	Dental	Retroflex	Palatal	Velar	Uvular	Glottal
Plosive	**voiceless unaspirated**	p		t̪	ʈ		k	(q)	
	voiceless aspirated	pʰ		t̪ʰ	ʈʰ		kʰ		
	voiced	b		d̪	ɖ		g		
Nasal		m		n̪	ɳ				
Tap or Flap				ɾ	ɽ				
Fricative	**voiceless**		f	s		ʃ	(x)		
	voiced			z		(ʒ)	(ɣ)		ɦ
Affricate	**voiceless unaspirated**					ʧ			
	voiceless aspirated					ʧʰ			
	voiced					ʤ			
Approximant			ʋ			j			
Lateral approximant				l	ɭ				

Table 3.2: Consonants of Panjabi (IPA representation)

Retroflex /ṇ/ and /ḷ/ (/ɳ/ and /ɭ/ in IPA) contrast with dental /n/ and /l/ in Lahore Panjabi, although this distinction is weakening with the younger generation of urban speakers. In this grammar we represent the retroflexion of nasals and laterals, while bearing in mind that in the current Panjabi orthography /ṇ/ is represented only sporadically, and /ḷ/ is not represented at all. Retroflexes in Hindko and Panjabi, as well as Saraiki, are not as strongly retroflexed as those in Hindi or the Dravidian languages.

Certain consonants have predictable variant pronunciations, or *allophones*, when they co-occur with other consonants. The dental nasal /n/ may be realized as a *velar* nasal [ŋ] when it occurs before velar plosives /k/, /kh/ or /g/, or as a *palatal* nasal [ɲ] when it occurs before palatal affricates /c/, /ch/, and /j/ (Shackle 2003: 590; Bhatia 1993: 333–334). Similarly, the voiceless *palatal* fricative /š/ may be realized as a voiceless retroflex fricative [ʂ] in clusters with the voiceless retroflex plosive /ṭ/ (Shackle 2003: 590), although this particular cluster is rare, occurring mostly in learned or Eastern Panjabi words. See also the discussion of consonant clusters in Section 3.5.

- رنگ 'color'

  Transcription: /rang/

  Pronunciation: [rɑŋg] before another vowel, [raŋ] in isolation

- چُنجھ 'beak'

  Transcription: /cúnj/

  Pronunciation: [cúɲj]

- مشٹنڈا 'rogue, hoodlum'

  Transcription: /mašṭanḍā/

  Pronunciation: [maʂʈanɖā]

In the text of this grammar, the consonants of Hindko, Panjabi, and Saraiki are transcribed using the Roman letters and combinations of letters shown in Table 3.3.

Sound in IPA	Transcription	Sound in IPA	Transcription
p	p	ɳ	ṇ
pʰ	ph	ɽ̃	ṛ̃
b	b	ɽ	ṛ
ɓ	ɓ	ɭ	ḷ
m	m	ʄ	ʄ
f	f	ʃ	š
ʋ	v	ʒ	ž
t̪	t	ʧ	c
t̪ʰ	th	ʧʰ	ch
d̪	d	ʤ	j
n̪	n	j	y
ɾ	r	k	k
s	s	kʰ	kh
z	z	ɡ	ɡ
l	l	ɠ	ɠ
ʈ	ṭ	x	x
ʈʰ	ṭh	ɣ	ɣ
ɖ	ḍ	q	q
ɗ	ɗ	ɦ	h

Table 3.3: IPA representation and transcription of consonant sounds

3.3.1.1 Hindko consonants

The only two analyses of Hindko phonology available to us are separated from today's (2018) Hazara Hindko by either time (Varma 1936) or space (Rashid and Akhtar 2012). Therefore, any statements about Hazara Hindko phonology made here must be understood as tentative. Clearly, instrumental study and both phonetic and phonological analysis are needed for (all varieties of) Hindko.

The consonant phonemes of Abbottabad Hindko are mostly the same as those of Panjabi, and are represented by the same Perso-Arabic letters that are used for Panjabi. However, the voiceless velar fricative /x/ appears to have become a native sound in Hindko, since in Hindko /x/ spontaneously appears in words which in Panjabi or Urdu have /kh/ (see Table 3.3). The retroflex /ṇ/ sound is perceived by many as a nasalized retroflex /ṛ̃/ and spelled by most writers of Abbottabad Hindko as ڑ (as is done in some areas for Pashto and Peshawar Hindko).[3] However some (for example, Sakoon 2002) use the character ݨ, which is regularly used for Saraiki retroflex /ṇ/. There is no retroflex /ḷ/ in Hazara Hindko.

3.3.1.2 Sound correspondences between Hindko and Panjabi

There are some regular sound correspondences between Panjabi and Hindko. For example, many words which have /v/ in Panjabi have /b/ in Hindko (Table 3.4).

Gloss	Panjabi	Hindko
'in'	وچ vic	بچ bic
'also'	وی vī	بی bī
'hours, o'clock'	وجے vaje	بجے baje
'bride'	وہوٹی ~ ووہٹی vɔ̃ṭī	بوہٹی bɔ̃ṭī

Table 3.4: Correspondences between /v/ and /b/ in Panjabi and Hindko

3 Shackle (1980: 500) cites the form اپڑا /apṛā/ 'one's own', which occurs in Abbottabad Hindko, as an instance of loss of nasalization from phonetic [ṛ̃].

Aspirated /kh/ in Panjabi often corresponds to /x/ in Hindko in word-medial position following a stressed vowel.[4] The words in Table 3.5, in which the stressed syllables are in boldface type, illustrate this.

Gloss	Panjabi	Hindko
'to see, look at'	ویکھنا **vekh**ṇā	دیخڑا **dex**ṛ̃ā
'to place, put, keep'	رکھنا **rakh**ṇā	رخڑا **rax**ṛ̃ā
'to say'	آکھنا **ākh**ṇā	آخڑا **āx**ṛ̃ā

Table 3.5: Correspondences between /kh/ and /x/ in Panjabi and Hindko

Word-initial /h/ in Hindko frequently corresponds to Panjabi /s/ or ∅, as exemplified in Table 3.6.

Gloss	Panjabi	Hindko
'one'	اک ikk	ہک hikk
'to be able'	سکنا sakṇā	ہکنڑا hakṇā

Table 3.6: Correspondences between word-initial vowel or /s/, and /h/ in Panjabi and Hindko

4 Varma (1936: 77) discusses the /kh/ > /x/ change, but mentions this change only before plosives; e.g. /likh ke/ ~ /lix ke/ 'having written' (Varma 1936: 82), /ˈākhda/ ~ /āxda/, 'saying', or /likh ca/ ~ /lix ca/ 'just write'. Perhaps this change has expanded its scope in Hindko since Varma's time. Nasir Abbas Syed (p.c.), hereafter abbreviated as NAS, comments that this does not happen in Multan Saraiki.

3.3.1.3 Saraiki consonants

There are significant differences between Saraiki phonology and that of Hindko and Panjabi. In the consonant system, shown in Table 3.7, the main points of difference are:

1. Saraiki has four voiced implosive stops: bilabial /ɓ/, alveolar /ɗ/, palatal /ʄ/, and velar /ɠ/. The pronunciation of implosives involves the larynx being lowered, creating negative pressure in the mouth, and the breath being very briefly drawn in before being released (Catford 1982: 73–77). None of these implosive stop consonant sounds occur in either Panjabi or Hindko, and since they are difficult for non-Saraiki speakers to pronounce they are the primary shibboleth for Saraiki, and are a major focus of many accounts of the language by Saraiki writers.

2. Retroflex /ḷ/ is not found in Saraiki.

3. Aspiration of voiced consonants (also known as "breathy voice") has not been lost in Saraiki, as it has in Hindko and Panjabi, and even the nasals, laterals, and semivowels have aspirated : unaspirated pairs. Aspiration in Saraiki shows many interesting features, including the loss of historical aspiration without the development of tone after a preceding aspirate, e.g. /ṭhaḍhā/ > /ṭhaḍḍā/ ٹھڈا 'cold (adj.)'; occasional spontaneous loss of historical aspiration, e.g. /caṛhaṇ/ > /caṛaṇ/ چڑݨ 'to climb'; and a tendency to transfer /h/ to adjacent voiced consonants to form voiced aspirates, e.g. /pandrãh/ > /pandhrã/ پندرھاں ~ پندھراں '15' (Shackle 1976: 30–36).[5]

4. Retroflex /ṇ/ is robustly present and is now represented consistently in the orthography with ݨ which emphasizes the phonemic contrast with ن rather than representing the phonetic nature of /ṇ/ as [ɽ̃], that is, a nasalized retroflex /ɽ/. Some earlier writers represented this phoneme by using the digraph نڑ, but this practice has lost ground to the use of ݨ.

According to Shackle (1976: 18), Shackle (2003: 590), Latif (2003: 94–95), and Syed and Aldaihani (2014), palatal and velar nasals are distinct phonemes in Saraiki. Contrastive pairs supporting this analysis include: velar vs. alveolar nasal, رنگ /raŋ/ 'color' vs. رن /ran/ 'woman, wife'; palatal vs. velar nasal, ونڄ /vãʄ-/ 'go' vs. وانگو /vāŋu/ 'like, similar to'. Compare also وڄ /vaʄ-/ 'strike'. This point has been debated among Saraiki writers, but the view advocating separate letters for these two sounds has not prevailed, and the currently accepted orthography does not include separate letters to

5 Shackle presents this as /pandhrã/, but Mughal (2010: 233) and Zahoor (2009: 79) give it as پندرھاں /pandarhã̄/

represent the palatal and velar nasals (see Shackle 2003: 598 for some of the proposed characters). This has resulted in some (according to the analysis in Shackle 1976, for example) phonologically inaccurate but forced spellings, e.g. the spelling of the stem of the verb 'go' as ونڄ /vãʄ-/, with the implosive palatal fricative, rather than as ونج representing actual /vãj-/ with a nasalized /a/ and the palatal fricative (in the absence of a unique character for the palatal nasal). This question is still not settled, but could perhaps be resolved by instrumental studies.

Table 3.7: Consonants of Saraiki, adapted from Shackle (1976) and Syed and Aldaihani (2014) (IPA representations)

		Bilabial	Labiodental	Dental	Alveolar	Retroflex	Palatal	Velar	Glottal
Plosive	**voiceless unaspirated**	p		t̪		ʈ	c	k	
	voiceless aspirated	pʰ		t̪ʰ		ʈʰ	cʰ	kʰ	
	voiced	b		d̪		ɖ	ɟ	g	
	voiced aspirated	bʰ		d̪ʰ		ɖʰ	ɟʰ	gʰ	
Implosive	**unaspirated**	ɓ			ɗ		ʄ	ɠ	
Nasal	**unaspirated**	m			n	ɳ	ɲ	ŋ	
	aspirated	mʰ			nʰ	ɳʰ			
Fricative	**voiceless**		f		s		ʃ	x	
	voiced		ʋ		z		ʒ	ɣ	ɦ
	voiced aspirated		ʋʰ						
Flap or Trill	**unaspirated**				r	ɽ			
	aspirated				rʰ	ɽʰ			
Lateral	**unaspirated**				l				
	aspirated				lʰ				
Approximant							j		

Minimal pairs for the implosive stops and for the palatal and velar nasals are given here (Latif 2003: 94–95; Kalanchvi 1979/1981). [6]

- /b/: /ɓ/
  بس /bas/ 'bus': ٻس /ɓas/ 'enough'
- /g/: /ɠ/
  گول /gol/ 'round': ڳول /ɠol-/ 'search'
- /j/: /ʄ/
  جالا /jālā/ 'niche or hole in a wall used as a cupboard': ڄالا /ʄālā/ 'cobweb'
- /ḍ/: /ɗ/: /d/
  ڈاہݨ /ḍāhaṇ/ 'to fall': ݙاٻ /ɗāɓ/ 'dust, soil': دابھ /dābh/ 'under the foot'
- /ɲ/: /ṇ/
  ونڄ /vaɲʄ-/ 'go!': وݨ /vaṇ/ 'a tree'
- /n/: /ŋ/
  رن /ran/ 'wife': رنگ /raŋ/ 'color'

Minimal pairs for unaspirated and aspirated labiodental approximants follow (Nasir Abbas Syed, p.c.):

- /v/: /vh/
  رواں /ravā̃/ 'running, functional': روھاں /ravhā̃/ 'cowpeas, a species of legume, Vigna unguiculata'
- /v/: /vh/
  نویں /navvẽ/ 'new pl.m': نوھیں /navvhẽ/ 'fingernails'

6 A very few words having an aspirated alveo-palatal nasal sound exist. The three such words found by Nasir Abbas Syed are کنڄھا /kañhā/ 'later variety of fruit; tree which yields fruit after the season', منڄھر /mañhar/ 'bull/ox which is impotent/castrated by birth'', and انڄھا /anñhā/ 'yet; still, until now'. The problem in representing words with this sound is that a unique Perso-Arabic character for the alveo-palatal nasal has not (yet) been accepted into the Saraiki alphabet in general use. The solution adopted, which is not unanimously accepted, is to spell the palatalized nasal with a Perso-Arabic digraph: نڄ as in the spelling of ونڄݨ /vāʄaṇ/ 'to go', for instance. No minimal pairs for these words are found. These are words from an agricultural society, and are still in use by rural Saraiki speakers. However, as NAS notes, with increasing cultural change, their frequency is likely to decline. Since these are the only words showing this sound that he was able to find, if these few words are lost, this sound will no longer be present in the language.

A phonetic development frequently observed in rapid or rural speech is that /m/ is followed by an intrusive [b], as in امبریکا /ambrīkā/ 'America', or جمبیلا /jambēlā/ 'Jamila'.

3.3.2 Vowels

The vowel segment inventories of all three languages under consideration are quite similar. Both Saraiki and Hindko show frequent elision of vowel sequences, which is often represented in writing.

3.3.2.1 Hindko vowels

Varma (1936: 55) finds that "Lahnda," which includes northern (Hazara) Hindko, has ten oral (that is, non-nasal) vowel phonemes: peripheral /i/, /e/, /a/, /ʌ/, /o/, and /u/; and centralized /ɪ/, /æ/, /ʊ/, and /ə/. In addition, according to Varma (1936: 90), all the oral vowels, plus some of the many diphthongs he identifies, can be nasalized. However, Varma makes no statement addressing the matter of whether nasalization is phonemic or not. (For nasalization, see also Section 3.4.1.1.1 below.) Varma's analysis is that of a native-speaker phonetician, and, although it was done almost eighty years ago, is still to be considered very reliable. The information in Varma's diagram of the tongue positions of these vowel sounds is represented in Table 3.8 and Table 3.9.

	Front	Central	Back
High (tense)	i		u
High (lax)	ɪ		ʊ
High-mid	e	ə	o
Low-mid	æ		ʌ
Low			ā

Table 3.8: Vowels of Hindko, adapted from Varma (1936: 55–59)

A recent study, Rashid and Akhtar (2012), based on phonetic analysis of the Hindko of Muzaffarabad and Pakistan-administered Kashmir using Praat software, finds nine oral vowels: /i/, /ɪ/, /e/, /ɑ/, /u/, /o/, /æ/, /ə/, and /ʊ/; and five nasal vowels: /ĩ/, /ẽ/, /ã/, /õ/, and /ũ/. They characterize these vowels with regard to frontness and backness, and closeness and openness. The information in Rashid & Akhtar's diagram of the

		Peripheral		
i				u
	ɪ	**Centralized**	ʊ	
e		ə		o
æ				ʌ
		ɑ		

Table 3.9: Centralized and peripheral vowels: Varma (1936: 55–59)

vowel space (Rashid and Akhtar 2012: 67) is represented in Table 3.10 and Table 3.11. For uniformity of presentation, we omit the nasal vowels.

	Front	**Central**	**Back**
High (closed)	i		u
High (half-closed)	ɪ		ʊ
Mid (half-closed)	e	ə	o
Mid (half-open)	æ		
Low (open)		ɑ	

Table 3.10: Vowels of Hindko: Rashid and Akhtar (2012: 67)

Vowel sandhi, often realized through elision, or coalescence, is a very salient feature of the spoken language in both Hindko and Saraiki. When two identical vowel sounds, or two similar sounds—for example, an oral vowel and a nasalized vowel—come together at a morpheme boundary, elision normally occurs. Vowel sandhi can result in a vowel intermediate to the original vowels, as in /ā/ + /e/ > /æ/, or in a vowel combining the features of both the elided vowels as in /ā/ + /ā̃/ > /ā̃/ and /ā/ + /n/ > /ā̃/. Elision is especially important in the pronunciation of some tense-aspect forms of verbs, especially those involving the present auxiliary. This is sometimes represented in writing and sometimes not—by different writers and even by the same writer. Elision is also heard in spoken Panjabi, but not usually represented in writing.

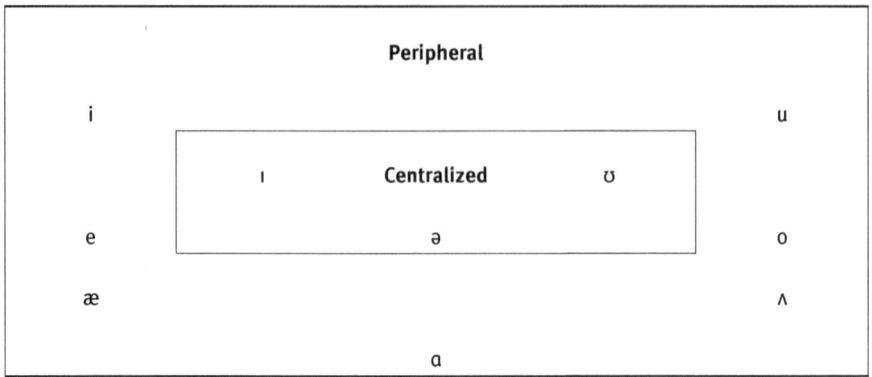

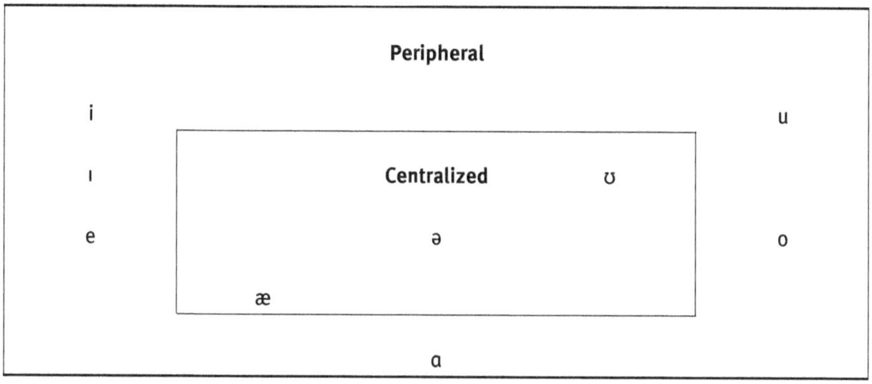

Table 3.11: Centralized and peripheral vowels: Rashid and Akhtar (2012)

3.3.2.2 Panjabi vowels

There are ten oral (non-nasal) vowels in Panjabi, as shown in Table 3.12. According to traditional terminology, seven of these are "long": /ā/, /e/, /ī/, /o/, /ū/, /æ/, and /ɔ/, and three are "short": /a/, /i/, and /u/. An alternate analysis, which we adopt here, categorizes these vowels in terms not of length, but of vowel type. In this grammar, we use the terms "centralized" in place of "short", and "peripheral" in place of "long" (following Shackle 1976: 12; Gill and Gleason 1969: 2; Shackle 2003: 587), shown in Table 3.12.

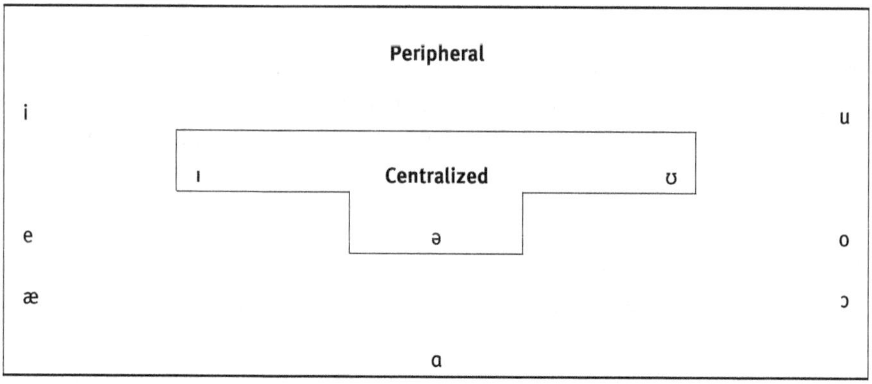

Table 3.12: Centralized and peripheral vowels of Panjabi (IPA representations)

In addition, /ə/ has an important allophone [ʌ], a lower-mid back unrounded vowel, which is more open and farther back than [ə] and which occurs in stressed syllables and before long (i.e. geminated) consonants and consonant clusters. It corresponds phonetically to the stressed vowel in the second syllable of the English word ‘above’ [ə.ˈbʌv], and is seen, for example, in the first, stressed, syllable of پتّا [pʌttā] ‘leaf’.

In this grammar, we transcribe the vowels of Hindko, Panjabi, and Saraiki using Roman letters as shown in Table 3.13.

Sound in IPA	Transcription	Sound in IPA	Transcription
i	ī	u	ū
ɪ	i	ʊ	u
e	e	o	o
æ	æ	ɔ	ɔ
ɑ	ā	ə/ʌ	a

Table 3.13: Vowels in transcription

3.3.2.3 Saraiki vowels

According to Shackle (1976: 12), there are nine primary vowels in Saraiki, which can, as for Panjabi and Hindko, be characterized as peripheral (“long”) and centralized (“short”). Shackle’s system can be diagrammed as in Table 3.14.

As with Hindko and Panjabi, a length distinction, which we have presented as the peripheral/centralized distinction, exists in Saraiki vowels. This distinction between peripheral and centralized vowels can in places better be characterized in terms of a difference of quality (Shackle 1976: 13). Syed and Kula (forthcoming) presents the same nine-vowel inventory. Short [ĕ] and [ŏ] allophones of /i/ and /u/, respectively are phonetically prominent in the language, and are dialectally distributed. The vowel /ə/ is considered as an allophone of /ʌ/ appearing in unstressed syllables by both Shackle and Syed. Both /ʌ/ and /ə/ are transcribed in this book as <a>.

The speech of our consultant has both long and short [e]. Compare the forms for the second person plural present of ‘be’ (also used as an auxiliary), تساں ہووے [tussã hivvē] ‘2PL are’ and اے ہن [ē hĕn] ‘3PL are’. These differences are sometimes reflected in the orthography (spelling), sometimes not. The vowel /o/ is phonemically long, but the centralized (short) back rounded vowel can vary between [ŏ] and [ŭ]. The Saraiki sound represented as /ʌ/ in Table 3.14 sometimes corresponds to a stressed [a] and sometimes to an unstressed [ə]. Our consultant characterizes some occurrences of (stressed) /ʌ/ as “tense, but not long.” This description of /ʌ/ seem to correspond to the

	Front unrounded				Back rounded
			Periph-eral		
High	i				u
			Centralized		
		ɪ		ʊ	
Mid	e	[ĕ]	[ə]	[ŏ]	o
			ʌ		
Low	æ		a		

Table 3.14: Saraiki vowels

distinction in Shackle (2001: 657), where he says: "There is a notable phonetic contrast between stressed [a] and the corresponding unstressed [ə]." Elsewhere he says: "accented /ʌ/ is markedly more open and low back than the centralized neutral vowel /ə/ of Panjabi, and nearer to /a/" (Shackle 1976: 13). Sometimes, because of Perso-Arabic spelling conventions, a tense (i.e. stressed but not long) vowel tends to be represented with a (long) vowel symbol, which can make for inconsistency in spelling.

Sometimes vowels which are peripheral in a Panjabi word are centralized but tense in some varieties of Saraiki, for example the word for 'eat', which is کھانا /khāṇā/, with a peripheral stem /ā/ in Panjabi, in some Saraiki varieties has a centralized but tense /ʌ/, i.e., [khʌn-], as in, for example ٻکری پترے کھندی پئی اے /ɓakrī patre khandī paī e/ 'the goat is eating leaves'. However, the infinitive of this word is spelled کھاوݨ /khāvaṇ/ in perhaps the most widely available and accepted Urdu-Saraiki dictionary (Mughal 2010), reflecting the pronunciation with the peripheral vowel.

The fronting of /a/ before /h/ which occurs in Panjabi (see Section 3.4.1.2.2) does not happen in Saraiki. So, for example, while Panjabi has ['ǽmad] for the name Ahmad (احمد), Saraiki has ['ahmad] (Shackle 1979: 203).[7]

Elision is an important feature of Saraiki. Short forms of the present auxiliary (see Section 8.5.3.1.1) frequently coalesce with preceding word-final vowels, especially when these are unstressed and follow a stressed syllable. These elisions are important in the formation (especially the pronunciation, and sometimes in the written form as

7 Some of the apparent differences we have noted between the Saraiki and the Panjabi vowel systems are at this point mainly anecdotal. Instrumental study remains to be done.

well) of periphrastic tenses, especially those formed with a participle plus the short form of the present auxiliary, like the present imperfect (referred to as the present in Shackle 1976: 99). Orthography is inconsistent in such cases: sometimes such forms are written as two words, sometimes as one. Elisions are written in some, but not all cases (Shackle 1976: 94). For example:

- After /-ā/:

  /-ā/ + /-ã̄/ > /-ã̄/, as in ٹُردا آں /ṭurdā ã̄/ '1SG.M walk' > ٹُرداں /ṭurdã̄/

  /-ā/ + /-e/ > /-e/ or /-æ/, as in ٹُردا اے /ṭurdā e/ '3SG.M walks' > ٹُردے /ṭurde/ or /ṭurdæ/

  /ā/ + /ẽ/ > /ẽ/ or /æ̃/, as in ٹُردا ایں /ṭurdā ẽ/ '2SG.M walk' > ٹُردیں /ṭurdẽ/ or /ṭurdæ̃/

- After /e/:

  /-e/ + /-o/ > /-io/ [yo], as in ٹُردے او /ṭurde o/ '2PL.M walk' > ٹُردیو /ṭurdio/

- After /-æ/:

  /-ae/ + /-ĕn/ > /-æn/, as in ڳئے اِن /ɠæ ĕn/ '3PL have gone' > ڳئیں /ɠæn/

3.3.3 Diphthongs

Identification and enumeration is more complicated for diphthongs than it is for simple vowels, since diphthongs involve movement of the articulators from one position to another. They are, however, a subset of the wider category of vowel sequences, which as a whole are characterized by movement from the position of an initial vowel sound to the position of a second vowel. The difference between diphthongs and other vowel sequences is that diphthongs function as single vowels in the nucleus of a single syllable, while other sequences are (usually) disyllabic. This difference, however, is not always clear, since complex vowel sounds may not be perceived or categorized in the same way by different observers and analysts. In fact, as Catford (1982: 215) points out, a diphthong may consist of two distinct elements with a rapid transition between them, or it may be a continuous gliding movement from a starting point to a finishing point. The frequency of elision in these languages further complicates the picture. Therefore, the descriptions of diphthong inventories in these languages are not strictly comparable and should be considered provisional, especially for Hindko and Saraiki.[8]

8 See Malik (1995: 21) for further discussion of the complexities of analyzing diphthongs and vowel sequences.

3.3.3.1 Hindko diphthongs

The problems of defining and identifying diphthongs apply most strongly to Hindko. Varma himself says that "These diphthongs vary in their degree of 'diphthongization', and in some cases it becomes difficult to determine whether they are diphthongs or two separate vowels" (Varma 1936: 61). He also notes that most of his diphthongs arise from "flexion"—that is, from adding grammatical endings to word stems. Concerning fifteen of them, Varma (1936: 63) says that "we cannot say definitely whether they are rising, falling, or 'even' diphthongs—the difference of perceptibility between the first and the second element being not very striking." Discussing Awankari, another variety of "Lahnda," Bahri (1963: 66) says: "There are no less than forty-one diphthongs in Awankari." He, too, stresses the difficulty of identifying diphthongs and distinguishing them from vowel sequences (Bahri 1963: 68). It appears that by "diphthong" Varma and Bahri may have meant what we are here calling "vowel sequence," which would include both monosyllabic diphthongs and disyllabic vowel sequences. In addition, importantly, various Hindko vowel sequences are subject to frequent elision, giving rise to phonetic diphthongs that are not phonemic.

Published lists of Hindko diphthongs vary considerably. Varma (1936: 61) lists 31: /ei/, /ai/, /ʌi/, /əi/, /oi/, /ui/, /ie/; /ɛe/, /ae/, /ʌe/, /əe/, /oe/, /ue/; /iɛ/, /īa/, /ia/, /ea/, /oa/, /ua/, /ūa/; /īo/, /io/, /eo/, /ao/, /ʌo/, /əo/; /iu/, /ɛu/, /au/, /ʌu/, /əu/. Other lists include the 41 listed by Bahri (1963: 65–69), and Rashid and Akhtar's three: /oɪ/, /āī/, and /uā/, as in the words/loɪ/ 'wool blanket', /kəsaɪ/ 'butcher', and /bʊa/ 'door' (Rashid and Akhtar 2012: 72).

The diphthongs of Hazara Hindko await detailed description and analysis.

3.3.3.2 Panjabi diphthongs

There is, by contrast, considerable consensus about the inventory of Panjabi diphthongs. According to Gill and Gleason (1969: 19), Bhatia (1993: 337), and Shackle (2003: 588), Panjabi has eight diphthongs, shown in Table 3.15.[9]

All of these begin with a centralized vowel and end with a peripheral vowel. In the diphthongs /ɪɑ/, /ɪɔ/, /ɪo/, /əi/, and /əe/, the first vowel is pronounced as an [ĕ] sound, similar to /e/, but of shorter duration. In other words, the vowel /ɪ/ lowers to [ĕ] before a non-high vowel, and the vowel /ə/ raises to [ĕ] before a non-low vowel. In the following examples, the transcriptions are in our transcriptional notation, and the pronunciations are given in IPA representation.

9 In Table 3.15, IPA <ə> represents our <a>, IPA <ɑ> represents our <ā>, IPA I represents our <i>, and IPA <ʊ> represents our <u>.

		Second vowel					
		i	e	ɑ	ɔ	o	u
First vowel	ɪ		ɪɑ	ɪɔ	ɪo		
	ə	əi	əe			əo	əu
	ʊ			ʊɑ			

Table 3.15: Diphthongs of Panjabi

- گیا 'go.PP-SG.M'

  Transcription: <gayā>

  Pronunciation: [gĕɑ]

- پیو 'father'

  Transcription: <piyo>

  Pronunciation: [pĕo]

- لیونا 'to bring'

  Transcription: <liyɔṇā>

  Pronunciation: [lĕɔɳɑ]

- گئی 'go.PP-SG.F'

  Transcription: <gaī>

  Pronunciation: [gĕi]

- گئے 'go.PP-PL.M'

  Transcription: <gae>

  Pronunciation: [gĕe]

These sound sequences are analyzed as diphthongs here.

Panjabi also permits sequences of two or three different peripheral vowels, excluding /æ/ and /ɔ/; for example کھائی /khā.ī/ 'eat.PP-SG.F'. Whereas diphthongs pattern as single vowels, each vowel in a sequence such as /ā.ī/ constitutes a separate syllable, and in this case a separate morpheme (Gill and Gleason 1969: 20).

3.3.3.3 Saraiki diphthongs

Shackle (1976: 13) lists 45 vowel sequences, of which he identifies the following five combinations of peripheral plus central vowel as disyllabic sequences in Central Saraiki:

- /īʌ/ as in بیئر /ˈbī.ʌr/ 'beer'
- /āi/ as in شائر /ˈšā.ir/ 'poet'
- /eu/ as in ڳیوم /ˈɠe.um/ 'I went'
- /ūʌ/ as in سوئر /ˈsū.ʌr/ 'pig'
- /oi/ as in کوئنہ /ˈkoi.nʌ/ 'not'

Shackle considered the following sequences to be diphthongs (Shackle 1976: 14–16)[10]:

Beginning with peripheral vowels:

- /āī/ as in مائی /māī/ 'mother'
- /āe/ as in بݨائے /bʌṇāe/ 'made.PL.M'
- /āæ/ as in بݨائیم /bʌṇāæm/ 'I made'
- /āo/ as in بݨاؤ /bʌṇāo/ 'make.IMP'
- /āũ/ as in بݨاؤں /bʌṇāũ/ 'let us make'
- /īã/ as in دھیاں /dhīã/ 'daughters'
- /īe/ as in بھتریے /bhʌtrīe/ 'nephews'
- /īæ/ as in دھیئیں /dhīæn/ 'they're daughters'
- /īũ/ as in پیوں/pīũ/ 'let us drink'
- /īo/ as in پیو/ˈpīo/ 'drink!'
- /eā/ as in ڳئیا or ڳیا /ɠeā/ 'went.SG.M'
- /eũ/ as in ݙیوں /ɗeũ/ 'let us give'

10 Whereas according to the criterion that diphthongs pattern as single vowels and vowel sequences consist of two distinct vowels, the classification would seem to us to be the reverse of what Shackle said.

- /eo/ as in ݙیو /ɗeo/ ‘give!’
- /ūā/ as in بُوا /būā/ ‘aunt’
- /ūæ/ as in بُوئے /būæ/ ‘it’s auntie’
- /ūī/ as in سُوئی /sūī/ ‘needle’
- /ūẽ/ as in بھُوئیں /bhūẽ/ ‘earth’
- /oæ/ as in چڑھوئے /cʌṛhoæ/ ‘he’s a washerman’
- /oā/ as in چڑھوئا /cʌṛhoā/ ‘washerman’
- /oe/ as in ٹوئے /ṭoe/ ‘pits’
- /oī/ as in چڑھوئی /cʌṛhoī/ ‘washerwoman’

Beginning with centralized vowels:

- /ʌī/ as in مئی /mʌī/ ‘May’
- /ʌo/ as in نوکر /nʌokʌr/ ‘servant’
- /iā̃/ as in کُتیاں /kuttiā̃/ ‘female dogs’
- /iʌ/ as in تربیئت /tʌrbiʌt/ ‘training’ (occurs in loans)
- /ie/ as in مرثیئے /mʌrsie/ ‘elegies’
- /iū/ as in وستیوں /vʌstiū̃/ ‘from the village’
- /io/ as in گھوڑیو /ghoṛio/ ‘O mares!’
- /ĕā̃/ as in کُتیئاں /kuttĕā̃/ ‘dogs’
- /ĕe/ as in ملئے /milĕē/ ‘they met’ (first element often dropped)
- /ĕu/ as in آکھیوم /ākhĕum/ ‘I said’
- /ĕū̃/ as in کھٻیوں /khʌɓĕū̃/ ‘from the left’
- /ĕo/ as in گھوڑیو /ghoṛĕo/ ‘O (male) horses’

- /uā/ as in دعا /duā/ 'prayer'
- /ue/ as in چُٹھ /ˈcueṭh/ 'sixty-four' (Shackle 1976: 16)
- /uī/ as in کوئی /kuī/ 'someone'

Note that with those diphthongs beginning with peripheral vowels the peripheral vowel occurs in a stressed syllable, while in those beginning with centralized vowels, except for /ʌī/ and /ʌo/, the centralized vowel elements are unstressed. Shackle's designation (Shackle 1976) of some sequences beginning with peripheral vowels as diphthongs appears to differ from the analysis he employs for Panjabi (Shackle 2003).[11]

3.4 Suprasegmentals

Suprasegmentals are features that occur simultaneously with segments but may involve more than one consonant or vowel segment. Suprasegmental features affecting vowels in these languages are nasalization, tone, and stress. We discuss these features separately for each of the three languages.

3.4.1 Suprasegmentals affecting vocalic segments and syllables

3.4.1.1 Nasalization

Phonemic nasalization is part of the vowel systems of all three of the languages discussed here. Nasalization is an articulatory feature produced mainly by the lowering of the velum (soft palate), thus allowing air to exit through the nasal passage and producing a nasalized vowel sound. We represent nasalized vowels by writing a tilde over the basic vowel symbol; for example, oral /ā/, nasal /ā̃/. Since nasalization is a feature that readily spreads either forward or backward from an inherently nasal segment, phonetic or automatic nasalization is also observed in all of these languages. However, automatic nasalization is not indicated in the transcriptions except in the phonetic (between square brackets) transcriptions where the nasalization is specifically being discussed.

11 NAS, (p.c.) notes 'If we have a sequence of two long vowels in underlying representation, either the first shortens, or they are treated as nuclei of two different syllables in very rare cases.' This analysis would rule out many of the sequences that Shackle calls diphthongs.

3.4.1.1.1 Nasalization in Hindko

Nasal vowels, both phonemic and phonetic, are perceptually very salient in spoken Hindko. According to Varma (1936: 90), all of the plain vowels and most of the diphthongs have nasal counterparts or can be contextually nasalized. Thus both peripheral and centralized vowels can be nasal in Hindko. Final vowels are frequently nasal, medial vowels less frequently. Varma analyzes nasal vowels in Hindko as either primary (independent) or secondary (dependent). Independent nasal vowels are those not induced by the presence of a nasal consonant in the same or an adjacent syllable. Dependent nasalization means nasalization induced by a preceding or succeeding nasal consonant either actually present in the same word or historically present (Varma 1936: 87)[12]. Because of the reference to historical conditions, this distinction is not necessarily equivalent to the difference between phonemic and phonetic nasalization in the modern language, and unfortunately Varma does not discuss the question of which oral/nasal vowel pairs are phonemically contrastive.

Independent nasalization generally occurs only in final position:

a. at the end of certain monosyllabic particles as یاں /yã̄/ 'or', تاں /tã̄/ 'then';

b. in some one-syllable content words, where inherent nasalization is inherited from MIA (Pk. chāyaṇa—n. 'covering' T5017[13]); for example, چھاں /chã̄/ 'shade'.

Dependent nasalization occurs in the vocalic endings of some words, the stems of which contain the nasal consonants /n/, /m/, and /ṛ̃/. In پراڑیں /purāṛ̃ī̃/ 'old', the feminine singular ending shows nasalization after the /ṛ̃/ in the stem. This happens frequently in Abbottabad Hindko. In addition, spontaneous nasalization arises in some polysyllabic words. For instance, with polysyllabic words, the final ا /ā/of some cardinal number names (see Section 5.1.4); and some feminine nouns can be phonetically nasalized. For example, two spellings, آپا /āpā/and آپاں /āpã̄/, are current for 'elder sister'. The reflexive pronoun اپڑا /apṛ̃ā/ is sometimes pronounced and spelled as اپڑاں /apṛã̄/, also showing secondary nasalization. Representation of such secondary nasalization in writing is variable and unpredictable. It seems that this (secondary) nasalization is perceived as so salient that it may have become reinterpreted as inherent nasalization.

The contrast between oral and nasal vowels is phonemically significant in some cases, including those of centralized vowels. The following examples of minimal or near-minimal pairs are taken from Sakoon's Hindko-Urdu dictionary.

- /a/ vs. /ã/

12 Nasalization induced by nasal spreading from inherently nasal consonants or vowels is referred to by various authors as "phonetic", "dependent", or "contextual" nasalization.

13 Notations of the form 'Tnnnn' refer to the entries in Turner's *Comparative Dictionary of the Indo-Aryan Languages* (Turner 1962–1966).

گڈ /gaḍ/ 'act of mixing, adulterating': گنڈھ /gã́ḍ/ 'knot' (Sakoon 2002: 207, 210)

لگ /lag/ 'loneliness, desertedness': لنگ /lãg/ 'line, row, rank' (Sakoon 2002: 219, 220)

- /ā/ vs. /ā̃/

باگ /bāg/ 'garden': بانگ /bā̃g/ 'call to prayer; rooster's crowing' (Sakoon 2002: 29, 31)

- /o/ vs. /õ/

پوچا/pocā/ 'clay wash for walls or floors': پونچا/põcā/ 'claws' (Sakoon 2002: 68, 69).[14]

3.4.1.1.2 Nasalization in Panjabi

Each of the seven peripheral vowels in Panjabi have phonemically nasalized counterparts; centralized vowels do not.

Nasalization is only contrastive in final position. Phonetic, or automatic, nasalization occurs in all positions, however. Nasalization can spread from inherently nasal segments either forward, i.e. progressively, or backward, i.e. regressively (Bhatia 1993: 337). It can even spread across syllables as in 'whether' below. The pronunciation of نہ /ná/ 'not, don't' as [nã́] is a case of progressive nasalization, and ٹنڈ /ṭinḍ/ 'earthen pot' as [ṭĩnḍ] illustrates regressive nasalization. In this grammar, however, we mark only phonemically nasal final vowels.[15]

- بھاویں 'whether'
  Transcription: /pàvẽ/
  Pronunciation: [pà̃vẽ]

---

14 Discussing Muzaffarabad Hindko, Rashid and Akhtar (2012: 70) find that all the peripheral (long) vowels except /æ/ have nasal counterparts, which they claim are phonemically distinct from the corresponding oral vowels (they do not, however, supply minimal pairs). They do not mention nasal centralized (short) vowels or discuss phonetic or secondary nasalization.

15 The word منہ /mū̃́/ 'mouth' is written without a long vowel letter, as though it contained only a short vowel, centralized /u/. However, this word definitely contains a peripheral, long /ū/, which is represented in its Gurmukhi spelling. Because the orthographically final ہ represents high tone, and the preceding ں represents nasalization, the vowel is actually the final segment of the word.

The above example shows that nasalization spreads backward in Panjabi until it encounters a blocking segment, and that semi-vowels do not block the spread of nasalization (Bhatia 1993: 337). Gill and Gleason (1969: 23) also say: "All types of nasalisation spread over any sequence of vowels not interrupted by a true consonant. /w/ does not limit the domain of nasalisation." Additionally, Zahid and Hussain (2012: 65) find that there is no significant difference in the strength of nasality between inherently nasal and contextually nasalized vowels.

According to Bhatia (1993: 347), vowels following nasal consonants are nasalized only if they have high or mid tone, thus نا /nã̄́/ 'no!' , ناں /nã̄ / 'name', but نھا /nā̀/ 'bathe!'

3.4.1.1.3 Nasalization in Saraiki

According to Shackle (1976: 12, 17), all six peripheral vowels have both oral and nasalized variants. He provides minimal pair examples for /e/ vs. /ẽ/ and /ā/ vs. /ā̃/. This nasalization contrast is phonemic, marking a difference in meaning. For example: ٹرے /ṭure/ 'go.SBJV.3SG': ٹریں /ṭurẽ/ 'go.SBJV.2SG'.

According to Latif (2003: 91) there are ten vowel phonemes: seven peripheral and three centralized, six of which have nasalized counterparts. According to Awan, Baseer, and Sheeraz (2012), Saraiki has ten vowel phonemes, eight of which have an oral/-nasal contrast. However, Nasir Abbas Syed (p.c.) states that he has not been able to find examples of phonemically nasal /õ/. Syed and Kula (forthcoming) has nine vowel phonemes, six peripheral and three centralized. All of these have nasalized counterparts, except for /o/. They consider [ə] as an allophone of /ʌ/, occurring in unstressed syllables.

Along with the oral/nasal contrast at the phonemic level, nasalization also spreads both backward and forward from an inherently nasal phoneme, either consonantal or vocalic, producing phonetically nasalized articulations which are not represented in writing, as also occurs in Hindko and Panjabi. Syed and Kula (forthcoming) is a detailed discussion of nasal spread in Saraiki. They find that semi-vowels and vowels are subject to nasalization, and liquids and less sonorous consonants block the spread of nasalization. A stressed syllable also blocks nasal spreading in Saraiki.

3.4.1.2 Tone

Many varieties of Panjabi, including the Lahore variety of Panjabi we describe here and all varieties of Hindko, are unusual among languages of the Indo-Gangetic plain in having phonemic tones, or characteristic differences in pitch that distinguish word meaning.[16] This feature, phonemic tone—its presence or absence, and its specific expression—is one of the most important differences in the phonologies of the three languages treated in this book. Both Hindko and Panjabi have phonemic tone, albeit with differing systems, but Saraiki does not.

3.4.1.2.1 Tone in Hindko

Tone in Abbottabad Hindko has not been discussed in previously published literature, except for a brief mention by Baart (2014: 5), who states that Abbottabad Hindko has three tones.[17] He presents the Hindko words for 'leper', 'horse', and 'bitter' as evidence of this. These words are given in Table 3.16, in which the Hindko forms are from our consultant. For the sake of comparison, the Panjabi, Saraiki, and Urdu counterparts of these words are also given. Neither the Urdu nor the Saraiki words have tone; hence they are separated from the tonal examples by a vertical line in the table.

Gloss	Tone	Hindko		Panjabi		Saraiki		Urdu	
		Roman	Perso-Arabic	Roman	Perso-Arabic	Roman	Perso-Arabic	Roman	Perso-Arabic
'leper'	high falling	kóṛā	کوڑہا	kóṛā	کوڑھا	koṛh	کوڑھ	koṛhī	کوڑھی
'horse'	low rising	kòṛā	کہوڑا	kòṛā	گھوڑا	ghoṛā	گھوڑا	ghoṛā	گھوڑا
'bitter'	level	koṛa	کوڑا	kɔṛā	کوڑا	kɔṛā	کوڑا	kaṛwā	کڑوا

Table 3.16: Tone comparison in Hindko, Panjabi, Saraiki, and Urdu

Notice that voiceless consonants resulting from the devoicing of initial voiced aspirates, as in 'horse,' are spelled differently in Hindko (with ہ *choṭī he*) than they are in

16 Tonal, or pitch accent, systems are common in the languages of the Hindukush and the Himalayan foothills (Baart 2014: 5).

17 Hindko has many dialects, each of which has slightly different phonology. Treatments of Awankari (Bahri 1963), and Peshawar and Kohat Hindko (Shackle 1980) describe systems which differ from that of Abbottabad Hindko. Those treatments indicate that Awankari and Kohat Hindko do not have the low-rising tone characteristic of Panjabi, but that Peshawar Hindko has low tone to a certain extent. Varma (1936) discusses tone in many varieties of "Lahnda", but does not focus on Hazara Hindko

Panjabi (which follows Urdu spelling and retains the ھ *do cašmī he* which represents historical aspiration).

These findings are confirmed by our own recordings of Abbottabad Hindko, although the low rising tone seems less pronounced than in Panjabi. In Abbottabad Hindko, inherited initial voiced aspirate sounds, for example /gh/, have become voiceless, but seem to retain a very slight aspiration in addition to developing low tone. The word for 'house, home,' for example, which in Panjabi is /kȁr/ and has developed a strong low tone and lost aspiration completely, is in Hindko /k(h)àr/ , with very slight, variable, non-distinctive aspiration, but spelled کھر <khar>, signalling its difference from Panjabi and Saraiki, as well as from Urdu. Similarly, تہیاں /tyȁn/ 'attention', spelled <tihyān>, corresponds to Panjabi دھیاں /tyȁn/ and Urdu دھیاں /dhyān/ (the latter two with identical spelling). It is the authors' impression that the low tone in Hindko is less pronounced than that of Panjabi, and that the retained aspiration mentioned above is very slight.

The high tone, on the other hand, is relatively salient. High tone has developed from non-initial voiced aspirates, as in the word اَنھاں /ánnā̃/ 'blind'. Compare Urdu اندھا /andhā/ and Panjabi انھا/ánnā/. In two-syllable words the high falling tone is always on the first syllable, and never on the second, as in [kóṛā] 'leper'. There is a small but significant number of minimal pairs for the high tone vs. toneless contrast; for example, as بڈی /baḍḍī/ 'large' but بڈھی /báḍḍī/ 'a bribe '; پا /pā/ 'put!' but پاہ /pā́/ 'manure', دا /dā/ 'of (m.sg.)' but داہ /dā́/ 'ten '.

3.4.1.2.2 Tone in Panjabi

Unlike that of frequently discussed tonal languages like Chinese or Thai, the tonal system of Panjabi is relatively simple, having three tones: level, high, and low. The level tone is the unmarked pitch contour of a stressed syllable; the labels *high* and *low* describe two marked pitch contours which contrast with it. The high tone starts at a high pitch and falls throughout the syllable, while the low tone starts at a low pitch and rises throughout the syllable. In this grammar, we do not use a special symbol for the unmarked level tone. The high tone is indicated with the acute accent, for example /ā́/, and low tone with the grave accent, for example /ȁ/. The following example, from Gill and Gleason (1969: 25), shows the three-way contrast between the tones:

- Level tone: چا /cā/ 'enthusiasm'
- Low tone: جھا /cȁ/ 'peep'
- High tone: چاہ /cā́/ 'tea'

As a rule, only stressed syllables bear high or low tone; however, not all stressed syllables have a high or low tone. High tone is usually accompanied by some phonetic shortening of the stressed vowel, while the low tone usually results in a phonetic lengthening of the vowel (Shackle 1979: 202). Both peripheral (long) and centralized (short) vowels can bear tone. The above examples illustrate the peripheral vowel case, while high and low tone on centralized vowels can be seen in کل /kál/ 'yesterday, tomorrow' and گھل /kàl-/ 'send', respectively.

In Panjabi and Hindko, before either ہ *choṭī he* or ح *baṛī he* (both of which represent (historical) /h/), historical /a/ is fronted to [æ], /i/ is lowered to [e], and /u/ is pronounced [o] or [ɔ] (Bhardwaj 1995: 70). High tone appears on these vowels as a reflex of the following /h/. These changes do not take place in Saraiki.

- کَہنا <kahṇā> /kǽṇā/ 'to say'
- کِہڑا <kihṛā> /kéṛā/ 'who, which one'
- کُہڑا <kuhṛā> /kóṛā/ 'leper'
- شَہِر <šahir> /šǽr/ 'city'
- پَہُنچنا <pahuncṇā> /pɔ́ncṇā/ 'to arrive, reach'

3.4.1.2.3 Tone in Saraiki

As stated above, Saraiki does not have phonemic tone.

3.4.1.3 Stress

Stress refers to the relative prominence of a given syllable relative to other syllables in a word. In this grammar, stress is represented, when required, with a short, raised line preceding the stressed syllable in the transcription field.

3.4.1.3.1 Stress in Hindko

For stress in Hindko we rely mainly on Bahri (1963), which, though it describes a Hindko variety different from that of Hazara, is considered by Shackle (1980: 487) "to be taken as typical of Hindko". Bahri (1963: 141) focuses on the strong stress accent in Hindko varieties, and considers the widespread elision of vowels found in Hindko to be due to this strong stress accent. Varma (1936: 92) further states that in "Lahnda" there is only one primary word stress; secondary word stress is not found.

As in Panjabi, stress interacts with other phonological features in multiple ways: (1) syllables uttered with high tone are always stressed (Bahri 1963: 191); (2) stress significantly affects the quality and length of vowels, so that vowels in syllables preceding or following the stressed syllable are shorter than normal (Varma 1936: 71); (3) stressed centralized vowels are followed by geminated consonants.

3.4.1.3.2 Stress in Panjabi

Every monomorphemic[18] word in Panjabi, except for unstressed clitics, carries lexical **stress**, which is realized through a combination of higher pitch, longer duration, and greater volume.[19] Stress placement in monomorphemic words is largely predictable. It depends on the **weight** of a syllable and its **position** in the word. Syllables can be **light** (consisting of one mora[20]) , **heavy** (consisting of two morae), or **superheavy** (consisting of three morae). Weight, in turn depends on vowel length and syllable structure. A syllable is light if it ends in a centralized (short) vowel, e.g. نہ /na/ 'NEG', or the first syllable in بچا /ba.cā/ 'save!'. Heavy syllables end in a peripheral (long) vowel, or consist of a consonant followed by a short vowel followed by a second consonant, e.g. the first and the second syllables in گاجر /gā.jar/ 'carrot', respectively. Syllables count as superheavy if they end in (a) a long vowel followed by a single consonant, e.g. the second syllable in مکان /ma.kān/ 'house' or آپ /āp/ 'self'; (b) a long vowel followed by two consonants, e.g. دوست /dost/ 'friend'; (c) two consonants followed by a long vowel, e.g. ترے /træ/ 'three'; (d) two consonants followed by a long vowel and another consonant, e.g. the final syllable of پروگرام /pro.grām/ 'plan'; or (e) a short vowel followed by two consonants, e.g. امب /amb/ 'mango'.

For purposes of stress placement, geminated consonants must be treated as a sequence of two identical consonants, occurring in sequences of the form VC.CV, as in the word بلی /ˈbil.lī// 'cat', which has the syllable pattern Heavy.Heavy, yielding stress on the penultimate (initial) syllable.

Stress assignment also depends on position. Stress is assigned to the penultimate (second to last) syllable, unless either (a) the ultimate (final) syllable is the heaviest, or (b) the antepenultimate (third from last) is heavier than the penultimate. For discussion see Bhatia (1993: 343), Malik (1995: 72, 79), and Dhillon (2007).

Monosyllabic words, except for certain clitics, carry inherent stress. Transitive/-causative derivations in which the stem ends in ا /ā/are regularly stressed on the stem-final /-ā/, in most cases consistent with the generalizations in Table 3.17; e.g., مروایا /marˈvā.yā/ 'caused to be killed', in which the dot in the transcription shows the location of the stem boundary. Further, stress correlates with tone, since only stressed syllables receive high or low tone, as well as with gemination, as discussed in Section 3.4.2.

18 Stress patterns in compound words are not treated here.

19 Stress is, however, not in itself contrastive in Panjabi.

20 A mora can be understood as a unit of time, i.e. how long a syllable takes to utter.

Antepenultimate syllable	Penultimate syllable	Ultimate syllable	Stress	Example
		2-syllable words		
——	Heavy	Heavy	Penultimate	مالی ˈmālī 'gardener'
——	Heavy	Heavy	Penultimate	گاجر ˈgājar 'carrot' دھوبݨ ˈtòbaṇ 'washerwoman'
	Light	Heavy	Ultimate	بچا baˈcā 'save!'
	Light	Superheavy	Ultimate	مکان maˈkān 'house'
	Heavy	Superheavy	Ultimate	شلوار šalˈwār 'šalwar'
		3-syllable words		
Heavy	Light	Heavy	Antepenultimate	پنجرا ˈpinjarā 'cage'
Heavy	Heavy	Heavy	Penultimate	چمکیلا camˈkīlā 'shining'

Table 3.17: Summary of Panjabi stress placement (Examples from Malik 1995: 73 and Bhatia 1993: 343)

In general, the relative prominence of a stressed syllable in Panjabi is greater than it is in either Urdu or Saraiki. Panjabi stress is forceful enough that vowels in unstressed syllables tend to be reduced preceding or following a stressed syllable. This results in predictable adaptations of borrowed words to native Panjabi phonology. For example, Urdu بازار /bāzār/ vs. Panjabi بزار /bazār/, in which the vowel in the syllable preceding the stressed syllable has been reduced from /ā/ to /a/; Urdu سوال /savāl/ 'question' vs. Panjabi سوال /svāl/, in which the centralized vowel of the first syllable has been elided; or Urdu اشارہ /išārā/ 'signal' vs. Panjabi شارہ /šārā/, in which the initial centralized vowel has been elided (Sharma 1971: 142).

Stress does to some extent help to distinguish the meanings of some words; with words one of which is a derived transitive stem including the inherently stressed transitive suffix /-ā/, we find pairs like:

- بچہ /ˈbaccā/ 'child' and بچا /baˈcā/ 'save' (Malik 1995: 73)

However, there are few such near minimal pairs and stress is not the only factor distinguishing these two words. In بچہ /ˈbaccā/ 'child' the consonant in the first syllable is geminated, while in بچا /baˈcā/ it is not. Therefore, as Shackle (2003: 592) cautions, it is problematic to consider stress to be phonemic in Panjabi.

3.4.1.3.3 Stress in Saraiki

Saraiki monosyllabic and disyllabic words, except for unstressed postpositional, emphatic, and elided present tense auxiliary elements, have one primary stressed syllable, which tends to be somewhat longer than any other, unstressed syllable in the word. The stressed syllable can be distinguished by having a long vowel, or by the occurrence of a geminated consonant following it. The most common word pattern is of a two-syllable word, with the stress on the first syllable; e.g., تُساں /ˈtussã/ 'you.PL'. All words have initial stress except for a few classes: (1) two-syllable words with a centralized vowel in the first syllable and either (a) a final peripheral vowel in the second, e.g., بھِرا /bhirā/ 'brother', (b) a peripheral vowel + consonant in the second, e.g., سوال /savāl/ 'question', (c) a centralized vowel + consonant in the second, e.g., گھسُن /ghasun/ 'punch (blow)'; (2) three-syllable words with a centralized vowel in the first syllable and either (a) a peripheral vowel, e.g., وچارا /vicārā/ 'poor fellow', or (b) a centralized vowel + geminate consonant, e.g., چُہتر /cuhattar/ 'seventy-four' in the second syllable, which have stress on the second syllable (Shackle 1976: 28–29).

The only pairs in which stress (partially) distinguishes meaning belong to the very small class of two-syllable words with a centralized vowel in the first syllable and a peripheral (long) vowel in the second syllable. Yet even in such pairs the vowel in the first syllable differs or the consonant is geminated. For instance:

- اطلاع /itt.ˈlā/ 'information, notification'

- اتلا /ˈit.lā/ 'so much'

- بھِرا /bhi.ˈrā/ 'brother'

- بھرا /ˈbha.rā/ 'fulfilled '(Shackle 1976: 29)

Words with three syllables which have stress on the initial syllable can also have a secondary stress on the third syllable, e.g. اَبڑغت /ub.baṛ.ˌɣut/ 'suddenly', where a short lower vertical line indicates the position of the secondary stress (example from Shackle, spelling from Mughal 2010: 43). Shackle (1976: 28) gives /aβarɣut/.

3.4.2 Suprasegmental features affecting consonants: Gemination

Consonants can be lengthened, or geminated. We treat this phenomenon as a suprasegmental feature, either as lengthening of or stress on a consonant, rather than as a cluster consisting of two identical consonants. Gemination is an important feature of all three languages described here. It arose historically from the simplification of Old Indo-Aryan (OIA) consonant clusters in Middle Indo-Aryan (MIA). For example, Sanskrit (OIA) *dughda* 'milk' > Pali (MIA) *duddha* > Panjabi دده /dúd(d)/ 'milk. 'This feature distinguishes these languages from more easterly languages, which have replaced this MIA gemination with vowel lengthening, e.g., Urdu and Hindi دودھ /dūdh/ 'milk'. Additionally, much more recently, some Perso-Arabic loans widely shared among all these three languages also have inherently geminate consonants, e.g., عزت /izzat/ 'respect'. Gemination is widespread and phonemic in all three of these languages; however, even when it is phonemic it is not usually indicated in writing, even in some dictionaries—even though the mechanism, the use of *tašdīd* ّ◌, is available and simple.

3.4.2.1 Gemination in Hindko

Gemination is phonemic, and very frequent, in Hindko; compare پتا ~ پتہ /patā/ 'information, knowledge' with پتا /pattā/ 'leaf, playing card'. Bahri (1963: 58) notes for Awankari that geminated consonants do not occur at the beginning of a word or in stressed syllables, but rather follow stressed syllables—the same situation that obtains in Panjabi and Saraiki.[21] He gives the examples وٹا /vaˈṭā/ 'exchange, change!' vs. وٹا /ˈ-vaṭṭā/ 'stone'. The corresponding pair in Abbottabad Hindko is بٹہ /ˈbaṭṭā/ 'stone' vs. بٹا /baˈṭā-/ 'change, exchange'.

3.4.2.2 Gemination in Panjabi

Gemination is also phonemic in Panjabi. This can be seen by comparing pairs like: سکا /ˈsukkā/ 'dry.SG.M' and سکا /suˈkā-/ 'dry'; سڈی /ˈsaḍḍī/ 'called, summoned' and صدی /ˈsadī/ ' century'; قصے /ˈkisse/ ' story, tale.OBL.SG', کسے /ˈkise/ ' someone'; or ہٹّی /ˈhaṭṭī/ 'shop' and ہٹی /ˈhaṭī/ 'moved.aside.SG.F'. From the examples of 'century' and 'someone', it can be seen that a stressed initial syllable does not necessarily correlate with gemination on the following syllable.

21 Although this is what Bahri says, presumably he means that geminates do not occur in the onsets of stressed syllables, as in these examples the initial element of the geminate falls in the coda, and hence in a stressed syllable.

Almost all consonant sounds in Panjabi can be geminated in word-medial or word-final position. Shackle (2003: 591–592) has stated that /r/, /ṛ/, /ṇ/, /ḷ/, /h/, and /v/ cannot be geminated in these positions, and Malik (1995: 46) lists only /p/, /b/, /t/, /ṭ/ /m/, /n/, /s/, /d/, /ḍ/, /c/ /j/, /k/, /g/, /v/ and /l/ as occurring geminated. Gemination does not occur word-initially. Geminated aspirates reduce to a cluster of an unaspirated consonant followed by its aspirated counterpart, e.g. /cch/. However, words such as پھلّنا /phuḷḷnā/ 'to flourish', نوّے /navve/ '90', تصوّر /tasavvur/ 'concept, idea', چِرّ /cirr/ 'sound of tearing cloth', درّا /darrā/ 'mountain pass/valley', and مسرّت /musarrat/ 'happiness' indicate that /r/, /ḷ/, and /v/ do, in fact, occur geminated in word-medial or final position. Interestingly, several words of this type are of Perso-Arabic origin, e.g. تصوّر /tasavvur/ 'concept, idea' and مسرّت /musarrat/ 'happiness', suggesting that with the increasing number of Perso-Arabic origin words used in Panjabi, generalizations about gemination need to be revised.

Gemination interacts with vowel quality and stress. In monosyllables, following a stressed short vowel, consonants are often pronounced with a force that causes a doubling of the consonant sound, as in ست /sat(t)/ 'seven', کن /kan(n)/ 'ear' (Bailey 1904a: 3). In polysyllabic words, gemination follows a stressed syllable containing a centralized vowel which precedes a disyllabic word with a peripheral vowel nucleus in the second syllable, or a trisyllabic word with a centralized vowel in the second syllable. For instance:

- ہٹّی /ˈhaṭṭī/ 'shop'
- مکھی /ˈmakkhī/ 'fly'
- کبا /ˈkubbā/ 'humpback'
- چکا /ˈcakkā/ 'wheel'
- اُکھڑنا /ˈukkhaṛnā/ 'to become loose, be uprooted'

This effect of stress is very strong, and some speakers also produce geminate consonants even following stressed peripheral vowels in polysyllabic words with no inherent or historical gemination, for example:

- پنجابی /panˈjābbī/ 'Panjabi'
- روٹی /ˈroṭṭī/ 'bread' (Shackle 2003: 591)

This relation between stress and geminaton is also the case for Saraiki (see Section 3.3.2.3) and for Hindko (Section 3.3.2.1).

In stem-final position, gemination is audible most clearly when the word inflects to add an extra syllable after the geminated segment, or if the word is followed by another word. In this grammar, gemination is represented by doubling the geminated element in the transcription, like this: تتّا /tattā/ 'hot'.

In the case of aspirated consonants, the plosive is written twice, but /h/ once, like this: ہتھ /hatth/ 'hand'.

3.4.2.3 Gemination in Saraiki

In Saraiki, according to Shackle (1976), all consonants except /h/ and /y/, /ṇ/, and /ṛ/ can be geminated.[22]

Gemination occurs only when a consonant follows a stressed central vowel; non-phonemic gemination can also occur in this environment. Consequently, gemination can never occur at the beginning of a word (Shackle 1976: 27). For example, the first and second person plural pronouns اساں /assā̃/ 'we' and تسّاں /tussā̃/ 'you.PL' have gemination of /s/ after a stressed first syllable. However, realization of gemination in Saraiki is weaker than it is in Panjabi (Shackle 1976: 27). So, according to Shackle (1976: 27) there is no real contrast in Saraiki between pairs like دلی /ˈdillī/ 'Delhi' and دلی /ˈdilī/ 'heartfelt'. In such pairs as وٹا /ˈvʌṭṭā/ 'clod' and وٹا /vʌˈṭā/ 'change', the contrast is one of stress more than of gemination. Compare this analysis with the treatment for Hindko immediately above.

3.5 Phonotactics

Phonotactics refers to the characteristic ways sounds combine to form syllables and words, and ways in which the occurrence of some sounds and syllable types is constrained to certain positions in a syllable or word. In the following two sections, syllable types and consonant clusters in these three languages are discussed. We employ a simple definition of syllable as an uninterrupted segment of speech consisting of a simple vowel or diphthong with or without preceding or following consonants, which is the domain to which stress may be assigned. A consonant cluster is a sequence of two different consonants pronounced together without an intervening vowel sound. Here, geminated consonants are not treated as consonant clusters.

22 Shackle (1976: 27) says that /ṇ/ and /ṛ/ cannot be geminated, but Nasir Abbas Syed disagrees, providing the following examples including these sounds: جنّاں /ʃaṇṇā̃/ 'person' and سڑّی /saṛṛī/ 'burned.PP.F'.

3.5.1 Hindko phonotactics

3.5.1.1 Hindko syllable types

Our data for Abbottabad Hindko yield the following syllable types, which are the same as those found for Panjabi:

- V, e.g., آں /ã̄/ 'ACC-DAT case ending, or marked feminine plural ending'
- CV. e.g., راہ /rā́/ 'way, path'
- VC, e.g., ات /it/ 'here'
- VCC, e.g., امب /amb/ 'mango'
- CVC, e.g., نک /nak/ 'nose'
- CCV, e.g., گراں /grã̄/ 'village'
- CVCC, e.g., دند /dand/ 'tooth'; کھنڈ /khanḍ/ ~ /khãḍ/ 'sugar'
- CCVC, e.g., پیاز /pyāz/ 'onion'.

3.5.1.2 Hindko consonant clusters

Consonant clusters occur syllable initially, as in ترے /træ/ 'three' or گراں /grã̄/ 'village'; medially, as in کتکا /kutkā/ 'pestle'. In syllable-final position the picture is less clear. Words like اگ /ag(g)/ 'fire', involving geminates, or borrowings like گوشت /gošt/ 'meat' are quite common. But if geminates are not considered as clusters, and borrowings are excluded, it appears that except for sequences involving a nasal + a dental, or labial plosive, e.g. /nd/ as in دند /dand/ 'tooth', or /mb/ as in امب /amb/ 'mango', which might also be analyzed as nasalized vowels preceding non-velar stops, Hindko does not allow syllable-final clusters in native words. This was the conclusion of Varma (1936: 84), who said that "Lahnda has no consonant-groups at the end of words."

3.5.2 Panjabi phonotactics

3.5.2.1 Panjabi syllable types

Panjabi syllables consist, at minimum, of a single vowel (V)—either central or peripheral. This vowel may be preceded or followed by up to two consonants (C), yielding the following syllable types:

- V, e.g., آ /ā/ 'come!'

- CV, eg., جا /jā/ 'go!'
- VC, e.g., آپ /āp/ 'self'
- CVC, e.g., وچ /vic/ 'in'
- CCV, e.g., بھرا /prā̀/ 'brother'
- VCC, e.g., امب /amb/ 'mango'
- CCVC, e.g., پروگرام /pro.grām/ 'plan' < 'program'
- CVCC, e.g., دوست /dost/ 'friend'

Phonemic nasalized vowels only occur in word-final position; however, according to Sharma (1971: 30), Panjabi shows a strong preference for (phonetic) nasalization with long, open syllables, e.g., Panjabi توں /tū̃/ versus Urdu تو /tū/ '2SG', Panjabi ناں /nā̃/versus Urdu نام /nām/ 'name', or Panjabi ماں /mā̃/ versus Saraiki ما /mā/ 'mother'.

Peripheral vowels generally do not occur in the first syllable of a disyllabic word in which the second syllable is closed and has a peripheral vowel. This phonotactic constraint accounts for the difference between; for example, Urdu بازار /bāzār/ and Panjabi بزار /bazār/ 'bazaar' or Urdu بیمار /bīmār/ and Panjabi بمار /bimār/ 'ill' (Sharma 1971: 12). Centralized vowels, as a rule, do not occur in word-final position. There are, however, some exceptions to this generalization:

1. A stressed vocative particle /-a/ sometimes occurs after a consonant-final name, e.g., سلیما /salīm-ˈá/ 'hey, Salim'.
2. A few high-frequency monosyllabic function words, e.g., کہ /ki/ 'that', کو /ku/ 'about, approximately' end in centralized vowels.
3. Another class of exceptions are words originating in Urdu (< Persian) that end in ہ *choṭī he*. While one would expect these words to end in /ā/, in fact the final vowel is "half-long" and closer to /a/, e.g., the adjectival form شادی شدہ /šādī šuda/ 'married'. In most cases nouns with this ending, e.g., نقشہ /nakša/ 'map', are treated as marked masculines—i.e., as though they ended in ا /ā/.

All consonants can occur in word-initial position except for the retroflex consonants /ṇ/, /ḷ/, /ṛ/, and /ṛh/. However, /ṇ/, /ḷ/, /ṛ/, and /ṛh/ can occur in syllable-initial position word medially, e.g., جاݨا /jāṇā/ 'to go'.

3.5.2.2 Panjabi consonant clusters

Consonant clusters can occur in syllable-initial, medial, and final positions. Initial clusters include /pr/, /kr/, /gr/, /ṭr/, /tr/, /sr/, /sy/, /sv/, /fr/, /sl/, /ky/, /khy/, /ty/, /py/, /by/, /vy/, /gv/. They occur in both indigenous words, e.g., تریڑ /treṛ/ 'dew', and borrowed words, e.g., ٹرک /ṭrak/ 'truck'. Initial clusters tend to occur when the syllable peak has a peripheral vowel, i.e., CCV̄, as in ویاہ /vyā̂/ 'wedding' (Sharma 1971: 57). Some initial clusters result from the elision of a centralized vowel preceding a stressed syllable, e.g., Panjabi سوال /svāl/, corresponding to Urdu سوال /savāl/ 'question'. The word صلاح 'advice', pronounced either as /slā̂/ or as /salā̂/, is an interesting case. In the first pronunciation it shows elision of a centralized /a/ preceding a stressed syllable in the borrowed Perso-Arabic word, originally /salāh/, yielding the syllable pattern CCV̄, as well as high tone induced by the post-vocalic /h/. The pronunciation retaining the centralized /a/ probably reflects knowledge of Urdu.

However, there is simultaneously a strong tendency to simplify some initial consonant clusters, especially those beginning with the sibilant /s/ plus a retroflex or velar plosive, i.e., /sṭ/ or /sk/ in loanwords. For example, in the English word *station* /sṭešan/ the initial /sṭ/ cluster is usually simplified to /ṭ/, yielding /ṭešan/; alternatively, an epenthetic vowel may break up the cluster, yielding /saṭešan/. However initial /sk/ in English loans is only sometimes treated in this way, since we have both /skūl/ and /sakūl/ سکول for 'school', but only سکنٹ /skinṭ/ for 'second'.

Medial clusters can occur in monomorphemic words, e.g., چسکا /caskā/ 'taste/craving for', or can arise at morpheme boundaries. A simple case of the latter is when a consonant-initial suffix is attached to a consonant-final stem. For instance, کر /kar/ 'do.STEM' + دا /-dā/ 'IP.SG.M' > کردا /kardā/ 'do-IP.SG.M', giving rise to the cluster /rd/. Another important source of such emergent clusters is the schwa-deletion rule. This rule plays an important part in Panjabi phonotactics. In the configuration CVCVC + V, which occurs in plural formation of polysyllabic unmarked feminine nouns, e.g. سڑک /saṛak/ 'road' + اں /-ā̃/ 'PL' > سڑکاں /saṛkā̃/ 'roads', the medial centralized vowel is deleted, giving rise to the cluster /ṛk/. In these two types of emergent clusters, the two consonants that have come together to form a cluster remain in separate syllables.

Final clusters consist of at most two consonants. Gill and Gleason (1969: 13–14) identify four patterns:

1. /l/ + plosive, sibilant, or nasal, e.g., پلس /puls/ 'police'
2. /r/ + plosive, sibilant, lateral, or nasal, e.g., مرچ /mirc/ 'pepper'
3. /ṛ + plosive, e.g., رڑک /riṛk/ 'trouble, enmity'
4. sibilant + plosive or nasal, e.g., مست /mast/ 'intoxicated'

Our own observations also include /nṭ/ in the English loan منٹ /minṭ/ 'minute'. Most of these occur in Lahore Panjabi, but for some of them in each class most speakers insert an epenthetic schwa between the two consonants. For example, in class (1) غلط /galt/ 'wrong' is usually pronounced as /galat/; in class (2) برف /barf/ is usually pronounced /baraf/; in class (3) رڑک /riṛk/ would be pronounced as /riṛak/ ; in class (4) رسم /rasm/ 'custom' is pronounced /rasam/. Some types of clusters, though, are not possible in word-final position. Kalra (1982: 102) finds that no clusters of the following four types are found in final position:

1. plosive + fricative/liquid/nasal/glide
2. fricative + nasal/liquid/glide
3. nasal + liquid
4. liquid + glide

3.5.3 Saraiki phonotactics

3.5.3.1 Saraiki syllable types

The following syllable types are attested in Saraiki:

- V, e.g., اے /e/ 'hey!' (vocative particle)
- VC, e.g., ات /it/ 'so much'
- VCC, e.g., امب /amb/ 'mango'
- CV, e.g., ما /mā/ 'so much; mother'
- CVC, e.g., بار /bār/ 'burden, weight'
- CVCC, e.g., کھنڈ /khanḍ/ 'sugar'
- CCV, e.g., ترے /træ/ 'three'
- CCVC, e.g., ترٹ /truṭ-/ 'break (intr. stem)'
- CVCCC, e.g., چندر /candr/ 'moon'
- CCVCC, e.g., سکتر /skutr/ 'stepson'[23]

23 Example courtesy of Nasir Abbas Syed, who also states that this is the only example of this syllable type that he could find.

3.5.3.2 Saraiki consonant clusters

Saraiki allows initial, medial, and final clusters—all of which can be found in indigenous words. The most frequent initial clusters are /tr/, /dr/, and /dhr/, as seen in ترٹݨ /truṭaṇ/ 'to break (intr.)', دربھ /drabh/ ' a kind of grass', and دھرکݨ /dhrukaṇ/ 'to run' (Shackle 1976: 24). Two-element medial clusters can involve almost any pair of consonants. Various types of final clusters occur in Saraiki, and are more frequent than initial clusters. They include:

1. dental plosive + /r/, پتر /putr/ 'son';
2. /n/ + dental plosive + /r/, چندر /candr/ 'moon';
3. nasal + sibilant, سیہنس /sæhins/ 'a thousand';
4. /ṇ/ + stop, وݨج /vaṇj ~ vaṇaj/ 'trade';
5. voiceless velar plosive + sibilant, نقش /nakš/ 'sign, pattern, impression'
6. voiceless fricative + voiceless plosive, دوست /dost/ 'friend'.

Implosives do not occur in final clusters (Shackle 1976: 24–26). Some other final clusters are also found in loans used in standard Saraiki, e.g., گارڈ /gārḍ/ 'guard', but most final clusters in borrowed words are subject to vowel epenthesis.

In the Saraiki of Multan, the choice of epenthetic vowel is frequently determined by progressive vowel-harmony from the stressed syllable. Thus, the Perso-Arabic loans گرم /garm/ 'hot', فکر /fikr/ 'worry', and شکر /šukr/ 'thanks' appear as Saraiki /ˈga.ram/, /ˈfi.kir/, and /ˈšu.kur/. This contrasts with consistent use of epenthetic /a/ in Panjabi, giving /garam/, /fikar/, /šukar/; and consistent use of epenthetic /u/ in the Awankari variety of Lahnda, yielding /gʌrum/, /fikur/, and /šukur/ (Shackle 1979: 206). See also Syed and Aldaihani 2014.

3.6 Orthography

Two aspects of the written language will be discussed here: (1) script, and (2) spelling. In Pakistan, all three languages—Hindko, Panjabi, and Saraiki—use the Perso-Arabic script. This script is based upon the original 28-letter Arabic alphabet, modified to include additional letters to represent sounds of Persian not found in Arabic (پ /p/, ژ /ž/, چ /c/, and گ /g/) , and then again later to include letters to represent grammatical and phonological distinctions present in Indo-Aryan languages: the introduction of ے to uniquely represent final /e/, the sign of masculine plural or oblique singular,[24] and the introduction of characters to represent aspirated and retroflex consonants. Writers of Panjabi, Hindko, and Saraiki apply most of the same modifications and general orthographic principles as do writers of Urdu, the national language of Pakistan. Many of the spelling patterns observed in Panjabi written in Perso-Arabic script are taken over directly from Urdu, which has, in almost all cases, retained historical spellings of Persian or Arabic loanwords.

Panjabi language users in India almost all write Panjabi in the Gurmukhi script, an Indic script related to Devanagari, the writing system used to represent Hindi. Gurmukhi and Devanagari are *abugidas*: almost all vowels are explicitly represented, with the exception of the centralized vowel /a/, which is left unwritten.

By contrast, the Perso-Arabic script is a modified *abjad*: peripheral vowels are explicitly represented, but the centralized vowels /a, i, u/ are usually left unrepresented. The Perso-Arabic script is written from right to left; numerals, however, are written from left to right. The script is inherently cursive, and letters may have up to four allographs, or different forms of the same symbol.

1. the **independent** form, which is unconnected to other letters;
2. the **initial** form, connected only on the left;
3. the **medial** form, connected on both sides; and
4. the **final** form, connected only on the right.

For those letters that do not connect leftward (as noted by "only joins right" in Table 3.18), the initial form is the same as the independent form, and the medial form is the same as the final form. After a letter that does not connect leftward a letter will be in its initial form.

Two types of Arabic calligraphy have been widely adopted for typography: *Naskh* and *Nastaʿlīq*. Naskh is characterized by a strictly horizontal orientation, and is used to print Arabic and (usually) Persian; in Pakistan, it is also used to print Pashto and Sindhi. In Nastaʿlīq, words or ligatures slope within each ligature from the top right to the bottom left; this is the most widely used typeface for printing Hindko, Panjabi, and Saraiki. This grammar follows the general practice in Pakistan and employs a Nastaʿlīq typeface wherever it is technically possible; exceptions are noted where they occur.

Table 3.18 lays out the letters of the Perso-Arabic script, as used for Hindko, Panjabi, and Saraiki. The table uses the Naskh style, as the font does a better job at showing where connecting letters attach (in all but the jīm class). The letters are shown in Nastaʿlīq style in Table 3.19. Letters used only in Saraiki will be discussed further in Section 3.6.5.

---

24 Its function later expanded to represent /e/ representing the izāfat following words ending in ا /ā/ or و /o, ū/ in Persian-influenced izāfat constructions.

Table 3.18: Letters of the Perso-Arabic script, as used for Hindko, Panjabi, and Saraiki

Name	Independent	Final	Medial	Initial	Note
alif madd	آ			آ	initial only
alif	ا	ـا		ا	only joins right
be	ب	ـب	ـبـ	بـ	
ɓe	ٻ	ـٻ	ـٻـ	ٻـ	Saraiki only
pe	پ	ـپ	ـپـ	پـ	
te	ت	ـت	ـتـ	تـ	
ṭe	ٹ	ـٹ	ـٹـ	ٹـ	
se	ث	ـث	ـثـ	ثـ	
jīm	ج	ـج	ـجـ	جـ	
ce	چ	ـچ	ـچـ	چـ	
ʄe	ڄ	ـڄ	ـڄـ	ڄـ	Saraiki only
baṛī he	ح	ـح	ـحـ	حـ	
xe	خ	ـخ	ـخـ	خـ	
dāl	د	ـد		د	only joins right
ḍāl	ڈ	ـڈ		ڈ	only joins right
ɗāl	ݙ	ـݙ		ݙ	Saraiki only; only joins right
zāl	ذ	ـذ		ذ	only joins right
re	ر	ـر		ر	only joins right
ṛe	ڑ	ـڑ		ڑ	only joins right
ze	ز	ـز		ز	only joins right

Table 3.18: (continued)

Name	Independent	Final	Medial	Initial	Note
že	ژ	ـژ		ژ	only joins right
sīn	س	ـس	ـسـ	سـ	
šīn	ش	ـش	ـشـ	شـ	
svād	ص	ـص	ـصـ	صـ	
zvād	ض	ـض	ـضـ	ضـ	
toë	ط	ـط	ـطـ	طـ	
zoë	ظ	ـظ	ـظـ	ظـ	
ˈain	ع	ـع	ـعـ	عـ	
ɣain	غ	ـغ	ـغـ	غـ	
fe	ف	ـف	ـفـ	فـ	
qāf	ق	ـق	ـقـ	قـ	
kāf	ک	ـک	ـکـ	کـ	
gāf	گ	ـگ	ـگـ	گـ	
ɠāf	ڳ	ـڳ	ـڳـ	ڳـ	Saraiki only
lām	ل	ـل	ـلـ	لـ	
mīm	م	ـم	ـمـ	مـ	
nūn	ن	ـن	ـنـ	نـ	
ṇūn	ݨ	ـݨ	ـݨـ	ݨـ	Saraiki only
vāv	و	ـو		و	only joins right
choṭī he	ہ	ـہ	ـہـ	ہـ	

Table 3.18: (continued)

Name	Independent	Final	Medial	Initial	Note
do chašmī he	ھ	ـھ	ـھـ		does not occur word initially
choṭī ye	ی	ـی	ـیـ	یـ	
baṛī ye	ے	ـے			final only, in medial and initial position is identical to ی

3.6.1 Segments in orthography

3.6.1.1 Consonants in orthography

Table 3.19 shows the representation of Hindko, Panjabi, and Saraiki consonant sounds in the orthography, presented in the order of standard phoneme charts.

Table 3.19: Consonant sounds in orthography

Transcription	Orthography
p	پ
b	ب
ɓ	ٻ
m	م
f	ف
v	و
t	ت ط
d	د
ɗ	ڋ
n	ن

Table 3.19: (continued)

Transcription	Orthography
r	ر
s	س ث ص
z	ذ ز ض ظ
l	ل
š	ش
ž	ژ
c	چ
ʄ	ڄ
j	ج
ṭ	ٹ
ḍ	ڈ
ṇ	Written in Saraiki as ڻ, in Panjabi as ن, and in Hindko as نڑ
ṛ	ڑ
ḷ	Not distinguished from ل
y	ی
k	ک
g	گ
ɠ	ڳ
x	خ
ɣ	غ
q	ق

Table 3.19: (continued)

Transcription	Orthography
h	ہ *choṭī he* is the usual representation of /h/. ھ *do cašmī he* represents aspiration in /ph/, /bh/, /th/, /dh/, /ṭh/, /ḍh/, /ch/, /jh/, /kh/, and /vh/, /mh/, /lh/, and nh/, and historic aspiration of voiced plosives in Panjabi. ح *baṛī he* represents /h/ in Arabic and Persian loanwords.

In the modification of the Perso-Arabic script used to write Panjabi, Hindko, and Saraiki a small ط *toë* is written over the Arabic letters ت *te*, د *dāl*, ر *re*, and sometimes ن *nūn* to represent the retroflex counterparts /ṭ/, /ḍ/, /ṛ/, and /ṇ/ of the dental sounds /t/, /d/, /r/, and /n/.

Several letters can correspond to a single consonant sound. For example, the four letters ظ *zoë*, ض *zvād*, ذ *zāl*, and ز *ze* all represent the /z/ sound. They have lost the distinct sounds they had in Arabic, since Indo-Aryan languages do not have those sounds, and the Arabic sounds have been assimilated to the perceived closest indigenous sounds. The letters ح *baṛī he*, ط *toë*, ص *svād*, ث *se*, ظ *zoë*, ض *zvād*, and ذ *zāl* are almost always retained in loanwords borrowed either directly from Arabic, or from Arabic via Persian, and thus preserve historical information.

The use and function of ھ *do cašmī he* varies among these languages. In all three languages, after the voiceless plosives پ *pe*, ت *te*, ٹ *ṭe*, and ک *kāf*, it represents aspiration, yielding the digraphs پھ، تھ، ٹھ and کھ for /ph/, /th/, /ṭh/, and /kh/, respectively. In Panjabi, it also represents historic aspiration of voiced plosives, now evolved into tone. In Saraiki, where historic aspiration is maintained for both voiceless and voiced plosives, it consistently represents aspiration.[25]

The letter ہ *choṭī he* is distinguished from ھ *do cašmī he* and is the default spelling of consonantal /h/ in all three languages. ح *baṛī he* is used in words of Arabic origin. In Panjabi, ہ *choṭī he* and ح *baṛī he* can also indicate high or low tone, depending on their position in a syllable, as in کھیہ /khé/ 'dust', or آرام دہ /ārām dé/ 'restful', where the ہ *choṭī he* indicates high tone, or in اصلاح /islā́/ 'reformation, correction', where ح

25 Since ھ *do cašmī he* is the initial form of ہ *choṭī he* in Arabic and the Naskh style, it often happens that writers of these languages in Pakistan who are familiar with Arabic and/or Naskh use ھ *do cašmī he* in initial position in words like ھے /hæ/ 'is'. This contradicts the generalizations above about the use of ھ *do cašmī he* for aspiration, but it is frequently encountered.

can indicate high tone for some speakers. In Hindko, ہ *choṭī he* appears in words with historically aspirated voiced plosives, similar to the way ھ *do cašmī he* functions in Panjabi. For example, the word for 'daughter', which historically has /dh/, is دھی /dhī/ in Saraiki, دھی /tī̀/ in Panjabi, and تہی /tī̀/ in Abbottabad Hindko.[26]

3.6.1.2 Vowels in orthography

The Perso-Arabic writing system has resources to represent both peripheral and centralized vowel sounds, and in cases where writers desire transparency and precision—for example, religious texts and books for young readers or foreign learners—they may partially or fully vocalize the text by writing all the vowels. Fully vocalized writing makes use of three diacritics which represent each of the three centralized vowels /a, i, u/ by one of the three vowel diacritics written over (for /a/ and /u/) or under (for /i/) the consonant that precedes it, as shown in Table 3.20.

In this section illustrating the use of these diacritics, examples are printed in a Naskh typeface rather than the Nastaʿlīq typeface used elsewhere in this grammar because vowel diacritics show up more clearly in horizontal Naskh than in sloping Nastaʿlīq. The small circles in Table 3.20 and Table 3.21 represent the characters to which the diacritics are attached.

Romanization	Orthography	Panjabi name
a	◌َ	zabar
i	◌ِ	zer
u	◌ُ	peš

Table 3.20: Centralized vowel diacritics

In order to unambiguously represent peripheral vowels, these diacritics are combined with the letters ی *ye*, و *vāv*, and ا *alif*, which in Arabic represent the vowels /ī/, /ū/, and /ā/ respectively. The peripheral vowel /ā/ in initial position is represented by ا *alif* with an extra top stroke, known as آ *alif madd*.

- آٹا /āṭā/ 'whole-wheat flour'

26 The possible reasons for this spelling convention are interesting. Perhaps it was adopted as a way of asserting Hindko identity, or perhaps it is intended to indicate a difference in the quality of Hindko and Panjabi low tone.

Romanization	Initial Position	Medial/Final Position
ī	اِی	◌ِی
e	ای	ی (medial) ے (final)
æ	اَی	◌َی (medial) ے (final)
ā	آ	ا
ū	اُو	◌ُو
o	او	و
ɔ/au	اَو	◌َو

Table 3.21: Representation of peripheral (long) vowels using diacritics

In medial position, /ā/ is represented by the centralized vowel diacritic ◌َ *zabar* followed by ا *alif*.

• پَانا /pāṇā/ 'to put'

However, in a few Arabic loanwords, for example the man's name Mustafa, /ā/ in final position is represented by a shortened version of ا *alif*, known as کھڑا الف /khaṛā alif/, written over the final form of ی *choṭī ye*.

• مُصطَفٰی /mustafā/ '[a proper name]'

The peripheral vowels /ī/ and /ū/ are represented in medial position by the centralized vowel diacritics ◌ِ *zer* and ◌ُ *peš*, followed by semivowel letters ی *baṛī ye* and و *vāv*, respectively. This graphically represents the analysis of /ā/, /ī/, and /ū/ as the "long" counterparts of /a/, /i/, and /ū/, respectively.

The peripheral vowels /e/ and /o/ are represented by ی *choṭī ye* and و *vāv* alone. Finally, the peripheral vowels /æ/ and /ɔ/ are represented by the centralized vowel diacritic ◌َ *zabar* followed by ی *baṛī ye* and و *vāv*, respectively.

The implementation of these principles depends on the position of the vowel within a word. In word-initial position, centralized vowels require a silent "carrier" letter. This letter is typically ا *alif*, but may also be ع *ain*, which represents an Arabic sound that is described as a pharyngeal fricative or epiglottal approximant [ʕ], but has no corresponding sound in any of these three Indo-Aryan languages, except in consciously Arabicized pronunciation. In word-medial position, centralized vowels are represented only with diacritics in fully vocalized writing. As noted above, centralized vowels do not occur in final position (except for a few unstressed particles); however, the diacritic ◌ِ *zer* is sometimes placed under the final consonant in a word to represent the *izāfat*, a linking vowel in Persian loanwords. (See Section 3.6.3).

A number of words that historically ended in /-ah/ have lost the final /h/, and the quality of the remaining vowel has changed to a half-long /a/, which most analyses treat as an allophone of /ā/. These words are often still spelled with their historical spelling as ◌َہ *zabar-choṭī he*; however, they are pronounced with a final /ā/ or /a/. Because spelling in vernacular writing is variable, some words ending in final /ā/ may be written either with ا *alif* or with ◌َہ *zabar-choṭī he*. In this grammar, we transcribe both spellings as /-ā/. Unless otherwise indicated, the examples that follow in this section are from Panjabi. Most of them are used, however, in all three languages.

- کمرہ ~ کَمرَا /kamrā/ 'room'
- بندہ ~ بَندَا /bandā/ 'man, person'

In word-initial position, all vowels require a carrier ا *alif* or ع *ain*. For /ī/, /e/, /o/, and /ū/, the presence of ا *alif* preceding ی *baṛī ye* or و *vāv* signals that the initial sound is a vowel, rather than a semivowel /y/ or /v/.

- عَربی /arbī/ 'Arabic'
- اَوکھا /ɔkhā/ 'difficult'
- عِیسائی /īsāī/ 'Christian'

In word-medial position, /ī/, /æ/, /ɔ/, and /ū/ are each represented in medial position by a diacritic followed by the medial forms of ی *ye* or و *vāv*, respectively, while /e/ and /o/ are represented by just the medial forms of ی *ye* and و *vāv* alone.

- بِیمہ /bīmā/ 'insurance policy'
- پَیر /pær/ 'foot'
- چَوداں /cɔdā̃/ 'fourteen'
- دُور /dūr/ 'far'
- کھیت /khet/ 'field'
- لوڑ /loṛ/ 'need'

In final position, /ɔ/ and /ū/ are again represented by ◌َ *zabar* or ◌ُ *peš*, respectively, followed by the final form of و *vāv*, while /o/ is represented by و *vāv* alone.

- نَو /nɔ/ 'nine'
- آلُو /ālū/ 'potato'
- دو /do/ 'two'

However, in word-final position, ے *baṛī ye* represents /e/ and /æ/, while ی *choṭī ye* represents /ī/.

- پانِی /pāṇī/ 'water'
- ساڑھے /sā̃ḍe/ '(an additional) one-half'

In Persian-origin words that contain the sequence خوا *xe-vāv-alif*, the letter و *vāv* represents centralized /u/ rather than the usual peripheral /ū/; for example خوش /xuš/ 'happy', as well as words derived from it.

In Section 3.3.3 we distinguish between diphthongs, which pattern as single sounds, and vowels which happen to occur together in a series. For both vowels in a series without an intervening consonant and for sounds perceived as diphthongs, the diacritic ٔ *hamza* is used. If the second vowel is ی *ye* representing /ī/, /e/ or /æ/, ٔ *hamza* appears above a "seat" in the line of script similar to the "seats" that support the dots in the medial forms of the letters ن *nūn* and ت *te*, like this: ئی. Representation of diphthongs using *hamza* occurs frequently in the representation of English words in these languages, something which is increasingly being done. For example, the English word high, would appear as ہائی.[27]

- گئی /gaī/ 'go.PP.SG.F'

If the second vowel is و *vāv*, the position of ٔ *hamza* depends on whether و *vāv* follows a letter to which it can join. If و *vāv* follows short vowel represented by hamza, the ٔ *hamza* occurs on a "seat," as in رئوف /raūf/ '[a proper name]'. If و *vāv* follows a non-joining letter, ٔ *hamza* occurs directly above و *vāv*, as in جاؤ /jāo/ 'go.IMP'.

As noted above, most written texts omit some or all centralized vowel diacritics, which requires the reader to supply the correct vowel from memory or context. This results in a certain degree of ambiguity, in which one letter or pair of letters can stand for more than one sound. These ambiguities are summarized in Table 3.22. Additional ambiguities arise from the fact that medial centralized vowels are generally not written at all.

From this point forward, we present examples as they normally appear in writing, without vowel diacritics.

---

27 Note the difference between the shape of the *hamza* in *naskh* or when quoted alone, ٔ, and the *hamza* in connected Nastaʿlīq, in the middle of ہائی.

Orthography	Transcription
initial آ	ā
initial ا	i, a, u
initial ای	ī, e, æ
initial او	ɔ, o, ū
medial ا	ā
medial ی	ī, e, æ
medial و	ɔ, au, o, ū
final ا	ā
final ی	ī
final ے	e, æ
final و	ɔ, o, ū

Table 3.22: Symbol-sound correspondences in writing without vowel diacritics

3.6.2 Suprasegmentals in orthography

3.6.2.1 Gemination in orthography

The Perso-Arabic script has a special symbol, ◌ّ *tašdīd*, which may be written over consonant and semi-vowel letters to represent gemination. However, use of the symbol is variable and sporadic not only in texts written in all three of the languages being described here, but even in dictionaries, as is also true of Urdu.

- ترقّی or ترقی /taraqqī/ 'progress, development'
- پتّھر or پتھر /patthar/ 'rock, stone'

3.6.2.2 Nasalization in orthography

As noted above, nasalization serves to distinguish meaning only in word-final position. Nasalization is indicated by placing the letter ں *nūn γunnā* (the letter ن *nūn* without a dot) after the word-final vowel.

- پہلاں /pǽlã̀/ 'before, earlier'

- لوکیں /lokĩ̄/ 'people'

Non-contrastive nasalized vowels do occur in word-initial and word-medial position; however, since ں *nūn γunnā* only occurs in final position, nasalization in these positions is written as a full ن *nūn*:

- بھانبڑ /pã̀baṛ/ 'large fire, blaze' pronounced as [pã̀baṛ] or [pàmbaṛ].

3.6.2.3 Stress and tone in orthography

Stress is not represented in the orthography of any of these three languages. However, since it is often associated with vowel length of a syllable and gemination of the onset of a following syllable, written forms can provide clues about syllable stress.

Panjabi and Hindko orthography does not explicitly represent tone. However, since tones in these languages are the reflexes of syllables that either historically had voiced aspirated plosives or in which an orthographic <h> is variably realized as /h/ or not pronounced, tone is represented indirectly in spelling. The Panjabi low tone occurs in syllables in which a voiced aspirated plosive or /h/ preceded the vowel in a stressed syllable. The high tone is the reflex of syllables in which a voiced aspirated plosive or /h/ followed the vowel in a stressed syllable.[28]

Historical voiced aspirated plosives are spelled with the letters ب *be*, د *dāl*, ڈ *ḍāl*, ج *jīm*, گ *gāf* followed by ھ *do cašmī he* to represent the sounds بھ /bh/, دھ /dh/, ڈھ /ḍh/, جھ /jh/, and گھ /gh/, respectively. While the voiced aspirate sounds are retained in Saraiki, in Panjabi all historical voiced aspirated plosives have lost their aspiration. Whether or not they have also lost their voicing depends on where they appear in the syllable: syllable-initially, historical voiced aspirated plosives are realized as voiceless unaspirated plosives; syllable-medially and finally, they are pronounced as voiced unaspirated plosives (see Table 3.23).

Recall that tone generally coincides with stress in Panjabi and Hindko: if a syllable is unstressed, it cannot carry a low tone, and usually does not carry a high tone. However, the historically aspirated consonant or /h/ need not occur immediately adjacent to the vowel of the stressed syllable. For example, if /h/ occurs anywhere before the stressed vowel, the tone will occur on the stressed syllable. For example, in گھبرانا /kabrã̀ṇā/ 'to worry, be upset', the low tone occurs on the stressed syllable following that in which the historical voiced /g/ occurred.

28 Apparent exceptions are the high tone on monosyllabic stem imperatives like دے /dé/ 'give!', جا /jấ/ 'go!', and future tenses of toneless stems, e.g. جاویگا /jấvegā/ 'he will go' (Shackle 2003: 593).

Position of historical voiced plosive	Voicing	Tone	Examples
Word-initial and before the stressed syllable	Voiceless	Low	بھرا <bhrā> [prà] 'brother'
Word-medial and before the stressed syllable	Voiced	Low	سدھار <sudhār> [sudàr] 'reform' کڈھوا <kaḍhvā> [kaḍvà] 'have taken out'
Word-medial and after the stressed syllable	Voiced	High	سادھو <sādhū> [sā́dū] 'saint, holy man' سانجھا <sānjhā> [sā́nja] 'common, shared'
Word-final and after the stressed syllable	Voiced	High	گنڈھ <ganḍh> [gánḍ] 'knot, bundle' لابھ <lābh> [lā́b] 'profit, benefit'

Table 3.23: Representation of Panjabi tones: historic voiced aspirated plosives (some examples from Bhardwaj 1995: 199–200.)

Consonantal /h/ is spelled ہ *choṭī he* or ح *baṛī he*. Pronunciation of orthographic <h> is variable by linguistic environment: it is much more likely to be pronounced word-initially than word-medially, where it usually indicates tone (Gill and Gleason 1969: 12). In syllable-final position, ہ *choṭī he* and ح *baṛī he* are hardly ever pronounced as /h/, but rather indicate tone. In syllable-initial position, these letters are more likely to be pronounced as /h/ in stressed syllables, either in monosyllabic words, such as ہار /hār/ 'necklace' or ہے /hæ/ 'is.EMPH', or polysyllabic words, such as آہو /āho/ 'yes'. In an unstressed initial syllable, /h/ is frequently dropped. For example, حیران /hærān/ 'surprised' is often pronounced as /rǟn/, with low tone replacing the dropped /h/ and elision of the vowel of the first syllable. This varies by idiolect: orthographic <h> is more likely to be pronounced by people whose speech is influenced by Urdu than by others. And it is variable by register: it is more likely to be pronounced in formal than in informal situations. When speakers pronounce orthographic <h>, they may also produce a tone; conversely, however, when speakers do not pronounce orthographic <h>, they consistently replace it with a tone. Examples of the variable pronunciation of <h> are shown in Table 3.24.[29]

29 In writing, the two words باہر /bāhar/ 'outside' and بہار /bahār/ 'spring' look quite different: The word باہر /bāhar/ 'outside' has peripheral /ā/ in the first syllable and is stressed on the first syllable, but بہار /bahār/ 'spring' has peripheral /ā/ in the second syllable and is stressed on the second syllable. In normal pronunciation, however, both words are monosyllabic and differ only in tone: /bā́r/ 'outside' vs. /bàr/ 'spring'. See Table 3.24.

Position of /h/	Pronounced	Tone	Examples
Word-initial and immediately before the vowel of the stressed syllable	Usually yes; tone without /h/ pronunciation stigmatized by some, particularly for Arabic and Persian loanwords	Low	ہتھ <hat(t)h> [hàt(t)h] **or** [ạ̀t(t)h] 'hand' حق <ha(k)k> [hàk(k)] **or** [àk(k)] 'right (legal, moral)'
Word-initial but not immediately before the vowel of the stressed syllable	Usually yes; in tone without /h/ pronunciation, unstressed centralized vowel after /h/ often omitted as well.	Low	ہلا <hilā> [hilā] **or** [hilā̀] **or** [lā̀] 'shake' حکیم <hakīm> [hakīm] **or** [hakī̀m] **or** [kī̀m] 'physician'
Word-medial and before the stressed syllable	Sometimes; /h/ without tone in Urdu-influenced pronunciation, tone without /h/, and /h/ with tone both possible.	Low	کہانی <kahāni> [kahā̀ṇī] **or** [kā̀ṇī] 'story' بہار <bahār> [bahār] **or** [bahā̀r] **or** [bā̀r] 'spring'
Word-medial and after the stressed syllable	Sometimes; tone without /h/ or /h/ without tone both possible, /h/ with tone impossible.	High	بوہا <būhā> [bū́ā] 'door' باہر <ˈbāhar> [bāhar] **or** [bā́r] 'outside'
Word-final and after the stressed syllable	No.	High	چاہ <cāh> [cā́] 'tea' منہ <munh> [mū̃́] 'mouth'

Table 3.24: Representation of Panjabi tones: the segment /h/ (after Bhardwaj 1995: 201–202)

3.6.3 Additional diacritics and spelling conventions

The Perso-Arabic script includes a number of additional diacritics, which are written above or below the consonant and semi-vowel letters. Some are optional; others are integral to the inherited spelling of the many Arabic and Persian loanwords.

In Persian, two words may be joined by a linking sound [e] known as *izāfat*, or 'addition'. Many Persian compounds with *izāfat* have been borrowed into Panjabi, and their spelling reflects the original Persian orthography. However, the use of diacritics is variable and sporadic, even in printed texts.

The spelling of *izāfat* compounds depends on the last letter of the first word in the compound. (1) If the first word ends in a consonant, the *izāfat* is spelled with a ◌ِ *zer*, written below the final consonant of the first word.

- وزیرِ اعظم /vazīr-e āzam/ 'prime minister'

Recall that Panjabi words do not end in centralized vowels; therefore, this final ◌ِ *zer* can only signal *izāfat*.

With some words including an izāfat construction, the izāfat is always pronounced, as in وزیرِ اعظم /vazīr-e āzam/ 'prime minister'. However, with others, as in طالبِ علم /tālib-e ilm/ 'student' , it is never pronounced. However, this spelling of *izāfat* is just as likely as other short vowels to be omitted in Panjabi texts; indeed, *izāfat* is usually not written, and, except in highly formal or religions registers, frequently not pronounced.

- طالبِ علم /tālib-e ilm/ 'student', always pronounced /tālib ilam/.

(2) If the last letter of the first word is ی /choṭī ye/ or ہ /choṭī he/ *choṭī ye*, *izāfat* is spelled by ◌ٔ *hamza* over that letter.

- ولیٔ کامل /valī-e kāmil/ 'perfect saint'

and (3) if the last letter of the first word is ا /alif/ or و /vāv/ *izāfat* is written as ے /baṛī ye/, with or without ◌ٔ /hamza/ above.

- روۓ زمین /rū-e zamīn/ 'surface of the ground'

A doubled form of ◌َ *zabar*, known as ◌ً *tanvīn*, appears over ا *alif* in a number of borrowed Arabic adverbs. This combination of symbols is pronounced /an/. *Tanvīn* is usually spelled consistently in those words in which it occurs.

- فوراً /fɔran/ 'immediately'

The diacritic ◌ْ *jazm* can be optionally written above a consonant letter to indicate that the letter is not followed by a centralized vowel—that is, that it is part of a consonant cluster. This diacritic is never written over a final consonant, since centralized vowels do not occur in word-final position. The use of ◌ْ *jazm* occurs only when full vocalization is employed; this particular symbol is mostly found in religious texts largely written in Arabic. Therefore, ◌ْ *jazm* is extremely infrequent in Hindko, Panjabi, or Saraiki texts.

3.6.4 Hindko orthography

Hindko employs the same alphabet and system of diacritics as does Panjabi. However, since Hazara Hindko is in the early stages of becoming a literary language, and there has been as yet little attention to the question of standardization, there is considerable variation in the way various writers spell certain Hindko words. For example, in the reflexive adjective, the retroflex nasal is spelled اپڑا /apṛā/, اپڑ̇اں /apṛ̃ā̃/, اپڑاں /apṛā̃/, اپݨا /apṇā/, or اپݨاں /apṇā̃/ by various people who write Hindko. An important Hindko-Urdu dictionary was published in 2002 (Sakoon 2002); in this dictionary, Sakoon usually uses the character ݨ for retroflex /ṇ/. This dictionary also helpfully presents variant spellings for some words like آپا /āpā/ and آپاں /āpā̃/ for 'elder sister' (Sakoon 2002: 1, note the phonetic nasalization in the second variant).

However, most publications available in Hindko represent the sound usually referred to as a retroflex /ṇ/ as ڑ̇, that is, as a nasalized retroflex /r/, or ṛ̃. Consequently, that representation is employed in this book.

The negative particle is spelled in various ways; for example, نیئھ (Sakoon 2009: 10), نینہ (AWT), or نئیں (AWT), all pronounced [nĩ̄]. This illustrates the fact that the distinction between the use of ھ *do cašmī he* and ہ *choṭī he* is also not always clear or consistently maintained. One type of inconsistency in the use of ھ arises from the fact that in Arabic ھ *do cašmī he* is the initial form of ہ *choṭī he*, whereas in Urdu (and languages whose spelling is influenced by Urdu orthographic conventions), it is reserved to indicate (historical or present) aspiration. This inconsistency is also found in other words involving the /h/ sound. The oblique form of the third person plural distal pronoun is attested variously spelled as انّاں /unnā̃/ and انہاں /unhā̃/ (AWT). Also, the oblique form of the third person singular distal pronoun, usually اس /is/, sometimes appears as ہس /his/. This is an example of a tendency to have an initial /h/ in forms which sometimes or elsewhere begin with vowels.

There is a tendency (even perhaps a preference) in Hindko spelling to write certain morphemes separately, even though according to the usual conventions of writing Perso-Arabic they could be written together (joined). For example: خوشبو آں /xušbūā̃/ 'fragrances', in which the feminine plural morpheme اں /-ā̃/ is written as though it were an independent word. In دو آ /dūā/ 'second, other.SG.M' and دوی آں /dūīā̃/ 'other.PL.F', in which the masculine singular adjectival ending and feminine plural endings, respectively, are written separately. This appears to be one solution to the problem of writing two consecutive long vowels, adopted by some writers. Similarly, the dative/accusative postposition اں /ā̃/ is usually written separately; for example, ادب آں /adab ā̃/ 'literature.ACC'.

3.6.5 Saraiki orthography

The Perso-Arabic representations of Saraiki consonants are largely the same as those for Hindko and Panjabi, with the important exceptions of the representation of the implosive consonants and of retroflex /ṇ/. After an initial period of orthographic uncertainty and debate (see Shackle 1976: 41 and Mughal 2002, passim), most writers have adopted five distinct, non-Urdu letters, which represent the four implosive consonants and retroflex /ṇ/:

- ٻ /ɓ/
- ݙ /ɗ/
- ڄ /ʄ/
- ڳ /ɠ/
- ݨ /ṇ/

These are the unique (non-Urdu) characters adopted in Mughal (2002) and Mughal (2004: 24–25), and usually employed since then, for example in Zahoor (2009). When necessary, this book will use these characters to normalize examples from earlier authors to fit into this system. The palatal nasal and the velar nasal are represented by the digraphs نج /ñ/ or نڄ /ɲ/, and نگ /ŋ/, respectively. Aspirated consonants are, as for Panjabi and Hindko voiceless aspirates, represented by digraphs consisting of the unvoiced member plus ھ *do cašmī he*, e.g., پھ /ph/.

Saraiki orthography is not yet completely standardized, especially the spelling of the vowel sounds, mainly for the following reasons. First, the vowel system of Saraiki is different from those of Hindko, Panjabi, and Urdu. Second, the Perso-Arabic writing system, especially as it is used for Urdu (the orthographic practices of which influence spelling practices in other languages influenced by it), does not usually differentiate centralized vowels. Third, there is much dialectal variation within the Saraiki-speaking region.

4 Nouns

4.1 The lexicon

Most words in Hindko, Panjabi, and Saraiki are inherited from Middle Indo-Aryan (MIA), which developed from Old Indo-Aryan (OIA). The Indo-Aryan (IA) base lexicon of these languages has been augmented by several centuries of borrowing from Persian and Arabic and more recently from Urdu and English. Hindko, Panjabi, and Saraiki have evolved in mutual contact with each other and with other local languages—Balochi, Sindhi, and Pashto—as well as with other, superstratal languages—Arabic, Persian, Urdu, and English. These numerous contact situations, of varying type, length, and intensity, have resulted in a large number of words being borrowed into these languages—at earlier stages more directly, and recently through Urdu. Many words for cultural items and government originated in Persian, words for religious concepts in Arabic, and words for technology and modern politics in English. In some cases, borrowed words have kept their original meaning, form, and orthography; in other cases, and over time, words have adapted to patterns native to these Indo-Aryan languages.

The three languages have rich derivational morphology which produces a range of nominal forms, to which inflectional information is then added. Nominal inflection and derivation depend on the origin of the word, and each of the languages have both inherited historical forms as well as forms borrowed from various other languages. We therefore begin with a discussion of the lexicon, and then move on to a discussion of derivational morphology in Section 4.2, before providing a detailed discussion of nominal inflection in Section 4.3 and Section 4.4.

Many speakers of all three languages are bi- or multilingual. Educated speakers will generally speak Urdu and English as well as Hindko, Panjabi or Saraiki. In addition, many will have some degree of command over other languages of Pakistan like Pashto, Sindhi, or Balochi. Hindko speakers often know and use Panjabi, Urdu, and Pashto; Saraiki speakers command Urdu, Panjabi, and often Sindhi or Balochi. The choice of which language to use in any given situation depends on the context and the other speakers involved.

Urdu has borrowed more heavily from Arabic and Persian than have Hindko, Panjabi, and Saraiki; and since Panjabi is more influenced by Urdu than are Hindko or Saraiki, more Perso-Arabic origin words are frequently used in Panjabi than in the other two languages. Depending on the educational level of a person and the specific interaction and discourse context, a speaker may incorporate more or fewer Urdu and Urdu-mediated Arabic items into their Hindko, Panjabi, or Saraiki. The following discussion, therefore, necessarily includes elements which are common to Urdu rather than uniquely belonging to any of these three indigenous languages.

https://doi.org/10.1515/9781614512257-004

4.1.1 Persian loans

Many Persian nouns, as well as many derivational elements that can be added to both indigenous and loan words to form nouns, have made their way into Hindko, Panjabi, and Saraiki. Many are very old borrowings (see Shackle 1978 on Persian elements in the Adi Granth), which had undergone phonological changes even by the time of the Adi Granth, e.g. Persian مسجد /masjid/ > Early Panjabi /masīti/> Modern Panjabi /masīt/ [1], while an increasing number are recent and have come via Urdu into all three of these languages. In some cases words have been borrowed multiple times, at different stages; for example Persian وقت /vaqt/ 'time' appears in the Adi Granth as /vakhatu/, whereas today it appears in Urdu as وقت /vaqt/, in modern Panjabi as وقت /vakat~ vaxat/, in Hindko as وخت /vaxt/, and in Saraiki to وقت /vakt~vaxt/.

4.1.2 Words incorporating Arabic definite articles

A few borrowings—phrases and proper names—that include the Arabic definite article ال /al-/ are used in all three languages. Although it is always written the same, ال /al-/ is frequently pronounced differently as a result of an Arabic assimilation rule whereby if the following word begins with a dental or alveolar consonant (or the palato-alveolar /š/) ت، ث، د، ذ، ر، ز، س، ش، ص، ض، ط، ظ، ل، ن /t, s d, z, r, š, l, or n/ (called "sun letters" in Arabic), then /l/ assimilates to that consonant and is pronounced as a geminated consonant. For example: شمس الدین /šams u**d**-dīn/ 'Shams ud-Dīn' (proper name; lit. 'sun of the faith'); بسم اللہ الرحمٰن الرحیم /b-ism illāh i**r**-rahmān i**r**-rahīm/ 'in the name of God, the Most Compassionate, Most Merciful' (often said when beginning something).

4.2 Derivational morphology

Derivational morphology is the process of adding affixes or other compounding elements to a word to derive another form class, in this case nouns. These languages have rich nominal derivational resources from various sources—Indo-Aryan, Persian, and Arabic. These elements vary in their current productivity; some can appear with any word, while others are restricted to a few fixed expressions. They also vary in frequency in the three languages being described here. Since adjectives are freely used as nouns in Hindko, Panjabi, and Saraiki, many of the elements described here can equally well be considered as deriving adjectives (see Chapter 5).[2]

1 Since the Adi Granth forms were written in an old form of Gurmukhi, not in Perso-Arabic, we have given them here in Roman representation only.

2 For more extensive lists of Panjabi derivational elements, see Bhatia (1993) and Malik (1995).

4.2.1 Suffixal elements

4.2.1.1 Agent noun-forming suffixes (Indo-Aryan)

The gender of nouns typically formed with each of these suffixes is indicated in parentheses after the suffix. The language(s) in which each word is attested are indicated after the item.

- **یا /-iyā/ (m)**

  This suffix forms nouns denoting agents, or persons associated with a specific thing, place, or characteristic. It is productive, appearing even on English loanwords.

  فروڈ /frɔḍ/ 'fraud'→ فروڈیا /frɔḍiyā/ 'fraudster' Pj

  گھل /kùl-/ 'wrestle' → گھلاٹیا /kulā̀ṭiyā/ 'wrestler' Pj

  ڈاک /ḍāk/ 'post, mail' → ڈاکیا /ḍākiyā/ 'postman' Pj

  لہور /lɔ̀r/ 'Lahore' → لہوریا /lɔ̀riyā/ 'person from Lahore' Pj

  گوگڑ /gogaṛ/ 'pot belly' → گوگڑیا /gogṛiyā/ 'pot-bellied person' Pj

  لکھ /lakkh/ '100 thousand' → لکھّیا /lakkhiyā/ 'person having hundreds of thousands of rupees' Hk

  کباڑ /kabāṛ/ 'scrap goods '→کباڑیا /kabāṛiyā/ 'dealer in scrap/second-hand goods' Pj

- **ان ~ نی ~ ݨی /-(a)ṇ ~ -nī ~ -ṇī/ (f)**

  This suffix denotes a female counterpart of a male person or animal. It frequently forms nouns referring to ethnic or national groups, or to the females of animal species.

  پنجابن/panjābaṇ/ Hk, Pj , پنجابݨ/panjābiṇ/ Sr 'Punjabi woman'

  شیرنی /šernī/ Pj شینہݨی /šĩhṇī/ Sr 'female lion'

  نین /næṇ/ 'wife of a barber' Pj

- **ی /-ī/ '(f)'**

  This suffix denotes either the female counterpart of a male person or animal, or the smaller version of an inanimate object. It behaves similarly in all three languages.

  بلّی /billī/ Hk, Pj , ٻلّی /ɓillī/ Sr 'female cat'

  چاچی /cācī/ 'father's younger brother's wife' Hk, Pj 'father's brother's wife' Sr

  ٹوکری /ṭokrī/ 'small basket' Pj

  روڈا /rauḍā/ 'shaven-headed male'→ روڈی /rauḍī/ 'shaven-headed female' Hk (Sakoon 2002)

- **ار ~ ارا ~ اری /-ār ~ -ārā ~ -ārī/ '(m)'**

  Variants of this suffix occur particularly in the domain of vocations and skilled trades. The suffix /-ār/ is found in some older formations, and appears not to be currently productive.

  /kumbhakāra/ 'potter' OIA → کمہیار /kumyȁr/ 'potter' Pj , کمبھار /kumbhār/ Sr

  سونا /sonā/ 'gold' → سنیارا /sunyārā/ 'goldsmith' Pj , سُنارا /sunārā/ Sr

  لکھ /likh-/ 'write' → لکھاری /likhārī/ 'writer' Pj, Sr

- **و /-ū/ (m)**

  The suffix /ū/ forms agentive nouns often denoting a person or thing that has the quality or does the action of a verb, adjective, or noun. This suffix is productive.

  ڈاکا /ḍākā/ 'robbery'→ ڈاکو /ḍākū/ 'robber' Hk, Pj, Sr

  گھوٹنا /kòṭṇā/ 'to pound, grab'→ گھوٹو /kòṭū/ 'grabber ' Pj

  اجاڑنا /ujāṛnā/ 'to waste, destroy'→ اجاڑو /ujāṛū/ 'wastrel, spendthrift ' Pj

  لادنا /lādṇā/ 'to load onto'→ لادُو /lādū/ 'a pack animal judged able to carry loads' Hk (Sakoon 2002: 214)

- **آکُو ~ آکا /-ākū ~ -ākā/ (m)**

  This suffix contains an (older) agentive suffix -ak, and is not currently productive.

  لڑاکا /laṛākā/ 'quarrelsome person' Pj (adj. form used as a noun)

  پڑھاکو /paṛȁkū/ 'studious person' Pj

- **یڑ ~ یرا /-eṛ ~ -erā/ (m)**

  Forms nouns referring to a person inclined to do an action related to the word (root):

  کہل /kȕl/ 'wrestle'→ کہلیڑ /kuleṛ/ 'person or animal inclined to fight' Hk (Sakoon 2002: 194)

  سپیرا /saperā/ 'snake charmer' Pj

  مچھیرا /macherā/ 'fisherman' Pj

4.2.1.2 Abstract noun-forming suffixes (Indo-Aryan)

- **اس /-ās/ Pj (f), اج /-āj/ Sr (f)**

  This suffix derives abstract nouns from adjectives. The resulting nouns denote a quality, as in:

مٹھا /miṭṭhā/ 'sweet'→ مٹھاس /miṭhās/ 'sweetness'

کھٹا /khaṭṭā/ 'sour'→ کھٹاس /khaṭās/ 'sourness' Pj , کھٹاج /khaṭāj/ Sr

تھندھا /greasy/→ تھندھاج ~ تھنداج /thindhāj ~ thindāj/ 'greasiness' Sr

This suffix also attaches to certain verbs to form abstract nouns indicating a need to perform a bodily function, as in:

پیݨا/pīṇā/ 'to drink' → پیاس /piyās/ 'a need to drink, thirst' Hk, Pj

روݨا /roṛā/ 'to cry'→ رواس /rawās/ 'weeping (as in mourning)' Hk (Sakoon 2002: 153)

- ک ~ کھ /-k ~ -kh/ (f) or (m)

Added to adjectives this element yields abstract nouns; these are older Indo-Aryan formations.

کالا /kāḷā/ 'black'→ کالکھ /kāḷakh/ 'blackness, soot (f)' Pj کالخ /kālax/ Hk (Sakoon 2002: 175)

سُ /su/ '(root meaning) good'→ سُکھ /sukh/ 'ease, comfort ' Hk, Pj, Sr (m)

دُ /du/ '(root meaning) bad'→دُکھ /dukh/ 'trouble, distress ' Hk, Pj (m), ڈکھ /ɗukh/ 'distress, pain, sorrow' Sr (Mughal 2010: 436)

اوکھ /aukh/ 'difficulty, hardship (f)' Pj

سوکھ /saukh/ 'ease, convenience (f)' Pj

- ن ~ ݨ ~ نا ~ ݨا ~ ڑا /-an ~ -aṇ ~ -nā ~ -ṇā ~ ṛā/ (m)

Added to verbal stems, this suffix forms the infinitive, or verbal noun, which is grammatically masculine singular. Hindko infinitives end in نا ~ ڑا /nā ~ ṛā/, Panjabi infinitives end in ݨا /ṇā ~ nā/, while Saraiki infinitives end in ݨ ~ ن /aṇ ~ an/. These verbal nouns denote the action of the verb (see Chapter 8).

کھا /khā-/ 'eat'→ کھاڑا /khā-ṛā/ Hk ; کھاݨا /khā-ṇā/ Pj ; > کھاوݨ /khāv-aṇ/ 'act of eating' Sr

لکھ /likh-/ 'write'→ لکھڑا /likh-ṛā/ Hk ; لکھݨا /likh-ṇā/ Pj ; لکھݨ /likkh-aṇ/ 'act of writing, to write' Sr

- پن ~ پݨ ~ پنا ~ پݨا ~ پا ~ پ /-pun ~ -paṇ ~ -puṇā ~ -paṇā ~ -pā ~ -p/ (m)

This suffix is added to various roots to form abstract nouns expressing a state or a condition. These are old formations.

سیاݨا /siāṇā/ 'wise'→ سیاݨپ /siāṇap/ 'wisdom' Pj

چھُوہر /chuhar/ 'boy'→ چھُوہرپ /chuharap/ 'childhood' Sr (Mughal 2010: 802)

چھوکرا /chokrā/ 'boy'→ چھوکراپنّا /chokrāpaṇṇā/ 'boyhood' Sr (Mughal 2010: 802)

بچّا ~ بچہ /baccā/ 'child'→ بچپن /bacpan/ 'childhood' Hk, Pj

کھوکھلا /khokhlā/ 'hollow'→ کھوکھلاپن /khokhlāpan/ 'hollowness, weakness' Pj

بُڈّھا /buḍḍhā/ 'biologically old'→ بُڈھیپا /ɓuḍhepā/ 'old age' Sr [3] (Mughal 2010: 124)

بُڑھاپا /buṛā̀pā/ 'old age' Pj

رنڈا /ranḍā/ 'widowed SG.M' →رنڈیپا /ranḍepā/ 'time/state of widowhood' Hk Sakoon 2002: 153

کسیلا /kasæḷā/ 'bitter, astringent '→ کسیلاپن /kasælāpaṇ/ 'bitterness, astringency' Pj

کوڑا /kauṛā/ 'bitter '→ کوڑاپن /kauṛāpaṇ/ 'bitterness' Pj

- **ت ~ اوٹ ~ وٹ ~ ٹ /-t ~ -āvaṭ ~ -vaṭ ~ -aṭ/ (f)**

  These suffixes form abstract nouns denoting the result of an action, or a lifestyle:

  بننا /baṇṇā/ 'to be made'→ بناوٹ /baṇ-āvaṭ/ 'structure, manufacturing; invention; artificiality' Pj, Sr

  رُکنا /rukṇā/ 'to stop'→ رکاوٹ /ruk-āvaṭ/ 'hindrance, obstruction' Pj

  گھلنا /kùḷṇā/ 'to wrestle'→ گھلٹ /kùḷ-aṭ/ 'fond of wrestling, wrestler' Pj (Malik 1995: 173)

- **اہٹ /-āhaṭ/ (f)**

  This suffix derives nouns indicating a state or quality.

  چکنا /ciknā/ 'greasy'→ چکناہٹ /ciknā̀ṭ/ 'greasiness' Pj

  کڑوا /kaṛvā/ 'bitter'→ کڑواہٹ /kaṛvāhaṭ ~ kaṛvā̀(ha)ṭ/ 'bitterness' Pj

  گھبرا /kabrā̀/ 'worry, anxiety'→ گھبراہٹ /kabrā̀ṭ/ 'nervousness, confusion, uneasiness' Pj

- **ا /-ā/**

  Added to verbal stems, /-ā/ forms abstract nouns denoting a state:

  سڑنا /saṛṇā/ 'to burn (intr.)'→ ساڑا /sāṛā/ 'burning, jealousy' Pj

  نبڑنا /nibaṛnā/ 'to complete'→ نباڑا /nibāṛā/ 'completion, settlement' Pj

3 Hindko has بُڈھیما /buḍhīmā/ 'old age', with /m/ rather than /p/ in this suffix (Sakoon 2002: 39).

- **ائی /-āī/ (f)**

  Added to verb stems, this suffix forms abstract nouns which denote an action, process, or payment for a specific type of work:

  پڑھ /páṛh-/ 'read'→ پڑھائی /paṛhā̀ī/ 'study, education' Hk, Pj, Sr

  بیج /bīj-/ 'sow'→ بجائی /bijāī/ 'sowing, payment for sowing' Pj

  سیُو /siū-/ 'stitch'→ سِلائی /silāī/ ~ سِوائی /sivāī/ 'stitching; charges for stitching' Pj

- **ت /-at/$_1$ (f)**

  This IA-origin suffix forms abstract nouns denoting a manner or style. This is to be distinguished from ت /-at/ $_2$, which is a frequently occurring Perso-Arabic suffix (see Section 4.2.1.3 below).

  لکھ /likh-/ 'write'→ لکھت /likhat/ 'penmanship; writing' Pj

  رنگ /rang/ 'color'→ رنگت /rangat/ 'coloring, hue, complexion' Pj

  آڑھت /ā́ṛt/ 'brokerage, agency' Pj

  سنگت /sangat/ 'association, company, congregation' Pj

- **ی /-ī/ (f)**

  This suffix, with multiple origins (Indo-Aryan, Perso-Arabic), forms abstract nouns from both adjectives and other nouns; it is very productive in all three languages. (See also Perso-Arabic ی /-ī/in Section 4.2.1.3.)

  adjective + /-ī/ → noun: اُچّا /uccā/ 'high' → اُچّائی /uccāī/ 'height' Hk, Pj

  noun + /-ī/ → noun: استاد /ustād/ 'teacher, expert' → استادی /ustādī/ 'expertise' Pj

4.2.1.3 Abstract noun-forming suffixes (Perso-Arabic)

- **ی /-ī/ , گی /-gī/ (f)**

  Added to adjectives, this suffix yields abstract nouns. گی /-gī/ appears after words that end in ہ /-ah/; /-ī/ is used elsewhere. Words with this suffix are found in all three languages and in Urdu, with generally the same meaning across languages. Examples:

  زندہ /zinda/ 'alive '→ زندگی /zindagī/ 'life'

  گرم /garam/ 'hot '→ گرمی /garmī/ 'heat'

- **ت /-at/ 2 (f)**

  Forms abstract nouns from adjectives denoting states.

  غریب /ɣarīb/ 'poor '→ غربت /ɣurbat/ 'poverty'

  ضروری /zarūrī/ 'necessary '→ ضرورت /zarūrat/ 'necessity'

- **یت /-iyat/ (f)**

  Adding the suffix یت /-iyat/ to nouns and adjectives forms a feminine abstract noun; adding it to an English word can impart a slang connotation in Panjabi. This suffix is productive, as can be seen by the last example below, where it has been added to the English word 'bore'.

  شخص /šaxs/ 'person '→ شخصیت /šaxsiyat/ 'personality'

  انسان /insān/ 'human being' → انسانیت /insāniyat/ 'humanity '

  اہم /æm/ 'important '→ اہمیت /æmiyat/ 'importance' Hk, Pj

  بور /bor/ ' boring ' → بوریت /bōriyat/ 'boredom'

4.2.1.4 Diminutives

- **ڑی /-ṛī/ '(f)' ڑا /-ṛā/(m) (Indo-Aryan)**

  When applied to a human child, this suffix usually has an affectionate tone.

  جاتک /jātak/ 'offspring, boy '→ جاتکڑی /jātakṛī/ 'little girl (affectionate)' Hk (Sakoon 2002)

  بال /ɓāl/ 'child '→ بالڑی /ɓalṛī/ 'little girl' Sr (Mughal 2010: 110)

  کوٹھا /koṭhā/ 'room, roof '→ کوٹھڑی /koṭhṛī/ 'small room; cell' Pj

  بچّا /baccā/ 'child '→ بچڑا /bacṛā/ 'child (affectionate)' Pj

- **یچہ /-īcah/ '(m)' ک /-ak/ (f) (Perso-Arabic)**

  These suffixes form nouns denoting a small object.

  باغ /bāgh/ 'garden, grove '→ باغیچہ /bāghīcā/ 'vegetable garden, private garden'

  عین /æn/ 'eye '→ عینک /ænak/ 'eye glasses (lit. little eye)'

4.2.2 Persian compounding elements

These are partially grammaticalized nominal elements—neither free morphemes nor suffixes.

4.2.2.1 Agent-noun forming

- **چی/-cī/ (m)**

  The element چی/-cī/ is originally Turkic, and was borrowed into Persian, thence into South Asian languages. It is not productive in contemporary Indo-Aryan languages.

  افیم /afīm/ 'opium '→ افیمچی /afīm-cī/ 'opium addict'

- **بان /-bān/, وان /-vān/ 'keeper, guardian ' (m)**

  میز /mēz/ 'table '→ میزبان /mēz-bān/ 'host'

  کوچ /kōc/ 'coach '→ کوچوان /kōc-vān/ 'coachman'

- **گر /-gar/ 'doer ' (m)**

  سودا /sɔdā/ 'merchandise '→ سوداگر /sɔdā-gar/ 'merchant'

  جادو /jādū/ 'magic '→ جادوگر /jādū-gar/ 'magician'

- **کار /-kār/ 'doer ' (m)**

  اہل /æl/ 'office, position'→ اہلکار /æl-kār/ 'official, office holder'

- **دان /-dān/$_1$ 'knower of' (m)**

  سیاست /syāsat/ 'politics'→ سیاستدان /syāsat-dān/ 'politician'

  زبان /zabān/ 'language '→ زباندان /zabān-dān/ 'language expert'

- **دار /-dār/ 'possessor/owner ' (m)**

  تھانا /thāṇā/ 'police station'→ تھانیدار /thāṇe-dār/ 'police station in-charge'

  صوبہ /sūbah/ 'province '→ صوبیدار /sūbe-dār/ 'rank in the military or police'

  دُکان /dukān/ 'shop '→ دُکاندار /dukān-dār/ 'shopkeeper'

4.2.2.2 Locative-noun forming

These elements form nouns referring to places where something happens or is kept, or which are characteristic of something.

- **دان /-dān/$_2$ (m) ~ دانی /-dānī/ 'container for' (f)**

  This element derives nouns with the meaning 'receptacle for X'. The masculine and feminine forms are more or less interchangeable in meaning except, perhaps, for a difference in size of the object. The element denoting X appears in the oblique case (visible only with marked masculine nouns); as in کوڑیدان /kūṛedān/ 'garbage can'

کوڑا /kūṛā/ 'garbage'. These Perso-Arabic origin suffixes are attached to both Perso-Arabic and Indo-Aryan origin words.

نمک /namak/ 'salt'→ نمکدانی /namak-dānī/ 'salt shaker' (f)

پھُل /phul/ 'flower'→ پھُلدان /phul-dān/ 'flower vase' (m)

کوڑا /kūṛā/ 'rubbish, trash'→ کوُڑیدان /kūṛe-dān/ 'rubbish bin, garbage can' (m)

- **گاہ /-gā/ 'place' (f)**

  چرا /carā-/ 'graze (tr.)'→ چراگاہ /carā-gā/ 'place for grazing'

  شکار /shikār/ 'hunting'→ شکارگاہ /shikār-gā/ 'place for hunting'

- **زار /-zār/ 'place where something abounds' (m)**

  Only a few borrowed words have this suffix. It is not productive in these languages.

  گُل /gul/ 'flower'→ گلزار /gul-zār/ 'garden'

  چمن /caman/ 'garden'→ چمنزار /caman-zār/ 'garden-like place'

- **آباد /-ābād/ 'a settlment; peopled' (m)**

  This element derives place names.

  اسلام /islām/ 'Islam'→ اسلام آباد /islāmābād/ 'city of Islam'

- **ستان /-(i)stān/ 'place' (m)**

  Nouns meaning a place characteristic of something specific are formed with this suffix. When the first element ends in a consonant, /i/ is inserted between the stem and the suffixal element.

  بلوچ /balōc/ 'a Baloch'→ بلوچستان /balōcistān/ 'Balochistan (province of Pakistan) (lit.'land of the Baloch')'

  ریگ /reg/ 'sand'→ ریگستان /registān/ 'desert (lit. 'sandy place')'

  قبر /qabar/ 'grave'→ قبرستان /qabristān/ 'graveyard'

4.2.3 Persian and Arabic conjunctive elements

These elements are used in a conjunctive process which yields collocations that function as single lexical elements. These elements generally appear first in Urdu and spread to the other languages of Pakistan.

4.2.3.1 و /-o-/ 'and'

The Arabic and Persian conjunction و /-o-/ 'and' is found in Urdu words and collocations used in Hindko, Panjabi, and Saraiki.

نظم و ضبط /nazm-o-zabt/ 'discipline'

امن و امان /amn-o-amān/ 'peaceful state of affairs'

4.2.3.2 The enclitic /e/ 'izāfat'

The اضافہ ezafeh or izāfat, /-e-/ , is a clitic which joins two nominals. The first element is always the thing referenced, and is either a noun, pronoun, or verbal participle. The second element modifies or qualifies the first and can be either a noun or an adjective. When two nouns are joined, the اضافہ izāfat conveys a possessive relationship: the first noun belongs to the second. As this construction is a borrowing from Persian, the اضافہ izāfat is generally used only to join words of Perso-Arabic origin, however in spoken usage it is occasionally also used with words of Indic origin. Increasingly, اضافہ izāfat is not pronounced in the spoken language, particularly when the first element ends in a short vowel + consonant, as in طالب علم /tālib ilm/ for /tālib-e-ilm/ ' student'. However, if the izāfat expression denotes a proper name or title, the izāfat is usually pronounced. Examples:

یومِ آزادی /yom-e-āzādī/ 'Independence Day'

وزیرِ آعظم /vazīr-e-āzam/ 'Prime Minister'

حکومتِ پاکستان /hukūmat-e-pākistān/ 'Government of Pakistan'

Compare this construction with the indigenous Indo-Aryan construction using a form of the genitive postposition دا /dā/: پاکستان دی حکومت /pākistān dī hukūmat/ 'Pakistan's government' . These Persian and indigenous constructions differ in both form and function. The word order is reversed, and the meanings differ: حکومتِ پاکستان /hukūmat-e-pākistān/ is a proper noun, referring to the Government of Pakistan as an official entity, while پاکستان دی حکومت /pākistān dī hukūmat/ is a common noun referring to the generic idea of governance of Pakistan.

4.3 Nominal categories

Hindko, Panjabi, and Saraiki all have partially morphologically marked distinctions for number[4], gender, and case.[5] They all have direct, oblique, and vocative case forms regularly; ablative singular forms occur fairly frequently, usually with inanimates, but ablative plural case endings are not attested; and locative forms, always with inanimates, exist to varying degrees in the three languages. The citation form for nouns is the nominative singular. Distinctions include: number (singular or plural), discussed in Section 4.3.1; gender (masculine or feminine), discussed in Section 4.3.2; and case (discussed in Section 4.3.3).

Not all grammatical relations, however, are marked by case suffixes. Some functions, such as genitive (possession), dative (indirect object), ergative (agentive); and (some) direct objects (accusative), are indicated by postpositions following nouns in their oblique case form. On the other hand, some adverbial relations are indicated by the oblique case without a postposition.

Possessive (genitive) forms of nouns and third person pronouns consist of the oblique case of the noun or pronoun plus the adjectival postposition دا /dā/ 'of', which agrees in number, gender, and case with the noun the possessive phrase modifies, e.g.:

اوُں دا بھرا /ṹ dā (m.sg.) bhirā (m.sg.)/ 'his/her brother' Sr

اُوں دے بھرا کول /ṹ de (m.sg.obl) bhirā kol/ 'with his/her brother' Sr

اوُں دی بھیݨ /ṹ dī (f.sg.) bhæṇ (f.sg.)/ 'his/her sister' Sr

Therefore, these possessive forms, which are actually postpositional phrases, have not been included in the declension paradigms for any of the three languages. First and second person pronouns, on the other hand, have marked adjectival genitive endings in را /-rā/.

Noun gender determines agreement with some adjectives and determiners (see Chapter 5), and some verb forms agree in gender and number with an argument of the sentence (see Chapter 9).

4.3.1 Number

Marked masculine and feminine nouns follow indigenous patterns of number marking showing a distinction between singular and plural, but an increasing number of words entering the languages through Urdu are unmarked. These either show no distinction in the direct case between singular and plural or take Persian and Arabic plural morphology.

4 While OIA had three number categories— singular, dual, and plural—all modern IA languages have only singular and plural.

5 *Case* refers to the different forms that nouns can take depending on their grammatical function in a sentence—subject, direct object, indirect object, possessor, or an adverbial function.

4.3.1.1 Persian and Arabic plural suffixes

There are two plural suffixes in Persian: (1) ان /-ān/ (with variants گان /-gān/, and یان /-yān/) originally for nouns that denote animate beings, and (2) ہا /hā/ for inanimates. Consonant-final animates take /-ān/; those ending in ہ /-a/ take گان /-gān/; and those ending in ا /-ā/ take یان /-yān/. Loanwords from Persian may take Persian plural endings, e.g. بزرگ /buzurg/ ' elder', plural بزرگان /buzurg-ān/. Commonly used Persian loanwords may also take indigenous plurals, in which case a word like بزرگ /buzurg/ is treated as an unmarked masculine. Using Persian plural forms signals a formal or literary style.

صاحب /sāhab/ 'gentleman'→ صاحبان /sāhabān/ 'gentlemen'

گمشدہ /gumšuda/ 'disappeared / lost person'→ گمشدگان /gumšudagān/ 'lost/disappeared people'

These Persian plural formations, as well as those in Arabic ات /-āt/ tend to have the sense of collective nouns.

4.3.1.1.1 ین /-æn/ Arabic dual ending

A very few words include these Arabic accusative/genitive dual forms, now understood as plurals. The only one in common use is the word for 'parents'.

والد /vālid/ 'father' → والدین /vāldæn/ 'parents'

طرف /taraf/ 'side' → طرفین /tarfæn/ 'the two sides (of), sides in a legal case'

4.3.1.1.2 ین /-īn/ Arabic plural

This suffix is affixed to adjectives or nouns:

متاثر /mutāsir/ 'affected ' → متاثرین /mutāsirīn/ 'affected ones'

مجاہد /mujāhid/ 'participant in a jihad ' → مجاہدین /mujāhidīn/ 'participants in a jihad'

4.3.1.1.3 ات /-āt/ Arabic plural

This suffix is affixed to nouns of either gender or to adjectives.

امتحان /imtyån/ 'examination '→ امتحانات /imtyånāt/ 'examinations' (m)

جنگل /jangal/ 'forest, wilderness area '→ جنگلات /janglāt/ 'forests' (m)

معلوم /mālūm/ 'known '[6] → معلومات /mālūmāt/ 'information (lit. 'known things')'

کاغذ /kāyaz/ 'paper'→ کاغذات /kāyzāt/ 'documents, documentation, paperwork' (m)

6 This is an adjective and has no singular form as a noun.

4.3.1.2 Arabic broken plurals

Arabic *broken plurals* form their plurals by altering the vowel pattern of the singular noun. Arabic broken plurals appear more frequently in Urdu than in the languages treated here. Two examples should suffice.

- خدمت /xidmat/ 'service'→ خدمات /xidmāt/ 'services' (f)

  خبر /xabar/ 'news '→ اخبار /axbār/ 'newspaper' [7]

Borrowed nouns used with their original Arabic or Persian plural (or Arabic dual) morphology do not simultaneously take Panjabi, Hindko, or Saraiki case endings when used with postpositions. When Persian or Arabic loanwords take native plural endings, however, the usual inflectional suffixes apply. For example:

كاغذ /kāɣaz/ 'paper (m.sg.dir)'
كاغذ /kāɣaz/ 'papers (m. pl. dir.) indigenous form'
كاغذاں وچ /kāɣzā̃ vic/ 'in the papers (m.pl.obl)'
كاغذات /kāɣzāt/ 'documents (m.pl.dir) Arabic plural'
كاغذات وچ /kāɣzāt vic/ 'in the documents'
* كاغذاتاں وچ /*kāɣzātā̃ vic/ 'in the documents'[8]

Loan words from other languages, such as English, do not usually bring their original morphology with them.[9]

رِکارڈ /rikārḍ/ 'record'
رِکارڈاں وچ /rikārḍā̃ vic/ 'in the records'

4.3.2 Gender

Old Indo-Aryan (OIA) had three genders—masculine, feminine, and neuter; only feminine and masculine classes remain in modern Hindko, Panjabi, and Saraiki. Many originally masculine or feminine Indo-Aryan words have remained masculine or feminine, respectively, in these languages, while originally neuter Indo-Aryan words have mostly become masculine, but occasionally feminine. For example, OIA /*ŕkṣa* / 'bear' (m) has developed into Hindko, Panjabi, and Saraiki رِچھّ /ricch/ 'bear' (m), and OIA /*rātra*/ 'night' (f.) (T10700) remains feminine in all three languages: رات /rāt/ (f).[10]

7 This word is feminine in Panjabi but masculine in Urdu.

8 An asterisk indicates an ungrammatical form.

9 In the case of some words that usually occur in the plural, like *matches*, the word is borrowed along with its plural suffix /-is/, but the word is treated as singular and in this case inflected as an unmarked feminine noun. However, there is also an increasing tendency to optionally use the English /s~z/ plurals when English loans are used in code-mixed discourse.

10 Notations of the form 'Tnnnn' refer to the entries in Turner's *Comparative Dictionary of the Indo-Aryan Languages* (Turner 1962–1966).

Middle Indo-Aryan (Pali) /pānīya/ 'water' (neuter) has become پاݨڑی /pāṛ̃ī/ Hk , پاݨی /pāṇī/ Pj , and پاݨی /pāṇī/ Sr (masculine) in these modern languages (T8082). The words for 'fire' are feminine in all three of these languages: Hindko and Panjabi اگّ /agg/ (f.), and Saraiki بھاہ /bhā/ (f). However OIA /*agnī*/ 'fire' was masculine (T55) while /*bhąsá*/ 'light', the source of Saraiki بھاہ /bhā/ 'fire', was masculine in both OIA and Prakrit (T9480). OIA /*nasta*/ 'nose' (m.) is masculine in Panjabi, نکّ /nakk/ (m.), and Hindko نک /nak/ (m.), but is feminine in Urdu.

Words borrowed from Arabic or Urdu usually maintain their original Arabic or Urdu genders; however, in some cases they can have different genders in these modern languages[11]. For example, اخبار /axbār/ 'newspaper' is masculine in Urdu but feminine in Panjabi'; conversely, میز /mez/ 'table' is masculine in Panjabi, but feminine in Urdu. English loanwords are assigned gender in various ways: sometimes influenced by the sound of the word and sometimes by the gender of a semantically related word. The indigenous words for 'vehicle, cart, car' are گڈّی /gaḍḍī/ Pj , گاڈی /gāḍī/ Hk , and گاڋی /gāɗī/ Sr , all of which are feminine. When the English word 'car' is used in these languages, as it increasingly is, it has feminine gender.

4.3.2.1 Semantic criteria

In all three languages, some semantic characteristics can be helpful in determining the gender of nouns. With animate entities, words denoting biological males are masculine, and those denoting females are feminine, regardless of their phonological form: ماں /mā̃/ 'mother' Pj (feminine), پیو /pyo/ 'father' Pj (masculine). With inanimate objects that can vary in size, the larger object is usually masculine and the smaller is feminine, for example the Hindko words نلّڑ /nallaṛ/ 'throat' (m.) and نلڑی /nalaṛī/ 'little throat' (f.) (Sakoon 2002: 243).

Importantly, it is not the case, for either animates or inanimates, that either gender is always the *unmarked* (default) term and the other the *marked* term (more restricted in meaning). For some word pairs, the feminine is the semantically unmarked term and the masculine form is semantically marked, while for others the masculine is the unmarked term and the feminine is marked. Consider the case of 'cat'. The feminine term بلّی /billī/ 'cat' Hk, Pj ٻلّی /ɓillī/ 'cat' Sr , the unmarked term, can refer to either female or male cats. If one wants to specify a specific cat as male, the form بلّا /billā/ 'tomcat' is used. Conversely, کُتا /kuttā/ 'dog' Hk, Pj, Sr (masculine) is the unmarked term, whereas کُتّی /kuttī/ 'bitch' (feminine) applies only to female dogs. With inanimate entities, in

11 Persian does not have grammatical gender.

Panjabi the word چھُری /churī/ 'knife' (feminine) is the unmarked term, and the corresponding masculine form چھُرا /churā/ refers to an unusually large knife. On the other hand, ڈبّا /ḍabbā/ 'box, tin (container)' (masculine) is the unmarked term, while ڈبّی /ḍabbī/ 'little box, container' (feminine) refers to a notably small box.

Other semantic criteria apply to small sets of nouns. The names of most metals and precious stones are masculine in Panjabi, for example سونا /sonā/ 'gold', لوہا /lóyā/ 'iron', and پکھراج /pukhrāj/ 'topaz' (Malik 1995: 208).

In Panjabi, nouns relating to the year, months, days of the week, cardinal directions, celestial bodies, and many species of trees are masculine (Malik 1995: 209, Bhatia 1993: 217).

سال /sāl/ 'year'
وار /vār/ 'day of the week'
سورج /sūraj/ 'sun'
چن /can/ 'moon'
جنوب /janūb/ 'south'

Some semantic classes consist of feminine nouns. For example, names of the lunar days, such as چَودویں /caudvī̃/ 'fourteenth (i.e. day of the full moon)', and Arabic forms of the pattern تفعیل /tafʕīl/ (tCCīC)[12], such as تحصیل /tæsīl/ 'administrative sub-division of a district', are feminine in all three languages.

4.3.2.2 Morphological criteria

Morphological patterns in some cases correlate with the gender of a noun; in others, there is no such correlation. The four patterns discussed in the following paragraphs originate in the IA stratum of these languages.

Generally in all three languages nouns ending in ا /-ā/ or اں /-ā̃/ in the singular direct case, are masculine, while nouns ending in ی /-ī/ or یں /ī̃/ are feminine. This is not an absolute rule, however, for any of the languages; consider چاہ /cā́/ 'tea',[13] which is feminine, and پاݨی /pāṛ̃ī/ ~ ہانی ~ پاݨی /pāṇī/ 'water', which is masculine in all three languages. Some nouns referring to humans behave as unmarked masculines with regard to case marking (that is, they have only one form for direct singular, direct plural, and oblique singular), but can take either masculine or feminine adjective and verb agreement depending on the sex of their referent. ڈاکٹر /ḍākṭar/ 'doctor' (< English) and دوست /dost/ 'friend' (< Persian) are two such cases. Note that neither of the source languages for these nouns has grammatical gender.

12 These are root patterns shown in the templatic morphology of Arabic, with a prototypical member to exemplify the pattern.

13 This word is also spelled as چاء by some writers of Hindko (Bashir and Kazmi 2012: 119).

Some nouns with animate referents have two forms, which depend on the sex of the referent. There are three important types of such pairs. The first type has the masculine ending in ا /-ā/ and the feminine ending in ی /-ī/. These are most common with some animals and kinship terms. For example, دادا /dādā/ 'paternal grandfather' (m.), and دادی /dādī/ 'paternal grandmother' (f.).

The second type includes masculines in /-ī/ or /āī/, often denoting occupational classes or some ethnic groups, which have feminine counterparts ending in Hindko /-ṛ̃/, Panjabi /-ṇ, -(a)ṇ, -āṇī/, or Saraiki /-iṇ, -āṇī/. For example:

تھوبی /tòbī/ Hk ,دھوبی /tòbī/ Pj , دھوبی /dhoɓī/ Sr 'washerman '

تھوبڑ /tòbaṛ̃/ Hk , دھوبن /tòbaṇ/ Pj , دھوبݨ /dhoɓiṇ/ Sr 'washerman's wife, washerwoman'

نائی /nāī/ 'barber' Hk, Pj, Sr

نین /næṇ/ Pj نواݨی /nivāṇī/ Sr 'barber's wife'

درزی /darzī/ 'tailor' Hk, Pj, Sr

درزن /darzaṇ/ Pj درزاݨی /darzāṇī/ Sr 'tailor's wife, female tailor '

پنجابی/panjābī/ 'Punjabi person' Hk, Pj, Sr

پنجابن/panjābaṇ/ 'Punjabi girl or woman' Pj

چودھری/cɔ̃drī/ 'village headman in Punjab' Pj

چودھرانی/cɔdrāṇī/ Pj , چُدھراݨی /cudhrāṇī/ Sr 'wife of the cɔ̃drī'

قصائی /kasāī/ 'butcher' Hk, Pj, Sr

قصین /kasæṇ/ Hk, Pj قصائݨ /kasāiṇ/ Sr 'butcher's wife' < Persian قصائی (Mughal 2010: 655)

Note that this alternation has also been applied to the Persian loanword for 'butcher'[14]. Masculine nouns not ending in ی /ī/ can also form feminine counterparts with this suffix, e.g. نوکر /nokar/ 'servant' and نوکراݨی /nokrāṇī/ 'maidservant'.

A third type of pair, which consists of masculines ending in /-ū/ with feminine counterparts in /-o/, is found in Panjabi. These can sometimes have slightly pejorative senses, as in:

لمبُو /lambū/ 'unusually tall male person' لمبو /lambo/ 'unusually tall female person'

بُدّھو /buddhū/ 'stupid/simple man' , بدّھو /buddho/ 'stupid/simple woman'.

Sometimes, though, these suffixes function as diminutives, with an affectionate sense, and frequently appear in nicknames for male or female persons, e.g. بِلّو /billū/, a nickname for a boy or a man named Bilaal, and بِلّو /billo/ a nickname for a girl, especially one viewed as pretty or who has brown or hazel (i.e. light-colored) eyes.

14 The original spelling of this Persian-origin word is retained here. It is possible that some writers of these languages may spell it as کسائی sometimes, reflecting its pronunciation.

However, although both masculine /-ū/ and feminine /-o/ endings exist, they often are not in a symmetrical relationship or are not used equally frequently. For example, چلاکو /calāko/ 'clever female person' appears in the frequently used Panjabi collocation چلاکو ماسی /calāko māsī/ 'clever girl/woman', often with an affectionate sense, whereas the masculine does not. The masculine form بدّھو /buddhū/ 'stupid/simple man' is relatively frequently used, but not its feminine counterpart.

A fourth type of pair is found in Saraiki, where there are a few masculine-feminine associations persisting from an older pattern. In such Saraiki pairs, nouns with back vowels /u/ or /a/ in the second, unstressed syllable are masculine, while those with the front vowel /i/ in this position are feminine. The following examples are from Shackle (1976: 43).

پنسِل /pinsil/ 'pencil' (f)

شُکر /šukur/ 'thanks' (m)

کُکڑ /kukuṛ/ 'cock, rooster' (m), and کُکڑ /kukiṛ/ 'hen' (f)

چھوہر /chohar/ 'boy' (m), and چھوہِر /chohir/ 'girl' (f)

In addition to the patterns of IA origin discussed above, a pattern originating in Arabic and transmitted through Persian and Urdu is found in these languages, most often in proper names and in a few pairs of common nouns. When a masculine name ends in a consonant other than ہ the feminine ends in ہ, for example, نجم /najam/ 'proper name for male' and نجمہ /najmā/ 'proper name for female'. Some commonly used common nouns exhibiting this pattern are: صاحب /sāb/ 'sir, gentleman (m)' and صاحبہ /sāiba/ 'Ms., Madame, lady (f)'; والد /vālid/ 'father (m)' and والدہ /vālda/ 'mother (f)'; محبوب /mæ(h)būb/ 'beloved (m)' and محبوبہ /mæ(h)būba/ 'beloved (f)'.

4.3.3 Case

Case is both a morphological and a syntactic/semantic category. Indication of case relations in all three languages is accomplished by a multi-layer system (following Masica 1991). Layer 1 consists of elements which attach directly to the stem; for these languages this means the oblique case. Layer 2 elements are added to the oblique case; the ablative and vocative cases, and simple postpositions, are such elements. Grammaticalized locative/oblique nominals which function as postpositions are Layer 3 elements.

All three languages have direct and oblique cases, and can theoretically form vocatives, for all nouns. The direct case is the default case; thus the citation form of nouns is the singular direct case form.

4.3.3.1 Direct

In all three languages the direct case[15] marks the grammatical subject of intransitive verbs, the subject of non-perfective tenses of transitive and ditransitive verbs, and most non-human, non-specific direct objects.

4.3.3.2 Oblique

In Panjabi and Saraiki, only marked masculines (Class I) show a distinct oblique case form in the singular.[16] With feminines and unmarked masculines, the singular oblique case has a zero ending; its underlying obliqueness becomes apparent when such a noun appears in construction with a marked adjective; for example وڈّے گھر وِچ /vaḍḍe (SG.M.OBL) kàr (SG.M.OBL) vic/ 'in the big house'. For this reason, all nouns and pronouns that are followed by a postposition are considered here to be in the oblique case—either overt or covert. Plural oblique case is marked on all nouns.

All postpositions follow nouns or pronouns in the oblique case; however, the converse is not true; not all oblique nouns and pronouns are followed by a postposition.

Hindko is unique in that all masculine nouns, both Class I (marked) and Class II (unmarked), have an overt oblique singular in /-e/, or /-ẽ/ for nouns ending in /-ā̃/. This includes Hindko infinitives, whose oblique form ends in /-ṛe ~ -ne/.

4.3.3.3 Vocative

The vocative case marks a person, animal, or personified inanimate entity directly addressed.[17]

Although vocatives are constructible for all nouns, only those for animates are generally produced. Vocative endings follow the oblique form. They are presented separately for Hindko, Panjabi, and Saraiki.

4.3.3.3.1 Hindko vocative case endings

This information on Hindko vocative usages is due to Abdul Wahid Tabassum, and are shown in Table 4.1.

15 This case is also sometimes called nominative case, e.g. in Cummings and Bailey (1912).

16 Some authors have referred to the oblique case as accusative, e.g. Malik (1995).

17 Although the vocative is most commonly used for animate nouns, it can also be used metaphorically, as in poetry.

Gender	Singular	Plural
Masculine	-ā	-o
Feminine	-e	-o

Table 4.1: Hindko vocative case endings

4.3.3.3.2 Panjabi vocative case endings

For the vocative endings in Panjabi, we follow Bhardwaj 2016: 109–112; these endings are shown in Table 4.2.

Gender	Stem	Singular	Plural
Masculine, marked		-ĕā	-ĕo
Masculine, unmarked	ā-final	-vā	-o
	ī-final	-ā	-o
	ū-final	-ā ~ Ø	-o
	consonant-final	-ā	-o
Feminine, marked		-e ~ Ø	-o
Feminine, unmarked	ā-final	-e ~ Ø	-o
	ā̃-final	-ẽ	-īyo
	ū-final	Ø	-o
	e-final	Ø	not attested
	o-final	-e	not attested
	consonant-final	-e	-o

Table 4.2: Panjabi vocative case endings

4.3.3.3.3 Saraiki vocative case endings

Vocative marking in Saraiki is quite complex. Variables like human vs. non-human addressee, common noun vs. proper name, and relative social status/relationship of the addressee as well as singular or plural number and gender are involved. With proper names, only singular number is involved.[18] The following information is due to Nasir Abbas Syed; common nouns are shown in Table 4.3, and proper nouns in Table 4.4.

18 The proper name Nur is chosen to illustrate these endings since it can be either a woman's or a man's name.

Characteristics of referent	Gender	Singular	Plural
Human common noun	Masculine	-ā ∼ Ø او چوہرا o chuhrā ‘o boy’	-o او چوہرو o chuhro ‘o boys’
	Feminine	-a ∼ Ø او چوہرا o chuhirā ‘o girl’	-ī̃ او چھوہریں o chuhirī̃ ‘o girls’
Non-human common noun	Masculine	اہ کھوتا o khotā ‘o male donkey’	اہ کھوتے o khote ‘o male donkeys’
	Feminine	او کھوتی o khotī ‘o female donkey’	-iyā̃ او کھوتیاں o khotiyā̃ ‘o female donkeys’

Table 4.3: Saraiki common noun vocative case endings

Gender	Nature of Relationship	Singular
Masculine	Unmarked, neutral	ø او نور o nūr 'o Nur'
	addressee of lower status/younger	-ā او نورا o nūrā 'o Nur'
	expressing hatred of addressee/very low status of addressee	-ī او نوری o nūrī 'o Nur'
	affection or some respect for addressee	-ū او نورو o nūrū 'o Nur'
	strong love for addressee	-aṇ او نورݨ o nūraṇ 'o Nur'
Feminine	unmarked, neutral	ø اڑی نور aṛī nūr 'o Nur'
	addressee of lower status/younger/expressing hatred of addressee	-ī اڑی نوری aṛī nūrī 'o Nur'
	for affection or love	-o اڑی نورو aṛī nūro 'o Nur'
	for a loved one	-ā̃ اڑی نوراں aṛī nūrā̃ 'o Nur'

Table 4.4: Saraiki proper name vocative case endings

4.3.3.4 Vocative particles

In addition to the case endings, addressees' names are often preceded by a vocative particle, again varying by the gender and relationship of the speaker to the addressee.

4.3.3.4.1 Hindko vocative particles

In Hindko, vocative particles which precede the name of the person/thing addressed include وا /vā/ and اوئے /oe/, which can be used with singular or plural male or female addressees, for instance اوئے کڑیو /oe kuṛiyo/ 'o girls', وا کڑیو /vā kuṛiyo/ 'o girls', اوئے جاتکا /oe jātakā/ 'o boy', or وا جاتکو /vā jātako/ 'o boys'. To show respect for an older person, one might say وا بڈیو /vā buḍeo/ 'o old man', using the plural vocative case ending.

4.3.3.4.2 Panjabi vocative particles

Panjabi vocative particles include:

- man to man/men: اوے /oe/
- woman/man to man or men (of junior status): وے /ve/
- man/woman to junior woman/women or girl/girls: نیں /nī̃/ ~ نی /nī /

4.3.3.4.3 Saraiki vocative particles

For addressing males, اے /e/ or او /o/ is used. For human females, اے /e/, او /o/, or اوئے /oe/'hey' are used. For non-humans, only او /o/ is used. Shackle (1976: 70) also gives اوئے /oe/ 'hey' , and a set of vocative particles which he says are characteristic of rural speech, as follows:

- man to a man: او /o/
- man to a woman: نیں /nī/ (used in areas adjoining Panjabi-speaking areas
- woman to a man: وے /ve/
- woman to a woman: وݨ /vaṇ/ ~ وݨے /vaṇe/ (used in areas adjoining Panjabi-speaking areas)

In addition, under the influence of Urdu, educated people often address a person without using any vocative suffix. In these cases, they slightly prolong the second vowel in words with (CVCV(C)) syllable structures. For example, if an educated speaker calls out to a person named Khalid, he will produce the name with a long vowel in a final, otherwise short, syllable, i.e. /xalīd/.

4.3.3.5 Ablative

Aside from the three cases regularly formed for all nouns (direct, oblique, and vocative), the ablative occurs most frequently–in all three languages. The ablative case ending occurs only with singular nouns (including infinitives), which generally refer to places, times, events, or conditions. It is formed by suffixing the ablative case ending /-õ/ (Pj, Hk) or /ũ̃/ (Sr) to the oblique singular, e.g. پاسا ~ پاسہ /pāsā/ 'side, direction (dir)' → پاسے /pāse/ 'side (obl)' → پاسیوں /pāseõ ~ pāseũ̃/ ' from the side (abl)'.

The most basic concrete meaning of the ablative is direction or motion away from (SOURCE), which develops into abstract meanings of displacement, change of condition, involuntary causation, or comparison; for example, ایس توں ودھ /æs tõ vád(d)/ 'more than this', lit. 'more from this'. With animates, ablative relations are usually indicated with postpositions, which themselves can take the ablative ending.

کول /koḷ/ Pj ~ /kol/ Hk, Sr → کولوں /kolõ/ Hk, کولوں /koḷõ/ Pj, کولوں /kolũ̃/ Sr 'from (a person)'

اندر /andar/ 'in, inside' Pj → اندروں /andrõ/ 'from inside'

بچ /bic/ Hk, وچ /vic/(Pj, Sr) 'in, at' → بچوں /bicõ/ Hk, وچوں /vicõ/ Pj, وچوں /vicũ̃/ Sr 'from inside; among'

The distinction in meaning between the form of a postposition or adverb with or without the ablative ending is sometimes minimal, as with پچھے /picche/ 'after, behind' with پچھوں /picchõ/ 'afterwards, later, from behind', or کد /kad/ 'when?' and کدوں /kadõ/ 'when?'. With plurals, postpositional expressions are always employed, as in example 4.1.

(4.1) کڑیاں منڈیاں نالوں زیادہ کم کیتا

kuṛiy-ā̃	*mũḍ-eā̃*	*nāḷõ*	*zyādā*	*kamm*	*kīt-ā*
girl-PL.DIR	boy-PL.OBL	than	more	work	do.PP-SG.M

'The girls did more work than the boys.' (Pj) (EB)

The ablative infinitive appears in constructions like those in the following examples, one from Panjabi and one from Saraiki.

(4.2) بس اک گلّ دسنوں رہندی اے

bas	*ik(k)*	*gall*	*das-ṇ-õ*	*rǽn-d-ī*	*e*
only	one	thing[F]	tell-INF.OBL-ABL	remain-IP-SG.F	be.PRES.SG

'There is just one thing left to tell.' (Pj) (Bashir and Kazmi 2012: 663)

(4.3) مینہ وسنوں کھڑ گیا

mīh	*vas-ṇ-ũ̃*	*khaṛ*	*ɠy-ā*
rain[M]	rain-INF.OBL-ABL	stop	go.PP-M.SG

'It stopped raining.' (Sr) (Shackle 1976: 134)

4.3.3.6 Locative

The locative case is no longer fully productive, only a few nouns in each of these languages having distinct locative forms. Some high-frequency nouns with original (older) locative singular forms are سویرے /saver-e/ 'in the morning' Pj , دنے /din-e/ 'by day' Hk, Pj / ڈِہاڑے /dīhāṛe/ 'by day' Sr , دھُپّے /tùpp-e/ 'in the sunshine' Pj , and کہرے /kàr-e/ Hk / گھرے /kàr-e/ 'at home' Pj .

However, the locative is still somewhat productive in Hindko and Panjabi, since the locative ending also occurs with some unmarked masculine nouns, e.g. بزارے /bazāre/ 'in/to the bazaar' some feminine nouns, e.g. مسیتے /masīte/ 'to/in the mosque', and even the English loanword 'school' in سکولے /skūl-e/ 'at/to school'. [19]

(4.4) ڈھائی کروڑ جاتک سکولے نہیں جاندے

ṭãī	*kroṛ*	*jātak*	*skūl-e*	*nī̃*	*jān-d-e*
2.5	ten-millions	children	school-LOC	not	go-IP-PL.M

'Twenty-five million children don't go to school.'[20] (Hk)

The locative plural is formed by suffixing ـیں /-ī̃/ or /ẽ/ to the stem; with vowel-final stems the final vowels merge with the ending. In Saraiki, usually /-ī̃/ appears with feminines and /-ẽ/ with masculines, but this is not necessarily the case in Panjabi or Hindko. A small number of nouns have both ablative singular and locative plural forms. Table 4.5 displays attested locative endings in Hindko, Panjabi, and Saraiki.

	Singular	**Plural**
Hindko	-e, -ī, -ī̃	-ī̃
Panjabi	-e, -ī	-ī̃
Saraiki	-e, -ẽ, -ī̃	-ẽ, -ī̃

Table 4.5: Locative endings in Hindko, Panjabi, and Saraiki

The locative case has several functions.

19 We do not have information about whether or not this is also the case in Saraiki.

20 Example from: http://www.wichaar.com/news/117 /ARTICLE/29863/2013-08-28.html

- spatial location:

  کھیت /khet/ 'field.SG.M.DIR' → کھیتیں /khet-ĩ/ 'field-PL.M.LOC, in the fields' Pj

  ہتھّ /hatth/ 'hand.SG.M.DIR' → ہتھیں /hatth-ĩ / 'hand-PL.M.LOC, in the hands' Pj

- temporal location, as in 4.5:

(4.5) ہر پنجیں ورھیں

har	*panj-ĩ*	*vâr-ĩ*
every	five-PL.LOC	year-PL.LOC

'every five years' (Pj) (Shackle 1972: 114)

- price for which something is obtained, as in 4.6:

(4.6) ایہ مینوں دسیں روپئیں ملیا

é	*mæ-nũ*	*das-ĩ*	*rūpa-ĩ*	*mil-iyā*
this	1SG-DAT/ACC	ten-PL.LOC	rupee-PL.LOC	be.obtained-PP.SG.M

'I got this for ten rupees!' (Pj) (Shackle 1972: 114)

The locative occurs in some common collocations with the verb پیݨا/pæṇā/ 'to fall', as in 4.7 and 4.8.

(4.7) سوچیں پیݨا

soc-ĩ	*pæṇā*
thought-PL.LOC	fall.INF

'to fall into thoughts (i.e. to become thoughtful, pensive)' (Pj) (EB)

(4.8) نظریں پیݨا

nazr-ĩ	*pæṇā*
sight-PL.LOC	fall.INF

'to fall into sight (i.e. to come suddenly into view)' (Bashir and Kazmi 2012: 583)

Adjectives, especially numerals, can also take the locative plural ending, as in 4.6. However, modifying adjectives increasingly tend to appear in the oblique singular before nouns marked with the locative plural.

4.4 Declension classes and paradigms

Some declension classes (I, II, and III) are common to all three languages. Class IV, which includes most feminines other than those in Class III is similar but not identical in Hindko, Panjabi, and Saraiki. Classes V and VI may be unique to Hindko; and Classes VII, VIII, and IX are found in Saraiki. Table 4.6 lays these classes out to facilitate comparison between the declension systems of the three languages. The numbers assigned to declension classes are used consistently across the three languages. Numbers assigned here to Saraiki declensional classes are compared for the reader's convenience with Shackle's (1976) classification.

From the table it can be seen that the simplest declension system is that of Panjabi, with both Hindko and Saraiki retaining some smaller classes of nouns which reflect older patterns. It seems likely that increasing convergence will lead to simplification in the direction of the Panjabi pattern.

Hindko	Panjabi	Saraiki
Class I (masculines with sg. direct in /-ā/ or /ā̃/)	Class I (masculines with sg. direct in /-ā/ or /ā̃/)	Class I (masculines with sg. direct in /-ā/ or /ā̃/) (compare Shackle's I)
Class II (all other masculines)	Class II (all other masculines)	Class II (all other masculines except those in Class VIII) (compare Shackle's II)
Class III (feminines with sg. direct in /-ī/ or /-ī̃/)	Class III (feminines with sg. direct in /-ī/ or /-ī̃/)	Class III (feminines with sg. direct in /-ī/ or /-ī̃/) (compare Shackle's IV)
Class IV (all other feminines except those in Classes V and VI) (declined the same as Class III)	Class IV (all other feminines; declined the same as Class III)	
Class V (feminines with oblique/agentive form in /ī/ and locative in /-ī̃/)		
Class VI (masculines and feminines with oblique/agentive case forms in /-ū/ ~ /-ū̃/		
		Class VII (feminines except those in Classes III, and IX); includes stems with stem-internal unstressed /i/). Has pl.dir/obl in /-ī̃/ and sg. loc. in /ī/; (compare Shackle's V)
		Class VIII (masculines with stem-internal unstressed /u/) (compare Shackle's III)
		Class IX (two exceptional feminines, ہنج hanj 'tear' and تند tand 'fiber' (compare Shackle's VI)

Table 4.6: Comparison of Hindko, Panjabi, and Saraiki declension classes

4.4.1 Hindko

4.4.1.1 Hindko declension classes

Hindko has marked masculines in unstressed /-ā/ (Class I), unmarked masculines (Class II), and marked feminines (Class III). However, it also has three additional classes—most other feminines (Class IV), feminines with oblique/agentive case forms in /-ī/ (Class V), and masculines and feminines with oblique/agentive case forms in /-ū/ ~ /-ū̃/ (Class VI). Unfortunately, our Hindko data so far are very limited, and this work must be considered an exploratory study. Identifying and refining the description of Hazara Hindko declension classes demands much more work.

4.4.1.2 Hindko noun paradigms

All masculine nouns in Hindko of both Class I and Class II have unique direct, oblique, and vocative (used mainly with humans) forms.[21] For some nouns, mainly inanimates denoting places, locative singular and ablative singular forms are also found. The locative seems to be employed with nouns signifying concrete place or time, or abstractions from these notions. It is sometimes used in the sense of an instrumental, as in ہتّھیں /hatthī̃/ 'in/by hand'. Locative and ablative plural relations are expressed with the oblique plural form plus a postposition. A small set of nouns have an oblique/agentive form in /-ī/ Class V. Hindko's Class V should be compared with Saraiki's Class VII, a task requiring further detailed work on Hindko. Another small group of nouns of both genders, mostly kinship terms it appears at this point, have an oblique/agentive form in /-ū̃/, for example ما ~ ماں، /mā ~ mā̃/ 'mother', تّھی /tī̀/ 'daughter', پھرا /prā̀/ 'brother', and پیو /pyo/ 'father' (Class VI). The oblique form precedes all postpositions. The postposition سُڑ /suṛ̃/, sometimes marks the subject/agent of perfective tenses of transitive verbs. Dative and accusative case relations are indicated by the Layer 2 element اں ~ آں /ā̃/, which follows the oblique form of the noun.

4.4.1.2.1 Masculine nouns (Classes I and II)

Marked masculine ا /-ā/ -final nouns (Class I):[22]

Where locative forms of ا /-ā/-final masculine nouns exist, they have the same form as the oblique singular. Thus a more economical synchronic analysis might be that the oblique form has oblique, locative, and instrumental functions.

---

21 The dative-accusative marker آں /ā̃/ is interesting; it seems to behave at some times like a postposition and at others like a Level 2 case ending—perhaps in a transitional stage from one status to another.

22 The forms in Table 4.7 and Table 4.12 were provided by our consultant, but not observed in actual usage.

	Singular	Plural
Direct	بُوہا bū̋-ā	بُوہے bū̋-e
Oblique	بُوہے bū̋-e	بوہیاں bū̋e-ā̃
Vocative	بُوہیا bū̋-eā	بوہیو bū̋-eo

Table 4.7: Marked masculine, ا /-ā/ -final (Class I) noun بُوہا /bū̋ā/ 'door'

An example of unmarked masculine nouns ending in vowels other than /-ā/ (Class II) is given in Table 4.8. Consonant-final, unmarked masculine nouns (Class II) are illustrated in Table 4.9. Consonant-final, unmarked masculine nouns having a singular locative and an ablative form (Class II) are illustrated in Table 4.10. For plurals and those nouns not having locative or ablative forms, however, a postposition attached to the oblique form serves these functions (see Table 4.10).[23]

	Singular	Plural
Direct (= nominative)	آلو ālū	آلو ālū
Oblique	آلوئے ālū-e	آلوآں ālū-ā̃
Vocative	آلوا ālū-ā	آلوؤ ālū-o

Table 4.8: Unmarked, vowel-final masculine noun آلو /ālū/ 'potato' (Class II)

23 With respect to Table 4.10, the spelling کہار /kȁr/, indicating a long vowel, appears when the word occurs in its direct case form (i.e. citation form). However, when it is followed by a case ending, the vowel sound shortens, and in the data in Table 4.10, this change is represented in the written forms of the word.

	Singular	Plural
Direct (= nominative)	پُتَّر puttar	پُتَّر puttar
Oblique/Agentive	پُتَّرے puttar-e	پُتَّراں puttar-ã
Vocative	پُتَّرا puttar-ā	پُتَّرو puttar-o

Table 4.9: Unmarked, consonant-final masculine noun پُتَّر /puttar/ 'son' (Class II)

	Singular	Plural
Direct (= nominative)	کہار kàr	کہار kàr
Oblique	کہرے kàr-e	کہراں kàr-ã
Ablative	کہروں kàr-õ	کہراں kàr-ã + postposition
Locative	کہرے kàr-e	کہراں kàr-ã + postposition
Vocative	کہرا kàr-ā	کہرو kàr-o

Table 4.10: Unmarked, consonant-final (Class II) masculine noun کہار /kàr/ 'house, home' (~کہر /kàr/)

4.4.1.2.2 Feminine nouns (Classes III, IV, V, and VI)

Marked feminine, /-ī/-final nouns (Class III) are illustrated in Table 4.11.

The direct and oblique singular forms for these Class III marked feminine nouns are the same, as are their direct and oblique plurals. This is the same as the Panjabi pattern. Class IV includes all other feminines except those in Classes V and VI. مَجھ /mā́j/ 'buffalo' is an example of a Class IV noun. Class IV nouns are declined like Class III nouns.

	Singular	Plural
Direct (= nominative)	کُڑی kuṛī	کُڑیاں kuṛiy-ā̃
Oblique		
Vocative	کُڑیے kuṛiy-e	کُڑیو kuṛiy-o

Table 4.11: Marked feminine, unstressed /-ī/-final noun کُڑی /kuṛī/ 'girl' (Class III)

Some unmarked (feminine) nouns have an oblique/agentive form ending in ی /-ī/ (Class V); a few also have a locative form in یں /-ī̃/; an example of a consonant-final Class V noun is اگ /agg/ 'fire', shown in Table 4.12. A vowel-final Class V noun is لَو /lao/ 'sunlight/daylight'.

	Singular	Plural
Direct (= nominative)	اگ agg	اگاں agg-ā̃
Oblique/Agentive	اگی agg-ī	اگاں agg-ā̃
Locative	اگیں agg-ī̃	اگاں agg-ā̃ + postposition
Vocative	اگے agg-e	اگو agg-o

Table 4.12: Consonant-final feminine noun اگ /agg/ 'fire' (Class V)

Example 4.9 shows the oblique form of the noun اگ /agg/ 'fire' as the subject/agent of a transitive sentence in a perfective tense.

(4.9) اگی میرا کہار برباد کیتا

agg-ī   mer-ā   kằr   barbād   kīt-ā
fire-SG.F.OBL   my-SG.M   house.SG.M   destroyed   do.PP-SG.M
'The fire destroyed my house.' (Hk) (AWT)

4.4.1.2.3 Class VI Hindko nouns (masculine and feminine)

A small class of Hindko nouns, most of our attested examples of which refer to male or female persons, have an oblique / agentive form ending in /-ū/ or /-ū̃/ (Class VI). They include ماں /mā̃/ 'mother'; تھی /tì/ 'daughter'; پیو/pyo/ 'father', پھرا /prà/ 'brother', and پہین /pæ̀n/ 'sister'. The paradigms for ماں /mā̃/ 'mother' and تھی /tì/ 'daughter' are given in Table 4.13 and Table 4.14, respectively.

	Singular	Plural
Direct (= nominative)	ماں mā̃	ماواں mā-vā̃
Oblique / Agentive	ماؤں mā-ū̃	ماواں mā-vā̃
Vocative	مائے mā-e	ماو mā-o

Table 4.13: Kinship noun ماں /mā̃/ 'mother' (Class VI)

	Singular	Plural
Direct (= nominative)	تھی tì	تھیاں tì-ā̃
Oblique / Agentive	تھیو tì-ū	تھیاں tì-ā̃
Vocative	تھیے tì-e	تھیو tì-o

Table 4.14: Kinship noun تھی /tì/ 'daughter' (Class VI)

Class VI includes both feminines and masculines. Example 4.10 illustrates the oblique/agentive form of پیو/pyo/ 'father' appearing as the agent of the simple perfect tense of the transitive verb کٹنڑا /kuṭṛ̃ā/ 'to beat'.

(4.10) اُس جاتکے دے پیوؤ اُس آں کُٹیا

us	*jātk-e*	*d-e*	*pyo-ū*	*us-ā̃*
that.OBL	boy-SG.M.OBL	GEN-SG.M.OBL	father-OBL	him.OBL-ACC

kuṭ-iyā
beat-PP.SG.M
'That boy's father beat him.' (Hk) (AWT)

4.4.2 Panjabi

4.4.2.1 Panjabi declension classes

All Panjabi nouns fall into one of four declension paradigms: marked masculine (Class I), unmarked masculine (Class II), marked feminine (Class III), and all other feminines (Class IV).

4.4.2.1.1 Marked masculine (Class I)

In the singular direct case form, masculine nouns in Class I end in an unstressed /-ā/, spelled with ا, ہ, ح, or ع, or less commonly, in unstressed اں /-ā̃/. The converse, however, is not true; not all nouns ending in /-ā/ or /-ā̃/ are masculine (see Section 4.4.2.1.3 below). Those ending in ح, or ع, are sometimes treated as unmarked, despite their final /-ā/. Such words are of Perso-Arabic origin. Examples of marked masculine nouns are:

منڈا /mũḍā/ 'boy'
حملہ /hamlā/ 'attack, invasion'
نکاح /nikā́/ 'Muslim marriage ceremony'
تنازع /tanāzā/ 'dispute, contention'
گنیاں /guṇiā̃/ 'T-square' (Malik 1995: 196)

4.4.2.1.2 Unmarked masculine (Class II)

Unmarked masculines end either in a consonant or any vowel other than unstressed /-ā/ or /-ā̃/. As noted above, unmarked nouns show no distinction in the direct case between singular and plural.[24] For example:

- consonant-final

  دن /din/ 'day'

  گھر /kàr/ 'house'

- /āī/-final

  نائی /nāī/ 'barber'

- /ī/-final

  دھوبی /tòbī/ 'washerman'

  پاکستانی /pākistānī/ 'Pakistani'

- /ī̃/-final

  دہیں /daī̃/ 'yogurt, curds'

- /ū/-final

  اُلّو /ullū/ 'owl'

  ڈاکو /ḍākū/ 'robber'

  کدّو /kaddū/ 'variety of summer squash; simpleton (slang)'

- /o/-final

  گھیو /kiyò/ 'ghee, clarified butter'

Two important classes of nouns ending in /-ī/ are masculine. These are (i) names for occupational classes, e.g. دھوبی /tòbī/ 'washerman' (m), and (ii) nouns derived with the adjective/noun-forming suffix /-ī/ as in پاکستانی /pākistānī/ 'Pakistani', as also discussed in Section 4.3.2.2.

24 A few words can take Persian or Arabic plural morphology, e.g. اخبار /axbār/ 'newspaper', the indigenous plural of which is the same as the singular, but which can sometimes occur as اخبارات /axbār-āt/ 'newspapers', often with a collective sense, as in 'the press'.

4.4.2.1.3 Feminine (Classes III and IV)

Feminine nouns characteristically end in ی /-ī/, e.g. کُڑی /kuṛī/ 'girl', or ـیں /-ī̃/, e.g. تیویں /tīvī̃/ 'woman' (Class III). However, many feminines also end in consonants and other vowels (Class IV). Examples of Class IV nouns include:

- consonant-final

  دُھپّ /tùpp/ 'sunshine'

- /o/-final

  گلو /glo/ 'species of vine'

  بگّو /baggo/ lit. 'little white one' (affectionate nickname for female child)

- /ū/-final

  آبرُو /ābrū/ 'honor, character, good reputation' (< Persian < Turkish)

- /æ/-final

  شے /šæ/ 'thing' (< Ar.)

Both Class III and IV feminine nouns are inflected in the same way (as opposed to Urdu). Saraiki and Hindko, however have additional feminine inflectional classes.

4.4.2.2 Panjabi noun paradigms

In this section, declensions of representative exemplars of each inflectional class identified in Panjabi are presented. As stated above, there are three completely productive cases in all three languages: direct, oblique, and vocative. All nouns will have possible forms in these cases (even if they are not generally produced). In addition, ablative and locative cases occur with some words (see Section 4.3.3.5 and Section 4.3.3.6 on their use). Note that forms for the ablative singular are provided for all words below; this is a more productive process than locative plural formation but ablative plural case endings are not found. Semantic relations not indicated by case endings are expressed with postpositions.

4.4.2.2.1 Marked masculine nouns (Class I)

The inflectional paradigm for منڈا /mũḍā/ 'boy', a typical Class I noun, is given in Table 4.15. All other masculine nouns ending in /-ā/ follow the same pattern.

	Singular	Plural
Direct	منڈا mũḍ-ā	منڈے mũḍ-e
Oblique	منڈے mũḍ-e	منڈیاں mũḍ-ĕã
Ablative	منڈیوں mũḍ-ĕõ	منڈیاں mũḍ-ĕã + postposition
Vocative	منڈیا mũḍ-ĕā	منڈیو mũḍ-ĕo

Table 4.15: Panjabi marked masculine noun مُنڈا /mũḍā/ 'boy' (Class I)

4.4.2.2.2 Unmarked masculine nouns (Class II)

This class includes all masculines other than those in Class I. The paradigms for vowel-final پاݨی /pāṇī/ 'water' and consonant-final دن /din/ 'day' are given in Table 4.16 and Table 4.17, respectively. All masculine nouns not ending in final unstressed /-ā/, including both those with final consonants and those with final vowels, follow this pattern.

	Singular	Plural
Direct	پاݨی pāṇī	پاݨی pāṇī
Oblique		پاݨیاں pāṇiy-ã
Ablative	پاݨیوں pāṇiy-õ	پاݨیاں pāṇiy-ã + postposition
Vocative	پاݨیا pāṇiy-ā	پاݨیو pāṇiy-o

Table 4.16: Paradigm for پاݨی /pāṇī/ 'water' (Class II)

	Singular	Plural
Direct	دن din	دن din
Oblique		دناں din-ā̃
Locative	دنے din-e	دنیں din-ĩ
Ablative	دنوں din-õ	دناں din-ā̃ + postposition
Vocative	دنا din-ā	دنو din-o

Table 4.17: Paradigm for دن /din/ 'day' (Class II)

4.4.2.2.3 Feminine nouns (Classes III and IV)

The inflectional paradigms of کُڑی /kuṛī/ 'girl' (Class III), and دھُپ /tùp(p)/ 'sunshine', and ہوا /havā/ 'wind' (Class IV) are given in Table 4.18, Table 4.19, and Table 4.20, respectively. Most feminine nouns end in /-ī/ and follow the pattern for کُڑی /kuṛī/ 'girl'. Nevertheless, there are many feminines that end in consonants or other vowels. They follow the patterns illustrated by دھُپ /tùpp/ 'sunshine' (Table 4.19) and ہوا /havā/ 'wind' (Table 4.20).

	Singular	Plural
Direct Oblique	کڑی kuṛī	کڑیاں kuṛiy-ā̃
Ablative	کڑیوں kuṛiy-õ	کڑیاں kuṛiy-ā̃ +postposition
Vocative	کڑیے kuṛiy-e	کڑیو kuṛiy-o

Table 4.18: Paradigm for کُڑی /kuṛī/ 'girl ' (Class III)

	Singular	Plural
Direct Oblique	دھُپ tùpp	دھپاں tùpp-ā̃
Locative	دھپے tùpp-e	دھپیں tùpp-ī̃
Ablative	دھپوں tùpp-õ	دھپاں tùpp-ā̃ + postposition
Vocative	دھپے tùpp-e	دھپو tùpp-o

Table 4.19: Paradigm for دھپ /tùpp/ 'sunshine' (Class IV)

	Singular	Plural
Direct Oblique	ہوا havā	ہواواں havā-vā̃
Locative	——	ہوئیں havā-ī̃
Ablative	ہواوں havā-õ	ہواواں havā-vā̃ + postposition
Vocative	ہوائے havā-e	ہواؤ havā-o

Table 4.20: Paradigm for ہوا /havā/ 'wind' (Class IV)

4.4.2.2.4 Panjabi Inflectional paradigms

Table 4.21– Table 4.24 show the inflectional affixes abstracted for each declension class identified. Table 4.21 through Table 4.22 show the inflectional endings for masculine marked and unmarked nouns, respectively. No unique locative singular forms are regularly attested for Class I marked masculines; and the ablative only occurs in the singular and the locative generally only in the plural.

	Singular	Plural
Direct	ا /-ā/	ے /-e/
Oblique	ے /-e/	یاں /-eā̃/
Ablative	یوں /-eõ/	––
Vocative	یا /-eā/	یو /-eo/

Table 4.21: Inflectional endings for marked masculine nouns (Class I)

Masculine nouns ending in اں /-ā̃/ also follow the paradigm in Table 4.21, with nasalization maintained in the direct plural and the oblique singular and plural. Unmarked masculine nouns (Class II) have the same form in the direct singular and plural, and oblique singular. The stem appears without any ending (Table 4.22).

	Singular	Plural
Direct	ø	ø
Oblique	ø	اں /-ā̃/
Locative	ے /-e/ rare	یں /-ī̃/ rare
Ablative	وں /-õ/	––
Vocative	ا /-ā/	و /-o/

Table 4.22: Inflectional endings for unmarked masculine nouns (Class II)

Table 4.23 gives the inflectional affixes for all feminine nouns in Panjabi. Although there is a formal distinction between two classes of feminine nouns—those with a thematic final /-ī/ (Class III), and all others (Class IV)—in Panjabi they are inflected uniformly, which we have recognized here.

	Singular	Plural
Direct	ی /ī/[25]	اں /-ā̃/
Oblique	ی /ī/	اں /-ā̃/
Locative	ے /-e/ rare	یں /-ī̃/ non-productive
Ablative	وں /-õ/	اں /-ā̃/ + postposition
Vocative	ے /-e/	و /-o/

Table 4.23: Inflectional endings for Panjabi feminine nouns (Class III and Class IV)

4.4.2.2.5 Some morphophonemic changes

When taking the inflectional endings in the above paradigms, some noun stems undergo phonological changes. Several general patterns can be identified. Masculine and feminine nouns ending in the long vowels ی /-ī/ and و /-ū/ shorten the long vowels to /-i/ and /-u/ respectively before the ending. A y-glide usually appears between a resulting short /i/ and the ending, and a v-glide sometimes appears between shortened /u/ and the ending. A semivowel (glide) /-v-/ intervenes between two/-ā/ vowels in succession, for example چاہ, /cā́/ 'tea', inserts a /-v-/ between the stem and the plural direct and oblique endings.

Singular	Plural
گاں gā̃ 'cow'	گانواں gā̃v-ā̃ 'cow'
چاہ cā́ 'tea'	چاہواں cā́v-ā̃ 'teas'

Table 4.24: Feminine nouns in /-ā̃/ /-ā́/ (Class IV)

If a two-syllable singular noun has an unstressed peripheral vowel in the final syllable, this is lost in the plural, e.g. نظر /nazar/ 'view' (f) and گدڑ /giddaṛ/ 'jackal' (m) become, respectively, نظراں /nazrā̃/ 'views' and گدڑاں /giddṛā̃/ in the oblique plural. This is an

25 Class IV direct and oblique singulars are zero marked.

instance of the automatic phonological process known as schwa-deletion, which can be summarized in the phonological rule /ə/ → Ø / (C)VC __ C V̄, that is, in the environment (C)VC __ C V̄, /ə/ is deleted (See Ohala 1974). This rule also operates in Hindko and Saraiki. Note that this change is not detectable in the Perso-Arabic script, which does not usually represent centralized vowels.

Feminine nouns ending in a nasalized vowel other than /-ã/ lose the stem-final nasalization in the plural:

- تیویں /tīvī̃/ 'woman' → تیویاں /tīviy-ã/ 'woman-PL'
- میہیں /mẽī̃/ 'water buffalo' → میہیاں /mẽiy-ã/ 'water buffalo-PL'

4.4.3 Saraiki

4.4.3.1 Saraiki declension classes

In addition to marked masculines (Class I), unmarked masculines (Class II), marked feminines (Class III), and most unmarked feminines (Class IV), Saraiki has a second class of feminines (Class VII), in which stem-internal /i/ indicates feminines, with direct and oblique plurals in /-ī̃/; a small class in which the back stem vowel /u/ marks masculines (Class VIII); and a vestigial class (IX) including only two (feminine) words. Classes VII, VIII, and IX are not found in Panjabi or, to our knowledge, in Hindko.[26] In such Saraiki pairs, nouns with back vowels /u/ or /a/ in the second (unstressed) syllable are masculine, while those with the front vowel /i/ in this position are feminine. For example:

- پنسِل /pinsil/ 'pencil' (f) (Class VII)
- شُکُر /šukur/ 'thanks' (m) (Class VIII)
- کُکُڑ /kukuṛ/ 'cock, rooster' (m) (Class VIII), and کُکِڑ /kukiṛ/ 'hen' (f) (Class VII)
- چھوہر /chohar/ 'boy' (m) (Class VIII), and چھوہِر /chohir/ 'girl' (f) (Class VII) (Shackle 1976: 43)

26 Shackle (1976: 43) says that pairs of this type are found in "some Northern Lahnda dialects," however we have not been able to verify this for current Abbottabad Hindko. Existence of this pattern in Saraiki is one reason why scholars (Grierson 1919: 1) have commented on the similarity of "Lahnda" and Sindhi to the Dardic languages, where vowel fronting or raising marks feminines (Bashir 2003: 823).

4.4.3.2 Saraiki noun paradigms

Since Saraiki has no unique agentive case form, agents (subjects of transitive verbs in perfective tenses) take the oblique form. The oblique form also precedes postpositions, and thus enters into the possessive, accusative/dative, and various locative and temporal expressions. The ergative (agentive) postposition نے /ne/ , which marks agents in Urdu and is used by most speakers in the third person in Panjabi, has not been traditionally used in Saraiki. However, Shackle (1976: 144) notes that نے /ne/ sometimes occurs in educated colloquial speech as an agentive (ergative) marker in imitation of Urdu and Panjabi, but that it is considered incorrect in careful speech and writing. Written forms provided by our consultant (2015) sometimes included نے /ne/ and sometimes did not.

Vocative case forms are, for practical purposes, restricted to animates. For a full discussion of Saraiki vocatives, see Section 4.3.3.3.3 and Section 4.3.3.4.3.

Locative and ablative forms exist for some but not all nouns. A few nouns referring to inanimates, from various declension classes, have locative case forms. Such nouns mostly denote place or time, and some such nouns have both singular and plural forms. Additionally, many adverbial forms ending in /-e/, which are now perceived as obliques of masculine nominals, were originally locatives. Ablative forms occur more frequently than locatives, and are not restricted to inanimates; however ablative plural forms do not exist. Ablatives are freely formed from infinitives and from most locative postpositions. However, since locatives and ablatives are not formed regularly for all nouns, some of the frequently occurring forms are presented here as lists, rather than as parts of regular paradigms (forms from Shackle 1976).

Ablative singular in -ū̃:

- گھروں /ghar-ū̃/ 'house-from' (m)
- ہتھوں /hath-ū̃/ 'hand-from' (m)

Locative singular in -e

- ڈِہاڑے /d̤ihāṛ-e/ 'daytime-in/during' (m)
- مسیتے /masīt-e/ 'mosque-in' (f)

Locative singular in -ī̃

- راتیں /rāt-ī̃/ 'night-at/in' (f)

Locative plural in -ẽ

- جنگلیں /jangl-ẽ/ 'jungles-in' (m)
- ہتھیں /hath-ẽ/ 'hands-in' (m)

- ڈِہاڑیں /dīhāṛ-ẽ/ 'daytimes-during/in' (m)

Locative plural in /-ī̃/

- راتیں /rat-ī̃/ 'nights-at/in' (f)
- مسیتیں /masīt-ī̃/ 'mosques-in' (f) (Shackle 1976: 50)

4.4.3.2.1 Masculine nouns (Classes I, II, VIII)

There are three form classes of Saraiki masculines: (i) those ending in unstressed /-ā/ (Class I), (ii) most others—both consonant- and vowel-final (Class II)—except for a few disyllabic nouns whose stems end in /r/, /ṛ/, or /l/ and which have /u/ in the unstressed second syllable (Class VIII). Classes I and II include the vast bulk of Saraiki masculine nouns. Class VIII represents an older pattern, no longer productive, in which stem-internal vowel alternation distinguished gender and number, and sometimes case. In modern Saraiki, nouns in this class have largely fallen together with Class II nouns (Shackle 1976: 46). Examples of Class VIII nouns are:

- شُکُر /šukur/ 'thanks' (m)
- کُکُڑ /kukuṛ/ 'rooster, cockerel' (m)
- چھوہر /chuhur/ 'boy' (m)

These are to be compared with the Class VII feminines.

This pattern, according to Shackle (1979: 195) was formerly also found in some other varieties of "Lahnda"; however, we have not yet found it in Abbottabad Hindko; very possibly, more detailed fieldwork could discover more information about it.

Marked, unstressed /-ā/-final masculine nouns (Class I) are the only ones with a direct plural and oblique singular form different from the direct singular. The oblique singular and the direct plural are the same, as is also the case in Panjabi and Hindko.

4.4.3.2.2 Saraiki masculine noun paradigms

An example paradigm of a Class I noun ending in -ā, چُوہا /cūhā/ 'rat' , is given in Table 4.25. An example of a vowel-final Class II noun, پیو /pyū/ 'father', is given in Table 4.26, and a very frequently used Class II consonant-final noun, گھر /ghar/ 'house, home', is given in Table 4.27.

Table 4.28 shows the conjugation of the Class VIII noun چھوہر /chūhar/ 'boy'. The forms in parentheses are from Shackle (1976: 46), and the others from UK.

27 Neither Shackle (1976) nor our consultant gave an ablative form for the word for boy.

Case	Singular	Plural
Direct	چوہا cūh-ā	چوہے cūh-e
Oblique	چوہے cūh-e	چوہیاں cūh-eā̃
Ablative	چوہیوں cūh-eū̃	چوہیاں cūh-eā̃ + postposition
Vocative	چوہا cūh-ā	چوہیو cūh-eo

Table 4.25: Saraiki masculine noun ending in -ā, چوہا/cūhā/ 'rat' (Class I)

Case	Singular	Plural
Direct	پیو pyū	پیواں pyu-(v)ā̃
Oblique		
Vocative	پیوا pyu-(v)ā	پیوو pyu-(v)o

Table 4.26: Saraiki masculine noun ending in a non-/ā/ vowel, پیو/pyū/ 'father' (Class II)[27]

Case	Singular	Plural
Direct	گھر ghar	گھر ghar
Oblique		گھراں ghar-ā̃
Ablative	گھروں ghar-ū̃	گھراں ghar-ā̃ + postposition
Vocative	n.a.	n.a.

Table 4.27: Saraiki consonant-final masculine noun گھر /ghar/ 'house, home' (Class II)

Case	Singular	Plural
Direct	چھوہر chuhar (chohur)	چھوہر chuhar (chohar)
Oblique	چھوہر chuhar (chohar)	چھوہراں chuhar-ā̃ (chorhā̃)
Ablative	چھوہروں chuhar-ū̃ (chorhū̃)	چھوہراں chuhar-ā̃ + postposition
Vocative	چھوہرا chuhar-ā (chorhā)	چھوہرو chuhar-o (chorho)

Table 4.28: Saraiki consonant-final masculine noun چھوہر /chuhar/ 'boy' (Class VIII)

4.4.3.2.3 Saraiki feminine noun paradigms

Saraiki feminine nouns fall into three declension classes.

Class III marked /-ī/-final feminine nouns such as ٻلّی /ɓillī/ 'cat', are exemplified in Table 4.29. Class IV includes all other feminine nouns except those in the smaller Classes VII and IX. As in Panjabi, Class IV feminines are declined in the same way as Class III feminines. A vowel-final Class IV feminine noun, ما /mā/ 'mother', and a Class IV consonant-final feminine noun, چھت/chat/ 'roof' are shown in Table 4.30 and Table 4.31, respectively.

Case	Singular	Plural
Direct Oblique	ٻلّی ɓill-ī	ٻلّیاں ɓilli-yā̃
Ablative	ٻلّیوں ɓilli-yū̃	––
Vocative	ٻلّیا ɓilli-yā	ٻلّیو ɓilli-yo

Table 4.29: Saraiki /-ī/-final feminine noun, ٻلّی /ɓillī/ 'cat' (Class III)

Case	Singular	Plural
Direct	ما mā	ماواں mā-vā̃
Oblique	ماؤ māo	ماواں mā-vā̃
Ablative	مائوں mā-ū̃ [28]	postpositional
Vocative	ما mā [29]	ماؤ mā-ō

Table 4.30: Saraiki /-ā/-final feminine noun, ما /mā/ 'mother' (Class IV)

Case	Singular	Plural
Direct Oblique	چھت chatt	چھتاں chatt-ā̃
Ablative	چھتوں chatt-ū̃	چھتاں chatt-ā̃ + postposition
Vocative	n.a.	n.a.

Table 4.31: Saraiki consonant-final feminine noun چھت /chatt/ 'roof' (Class IV)

4.4.3.2.4 Class VII (feminine) noun paradigm

A third feminine declension includes some words for female persons (especially relatives), and some other frequently occurring nouns. This class is distinguished by its direct and oblique plural forms in یں /-ī̃/ (Class VII). بھیݨ /bheṇ/ 'sister' and چھوہِر /chuhir/ 'girl', illustrated in Table 4.32 and Table 4.33, respectively, belong to this class.[30]

Case	Singular	Plural
Direct Oblique	بھیݨ bheṇ	بھیݨیں bheṇ-ī̃
Vocative	بھیݨا bheṇ-ā	بھیݨو bheṇ-ō

Table 4.32: Saraiki feminine noun بھیݨ /bheṇ/ 'sister' (Class VII) (forms from Shackle 1976: 48)

28 This is an ablative form from Shackle (1976: 48), Nasir Abbas Syed, however, does not accept ablative case forms for any animate feminines.

29 With /ā/-final ما /mā/ the vocative ending /-ā/ merges with the stem-final /ā/.

30 A third feminine class (Class IX) includes only two words, ہنج /hanj/ 'tear (from eye)' and تند /tand/ 'fiber' (Shackle 1976: 47) and will not be treated here.

31 This ablative form is from Shackle (1976: 48). Our consultant expressed the ablative singular relationship with a postposition in its ablative form.

Case	Singular	Plural
Direct	چھوُہِر chuhir	چھوُہِریں chuhir-ī̃
Oblique		
Ablative	چھوُہِروں chuhir-ū̃ [31]	چھوُہِریں chuhir-ī̃ + postposition
Vocative	چھوہِراں (æ) chuhir-ā̃	چھوُہِریں chuhir-ī̃

Table 4.33: Saraiki feminine noun چھوُہِر /chuhir/ 'girl' (Class VII)

4.4.3.2.5 Class VIII (masculine) noun paradigm

Class VIII is small class of masculine nouns in which stem-vowel alternation signals changes in gender, number, and case. چھوُہِر /chuhir/ 'girl' (Table 4.33) is a feminine noun of Class VII and چھوُہر /chuhar/ 'boy' (shown in Table 4.28 above) is an example of a Class VIII noun.

5 Adjectival and adverbial modification

Adjectival modifiers are elements which restrict or refine the meaning of nouns. Adverbial modifiers are semantically more various and complex; they can modify adjectives, other adverbs, verbs, or entire sentences. In Hindko, Panjabi, and Saraiki both adjectival and adverbial modifiers can consist of single words, phrases, or clauses. This chapter discusses, for each language, the sources of adjectives and adverbs, the form classes (inflecting or invariant) into which adjectives fall, and the semantic classes of adverbs. For discussion of clausal adjectival and adverbial modification, see Chapter 9. A sentence can contain multiple modifiers, of various types. For discussion of word-order considerations in such cases, see Chapter 9, Section 9.1.1.2.

5.1 Adjectives and adjectival expressions

5.1.1 The adjectival lexicon: sources and derivation of adjectives

As with nouns, the adjectival lexicon consists of its inherited Indo-Aryan base and incremental additions from various languages at different time depths, including both words and derivational elements. Some derivational processes are synchronically productive in all three languages, yielding new adjectives—notably those employing the suffix آلا ~ والا /-vāḷā/ ~ /vālā/ ~ /āḷā/ ~ /ālā/ and the denominal suffix ی /-ī/. Adjectives share much of their morphology with nouns, and most of them can also be used as nouns. Adjectives can be derived from nouns, adverbs, other adjectives, or verbs. The most productive derivational processes are suffixal.

5.1.1.1 Indo-Aryan suffixal element: والا /-vāḷā/~ /-vālā/; آلا /āḷā/ ~ /ālā/

The adjective-forming suffix والا /-vāḷā/ ~ /-vālā/(< OIA pāla 'keeper of'), with the alternate form آلا /āḷā/~ /ālā/ which appears frequently in Hindko and Saraiki, is the only productive derivational element which produces inflecting ("black") adjectives (for which see Section 5.1.1.6). It is one of the most versatile and widely used elements in these languages, especially in the spoken language. It makes inflecting, or marked, adjectives/nouns from a great variety of words or constructions. Suffixed to the oblique case of a lexical noun it denotes a person or thing connected in some way to that noun. Added to the oblique infinitive of a verb it generates forms which can function adjectivally, as agentive nouns, or in constructions which function as relative clauses. In all of these constructions, a modified noun, either expressed when the usage is adjectival or unexpressed when the usage is nominal, is part of the conception.

https://doi.org/10.1515/9781614512257-005

- noun + والا /-vāḷā/

  گھر /kàr/ 'house' → گھر والا /kàr vāḷā/ 'of the house (adj.); husband, man of the house (n.)' Pj

  کوٹ /koṭ/ 'coat' → کوٹ والا /koṭ vāḷā/ 'pertaining to a coat; masculine entity connected in some way with a coat/coats.' Pj

  کڈھائی آلا /kaḍhāī ālā/ 'embroidered' Sr

  گھر آلے /ghaṛ āle/ 'family' Sr

  امب آلا باغ /amb ālā bāɣ/ 'mango orchard' Sr

- adjective + والا /-vāḷā/:

  چنگے والے کپڑے /cãge vāḷe kapṛe/ 'the good clothes (as opposed to the inferior ones)'

- adverb + والا /-vāḷā/:

  اتّے والا /utte vāḷā/ 'upper; the one on top' Pj

  پچھے والا /piche vāḷā/ 'the one behind/ in back' Pj

  سب توں تھلے والا /sab tõ thalle vāḷā/ 'the bottom-most one' Pj

  نال آلا کمرہ /nāl ālā kamrā/ 'adjacent room' Hk

- oblique infinitive + والا /-vāḷā/:

  چلنا /calṇā/ 'to go, move' → چلن والا /calaṇ vāḷā/ Pj ; چلنڑے آلا /calṛ̃e ālā/ Hk 'one that moves; mover, goer; about to go'

The oblique infinitive of a verb followed by والا /vāḷā/ forms: (1) agent nouns, (2) verbal constructions meaning 'about to V', e.g. جان والا /jāṇ vāḷā/ 'about to go' (Pj), (3) adjectives from clauses, which function as relative clauses (5.1). This suffix is attached to the oblique infinitive of the verb, often preceded by other elements of the underlying adjectivalized clause, as in 5.1, where it is glossed as "NMLZ".

(5.1) گھوڑا گھاہ کھان والا جانور اے

kòṛ-ā	*kầ*	***khāṇ-vāḷā***	*jānvar*	*e*
horse-SG.DIR	grass	**eat.INF.OBL-NMLZ.SG.M**	animal	be.PRES.3SG

'The horse is a grass-eating animal. (an animal [which eats grass])' (Pj) (EB)

5.1.1.2 Suffixal elements: Persian

A number of suffixes which form adjectives from nouns are of Persian and/or Arabic origin.

5.1.1.2.1 ی /-ī-/

The suffix ی /-ī/ is identical to that found in some Arabic borrowings; it derives adjectives from nouns, with meanings corresponding roughly to the English suffixes -al, -ous, or -ish. It may be used with both indigenous Indo-Aryan and borrowed Persian or Arabic lexical items. In the following examples, دیس /des/ 'homeland, country' is a native Indic word, and کتاب /katāb/ 'book' is from Arabic.[1]

- دیس /des/ 'country' + /-ī/ → دیسی /desī/ 'indigenous'
- کتاب /katāb/ 'book' + /-ī/ → کتابی /katābī/ 'bookish, intellectual'
- ہمت /himmat/ 'courage' + /-ī/ → ہمتی /himmatī/ 'courageous'
- آخر /āxar/ 'end, limit' + /ī/ → آخری /āxarī/ 'final, last'
- پاکستان /pākistān/ 'Pakistan'+ /ī/ → پاکستانی /pākistānī/ 'Pakistani'
- نام /nām/ 'name'+ /ī/ → نامی /nāmī/ 'famous'

The ی /ī/ suffix may also derive secondary adjectives from existing adjectives, such as اندرونی /andarūnī/ 'interior' (adj.) from اندرون /andarūn/ 'inner' (adj.), or from adverbs, e.g. اوپر /ūpar/ 'above' + /ī/ → اوپری /ūparī/ 'superficial, external'

5.1.1.2.2 آنہ /ānā/

The suffix آنہ /-ānā/ derives adjectives of quality from nouns; it is similar in function to the English suffix /-ly/. Adjectives in آنہ /-ānā/ are not used to describe humans; rather, they are formed from nouns referring to people or types of people and describe characteristic behaviors or events, for example:

- دوست /dost/ 'friend' → دوستانہ /dostānā/ 'friendly (relationship, meeting)'
- مرد /mard/ 'man' → مردانا /mardānā/ 'masculine (clothes, behavior)'
- سال /sāl/ 'year' سالانہ → /sālānā/ 'yearly, annual (event)'

---

1 Prescriptively, this word is /kitāb/ in Urdu as well as in educated, urban Panjabi pronunciation, but it is often pronounced with /i/ changed to /a/. Some authors (e.g. Bhatia 1993) show this reduction of /i/ to schwa. The same thing is found in /āxar/ instead of /āxir/ 'finally'.

5.1.1.2.3 ناک /-nāk/ and گین /-gīn/

The suffixes گین /-gīn/ and ناک/-nāk/ correspond roughly to English /-ful/; they create adjectives of quality from abstract nouns. Neither is currently productive.

- خطرہ /xatarā/ 'danger' → خطرناک /xatarnāk/ 'dangerous'
- خوف /xɔf/ 'fear, terror' → خوفناک /xɔfnāk/ 'terrifying'
- شرم /šarm/ 'shame' → شرمناک /šarmnāk/ 'shameful'
- غم /ɣam/ 'sorrow, grief' → غمگین /ɣamgīn/ 'depressed, grief-stricken'

In general, words with ناک /-nāk/ refer to the cause of the resulting description (usually referring to something harmful), and those with گین /-gīn/ refer to its sufferer. Thus شرمناک /šarmnāk/ means 'causing shame', while شرمگین /šarmgīn/ 'bashful' means 'experiencing shame'. This example is offered only to contrast the general meaning of these two suffixes; the usual words for 'bashful' in these languages have indigenous morphology: سرمیلا /šarmīlā/ (Pj), شرماؤ /šarmāo/ (Sr), شرموکشرمی /šarmokašarmī/ (Hk Sakoon 2002: 169).

5.1.1.2.4 دار /-dār/; آوار /-āvār/, وار /-vār/, ور /-var/; and مند /-mand / ~ وند /-vand/ Sr

These suffixes form denominal adjectives, all with the general meaning of 'possessing X, characterized by X'. The forms are found in all three languages, except وند /vand/, which occurs mostly in Saraiki. Words formed with them sometimes represent a more formal register than synonymous words formed with the suffix ی /-ī/, e.g. دولتمند /dɔlatmand/ and دولتی /dɔlatī/, both meaning 'wealthy', or نامور /nāmvar/ and نامی /nāmī/ 'famous'. Other examples include:

- ایمان /imān/ 'faith, integrity' → ایماندار /imāndār/ 'faithful, trustworthy' Hk, Pj, Sr
- نام /nām/ 'name' → نامور /nāmvar/ 'renowned, famous' Pj ;
- ناں /nā̃/ 'name' → ناں ور /nā̃war/, ناں دار /nā̃dār/ 'famous, renowned' Sr (Mughal 2010: 857, 910)
- ہنر /hunar/ 'skill' → ہنرمند /hunarmand/ 'skilled' Pj
- دولت /dɔlat/ 'wealth' → دولتمند /dɔlatmand/ 'wealthy' Hk, Pj

- عقل /akal/ 'intelligence, sense' → عقل وند /akalvand/ 'intelligent' Sr (Mughal 2010: 269)

There is no predictable difference in meaning between these suffixes; where a stem may form adjectives with more than one of them, the precise meanings of the derived words have developed independently. Some words with the ور /-var/ suffix have been reanalyzed as nouns, such as جانور /jānvar/ 'animal (lit. possessing life)'. مند /-mand/ is not currently productive, but دار /-dār/ is used in new compounds with all classes of words—Indic and Perso-Arabic. Some of these are mostly used as nouns.

- زمین /zamīn/ 'land' → زمیندار /zamīndār/ 'landowner' (adj./n.)
- پیدا /pædā/ 'born, created' → پیداوار /pædāvār/ 'production' (n.)
- پھل /phal/ 'fruit' → پھلدار /phaldār/ 'fruit-bearing' (adj.)

Perso-Arabic origin suffixes derive unmarked (non-inflecting) adjectives—mostly from non-Indic borrowings. Since new adjectives are increasingly being borrowed, including from English, the class of unmarked adjectives is growing.

5.1.1.2.5 The exclamation/exhortation باد /-bād/ 'let it be, so be it'

Added to adjectives denoting a state, باد /-bād/, a Persian subjunctive form meaning 'let it be', yields terms meaning 'may X be/remain in state Y'.

- زندہ /zindā/ 'alive' → زندہ باد /zindā-bād/ 'long live X'
- مردہ /murdā/ 'dead ' → مُردہ باد /murdā-bād/ 'death to X'

5.1.1.3 Prefixal elements – Indo-Aryan اݨ ~ان ~ ا /a/ ~ /aṇ/ 'not'

This old inherited negative element occurs prefixed to IA roots in many words in these three languages. Examples include:

- انپڑھ /aṇpáṛ/ 'illiterate' Pj
- انہونی /aṇhoṇī/ 'rare, unusual, impossible' Pj
- انجان /aṇjāṇ/ 'ignorant, innocent' Pj
- اݨہووݨاں /aṇhovaṇā̃/ 'unusual' Sr (Mughal 2010: 632)
- اݨسچیتا /aṇsucetā/ 'unaware, unconscious' Sr (Mughal 2010: 631)
- اڑسنی /af̣suṇī/ 'unheard (of)' Hk (Sakoon 2002: 23)
- انسیتا /aṇsītā/ 'unstitched (m.sg.)' Pj , or اڑسیتا /af̣sītā/ 'unstitched' Hk (Sakoon 2002: 23)

5.1.1.4 Prefixal elements – Perso-Arabic

Most of the prefixal elements now productive in these languages are of Perso-Arabic origin. Most words containing these elements have entered the languages through Urdu, and are found in all three languages, with perhaps minor spelling differences. The most frequently occurring of these are negative elements:

غیر /ɣær/ 'not' (< Arabic, Persian)

- غیرملکی /ɣærmulkī/ 'foreign (lit. 'not national')' Hk, Pj, Sr
- غیراخلاقی /ɣæraxlākī/ 'amoral, immoral' Hk, Pj, Sr
- غیرحاضر /ɣærhāzar/ 'absent (lit. 'not present') ' Hk, Pj, Sr

لا /lā/ 'not' (< Arabic)

- لاجواب /lājavāb/ 'the very best, irrefutable' Hk, Pj, Sr (جواب /javāb/ 'answer')
- لاقنونیت /lākanūniyat/ 'lawlessness' Hk, Pj, Sr (قنونیت /kanūniyat/ 'legality')
- لاپتا /lāpatā/ 'lost' Hk, Pj, Sr (پتا /patā/ 'trace; information; address')

نا /nā/ 'not' (< Persian)

- ناپسند /nāpasand/ 'displeasing, disliked' Pj
- ناساپیاں /nāsāpiyā̃/ 'suddenly; unstructured' Hk (Sakoon 2002:239)
- ناسمجھ /nāsamaj/ 'ignorant, foolish' Pj

بے /be/ 'without' (< Persian)

- بیوقوف /bevkūf/ 'stupid (lit. without knowledge)' Pj
- بےللّا /belallā/ 'stupid' Hk (Sakoon 2002: 51)
- بےسمجھ /besamajh/ 'without understanding' Sr (Mughal 2002: 902)

ہم /ham/ 'same, with' (< Persian)

ہم /ham/ is a compounding morpheme, rather than a prefix. The result is an adjective that can, as can all adjectives, also be used as a noun. The three words shown here are used in all three languages.

- عمر /umur/ 'age' → ہمعمر /ham-umur/ 'of the same age'
- سایہ /sāyā/ 'shade' → ہمسایہ /ham-sāyā/ 'neighbor (sharing the same shade)'
- وطن /vatan/ 'country' → ہموطن /ham-vatan/ 'compatriot'

5.1.1.5 Persian past participles

Some nouns and adjectives, many of them Persian past participles, end in a 'silent' ہ *choṭī hē*.[2] Masculine nouns ending in ہ *choṭī hē* usually inflect according to the marked (Class I) paradigm. Adjectives with this ending, however, are generally unmarked:

- میرا پسندیدہ گانا /merā pasandīdā gāṇā/ 'my favorite song' (M)
- میری پسندیدہ کتاب /merī pasandīdā katāb/ 'my favorite book' (F)

Some of these Persian past participles are used only as attributive adjectives, e.g. پسندیدہ /pasandīdā/ 'favorite', while others, e.g. شادی شدہ /šādī šudā/ 'married' can be used either attributively or predicatively.

However, a few adjectives ending in ہ, for example تازہ /tāzā/ 'fresh', have been reanalyzed by many people as marked adjectives, and can thus behave either as marked or unmarked adjectives. This word is usually treated as a marked adjective in these three languages. It is difficult to generalize about which adjectives will be reanalyzed as marked adjectives; however, in general, words which have developed in this way tend to be high-frequency words referring to concrete things in daily life.

- تازا امب/ تازہ امب /tāzā amb (M)/ 'a fresh mango' Pj
- تازی خرمانی /tāzī xurmānī (F)/ 'a fresh apricot' Pj
- تازی روٹی /tāzī roṭī (F)/ 'fresh bread' Pj

5.1.1.6 Classes of adjectives

All three languages have two classes of adjectives, which have conventional, mnemonically motivated labels: (1) marked, or inflecting, adjectives that change their form to agree with the noun they modify, i.e. carry a distinctive mark of their gender and number (called by Shackle 1972: 25 "black" adjectives after کالا /kālā/ 'black', a prototypical member of this class), and (2) unmarked, or non-inflecting, adjectives that are invariant in form (called "red" adjectives after لال /lāl/ 'red', a prototypical member of the class). Saraiki alone has a unique, third class of adjectives, called by Shackle (1976: 50) پھٹوکر /phiṭokar/ 'unfast', maintaining the color-terms mnemonic nomenclature.

---

2 See the discussion of nouns of this form in Chapter 4, and the note on transcription in Section 3.6.1.2.

5.1.1.6.1 Marked ("black") adjectives

Marked adjectives agree in gender, number, and case with the noun they modify; their citation form is the masculine singular direct case, as in کالا /kāḷā/(Pj) ~ /kālā / 'black' (Hk, Sr). The declension of marked ("black") adjectives is the same in all three languages. Marked adjectives take the same endings as marked masculine nouns (Class I) and marked ی /ī/-final feminines (Class III). Unmarked adjectives have a single form regardless of the gender, number, or case of the nouns they modify.

One example of a typical, commonly used marked adjective is presented for each language (Table 5.1 for Hindko, Table 5.2 for Panjabi, and Table 5.4 for Saraiki). Note that the table for Hindko provides only those forms given explicitly in Sakoon (2002), since we do not want to give unattested (n.a.) forms even though we have a high degree of confidence that they exist. Feminine plural endings are given as /-iyā̃/ instead of the underlying /īā̃/ because the long /ī/ preceding the long vowel /ā̃/ of the plural suffix is shortened and an audible /y/-glide appears. This /y/-glide is consistently represented in the Perso-Arabic orthography.

Case	Gender	Singular	Plural
Direct	Masculine	نکڑا nikkṛā	نکڑے nikkṛe
	Feminine	نکڑی nikkṛī	نکڑیاں nikkṛiyā̃
Oblique	Masculine	n.a.	n.a.
	Feminine	n.a.	n.a.

Table 5.1: Marked Hindko adjective نکڑا /nikkṛā/ 'small' (Sakoon 2002: 243)

Shackle (1972: 43) notes that in Panjabi, while marked adjectives used to agree with masculine nouns in the oblique plural, it is becoming common (under the influence of Urdu) for the adjective to appear in the oblique singular in such cases. Both of the following constructions are found:

- چنگیاں بندیاں نال /cãgĕā̃ (OBL.PL.) bandĕā̃ nāḷ/ 'with good men/persons'
- چنگے بندیاں نال /cãge (OBL.SG) bandĕā̃ nāḷ/ 'with good men/persons'

Gender	Case	Singular	Plural
Masculine	Direct	میرا merā	میرے mere
	Oblique	میرے mere	میریاں ~ میرے merĕā̃ ~ mere
Feminine	Direct	میری merī	میریاں meriyā̃
	Oblique	میری merī	میریاں meriyā̃

Table 5.2: Marked Panjabi possessive adjective میرا 'my, mine'

Case	Gender	Singular	Plural
Direct	Masculine	نواں navā̃	نویں navē
	Feminine	نویں navī̃	نویاں naviyā̃
Oblique	Masculine	نویں navē	نویں navē نویاں navĕā̃
	Feminine	نویں navī̃	نویاں naviyā̃

Table 5.3: Nasal /-ā̃/-ending adjective نواں /navā̃/ 'new' Hk, Pj, Sr

Marked adjectives that end in a nasalized آں آ /-ā̃/, e.g. نواں /navā̃/ 'new' maintain their nasalization throughout the declension in all three languages; otherwise they follow the normal paradigm. Table 5.3 shows the marked adjective نواں /navā̃/ 'new'.

Saraiki marked adjectives ending in /-ā̃/ maintain the nasalization in the feminine singular ending in /-ī̃/, as well as in the masculine plural and oblique singular ending in /-ē̃/. An important member of this class is the adjective کیہاں /kehā̃/ 'what kind of', which also has stem-vowel modifications. Its forms are shown in Table 5.5.

Case	Gender	Singular	Plural
Direct	Masculine	کالا kālā	کالے kāle
	Feminine	کالی kālī	کالیاں kāliyā̃
Oblique	Masculine	کالے kāle	کالیاں ~ کالے kālĕā̃ ~ kāle
	Feminine	کالی kālī	کالیاں kāliyā̃

Table 5.4: Marked Saraiki ("black") adjective کالا /kālā / 'black'

Case	Gender	Singular	Plural
Direct	Masculine	کیہاں kehā̃	کہیں kahẽ
	Feminine	کہیں kahī̃	کہیاں kehiyā̃
Oblique	Masculine	کہیں kahẽ	کہیں kahẽ
	Feminine	کہیں kahī̃	

Table 5.5: Marked Saraiki ("black") adjective with nasalization and stem-vowel alternation کیہاں /kehā̃ / 'what kind of'

5.1.1.6.2 Unmarked ("red") adjectives

All three languages have a second main adjective type, invariant adjectives, which have only one form—in both genders and numbers, and in all cases. Like the marked adjectives, this class of adjectives is sometimes named for one of its prototypical members, the adjective لال /lāl/ 'red'.

5.1.1.6.3 Saraiki stem-vowel alternating ("unfast") adjectives

A distinguishing feature of Saraiki is its third class of adjectival declension. Employing Shackle's color-term nomenclature system for adjective classes, this class is named for its prototypical member, the adjective پھٹوکر /phiṭokar/ 'non-fast (of color, dye)' (Shackle 1976: 50). There are only a few members of this class, which in the Multan variety of Saraiki inflect only for gender and thus have only two forms. These adjectives follow the same (archaic) gender marking pattern as the Class VII Saraiki nouns (e.g. 'boy' and 'girl', see Section 4.4.3.2.5), having /a/as the final stem vowel in the masculine form and /i/ in the feminine. This pattern is currently weakening in the language.

	Masculine	**Feminine**
Direct and oblique (singular and plural)	پھٹوکر phiṭokar 'unfast'	پھٹوکر phiṭokir 'unfast'

Table 5.6: Saraiki stem-vowel alternating ("unfast") adjectives

5.1.2 Adjectives in construction with nouns

When adjectives of any type occur in construction with nouns of any type, each element obeys the rules of the class (adjectival or nominal) to which it belongs. This holds true in all three languages.

5.1.2.1 Hindko example

The paradigm shown in Table 5.7, for a Hindko example, demonstrates that the unmarked adjective بیمار /bimār/ 'sick' obeys one sets of rules, remaining invariant, while the marked masculine noun گھوڑا /kòṛā/ 'horse' follows another.[3]

3 The word بیمار /bimār/ 'sick' is spelled here as it usually is in Panjabi (< Urdu). It is possible that some Hindko writers may choose to spell it بمار /bimār/ to reflect its actual pronunciation.

Case	Singular	Plural
Direct	بیمار گھوڑا bimār kòṛā 'sick horse'	بیمار گھوڑے bimār kòṛe 'sick horses'
Oblique	بیمار گھوڑے bimār kòṛe 'sick horse'	بیمار گھوڑیاں bimār kòṛĕã̄ 'sick horses'

Table 5.7: Unmarked adjective with marked (Class I) noun (Hindko)

5.1.2.2 Panjabi example

The inflection of a marked Panjabi adjective چنگا /cãgā/ 'good' in construction with the Class I masculine noun منڈا /mũḍā/ 'boy' is shown in Table 5.8, and in Table 5.9 with the marked ی /-ī/-final feminine noun کڑی /kuṛī/ 'girl'.

	Singular	Plural
Direct	چنگا منڈا cãg-ā mũḍ-ā	چنگے منڈے cãg-e mũḍ-e
Oblique	چنگے منڈے cãg-e mũḍ-e	چنگیاں منڈیاں cãg-ĕyã̄ mũḍ-ĕyã̄[4]
Vocative	چنگیا منڈیا cãgĕ-a mũḍĕ-a	چنگیو منڈیو cãgĕ-o mũḍĕ-o

Table 5.8: Panjabi modified masculine noun چنگا منڈا /cãgā mũḍā/ 'good boy'

4 The pronunciation of orthographic /i/ here is close to ĕ (short e).

	Singular	Plural
Direct Oblique	چنگی کڑی cãg-ī kuṛī	چنگیاں کڑیاں cãg-iyā̃ kuṛiy-ā̃
Vocative	چنگیے کڑیے cãg-iye kuṛiy-e	چنگیو کڑیو cãg-iyo kuṛiy-o

Table 5.9: Panjabi modified feminine noun چنگی کڑی /cãgī kuṛī/ ‘good girl’

5.1.2.3 Saraiki examples

Table 5.10 and Table 5.11 show the “black” adjective لمبا /lambā/ ‘long, tall’ in construction with the Class VII-feminine noun چھوہر /chuir/ ‘girl’ in Table 5.10, and with the Type VII-masculine noun چھوہر /chuar/ ‘boy’ in Table 5.11. The pronunciation of the stem vowel in these two words varies dialectally between [ŏ] (Central, Shackle) and [u] (UK). Similarly, /h/ is dialectally pronounced (Central, Shackle) or not (Southern, UK). The forms in Table 5.10 and Table 5.11 are those supplied by UK.[5] Sometimes the /h/-less pronunciation is spelled with ء *hamza* instead of ہ /h/.

Case	Singular	Plural
Direct / Oblique	لمبی چھوہر lambī chuir	لمبیاں (لمبی) چھوہریں lambiyā̃ (lambī) chuirĩ
Vocative	لمبی چھوہر lambī chuir	لمبیاں (لمبی) چھوہریو lambiyā̃ (lambī) chuireo

Table 5.10: Saraiki modified feminine noun لمبی چھوہر /lambī chuir/ ‘tall girl’

Note that (under influence from Urdu), feminine plural nouns may sometimes be modified by a singular (invariant) feminine adjectival form, as shown in the parenthetical forms in Table 5.10.

For discussion of the order of multiple adjectival modifiers in a noun phrase, see Section 9.1.1.2.

5 For the vocative of چھوہر /chohir/ ‘girl’, Shackle (1976: 48) has چھوہرا /chohirā/.

Case	Singular	Plural
Direct	لمبا چھوہر lambā chuar	لمبے چھوہر lambe chuar
Oblique	لمبے چھوہر lambe chuar	لمبے چھوہراں lambe chuarā̃
Vocative	لمبیا چھوہرا lambe chuarā	لمبے چھوہرو lambe chuaro

Table 5.11: Saraiki modified masculine noun لمبا چھوہر /lambā chuar/ ‘tall boy’

5.1.3 Comparative and superlative constructions

A few marked adjectives display an older, morphological mechanism for forming comparatives. However, syntactic comparison is the main way of expressing comparison in all three of the modern languages.

5.1.3.1 Morphological comparison

The Indo-Aryan origin suffix /-ˈerā/ can be added to some marked adjectives, in all three languages, to convey a relative comparative sense.[6] Addition of this suffix with its initial stressed vowel results in a peripheral stem vowel being “weakened” to a centralized vowel.

- چھوٹا /choṭā/ ‘small’ → چھُٹیرا /chuṭerā/ ‘rather small, younger, lesser’ Pj, Sr

From words for ‘big’, there are the following:

- بڈّا /baḍḍā/ ‘big’ → بڈیرا /baḍerā/ ‘elder male’ Hk
- وڈّا /vaḍḍā/ ‘big’ → وڈیرا /vaḍerā/ ‘elder, ancestor, feudal landlord’ Pj
- وݙا /vaɗɗā/ ‘big’ → وݙیرا /vaɗerā/ ‘feudal (lit. ‘big’) landlord, father, family elder’ Sr

Other Panjabi forms with this suffix include:

- جیٹھا /jeṭhā/ ‘oldest male child’ → جِٹھیرا /jiṭherā/ ‘elder, ancestor’
- بہت /bɔ̃t/ ‘much’ → بہتیرا /batérā/ ‘much, plenty of’.

6 See Markey (1985) on the distinction between absolute and relative comparison.

Additionally, in educated speech, various loan words from Urdu employing the Persian-origin comparative suffix تر /-tar/ are used, e.g. بہتر /behtar/ with the meaning 'very good, better, preferable', and the superlative element ترین /-tarīn/, e.g. بہترین /bé-tarīn/ 'excellent, top quality'. For example: ایہہ بہترین سکول اے /é bétarīn skūl e/ 'This is an excellent school.' These relative comparative forms can be understood as conveying a type of emphatic meaning.

5.1.3.2 Syntactic comparison

In all three languages, comparisons are usually constructed syntactically. All three languages form their syntactic comparative and superlative constructions in parallel ways, employing the ablative case of postpositions with the oblique case of the noun naming the standard of comparison, i.e., the thing to which another thing is being compared, and the positive (base) form of the adjective. These constructions yield absolute comparisons, of the type *big, bigger, biggest*.

Comparative meaning in Hindko is achieved by using the postposition کولوں /kolõ/ 'than' with the noun naming the standard of comparison, as in 5.2:

(5.2) میری پہنڑ تیری پہنڑوں کولوں لمی اے

mer-ī	*pæ̀ṛ̃*	*ter-ī*	*pæ̀ṛ̃-ũ*	***kolõ***	*lamm-ī*
1SG.GEN-SG.F	sister.SG.F	2SG.GEN-SG.F	sister-OBL	**than**	tall-SG.F

e
be.PRES.3SG

'My sister is taller **than** your sister.' (Hk) (AWT)

Superlative meaning, e.g. 'biggest', is achieved by using the postpositions بچوں/bicõ/(Hk), /vicõ/ (Pj), /vicũ/ (Sr), or کولوں /kolõ/ 'from among, of' with ساریاں /sār-iyā̃/ 'all-OBL.PL.F' for feminines as in 5.3 or ساریاں /sār-ĕā̃/ 'all-OBL.PL.M' for masculines, as in 5.4. Notice that the Perso-Arabic spelling of both the feminine and the masculine forms of the oblique plural of سارا /sārā/ 'all' is the same; the difference shows up only in pronunciation and in the agreement context of the sentence.

(5.3) ایہہ اس عورت دی ساریاں بچوں نکی تہی اے

é	*us*	*ɔrat*	*d-ī*	***sār-iyā̃***	***bicõ***
this	that.OBL	woman.SG.F.OBL	GEN-SG.F	**all-F.PL.OBL**	**among**

nikk-ī	*tì̃*	*e*
little-SG.F	daughter.SG.F	be.PRES.3SG

'This is that woman's youngest daughter.' (Hk) (AWT)

(5.4) ساریاں کولوں بڈا پتر

sār-ẽã	***kol-õ***	*baḍḍ-ā*	*puttar*
all-M.OBL.PL	**from**	big-SG.M.	son.SG.M

'oldest (lit. 'biggest son')' (Hk) (AWT)

In Panjabi, to form comparatives, the standard of comparison—which will be a noun in the oblique case (as in 5.5) or a personal pronoun in the genitive form (as in 5.6)—is followed by the postposition توں /tõ/ 'than' or نالوں /nāḷõ/ 'than', which is then followed by the adjective in its positive form.

(5.5) منڈا کڑی توں لما اے

mũḍ-ā	*kuṛ-ī*	***tõ***	*lamm-ā*	*e*
boy-SG.M.DIR	girl-SG.F.OBL	**than**	tall-SG.M.DIR	be.PRES.3SG

'The boy is taller **than** the girl.' (Pj) (EB)

(5.6) اوہ میرے نالوں تگڑا اے

ó	*mer-e*	***nāḷõ***	*tagṛā*	*e*
3SG	1SG.GEN-SG.M.OBL	**than**	strong.SG.M	be.PRES.3SG

'He is stronger **than** me.' (Pj) (EB)

Additionally, the compound postposition دے مقابلے /de mukāble/ 'in comparison with' (optionally extended with وچ /vicc/ 'in') can be used to mark the standard of comparison.

(5.7) حمزہ علی دے مقابلے وچ چنگا اے

hamzā	*alī*	***d-e***	***mukābl-e***	***(vicc)***	*cãgā*
Hamzah	Alī	**GEN-SG.M.OBL**	**comparison-SG.M.OBL**	**(in)**	good

e
be.PRES.3SG

'Hamzah is better **than** Ali.' (Bhatia 1993: 140)

In another construction, which names the items being compared in a compound noun phrase rather than designating one of them as a standard of comparison, this compound noun phrase can be followed by the postposition وچ /vicc/ 'between' or 'among', then followed by the adjective naming the quality with respect to which they are being compared. This construction differs from those with توں /tõ/ 'than', /nāḷõ/ 'than', and دے مقابلے /de muqāble/ 'in comparison with', in that neither of the items is presented as the standard of comparison; thus وچ /vicc/ 'between' applies to both or all the items in the compound noun phrase.

(5.8) حمزہ تے علی وچ حمزہ چنگا اے

hamzā	*te*	*alī*	***vicc***	*hamzā*	*cãgā*	*e*
Hamzah	and	Ali	**between**	Hamzah	good	be.PRES.3.SG

'Hamzah is better than Ali. (lit. 'Between Hamzah and Ali, Hamzah is better.')' (Bhatia 1993: 140)

Comparison stating that two items are equal or unequal in some respect can be accomplished by a relative-correlative construction using the pair جنا --- اوہنا /jinnā ... ónnā/ 'as much as ... so much', as in example (5.9) where they appear in reverse order in a focus construction.

(5.9) میرے کول اوہنے پیسے نہیں جنّے سلیم کول نیں

mer-e	*koḷ*	***ónne***	*pæse*	*nĩ̄*
1SG.GEN-SG.M.OBL	with	**that.much.PL.M**	money.PL.M	are.not

jinne	*salīm*	*koḷ*	*nẽ*
as.much.as.PL.M	Salim.OBL	with	be.PRES.3PL

'I don't have **as much** money **as** Salim does.' (Pj) (EB)

In the superlative construction, the phrases سبھ توں /sáb tõ/ and سبھاں توں /sábā̃ tõ/ for both genders, and ساریاں توں /sārĕā̃ tõ/ for masculines, or ساریاں توں /sāriyā̃ tõ/ for feminines – all meaning 'than all' are used, as in 5.10.

(5.10) ایہہ کڑی سبھ توں سوہنی اے

é	*kuṛī*	***sâb***	***tõ***	*sóṇ-ī*	*e*
this	girl-SG.F.DIR	**all**	**than**	pretty-SG.F.DIR	be.PRES.3SG

'This girl is the prettiest **of all.**' (Pj) (EB)

An alternate way to express superlative meaning is through the use of نالوں کوئی نہیں /nāḷõ koī naĩ̄/ 'than X, there isn't anyone/anything else', as in 5.11.

(5.11) اوہ دے نالوں سیانا کوئی نہیاں (اے)

ó	*d-e*	***nāḷõ***	*syāṇ-ā*	*koī*	***naĩ̄***	*(e)*
3SG.OBL	GEN-SG.M.OBL	**than**	wise-SG.M	anyone	**NEG**	(be.PRES.3SG)

'There **isn't** anyone wiser **than** him. (i.e., He is the wisest of all.)' (Pj) (EB)

A superlative sense can also be expressed by using an adjective twice, separated by the postposition توں /tõ/. The first adjective, followed by the postposition, appears in the oblique, and the second is in the case required by its position in a sentence, as shown in 5.12 and 5.13.

(5.12) چنگے توں چنگا

cãg-e	*tõ*	*cãg-ā*
good-SG.M.OBL	from	good-SG.M.DIR

'the best (of a masculine entity)' (Pj) (EB)

(5.13) چنگی توں چنگی

cãg-ī	*tõ*	*cãg-ī*
good-SG.F.OBL	from	good-SG.F.DIR

'the best (of a feminine entity)' (Pj) (EB)

The Saraiki comparative construction consists of the standard of comparison followed by the postposition کنوں /kanũ/ 'from' or کولوں /kolũ/ 'from' and the positive (base) form of the adjective, as in example 5.14.

(5.14) اوندا بھرا اوندی بھیݨ کنوں لمبا ہے

ũ-d-ā	*bhirā*	*ũ-dī*	*bheṇ*	***kanũ***
3SG.OBL-GEN-SG.M	brother.SG.M	3SG-GEN.SG.F	sister.SG.F	**than**

lambā	*he*
tall.SG.M	be.PRES.3SG.

'His brother is taller than his sister.' (Sr) (UK)

The superlative construction consists of the phrase سبھ کنوں /sabh kanũ/ 'of all' or سبھیں کنوں /sabhĩ kanũ/ 'of all' followed by the adjective, as in examples 5.15 and 5.16.

(5.15) سبھ کنوں وݙی عمارت

sabh	***kanũ***	*vadd-ī*	*imārat*
all	**than**	big-SG.F	building.SG.F

'the biggest building **of all**' (Shackle 1976: 112)

(5.16) اے اوں تریمت دی سبھیں کنوں ننڈھی دھی ہے

e	*ũ*	*trīmat*	*d-ī*	*sabhĩ*	*kanũ*	*nanḍh-ī*
this.DIR	that.SG.OBL	woman.SG.OBL	of-SG.F	all.OBL	than	little-SG.F

dhī	*he*
daughter.SG.F	be.PRES-3SG

'This is the youngest daughter of that woman.' (Sr) (UK)

Table 5.12 summarizes comparative and superlative marking ablative postpositions most often used in the three languages.

Language	Postpositions used
Hindko	کولوں kolõ بچوں bicõ
Panjabi	توں tõ نالوں nāḷõ
Saraiki	کنوں ~ کن ~ کنو kanũ ~ kanū ~ kan کولوں ~ کولو kolũ ~ kolū

Table 5.12: Comparative and superlative marking postpositions

5.1.3.3 Demonstrative, relative, and interrogative elements

In all three languages, demonstratives (this/that), relatives (that/who/which), and interrogatives (what/which?) can function as either adjectives or pronouns. When they function as adjectives, these words precede the noun they modify; if they are marked adjectives, they will agree with their noun in gender, number, and case. When they function as pronouns, they take the place of a noun or noun phrase and are case-marked according to their function in their clause.

5.1.3.3.1 Demonstrative adjectives

Since the demonstrative forms function as third-person pronouns in the pronominal system, they are introduced here as adjectives and then presented again in Chapter 6 in their pronominal function (and cross-referenced to this section). Table 5.13 presents the adjectival demonstrative forms for Hindko, Panjabi, and Saraiki.

		Hindko	Panjabi	Saraiki
Proximal - Direct	Singular 'this'	ایہہ é	ایہہ é ~ áe	اے e ~ æ
	Plural 'these'	ایہے é	ایہہ é ~ áe	اے e ~ æ
Proximal - Oblique	Singular 'this'	اِس is	ایس és ~ æs	اِیس ī ~ hī
	Plural 'these'	اِنہاں ínā̃	ایہناں énā̃ ~ ǽnā̃	اِنہاں inhā̃
Distal - Direct	Singular 'that'	اوہ ó	اوہ ó	او o
	Plural 'those'	اوہ ó	اوہ ó	او o
Distal - Oblique	Singular 'that'	اُس us	اوس ~ اوہ ós ~ ó	اُوس ū̃ ~ hū̃
	Plural 'those'	اُنہاں únā̃	اوہناں ónā̃	اُنہاں unhā̃

Table 5.13: Demonstrative adjectives - Hindko, Panjabi, Saraiki

5.1.3.3.2 Relative adjectives

Relative adjectives also function substantively in the pronominal system in all three languages. Table 5.14 lays out the masculine forms of relative adjectival elements for Hindko, Panjabi, and Saraiki; these are marked adjectives, and inflect for number, gender, and case, depending on the noun they modify. Their feminine forms are constructed as for marked adjectives.

A second relative form, جو /jo/, functions mainly in the pronominal system in all three languages. It will be discussed in Section 6.7. For the syntax of relative-correlative clauses, a structure common to all three languages, and examples from all three languages, see Chapter 9.

	Singular	Plural
Hindko		
Direct	جیہڑا jéṛā 'which…'	جیہڑے jéṛe 'which…'
Oblique	جیہڑے jéṛe 'which…'	جیہڑیاں jéṛĕā̃ 'which…'
Panjabi		
Direct	جیہڑا jéṛā 'which…'	جیہڑے jéṛe 'which…'
Oblique	جیہڑے jéṛe 'which…'	جیہڑے ~ جیہڑیاں jéṛe ~ jéṛĕā̃ 'which…'
Saraiki		
Direct	جیرھا ~ جیڑھا ~ جہڑا jerhā ~ jeṛhā 'which…'	جہڑے ~ جیرھے ~ جیڑھے jerhe ~ jeṛhe 'which…'
Oblique	جہڑے ،~ جہرھے ~ جیڑے jerhe ~ jeṛhe 'which…'	جہڑیاں ~ جہڑے jerhĕā ~ jeṛhe 'which…'

Table 5.14: Relative adjectives - Hindko, Panjabi, Saraiki (masculine forms)

5.1.3.3.3 Interrogative adjectives

All three languages have marked interrogative adjectival forms which can also function substantively. Their masculine forms are given in Table 5.15. For specifically pronominal forms, see Section 6.5.

7 The interrogative adjectives for Hindko and Panjabi are spelled in two ways, illustrated by کہڑا ~ کیہڑا in the Hindko paradigm. A rough Google search on March 2, 2017 shows that the کیہڑا spelling is more frequently encountered.

	Singular	Plural
Hindko		
Direct	کہڑا ~ کیہڑا kéṛā 'which?'	کیہڑے kéṛe 'which?'
Oblique	کیہڑے kéṛe 'which?'	کیہڑیاں kéṛĕã̄ 'which?'
Panjabi		
Direct	کیہڑا kéṛā 'which?'	کیہڑے kéṛe 'which?'
Oblique	کیہڑے kéṛe 'which?'	کیہڑے ، ~ کیہڑیاں kéṛe ~ kéṛĕã̄ 'which?'
Saraiki		
Direct	کیرھا ، ~ کیڑھا، ~ کہڑا kerhā ~ keṛhā 'which?'	کیرھے، ~ کہڑے، ~ کیڑھے kerhe ~ keṛhe 'which?'
Oblique	کیرھے، ~ کہڑے، ~ کیڑھے kerhe~ keṛhe 'which?'	کہڑیاں ~، کہڑے kerhĕā ~ keṛhe 'which?'

Table 5.15: Interrogative adjectives - Hindko, Panjabi, Saraiki[7]

The interrogative کیہڑا /kéṛā/ Hk, Pj ~ کیڑھا /keṛhā/ Sr [8], is a marked adjective, meaning 'which?' when it seeks specification of an item within a known finite set; when questioning the existence of something, it can also mean 'what?' ; for instance, کیہڑا بھرا /kéṛā prā̀/ can mean either 'which brother?' or 'what brother?!' (implying lack of knowledge of any brother, or questioning the existence of any brother), depending on intonation and word order, or as in example 5.17, which shows it in adjectival function.

8 There are several spellings of this word in use.

In the meaning 'what', questioning existence, these forms are often used in rhetorical questions, which have a strong negative implication, as in 5.18.

(5.17) اوہ کیہڑے کمرے وچ ہوندی اے

ó	***kéṛ-e***	*kamr-e*	*vic*	*hon-d-ī*	*e*
3SG	**which-OBL**	room-OBL	in	stay-IP-SG.F	be.PRES.3SG

'**Which** room is she usually in?' (Pj) (EB)

(5.18) اوہ کیہڑا کم اے

ó	***kéṛā***	*kamm*	*e*
3SG	**what-SG.M**	work[M]	be.PRES.3SG

'**What** work is that? (i.e., That is no work at all.)' (EB)

For its pronominal function, see Section 6.5.2.

5.1.3.3.4 Adjectival-adverbial, declarative, interrogative, and relative sets

Each of these languages has a series of words which have systematically related forms and functions. These form four-word sets, with relative, interrogative, proximal demonstrative, and distal demonstrative members, each of which is indicated by its initial sound. The interrogatives have initial /k/; the proximal demonstratives /i/ or /e/; the distal demonstratives /o/, /w/, or, in a few cases, /t/; and the relatives /j/. These sets include words with meanings of time, location, direction, manner, and quantity. In many cases, oblique singular forms of the marked adjectival words serve as adverbs.

The sets are shown in Table 5.16, Table 5.17, and Table 5.18. In Table 5.16, forms from Sakoon (2002) are indicated by a superscript 2, and forms from AWT by a superscript 1. In Table 5.18, forms from Mughal (2010) are indicated with a superscript 1, forms from Shackle (1976) with superscript 2, forms from Zahoor (2009) with superscript 3, and forms from UK with superscript 4. Adjectival forms appear in their masculine singular forms.

	Time (adv.)	Place (adv.)		Manner (adv.)	Manner (adj.)	Quantity (adj.)
		Location	Direction			
Proximal	ہونڑ huṇ 'now' [1]	اتھے ithe 'here' [1]	ادہر ídar 'to here' [1]	انجو injū [1,2] اینویں ĩvẽ 'in this way' [2]	اہجیا ehajiyā 'of this kind' [1]	ایڈا eḍḍā 'this much/ many' [2]
Distal	تد tad [1,2] تدوں taddõ 'then'	اُتھے uthe 'there' [1]	اُتھے uthe 'to there' [1]	اُنجو unjū [2] ہُنجو hunjū 'in that way' [2]	اوہجیا ohajiyā 'of that kind' [2]	اوڈّا oḍḍā 'that much/ many'
Interrog-ative	کدوں kadõ 'when?' [2] کد kad 'when?' [2]	کھتے kithe [1] [2]	کت kut [2] کتھا kutthā [2] کِنگا kingā 'to where?' [2]	کنجو kinjū [1] کتھا kitthā [2] کیاں kiyā̃ 'how?' [2]	کہجیا kihajiyā [1] کیہجیا kĩjiyā 'what kind of?' [2]	کتنا kitnā [1] کیڈا keḍā 'how much/ many?' [2]
Relative	جد jad [2] جدوں jaddõ جاں jā̃ 'time at which' [2]	جتھے jithe 'place at which' [1,2]	جتھا jithā 'direction in which' [2]	جیہاں jehā̃ [2] جیئوں jeũ [2] جِویں jivẽ [2] جنجو jinjū 'way in which' [1]	جیہا jehā 'the kind which, like' [2]	جت jit [2] جڈّا jiḍḍā 'as much/ many as' [2]

Table 5.16: Hindko demonstrative, interrogative, relative forms

	Time (adv.)	Place (adv.)		Manner (adv.)	Manner (adj.)	Quantity (adj.)
		Location	Direction			
Proximal	ہون huṇ 'now'	ایتھے etthe 'here' ارے ure 'over here, hither'	ایدھر édar 'to here' اورھاں úrā̃ 'here, hither'	ایویں evẽ 'in this way'	ایہو جیہا éo jéā 'of this kind, like this'	اینا ennā 'this much'
Distal	تد tad 'then'	اوتھے otthe 'there' پرے pare 'over there'	اودھر ódar 'to there' پرھاں párā̃ 'over there, thither'	اوویں ovẽ 'in that way'	اوہو جیہا óo jéā 'of that kind, like that'	اونا onnā 'that much'
Interrog-ative	کد kad 'when?'	کتھے kitthe 'where?'	کیدھر kíddar 'to where?'	کیویں kīvẽ 'how?'	کیہو جیہا kéo jéā 'what kind of?'	کنا kinnā 'how much?'
Relative	جد jad 'time at which'	جتھے jitthe 'place at which'	جدھر jíddar 'direction in which'	جیویں jīvẽ 'way in which'	جیہو جیہا jéo jéā 'the kind which'	جنا jinnā 'as much as'

Table 5.17: Panjabi demonstrative, interrogative, relative forms

	Time (adv.)	Place (adv.)		Manner (adv.)	Manner (adj.)	Quan-tity (adj.)
		Loca-tion	Direction			
Proxi-mal	ہُݨ huṇ 'now'[1, 2, 3, 4]	اِتھ ith[2] اِتھاں ithã̄ 'here'[2, 4]	اِیݙے eɗe ~ iɗɗe [2] اِیں پاسے ī̃ pāse 'to here' [2]	ایں ī̃ ایویں īvẽ 'in this way'[2, 4]	اِہجاں ihajã̄ یہجاں īhajã̄ ایجھاں ejhã̄ [2] اینجھا ī̃jhā 'of this kind, like this' [4]	اِتلا itlā [2] اِتّی ittī 'this many' [2]
Distal	تݙاں taɗã̄ 'then'[1, 2]	اُتھ uth[2] اُتھاں uthã̄ 'there'[4]	اوݙے uɗɗe [2] اوں پاسے ũ̄ pāse 'to there' [2]	اوں ũ̄ اوویں ūvẽ 'in that way'[2]	اوہو جیہاں oho jeã̄ اوجھاں ojhã̄[2] اونجھا ũ̄jhā 'of that kind, like that'[4]	اُتلا utlā [2] اُتّی uttī 'that many' [2]
Inter-rogative	کݙاں kaɗã̄ 'when?'[1, 3]	کتھ kith[2] کِتھاں kithã̄[1, 3] کِن kin 'where?'[1]	کیݙے keɗe[2] کِݙے kiɗe 'to where?' [2]	کیویں kivẽ 'how?'[3]	کِہجاں kihajã̄[1] کیجھاں kejihã̄[2] کیہاں kehã̄[2] کِہاں kihã̄ 'what kind of?'[2]	کِتلا kitlā [2] کِتّی kittī [2] چوکھے cokhe 'how many?' [4]
Rela-tive	جݙاں jaɗã̄ 'time at which'[2]	جِتھ jith [2] جِتھاں jithã̄ 'place at which' [2]	جیݙے jeɗe[2] جِݙے jiɗe 'direction in which'[2]	جیویں jivẽ 'way in which'[1]	جیہاں jehã̄[2, 4] جھیاں jheã̄[2] جیجھیاں jejheã̄[2] جیجھاں jejhã̄ 'the kind which'[2]	جِتلا jitlā [2] جِتّی jittī 'as many as' [1, 2]

Table 5.18: Saraiki demonstrative, interrogative, relative forms

5.1.3.4 Quantifiers

Quantifiers are words that express quantity or number, such as 'many', 'some', 'all', and the cardinal numerals. These elements can function adjectivally, adverbially, or nominally. The most important basic quantifiers for Hindko, Panjabi, and Saraiki are listed below. Several of them are common to all three languages, and others are very close in form. Those ending in a final ا /-ā/ are marked adjectives and agree with the noun they modify in gender, number, and case. The others are unmarked adjectives and are invariant in form.

5.1.3.4.1 Hindko quantifiers

In the following list, forms from Sakoon (2002) are marked with a superscript 2; those from AWT with a superscript 1.

- سارا /sārā/ 'entire (sg.), all (pl.)'[1,2]
- تھوہڑا ~ تھوڑا /thóṛā/ 'little (sg.), few (pl.)'[2]
- تھوہڑا جا /thóṛā jā/ 'a little (with mass nouns)'[1]
- کوئی ~ کُئی /kuī/ ~ /koī/ 'any, some'[1]
- کجھ /kúj/ 'some (quantitative, with count nouns)'[1, 2]
- کئی /kaī/ 'many'
- ہر /har/ 'each, every'[2]

5.1.3.4.2 Panjabi quantifiers

- سارا /sārā/ 'entire (sg.), all (pl.)'
- تھوڑا /thoṛā/ 'little (sg.), few (pl.)'
- تھوڑا جیہا /thoṛā jéā/ 'a little (mostly with mass nouns)'
- کوئی /koī/ 'any, some'
- کجھ /kúj/ 'some (but not all)'
- کئی /kaī/ 'many, several'
- سبھ /sáb/ 'all, entire'
- ہر /har/ 'each, every'

5.1.3.4.3 Saraiki quantifiers

These forms are from Shackle (1976).

- سارا /sārā/ 'entire (sg.), all (pl.)'
- تھوڑا ~ تھولا /thoṛā/ ~ /tholā/ 'little (sg.), few (pl.)'
- کئی /kuī/ 'any, some'
- کجھ /kujh/ 'some'
- ہک /hik/ 'some, somewhat (adv.)'
- کئی /kaī/ 'many, several'
- سبھ /sabh/ 'all, entire'
- ہر کئی /har kuī/ 'each, every'
- یکا /yakā/ 'all, whole'

The words سبھ /sabh/ 'all, entire' and ہک /hik/ 'some' have emphatic forms which have distinct forms for masculine and feminine singular direct case. Oblique singular and plural direct are the same for both masculine and feminine. Plural oblique forms consist of the oblique singular plus /ī/. These two words pattern similarly; their forms are: سبھو /sabho/ '(SG.M.DIR)', سبھا /sabhā/ '(SG.F.DIR)', سبھے /sabhe/ '(PL.DIR; SG.OBL)', سبھے ای /sabheī/ '(PL.OBL.)'; ہکو /hiko/ '(SG.M.DIR)', ہکا /hikā/ (SG.F.DIR), ہکے /hike/ '(PL.DIR; SG.OBL), 'ہیکے ای /hikeī/ '(PL.OBL.)' (Shackle 1976: 61).

5.1.3.5 Indefinite adjectival expressions

All three languages have variants of two basic indefinite elements, both of which can function either as adjective or pronoun. These elements are کوئی ~ کئی /kuī/ ~ /koī/ 'any, some', and کجھ /kúj/ Hk Pj ~ کجھ /kujh/ Sr 'some'. There is a difference between these two elements: کئی ~ کوئی /kuī ~ koī/ is a non-specific indefinite element. کجھ /kúj/ ~ /kujh/ 'some', in the singular, usually has a quantitative sense, i.e., 'some but not all', but in the plural, this distinction is sometimes neutralized, so that کجھ /kúj/ serves as the plural of کوئی in Hindko and Panjabi, meaning 'some' (pl.). This does not happen in Saraiki. In addition, کجھ also functions adverbially in all three languages, with a sense of 'somewhat, rather' (5.27 below). When these forms function pronominally, کوئی /koī/ usually means 'someone', and کجھ /kúj/ ~ /kujh/ means 'something'. Table 5.19 and Table 5.20 give the forms of these two elements in the three languages.

	Hindko		Panjabi		Saraiki[9]	
	Singular	**Plural**	**Singular**	**Plural**	**Singular**	**Plural**
Direct	کوئی ~ کئی kuī ~ koī	کئی kaī کجھ kúj	کوئی koī	کجھ kúj کوئی koī کئی kaī	کوئی koī ~ kuī$_{M}$ کئی kaī$_{F}$	کئی kaī$_{M/F}$
Oblique	کسے kise	کجھ kúj	کسے kise کسی kisī	کئیاں kaiyā̃ کجھ kúj	کہیں kahī̃	کنہاں kinhā̃ کئیاں kaīā̃
Locative	کسی kisī					

Table 5.19: Non-specific indefinite adjective کوئی ~ کئی /kuī/ ~ /koī/ 'a, any, some'– Hindko, Panjabi, Saraiki

Plural کئی /kaī/, with oblique form کئیاں /kaiyā̃/, has the sense of 'several, many'.

9 Saraiki forms are from Shackle (1976: 61).

	Hindko		Panjabi		Saraiki	
	Singular	Plural	Singular	Plural	Singular	Plural
Direct	کُجھ kúj	کُجھ kúj	کُجھ kúj	کُجھ kúj	کُجھ kujh	کُجھ kujh
Oblique	کُجھ kúj	کُجھ kúj	کُجھ kúj	کُجھ kúj	کُجھ kujh	کُجھ kujh

Table 5.20: Indefinite adjective کُجھ /kúj/ ~ /kujh/ 'some (quantitative)'– Hindko, Panjabi, Saraiki

5.1.3.5.1 Indefinite adjectives – Hindko

Examples 5.19, 5.20, 5.21, 5.22 and 5.23 illustrate the use of the indefinite adjective in Hindko. For its pronominal use, see Section 6.6.

(5.19) کونڑ ایہا ؟ ماہنہ نیئں پتا کوئی جنڑاں ایہا

kɔr̃ éy-ā mā̃́ nī̃́ patā ***koī*** *jar̃-ā̃ éy-ā*

who be.PST-SG.M 1SG.OBL not known **some** man-SG.M be.PST-SG.M

'Who was it? I don't know - it was **some** man.' (Hk) (AWT)

(5.20) ماہنہ نیئں پتا کجھ جنڑے ایہے

mā̃́ nī̃́ patā ***kúj*** *jar̃-e éy-e*

1SG.OBL not known **some** man-PL.M be.PST-PL.M

'I don't know – it was **some** men.' (Hk) (AWT)

(5.21) کجھ لوکاں سکولے آں تباہ کیتا اے

kúj *lok-ā̃ skūl-e-ā̃ tabā́ kīt-ā*

some.PL people-PL.OBL school-OBL-ACC destroy do.PP-SG.M

e

be.PRES.3SG

'**Some** persons have destroyed the school.' (Hk) (AWT)

(5.22) کئی لوک آئے ایہے

kaī	*lok*	*āe*	*éye*
several	people	come.PP.PL.M	be.PST.PL.M

'**Several** people came/had come.' (Hk) (AWT)

کوئی /koī/ 'any, some' has a locative (or oblique) form کسی /kisī/, which appears in example (5.23).

(5.23) میں کسی جائی پڑھیا

mæ̃	***kis-ī***	*jā-ī*	*paṛh-iyā*
I	**some-OBL/LOC**	place-OBL/LOC	read-PP.SG.M

'I read it **some**where.' (Hk) (AWT)

5.1.3.5.2 Indefinite adjectives – Panjabi

The adjectival functions of کوئی /koī/ 'any, some' and کجھ /kúj/ 'some' are illustrated in examples (5.24), and (5.25), (5.26), and (5.27) respectively. For examples of their pronominal use, see Section 6.6.

(5.24) کوئی منڈا ایتھے نہیں آیا

koī	*mũḍā*	*étthe*	*nĩ́*	*ā-yā*
any	boy	here	not	come.PP-SG.M

'**No** boy came here.' (Pj) (Bhatia 1993: 189)

(5.25) کُجھ لوکاں دا خیال اے کہ پاکستان اچ ہجے وی وڈیرا بادشاہ دی حیثیت رکھدا اے

kúj	*lok-ā̃*	*d-ā*	*xyāl*	*e*	*ki*	*pākistān*
some	people-OBL.PL	GEN-SG.M	opinion	be.PRES.3SG	that	Pakistan
icc	*haje-vī*	*vaḍerā*	*bādšā*	*d-ī*	*hæsiyat*	*rakh-d-ā*
in	still-EMPH	feudal.lord	king	GEN-SG.F	status.F	keep-IP-SG.M
e						
be.PRES.3SG						

'**Some** people think that a feudal landlord still maintains the status of king in Pakistan.' (Pj) (Bashir and Kazmi 2012: 610)

(5.26) کجھ لوک آئے - کجھ نہیں آئے

kûj	*lok*	*ā-e*	–	***kûj***	*nī̃*	*ā-e*
some	people	come.PP-PL.M	–	**some**	not	come.PP-PL.M

‘**Some** people came –**some** didn’t.’ (Pj) (EB)

(5.27) اج تسی کجھ پریشان لگدے او

ajj	*tussī*	***kûj***	*parešān*	*lag-d-e*	*o*
today	you	**somewhat**	worried	seem-IP-PL.M	be.PRES.2PL

‘You seem **somewhat** worried today.’ (Pj) (EB)

5.1.3.5.3 Indefinite adjectives – Saraiki

Adjectival uses of the indefinite adjectives in Saraiki are shown in examples (5.28) and (5.29). For pronominal uses, see Section 6.6.

(5.28) میکوں کہیں شے کنوں ڈر نہیں لگدا

mæ-kū̃	***kahī̃***	*šæ*	*kanū̃*	*ɗar*	*nahī̃*	*laɠ-d-ā*
1SG-DAT	**any.OBL**	thing	from	fear	not	attach-IP-SG.M

‘I am not afraid of **anything.**’ (Sr) (UK)

(5.29) تاں جو کجھ تجربہ حاصل کر سگاں

tā̃jo	***kujh***	*tajarbā*	*hāsal kar*	*saɠ-ā̃*
so.that	**some.DIR**	experience	get	be.able-SBJV.1SG

‘...so that I can get **some** experience’ (Zahoor 2009: 62)

5.1.3.6 Reflexive adjectives

When a possessive adjective in a clause refers back to the subject of the clause, a reflexive adjective is used. The reflexive adjectives in all three languages have developed from the Old Indo-Aryan form *ātmán* ‘breath, soul’. In all three languages, the reflexive adjectives function also as an emphatic element. There are also pronominal reflexive elements, which are discussed in Section 6.3.

5.1.3.6.1 Reflexive adjective – Hindko

The reflexive adjective in Hindko, اپڑا ~ اپڑاں ~ اپنڑا /apṛā ~ apṛā̃ ~ apṛ̃ā/ 'self's', is found with varying spellings, as noted. Example 5.30 illustrates coreference with the subject, while 5.31 illustrates the emphatic usage.

(5.30) میں کتاب اپڑے دادے آں دیساں

mæ̃	*kitāb*	***apṛ-e***	*dād-e-ā̃*	*de-s-ā̃*
I	book	**self's-SG.M.OBL**	grandfather-OBL-DAT	give-FUT-1SG

'**I** will give the book to **my** grandfather.' (Hk) (AWT)

(5.31) ایہہ میری اپڑی کتاب اے

é	***mer-ī***	***apṛ-ī***	*kitāb*	*e*
this	**my-SG.F**	**EMPH-SG.F**	book[F]	be.PRES.3SG

'This is **my own** book.' (Hk)

5.1.3.6.2 Reflexive adjective – Panjabi

The reflexive adjective in Panjabi is آپنا /āpṇā/. Example 5.32 illustrates subject coreference, and 5.33 illustrates the emphatic usage. Note that under the influence of Urdu, some writers of Punjabi spell this adjective and forms derived from it as اپ /ap/, with a short initial vowel ا /a/ instead of آ /ā/. In the discussion that follows, in our own examples we spell the Punjabi forms with آ *alif madd* and romanize them with /ā/; however, we do not change/normalize instances of ا /alif/ in authentic examples taken directly from other sources.

(5.32) میں سلیم نوں آپنی کتاب دِتی

mæ̃	*salīm-nū̃*	***āpṇ-ī***	*katāb*	*dit-ī*
1SG	Salim-DAT	**self's-SG.F**	book[F]	give.PP-SG.F

'**I** gave Salim **my** book.' (Pj) (EB)

(5.33) ایہہ میری آپنی کتاب اے

é	***merī***	***āpṇ-ī***	*katāb*	*e*
This	**1SG.GEN-SG.F**	**EMPH-SG.F**	book[F]	be.PR.3SG

'This is **my own** book.' (Pj) (EB)

5.1.3.6.3 Reflexive adjective – Saraiki

The reflexive adjective in Saraiki is آپݨا ~ اپݨا /apṇā ~ āpṇā/. It functions in the same ways as the reflexive adjective in Hindko and Panjabi. Subject coreference is illustrated in 5.34, and the emphatic usage in 5.35.

(5.34) ساڈے لوک زیادہ تر اپݨے ٹبر وچ ای شادی کریندن

sāɗe	*lok*	*zyādatar*	*apṇe*	*ṭabar*	*vic*	*ī*
our	people	mostly	self.SG.M.OBL	relatives	among	EMPH

šādī	*kare-nd-ĕn*
marriage	do-IP-PRES.3PL

'Our people mostly marry among their (own) relatives.' (Sr) (Zahoor 2009: 65) (UK)

(5.35) اوندے آپݨے ٻال کینھی

ū̃-d-e	***āpṇ-e***	*ɓāl*	*kænhī*
3SG.OBL-GEN-PL.M	**EMPH-PL.M**	children	are.not

'She has no children of **her own**.' (Sr) (UK)

5.1.4 Numbers

The number systems and names in Hindko, Panjabi, and Saraiki share several features. The following statements apply to the number systems of all three languages.

5.1.4.1 Common features

Cardinal numbers can function as both adjectives and nouns. The teen numerals are formed on the inherited [n + 10] pattern; that is, the part of the number specifying the units place precedes the element meaning ten, e.g., in پندراں /pandarā̃/ Pj , پندھراں /pandharā̃/ 'fifteen' Sr the structure represents [5 + 10]. Numbers between twenty and one hundred are formed on the pattern [n + multiple of 10], as in پینتی /pæntī/ Pj , پینتریہہ /pæntrīh/ 'thirty-five' Sr , i.e., [5 + (3 x 10)]. The set of 'nines' other than 'nine' itself and 'ninety-nine', i.e., 19, 29, ... 89, is consistently represented by [one less than x] where x is a multiple of ten, e.g., اُنتی /unnattī/ Pj , اُنتریہہ /untrīh/ 'twenty-nine' Sr = [1 less than 30], and so on.

5.1.4.1.1 Large numbers

In all three languages, numbers greater than one thousand are generally expressed in multiples of one thousand ہزار /(ha)zȁr/, one hundred thousand لکّھ /lakkh/, ten million کروڑ /kroṛ/, 'one billion' ارب /arab/, and one hundred billion کھرب /kharab/. In this system, the periods are demarcated in multiples of one hundred, rather than one thousand as in the international system. Thus there is no single word for one million, and this number is expressed by دس لکّھ /das lakkh/ 'ten lakhs' [10 x 100,000]. So, for example, 20,406,000 is expressed as: دو کروڑ چار لکّھ تے چھ ہزار /do kroṛ cār lakkh te che (ha)zȁr/ 'two crores, four lakhs, and six thousands'.[10] These terms are also frequently used in South Asian English. Large numbers are shown in Table 5.21.

100	سو sau ~ so$_{Hk, Pj}$ sɔ$_{Sr}$
1,000	ہزار (ha)zār ~ zȁr$_{Hk, Pj}$ hazār$_{Sr}$
1,00,000	لکّھ lakkh
1,00,00,000	کروڑ kroṛ
1,00,00,00,000	ارب arab
1,00,00,00,00,000	کھرب kharab

Table 5.21: Large numbers

In Pakistan, numbers are more commonly written in western Arabic numerals, 1, 2, 3, . . .; however, the eastern Arabic numerals ۱، ۲، ۳ ـ ـ ـ based on the Persian forms, are also used. It is common for large numerals to be written with commas separating the first three zeros, and each subsequent pair of zeros in the number, as shown in the table above.

10 The word for 'six' is always pronounced /che/, but under the influence of Urdu, spelling is more frequently چھ rather than چھے. However, a large number of people writing on the internet do spell it as چھے.

In rural areas, a vigesimal system, based on multiples of twenty, has traditionally been used. Though now rarely found in urban centers, the vigesimal system was previously used over a wide swath of South Asia. In this system, one counts the number of 'twenties', with ویہہ /vī́/ 'twenty' in the plural ویہاں /vī́ā̃/. For example, in this system, forty is دو ویہاں /do vī́ā̃/ 'two twenties'; and one hundred twenty is چھ ویہاں /che vī́ā̃/ 'six twenties'. It is rare to find 'five twenties', سو /sau/ 'one hundred' being more common. A number exceeding a multiple of twenty by one to ten is expressed by adding the number by which the multiple of twenty is exceeded to the multiple of twenty, so that 'seventy' is تن ویہاں تے دس /tin vī́ā̃ te das/ 'three twenties and ten.' For numbers one to nine less than a multiple of twenty, that number is subtracted from the multiple of twenty, so that, for example, 'fifty-nine' could be expressed (in Panjabi) as اک گھٹ تن ویہاں /ikk kàṭ tin vī́ā̃/ 'one less than three twenties'.

5.1.4.1.2 Fractional numbers

Some frequently used fractional numbers are expressed with non-compositional terms, which are very similar in the three languages. There are unique words for one-and-a-half and two-and-a-half, and words for one quarter more than number, one quarter less than a number, and a number plus one half, e.g., Panjabi ڈیڑھ /ḍéṛ/ 'one and a half' and ڈھائی /ṭā̀ī/ 'two and a half'. These words can also be used with the larger numbers, for example, ڈھائی ہزار /ṭā̀ī hazār/ 'two and a half thousand, i.e., 2,500'; پونے ترے لکھ /pɔṇe træ lakkh/ 'one quarter less than three x hundred thousand, i.e., 275,000'; ساڈھے پنج کروڑ /sā́ḍhe panj kroṛ/ 'five and a half × ten million, or 55,000,000'. A similar pattern is found in Hindko and Saraiki. These terms are compared in Table 5.22.

All five of these words precede the number they apply to. The word for 'one-half', e.g. اڈّھا /áddā/, e.g., اڈھا گھنٹا /áddā kæ̀nṭā/ 'half an hour' Pj , is distinct from both ڈیڑھ /ḍéṛ/ 'one and a half', and ساڈھے /sā́ḍe/ 'some number plus a half'. A prefixal element ادھ /ádd/ also exists, e.g., ادھ کلو /ádd kilo/ 'half a kilogram' Pj, Sr . The 'half' morpheme also occurs in the phrase ادھو ادھ /áddo ádd/ 'fifty-fifty, half-half, in two equal shares' Pj , ادھو ادھ /addho addh/ Sr . When used meaning 'three quarters of a singular entity' /pɔṇā/ is singular but otherwise it takes the plural, e.g., پونا گھنٹا /pɔṇā kæ̀nṭā/ '1/4 less than an hour' Pj . A unique word for 'three quarters', منّا /munnā/ used with measure nouns, e.g., منا سیر /munnā ser/ '3/4 seer (a unit of weight equivalent to about 933 grams)' is used in Saraiki and Panjabi.[11] The word پا /pā/ '1/4 of' is frequently used with units

11 It occurs in the title of a well-known collection of short stories, *Munnā Koh Lahore* [Three quarters of a koh to Lahore] by Afzal Ahsan Randhava (Randhava 2007). A کوہ /kó/ is a measure of distance equivalent to about 2.4 kilometers.

	Hindko	Panjabi	Saraiki
1½	ڈیڈھ ḍéḍ	ڈیڑھ ḍéṛ	ڈِڈھ ɗiḍh
2½	ٹھائی ṭā̃ī	ڈھائی ṭā̃ī	اڈھئی aḍhaī
number + ¼	سوا savā e.g. سوا دو savā do '2¼'	سوا savā e.g. سوا دو savā do '2¼'	سوا savā e.g. سوا ڋو savā ɗū '2¼'
number - ¼	پونیں pɔṇẽ e.g. پونیں یاراں pɔṇẽ yārā̃ '10¾'	پونے pɔṇe e.g. پونے دو pɔṇe do '1¾'	پونے paoṇe e.g. پونے ترے paoṇe træ '2¾'
number (≥3) + ½	ساڈھے sā̃ḍe e.g. ساڈھے ترے sā̃ḍe træ '3½'	ساڈھے sā̃ḍe e.g. ساڈھے تِن sā̃ḍe tin '3½'	ساڈھے sāḍhe e.g. ساڈھے ڋہ sāḍhe ɗah '10½'

Table 5.22: Special fractional numbers terms – Hindko, Panjabi, Saraiki

of weight, formerly سیر /ser/ and now کِلو /kilo/ 'kilogram'. So, for example, پا آلو /pā ālū/ means 'a quarter kilo of potatoes', or '250 grams of potatoes'.

The expression of fractional numbers other than the special cases discussed above follows a similar pattern in all three languages. Unique forms exist for 'one-half', 'one-third', and 'one-fourth'; their forms in Hindko, Panjabi, and Saraiki are shown in Table 5.23. The words for 'one-fourth' and 'one-third' are marked feminine nouns; 'one-half' is an unmarked masculine noun.

For other fractions, the ordinal number is used with the word حصّہ /hissā/ 'part[M]', e.g., اٹھواں حصا /aṭhwā̃ hissā/ 'eighth part, i.e., one-eighth'. For fractions with a numerator greater than one, expressions of the form [out of every n, x], as in Panjabi ہر تِن وِچوں دو /har tinn vicõ do/ 'out of every three, two', i.e., 'two-thirds of'; or [out of n parts, x], as in تِن حصیاں وِچوں دو. /tinn hisseā̃ vicõ do/ 'two out of three parts; two-thirds of ' are also used.

Fraction	Hindko	Panjabi	Saraiki
½	اَدّھ ádd	اَدّھ ádd	اَدّھ addh
⅓	ترِہائَی trihāī	تہائَی tihāī	ترِہائَی trihāī
¼	چتھائَی cuthāī	چتھائَی cuthāī	چتھائَی cuthāī

Table 5.23: 'half', 'third', 'quarter, fourth'– Hindko, Panjabi, Saraiki

5.1.4.2 Cardinal numbers

Since the specific forms of both cardinal and ordinal numerals vary among the three languages, they are presented separately for each language.

5.1.4.2.1 Hindko cardinal numbers

The Hindko cardinal numbers are similar to those of Panjabi, but note the clearly pronounced /h/ in ہِک /hikk/ 'one'. For the numbers 11 to 19, Hindko nasalizes the final vowels, for example, یاراں /yārā̃/ 'eleven', while most of the other numbers do not have this nasalization. The transcriptions in Table 5.24 represent AWT's pronunciation, and the Perso-Arabic spellings represent these pronunciations.

1	ہِک hikk	11	یاراں yārā̃
2	دو do	12	باراں bārā̃
3	ترَیہہ trǽ	19	اونی unnī
4	چار cār	20	بی bī
5	پنج panj	25	پنجی panjī
6	چھے che	30	تری trī
7	سَت sat	40	چالی cālī
8	اَٹھ aṭh	50	پنجاہ panjā́
9	نوں nõ	90	نوّے navve
10	دہ dah	100	سو so

Table 5.24: Hindko cardinal numbers (AWT)

5.1.4.2.2 Panjabi cardinal numbers

Panjabi cardinal numbers from one to ten are shown in Table 5.25. Oblique and locative forms largely follow Malik (1995: 205–206).

Cardinal numbers from two to ten are inflected for case; no cardinal numbers are inflected for gender. The numbers one, two, and four have the same forms for both the oblique and the locative (see Table 5.25). These forms are seen in اک دنی /ikk dinī/ 'on one day' (locative) and دوں کڑیاں نوں /dũ kuṛiyā̃ nū̃/ (oblique) 'to two girls'. Compare تِنّیں انّیں /tinnī̃ annī̃/ 'for three annas' (locative) (Malik 1995: 205).

Table 5.26 shows the Panjabi cardinal numbers from eleven to one hundred.

---

12 When used as a noun, وِیہہ /vī́/ 'score' is feminine.
13 The word for '25' presents an interesting development. In Gurmukhi, this word is spelled with ਝ, the character for aspirated j. This lost aspiration is the source of the perceptible tone on the first syllable of this word. However, in Perso-Arabic representation, this word is more frequently spelled with unaspirated ج rather than جھ. This influence of spelling is likely to result in the weakening of the tonal system in Pakistani Panjabi. The effects of spelling on language change are well documented, e.g. Polomé (1994) and Wang (1979).

Number	Direct	Oblique	Locative
1	اک ikk	اک ikk	اک ikk
2	دوں ~ دو do ~ dū̃	دوں ~ دُواں dū̃ ~ dūā̃	دوں dū̃
3	تن ~ ترے tinn ~ træ	تناں tinnā̃	تنیں tinnī̃
4	چئوں ~ چار caū̃ ~ cār	چئوں ~ چواں caū̃	چئوں caū̃
5	پنج panj	پنجاں panjā̃	پنجیں panjī̃
6	چھ ~ چھے che	چھیاں cheā̃	چھیئیں ~ چھیں cheī̃ ~ chī̃
7	ست satt	ستاں sattā̃	ستیں sattjī̃
8	اٹھ aṭṭh	اٹھاں aṭṭhā̃	اٹھیں aṭṭhī̃
9	نو ~ نوں nɔ ~ nɔ̃	نوواں nɔvā̃	نوویں nɔvī̃
10	دس das	دساں dasā̃	دسیں dasī̃

Table 5.25: Panjabi number names 1–10

The numbers '2', '3', and '4' have special multiplicative forms: دُگنا /dugṇā/ ~ دوہرا /dórā/ ~ دونا /dūṇā/ 'double, two-fold', تیہرا /tī́rā/ ~ تینی /tīṇī/ 'triple, three-fold', and چوہرا/cɔ́rā/ ~ چونا/cɔnā/ 'quadruple, four-fold' (Gill and Gleason 1969).

11	یاراں yārā̃	31	اِکتی (i)kattī
12	باراں bārā̃	32	بتی battī
13	تیراں terā̃	33	تیتی tettī
14	چوداں cɔdā̃	34	چونتی ∼ چوتی cɔntī ∼ cɔttī
15	پندراں pandarā̃	35	پینتی pæntī
16	سولاں solā̃	36	چھتی chattī
17	ستاراں satārā̃	37	سینتی sæntī
18	اٹھاراں aṭhārā̃	38	اٹھتی aṭhattī
19	اُنّی unnī	39	اُنتالی untālī
20	وِیہہ vī́ [12]	40	چالی cālī
21	اِکی ikkī	50	پنجاہ pãjá̃
22	بائی bāī	60	سٹھ saṭṭh
23	ترئی ∼ تیی traī ∼ teī	70	ستر sattar
24	چویہ ∼ چھوی cávī	80	اسی assī
25	پنجھی ∼ پنجی pánjī[13]	90	نوے ∼ نبے navve ∼ nabbe
26	چھبی chabbī	100	سو so ∼ sau
27	ستائی sattāī		
28	اٹھائی aṭhāī		
29	اُنتی uṇattī		
30	تریہہ ∼ تیہہ trī́ ∼ tī́		

Table 5.26: Panjabi cardinal numbers 11–100 (Bashir and Kazmi 2012)

5.1.4.2.3 Saraiki cardinal numbers

Saraiki cardinal numbers are presented in Table 5.27 and Table 5.28. The Perso-Arabic Saraiki spellings are from Zahoor (2009) and the Central variety pronunciations from Shackle (1976: 52–53). The number for 'one' shares the clear initial /h/ with Hindko. Of the cardinal numbers from one to ten, shown in Table 5.27, the words for 'three', 'four', 'five', 'six', 'seven', 'eight', and 'ten' have distinct direct and oblique forms. None of our sources mentions locative forms for these numbers.

Number	Direct	Oblique
1	ہِک hik	ہِک hik
2	ݙُو ɗū	ݙُو ɗū
3	ترَے træ	تریں trĩ
4	چار cār	چَوں caũ
5	پنج pãj	پنجاں pãjã
6	چھ chi	چھِہاں chihã
7	سَت sat	سَتاں satã
8	اَٹھ aṭh	اَٹھاں aṭhã
9	نَوں naũ	نَوں naũ
10	ݙَہ ḍah	ݙَہاں ḍahã

Table 5.27: Saraiki cardinal number names 1–10

The numbers from eleven to one hundred, however, do not have distinct oblique forms. These are presented in Table 5.28. [14]

Table 5.28: Saraiki cardinal number names 11–100

11	یارھاں yārhã ~ yārãh	41	اِکتالیہ iktālī	71	اِکہتّر ikhattar
12	ٻارھاں ɓārhã ~ bārãh	42	ٻتالیہ ɓitālī	72	ٻہتّر ɓahattar
13	تیرھاں terhã ~ terãh	43	ترتالیہ tirtālī	73	تہتّر tihattar
14	چوݙھاں cauɗhã ~ cauɗãh	44	چوتالیہ cutālī (Shackle 1976)	74	چوہتّر cuhattar

14 The spellings of some number names vary. For example, the words for 'six' and 'ten' appear as چھی /chī/ and ݙاہ /ɗāh/, respectively, in Parvez (1992: 37).

Table 5.28: (continued)

15	پندرھاں pandrhā̃ ~ pandrāh ~ pandhrā̃	**45**	پینتالیہ pæ̃tālī	**75**	پنجھتّر panjhattar
16	سولھاں solhā̃ ~ solāh	**46**	چھتالیہ chitālī	**76**	چھہتّر chihattar
17	ستارھاں satārhā̃ ~ satārāh	**47**	ستالیہ satālī	**77**	ستتّر satattar
18	اَٹھاراں aṭhārā̃ ~ aṭhārāh	**48**	اٹھتالیہہ aṭhtālī	**78**	اَٹھتّر aṭhattar
19	اُنویہہ unvī	**49**	اُنوِنجھا unvanjhā	**79**	اُناسی unāsī
20	وِیہہ vīh	**50**	پنجھا panjhā ~ panjāh	**80**	اَسی asī
21	اِکویہہ ikvī	**51**	اکونجھا ikvanjhā	**81**	اِکاسی ikāsī
22	باوِیہہ ɓāvī	**52**	بونجھا ɓavanjhā	**82**	بیاسی ɓiāsī
23	تریَویہہ trevī	**53**	ترونجھا tirvanjhā	**83**	تِراسی tirāsī
24	چویہہ cavī	**54**	چُرونجھا curvanjhā ~ curanjhā	**84**	چُوراسی curāsī
25	پنجویہہ panjvī	**55**	پچونجھا pacvanjhā	**85**	پنجاسی panjāsī
26	چھوّیہہ chavī	**56**	چھونجھا chivanjhā	**86**	چھیاسی chiāsī
27	ستاوِیہہ satāvī	**57**	ستونجھا satvanjhā	**87**	ستاسی satāsī
28	اَٹھاوِیہہ aṭhāvī	**58**	اَٹھونجھا aṭhvanjhā	**88**	اَٹھاسی aṭhāsī
29	اُنترّیہہ unattrī	**59**	اُنیٹھ unæṭh	**89**	اُنانوے unānve

Table 5.28: (continued)

30	تریہہ trīh	60	سٹھ saṭh	90	نوّے navve
31	اِکتریہہ ikatrī	61	اِکیٹھ ikæṭh	91	اِکانوے ikānve
32	بتریہہ ɓatrī	62	بیٹھ ɓæṭh	92	بیانوے ɓiānve
33	تینتریہہ ~ تیتریہہ tẽtrī ~ tetrī	63	تریٹھ treṭh	93	تِریانوے triānve ~ tirānve
34	چوِنتریہ ~ چوَتریہہ caɔ̃trī ~ cautrī	64	چُنٹھ cũṭh (Zahoor 2009) چُیٹھ cueṭh (Shackle 1976)	94	چورانوے curānve
35	پینتریہہ pæntrī	65	پنجیٹھ panjæṭh	95	پنجانوے panjānve
36	چھتریہہ chatrī	66	چھیٹھ chiæṭh	96	چھیانوے chiānve
37	ستتریہہ satattrī	67	ستیٹھ satæṭh	97	ستانوے satānve
38	اَٹھتریہہ aṭhattrī	68	اَٹھیٹھ aṭhæṭh	98	اِٹھانوے aṭhānve
39	اُنتالیہ untālī	69	اُنہتّر unhattar	99	نِرنوے niranve ودھانوے vadhānve (Zahoor 2009)
40	چالیہ calī	70	ستّر sattar	100	سو sao

5.1.4.3 Ordinal numbers

Ordinal numbers represent the position of a term in an ordered set: 'first', 'second', 'third', etc. All ordinal numbers are marked adjectives, and thus inflect for gender, number, and case. In all three languages, the word for 'first' is suppletive, being a reflex of OIA *prathila* 'first' (T8652).[15] The words for 'second', 'third', and 'fourth' are slightly irregular in all three languages. The ordinal numbers are formed regularly from the cardinal numbers by adding the suffix واں /-vā̃/ directly to the cardinal number; for example, 'sixth' is چھیواں /chevā̃/ in all three languages.

5.1.4.3.1 Hindko ordinal numbers

Ordinal terms from 'fifth' and above are formed by adding the marked adjectival suffix واں /-vā̃/ to the base of the cardinal number word. The Hindko ordinal numerals for 'first' through 'twelfth' are given in Table 5.29.

first	پہلا pælā	**seventh**	ستواں satvā̃
second	دُوّا duwwā (Sakoon 2002) دوآ dūā (AWT)	**eighth**	اٹھواں aṭhvā̃
third	ترِیّا trīyā	**ninth**	نوواں novā̃
fourth	چوتھا cothā	**tenth**	دسواں dasvā̃
fifth	پنجواں panjvā̃	eleventh	یارھواں yā́rvā̃
sixth	چھیواں chevā̃	**twelfth**	بارھواں bā́rvā̃

Table 5.29: Hindko ordinal numbers

15 Notations of the form 'Tnnnn' refer to the entries in Turner's *Comparative Dictionary of the Indo-Aryan Languages* (Turner 1962–1966).

5.1.4.3.2 Panjabi ordinal numbers

The first four ordinal numbers are:

- پہلا ~ پہلاں /pǽlā/ ~ /pǽlā̃/ 'first'
- دوجا ~ دوسرا /dūjā/ ~ /dūsrā/ 'second' (< Urdu)
- تیجا ~ تیسرا /tījā/ ~ /tīsrā/ 'third' (< Urdu)
- چوتھا /cɔthā/ 'fourth'

To form the ordinals from 'fifth' to 'tenth', the suffix واں /-vā̃/ is added directly to the cardinal number. For the ordinals from 'eleventh' on, the final /-ā/ of the root is dropped before adding واں /-vā̃/, so that یاراں /yā́rā̃/ 'eleven' becomes یارھواں /yā́rvā̃/ 'eleventh'. A high tone is present for most speakers in the ordinals from eleventh to nineteenth, which is reflected in the Perso-Arabic script by the presence of ھ *do cašmī he*. Note that when 'first', 'second', 'third', or 'fourth' is used in combination with other numbers these four words follow the regular pattern for ordinals; thus اکواں /ikkvā̃/ 'n + first' is used, and not پہلا /pǽlā/ 'first'; thus اک سو اکواں /ikk sɔ ikkvā̃/ 'one hundred and first', and so on.

5.1.4.3.3 Saraiki ordinal numbers

The Saraiki ordinals for the numbers one to twelve and selected higher ordinals are presented in Table 5.30. The ordinal-forming suffix is واں /-vā̃/following numbers with an aspirated consonant in the stem, e.g. '60th'. With numbers ending in /h/, metathesis can occur, yielding a suffix وھاں /-vhā̃/, as in '20th'. Additionally, forms ending in /-vhā̃/ do also occur as alternates sometimes.

first	پہلا pahlā ~ pæhlā ~ pælhā̃	**nineteenth**	انویوھاں unvīvhā̃
second	ݙُوجھا ɗūjhā	**twentieth**	ویہواں ~ ویوھاں vihvā̃ ~ vīvhā̃
third	تریجھا trījhā	**thirtieth**	تریوھاں ~ تریہواں trīvhā̃ ~ trihvā̃
fourth	چَوتھا caothā	**fortieth**	چلیوھاں calīvhā̃
fifth	پنجواں ~ پنجوھاں pañjvā̃ ~ pañjvhā̃	**fiftieth**	پنجاوھاں panjāvhā̃
sixth	چھیواں ~ چھیوھاں chevā̃	**sixtieth**	سٹھواں saṭvā̃ ~ saṭhvā̃
seventh	ستواں ~ ستوھاں satvā̃ ~ satvhā̃	**seventieth**	ستروھاں satarvā̃ ~ satarvhā̃
eighth	اٹھواں aṭhvā̃	**eightieth**	اسیوھاں assīvā̃ ~ asīvhā̃
ninth	ناواں nāvā̃	**ninetieth**	نویوھاں navvevā̃ ~ navevhā̃
tenth	ݙاہواں ɗāhvā̃	**hundredth**	سوھاں ~ سویوھاں savā̃ ~ savīā̃ ~ savhā̃ ~ savīvhā̃
eleventh	یارھواں yārhvā̃		
twelfth	ٻارھواں ɓārhvā̃		

Table 5.30: Saraiki ordinal numbers

5.1.4.4 Indefinite numerical expressions

Regularly formed indefinite numbers consist of the oblique plural of the words for large numbers, for example, ہزاراں, /hazārā̃/ 'thousands of', or لکھاں /lakkhā̃/ 'hundreds of thousands'. A common idiomatic expression in Panjạbi for an inappropriately large, indefinite number, with a sense something like 'a lot of, far too many' is چھتی سو /chattī sɔ/, lit. 'thirty-six hundred' (Gill and Gleason 1969: 13). This negative connotation is not shared by the regularly formed indefinite numbers.

(5.36) اوہ چھتی سو بماریاں دی کھادی اے

ó	***chattī***	***sɔ***	*bimāriy-ā̃*	*d-ī*	*khā́d-ī*
3SG	**thirty-six**	**hundred**	illness-PL.F	GEN-SG.F	eat.PP-SG.F

e
be.PRES.3SG

'She is afflicted with **too many** illnesses.' (Pj) (EB)

Another way to express approximation is by juxtaposing two sequential or close numbers; for example دوچار منڈے /do cār mũḍe/ 'a few boys'. Another, rather vaguer, way of expressing an approximate number is with the indefinite adjective کوئی /kuī/ 'some', as in کوئی ویہہ بندے /kuī vī́ bande/ 'some twenty men/people'. A variant of this pattern in Panjabi involves the suffixal particle کُہ[16] /ku/ 'about, approximately', as in ویہہ کُہ بندے /vī́ ku bande/ 'about twenty men/people'. Saraiki has a similar construction with کھن /khun/ 'about', used with large round numbers, e.g. ہزار کھن سال /hazār khun sāl/ 'about a thousand years' (Shackle 1976: 112).

5.1.4.5 Totalizing (aggregating) suffixes

All three languages employ totalizing suffixes, having largely similar forms. The Hindko direct case and oblique forms are exemplified in 5.37 and 5.38, respectively.

(5.37) چوئے / چارے جاتک اج آئین

*cau-**e*** /	*cār-**e***	*jătak*	*ajj*	*ā-e-n*
four-**TOT** /	four-**TOT**	boy.PL.M	today	come-PP.PL.M-PRES3PL

'**All** four boys are present (lit. 'have come') today.' (AWT)

---

16 Spelling of this element is problematic in Perso-Arabic, since most words do not end in short vowels. The Gurmukhi spelling ਕੁ /ku/ shows the short vowel easily.

(5.38) انہاں چوہاں جاتکاں روٹی دیئیں

én-ã̃	*cau-**ã̃***	*jātk-ã̃*	*roṭī*	*de-ĩ*
these-OBL.PL	four-**TOT.OBL**	boy.PL.M-DAT	food	give-IMP.2SG

'Give food to **all** four of these boys.' (AWT)

In Panjabi, direct case number terms meaning 'all n' are formed by adding the totalizing suffix ے /e/ ~ ـیں /ẽ/, or recently اوں /õ/ (<Urdu) to the cardinal numbers up to ten; for example, چارے کڑیاں /cār-e kuṛiã̃/ 'all four girls'. The oblique forms add اں /ã̃/, for example چوّاں کڑیاں نوں /cau-ã̃ kuṛiã̃ nũ̃/ 'to all four girls'.

For numbers greater than ten, the pattern 'n of n' applies, e.g., باراں دے باراں منڈے /bārã̃ de bārã̃ mũḍe/ 'all twelve boys'.

The number 'one' has a unique, 'emphatic', form, اکو ~ اکوئی /ikko/ ~ /ikkoī/ 'only one'. For numbers without a unique totalizing form, the emphatic particle ای /-ī/ can be added to the oblique form, e.g. چھیاں ای نوں /cheã̃ ī nũ̃/ 'to all six' (Malik 1995: 206).

In Saraiki, totalizing elements can take several variant forms. The direct and oblique forms of the cardinals from 2 to 10 are shown in Table 5.31, based on Shackle (1976: 51–52), who refers to them as "emphatic."

17 * The form marked with an asterisk in Table 5.31, given by Shackle, is not accepted by Nasir Abbas Syed, who says that in actual practice, the expression نوٗ دے نوٗ /nau de nau/ 'nine of nine' is used in this sense. He thinks that there is no totalizing form for 'all nine'.
** The form marked with a double asterisk is rare.

	Direct	Oblique
2–'both'	ݙُوہیں ɗūhẽ ~ ݙُہیں ɗuhẽ ~ ݙُہائیں ɗuhāẽ	ݙُہاں ɗuhā̃
3–'all three'	تِریہے trihe	تِرہاں trihā̃ ~ تِرہیں trihaẽ
4–'all four'	چارہے cārhe	چوہاں cavhā̃ ~ چوانہہ cavā̃h ** ~ چوھیں cavhaẽ ~ چارہیں carhẽ
5–'all five'	پنجے panje	پنجھاں panjhā̃ ~ پنجانہ panjā̃h ~ پنجائیں panjāẽ
6–'all six'	چھیہے chīhe	چھیہاں chihā̃ ~ چھہیں chihāẽ
7–'all seven'	ستے sate	ستاں satā̃ ~ ستیں satẽ
8–'all eight'	اٹھے aṭhe	اٹھاں aṭhā̃ ~ اٹھیں aṭhẽ
9–'all nine'	نوھیں nauhẽ * (Shackle 1976: 52)	نواں navā̃ ~ نویں navẽ
10–'all ten'	ݙہے ɗahe	ݙہاں ɗahā̃ ~ ݙہیں ɗahẽ

Table 5.31: Saraiki totalizing/aggregative forms of numbers 2–10[17]

5.2 Adverbs and adverbial expressions

Adverbial relations can be expressed with simple, single-word adverbs; oblique or locative forms of nouns occurring without a postposition; full postpositional phrases expressing relations of time, place, or manner; or subordinate clauses. In these sections, some frequently appearing simple adverbs, examples of oblique noun phrases used in adverbial function, and a few postpositional phrases functioning adverbially will be listed for each language separately. For adverbial subordinate clauses, see Chapter 9.

5.2.1 Hindko adverbs and adverbial expressions

5.2.1.1 Simple adverbs – Hindko

The following subsections list some common adverbs and adverbial expressions in Hindko. Unless otherwise indicated, these adverbs are as provided by AWT.

5.2.1.1.1 Quantity

- بونہہ ~ بہوں /baū̃/ ‘very’
- زیادہ /zyāda/ ‘much, too much, very’
- اکّا /ukkā/ ‘completely’ (Sakoon 2002: 17)

5.2.1.1.2 Time

- کدوں /kadõ/ ‘when?’
- کدے /kadde/ ‘ever’; also used as a conjunction meaning ‘if’
- کدے نہ ~ کدے نینہ /kadde na, kadde nī̃/ ‘never’
- ہمیشہ /hamešā/ ‘always’
- کل /kal/ ‘yesterday’
- آخر /āxir/ ‘finally’
- روز /roz/ ‘daily, every day’

5.2.1.1.3 Place

- کتھے /kithe/ ‘where?’
- اُتھے /uthe/ ‘there’
- اِتھے /ithe/ ‘here’
- اِدہر /idhar/ ‘here, hither’
- سامنڑے /sā̃mṛ̃e/ ‘opposite, in front of, facing’

5.2.1.1.4 Reason

- کیوں /kyȭ/ 'why?'

5.2.1.1.5 Manner

- جلدی /jaldī/ 'quickly, early'
- ہولیاں /hɔliã̄/ 'slowly' (Sakoon 2002: 256)
- سدھے /siddhe/ 'straight'

5.2.1.2 Oblique noun phrases – Hindko

Oblique forms of nouns without a postposition frequently fulfill adverbial (temporal, spatial, manner) functions. For example:

(5.39) اسے وقت

us-e *vaxt*
that.OBL-EMPH time.OBL
'at that very time' (Hk) (AWT)

(5.40) کس ویلے

kis *vel-e*
what.OBL time-OBL
'at what time, when?' (Hk) (AWT)

(5.41) کسے جائی

kis-e *jā́-ī*
some.OBL-EMPH place-LOC
'in some place' (Hk) (AWT)

Also, for those nouns which retain locative or ablative case endings, those endings inherently convey adverbial meanings. See the locative form of the noun جاہ /jā́/ 'place' in (5.41) immediately above for an example of this.

5.2.1.3 Indefinite adverbials – Hindko

Some indefinite Hindko adverbials are shown in Table 5.32. Since indefinites are closely related to interrogatives, these are also shown for comparison. (See also Table 5.16 for the interrogative forms.)

Form	Place	Time
Interrogative (INT)	کتھا kuthā 'where, whither?' کتھے kithe 'where?'	کد kad کدوں kaddõ 'when?'
Indefinite (INDEF)	کتھے بی kithe bī 'anywhere, somewhere'	کدے kadde 'ever' کدھرے kidhare 'ever'
INDEF (reduplicated)	کتھے کتھے kithe kithe 'here and there', 'from place to place'	کدے کدے kadde kadde 'sometimes, from time to time'
INDEF + نہ + INDEF	کتھے نہ کتھے kithe na kithe 'somewhere or other'	کدے نہ کدے kadde na kadde 'sometime or other'

Table 5.32: Interrogative-indefinite adverbs – Hindko

5.2.2 Panjabi adverbs and adverbial expressions

5.2.2.1 Simple adverbs – Panjabi

5.2.2.1.1 Quantity

- بہُت /bɔ̃t/ 'much, very'
- گھٹ /kə̀ʈ/ 'little, less'

5.2.2.1.2 Time

Many of the words which now are perceived as and function as simple temporal adverbs are originally oblique or locative forms of nouns referring to units or periods of time. Several originally spatial adverbs are also used with temporal reference. Interestingly, the root اگ /ag-/ can refer to either future or past time.

- اگے /agge/ 'formerly; going forward (future)'

- اگے نوں /agge nū̃/ 'in future'
- اج /ajj/ 'today'
- اجے /aje/ 'as yet; still; right now; to this day'
- ایدکی ~ ایتکی /ædkī ~ ætkī/ 'this time; this year'
- ایس سال /æs sā́l/ 'during this year'
- کل /kál/ 'yesterday; tomorrow'
- پرسوں /parsõ/ 'day before yesterday; day after tomorrow'
- بھلکے /pàlke/ 'tomorrow'
- پہلاں /pǽlā̃/ 'first; at first; formerly'
- حالے ~ حالی /hāle/ ~ /halī/ 'at present; now; still'
- دنے /dine/, دیہاڑے /deā̀ṛe/ 'by day, during the day'
- راتی /rātī/ 'by night; during the night'
- شامی /šāmī/ 'in the evening'
- سویلے~سویرے /savele ~ savere/ '(early) in the morning'
- ویلے سر~ وقت سر /veḷe sir ~ vakat sir/ 'in time; at the proper time'
- اینے وِچ /enne vicc/ 'in the meantime'
- پچھوں ~ پچھے /picchõ/ ~ /picche/, مگروں /magarõ/ 'afterwards'

5.2.2.1.3 Place

Several of these spatial adverbs can combine with دے /de/ 'of' to form complex postpositions (see Chapter 7). Several are also used with temporal meaning. See also table 5.17.

- نیڑے /neṛe/ 'near',
- اُرھاں /úrā̃/ 'hither, here'
- دور /dūr/ 'far'

- پرھاں /párã̄/ 'the other side, away, at a distance'
- اتے /utte/ 'above, over, on'
- اُتانہ ~ اُتانھ /utã̄/ 'upwards'
- ہیٹھاں /héṭhã̄/, تھلے /thalle/ 'below, downstairs'
- ساھمنے /sā́mṇe/ 'facing, in front of'

5.2.2.1.4 Reason

- کیوں /kyȭ/ 'why?'
- تاں /tã̄/ 'therefore, for this reason'

5.2.2.1.5 Manner

Several manner adverbial phrases involve reduplicative processes.

- دھڑا دھڑ /tàrātàr/ 'in rapid succession'
- فٹافٹ /faṭāfaṭ/, چھیتی /chetī/ 'quickly'
- ہولی ہولی /hɔḷī hɔḷī/ ~ /hɔlī hɔlī/ 'slowly, gradually, carefully'
- گھڑی مڑی /kàṛī muṛī/, بار بار /bār bār/ 'repeatedly'
- پھر، فیر /fir/ 'again'
- کیویں ~ کویں /kīvẽ ~ kivẽ/, کنج /kinj/ 'how?'
- مُڑ مُڑ /muṛ muṛ/ 'again and again'

5.2.2.2 Indefinite adverbials – Panjabi

Indefinite adverbials are closely related to the interrogative and in some cases the relative forms (Table 5.17). Table 5.33 displays interrogative, relative, and indefinite forms of locative and temporal adverbials for Panjabi. Emphatic forms add the inclusive particle وی /vī/ 'also, even' to the basic relative or indefinite forms. Reduplicated indefinite or relative forms convey a distributive rather than a stipulative sense.

Table 5.33: Interrogative, indefinite, relative spatial and temporal adverbs – Panjabi

Form	Place	Time
Interrogative (INT)	کتھے kitthe 'where?'	کد ~ کدوں kad ~ kadõ 'when?'
Relative (REL)	جتھے jitthe 'where ...'	جدوں jadõ 'when ...'
Indefinite (INDEF)	کتے kite 'somewhere'	کدی ~ کدے kadī ~ kade 'sometimes'
REL + وی (EMPHATIC)	جتھے وی jitthe vī 'wherever ...'	جدوں وی jadõ vī 'whenever ...'
INDEF + وی (EMPHATIC)	کتے وی kite vī 'anywhere'	کدی وی ~ کدے وی kadī vī ~ kade vī 'at any time'
REL + INDEF	جتھے کتے jitthe kite 'wherever ...'	جدوں کدے jadõ kade 'whenever ...' جدوں کدی jadõ kadī 'whenever ...'
INDEF reduplicated	کتے کتے kite kite 'here and there'	کدی کدی kadī kadī 'now and then; from time to time'
REL reduplicated	جتھے جتھے jitthe jitthe 'wherever ...'	جدوں جدوں jadõ jadõ 'whenever ...'
INDEF + نہ na + INDEF	کتے نہ کتے kite na kite 'somewhere or other'	کدی نہ کدی kadī na kadī 'sometime or other'
INDEF + NEG	کتے نہیں kite naĩ 'nowhere'	کدی نہیں kadī naĩ 'never'

Table 5.33: (continued)

Form	Place	Time
INDEF + وی vī + NEG (EMPHATIC)	کتے وی نہیں kite vī naĩ 'not anywhere; nowhere'	کدی وی نہیں kadī vī naĩ 'at no time, never'

5.2.3 Saraiki adverbs and adverbial expressions

Saraiki adverbs fall into the same classes as do Hindko and Panjabi forms.

5.2.3.1 Simple adverbs – Saraiki

The following are a few of the most frequently occurring simple adverbs. Unless otherwise indicated, transcriptions are based on Shackle 1976, and our Perso-Arabic spellings reflect those pronunciations.

5.2.3.1.1 Quantity

- ٻہوں /ɓaũ/ 'much, very'
- ڈاڈھی /ɗāḍhī/ 'very, extremely'
- ڈھیر /ḍher/ 'very'
- گھٹ /ghaṭ/ 'less'
- ودھ /vadh/ 'more'
- صرف /sirif/, سکھݨی /sakhṇī/ 'only'

5.2.3.1.2 Time

- ہݨ /huṇ/ 'now'
- ہݨے /huṇe/ 'right now'
- اڄ /aʄ/ 'today'
- کلھ /kalh/ 'yesterday'
- کلتّھوں /kalatthū̃/ 'day before yesterday'
- سدا /sadā/, یکا /yakā/, ہمیشہ /hamešā/ 'always', نِت /nit/ 'always' (Mughal 2010: 550)
- اڄاں /aʄā̃/ , اڄاݨ /aʄāṇ/ 'still, yet'
- صبائیں /sabāhī̃/ 'tomorrow (lit. 'in the morning')'
- سویلے /savele/ 'early'
- ول /val/ 'then, again'
- وت /vat/ 'then (at that time)'
- بعد اِچ /bād ic/ 'later'
- اوڑک /oṛik/ ~ /oṛek/ 'finally'

5.2.3.1.3 Place

- اتے /utte/ 'above'
- تلے /talle/, ہیٹھ /heṭh/ 'below'
- نال /nāl/, سنگ /sang/, کول /kol/, نیڑے /nere/ 'near, nearby'
- پرے /pare/~ پریں /parẽ/ 'far away, beyond, removed; on that side'
- اُرے /ure/ 'on this side'
- ساہمݨے /sāmhṇe/ 'in front of'
- پچھلے پاسے /pichle pase/, پچھوں /pichõ/ 'behind'

5.2.3.1.4 Reason

- کیوں /kyū̃/ 'why?'

5.2.3.1.5 Manner

- مساں /masã̄/ 'hardly, barely'
- ہولے /hɔle/ 'slowly'
- کیویں /kīvẽ/ 'how?'

5.2.3.2 Indefinite adverbials – Saraiki

Saraiki indefinite adverbials formed in various ways are shown in Table 5.34, based on information in Shackle (1976). See Table 5.19 for relative and interrogative forms with which some indefinite forms are constructed. Blank cells indicate that the authors do not have enough information to determine whether or not such forms exist.

Form	Place	Time	Manner
Indefinite (INDEF)	کہیں جاہ / جاء تے kahī̃ jah te 'at some place'	کہیں ویلے kahī̃ vele 'sometime'	کہیں طرح kahī̃ tarah 'in some way'
Indefinite emphatic (INDEF EMPH)	کتھاہیں kithāhī̃ 'wherever'	کڈاہیں kaɗāhī̃ 'whenever'	
REL + INT	جتھاں کتھاں jithā̃ kithā̃ 'wherever …' جیڈے کیڈے jeɗe keɗe 'in whichever direction'		
REL + DISTAL			جیویں تیویں jīvẽ tīvẽ 'somehow or other'
REL + INDEF EMPH		جڈاں کڈاہیں jaɗā̃ kaɗāhī̃ 'whenever …'	
INDEF + نہ + INDEF	کتھاہیں نہ کتھاہیں kithāhī̃ na kithāhī̃ ' somewhere or other'	کڈاہیں نہ کڈاہیں kaɗāhī̃ na kaɗāhī̃ 'sometime or other'	کِوھیں نہ کِوھیں kivhẽ na kivhẽ (Shackle 1976: 66) کہیں نہ کہیں طرحے kahī̃ na kahī̃ tarhe 'somehow or other' (Nasir Abbas Syed)
INDEF + NEG	کتھاہیں نیں kithāhī̃ n(a)ī̃ 'nowhere'	کڈاہیں نیں kaɗāhī̃ n(a)ī̃ 'never'	کِوھیں نیں kivhẽ nī̃ (Shackle 1976: 66) کہیں طرحے نیں kahī̃ tarhe nī̃ 'in no way' (NAS)

Table 5.34: Interrogative, indefinite, relative adverbs – Saraiki

6 Pronouns

6.1 Introduction

Pronouns are words that refer to some nominal element mentioned elsewhere in a discourse or recoverable from context; they take the place of common or proper nouns, noun phrases, or nominal clauses. The general observations in Section 6.1 apply to Hindko, Panjabi, and Saraiki.

6.1.1 Person and number

Person refers to the participants in a verbal interaction: first person refers to the speaker, 'I', second person to the addressee, 'you', and third person to anyone or anything else. Third person pronouns can be either demonstrative (pointing out things), such as English *this*, *these*, *that*, *those* or anaphoric, like *she*, *he*, *it*, *they*, referring to nominal arguments mentioned elsewhere in discourse or recoverable from surrounding context. All three languages have first and second-person personal pronouns. The function of third-person pronouns in Hindko, Saraiki, and Panjabi is filled by the demonstrative pronouns. All three languages have two degrees of distance in their deictic systems and thus have proximal and distal demonstrative pronouns. As in many South Asian languages, plural pronouns and agreement patterns are used to indicate formality or respect. Hindko, Panjabi, and Saraiki each have one second-person plural pronoun, with the following direct case forms: تُسّیں /tussī̃/ Hk, تُسیں /tusī̃/ ~ تُسی /tusī/ Pj, and تُسّاں /tussā̃/ ~ /tusā̃/ Sr.[1] These second-person plural forms are used either with plural reference or as a deferential form of address for individuals in both formal and familiar situations. They are typically used to address elders, adults with whom one is not acquainted, social or professional superiors, as in (6.1), and sometimes by wives to their husbands.

(6.1) تُسی کِتھوں دے او ڈاکٹر صاحب

tusī	*kitth-õ*	*d-e*	*o*	*ḍākṭar*	*sáb*
2PL.DIR	where-ABL	GEN-PL.M	be.PRES.2PL	doctor	sir

'Where are **you (pl.)** from, doctor?' (Pj)

---

[1] The /s/ in the Saraiki forms appears as non-geminated in Shackle (1976) but as geminated in Grierson (1919). Our consultant, UK, maintains that it should be geminated.

The second-person singular pronoun توں /tũ/, used in all three languages, implies minimal social distance, and thus can convey intimacy, informality, or disrespect, depending on the interactional and social context. Typical contexts of use are by parents addressing their children, between close friends, between husband and wife, in song and poetry, or to address God or a beloved person.[2]

6.1.2 Case

As with the form of nouns, the form of pronouns depends on their grammatical function in a sentence—whether subject, direct object, indirect object, or other oblique argument marked by a postposition. In all three languages pronouns have at least direct and oblique forms. Other case relations are usually indicated by postpositions which follow either the oblique or the genitive form. Such functional case marking is accomplished by various postpositions; for example locative relations are usually expressed with the postposition وچ /vic/ ~ /vicc/‘in’, which usually follows the genitive form of the pronoun, for example, اوہ دے وچ /ó de vicc/ ‘in it/him/her’ Pj . With most pronouns, ablative case relations are expressed by oblique or genitive pronominal stems followed by the postposition توں /tõ/ ‘from’ or کولوں /kolõ/ (Pj, Hk, Sr), and have the basic meaning of ‘from X’, e.g. تیرے کولوں /tere kolõ/ ‘from you (SG)’.

Genitive (possessive) forms mark relationships between two nominal arguments—noun and noun, or pronoun and noun—as with میری گڈی /merī gaḍḍī/ ‘my car’ (Pj). In all three languages, genitive forms for both nouns and pronouns are morphologically marked (“black”) adjectives, which change their form to agree with the gender and number of the “possessed” noun that follows them. Thus, even if a speaker is female, for example, she would say میرا گھر /merā kàr/ ‘my house’ (Pj), since گھر /kàr/ ‘house’ is a singular masculine noun. Similarly, a male speaker will say میریاں کتاباں /meriyā̃ katābā̃/ ‘my books’ because کتاباں /katābā̃/ ‘books’ is a feminine plural noun. (For paradigms of marked adjectives, see Section 5.1.1.6).

2 Formality distinctions are observed less in these languages than they are in Urdu, which has three second-person pronouns تُو /tū/(intimate), تم /tum/(familiar), and آپ /āp/(formal, respectful), while these three language have two. The functions of Urdu آپ /āp/ are fulfilled by تُسّیں /tussī̃/ Hk , تُسّی /tusī/ Pj , and تُسّاں /tussā̃/ ~ /tusā̃/ Sr . In these languages the functions that تم /tum/ has in Urdu are distributed between توُں /tū̃/ and تُسّیں /tussī̃/ Hk , تُسی ~ تُسیں /tusī ~ tusī̃/ Pj , and تُسّاں /tussā̃/ ~ /tusā̃/ Sr .

6.2 Personal pronouns

6.2.1 Hindko personal and third person pronouns

Direct, oblique/agentive, and dative/accusative forms of Hindko first, second, and third-person pronouns are given in Table 6.1.[3]

Table 6.1: Hindko personal pronouns

Person	Case	Singular	Plural
1st	Direct	میں mæ̃ 'I'	اسی assī 'we'
	Oblique/Agentive	میں mæ̃ 'I'	اساں assā̃ 'us, we'
	Dative/Accusative	مانہہ mā́̃ 'I, me'	اساں assā̃ 'us'
2nd	Direct	تُوں tū̃ 'you'	تُسی tussī 'you'
	Oblique/Agentive	تُد tud 'you' [4]	تُساں tussā̃ 'you'
	Dative/Accusative	تُداں tudā̃ 'you'	تُساں آں tussā̃ ā̃ 'you'
3rd proximal	Direct	ایہہ é 'he/she/it/this'	ایہے ḗ 'these/they'
	Oblique/Agentive	اِس is 'he/she/him/her/it/this'	اِنہاں ínā̃ 'these/them'

3 Alternate spellings encountered for the third person plural proximal pronoun are ایہ and ایہہ, which are identical to those for the singular form. AWT hears a difference in length between the third person singular proximal pronoun ایہہ /é/ and the third person plural proximal form ایّے /ḗ/. We have represented this in the paradigm in table Table 6.1.

Table 6.1: (continued)

Person	Case	Singular	Plural
	Dative/Accusative	اِس آں isã̄ 'him/her/it/this'	اِنہاں ínã̄ 'these/them'
3rd distal	**Direct**	~ او اوہ o 'he/she/it/that'	او~ اوہ o 'those/them'
	Oblique/Agentive	اُس us 'he/she/him/her/it/that'	اُنہاں únã̄ 'those/them'
	Dative/Accusative	اُس آں usã̄ 'him/her/it/that'	اُنہاں únã̄ 'those/them'

Genitive forms of Hindko personal pronouns are given in Table 6.2. The first and second person singular pronouns have special genitive forms ending in را /-rā/. Genitive forms of first and second person plurals and the third-person (demonstrative) pronouns are formed exactly as for nouns, that is with the postposition دا /dā/ 'of' following the oblique form, forming marked adjectives. For example, اُس دا پُتّر /us dā puttar/ 'his/her son' and اُس دی تِھی /us dī tì̄/ 'his/her daughter'.[5] Alternate forms of the first-person plural possesive forms (see Table 6.2) are found in Sakoon (2002: 163). These are based on an alternate oblique stem سہا- سوُا-~-. The masculine singular form is سُہاڈا ~ سہاڈا /suā̀ḍā ~ sā̀ḍā/ 'our, ours'. All the genitive forms are marked adjectives.

4 Sakoon (2002: 77) gives the second-person singular oblique form as تُدھ /tudh/.

5 Speakers of some other Hindko varieties have the genitive postposition نا /nā/ 'of'.

	Masculine singular	Masculine plural	Feminine singular	Feminine plural
1st person singular	میرا merā 'my, mine'	میرے mere 'my, mine'	میری merī 'my, mine'	میریاں meriyā̃ 'my, mine'
1st person plural	اساں دا assā̃ dā 'our, ours'	اساں دے assā̃ de 'our, ours'	اساں دی assā̃ dī 'our, ours'	اساں دیاں assā̃ diyā̃ 'our, ours'
2nd person singular	تیرا terā 'your, yours'	تیرے tere 'your, yours'	تیری terī 'your, yours'	تیریاں teriyā̃ 'your, yours'
2nd person plural	تُساں دا tussā̃ dā 'your, yours'	تُساں دے tussā̃ de 'your, yours'	تُساں دی tussā̃ dī 'your, yours'	تُساں دیاں tussā̃ diyā̃ 'your, yours'

Table 6.2: Hindko possessive pronouns

6.2.2 Panjabi personal and third person pronouns

Direct, oblique, dative-accusative, and ablative case forms of the personal and third person pronouns are given in Table 6.3. The oblique forms are the base to which most simple postpositions attach. The dative-accusative forms consist of the oblique base followed by the postposition نوں /nū̃/, which marks both indirect objects and the logical subjects of a class of verbs which take experiencer, or non-agentive, subjects; as well as some direct objects.[6] The dative-accusative element is enclitic (unstressed and phonologically dependent on the word it attaches to) in all three languages, hence the tendency to write them together sometimes with pronominal forms, which may foreshadow a development into new case endings. Ablative forms for personal pronouns combine the oblique forms of the pronoun with the postposition توں /tõ/ 'from', giving meanings of 'from me', 'from you, 'from him', etc. Ablative case forms for the first and second-person pronouns are included here; however, they are mostly archaic and currently found mostly in songs and poetry (see 6.2), rather than in everyday prose speech or writing.[7]

6 See Section 9.1.4 for discussion of direct object marking.

7 They do not occur at all in Bashir & Kazmi's (2012) dictionary of contemporary Pakistani Panjabi. Bhatia (1993: 229) points out that in some dialects, the postposition توں /tõ/ appears as تھوں /thõ/ when combined with pronouns (Bhatia 1993: 229). A 2016 internet search indicated

(6.2) کیہڑی گل توں رُسیا ایں میتھوں ، ایسی کیہہ گل ہوئی

kéṛī	*gal*	*tõ*	*rus-iyā*	*ẽ*	***mæ-thõ***	*æsī*
which	matter	from	annoyed-PP.SG.M	be.PRES.2SG	**1SG-ABL**	such-SG.F

kī́	*gal*	*hoī*
what	matter	become.PP.SG.F

'What are you annoyed **with me** for; what happened?' (Pj) (http://www.hamariweb.com/poetries/Poetry.aspx?id=41699)

Table 6.3: Panjabi direct, oblique, and ablative case forms of personal pronouns

Person	Case	Singular	Plural
1st	Direct	میں mæ̃	اسی ~ اسیں asī ~ asī̃
	Oblique	مے mæ	اساں ~ سا sā ~ asā̃
	Dative/accusative	میٹوں mænū̃	سانوں sānū̃
	Ablative	میتوں ~ میتھوں mætõ ~ mæthõ	ساتوں ~ ساتھوں sātõ ~ sāthõ
2nd	Direct	توں tū̃	تُسی ~ تُسیں tusī ~ tusī̃
	Oblique	تے tæ	تُہا ~ تُساں tuȁ- ~ tusā̃
	Dative/accusative	تینوں tænū̃	تُہانوں tuȁnū̃
	Ablative	تیتوں ~ تیتھوں tætõ ~ tæthõ	تُہاتوں ~ تُہاتھوں tuȁtõ ~ tuȁthõ
3rd proximal	Direct	ایہ ~ ایہہ é	ایہ ~ ایہہ é

that the variants with aspirated تھوں /thõ/ occur more frequently than those with unaspirated توں /tõ/.

Table 6.3: (continued)

Person	Case	Singular	Plural
	Oblique	ایہ ~ ایہہ ~ ایس é ~ æs	ایہناں énā̃
	Dative/accusative	ایہنوں énū̃	ایہناں نوں énā̃nū̃
	Ablative	ایس توں æs tõ	ایہناں توں énā̃ tõ
3rd distal	**Direct**	اوہ ó	اوہ ó
	Oblique	اوہ ~ اوس ó ~ os	اوہناں ónā̃
	Dative/accusative	اوہنوں ~ اوس نوں os nū̃ ~ ónū̃	اوہناں نوں ónā̃ nū̃
	Ablative	اوس توں os tõ	اوہناں توں ónā̃ tõ

The alternations between oblique ایہہ /é/ vs. اس /æs/ and اوہ /ó/ vs. اوس /os/ are frequent in Panjabi. Shackle (1972) notes that the اس /æs/ and اوس /os/ forms appear primarily in written Panjabi. There is disagreement about the presence of tone in the اس /æs/ and اوس /os/ forms.

Ablative spatial relations in Panjabi are usually expressed with a genitive form followed by the postposition کولوں /kolõ/ 'from X'.

Although in Lahore Panjabi the first and second-person plural direct forms are usually اسی /assī/ and تُسی /tussī/, respectively, اساں /asā̃/ 'we.OBL' and تُساں /tusā̃/ 'you.OBL' sometimes occur. These forms are usually associated with more westerly varieties. These full oblique pronouns are distinct from the oblique bases سا /sā-/ '1PL' and توا /tuā̀-/ '2PL' to which Level II postpositions are attached.

In Panjabi, اوہ /ó/ 'he, she, that, it, they' and اوہناں /ónā̃/ 'him, her, them' are the distal (remote) singular and plural direct, and plural oblique demonstrative forms, respectively; while ایہہ /é/ 'he, she, this, they', and ایہناں /énā̃/ 'these, them' are the proximal (near) forms. They take the same case-marking postpositions as the personal pronouns. For more on the uses of various postpositions, see Chapter 7; for more on dative subjects, see Section 9.1.3.2.

In tenses constructed on the perfective participle, Panjabi sometimes uses the grammatical postposition نے /ne/ to mark a third-person agent/subject of a transitive clause. If نے /ne/ occurs, the noun or pronoun it precedes is in the oblique case. When the agent/subject is marked with نے /ne/, the verb agrees with the direct object, as in 6.3, provided that it is not marked with the dative-accusative postposition نوں /nū̃/. If it is so marked, the verb takes default masculine singular agreement. This pattern of case marking is referred to as split-ergative (see Section 9.1.2.2). This happens only with third-person subjects; first and second-person subjects remain in their direct case form.

(6.3) اوہ نے گڈّی کرائے تے لتّی

ó	*ne*	*gaḍḍī*	*kirāy-e*	*te*	*litt-ī*
3SG	ERG	cart[F]	rent-OBL	on	take.PP-SG.F

'He rented a cart.' (Pj) (Bhatia 1993: 223)

This use of نے /ne/ to mark third-person agents in ergative contexts appears to be an influence of Urdu or (in India) of Hindi, as it is found only sometimes in Lahore Panjabi, and is not at all characteristic of Hindko or Saraiki. According to Bashir and Kazmi 2012: 655, fn 12, "The 3rd person singular oblique pronoun + postposition نے combination ایہنے and اوہنے are commonly replaced with the oblique pronouns ایس and اوس. The 3rd person plural oblique pronouns ایہناں and اوہناں are also commonly used without the postposition نے."

Genitive forms of pronouns are marked adjectives (as described in Section 5.1.1.6), which agree in number, gender, and case with the noun modified (the "possessed" noun). In the third person, the oblique pronominal stem combines with the genitive postposition دا /dā/ 'of' just as with nouns, with the postposition دا /dā/ inflecting as a marked adjective. These adjectival genitive forms are presented in Table 6.4.

	Masculine noun modified		Feminine noun modified	
	Singular	**Plural**	**Singular**	**Plural**
1st person singular	میرا merā	میرے mere	میری merī	میریاں meriyā̃
1st person plural	ساڈا sāḍā	ساڈے sāḍe	ساڈی sāḍī	ساڈیاں sāḍiyā̃
2nd person singular	تیرا terā	تیرے tere	تیری terī	تیریاں teriyā̃
2nd person plural	تُہاڈا tuȁḍā	تُہاڈے tuȁḍe	تُہاڈی tuȁḍī	تُہاڈیاں tuȁḍiyā̃
3rd person proximal, singular	ایہ دا ~ ایہدا ~ ایس دا édā ~ æs dā	ایہ دے ~ ایہدے ~ ایس دے éde ~ æs de	ایہدی ~ ایس دی ǽdī ~ æs dī	ایہدیاں ~ ایس دیاں ǽdiyā̃ ~ æs diyā̃
3rd person proximal, plural	ایہناں دا ǽnā̃ dā	ایہناں دے ǽnā̃ de	ایہنان دی ǽnā̃ dī	ایہنان دیاں ǽnā̃ diyā̃
3rd person distal, singular	اوہ دا ~ اوہدا ~ اوس دا os dā ~ ódā	اوہدے ~ اوہ دے ~ اوس دے os de ~ óde	اوہ دی ~ اوہدی ~ اوس دی os dī ~ ódī	اوہ دیاں ~ اوہدیاں ~ اوس دیاں os diyā̃ ~ ódiyā̃
3rd person distal, plural	اوہناں دا ónā̃ dā	اوہناں دے ónā̃ de	اوہناں دی ónā̃ dī	اوہنان دیاں ónā̃ diyā̃

Table 6.4: Genitive forms of pronouns, Panjabi

6.2.3 Saraiki personal and third person pronouns

Saraiki personal pronouns are presented in Table 6.5. According to our consultant, the final vowel of the second person plural pronoun تساں /tussā̃/is pronounced as short, tense, and nasalized /ã/. Perso-Arabic spelling conventions, however, force this to be represented with ا /alif/, which usually represents a long /ā/. We represent it in Roman with the long vowel as shown in the table following the established tradition, both with writers who have written Saraiki forms in roman representation and those who write Perso-Arabic forms.

For full pronouns, dative-accusative relations are indicated by the postposition کوں /kū̃/, which follows the oblique form of the pronoun. Notice that the nasalization present in the full first and second-person singular direct forms is absent in the oblique stem used before postpositions, e.g. میکوں /mæ-kū̃/'(to) me'. Ablative meaning is generally conveyed by the genitive form of the pronoun followed by the postposition کولوں /kolū̃/, which consists of the nominal form کول /kol/ 'vicinity' plus the ablative ending وں /-ū̃/. Various adverbial relations are indicated by distinct postpositions. For the first and second-person singular and plural pronouns, the direct and agentive forms are the same. For the third-person pronouns, however, the agentive form is the same as the oblique. The possessive (genitive) forms are adjectival.

Table 6.5: Saraiki personal pronouns

Person	Case	Singular	Plural
1st	**Direct**	میں mæ̃ 'I'	اساں ~ آپاں assã ~ āpã (Southern Bahawalpur) 'we'
	Oblique	مے mæ 'I'	اساں ~ سا assã ~ sā 'us'
	Agentive	میں mæ̃ 'I'	اساں assã 'we'
	Possessive	میڈا meɗā 'my, mine'	ساڈا ~ اساڈا sāɗā ~ asāɗā 'our, ours'
2nd	**Direct**	توں tū̃ 'you'	تُساں tussã 'you'
	Oblique	تے tæ 'you'	تُہا tuhā 'you'
	Agentive	توں تیں tū ~ tæ̃ 'you'	تُساں tussã 'you'

Table 6.5: (continued)

Person	Case	Singular	Plural
	Possessive	تیڈا teḍā 'your, yours'	تُہاڈا tuhāḍā 'your, yours'
3rd proximal	Direct	اے e ~ æ 'he/she/it'	اے e ~ æ 'they'
	Oblique	ہیں ~ ایں hĩ ~ ĩ 'he/she/it'	اِنہاں inhā̃ 'they, these'
	Agentive	ایں ĩ 'he/she/it'	اِنہاں inhā̃ 'they'
	Possessive	ایں دا ĩ dā 'his/hers/its'	اِنہاں دا inhā̃ dā 'theirs'
3rd distal	Direct	او o 'he/she/it'	او o 'they'
	Oblique	ہُوں ~ اوں hũ ~ ũ 'he/she/it'	اُنہاں unhā̃ 'they, these'
	Agentive	اوں ũ 'he/she/it'	اُنہاں unhā̃ 'they'
	Possessive	اوں دا ũ dā 'his/hers/its'	اُنہاں دا ~ اُنہیں دا unhā̃ dā ~ unhē̃ dā 'theirs'

6.3 Reflexive pronouns

A basic reflexive pronominal element occurring in all three languages is based on the element آپ /āp/ 'self'. This element can function either as a true reflexive pronoun or as an emphatic marker. In addition, the Persian-origin خود /xud/ 'self' is increasingly used in all three languages in urban contexts.

See Section 5.1.3.6 for discussion of reflexive adjectives.

6.3.1 Hindko reflexive pronoun

In Hindko the following forms are found: آپ /āp/, آپا ~ آپاں /āpā ~ āpā̃/, and آپے /āp-e/ 'self-OBL'. For some case functions, postpositions following the adjectival form are used, as in examples 6.4 and 6.5. In addition to آپ /āp/, emphatic forms include, آپو /āpo/, آپو آپ /āpo āp/, آپے /āpe/, and آپئی /āpaī/ (Sakoon 2002: 1). Example 6.6 illustrates the emphatic function of آپ /āp/ 'self'.

(6.4) اُس اپڑے اسطے بوہا کھولیا تے اندر آیا

us	***apṛe***	*āste*	*bū́ā*	*khol-iyā*	*te*	*andar*
3SG.OBL	**REFL.GEN**	for	door	open-PP.SG.M	and	inside

ā-yā
come-PP.SG.M

'He opened the door for **himself** and came in.' (Hk) (AWT)

(6.5) اُناں معاملہ آپے بچ رخیا

únā̃	*māmlā*	***āp-e***	*bic*	*rax-iyā*
3PL.OBL	matter	**REFL-SG.M.OBL**	among	keep-PP.SG.M

'They kept the matter among **themselves**.' (Hk) (AWT)

(6.6) میں آپ دیخ رہیاں

mǣ̃	***āp***	*dex-ryā̃*
1SG	**REFL**	see-CONT.II.PRES.SG.M.1SG

'I am seeing it **myself**.' (Hk) (AWT)

6.3.2 Panjabi reflexive pronouns

Panjabi has several forms from the reflexive element آپ /āp/ 'self', for instance آپی، آپے، آپو، آپوں /āpī, āpe, āpo, āpõ/, the meaning of which is controlled by the grammatical or semantic subject of the sentence. It is used both as a reflexive pronoun (as in 6.7 and 6.8) and as an emphatic element (as in 6.9 and 6.10). In oblique contexts آپنے آپ /āpṇe āp/ usually appears with postpositions in Panjabi and Saraiki.

The genitive, or possessive, form of آپ /āp/ is آپنا /āpṇā/ 'self's'. Like all marked adjectives, the genitive reflexive declines for number, gender, and case, but not for person. (See Section 5.1.3 for forms and examples.) Repeating the reflexive pronoun after its genitive form, as in آپنے آپ /āpṇe āp/ 'oneself', gives an emphatic meaning, indicating that someone did something as a result of his own action, as in 6.7.

(6.7) اوہ نے آپنے آپ نوں بدنام کیتا سی

ó	*ne*	***āpṇe.āp***	*nū̃*	*badnām*	*kīt-ā*	*sī*
he	ERG	**REFL**	ACC	disgraced	do.PP-SG.M	be.PST.3SG

'He disgraced **himself.**' (Pj) (EB)

When followed by most postpositions, including توں /tõ/ 'from', and نال /nāḷ/ 'with', reflexive pronouns appear in the genitive oblique form, as do other nouns and pronouns. An example is shown in 6.8.

(6.8) منڈے تے کڑیاں کمپیوٹر نوں آپنے نال رکھدے نیں

mū̃ḍ-e	*te*	*kuṛiy-ā̃*	*kampyūṭar*	*nū̃*	***āpṇ-e***	*nāḷ*
boy-PL.M	and	girl-PL.F	computer	ACC	**REFL-SG.M.OBL**	with

rakkh-d-e	*nẽ*
keep-IP-PL.M	be.PRES.3PL

'Boys and girls keep (the) computers with **themselves.**' (Pj) (Chaudhry 1999: 15)

(6.9) میں آپی کرانگا

mæ̃	***āp-ī***	*kar-ā̃-g-ā*
1SG	**REFL-EMPH**	do-SBJV.1SG-FUT-SG.M

'I (M) will do it **myself.**' (Pj) (EB)

(6.10) سلیم آپی آیا

salīm	***āp-ī***	*ā-yā*
Salim	**REFL-EMPH**	come-PP.SG.M

'Salim came **himself** [rather than sending someone else].' (Pj) (EB)

خود /xud/ 'self', of Persian origin, has a similar function; like آپ /āp/, it is often used in conjunction with the emphatic particle ای /-ī/, as in 6.11, and can sometimes be used as a true reflexive, as in 6.12.

(6.11) میں خود ای آواں گا

mæ̃	***xud-ī***	*ā-vã-g-ā*
1SG	**REFL-EMPH**	come-SBJV.1SG-FUT-SG.M

'I will come **myself** [without assistance, or sending someone else].' (Pj) (EB)

(6.12) دور رہ کے خود نوں سزاواں دتیاں

dūr	*ræ̃*	*ke*	***xud***	***nū̃***	*sazā-vã̄*	*ditt-iyã̄*
far	live	CP	REFL	ACC	punishment-PL.F	give.PP-PL.F

'Staying far away (someone) has punished **himself.**' (Pj) (http://www.hamariweb.com/poetries/Poetry.aspx?id=40257"www.hamariweb.com/poetries/Poetry.aspx?id=40257)

6.3.3 Saraiki reflexive pronouns

Shackle (1976: 59) gives the following forms for the Saraiki reflexive pronoun: آپ /āp/(direct), آپݨے آپ /āpṇe āp/ (oblique), آپت /āpat/(locative plural), as well as آپے /āpe/(emphatic). Example 6.13 illustrates both the direct form آپ /āp/ in its emphatic function and the adjectival genitive form اپݨا /apṇā/ 'self's'.[8]

8 This example is given as in Zahoor 2009, showing the full form of the present tense of 'be', yielding a somewhat emphatic sense. Usually the short form appears as auxiliary, in non-emphatic contexts.

(6.13) میں اپݨے کپڑے آپ بݨیندی ہاں

mæ̃	***apṇ-e***	*kapṛ-e*	***āp***	*baṇ-e-nd-ī*	*hā̃*
1SG	**REFL-PL.M**	clothes-PL.M	**EMPH**	make-PF-IP-SG.F	be.PRES.1SG

'I make **my** clothes **myself.**' (Sr) (Zahoor 2009: 49)

The Persian-origin خود /xud/ 'self' is also used in Saraiki, as shown in 6.14.

(6.14) میں خوُد بݨیساں

mæ̃	***xud***	*baṇ-e-s-ā̃*
1SG	**REFL**	make-PF-FUT-1SG

'I will make (them) **myself.**' (Sr) (Shackle 1976: 171)

6.4 Reciprocals

Two constructions to express reciprocal states or actions are used in all three languages. The first consists of the pronouns آپے /āpe/ Hk , آپس /āpas/ Hk Pj , آپو /āpo/ Pj , and آپت /āpat/ Sr , which are developments of the reflexive pronoun آپ /āp/ 'self'. The second construction involves the words 'one ... other' in forms specific to each language.

6.4.1 Hindko reciprocal pronouns

The first type appears in example 6.15.

(6.15) آپے بچ لڑنا جھگڑنا

āp-e	*bic*	*laṛnā*	*càgaṛnā*
self-OBL	among	fight-INF	quarrel-INF

'To fight among **(one's)selves.**' (Hk) (bugyaran.blogspot.com/2007/11/blog-post.html)

Examples 6.16 and 6.17 show two examples of the type based on 'one' and 'the other': ہکی دوُے /hikī dūe/ ~ ہکی دوُہے /hikī dū́e/ 'each other'.

(6.16) اسی ہکی دوہے آں دیخ رہے ایہے آں

assī	***hikī***	***dū̃e***	*ā̃*	*dex*	*ré*	*éye-ā̃*
1PL.DIR	**one**	**other**	ACC	look	remain.PP.PL.M	be.PST.PL.M-1PL

'We were looking at **each other**.' (Hk) (AWT)

(6.17) اساں ہکی دوہے دی مجبوری آں سمجھنڑا چاہی دے

ass-ā̃	***hikī***	***dū̃e***	*d-ī*	*majbūrī*	*ā̃*	*samaj-ṛ̃-ā*
1PL-OBL	**one**	**other**	GEN-SG.F	constraint[F]	ACC	understand-INF-SG.M

cāh-ī-d-æ
want-PASS-IP-SG.M+be.PRES

'We should understand **each other's** constraints.' (Hk) (AWT)

6.4.2 Panjabi reciprocal pronouns

The pronoun آپو /āpo/ 'selves' or آپس /āpas/ 'each other, ourselves' appears in contexts of mutually affecting states or mutually conducted actions. A frequent collocation involving a reciprocal state is آپس دی گل /āpas dī gal/ 'a matter among ourselves', as in example 6.18.

(6.18) آپس دی گل سب دے سامھنے نئیں کریدی

āpas	*d-ī*	*gal*	*sáb*	*de*	*sā̃mṇ-e*	*nī̃*
REFL	GEN-SG.F	matter[F]	all	GEN-SG.M	presence-OBL	NEG

kar-ī-d-ī
do-PASS-IP-SG.F

'One shouldn't discuss **private** matters in front of others.' (Pj) (www.urduweb.org/mehfil/threads/54043)

In some cases, it is used with a sense of reciprocal action, as in 6.19.

(6.19) اوآپس وچ نہیں بولدے

    ó   **āpas**   vicc   nī̃   bol-d-e
    3PL **REFL** in   NEG speak-IP-PL.M

    'They do not talk with **each other**.' (Pj) (Bhatia 1993: 138)

Example 6.20 illustrates use of آپو /āpo/.[9]

(6.20) امریکا پاکستان دا پیار تے نہیں خرید سکدا پر آپو وچ عزت دا رشتہ بن سکدا ہے

    amrīkā   pākistān   d-ā   pyār   te   nā̃ī   xarīd   sak-d-ā
    America Pakistan GEN-M.SG love TOP NEG buy   be.able-IP-SG.M

    par   **āpo**   vic   izzat   d-ā   rištā   ban
    but   **REFL** in   respect GEN-M.SG relationship be.made

    sak-d-ā   e
    be.able-IP-SG.M be.PRES.3SG

    'America cannot buy Pakistan's love, but a relationship of **mutual** respect can be established.' (Pj) (http://www.wichaar.com/news/117/ARTICLE/11785/2009-01-29.html)

Reciprocity can also be expressed using the phrase اک دوجے /ikk dūjje/ 'one another' followed by a postposition, as in 6.21 and 6.22.

(6.21) اک دوجے نال بھائی چارہ رکھنا چاہیدا اے

    ikk   **dūj-e**   nāḷ   pāīcāra   rakh-ṇ-ā
    one **other-OBL** with brotherhood[M] keep-INF-SG.M

    cā̃-ī-d-ā   e
    want-PASS-IP-SG.M be.PRES.3SG

    'People should maintain brotherly relations with **one another**.' (Pj) (https://pnb.wikipedia.org/wiki/%D8%A7%D9%86%D8%B3%D8%A7%D9%86%DB%8C_%D8%AD%D9%82)

---

[9] Based on its frequent appearance with وچ /vicc/ 'in', Cummings and Bailey (1912: 53) consider آپو /āpo/ as a locative plural. The same reasoning apparently underlies Shackle's designation of Sr آپت /āpat/ as a locative plural.

(6.22) دوویں ہر ویلے اک دوجے دیاں غلطیاں لبھدے رہندے نیں

do-vẽ	*har*	*veḷ-e*	***ikk***	***dū-je***	*d-iyā̃*	*galti-yā̃*
two-all	each	time-OBL	**one**	**other-OBL**	GEN-PL.F	error-PL.F

lắb-d-e	*rǽn-d-e*	*nẽ*
find-IP-PL.M	remain-IP-PL.M	be.PRES.3PL

'Both of them are always finding fault in **each other.**' (Pj) (Bashir and Kazmi 2012: 44)

6.4.3 Saraiki reciprocal pronouns

In Saraiki, the reciprocal pronoun is آپت /āpat/ (Mughal 2010: 19). It occurs most frequently in the collocation آپت وِچ /apat vic/, or /apatic/in colloquial speech, 'among selves', as in 6.23.[10]

(6.23) اساں جڈاں آپت وچ علمی ڳالھیں کریندے ہئیں تاں اپݨی زبان استعمال کریندے ہئیں

assā̃	*jaɗā̃*	***āpat***	***vic***	*ilmī*	*ɠālh-ī̃*	*kar-e-nd-e*
1PL	when	**REFL**	**among**	scholarly	word-PL	do-PF-IP-PL.M

haī̃	*tā̃*	*apṇ-ī*	*zabān*	*istemāl*	*kar-e-nd-e*
be.PRES.1PL	then	REFL.GEN-SG.F	language[F]	use	do-PF-IP-PL.M

haī̃
be.PRES.1PL

'When we discuss scholarly matters **among ourselves,** (then) we use our own language.' (Sr) (http://sunjjan.blogspot.com/2015_02_01_archive.html)

Forms based on 'one' and 'the other' are also employed, as shown in 6.24, 6.25.

(6.24) ہک دوجھے نال نہ بھڑو

hik	***dūjh-e***	*nāl*	*na*	*bhiṛ-o*
one	**other-OBL**	with	NEG	quarrel-IMP.2PL

'Don't quarrel with **each other.**' (Sr) (UK)

10 This form also appears in Wagha (1998: 316) and Shackle (1972: 117). Shackle (1976: 59) considers it the locative plural of the reflexive pronoun آپ /āp/.

(6.25) او ہمیشہ ہک مے اچ نقص کڈھے دے رہندن

o	*hameša*	***hik***	***mæ***	*ic*	*nuks*	*kaḍh-e-d-e*	*rahn-d-ĕ-n*
3PL	always	**one**	**other**	in	fault	find-PF-IP-PL.M	remain-IP-PL.M-3PL

'They are always finding fault with **each other.**'[11] (Sr) (UK)

(6.26) او ہمیشہ ہک ٻئے دییں غلطییں دی ڳول اچ رہ ویندن

o	*hameša*	***hik***	***ɓæ***	*d-iyĩ*	*ɣalti-yĩ*	*d-ī*	*ɠol*
3PL	always	**one**	**other**	GEN-PL.F	mistake-PL.F	GEN-SG.F	search[F]

ic	*rah*	*ven-d-ĕn*
in	remain	go-IP-3PL

'They are always finding fault with **each other.**' (Sr) (NAS)

Nasir Abbas Syed (p.c.) points out that many speakers have the form of 'other' with an initial implosive bilabial /ɓ/ , as in 6.26. This form is derived etymologically from Saraiki ɓiā ∼ ɓiyā or Sindhi ɓā, '2'.

6.5 Interrogative pronouns

All interrogative pronouns and other question words in these languages begin with ک /k-/. Where sources differ on orthography or pronunciation, variants are given in the tables.

6.5.1 Hindko interrogative pronouns

The forms for کوڑ /kɔɽ̃ / 'who' and کے /ke/ 'what' are given in Table 6.6 and Table 6.7, respectively.

Sentences 6.27, 6.28, and 6.29 illustrate the direct form, the oblique singular, and the oblique plural of کوڑ /kɔɽ̃ / 'who'. Notice that the agents of these perfective transitive sentences occur in the oblique form with no postposition.

11 The vowel sound in the final syllable of ویندن in example 6.26and رہندن in example 6.25, is a phonetically short /ĕ/, represented in Perso-Arabic as /i/ because of Perso-Arabic writing conventions.

Case/Number	Singular	Plural
Direct (= nominative)	کونڑ kɔr̃ 'who?'	کونڑ kɔr̃ 'who?'
Oblique	کِس kis 'who, whom?'	کِنہاں kínã̄ 'who, whom?'

Table 6.6: Hindko interrogative pronoun کونڑ /kɔr̃/ 'who'

Case/Number	Singular	Plural
Direct (= nominative)	کے ke 'what?'	کے ke 'what?'
Oblique	کِس kis 'what?'	کِنہاں kínã̄ 'what?'

Table 6.7: Hindko interrogative pronoun کے /ke/ 'what'

(6.27) کونڑ ایہا

kɔr̃ *éy-ā*
who.DIR be.PST-SG.M
'**Who** was it?' (Hk) (AWT)

(6.28) او تد کِس کولوں کہدا ایہا

o *tud* ***kis*** *kolõ* *kì-dā* *éyā*
that 2SG.OBL **who.SG.OBL** from take-PP.SG.M be.PST.SG.M
'From **whom** did you get/buy that?' (Hk) (AWT)

(6.29) پولیس چوکی تے کنہاں حملہ کیتا

polīs	*cokī*	*te*	***kínā̃***	*hamlā*	*kīt-ā*
police	post	on	**who.PL.OBL**	attack[M]	do.PP-SG.M

‘**Who** (PL) attacked the police post?’ (Hk) (AWT)

Example 6.30 illustrates the use of کے /ke/ ‘what?’.

(6.30) توں کے کرسیں جے تیرا جہاز لیٹ ہو گیا

tū̃	***ke***	*kar-s-ǣ*	*je*	*ter-ā*	*jàz*	*leṭ*	*ho*
2SG	**what**	do-FUT-2SG	if	2SG.GEN-SG.M	plane[M]	late	become

ga-yā
go-PP.SG.M

‘**What** will you do if your flight is late?’ (Hk) (AWT)

6.5.2 Panjabi interrogative pronouns

The interrogative pronoun کون /kauṇ/ ‘who’ inflects for number and case, as does its impersonal counterpart, کیہہ ~ کیہ /kī́/ ‘what’. The forms are shown in Table 6.8.

Case marking for the interrogative pronouns functions the same as for personal pronouns. Example 6.31 illustrates the direct singular form of کون /kauṇ ~ kɔṇ/ ‘who’. Pronunciation of the vowel varies between the simple vowel /ɔ/ and the diphthongal /au/.

(6.31) لکھے نوں کون ٹال سکدا اے

likh-e	*nū̃*	***kɔṇ***	*ṭāl*	*sak-d-ā*	*e*
write-PP.SG.M.OBL	ACC	**who**	avoid	be.able-IP-SG.M	be.PRES.3SG

‘**Who** can avoid what is written?’ (Pj) (Bashir and Kazmi 2012: 201)

Like third-person personal pronouns, interrogative pronouns can also take the ergative case marker نے /ne/ to mark the agent in perfective forms of transitive verbs, as in 6.32. In both examples 6.31 and 6.32 the interrogative word forms a rhetorical question with a strong negative implication. Example 6.33 below, however, is a genuine information-seeking question.

	Personal		Impersonal	
	Singular	**Plural**	**Singular**	**Plural**
Direct	کون kauṇ ~ kɔṇ	کون kauṇ ~ kɔṇ	کیہ ~ کیہہ kī̃	کیہ ~ کیہہ kī̃
Oblique	کس kis کہ kí	کہناں kínā̃	کہ kah	کہن kán
Ergative	کہنے kíne کس نے kis ne	کہناں نے kínā̃ (ne)	کہنے káne کس نے kas ne	
With نوں **nū̃**	کہنوں kínū̃ کسنوں kisnū̃	کہناں نوں kínā̃ nū̃	کہنوں kánū̃	کہنوں kánū̃

Table 6.8: Interrogative pronouns کون /kauṇ ~ kɔṇ/ 'who' and کیہ ~ کیہہ /kī̃/ 'what'

(6.32) بھلک کہنے دیکھی اے

pàlak	***kí-ne***	*dekh-ī*	*e*
future[F]	**who.OBL-ERG**	see.PP-SG.F	be.PRES.3SG

'**Who** has seen the future?' (Pj) (Bashir and Kazmi 2012: 124)

The interrogative adjective کیہڑا /kéṛā/ 'who, what, which' is also frequently used substantively as a pronoun, meaning 'who'. It has the same distribution as the interrogative pronoun کون /kauṇ/ 'who', but only کیہڑا /kéṛā/ declines for both gender and number as well as case. See Example 6.33.

(6.33) اوہ کیہڑیاں نیں

ó	***kéṛ-iyā̃***	*nẽ*
those	who-PL.F	be.PRES.3.PL

'**Who** are they (those girls/women)?' (Pj) (EB)

6.5.3 Saraiki interrogative pronouns

Table 6.9 and Table 6.10 list the Saraiki personal and impersonal interrogative pronouns. The nasalization present in کیں /kæ̃/, the oblique singular form of کون /kaon/ 'who', disappears before the dative/accusative postposition کوں /kū̃/. Consequently, spelled-out forms with the dative/accusative postposition کوں /kū̃/ and the genitive (possessive) form of the pronoun, are given. As in Panjabi, the interrogative adjective کیڑھا ~ کیرھا /keṛhā ~ kerhā/ frequently functions pronominally.

Case/person-number	Singular	Plural
Direct	کون kaon	کون kaon
Oblique	کیں kæ̃	کِنہاں ~ کنھاں ~ کِنہیں kinhā ~ kinhẽ̃
Dative/accusative (marks some direct objects)	کیکوں / کے کوں kæ kū̃	کِنہاں کوں ~ کِنہیں کوں kinhā̃ kū̃ ~ kinhẽ kū̃
Genitive	کیں دا kæ̃ dā	کنھاں ~ کنہاں دا ~ کِنہیں دا kinhā̃ dā ~ kinhẽ dā

Table 6.9: Interrogative pronoun کون /kon (~kaon)/ 'who' (Shackle 1976: 60)

Case/person-number	Singular	Plural
Direct (= nominative)	کیا kyā	کیا kyā
Oblique	کیں kæ̃	کنھاں ~ کنہاں kinhā̃

Table 6.10: Interrogative pronoun کیا /kyā/ 'what'

Example 6.34 illustrates the direct case form of کون /kaon/ 'who'; 6.35 shows the oblique case form marking the agent of a transitive perfective[12]; and 6.36 shows the oblique form with a postposition.

(6.34) کون آ ڳے

kaon	*ā*	*ɠæ*
who.DIR	come	go.PP.be.PRES+3SG.M

'**Who** has come?' (Sr) (UK)

(6.35) میچ کئیں جیتے

mæc	***kaĩ/kæ̃***	*jī-tæ*
match(M)	**who.OBL**	win-PP-SG.M+be.PRES

'**Who** won the match?' (Sr) (Zahoor 2009: 46)

(6.36) اے کیندے کنوں گھدی

e	***kæ̃-de***	*kanū̃*	*ghi-d-ī*
this	**who.OBL-GEN**	from	take-PP-SG.F

'From **whom** did you buy this?' (Sr) (UK)

Sentence 6.37 shows کیا /kyā/ 'what' as a direct object.

(6.37) توں کیا کریسیں جے تیڈی فلایٹ چرکیں ہووے

tū̃	***kyā***	*kar-e-s-æ̃*	*je*	*teɗ-ī*	*flāiṭ*	*cirkī̃*
2SG	**what**	do-PF-FUT-2SG	if	2SG.GEN-SG.F	flight[F]	late

ho-ve
be-SBJV.3SG

'**What** will you do if your flight is late?' (Sr) (UK)

6.6 Indefinite pronouns

The basic indefinite pronouns in all three languages begin with ک /k/, since they have developed from the OIA interrogatives.[13]

12 Nasir Abbas Syed suggests that this is Urdu-influenced usage. He suggests jītie and jittie 'won' as more characteristically Saraiki forms.
13 See Masica (1991: 255).

6.6.1 Hindko indefinite pronouns

The Hindko indefinite pronoun/adjective کُئی /kuī/ 'a, some, any' is presented in Table 6.11. The form کِسی /kisī/ appears to be an emphatic form of the oblique form, کِسے /kise/. Additionally, AWT gives the form کِرے /kire/ as an alternate for کِسے.

Case/Number	Singular	Plural
Direct (= nominative)	کُئی kuī 'a, some'	کُجھ kúj 'some'
Oblique	کِسے ~ کِرے kise ~ kire 'a, some'	کُجھ kúj 'some'

Table 6.11: Indefinite pronoun/adjective کُئی /kuī/ 'a, some, any'

The direct form کُئی /kuī/ appears as the subject of an intransitive sentence in 6.38. The oblique form کِسے /kise/ is used as the agent of the transitive verb 'steal' in the present perfect tense in example 6.39, and as the object of the dative postposition آں /ã/ in 6.40. Example 6.40 also illustrates the compound verb دے چھوڑ /de choṛ/ 'give-leave' in the future/presumptive perfect.

(6.38) جُدوں تُسی بیمار ایہیوتُساں دیکھڑے آں کُئی نئیں آیا

judõ	*tussī*	*bimār*	*éye-o*	*tussā̃*	*dex-ṛ-e*	*ā̃*
when	2PL	ill	be.PST.PL.M-2PL	2PL.OBL	see-INF-OBL	DAT

kuī	*naĩ*	*ā-yā*
anyone.DIR	NEG	come-PP.SG.M

'When you were ill, **no one** came to visit you.' (Hk) (AWT)

(6.39) کِسے میری منجھ چُھپائی اے

kise	*mer-ī*	*mā̃j*	*chupā-ī*	*e*
someone.OBL	1SG.GEN-SG.F	buffalo.SG.F	steal.PP-SG.F	be.PRES.3SG

'**Someone** has stolen my buffalo.' (Hk) (AWT)

(6.40) تُد ضرور کِسے آں کتاب دے چھوڑی ہوسی

tud *zarūr* ***kise*** *ā̃* *kitāb* *de* *choṛ-ī*
2SG.OBL definitely **someone.OBL** DAT book[F] give leave-PP.SG.F

ho-s-ī
be-FUT-3SG

'You must have given the book to **someone**.' (Hk) (AWT)

Examples 6.41 and 6.42 illustrate the use of indefinite pronouns with inclusive meaning جو کُجھ /jo kúj/ 'whatever' and جو وی ~ جو بی /jo vī ~ jo bī/ 'whatever (at all)'

(6.41) اُس جو کُج ٹہاکیاں بچ دیکھیا بُہوں ڈراوڑا ایہیا

us ***jo.kúj*** *ṭȁk-eā̃* *bic* *dex-iyā* *báū̃*
3SG.OBL **whatever** mountain-PL.OBL in see-PP.SG.M very

ḍarāuṛ-ā *éy-ā*
frightening-SG.M be.PST-SG.M

'**Whatever** he saw in the mountains was very frightening.' (Hk) (AWT)

(6.42) تُداں ہس طرحاں نیئں کرناں چاہی دا پہانویں لوک جووی آخن

tud-ā̃ *his* *tarā̃* *nī̃* *karnā̃* *cā̃-ī-d-ā* *pā̃vẽ*
2SG.OBL-DAT this way not do.INF want-PASS-IP-SG.M whether

lok ***jo.vī*** *āx-an*
people **whatever** say-SBJV.3PL

'You shouldn't do like this, **whatever** people may say.' (Hk) (AWT)

6.6.2 Panjabi indefinite pronouns

Panjabi's two indefinite pronouns, کوئی /koī/ 'anybody, anyone; somebody, someone'; and کُجھ /kúj/ 'something', also function adjectivally. As a pronoun, کوئی /koī/ can be translated as 'anybody', 'anyone', 'somebody', 'someone', with non-specific indefinite meaning. Co-occuring with a negative element, it means 'no one' or 'nobody'. کوئی /koī/ and the negative element do not need to be immediately adjacent, and, in fact, are often found at a distance in the clause. As an adjective, کوئی /koī/ means 'any' or 'some', and کُجھ /kúj/ means 'some' with a partitive sense. In these cases, the adjective must appear within its noun phrase, though not necessarily adjacent to the head noun. Example 6.43 illustrates کوئی /koī/ in its pronominal function, and 6.44 in its adjectival use, both in direct case and oblique forms. See also Section 5.1.3.5.2 for more examples of adjectival use.

(6.43) کمرے وچ کوئی نہیں اے

kamr-e	*vic*	***koī***	*nī̃*	*e*
room-OBL	in	**anyone**	not	be.PRES.3SG

'There isn't **anyone** in the room.' (Pj) (EB)

(6.44) اسیں کوئی بہانہ بنا کے اوہدے کولوں کھسک جانا تے کسی ہور تھاں تے بہہ کے گپ شپ لاؤنی

asī̃	***koī***	*bā̃nā*	*baṇā-ke*	*ó-de*	*kolõ*	*khisak*	*jā-ṇā*
1PL	**some.DIR**	excuse	make-CP	3SG.OBL-GEN	from	slip.away	go-INF

te	*kisī*	*hor*	*thā̃*	*te*	*bǽ-ke*	*gap.šap*	*lāo-ṇī*
and	some.OBL	other	place	at	sit-CP	chatting[F]	bring-INF.SG.F

'We would make **some** excuse and slip away from him, and sit somewhere else and chat.' (Pj) (http://a-shahkar.blogspot.com/2009/12/blog-post_02.html)

Example 6.45 shows کجھ /kúj/ 'some, something' functioning as a pronoun, and 6.46 shows it functioning adjectivally (as a quantifier).

(6.45) میرے کول کجھ نہیں

mer-e	*koḷ*	***kúj***	*nī̃*
1SG.GEN-SG.M.OBL	near	**something**	NEG+be.PRES.3SG

'I don't have **anything**.' (Pj) (EB)

(6.46) سانوں کجھ سخت فیصلے کرنے پین گے

sā-nū̃	***kúj***	*saxt*	*fæsl-e*	*kar-n-e*	*pæṇ-g-e*
1PL.OBL-DAT	**some**	hard	decision-PL.M	do-INF-PL.M	fall-FUT-PL.M

'We will have to make **some** hard decisions.' (Pj) (Bashir and Kazmi 2012: 451)

In addition to its pronominal and adjectival uses, کجھ /kúj/ can also function as an adverb meaning 'rather, somewhat'. Example 6.47 illustrates this.

(6.47) کاکا کجھ وڈا ہو گیا اے

kākā	***kúj***	*vaḍḍ-ā*	*ho*	*ga-yā*	*e*
little.boy	**somewhat**	big-SG.M	become	go.PP-SG.M	be.PRES.3SG

'The (little) boy has gotten **a bit** bigger.' (Pj) (EB)

6.6.3 Saraiki indefinite pronouns

Saraiki has the same two types of basic indefinite pronoun as Hindko and Panjabi, the non-specific indefinite کُوئی /kuī/ 'some, any; someone, anyone' and کُجھ /kujh/ 'something'. Table 6.12 gives the direct and oblique forms of کُوئی /kuī/. کُجھ /kujh/ 'something' has only one form for direct and oblique, singular and plural.

Case/person-number	Singular	Plural
Direct	کوئی kuī 'some, any (m.)' کئی kaī 'some, any (f.)'	کئی kaī ~ kĕī 'some, any persons'
Oblique	کہیں kahī̃ 'some, any'	کنہاں kinhā̃ کنہیں kinhẽ کئیاں kaiyā̃ 'several'

Table 6.12: Saraiki indefinite pronoun کوئی /kuī/ 'someone, anyone'

Pronominal use of Saraiki کُوئی /kuī/ 'someone, anyone' is illustrated in 6.48, which includes both the direct and the oblique case forms.

(6.48) کہیں کنوں پچھ ۔ کُوئی ہی تیکوں ڈِس سگدے

kahī̃	*kanū̃*	*puch*	–	***kuī***	*hī*	*tæ-kū̃*	*ɗas*
someone.OBL	from	ask	–	**anyone.DIR**	EMPH	2SG-DAT	tell

saɠ-d-e
be.able-IP-be.PRES+3SG.M
'Ask **someone. Anyone** can tell you.' (Sr) (UK)

Compound pronominal forms with کُوئی /kuī/ are: کُوئی نہ کُوئی /kuī na kuī/ 'someone or other', ہرکُوئی /har kuī/ 'everyone, anyone' and سبھ کُوئی /sabh kuī/ 'everyone' (Shackle

1976: 63). Compound pronominal forms with کجھ include: کجھ نہ کجھ /kujh na kujh/ 'something or other'; سارا کجھ /sārā kujh/, سبھ کجھ /sab kujh/, or سبھو کجھ /sabho kujh/ 'everything'; and بیا کجھ /ɓiyā kujh/ 'something/anything else', which is illustrated in 6.49:[14]

(6.49) بیا کجھ چہیدا اے

ɓiyā ***kujh*** *cah-ī-d-ā* *e*
more **anything** want-PASS-IP-SG.M be.PRES.3SG
'Do (you) need/want **anything** else? (lit. Is anything else needed?)' (Sr) (Zahoor 2009: 53)

6.7 Relative pronouns

In all three languages two forms are employed as relative pronouns. One is the pronominal form جو /jo/ 'who, which', which is common also to Urdu and Hindi. The forms of جو /jo/ 'who, which' in the three languages are shown in Table 6.13 (below). The second is the relative adjective جہڑا ~ جیہڑا /jéṛā/ 'which', used (as most adjectives can be) substantively (in nominal function). Of these, the relative adjective جہڑا ~ جیہڑا /jéṛā/ (Pj, Hk) and جیڑھا ~ جیرھا /jeṛhā ~ jerhā/ (Sr) 'which', is far more frequent. This is a marked ("black") adjective whose forms have previously been given for all three languages in Table 5.14.[15] Examples of various types of relative clauses in all three languages will be found in Chapter 9. The forms of the Hindko, Panjabi, and Saraiki relative pronoun جو /jo/ 'who, which' are found in Table 6.13 below.

Regarding the Saraiki forms in Table 6.13, notice that the nasalization of the singular oblique form tends to be omitted preceding the dative-accusative postposition کوں /kū̃/. Forms marked with ** are from our consultant, UK. Otherwise, the forms are from Shackle (1976: 60). The form جت /jit/ oblique sg. of جو /jo/occurs in our small corpus with the postpositions نال /nāl/ 'with' and اِچ /ic/ 'in'.

14 This sentence would normally be written, and spoken, with elipsis between the masculine singular ending -ā and the present tense of 'be', thus چاہیدے /cāhīde/. Also, an original Saraiki expression of this meaning would use the verb لوڑیندے /loṛīnde/ 'is needed'.

15 Sakoon (2002: 109) spells the Hindko relative adjective forms with the short vowel /i/, and with /h/ following rather than preceding /ṛ/, as: جڑھے، جڑھی، جڑھا /jíṛe, jíṛī, jíṛā/, respectively, for the masculine plural, feminine singular, and masculine singular of the relative adjective.

Case/ Number	Singular	Plural
Hindko		
Direct	جو jo	جو jo
Oblique	جِس jis	جِنہاں jínā̃
Panjabi		
Direct	جو jo	جو jo
Oblique	جِس ~ جِہ- jis / jí-	جِنھاں ~ جِنہاں jínā̃
Saraiki		
Direct	جو jo	جو jo
Oblique	جئیں ~ جیں ~ جِت ** jæ̃ ~ jit**	جنھاں ~ جنھیں** jinhā̃ ~ jinhẽ**
Genitive	جیندا jæ̃dā	جِنھاں دا jinhā̃ dā
Dative/accusative	جیکوں jækũ	جِنھاں کوں jinhā̃ kũ

Table 6.13: Relative pronoun جو /jo/ 'who, which' in Hindko, Panjabi, and Saraiki

6.8 Pronominal suffixes

Affixal elements which index (or point to) sentence elements that can also be expressed with separate personal or demonstrative pronouns are referred to here as pronominal suffixes. Pronominal suffixes have a number of functions in several South Asian languages (see Emeneau 1980). In the languages examined here, they appear in the following functions, indexing:

- accusative-marked direct object
- agent of perfective transitive verbs

- indirect object (dative)
- possessor
- "dative subject"/ "ethical dative"
- addressee

Pronominal suffixes, sometimes referred to as pronominal clitics because of their phonological behavior, are a feature which used to be more widespread and were frequently used in the continuum of languages once named "Lahnda". They were not found in eastern varieties of Panjabi.[16] Now, however, some use of pronominal suffixes is found in the Panjabi of Lahore, which, as discussed earlier, has incorporated some features of more westerly varieties and of Hindko and Saraiki. Since the pronominal suffix system has its fullest expression in Saraiki, the pronominal suffixes for Saraiki will be discussed first, followed by Panjabi, and then by Hindko.

6.8.1 Pronominal suffixes in Saraiki

The system of pronominal suffixes is one of the most distinctive elements of Saraiki. Shackle (1976: 101) presents an extensive discussion of pronominal suffixes as they were in use at that time. He identifies two sets of suffixes: a direct set appearing when the argument indexed has a direct case function, and an oblique set appearing when the argument indexed has an oblique case function. These are shown here in Table 6.14 (based on Shackle 1976: 103).

The existence of the direct forms means that in sentences with first- or second-person subjects, direct-case arguments too can be indicated by a pronominal suffix as well as by independent pronouns, as in 6.53. This is a key difference between Saraiki and both Panjabi and Hindko, where only oblique arguments can be indexed by pronominal suffixes. Importantly, (i) there are no third-person direct forms, and (ii) direct and oblique forms differ only in the second-person singular. The direct forms are used only in those tenses which consist of a bare participle, that is the simple perfect (= perfective participle) and the simple irrealis (= imperfective participle). Their most frequent occurrence is with the simple perfect (conveying past time reference), as in example 6.54, in which the pronominal suffix expresses the direct-case subject 'we' of a perfective intransitive.

First and second-person arguments that are indexed by pronominal suffixes are necessarily human; regarding the third-person suffixes, Shackle (1976: 150) says that they "normally relate to persons or animates". Example 6.50 illustrates the use of the

16 Their use in "Lahnda", Sindhi, Pashto and some of the Dardic languages has been discussed in the wider geographical context of a South Asian linguistic area in Emeneau (1980).

Person	Case	Singular	Plural
1st	**Direct**	-m	-se
	Oblique	-m	-se
2nd	**Direct**	-õ	-he / -ve
	Oblique	-ī ~ ĩ / -hī / -ā / -o	-he / -ve
3rd	**Direct**	none	none
	Oblique	-s	-ne

Table 6.14: Saraiki pronominal suffixes

third person singular suffix to index a non-human animate. For example, in response to the question, "Have you seen my buffalo?", sentence 6.50 can occur. Sentence 6.50 expresses both the first-person agent 'I' and the third-person object 'it' with pronominal suffixes; the suffix for the agent precedes the suffix for the object.

(6.50) ڈٹھمس

*ḍiṭh-im-**is***
see.PP-PS1SG-**PS3SG**
'I saw **it**.' (Sr) (Nasir Abbas Syed, p.c.)

Although pronominal suffixes are usually used to refer to animate entities, it is possible for the third person suffix to refer to an inanimate object in a situation which involves strong emotional affect of a speaker, either negative or positive. An example scenario is the following. Suppose a thorny bush near the doorway of a person's house repeatedly catches and rips his clothes and pricks him, so he cuts it down angrily. One day his neighbor asks him, "What happened to your bush?" The person might reply as in example 6.51:

(6.51) روز روزتنگ کریندی ہئی، گھتیمس کہاڑا۔کپ کے ولا رکھیمس

roz	*roz*	*tang*	*kar-end-ī*	*haī*	*ghatye-m-**is***
day	day	tight	do-IP-F.SG	be.PST.3SG.F	strike.PP-PS1SG-**PS3SG**

kuhāṛā	*kap*	*ke*	*valā*	*rakhye-m-**is***
axe	cut	CP	again	keep.PP-PS1SG-**PS3SG**

'It (the bush) was tormenting me every day. I struck **it** (with an) axe (and) cut **it** down once and for all.' (Sr) (Nasir Abbas Syed, p.c.)

According to (Shackle 1976: 101), in Saraiki these suffixes attach only to finite verb forms. Shackle contrasts this with the situation in Sindhi, where pronominal suffixes can attach to certain nouns and postpositions. Wilson (1899), writing about the Panjabi of Shahpur (District Sargodha), gives examples of pronominal suffixes referring to a genitive argument and replacing the present tense of 'be', as in 6.52.

(6.52) گھر کتھے نے

ghar *kithe* ***ne***
house where **PS3PL**
'Where is **their** house?' (Sr) (Wilson 1899: 24)

Some simple sentences can have two types of expression: (1) all major constituents are expressed with full pronouns, as in 6.53, or (2) a major constituent is expressed by a pronominal suffix, as in 6.54, in which the first-person plural suffix سے /-se/ expresses the subject, 'we', of this intransitive sentence. Full pronouns and pronominal suffixes referring to the same argument can co-occur in perfective tenses of intransitives. Thus in sentences like 6.54, it is also possible (but rarely done) to include the full pronoun اساں /assā̃/ 'we'.

(6.53) اساں ملتان ڳئے

assā̃ *multān* *ɠæ*
we Multan go.PP.PL.M
'**We** went to Multan.' (Sr) (Shackle 1976: 147)

(6.54) ملتان ڳیوسے

multān *ɠy-**ose***
Multan go.PP-**PS1PL**
'**We** went to Multan.' (Sr) (Shackle 1976: 151)

With transitives, however, a full pronoun and a pronominal suffix referring to the same argument do not co-occur. Examples with the transitive verb آکھݨ /ākhaṇ/ 'to say', are shown as 6.55 and 6.56. These transitive examples are significant in that they show a perfective tense of a transitive verb marked for the agent, thus in effect "agreeing" with the agent of the sentence. This complicates the picture of (split-) ergativity in South Asian languages.

(6.55) آکھیُوم

*ākh-i-**um***
say-PP-**PS1SG**
'I said.' (Sr) (Shackle 1976: 15)

(6.56) آکھیُوس

*ākh-i-**us***
say-PP-**PS3SG**
'He/she said.' (Sr) (Shackle 1976: 118)

Example 6.57, with the intransitive verb ٹُرݨ /ṭuraṇ/ 'to walk, go, leave' is constructed in the same way as 6.55.

(6.57) ٹُریُوم

*ṭur-i-**um***
walk-PP-**PS1SG**
'I left.' (Sr) (Shackle 1976: 103)

Examples 6.58–6.62 show a few possible combinations of the transitive verb پیوݨ/pī-vaṇ/ 'to drink' and various combinations of masculine or feminine direct object with first, second, and third-person subjects (agents). In each of these examples, all of which are in the (present) perfect form, the pronominal suffix refers to the subject (agent). The gender of the direct object is indicated on the perfective participle.

(6.58) پیتُم~پیتوم

*pīt-u-**m***
drink-PP.SG.M-**PS1SG**
'I drank it (SG.M.OBJECT)' (Sr) (Nasir Abbas Syed, p.c.)

(6.59) پیتئی

*pīt-a-**ī***
drink-PP.SG.M-**PS2SG**
'You (sg.) drank it (SG.M.OBJECT).' (Sr) (Shackle 1976: 105)

(6.60) پیتیس

*pīt-æ-**s***
drink-PP.SG.M-**PS3SG**
'**He/she/it** drank it (SG.M.OBJECT)' (Sr) (Shackle 1976: 105)

(6.61) پیتم ~ پیتیم

*pīt-i-**m***
drink-PP.SG.F-**PS1SG**
'**I** have drunk it (SG.F.OBJECT)' (Sr) (Nasir Abbas Syed, p.c.)

(6.62) پیتنس

*pīt-in-**is***
drink-PP.PL.M-**PS3SG**
'**He/she/it** drank them (PL.M.OBJECT).' (Sr) (Shackle 1976: 105)

Some recent examples include 6.63 and 6.64, both of which include two pronominal suffixes. In 6.63 the suffix م /m/ referring to the agent 'I', precedes the suffix /ī/ which indexes the indirect object 'you'. Notice that here the verb is marked with the subject and indirect object, but not the direct object, which in this sentence is expressed with the full pronoun اوکوں /ū-kū̃/. In 6.64 a first-person agent, 'we', affects a third-person indirect object, 'them'. As in 6.63, the suffix expressing the agent precedes the one expressing the indirect object. In this recent example, the second person singular argument is expressed by both the full pronoun تیں /tæ̃/ and the second person singular suffix ی /ī/. If تیں کنیں /tæ̃ kanẽ/ is understood as an indirect object, this may show a weakening of the earlier constraint on co-occurrence of both full pronouns and pronominal suffixes. If, however, it is perceived as a goal of motion, this comment would not apply.

(6.63) اوکوں تیں کنے پٹھیمی

ū-kū̃	*tæ̃*	*kan-e*	*paṭhiē-**m-ī***
3SG-ACC	2SG.OBL	vicinity-LOC	send.PP-**PS1SG-PS2SG**

'**I** sent him/her to **you**.' (Sr) (UK)

(6.64) آپݨی کالی ٻکری ݙکھالیسینے

āpṇ-ī	*kāl-ī*	*ɓakr-ī*	*ɗikh-āl-ī-**se-ne***
REFL.GEN-SG.F	black-SG.F	goat-SG.F	see-CS-PP.SG.F-**PS1PL-PS3PL**

'**We** showed **them** our black goat.' (Sr) (UK)

There is, in addition to language change since Shackle's time, apparently considerable dialectal and idiolectal variation in the use of Saraiki pronominal suffixes. For example, Nasir Abbas Syed does not accept the use of both pronominal suffixes in 6.64, and offers the following sentence for the same meaning, in which only the pronominal suffix for the agent appears: آپݨی کالی ٻکری ݙکھائی سے /āpnī kalī ɓakrī ɗikhāī se /. Such questions require fresh detailed research specifically focused on dialectal variation in the usage of pronominal suffixes.

Pronominal suffixes indexing (potentially accusative marked) direct objects are relatively rarer. Examples 6.65, 6.66, and 6.67[17] are three such instances.[18]

(6.65) ماریومس

*māri-**ŏ/um-is***
beat/kill.PP-**PS1SG-PS3SG**
'**I** beat/killed **him/her/it.**' (Sr) (Nasir Abbas Syed, p.c.)

(6.66) مارِس

*mār-**is***
beat/kill.IMP.SG-**PS3SG**
'Beat/kill **him/her/it!**' (Sr) (Shackle 1976: 102)

(6.67) ݙٹھومس

*ɗiṭh-**om-is***
see.PP-**PS1SG-PS3SG**
'**I** saw **him.**' (Sr) (Shackle 1976: 152)

The dative subject of a gerundive may also appear as a pronominal suffix, as in example 6.68, where the experiencer, i.e. the person who had to go somewhere, is indexed by the third-person singular suffix/-s/.

17 Compare 6.50 and 6.67 for an example of dialectal and individual variation in the use of pronominal suffixes.

18 It is important to note that all three of these examples involve a first- or second-person agent acting on a third-person patient/object. Whether it is possible to index a first-person patient acted on by a second- or third-person agent with a pronominal suffix is not yet clear to us.

(6.68) کڈاہیں ونڄݨا ہس

kiɗāhĩ	*vãf-ṇā*	*ha-**s***
somewhere	go-GRDV.SG.M	be.PST-**PS3SG**

'He/she had to go somewhere.' (Sr) (Shackle (1976: 151), cited from Lashari (1971: 3))

A pronominal suffix may index a genitive argument, as in 6.70, which expresses the same meaning as 6.69.

(6.69) اُوں دیاں ڈُوہے دھیاں آیاں ہن

ũ	***d-iyã***	*ɗūhe*	*dhiyã*	*āiyã*	*han*
3SG.OBL	**GEN-PL.F**	both	daughter.PL	come.PP.PL.F	be.PST.3PL

'Have both of **his** daughters come?' (Sr) (Shackle 1976: 152)

(6.70) ڈُوہے دھیاں آیاں ہانس

ɗūhe	*dhiyã*	*āiy-ã*	*hān-**is***
both	daughter.PL.F	come.PP-PL.F	be.PST.3PL-**PS3SG**

'Have both of **his** daughters come?' (Sr) (Shackle (1976: 152), cited from Lashari (1971: 3))

Sentence 6.71 shows a pronominal suffix cliticized to the negative particle. At first glance, this appears at variance with the statement by Shackle (1976: 101) that pronominal suffixes attach only to finite verbs. However, Shackle (1976: 107) discusses "personal negative forms clearly cognate with the pronominal suffixes." Example 6.71 appears to be a case of this. Additionally, if the negative particle نہیں /naĩ/ is analyzed as a negative verb '-is/are not', then this is also an instance of cliticization to the verb auxiliary. The formation of negative auxiliaries in Saraiki is discussed by Shackle (1976: 107).

(6.71) تیکوں اوں کنے کینہ ما پٹھیا

tæ-kũ	*ũ*	*kane*	*kæna-**mā***	*paṭh-iyā*
2SG-ACC	3SG.OBL	near	NEG-**PS1SG**	send-PP.SG.M

'**I** did not send you to him.' (Sr) (UK)

Shackle (1976: 101) noted that the use of pronominal suffixes seemed at that time to be decreasing in formal speech and writing. The extent to which the trend he observed has continued is a topic for further research. Our hypothesis is that the trend will have accelerated, probably more in urban than in rural areas, but we have no quantitative data to support this idea.

6.8.2 Pronominal suffixes in Panjabi

Since most published descriptions of Panjabi to date have been of eastern varieties, the use of pronominal suffixes in Panjabi has been one of its least documented phenomena. While pronominal suffixes are one of the most distinctive features of Saraiki; they also appear, though to a lesser extent, in Hindko and the more westerly dialects of Panjabi, including the districts of Sialkot, Gujranwala, Lahore, Gujrat, and Ferozepur (Cummings and Bailey 1912). Cummings and Bailey note specifically that their work does not describe the Panjabi of the Sikhs. Bhatia (1993) notes that pronominal suffixes are not found in Majhi. However, he lists forms he says are found in the Panjabi of Shahpur, in Sargodha District (about 253 kilometers northwest of Lahore). Akhtar (1997), a study on pronominal suffixes in Panjabi, is based on the dialect of Gujrat District (about 116 kilometers north-northwest of Lahore), and the Panjabi-speaking informant mentioned by Butt (2007: 2) was originally from Hafizabad (also about 116 kilometers northwest of Lahore).

The appearance of pronominal suffixes in Lahore Panjabi is one effect of the increasing inflow of people from other parts of Punjab and Pakistan into this urban center. In today's Panjabi in Lahore, these suffixes occur sporadically and only in the second and third persons (see Table 6.15). The forms that occur are considerably mixed, including forms previously found only in more westerly varieties of Panjabi or in Saraiki. This situation has significantly complicated their documentation and description.

Person	Singular	Plural
2nd	اوں -ũ CB ای -ī ا -ā CB ایں -ĩ	جے je
3rd	س -s سو -sū سوں -sũ CB	نے ne

Table 6.15: Pronominal suffixes found in Lahore Panjabi[19]

There are questions about how to classify these pronominal elements; most are attached at the end of words and thus are referred to as suffixes. However, in future tense forms they appear between the verb stem and the future morpheme /g/. In some cases

19 These forms are attested in Cummings and Bailey (1912), Akhtar (1997), Akhtar (1999), Butt (2007), and Bashir and Kazmi (2012). Those noted with (CB) are found only in Cummings and Bailey.

they appear to function as separate words, while in other cases they are phonologically closely bound to their hosts and can be considered clitics. Despite these differences in how they appear, we are labelling these elements consistently as "PSperson.number". But their appearance sometimes as clitics and sometimes as what seem to be separate words demands further analysis. The use of pronominal suffixes is idiomatic but entirely non-obligatory.

There is variation among speakers and age groups in the frequency and distribution of the pronominal suffixes. In general, they are more frequently used by older persons or those with rural backgrounds. Akhtar (1997) confirms the use of ی /-ī/, سو /-s(ū)/, جے /je/, and نے /ne/, but makes no mention of the other forms reported by Cummings and Bailey, a much older source. The most recent work on this topic, Butt (2007), additionally confirms the use of ا /-ā/ and وں /-ū̃/ by a Lahore Panjabi speaker from a family originally from Hafizabad. Neither Butt nor Akhtar document ی /-ī/ or اِیں /-ī̃/ as second-person singular suffixes; however Bashir and Kazmi (2012) provide several examples of ی /-ī/, (see examples below); and اِیں /-ī̃/ appears frequently, functioning to attract the attention of an addressee.

It appears that the current (2018) situation is simpler than that described by Cummings and Bailey (1912), in which the form used depended on several factors, including the number and person of the subject of the verb.[20] While the second and third-person singular suffixes are usually written attached to verb stems, the plural suffixes جے /je/ and نے /ne/ are mostly written as separate orthographic words. In contemporary Panjabi they do not index direct-case arguments (subject or unmarked direct object), and (unlike Saraiki and Sindhi) only second and third-person forms are found (Table 6.15).

Interpretation of reference and grammatical function is straightforward in most cases. Since there are no first-person forms, we only have to deal with second and third-person arguments. Second-person forms can fulfill any of the six functions listed above (at the beginning of Section 6.8), and in many cases seem to perform more than one role simultaneously. Interpretation of third-person forms is relatively simpler, since they cannot index an addressee.

20 Cummings and Bailey 1912 suggest that the second-person singular suffix is /ū̃/ when the subject of the verb is in the first person singular or plural, /ī/ when the subject is in the third-person singular, and /ī̃/ or /ā̃/ when the subject is in the third-person plural. For the third-person singular and the second and third-persons plural, all forms are equally frequent. Cummings and Bailey also say that the form of the suffix used depends on the tense, aspect, and transitivity of the verb. Thus the verb ہونا /hoṇā/ 'to be' is replaced by the suffixes in the present tense, whereas in the past tense, the suffixes contract with the ordinary past tense form of ہونا /hoṇā/ 'to be' سی / ساں / سن سیں / /sī/sā̃/san/sæ̃ 'was/were'. Past-tense forms of this type include ساسوں /sāsū̃/, ساجے /sāje/, and so on (Cummings and Bailey 1912: 352). However, these forms are as yet unattested in modern Panjabi and require further investigation.

One function of pronominal suffixes is to indicate a direct object of the verb, provided that it is one which would, if expressed with a full pronoun, be marked with the accusative postposition نوں /nū̃/, as in 6.72, the meaning of which is expressed with a pronominal suffix in 6.73. Akhtar (1997: 3, 5) shows that a non-accusative marked direct object can not be indexed by the pronominal suffix سُو /sū/. Thus سُو /sū/ in 6.74 cannot be used to refer to a direct case object, like ‘a book’.

(6.72) فواد نے اوہنوں ماریا

fawād-ne ***ó-nū̃*** *mār-iyā*
Fawad-ERG 3.SG.OBL-ACC beat-PP.SG.M
‘Fawad beat **him/her.**’ (Pj) (Akhtar 1997: 4)

(6.73) فواد نے ماریا سو

fawad-ne *mār-iyā-**s(ū)***
Fawad-ERG beat-PP.SG.M-**3SG**
‘Fawad beat **him/her.**’ (Pj) (Akhtar 1997: 4)

(6.74) فواد نے سمبل نوں دتی سو*

fawād* *ne* *sumbal* *nū̃* *ditt-ī* ***sū*
Fawad ERG Sumbal DAT give.PP-SG.F **PS3SG**
‘*Fawad gave **it** to Sumbal.’ (Pj) (Akhtar 1997: 4)

Pronominal suffixes can also mark the agent of transitive verbs, as in 6.75, 6.76, and 6.77.

(6.75) درخواست دے دتی نیں تے اک ہفتے بعد جواب ملے گا

darxāst *de* *dit-ī* ***nẽ*** *te* *ikk* *hafte* *bād*
application[F] give give.PP-SG.F **PS3PL** and one week after

jawāb *mil-e-g-ā*
reply[M] be.received-SBJV.3SG-FUT-SG.M
‘**He** has submitted the application and will receive an answer in a week.’[21] (Pj) (Bashir and Kazmi 2012: 594)

21 The third-person plural is used here with deferential reference to a single, specific male individual. Otherwise, without specific context, it could also mean ‘they’ or ‘she’.

(6.76) جان توں پہلاں تہاڈے کولوں پچھیا سو

jā-ṇ tõ pǽlā̃ tuā̀ḍ-e kol-õ puch-iyā ***sū***
go-INF ABL before 2SG.GEN-OBL vicinity-ABL ask-PP.SG.M **PS3SG**
'Did **she/he** ask you before going?' (Pj) (Bashir and Kazmi 2012: 377)

(6.77) مینوں ایہہ خبر آپے دسی سُو

mæ-nū̃ é xabar āp-e das-ī ***sū***
1SG-DAT this news[F] REFL-EMPH tell.PP-SG.F **PS3SG**
'**She/he** herself/himself told me the news.' (Pj) (Bashir and Kazmi 2012: 377)

Pronominal suffixes can refer unambiguously to an indirect object, as in example 6.78.

(6.78) خبر مل گئی نیں

xabar mil ga-ī ***nẽ***
news[F] be.received go.PP-SG.F **PS3PL**
'Have **they** gotten the news?' (Pj) (Bashir and Kazmi 2012: 594)

Since pronominal suffixes can refer to an agent (ergative subject), as in 6.79, or an indirect object, as in 6.80, if neither agent nor indirect object is expressed, as in 6.81, the pronominal suffix can refer to either of these two arguments and the meaning must be disambiguated by context.

(6.79) سمبل نوں کتاب دِتیس

*sumbal nū̃ katāb ditt-ī-**s(ū)***
Sumbal DAT book[F] give.PP-SG.F-**PS3SG**
'**She/he** gave a book to Sumbal' (Pj) (Akhtar 1997: 2)

(6.80) فواد نے کتاب دتی سو

*fawad-ne katāb ditt-ī-**s(ū)***
Fawad-ERG book[F] give.PP-SG.F-**PS3SG**
'Fawad gave **her/him** a book.' (Pj) (Akhtar 1997: 2)

(6.81) کتاب دتّی سو

    katāb   ditt-ī-**s(ū)**
    book.SG.F give.PP-SG.F-**PS3SG**
    '**He/she** gave the book (to someone).'
    '(Someone) gave the book to **him/her**.' (Pj) (Akhtar 1997: 2)

A genitive argument ("possessor") can also be indexed by a pronominal suffix, as in (6.82), where سُو /sū/ refers to the person whose sons work.

(6.82) منڈے کم کردے سو

    mū̃ḍ-e   kamm   kar-d-e-**s(ū)**
    boy-PL   work   do-IP-PL.M-**PS3SG**
    '**His/her** sons work.' (Pj) (Akhtar 1997: 4)

In 6.83 سُو /sū/ seems clearly to indicate an "ethical dative", i.e. a person affected by an event or circumstance.

(6.83) بُھل ہو گئی سُو

    pùl   ho   ga-ī   **s(ū)**
    mistake[F] be go.PP-SG.F **PS3SG**
    '**She/he** made a mistake (or forgot).' (Pj) (Akhtar 1997: 9)

Perhaps the most common usage of the second-person elements today in Panjabi is to gain the attention of an addressee. In the contemporary language (2019), the second-person singular form ای /ī/ is frequently encountered in this function. In example 6.84, the suffix indexes the addressee and possibly an implied "possessor."

(6.84) میں پچھ رہی آں کہ بستہ کتھے ای

    mæ̃   puch ra-ī   ā̃   ki   bastā   kitthe **ī**
    1SG   ask   CONT.II-SG.F be.PRES.1SG that book.bag where **PS2SG**
    'I(F) am asking **you** where **your** book bag is.' (Pj) (Bashir and Kazmi 2012: 72)

The interpretation of sentences 6.85 and 6.86 is complex. Since both are questions, addressed to a second person 'you', the second-person singular element ای /ī/ simultaneously indexes the addressee and the agent in 6.85, or the addressee and the "ethical dative" argument in 6.86.

(6.85) کتاب لین توں پہلاں اوہنوں دسیا ای

katāb	*læṇ*	*tõ*	*pǽlā̃*	*ó-nū̃*	*das-iyā*	*ī*
book	take.INF.OBL	ABL	before	3SG-DAT	tell-PP.SG.M	**PS2SG**

'Did **you** tell him before taking the book?' (Pj) (Bashir and Kazmi 2012: 72)

(6.86) بس کلینر نے پچھیا ، مائی کتھے جانا ای

bas	*klīnar*	*ne*	*puch-iyā*	*māī*	*kitthe*	*jā-ṇā*	*ī*
bus	cleaner	ERG	ask-PP.SG.M	old.lady	where	go-INF	**PS2SG**

'The bus cleaner asked, "Old lady, where do **you** want to go?"'[22] (Pj) (Bashir and Kazmi 2012: 72)

In examples 6.87, 6.88, and 6.89, indexing the addressee, the second-person plural suffix جے /je/ directs the question to the addressee, who is also the agent of the action.

(6.87) ساریاں چیزاں سوٹکیس اچ رکھ لیاں جے

sāriyā̃	*cīz-ā̃*	*sūṭkes*	*ic*	*rakh*	*li-yā̃-**je***
all.PL.F	thing-PL.F	suitcase	in	put	take-PP.PL.F-**PS2PL**

'Have **you (pl.)** put everything in the suitcase?' (Pj) (Bashir and Kazmi 2012: 232)

(6.88) میں تعریف کردیاں کہیا ، بڑی سوہنی چادر لئی ہوئی جے

mæ̃	*tārīf*	*kar-d-eā̃*	*ky-ā́*	*baṛ-ī*	*sóṇ-ī*
1SG	praise	do-IP-SG.M.OBL	say.PP-SG.M	very-SG.F	pretty-SG.F

cāddar	*l-aī*	*ho-ī*	***je***
shawl[F]	take-PP.SG.F	be-PP.SG.F	**PS2PL**

'I said admiringly, **"You** are wearing a very pretty shawl."' (Pj) (Bashir and Kazmi 2012: 232)

22 Panjabi مائی /māī/ 'old lady' (< the root for 'mother', 'elder woman') does not have the somewhat negative and rude connotation that 'old lady' or 'old woman' do in English.

(6.89) اوئے بچیو اتھے کیہہ کیتا جے

oe	*bacc-eo*	*ethe*	*kĩ́*	*kīt-ā*	***je***
hey	child-PL.VOC	here	what	do.PP-SG.M	**PS2PL**

'Hey kids, what have **you** done here?' (Pj) (Bashir and Kazmi 2012: 232)

When the second-person addressee is not the subject/agent of the clause, the pronominal element has different overlapping functions, as in 6.90, 6.91, 6.92, and 6.93, where جے /je/ functions simultaneously to attract the attention of the addressee, and to index a possessor or "ethical dative" (cf. "dative subject"), as in 6.90. Example 6.90 is from 1904, but the same type is still found today, as in 6.91.

(6.90) کیہ جے

kĩ́	***je***
what	**PS2PL**

'What has happened to **you**?'
'I ask **you** what has happened.' (Pj) (Bailey 1904b: 22)

(6.91) تے اگلی واری پتر کدوں آوے گا جے

te	*agalī*	*vārī*	*puttar*	*kadõ*	*ā-ve-gā*	***je***
and	next	time	son	when	come-SBJV.3SG-FUT.SG.M	**PS2PL**

'So, when will **your (pl.)** son come next time?' (Pj) (Bashir and Kazmi 2012: 232)

(6.92) کل تک گڈی ٹھیک ہو جائے گی سو

kál	*tak*	*gaḍḍī*	*ṭhīk*	*ho*	*jā-e-g-ī*	***sū***
tomorrow	by	car[F]	fixed	become	go-SBJV.3SG-FUT-SG.F	**PS3SG**

'Will **his/her** car be fixed by tomorrow?' (Pj) (Bashir and Kazmi 2012: 377)

(6.93) ہور کنے دناں اچ گھر مک جائے گا نیں

hor	*kinne*	*din-ā̃-c*	*kȁr*	*muk*
more	how.many	day-PL.OBL-in	house	be.finished

*jā-e-g-ā-**nẽ***
go-SBJV.3SG-FUT-SG.M-**PS3PL**

'In how many more days will **their** house will be finished?' (Pj) (Bashir and Kazmi 2012: 594)

The second-person singular element اس‎ /-ī̃/ raises interesting questions. It may be that this form is in free variation with ی /-ī/, as suggested in Bailey (1904b: 20). However, another possible analysis of اس‎ /-ī̃/ emerges from the fact that it appears in several published grammars analyzed as a "singular polite imperative" ending (Bailey 1904b: 43); Cummings and Bailey 1912: 77; Gill and Gleason 1969: 37; Bhatia 1993: 35; Singh et al. 2011: 82). (See also Section 8.4.4.1.2) This apparent reanalysis of a second-person singular pronominal suffix (with the addition of nasalization) as an imperative verbal ending is consistent with Butt's (2004: 23) proposed diachronic scenario, in which pronominal suffixes are in the process of being integrated into the verbal paradigm as agreement markers.[23] Further evidence in support of this hypothesis is Bailey's (1904: 43) statement that the plural polite imperative in /ĕo/ ~ /iyo/ is nearly always used with جے /je/, as اُٹھیو جے /uṭṭhiyo je/ 'please get up', in a way parallel to the singular polite imperative اُٹھیں /uṭṭh-ī̃/.

This is an extremely common usage, interpreted by an addressee as a simple imperative followed by an attention-getting suffix, as in 6.94.

(6.94) ویکھیں ٹُٹ نہ جاوے

vekh-ī̃	-	*ṭuṭ*	*na*	*jā-ve*
look-**PS2SG**	–	break	NEG	go-SBJV.3SG

'Watch out – don't let it break!' (Pj) (EB)

These pronominal elements are not always suffixed to the verb root. Two important cases involve (i) negative sentences, and (ii) future tense forms. In the negative sentences 6.95, 6.96, and 6.97, سو /sū/ cliticizes to the negative نہیں /naī̃/.[24] This is parallel to the behavior of the past tense auxiliary in negative sentences (see Chapter 9 on this point).

(6.95) کم نہیں سو کیتا

kamm	*naī̃-**s(ū)***	*kīt-ā*
work	NEG-**PS3SG**	do.PP-SG.M

'**She/he** did not do the work.'
'(someone) did not do the work **for him/her.**'[25] (Pj) (Akhtar 1997: 7)

23 Ali Hussain Birahimani has independently proposed (p.c.) such an analysis for some of the Saraiki negative forms of 'be' that appear in some of our paradigms.

24 If the negative particle نہیں /naī̃/ is analyzed as a negative verb '-is/are not', then this is also an instance of cliticization to the verb auxiliary. The formation of negative auxiliaries in Saraiki is discussed by Shackle (1976: 107).

25 The suffix here can refer either to the agent or to the ethical dative object.

(6.96) تہانوں کوئی خط نئیں سو دتا ؟

tuā̀-nū̃ *koī* *xat* *nī́-***sū** *dit-ā*
2SG.OBL-DAT any letter[M] NEG-**PS3SG** give.PP-SG.M
'Didn't **he/she** give you any letter?' (Pj) (Bashir and Kazmi 2012: 377)

(6.97) میں کم نہیں سو کیتا

mæ̃ *kamm* *nī́-***sū** *kīt-ā*
1SG work NEG-**PS3SG** do.PP-SG.M
'I didn't do **his/her work** / the work **for him/her.**'[26] (Pj)

Another case when a pronominal affix need not attach to a verb is illustrated in 6.98, where سو /sū/ follows the interrogative word کیہہ /kī́/ 'what' in an emphatic word order in a rhetorical question with negative implication.

(6.98) لبھیا کیہ سو

láb-iyā *kī́* ***sū***
find-PP.SG.M what **PS3SG**
'What did **s/he** get?!'[27] (Pj) (www/sanjhaPunjab.net/ghazal-qamar-uz-zaman/)

In future tense forms, as in examples 6.100, 6.101, and 6.102 the pronominal affix can appear between the verb stem and the future suffix گا /gā/. Notice that in this case the pronominal affix referring to the direct object replaces the (subject-agreeing) subjunctive morpheme which usually appears between the stem and the future morpheme گا /gā/. Compare 6.99, the usual contemporary Panjabi expression, with 6.100. Example 6.99 expresses the direct object with the full second-person pronoun in the oblique case marked with the accusative postposition, تینوں /tæ-nū̃/ 'you', and the verb ماراں گا /marā̃-gā/ 'I will beat/kill' agrees with the first person singular subject. In 6.100, however, the second-person pronominal suffix اوں /ū̃/ 'PS.2SG' indicates the direct object

26 The suffix refers to either the possessor or the ethical dative argument. Example adapted from Butt (2007: 14).
27 Implied meaning: 'S/he did not get anything.'

of the verb 'kill', that is, 'you'.[28] In Bailey's time (1925) appearance of both the full pronoun and the pronominal suffix did not occur, hence the unacceptability of 6.101 at that time. This was apparently still the case in 1997, as Akhtar says: "The affixation of the formative /-s(ū)/ is prohibited when all the constituents are in their places." We understand this to mean that a full pronoun and سُو /sū/ do not co-occur.

(6.99) میں تینوں مارانگا

mǣ ***tæ-nū̃*** *mār-ā̃-g-ā*
1SG **2SG.OBL-ACC** beat-SBJV.1SG-FUT-SG.M
'I (M) will beat/(kill) **you.**' (Pj) (EB)

(6.100) میں مارونگا

mǣ *mār-**ū̃**-g-ā*
1SG kill-**PS2SG**-FUT-SG.M
'I (M) will beat/kill **you.**' (Pj) (Cummings and Bailey 1912: 349)

(6.101) میں تینوں مارونگا

mǣ* ***tæ-nū̃* *mar-**ū̃**-g-ā*
1SG **2SG-ACC** beat-**PS2SG**-FUT-SG.M
NOT: 'I will beat **you.**' (Pj) (Cummings and Bailey 1912: 349)

A modern example, 6.102, shows the same order of elements in future tense forms as earlier reported by Cummings & Bailey.

(6.102) خط ملسو گا تے فوراً آویگا

xat *mil-**sū**-g-ā* *te* *foran*
letter[M] be.received-**PS3SG**-FUT-SG.M then immediately

ā-ve-g-ā
come-SBJV.3SG-FUT-SG.M
'He will come immediately when **he** gets the letter.' (Pj) (Bashir and Kazmi 2012: 377)

---

28 In 2016, 6.100 is virtually identical to the Urdu sentence with the same meaning, and would probably be understood as an Urdu-influenced Panjabi sentence, with Urdu first-person singular اوں /ū̃/ instead of Panjabi آں /ā̃/, the only difference being that in the Urdu sentence the direct object must be inferred from context. Perhaps this homophony between the Panjabi second-person singular pronominal suffix اوں /ū̃/ and the Urdu first-person singular subjunctive is a factor leading to the disuse of this pronominal suffix in future forms.

Co-occurrence of pronominal suffixes with auxiliaries is another area which needs exploration. The contemporary examples 6.104 and 6.105 show that the element سُو /sū/ does not co-occur with the present tense auxiliary (compare 6.103). Additionally, Bailey 1904b: 20–22 has many examples in which the pronominal suffix, in its function of indicating an addressee, appears to make a present tense auxiliary redundant, e.g. 6.106.

(6.103) فواد ماردا اے

fawād	*mār-d-ā*	*e*
Fawad	beat-PP-SG.M	be.PRES.3SG

'Fawad beats him/her/it.' (Pj) (Akhtar 1997: 8)

(6.104) فواد ماردا سُو

fawād	*mār-d-ā*	***s(ū)***
Fawad	beat-PP-SG.M	**PS3SG**

'Fawad beats **him/her/it**.' (Pj) (Akhtar 1997: 8)

(6.105) فواد ماردا اے سُو

**fawād*	*mār-d-ā*	*e*	***s(ū)***
Fawad	beat-PP-SG.M	be.PRES.3SG	**PS3SG**

'*Fawad beats **him/her**.' (Pj) (Akhtar 1997: 8)

(6.106) کتھے ای

kitthe	***ī***
where	**PS2SG**

'(**I ask thee**) where is it?' (Pj) (Bailey 1904b: 21)

Pronominal suffixes could, however, in 1904 co-occur with past tense auxiliaries, as shown in example 6.107. Whether this sentence type is still possible requires investigation.[29]

(6.107) کتھے جانا سا جے

kitthe	*jā-ṇā*	*sā*	***je***
where	go-INF	be.3SG.PST	**PS2PL**

'Where did **you** have to go?'[30] (Pj) (Bailey 1904b: 22)

29 In Butt's (2007) discussion of pronominal suffixes in Panjabi, following Akhtar (1997: 6) who characterizes arguments represented by the suffix سُو /sū/ as "unstressed", she proposes that pronominal suffixes in Panjabi represent backgrounded information.

30 Before the pronominal affix, سی /sī/ becomes سا /sā/ (Cummings and Bailey 1912: 11). This equals the modern sentence /tusā̃ ~ tuānū̃ kitthe jāṇā sī./

6.8.3 Pronominal suffixes in Hindko

Some uses of pronominal suffixes are attested in contemporary Abbottabad Hindko, though their use appears to be decreasing. Most of our attested examples involve the third-person singular suffix س /s/, which is cognate with the third-person singular oblique suffix of Saraiki and the affix سو /sū/ used in Panjabi. In all of these languages س /s/ occurs in oblique functions. According to discussions with people in Abbottabad in 1989, there are no pronominal suffixes in use for first and second persons, or for third-person plural. However, 6.109 seems to involve a third person plural pronominal suffix نے /-ne/ indexing the third-person plural agent 'they'. Also, 6.108 seems to include the second person suffix ای /ī/, functioning either to address someone or to index the agent 'you(SG)'.

(6.108) کے آخیا ای

kæ *āx-iyā* ***ī***
what say-PP.SG.M **PS2SG**
'What did **you** say?!' (Hk) (Soz 2011: 99)

(6.109) اساں کہروں کڈ چھوڑیا ایہا نے

asā̃ *kàr-õ* *kaḍ* *choṛ-iyā* *éyā-**ne***
1PL.OBL house-ABL remove leave-PP.SG.M be.PST.SG.M-**PS3PL**
'**They** threw us out of the house.' (Hk) (AWT)

In sentence 6.110, the pronominal suffix س /s/ appears only if its referent is not present in the speech act situation. The absence of pronominal suffixes for first and second-person arguments in Hindko may be related to this constraint.[31] Note that in Saraiki (ca. 1976), it was possible for a full pronoun and a pronominal suffix referring to the same individual to co-occur, but generally only with the direct suffix and the perfective participle of intransitive verbs, as in 6.54 above. Contrast this situation with the constraint mentioned by Cummings and Bailey (1912: 349) and illustrated in example 6.101 above.

---

31 It may be that the third person pronominal suffix can be characterized as functioning (only) anaphorically.

(6.110) بڑی سوہنڑی کتاب لکھیس

baṛī	*sóṙī*	*kitāb*	*likh-ī-**s***
very	nice	book[F]	write-PP.SG.F-**PS3SG**

'**He/she (absent)** wrote a very fine book.' (Hk) (AWT)

In examples 6.111, 6.112, and 6.113, س /s/ is the third-person singular suffix indexing an agent. In 6.112 and 6.113, it indexes the agent function in the correlative (matrix) clause.[32] Example 6.113 should be compared to example 9.43, both of which are Hindko renderings of the same sentence, 6.113 in 1989, and 9.43 in 2015. Note that the earlier sentence 6.113 uses the pronominal suffix, while the later one (9.43) does not.

(6.111) کپڑے جاتکے آں لوائس

kapṛ-e	*jātk-e-ā̃*	*lawā-e-**s***
clothes-PL.M	boy-OBL-DAT	put.on-PL.M-**PS3SG**

'**She/he** (previously mentioned, but now absent) put the clothes on the boy.' (Hk) (AWT)

(6.112) او آدمی جس آں مل کے میں کہر آیاں میرا کم نئیں کیتا س

o	*ādmī*	*jis-ā̃*	*mil-ke*	*mǣ̀*	*kàr*	*ā-yā̃*
that	man	who.OBL-ACC	meet-CP	1SG	home	come-PP.SG.M+1SG

mer-ā	*kamm*	*nī̃*	*kīt-ā-**s***
1SG.GEN-SG.M	work.SG.M	not	do.PP-SG.M-**PS3SG**

'**The man,** whom after having met I came home, didn't do my work.' (Hk) (AWT)

(6.113) اوہی آدمی جس ساڈی مجھ چپائی اُس گراں ای بچوں کھوڑا چپایاس

ó-ī	*ādmī*	*jis*	*sāḍ-ī*	*májj*	*cupā-ī*
that-EMPH	man	who.OBL	1PL.GEN-SG.F	buffalo[F]	steal.PP-SG.F

us	*grā̃-ī*	*bic-õ*	*kòṛ-ā*	*cupā-yā-**s***
that.OBL	village-LOC/OBL	in-ABL	horse-SG.M	steal-PP.SG.M-**PS3SG**

'**The same man** who stole our buffalo stole a horse in that village.' (Hk) (EB field notes 1989)

32 In the standard relative-correlative structure, this function is accomplished by a correlative demonstrative pronoun (see Chapter 9).

In 6.114, 6.115, and 6.116 below, the third-person singular suffix س /s/ indexes the indirect object; and in 6.117 it indexes a "dative subject" (i.e. "ethical dative" if that category is employed).[33]

(6.114) اللہ زندگی دیس

allah *zindagī* *de-**s***
God life give-**PS3SG**
'May God give **her** long life.' (Hk) (https://www.youtube.com/watch?v=HwFIj5GODds_Accessed_May_21,_2016)

(6.115) آخدس

*āx-d-a-**s***
say-IP-SG.M-**PS3SG**
'He says to **him/her**' (Hk) (Sakoon 2002: 2)

(6.116) آخُس

*āx-**us***
say-**PS3SG**
'Say to **him/her.**' (Hk) (Sakoon 2002: 2)

(6.117) اُس پینڈی جُولنیس

us *pinḍī* *jul-n-æ-**s***
3SG.OBL Pindi go-INF-be.PRES.3SG-**PS3SG**
'**S/he** has to go to Pindi.' (Hk) (EB field notes 1989)

In 6.118, س /s/ could be interpreted as having either a possessive or ethical dative sense.

(6.118) ایہہ کتاب اُس کول نیس

é *kitab* *us* *kol* *nī-**s***
this book 3SG-OBL with is.not-**PS3SG**
'**S/he** doesn't have (a copy of) this book.' (Hk) (EB field notes 1989)

In 6.119, س /s/ indexes the direct object 'boy'.

33 Such constructions are alternatively analyzed as indirect objects.

(6.119) اُس جاتکے دے پیونو کُٹیاس

us	*jātk-e*	*d-e*	*pyo-ū*	*kuṭ-iyā-***s**
3SG.OBL	boy-OBL	GEN-SG.M.OBL	father-OBL	beat-PP.SG.M-**PS3SG**

'That boy's father beat **him** .' (Hk) (AWT)

6.8.4 Comparison of functions of pronominal suffixes

Table 6.16 and Table 6.17 summarize information presented so far in this chapter. Table 6.16 compares the attested occurrence of pronominal suffixes for persons and numbers found in Saraiki, Panjabi, and Hindko.

Person/number	Saraiki	Panjabi	Hindko
1st singular	yes (dir = obl)	no	no
1st plural	yes (dir = obl)	no	no
2nd singular	yes (dir ≠ obl)	yes (only obl)	yes ?
2nd plural	yes (dir = obl)	yes (only obl)	no ?
3rd singular	yes (only obl)	yes (only obl)	yes (only obl)
3rd plural	yes (only obl)	yes (only obl)	yes (only obl)

Table 6.16: Pronominal suffixes found in Saraiki, Panjabi, and Hindko

Table 6.17 summarizes information available to us about the functions in which pronominal suffixes are attested in these languages and lists at least one relevant example for each. Notably, only in Saraiki can a direct-case subject be indexed by a pronominal suffix.

34 Shackle (1976: 103) says that the oblique suffixes may be used in senses corresponding to a dative-accusative or a possessive pronoun. However he provides no example of a suffix conveying the possessive meaning. Our current fieldwork also yields no such example, leaving the situation unclear.

Function	Saraiki	Panjabi	Hindko
Direct case subject	attested 6.54, 6.57	no	no
Ergative agent	attested 6.55, 6.56	attested 6.75, 6.76	attested 6.110, 6.108
Direct object (acc. marked)	attested 6.65, 6.66	attested 6.73, 6.104	attested 6.119
Indirect object	attested 6.63, 6.64	attested 6.78	attested 6.115, 10.8?
Possessive	attested ?[34]	attested 6.81	attested 6.118
"Dative subject" / "Ethical dative	attested 6.68	attested 6.83	attested 6.117, 6.118
Addressee	not attested	attested 6.84,	attested 6.108, 10.8?

Table 6.17: Functions of pronominal suffixes in Saraiki, Panjabi, and Hindko

7 Postpositions

Various relations between words in a sentence, including both core grammatical relations (subject, direct object, indirect object) and adjunct spatial, temporal, manner, or causal relations, can be indicated by postpositions, as well as by case suffixes. The grammatical postpositions mark the relation of the nominal argument they follow to the verb; in this way, they function like case markers. Unlike the oblique and ablative case endings, however, they do not always orthographically attach to the nouns they affect.

Following Masica (1991: 231), we discuss case-marking functions in terms of Layer I, Layer II, and Layer III, or Layer IV elements. Hindko, Panjabi, and Saraiki have a multi-layered case marking system consisting of at least four layers. Layer I consists of the basic DIRECT : OBLIQUE case distinction, and in some instances ablative. All nouns, pronouns, and adjectives modifying them occur in the oblique case when followed by a postposition. Layer II includes the simple, monomorphemic postpositions which attach to the Layer I OBLIQUE form of a nominal. Layer II includes the grammatical postpositions marking agent, indirect object, and direct object; a few adjectival postpositions; and some of the simple postpositions expressing spatial and temporal relations. Layer III consists of complex postpositions that consist of more than one morpheme. Many of these are themselves oblique forms of nouns or include a genitive or ablative element, either obligatory or optional. Some postpositions can behave either as Layer II or Layer III elements, depending on whether the nominal they follow is a noun or a pronoun. Layer IV elements include complex postpositions consisting of OBL + GEN + 'near' + ABL like اوہ دے کولوں /ó de koḷõ/ 'from him/her' Pj and اوں دے کنوں /ũ̃ de kanũ̃/ 'from him/her' Sr .

7.1 Layer II postpositions

7.1.1 Grammatical postpositions

All three languages have a dative-accusative postposition used to mark indirect objects and some direct objects. This postposition also functions in all three languages to mark "dative subjects,"[1] i.e. entities (usually human) which are affected by some condition or event. In all three languages, the basic function of this postposition is to mark a physical, temporal, abstract, or metaphorical GOAL.

In Panjabi and marginally in Saraiki a third person agent of a transitive verb in a perfective tense is sometimes marked by the postposition نے /ne/, known as the

1 The term "ethical dative" is used in some literature for the meanings which we indicate with "dative subject."

https://doi.org/10.1515/9781614512257-007

ergative marker. The extent to which this ergative postposition is used differs between Panjabi and Saraiki, occuring more freqently in Panjabi than in Saraiki. Within a language, speakers also differ with regard to their use of this element; in general, older persons with a rural background tend to use it less than younger, urban dwellers, who are more influenced by Urdu. Hindko sometimes uses the agentive postposition سڑ /suṛ/.

These grammatical postpositions immediately follow the oblique case form of the noun or pronoun they mark. When directly attached to a noun or pronoun they are enclitic—unstressed and pronounced as part of the preceding word.

7.1.1.1 Hindko grammatical postpositions

The most important grammatical postposition is the dative-accusative marker آں /ã/, which marks all indirect objects (e.g., example 7.1) and some direct objects (usually those which are specific and animate), as in example 7.2. Its functions can be compared with those of Panjabi نوں /nũ/ and Saraiki کوں /kũ/. It also occurs sometimes with the spatial meaning of 'to' or the temporal sense of 'on', as in example 7.3.

(7.1) میرے پہراؤ سلیم آں خط لکھیا ایہا

mer-e	*prā̀-ū*	***salīm***	***ã***	*xat*	*likh-iyā*
1SG.GEN-M.SG.OBL	brother-OBL	**Salim**	**DAT**	letter	write-PP.SG.M

éy-ā
be.PST-SG.M

'My brother wrote a letter **to Salim.**' (Hk) (AWT)

(7.2) میں تداں اس در پیجھ ساں

mæ̃	***tud-ã***	*us*	*dar*	*pèj-s-ã*
1SG	**2SG-ACC**	3SG.OBL	near	send-FUT-1SG

'I will send **you** to him/her.' (Hk) (AWT)

(7.3) ہفتے آں میٹنگ اے

haft-e	***ã***	*mīṭĩg*	*e*
Saturday-OBL	**on**	meeting	be.PRES.3SG

'There's a meeting **on Saturday.**' (Hk) (AWT)

The agentive postposition نے /ne/ is not found (natively) in Abbottabad Hindko; it did not occur in any of the sentences collected by E. Bashir in 1989 or in 2015. For instance, the sentence in example 7.4, which, since it has a third person singular agent (mother) of a transitive verb in a perfective tense would be a candidate for نے /ne/ in Panjabi, does not contain نے /ne/ in Hindko. Its third person singular subject occurs in the oblique case form. All agents of transitive verbs in perfective tenses, including third person, occur in their oblique or agentive case form (see Chapter 4 on nouns).[2] Additionally, there is an agentive postposition سنڑ /suṛ̃/ which is sometimes used by some speakers of Abbottabad and Mansehra Hindko with first and second person plural and third person singular and plural subjects, shown in 7.5 (also Sakoon 2002: 163).[3]

(7.4) میری ماؤ کجھ نویں کپڑے کہد ین

mer-ī	***maũ***	*kúj*	*nav-ẽ*	*kapṛ-e*
1SG.GEN-SG.F	**mother.OBL**	some	new-PL.M	clothes-PL.M

kìd-e-n
buy.PP-PL.M-be.PRES.3PL

'My **mother** bought some new clothes.' (Hk) (AWT)

(7.5) اس سنڑ ایہہ گل کیتی

us	***suṛ̃***	*é*	*gal*	*kīt-ī*
3SG.OBL	**ERG**	this	speech.SG.F	do.PP-SG.F

'**He/she** said this.'
'**He/she** told (me) about this.' (Hk) (AWT)

7.1.1.2 Panjabi grammatical postpositions

The dative-accusative postposition نوں /nū̃/ has a wide range of functions generally relating to GOAL marking. In Panjabi, all indirect and some direct objects, as well as a wide range of dative subjects, are marked by نوں /nū̃/, as in example 7.6. Third person (singular) agents of transitive verbs in perfective tenses are often marked by the

2 نے /ne/ is, however, sometimes seen in the writing of those writers whose style is influenced by Urdu, and fairly frequently in the Hindko of Peshawar. Agent marking and the ergative construction are discussed in Chapter 9.

3 Bailey (1920: 89), discussing the language of the Kaghan Valley, says, "The agent preposition suN which is not used with the 1st and 2nd singular pronouns, is interesting. Its use is optional, as the simple oblique is sufficient. The commonest ending for the obl. sg. is -e or -u, for the plural it is always aaN." This description fits the situation in present-day Hazara Hindko very closely.

postposition نے /ne/, known as the ergative marker, as in example 7.7. However, despite statements in some descriptions of Panjabi, the use of نے /ne/ is by no means obligatory or universal. [4]

Usually these grammatical postpositions directly follow the oblique form of a nominal without any intervening material. It is, however, possible for the emphatic element ی /ī/ to intervene between an oblique nominal and either the dative-accusative postposition نوں /nū̃/ or the ergative postposition نے /ne/, yielding اُسی نوں /us-ī nū̃/ '3SG-EMPH ACC' and اُسی نے /us-ī ne/ '3SG-EMPH ERG'. These grammatical postpositions are sometimes written as separate words and sometimes not.

(7.6) اوہنوں انگریزی بالکل نئیں آندی

ó-nū̃	*angrezī*	*bilkul*	*naī̃*	*ā-nd-ī*
3SG-DAT	English.SG.F	completely	NEG	come-IP-SG.F

'**He/she** doesn't know English at all.' (Pj) (Bashir and Kazmi 2012: 8)

(7.7) سب امیدواراں نے اپنیاں درخواستاں جمع کرا دتیاں نیں

sáb	***umīdwār-ā̃***	***ne***	*apṇ-iyā̃*	*darxāst-ā̃*	*jamā*
all	**candidate-PL.OBL**	**ERG**	self's-PL.F	application-PL.F	submitted

kar-ā	*ditt-iyā̃*	*nẽ*
do-CS	give.PP-PL.F	be.PRES.3PL

'All the **candidates** have submitted their applications.' (Pj) (Bashir and Kazmi 2012: 593)

7.1.1.3 Saraiki grammatical postpositions

The only postposition in Saraiki which can properly be said to mark a core grammatical constituent is the dative-accusative کوں /kū̃/, which marks all indirect objects, some direct objects (usually those which are definite or specific, also usually animate or human), and many dative subjects, as in example 7.8. Importantly, the postposition نے /ne/ 'ergative marker', used regularly in Urdu and by some Panjabi speakers with third person singular agents, is not original in Saraiki. According to Shackle (1976: 144), "the p[ost]p[ositio]n /ne/ is occasionally used as a marker of E[rgative] in imitation of

4 The use of نے /ne/ to mark some third person agents of perfective transitive verbs in Panjabi seems (to E. Bashir) to be an influence of Urdu; the relation between the use of this element in Urdu and Panjabi (in various functions) is a complicated question.

U[rdu] P[anjabi] usage: this is quite frequent in educated colloquial speech but is considered incorrect in careful speech and writing." No examples of نے /ne/ were found in our field data, and Nasir Abbas Syed confirms that monolingual Saraiki speakers never use نے /ne/; but example 7.9 occurs in Zahoor (2009), a conversation manual for Urdu and English speakers learning Saraiki. Object and agent marking are discussed in detail, with examples, in Chapter 9.

(7.8) تیکوں آپݨا چھوٹیلا یاد ہے

tæ-kũ̄	*āpṇ-ā*	*choṭ-e-lā*	*yād*	*he*
2SG-DAT	self's-SG.M	small-M.SG.OBL-time.of	memory	be.PRES.3SG

'Do **you** remember your childhood?' (Sr) (Nasir Abbas Syed)

(7.9) انھاں ݙیہاڑیاں اچ او نے بی اے کیتے

inhā̃	*ɗīhāṛ-ĕā̃*	*ic*	***o***	***ne***	*bī*	*e*
3PL.OBL	day-PL.OBL	in	**3SG.OBL**	**ERG**	B	A

kīt-æ
do.PP-M.SG.3SG+be.PRES.3SG

'**He/she** did his/her B.A. recently.' (Sr) (Zahoor 2009: 51)

Table 7.1 compares the dative-accusative and the ergative postpositions for Hindko, Panjabi, and Saraiki. Parentheses around an element indicate that it is restricted in occurrence or optional. Square brackets around an element indicate an Urdu-influenced usage.

Language/Form	Dative-accusative	Ergative
Hindko	آں /ā̃/	(سڑ suṛ̃), [(نے /ne/)]
Panjabi	نوں /nū̃/	[(نے /ne/)]
Saraiki	کوں /kū̃/	[(نے /ne/)]

Table 7.1: Dative-accusative and ergative postpositions in Hindko, Panjabi, and Saraiki

7.1.2 Adjectival postpositions

Most postpositions are invariant—they do not inflect to agree with either with the noun they follow or the noun they precede. However, a few display both postpositional properties (in that they cause the nominal they follow to be in its oblique form) and adjectival properties (in that they agree with the noun they precede). These are Layer II case-marking elements. In their adjectival function, they behave as marked ("black") adjectives. The primary example of this class is the genitive postposition دا ~ نا /dā ~ nā/ (Hk), دا /dā/ (Pj, Sr), 'of' , which inflects for gender, number, and case to agree with the noun it precedes, i.e. the thing "possessed".

7.1.2.1 The genitive postposition

Genitive, or possessive, relations for all but first and second person pronouns are marked by the adjectival postposition دا /dā/ in all three languages.[5] دا /dā/ functions both as a postposition, in that it requires the noun it follows to be in the oblique case, and as a marked adjective since it agrees with the noun that the possessive phrase modifies. When it follows a noun, it forms a construction which is formally a postpositional phrase but functionally an adjectival phrase. A few simple examples follow—for Hindko, in 7.10 and 7.11, Panjabi, in 7.12 and 7.13, and Saraiki, in 7.14.

(7.10) اس دا کھوڑا

us	***d-ā***	*kòṛ-ā*
3SG.OBL	**GEN-SG.M**	horse-SG.M

'his/her horse' (Hk) (AWT)

(7.11) اس دی بلی

us	***d-ī***	*bill-ī*
3SG.OBL	**GEN-SG.F**	cat-SG.F

'his/her cat' (Hk) (AWT)

(7.12) آدمی دا گھر

ādmī	***d-ā***	*kàr*
man.SG.M.OBL	**GEN-SG.M.DIR**	house.SG.M.DIR

'the/a man's house' (Pj) (EB)

5 Some varieties of Hindko have نا /nā/ instead of دا /dā/.

(7.13) عورت دا گھر

ɔrat	***d-ā***	*kàr*
woman.SG.F.OBL	**GEN-SG.M.DIR**	house.SG.M.DIR

'the/a woman's house' (Pj) (EB)

(7.14) اوں عورت دا پتر

ū̃	*ɔrat*	***d-ā***	*putr*
3SG.OBL	woman.SG.F.OBL	**GEN-SG.M**	son.SG.M

'that woman's son' (Sr) (UK)

In addition, other close relations between entities, for instance the material of which something is made, are expressed as a genitive relation, as in example 7.15.

(7.15) اک لکڑی دا کھوکھلا گھوڑا

ikk	*lakṛī*	***d-ā***	*khokhl-ā*	*kòṛ-ā*
one/a	wood.OBL	**GEN-SG.M**	hollow-SG.M	horse-SG.M

'a hollow wooden horse (lit. horse **of** wood)' (Pj) (https://pnb.wikipedia.org/wiki/اوڈیسی)

7.1.2.2 والا~آلا /-ālā ~ -vālā ~ -vāḷā ~ -āḷā/

This element, found in all three languages, has been previously discussed as an adjective-forming element (Section 5.11), but it could equally well be analyzed as an adjectival (Level II) postposition, since it follows the oblique form of a nominal, and it is adjectival. In some cases, it can convey the same or similar meaning as دا /dā/ 'of'. For example, پھل والی دکان /phal vālī dukān/ and پھل دی دکان /phal dī dukān/ both mean 'fruit shop'.

7.1.2.3 جوگا /jogā/ Hk, Pj ; جوڳا /joɠā/ Sr 'capable of, worthy of'

The postposition جوگا /jogā/ 'capable of, worthy of' in Hindko is illustrated below in example 7.16 (see also 7.77 below). Example 7.17 is from Panjabi, and 7.18 is from Saraiki.[6]

(7.16) ایہہ کتاب پڑھنے جوگی نئیں

é	*kitāb*	*páṛ-n-e*	***jog-ī***	*naī̃*
this	book.SG.F	read-INF-OBL	**worthy.of-SG.F**	is.not

'This book isn't **worth** reading.' (Hk) (AWT)

(7.17) اللّٰہ جانے ایہہ مرن جوگے دہشت گرد کدوں ساڈے ملک اچوں جان گے

Allah	*jān-e*	*é*	*mar-an*	***jog-e***
God	know-3SG.SUBJ	these	die-OBL.INF	**deserving.of-PL.M**

déšatgard	*kadõ*	*sāḍ-e*	*mulk*	*ic-õ*
terrorist.PL.M	when	1PL.GEN-SG.M.OBL	country.SG.M.OBL	in-ABL

jā-ṇ-ge
go-3PL-FUT.PL.M

'God knows when these cursed terrorists will leave our country.' (Pj) (Bashir and Kazmi 2012: 534)

(7.18) اوہ ایں کم جوڳا کینہی

o	*ī̃*	*kamm*	***joɠ-ā***	*kænhī*
3SG	this.OBL	work.SG.OBL	**capable.of-SG.M**	is.not

'He is un**able** to do this work.' (Sr) (UK)

6 There may be more such postpositions in Hindko, but time has not permitted us to find them.

7.1.2.4 جیہا /jiā̃́/ Hk, Pj ; جیہاں ~ جھیاں /jehā̃ ~ jheā̃/ 'like, similar to' Sr [7]

This element is indigenous to all three languages, occurring with slightly differing spellings. In Hindko and Panjabi, it follows the genitive of first and second person pronouns and the genitive or oblique of third person pronouns and nouns; in Saraiki, it follows the oblique form of all pronouns and nouns. A Hindko example is 7.19; Panjabi sentences are 7.20 and 7.21; and Saraiki are 7.22, 7.23, and 7.24.

(7.19) جنہاں کہڑیاں بچ ہک جہیا ٹیم ایں اُنہاں لینڑاں لا کے ملاتو

jí-nā̃	*kàṛyi-ā̃*	*bic*	*hikk*	***ji-ā̃́***	*ṭem*	*ẽ*
REL-OBL.PL.F	clock-OBL.PL.F	in	one	**like-SG.M**	time	be.PRES.3PL

un-ā̃	*læṛ̃-ā̃*	*lā*	*ke*	*milā-o*
3PL.DIST.OBL-ACC	line-PL.F	put	CP	connect-IMP.2PL

'Connect those clocks which have the **same** time with a line.' (Hk) (http://www.hindko.org/en/text-books)

(7.20) تیرے جیہا کوئی نہیں

te-re	***ji-ā̃́***	*koī*	*naĩ́*
2SG.GEN-SG.M.OBL	**like-SG.M**	any	is.not

'There is no one **like** you' (Pj) (http://alqlm.org/xen/threads/)

(7.21) اوہدے جیہا ڈاڈھا بندہ اپنی گل منوا ای لیندا اے

ó-de	***ji-ā̃́***	*ḍā́ḍ-ā*	*bandā*	*āpṇ-ī*	*gal*
3SG.OBL-GEN.SG.M.OBL	**like-SG.M**	firm-SG.M	person	self's-SG.M	word

man-vā	*ī*	*le-nd-ā*	*e*
agree-CS	EMPH	take-IP-SG.M	be.PRES.3SG

'A firm person **like** him eventually has his way' (Pj) (Bashir and Kazmi 2012: 319)

7 Shackle (1976: 55–62) gives these forms with the final /a/ nasalized, an observation confirmed by Nasir Abbas Syed, while some of our examples do not show nasalization. Syed comments that, in general rural Saraiki speakers tend to use more nasalized forms than do urban dwellers, who are influenced by Urdu and Panjabi pronunciation, which, according to Syed, is less inclined to nasalization.

(7.22) میکوں اینجھے کھانڑے پسند آندن

mæ-kũ	***ĩ-jh-e***	*khāṇ-e*	*pasand*
1SG-DAT	3SG.PROX.OBL-like-PL.M	food-PL.M	pleasing

ā-nd-ĕn
come-IP-PL.M+be.PRES.3PL

'I like this kind of dishes (food)' (Sr) (UK)

(7.23) تیں جہیں چوہر

tæ̃	***jah-ĩ***	*cūhir*
2SG.OBL	**like-SG.F**	girl.SG.F

'a girl **like** you' (Sr) (Shackle 1976: 110)

(7.24) انہاں ڈی سی او کوں آکھیا جو تساں جیہے محنتی افیسرز

inhā̃	*ḍī*	*sī*	*o*	*kũ*	*ākh-iyā*	*jo*	*tussā̃*	***jih-e***
3PL.OBL	D	C	O	DAT	say-PP.SG.M	that	2PL.OBL	**like-PL.M**

mehntī	*āfisarz*
hard-working	officers[PL.M]

'They said to the District Coordination Officer that hard-working officers **like** you …' (Sr) (http://saraiki.app.com.pk/saraiki/2016/09/)

7.1.2.5 ورگا /vargā/ 'like' Pj

The adjectival postposition ورگا /vargā/ 'like' follows the genitive of first, second, and third person pronouns and the oblique of nouns. See the Panjabi examples 7.25 and 7.26.

(7.25) تیرے ورگی بدتمیز کڑی نال میں نہیں رہ سکدا

ter-e	***varg-ī***	*badtamīz*	*kuṛī*	*nāḷ*	*mæ̃*	*naĩ*
2SG.GEN-SG.M.OBL	**like-SG.F**	bad.mannered	girl.SG.F	with	1SG	NEG

ræ̃	*sak-d-ā*
live	be.able-IP-SG.M

'I can't live with a bad mannered girl **like** you.' (Pj) (http://www.wichaar.com/news/184/ARTICLE/5360/2008-05-23.html)

(7.26) کوئی ساگ نہیں ماں دے ساگ ورگا

koī	*sāg*	*naĩ*	*mā̃*	*d-e*	*sāg*
any	greens.SG.M	is.not	mother	GEN-SG.M.OBL	greens.SG.M.OBL

varg-ā
like-SG.M

'There are no greens **like** (those prepared by) a mother. (i.e. nothing is like a mother's love and care)' (Pj) (http://fbdio.com/video/1364567/)

7.1.2.6 Other adjectival postpositions

Shackle (1976: 55) lists several other adjectival postpositions in Saraiki. They include جتلا / جتنا /jitlā ~ jitnā/ 'as much as', and جیڈا /jeɗā/ 'as big as' (Shackle 1976: 56).

7.2 Layer III and complex postpositions

7.2.1 Sources of derived postpositions

Postpositions can be derived from various parts of speech, including nouns, adverbs, and verbs; but not from adjectives. With postpositions derived from nouns, the noun can either appear in the oblique, or a Layer I case ending can be incorporated, as in Panjabi ہتھوں /hath-õ/ 'hand-ABL > from the hand, by the hand of'.

In all three languages some postpositions are optionally preceded by the genitive postposition, when they occur with third person pronouns or with nouns. With first and second person pronouns, these pronouns obligatorily follow the genitive form. For example, with Panjabi وچکار /vickār/ 'between; in the middle', both بھراواں وچکار /prā̀vā̃ vickār/ and بھراواں دے وچکار / /prā̀vā̃ de vickār/ 'among the brothers' occur. The same applies to ہیٹھ ~ ہیٹھاں /heṭh-heṭhā̃/ 'below; underneath', as in منجی (دے) ہیٹھاں /manjī (de) heṭhā̃/ 'under the bed'; (دے) تھلے /(de) thalle/ 'below; under', as in رکھاں دے تھلے /rukkhā̃ (de) thalle/ 'under the trees'; (دے) اگے /(de) agge/ 'before; in front of'; as in گھر (دے) اگے /kàr (de) agge/ 'in front of the house'; (دے) واستے /de vāste/ 'for the sake of, for the purpose of', as in گھر (دے) واستے /kàr (de) vāste/ 'for the house'. نیڑے /neṛe/ 'near' also falls in this category.

Hindko (دے) بغیر /(de) bayær/ 'without' and (دے) بعد /(de) bād/ 'after' follow the same pattern, as do most Saraiki postpositions (Shackle 1976: 57).

Some postpositions are obligatorily preceded by a genitive element, e.g. دی تراں ~ دی طراں /dī tarā̃/ 'like'[8], as in چور دی طراں /cor dī tarā̃/ 'like a thief' or میری طراں /merī tarā̃/ 'like me' (Pj Sr); or طرف /taraf/ 'direction, as in میری طرف /merī taraf/ (Pj, Hk), میڈی طرف /meḍ̄ī taraf/ 'toward me' (Sr); or دے پاسے /de pāse/, as in دریا دے شمال دے پاسے /daryā de šimāl de pāse/ 'on the north side of the river' (Pj). These are Layer III formations. Many of these postpositions were originally nouns which have undergone varying degrees of grammaticization. The gender of the genitive postposition depends on the gender of the original noun. The form دے /de/, masculine singular oblique, occurs when that noun is masculine, and دی /dī/, feminine, when the original noun is feminine.

Some postpositions are also derived from verbs. In the cases shown below, the postposition is formed from the verb stem with the conjunctive participial ending کے /-ke/ (see Section 8.4.2.3) for discussion of the conjunctive participle). The following examples are from Panjabi, but are commonly used and understood in Hindko and Saraiki as well. ملا /milā-/ 'meet.CAUS' > ملاکے /milāke/ 'including' , چھڈ /chaḍḍ-/ 'leave, abandon' > /chaḍḍke/ 'excepting, leaving aside' کر /kar-/ 'do' > کرکے /karke/ 'on account of, because of',

7.2.2 Locative relations – spatial and temporal

A large number of postpositions denote adjunct relations—elements of meaning other than the grammatical relations subject, direct object, and indirect object which are essential to the basic structure of a sentence. These other elements include spatial, temporal, causal, and manner relations. In earlier forms of Indo-Aryan (Sanskrit and various forms of Middle Indic), many of these relations were indicated by case inflection. Over time, the case system has evolved into a system in which such relations are mainly indicated by postpositions. Each language has been affected somewhat differently in this process.

7.2.2.1 Locative postpositions – Ḥindko

Three of the most frequently used Hindko postpositions are exemplified here. The basic idea of physical proximity, with its extended meanings, is expressed by کول /kol/

8 This word occurs spelled in either of these ways. The spelling with ط reflects a partial carryover of Urdu spelling into Panjabi. This is the usual practice with Panjabi and Saraiki writers, but not all agree with it. Also, the prominent non-phonemic nasalization is reflected here in both spellings. Since the originally Arabic noun طرح /tarah/ 'way, method' is feminine, the feminine form of the genitive occurs.

'near, in the vicinity of'. With nouns and pronouns except for the first and second person singular, کول /kol/ follows the oblique, as in example 7.27; with the first and second person singular pronouns, it follows the genitive, as in example 7.28.

(7.27) تُوں اس با بے کول بیٹھے دا ایہیا ایں، جس آں میں اپڑی کہانی دسی ایہی

tũ	*us*	*bāb-e*	***kol***	*bæṭhe-d-ā*	*éy-ā-ẽ*
2SG	that	old.man-OBL	**near**	sit.PP-STAT-SG.M	be.PST-SG.M-2SG

jis-ā̃	*mæ̃*	*apṛ-ī*	*kàṇī*	*das-ī*	*éy-ī*
whom.OBL-DAT	1SG	self's-SG.F	story.SG.F	tell.PP-SG.F	be.PST-SG.F

'You were sitting **with** the old man to whom I had told my story.' (Hk) (AWT)

(7.28) اس تداں میرے کول پہیجیا

us	*tud-ā̃*	*mer-e*	***kol***	*pèj-iyā*
3SG.OBL	2SG.OBL-ACC	1SG.GEN-SG.M.OBL	**near**	send-PP.SG.M

'He/she sent you **to** me.' (Hk) (AWT)

Accompaniment is expressed by نال /nāl/ 'with', as shown in examples 7.29 and 7.30. With nouns it follows the oblique, as in 7.29, behaving as a Layer II element, and with first and second singular pronouns it follows the genitive, as in 7.30, forming a Layer III construction.

(7.29) جس جڑیں نال توں پیا گلاں کرنا ایہیا ایں او میرا رشتہ دار اے

jis	*jaṛ-ẽ*	***nāl***	*tũ*	*p-yā*	*gall-ā̃*	*kar-n-ā*
which.OBL	man-OBL	**with**	2SG	CONT.I-SG.M	word-PL.F	do-IP-SG.M

éy-ā-ẽ	*o*	*mer-ā*	*ristadār*	*e*
be.PST-SG.M-2SG	3SG	1SG.GEN-SG.M	relative	be.PRES.3SG

'The man **with** whom you were talking is related to me.'[9] (Hk) (AWT)

(7.30) میں تیرے نال پشاور نہ جل ہکدا

mæ̃	*ter-e*	***nāl***	*pišāwar*	*na*	*jul*	*hak-d-ā*
1SG	2SG.GEN-SG.M.OBL	**with**	Peshawar	NEG	go	be.able-IP-SG.M

'I cannot go **with** you to Peshawar.' (Hk) (AWT)

The meaning of 'opposite, in front of' is expressed with سامڑے /sāmṛe/, as in example 7.31.

9 The form پیا /pyā/, glossed here as CONT(INUOUS) is the grammaticalized masculine singular perfective participle of پیڑا /pæṛā/ 'to fall, lie'. See Section 8.4.5.2.2, Section 8.3.1.6.7, and Section 8.5.6.3 for its use in Panjabi, Hindko, and Saraiki, respectively.

(7.31) میرے سامنڑے ٹُر

mer-e **sāmṛe** *ṭur*
1SG.GEN-SG.M.OBL **in.front.of** walk
'Walk **in front of** me!' (Hk) (AWT)

7.2.2.2 Locative postpositions – Panjabi

Some common postpositions marking stative temporal and spatial relations are: وچ /vic/ 'in, at', اتّے ~ تے /utte ~ te/ 'on', and کول /koḷ/ 'near, to'. When these postpositions follow a first, second, or third person singular pronoun, the pronoun usually appears in its genitive form: اوہ دے وچ /ó de vic/ 'in 3SG', اوہ دے اتّے /ó de utte/ 'on (top of) 3SG', اوہ دے کول /ó de koḷ/ 'near 3SG'; but the third person plural pronoun can appear without the genitive element: اوہناں وچ /ónā̃ vic/ 'in 3PL'. With nouns, they usually (but not always) occur with the oblique but without the genitive element, e.g. گھر وچ /kàr vic/ 'in the house'.

وچ /vic/ 'in, at' and اتّے /utte/ 'on' are often found in a phonologically reduced form both in speaking and writing. وچ /vic/ ~ اچ /ic/ ~ چ /c/ 'in'. Often, but not necessarily, اچ /ic/ appears with consonant-final nouns and وچ /vic/ with words ending in vowels or consonant clusters. چ /c/ appears with either vowel- or consonant-final words, e.g. کمرےچ /kamre-c/ 'in the room', گھرچ /kàr-c/ 'in the house', but not with words ending in چ /c/, ج /j/, or consonant clusters. Thus, سوچ وچ /soc vic/ 'in thought', فرج وچ /frij vic/ 'in the fridge', or پنڈ وچ /pinḍ vic/ 'in the village'. Thus we can have: گھر دے وچ /kàr de vic/, گھروچ /kàr vic/, گھراچ /kàr ic/ and گھرچ /kàrc/, but not گھر دےچ * /kàr de c/ or گھر دے اچ * /kàr de ic/ for 'in the house'.

Similarly, we can have, for example: کرسی دے اتّے بیٹھو /kursī de utte bæṭho/, کرسی اتّے بیٹھو /kursī utte bæṭho/, or کرسی تے بیٹھو /kursī te bæṭho/ 'sit on the chair', but not کرسی دے تے بیٹھس * /*kursī de te bæṭho/ (Gill and Gleason 1969: 55).

Some adverbs can follow a noun or pronoun in the ablative or genitive case, thus forming Layer II (with the ablative case ending) or Layer III (with توں or the genitive) postpositional elements.[10] They include the following:

10 That these items are basically adverbs can be seen in the following example: باہر بیٹھو /bā̃r bæṭho/ 'sit outside!' and similar sentences with the other elements.

باہر /bā̃r/ 'outside (of)', e.g. شہروں باہر /šǽr-õ bā̃r/ or شہرتوں باہر /šǽr tõ bā̃r/ 'outside the city'

دور /dūr/ 'away from; at a distance from', e.g. گھروں دور /kàr-õ dūr/; گھرتوں دور /kàr tõ dūr/ 'far from the house'

اگے /agge/ 'before; in front of; beyond', e.g. دکان توں اگے /dukān tõ agge/ 'beyond the shop'; میرے اگے /mere agge/ 'ahead of me'

ارے /ure/ 'on this side of, on the near side of', e.g. سکول دے ارے /skūl de ure/ 'on this side of the school'

پرے /pare/ 'on that side of, beyond; at a distance from', e.g. پنڈوں پرے /pinḍ-õ pare/; پنڈ توں پرے /pinḍ tõ pare/ 'beyond the village'

پار /pār/ 'across, on the far side of', e.g. دریا دے پار /daryā de pār/; دریائوں پار /daryā-õ pār/ 'across the river'; دریا توں پار /daryā tõ pār/ 'across the river'.

7.2.2.3 Locative postpositions – Saraiki

Some basic locative postpositions in Saraiki, many of which are shared with Hindko and Panjabi, are the following:

وچ /vic/ ~ اچ /ic/ 'in' (II/III)

کن /kan/ ~ کول /kol/ 'to, near, in possession of' (II with nouns, III with pronouns)

تے /te/ 'on, to' (II with nouns; III with pronouns)

ہیٹھ /heṭh/ 'beneath, below'

اندر /andar/ 'inside'

باہر /ɓāhar/ 'outside'

As in Panjabi, many words function as adverbs in verbal phrases and as postpositions in nominal phrases (Shackle 1976: 56). Many of these items—the forms ending in /e/—are originally the oblique or locative form of nouns. These postpositions follow the oblique or genitive form of the noun or pronoun, as in examples 7.32 and 7.33, which uses the postposition تلے /talle/ 'under' and کنے /kane/ 'near'. Some other frequently used members of this class are as follows:

اگے /aɠe/ 'before, ahead of'; اتے /utte/ 'above'; پہلے/pehle/ ~ /pelhe/ 'before'; پچھے /piche/ 'behind'

(7.32) اوں وݨ تلے

ũ	*vaṇ*	***talle***
3SG.OBL	tree.OBL	**under**

'**under** that tree' (Sr) (UK)

(7.33) اوکوں میں کنے پٹھیئی

ū-kũ̃ *mæ̃* ***kane*** *paṭhĕ-ī*
3SG.OBL-ACC 1SG.OBL **to** send.PP-PS2SG
'You sent him/her **to** me.'[11] (Sr) (UK)

Many postpositions can take the ablative ending /-ũ̃/ to add the meaning 'from' to the basic meaning, e.g. کنو /kanũ̃/ (from کن /kan/ 'nearby' + وں /ũ̃/ 'ABL'), in examples 7.34 and 7.35. Some adverbs, e.g. پہلے /pehle/ 'before' can combine with an ablative postposition, for example, کنوں /kanũ̃/ 'from', to function as a complex (Layer IV) postposition, کنوں پہلے /kanũ̃ pehle/ 'before', as in 7.35.

(7.34) میں اے ھک ھٹی آلے کنوں گھدے

mæ̃ *e* *hik* *haṭṭī-āl-e* ***kanũ̃***
1SG this a/one shop.SG.F.OBL-NMLZ-OBL **from**

ghi-d-e
take-PP-SG.M+3SG.PRES
'I got this **from** a shopkeeper.' (Sr) (UK)

(7.35) پیو کمبرے اچ آوݨ کنوں پہلے کھنگیے

pyū *kambr-e* *ic* *āv-aṇ* ***kanũ̃*** ***pelhe***
father room-OBL in come-INF.OBL **ABL** **before**

khang-iye
cough.PP-SG.M+PRES.3SG
'Father coughed **before** coming into the room.' (Sr) (UK)

The temporal postposition سیت /set/ 'at the same time as' is illustrated in example 7.36 following an infinitive in its oblique form, which is identical to the direct form in Saraiki.[12]

11 Nasir Abbas Syed has nasalized ایں /ĩ/ for the second person singular pronominal suffix
12 Example 7.36 is interesting in that it employs both the (original) morphological passive in -j- and the (later) analytical passive formed with 'go'.

(7.36) سٹیشن تے پوہچن سیت مفرور سنجنیج گے

sṭešaṇ	*te*	*pohc-aṇ*	***set***	*mafrūr*	*sũfṇe-j*
station	at	arrive-INF.OBL	**at.the.same.time.as**	fugitive	recognize-PASS

gˊ-ae
go.PP-SG.M

'**As soon as** (he) reached the station the fugitive was recognized.' (Sr) (UK)

7.2.3 GOAL and direction of motion

The relations of GOAL (end point) and SOURCE (point of origin) are so basic in conceptualizing an event or action that they sometimes straddle the categories of case ending (Layer I) and grammatical postposition (Layer II). Thus, to express SOURCE relations, all three languages still have a productive ablative case ending (Layer I) (see Chapter 4 on nouns and Chapter 6 on pronouns), while at the same time expressing some ablative relations by means of basic postpositions (Layer II). Similarly, GOAL is sometimes expressed with a simple oblique (Layer I), and sometimes with the dative-accusative postposition (Layer II), which, in addition to marking direct and indirect objects, can also be used to mark motion toward (usually something inanimate). The basic spatial relations of GOAL and SOURCE are extended to apply to temporal and other abstract relations as well.

7.2.3.1 Goal and direction of motion – Hindko

Often the goal of motion is indicated by the dative-accusative postposition آں /ã/ 'to', as in example 7.37. Goal and direction of motion can also be indicated with در /dar/ ~ دار /dār/ 'to, toward' (Sakoon 2002: 138), as in example 7.38.

(7.37) میں کہرے آں جلساں

mæ̃	***kàr-e-ã***	*jul-s-ã*
1SG	**home-OBL-to**	go-FUT-1SG

'I will go **home**.' (Hk) (EB 1989, unpublished field notes, Abbottabad)

(7.38) میں تداں اس در نہ پیہج ساں

mæ̃ tud-ā̃ us ***dar*** *na pèj-s-ā̃*
1SG 2SG.OBL-ACC 3SG.OBL **to** NEG send-FUT-1SG
'I will not send you to **him/her.**' (Hk) (AWT)

تک /tak/, shared with Panjabi and illustrated in 7.39, and تاڑی /tāṛī/ 'until, up to', as in example 7.40 (Sakoon 2002: 76), indicate distance and endpoint.

(7.39) اِتھے اس ویلے تک انتظار کرکہ او تداں میرا خط دیوے

ithe us vel-e ***tak*** *intazār kar ki o tud-ā̃*
here that.OBL time-OBL **until** wait do when 3SG 2SG.OBL-DAT

mer-ā xat de-ve
1SG.GEN-SG.M letter.SG.M give-SBJV.3SG
'Wait here **until** he/she gives you my letter.' (Hk) (AWT)

(7.40) او پشور گئے دے تے ہونڑ تاڑیں اتھے ہی اے

o pišɔr g-ae-de te
3SG Peshawar go.PP-SG.M+be.3SG.PRES-STAT.SG.M+be.3SG.PRES and

huṛ̃ tāṛ̃ī *uthe hī e*
now until there EMPH be.PRES.3SG
'He has gone to Peshawar and is **still** there.' (Hk) (AWT)

Notice that the type of 'until' clause in 7.39, employing a کہ /ki/ clause and a subjunctive verb, does not involve a negative element, as is virtually obligatory in Panjabi or Urdu 'until' clauses employing a relative-correlative construction. An 'until' clause including a negative element is given in example 7.41.

(7.41) میں اُس ویلے تک نہ کھاندا جد تک توں نہ آسیں

mæ̃ us vel-e tak na khā-nd-ā jad ***tak*** *tū̃ na*
1SG 3SG.OBL time-OBL until NEG eat-IP-SG.M REL **until** 2SG NEG

ā-s-ẽ
come-FUT-2SG
'I won't eat **until** you come.' (Hk) (AWT)

7.2.3.2 Goal and direction of motion – Panjabi

In Panjabi, the goal of motion is usually indicated by a simple oblique form, as in example 7.42.

(7.42) اوہ آپنے گھر گیا اے

ó	āpṇ-e	**kår**	gy-ā	e
3SG	self's-SG.M.OBL	**house.OBL**	go.PP-SG.M	be.PRES.3SG

'He has gone **to** his (own) **house.**' (Pj) (EB)

Direction of motion, however, is usually expressed with the postposition ول /vall/ 'in the direction of, toward', as in example 7.43.

(7.43) اوہ پچھلی گلی ول نس گیا سی

ó	pichḷī	gaḷī	**vall**	nas	gy-ā	sī
3SG	back	street	**towards**	run.away	go.PP-SG.M	be.PST.3SG

'He ran (away) **toward** the back street.' (Pj) (Adapted from Bashir and Kazmi 2012: 48)

In addition to the grammatical postpositions نوں /nū̃/ and نے /ne/, some other Layer II postpositions do not occur with the genitive postposition with nouns, for instance تک /tak/ 'up to, until', which expresses an interval up to a specified point (both spatial and temporal), for example سڑک تک /saṛak tak/ 'up to the road', but not *سڑک دے تک /*saṛak de tak/; and توں /tõ/ 'from', for example سکول توں /skūl tõ/ 'from (the) school' but not *سکول دے توں /*skūl de tõ/.

7.2.3.3 Goal and direction of motion – Saraiki

The goal of motion, for example, 'city' in 7.44, can be expressed with the oblique form of a nominal. Since the oblique form of many nouns is identical to the direct form, this is not obvious, except with marked masculine nouns.

(7.44) او ٻہوں جلدی شہر ویسی پئی

o	ɓahū̃	jaldī	**šahar**	væ-sī	pa-ī
3SG	very	soon	**city.OBL**	go-FUT.3SG	fall.PP-SG.F

'She will be going **to the city** very soon.'[13] (Sr) (Shackle 1976: 132)

13 In Shackle (1976: 132) this example is cited from Lashari (1971: 65). The verb form in this sentence is a future augmented with the perfective participle of پووݨ /povaṇ/ 'to fall', which lends a sense of immediacy to the future action. Compare this form to other progressive tenses discussed in Chapter 8.

An inanimate destination can also be expressed with the postposition تے /te/ 'to', as in 7.45. With an animate goal, e.g. 'doctor', as in 7.46, the postposition کنے /kane/ 'to', which is the oblique of کن /kan/ 'in the vicinity of', appears.

(7.45) دکان تے ونج

dukan **te** *vãʄ*
shop.OBL **to** go
'Go **to** the shop.' (Sr) (UK)

(7.46) میکوں ڈاکٹر کنے ونجنا ھا

mæ-kũ *ḍākṭar* ***kane*** *vãʄ-ṇ-ā* *h-ā*
1SG-DAT doctor **to** go-GRDV-SG.M be.PST-SG.M
'I had to go **to** the doctor.' (Sr) (UK)

Direction of motion is expressed with several postpositions, all of which are unstressed. تئیں /taĩ/ 'up to, until' (Shackle 1976: 65); توݨی /toṇī/ ~ تاݨی /tāṇī/ 'up to, until' (see example 7.47); پاسے /pāse/ 'toward', Layer III, following genitive, e.g. اوں پاسے /ũ pāse/ 'in that direction' (Shackle 1976: 67); طرف /taraf/ 'direction' [F], Layer III, with feminine genitive form of noun or pronoun > 'toward', e.g. میڈی طرف /meɗī taraf/ 'toward me'; دو /do/ ~ ڈے /ɗe/ ~ ڈو /ɗo/ 'to, toward' (Shackle 1976: 55) (see example 7.48).

(7.47) اتھاں جمب جے تاݨی او میڈی چٹھی ڈیندے

itthã *jamb* *je* *tāṇī* *o* *meɗ-ī* *ciṭṭh-ī*
here wait.patiently when.REL until 3SG 1SG.GEN-SG.F letter-SG.F

ɗe-nd-e
give-IP-SG.M+be.3SG.PRES
'Wait here until he gives (you) my letter.'[14] (Sr) (UK)

(7.48) اختر پیو دو تار بھیج ڈتی

axtar ***pyū*** ***do*** *tār* *bhej* *ɗitt-ī*
Akhtar **father.OBL** **to** telegram[F] send give.PP-SG.F
'Akhtar sent his **father** a telegram.' (Sr) (Shackle (1976: 131), cited from Lashari 1971: 320.)

14 Note the absence of a negative element in this Saraiki 'until' clause.

7.2.4 SOURCE (Ablative)

The ablative indicates a generalized notion of SOURCE, including spatial, temporal, and abstract senses including cause or reason, and the standard of comparison in comparative constructions (see Chapter 5). The ablative relation, indicating direction from, is marked by either the Layer I ablative case ending وں /õ/ Hk, Pj وں /ũ̃/ Sr , the Layer II postposition توں /tõ/ 'from' Hk, Pj توں /tũ̃/ Sr , or other complex postpositions with more specific meanings. Complex postpositions consisting of a simple postposition plus the ablative ending are regularly formed in all three languages.

7.2.4.1 Ablative relations – Hindko

Most Hindko postpositions can add the ablative ending وں /õ/ directly to the postposition, adding the meaning of SOURCE to the basic meaning and forming a Layer III element, as with کول /kol/ 'in the vicinity of, with' > کولوں /kolõ/ 'from'. This is used for actions of transferring something physical from a person, as in examples 7.49 and 7.50, as well as for an abstract source such as a feared object, as in example 7.51.

(7.49) او تدکس کولوں کہدا ایہا

o	*tud*	*kis*	***kolõ***	*kìd-ā*	*éy-ā*
3SG	2SG.OBL	who.OBL	**from**	take.PP-SG.M	be.PST-SG.M

'**From** whom did you buy that?' (Hk) (AWT)

(7.50) او پیسے اس کولوں چا کہن

o	*pæse*	*us*	***kolõ***	*cā*	*kìn*
that	money	3SG.OBL	**from**	lift	take

'Take that money **from** him/her!'[15] (Hk) (AWT)

(7.51) میں کسی چیزاں کولوں نہ ڈردا

mæ̃	*kisī*	*cīz-ā̃*	***kolõ***	*na*	*ḍar-d-ā*
1SG	any.PL.OBL	thing-PL.OBL	**from**	NEG	fear-IP-SG.M

'I (m.) am not afraid **of** anything.' (Hk) (AWT)

Similarly, توں /tõ/ 'from, since, than, because of' is the ablative form of the simple locative postposition تے /te/ 'on, at'. Hindko employs توں /tõ/, shared with Panjabi,

15 See Section 10.1.3 for discussion of constructions with چا /cā-/ 'lift'.

in spatial, temporal, causal, and comparative senses, shown in examples 7.52 through 7.55, respectively. Additionally, Sakoon (2002: 90) gives the postposition تھیں /thī̃/ ~ تھی /thī/ ~ تی /tī/ 'from', e.g. اُس تھیں /us thī̃/ 'from him/her/it'.[16]

(7.52) ام دا باغ لاہورتوں داہ میل ا یہیا

am	*d-ā*	*bāy*	*lahɔr*	***tõ***	*dāh*	*mīl*	*éy-ā*
mango	GEN-SG.M	orchard.SG.M	Lahore	**from**	ten	miles	be.PST-SG.M

'The mango orchard was ten miles **from** Lahore.' (Hk) (AWT)

(7.53) ادھوانڑا کھانڑے توں بعد

adwā̀ṛ̃ā	*khā-ṛ̃-e*	***tõ***	***bād***
watermelon	eat-INF-OBL	**from**	**after**

'**after** eating watermelon' (Hk) (AWT)

(7.54) کہڑیاں گلاں توں جنگ ہوئی

kíṛ-iyā̃	***gall-ā̃***	***tõ***	*jang*	*ho-ī*
which-PL.F.OBL	**matter-PL.F.OBL**	**because.of**	war[F]	become.PP-SG.F

'**What** caused the war?' (Hk) (AWT)

(7.55) ایہہ کپڑا اس کپڑے توں چنگا اے جہڑا جمیلہ آندے

é	*kapṛ-ā*	*us*	*kapṛ-e*	***tõ***	*cā̃g-ā*
this	cloth-SG.M	that.OBL	cloth-SG.M.OBL	**than**	good-SG.M

e	*jéṛ-ā*	*jamīla*	*ānd-æ*
be.PRES.3SG	which-SG.M	Jamila	bring.PP-SG.M+be.PRES.3SG

'This cloth is better **than** that which Jamila brought.'[17] (Hk) (AWT)

16 See Section 8.5.3.2 for discussion of this verb, and whether these forms could be grammaticalized reflexes of the verb تھی /thī-/ 'become', still found in Saraiki.

17 The verb form آندے /andæ/ reflects the elision which is so widespread in Hindko and Saraiki. The ā-final m.sg. perfective participle and the present tense form of 'be' coalesce. In fact, this elision is also heard in Panjabi, but it is not represented in writing.

7.2.4.2 Ablative relations – Panjabi

As in Hindko, Panjabi also employs ablative expressions for a variety of SOURCE concepts: spatial, in examples 7.56 and 7.57, temporal, in examples 7.58 and 7.59, abstract, in example 7.60, and causal, in examples 7.61 and 7.62.

(7.56) کتھوں آئے او

kith-õ	*ā-e*	*o*
where-ABL	come-PP.PL.M	be.PRES.2PL

'**Where** have you come **from**?' (Pj) (EB)

(7.57) اے اسلام آباد توں ۱۰۰ کلومیٹر دور اے

e	*islāmābād*	***tõ***	*100*	*kilomīṭar*	*dūr*	*e*
3SG	Islamabad	**from**	100	kilometers	distant	be.PRES.3SG

'It is 100 kilometers **from** Islamabad.' (Pj) (https://pnb.wikipedia.org/wiki/%D8%A7%DB%8C%D8%A8%D9%B9_%D8%A2%D8%A8%D8%A7%D8%AF)

(7.58) دوجی جنگ عظیم توں بعد سرد جنگ بتھیرے چر تک چلدی رہی

dūjī	*jang*	*e*	*azīm*	***tõ***	***bād***	*sard*	*jang*	*bathere*	*cir*	*tak*
second	war	EZ	great	**ABL**	**after**	cold	war	great	time	until

cal-d-ī	*rá-ī*
movie-IP-SG.F	remain-PP.SG.F

'After the Second World War, the Cold War continued for quite some time.' (Pj) (Bashir and Kazmi 2012: 89)

(7.59) رات دس وجے توں بعد میں بچیاں نوں باہر نئیں جان دیندی

rāt	*das*	*vaj-e*	***tõ***	***bād***	*mæ̃*	*bac-ĕã*	*nũ*	*bā́r*
night	ten	o'clock-OBL	**ABL**	**after**	1SG	child-PL.OBL	ACC	outside

naī̃	*jāṇ*	*de-nd-ī*
NEG	go.INF.OBL	give-IP-SG.F

'I (f) do not allow the children to go out **after** ten at night.' (Pj) (Bashir and Kazmi 2012: 317)

(7.60) دنداں تے مسوڑھیاں نوں خراب ہون توں بچان لئی دہی ورتنا چاہیدا اے

dand-ā̃	*te*	*masū́ṛe-ā̃*	*nū̃*	*xarāb*	*hoṇ*	***tõ***
tooth-PL.F.OBL	and	gums-PL.M.OBL	ACC	spoiled	be.INF.OBL	**from**

bacā-ṇ	*laī*	*daī́*	*vart-ṇā*	*cā́i-d-ā*	*e*
save-INF.OBL	for	yogurt.SG.M	use-INF	be.wanted-IP-SG.M	be.PRES.3SG

'One should consume [lit. use] yogurt to protect the gums and teeth **from** becoming rotten.' (Pj) (Bashir and Kazmi 2012: 610)

(7.61) اوہ دے آن توں میں خوش ہویا

ó	*d-e*	*ā-ṇ*	***tõ***	*mæ̃*	*xuš*	*ho-iyā*
3SG.OBL	GEN-SG.M.OBL	come-INF.OBL	**ABL**	1SG	happy	be-PP.SG.M

'**Because of** his/her arrival, I (M) became happy.' (Pj) (Bhatia 1993: 79)

توں /tõ/ 'from' can also participate in complex postpositions (Layer III) as in example 7.59 above, in which an oblique element (Layer I) is followed by the basic ablative postposition توں /tõ/ (Layer II) and a second postposition بعد /bād/ 'after' to form the complex postposition توں بعد /tõ bād/ 'after' (Layer III).

In example 7.62, the ablative postposition توں /tõ/ (Layer II) is preceded by the third person singular pronoun اس /os/ in the oblique, not the genitive, to form the Layer III complex postposition توں علاوہ /tõ alāva/ 'besides, in addition to'.

(7.62) اوس توں علاوہ نوے مادیاں دی دریافت توں سیکلاں نوں ہلکا بنایا گیا اے

os	***tõ***	***alāva***	*nav-e*	*mād-ĕā̃*	*dī*
3SG.OBL	**ABL**	**in.addition**	new-PL.M.OBL	material-PL.M.OBL	of

daryāft	*tõ*	*sækl-ā̃*	*nū̃*	*halk-ā*	*banā-yā*
invention	ABL	bicycle-PL.OBL	ACC	light-SG.M	make-PP.SG.M

gyā	*e*
go.PP.SG.M	be.PRES.3SG

'**In addition to** that, with the invention of new materials bicycles have been made lighter.' (Pj) (https://pnb.wikipedia.org/wiki/سیکل)

Some adverbs can follow either the ablative case ending وں /õ/ or the ablative postposition توں /tõ/. One such adverb is باہر /bā́r/ 'outside (adv.)', which may appear as شہروں باہر شیرتون باہر /shǽrõ bār/ or شیرتون باہر /shǽr tõ bār/ 'outside the city'. Another such adverb is پار /pār/ 'across, on the far side of (adv.)', which may occur as سڑکوں پار /saṛkõ pār/, سڑک توں پار /saṛak tõ pār/, or سڑک دے پار /saṛak de pār/.

Some complex postpositions (Layer III) including an ablative element, are shown in Table 7.2 for Panjabi, with the words from which they are derived shown at the left.

وچ vicc 'inside'	وچوں viccõ 'from inside/among'
نال nāḷ 'with'	نالوں nāḷõ 'from the company of' or 'than' in comparative constructions
ول vall 'towards'	ولوں vallõ 'from the direction of'
اگے agge 'front'	اگوں aggõ 'from now on'
تھلے thalle 'under'	تھلیوں / تھلئوں thallĕõ 'from below'
کول koḷ 'near'	کولوں koḷõ 'from the vicinity of'

Table 7.2: Complex Panjabi postpositions with -وں /-õ/

7.2.4.3 Ablative relations – Saraiki

As in Hindko and Panjabi, simple Saraiki postpositions can be augmented with the ablative ending اوں /ũ/. The following postpositions consist of an ablative case marked form of a simple locative postposition, and are thus Layer III elements :

کنوں /kanũ/ 'by' (secondary agent marker); 'than (comparative); from' (at a distance from; because of) consists of the ablative form of the locative postposition کن /kan/ 'near, in the possession of'. When it includes a genitive element, it becomes a Layer IV expression. For example, اوں دے کنوں /ũ de kanũ/ '3SG.OBL GEN.SG.M.OBL by 'by him/her''.

کولوں /kolũ/ 'from (the vicinity of)' is often equivalent to کنوں /kanũ/.

توں /tũ/ 'from' is the ablative form of تے /te/ 'on'.

اچوں /icũ/ 'from in(side)' is the ablative form of اچ /ic/ 'in'.

لا کانوں /lā kanũ/ 'since' consists of لا /lā/ 'time during which' plus the ablative element کنوں /kanũ/(Shackle 1976: 56).

An example including کنوں /kanū̃/ is given in 7.63.

(7.63) اوندے کنو او پیسے گھن

ū̃-de	***kan-ū***	*o*	*pæse*	*ghin*
3SG.OBL-GEN.SG.M.OBL	**vicinity-ABL**	3.PL	money	take

'Take that money **from** him!' (Sr) (UK)

7.2.5 Spatial/temporal postpositions – Comparison

Table 7.3 compares some basic spatial/temporal postpositions in Hindko, Panjabi, and Saraiki.

Table 7.3: Some basic spatial-temporal postpositions in Hindko, Panjabi, and Saraiki

Meaning	Hindko	Panjabi	Saraiki
in	وچ /vic ~ ic/	وچ ~ وچے ~ اچ ~ چ /vicc ~ vice ~ ic ~ c/	وچ /vic ~ ic/
on, above; at	تے ~ اتے /te ~ utte/	تے ~ اتے /te ~ utte/	تے ~ اتے /te ~ utte/
below, beneath, under	تلے /talle/	تھلے genitive + /thalle/, or ہیٹھ genitive + /heṭh/	تلے /talle/, or ہیٹھ /heṭh/
with	نال /nāl/	نال /nāḷ/	نال /nāl/
inside	اندر /andar/	اندر /andar/	اندر /andar/
outside	وں باہر ablative + /bā̃r/	توں باہر ablative + /bā̃r/, or دے باہر genitive + /bā̃r/	ٻہر /ɓahar/ ~ /ɓæhir/, or توں ٻاہر ~ ٻاہر /ɓāhir/ ~ ablative + /ɓāhir/
across	پار /pār/	پار /pār/	پار /pār/

Table 7.3: (continued)

Meaning	Hindko	Panjabi	Saraiki
up to, until	تک /tak/, or تاڑی /tāṛ̃ī/	تک /tak/, تائیں /tāī̃/, تیک /tīk/, or تیکر /tīkar/	تئیں~تائیں taĩ ~ tāĩ, or تاݨی ~ توݨی /tāṇī ~ toṇī/
towards	ول genitive + /val/or در /dar/	ول genitive + /vall/	پاسے /pāse/,or دو /do/
facing, in front of	سامنڑے genitive + /sā̃mṛ̃e/	سامہنے ~ سامھنے genitive + /sā̃mṇe/	سامھݨے genitive + /sāmhṇe/
ahead of, in front of	اگے /agge/	اگے /agge/	اڳوں /aɠɠū̃/
near	در /dar/, or کول /kol/	کول /koḷ/	کولھ /kolh/, or کن /kan/

7.2.6 Accompaniment, instrument, cause, manner

These relationships are expressed with the postposition نال /nāl/ Hk, Sr , /nāḷ/ Pj in all three languages.

7.2.6.1 Accompaniment, instrument, cause, manner – Hindko

In example 7.64 we have a melded manner + cause meaning, and in 7.65 the meaning has elements of both accompaniment and cause. Example 7.66 shows a clear causal sense.

(7.64) بچہ خوشی نال ہنسیا

bacc-ā *xušī* ***nāl*** *hãs-iyā*
child-SG.M happiness.OBL **with** laugh-PP.SG.M
'The baby laughed **with** pleasure.' (Hk) (AWT)

(7.65) میں اس نال ناراض آں

mæ̃ *us* ***nāl*** *nārāz* *ā̃*
1SG 3SG.OBL **with** angry be.PRES.1SG
'I am angry **with** him/her.' (Hk) (AWT)

(7.66) او تاپے نال مریا

o *tāp-e* ***nāl*** *mar-iyā*
3SG.DIR fever-OBL **with** die-PP.SG.M
'He died **of** a fever.' (Hk) (AWT)

7.2.6.2 Accompaniment, instrument, cause, manner – Panjabi

The Panjabi postposition نال /nāḷ/ 'with, by' indicates relations of accompaniment, as in example 7.67, instrumental, as in 7.68, and manner, as in 7.69. The instrument can be a concrete object, as in 7.68, denoting the means by which an action is performed, or an non-physical concept indicating the manner in which it is performed (7.69). نال /nāḷ/ 'with, by' can behave as either a Layer II or III postposition with nouns, as in 7.68 and 7.69, and pronouns 7.67. Example 7.68 has an instrument meaning, and 7.69 shows a manner sense. 7.70 shows a clearly causal sense.

(7.67) سلیم ساڈے نال آویگا

salīm *sāḍ-e* ***nāḷ*** *ā-ve-g-ā*
Salim 2PL.GEN-SG.M.OBL **with** come-SBJV.3SG-FUT-SG.M
'Salim will come **with** us.' (Pj) (EB)

(7.68) میں کیلا چاکو دے نال کٹیا

mæ̃ *kelā* *cākū* *d-e* ***nāḷ*** *kaṭ-iyā.*
1SG banana.SG.M knife GEN-SG.M.OBL **with** cut-PP.SG.M
'I cut the banana **with** a knife.' (Pj) (Bhatia 1993: 180)

(7.69) اوہ نے مینوں زور نال واج ماری

ó-ne	*mæ-nũ*	*zor*	***nāḷ***	*vāj*	*mār-ī*
3SG.OBL-ERG	1SG-DAT	force	**with**	voice.SG.F	hit.PP-SG.F

'He/she called me loudly.' (Pj) (EB)

(7.70) ایہناں وچوں دو دے علاوہ باقی سارے گرمی نال مر گئے

énã	*vic-õ*	*do*	*de*	*alāva*	*bākī*	*sāre*	*garmī*
3PL.OBL	among-ABL	two	GEN.SG.M	excepting	rest.of	all	heat

nāḷ	*mar*	*ga-e*
with	die	go.PP-PL.M

'Except for two of them, all the rest died **of** heat.' (Pj) (https://pnb.wikipedia.org/wiki/سلطنت, غوریہ) (EB)

The instrumental or secondary agent relation can also be expressed with the denominal postposition ہتھے /hatth-e/ 'at the hand of' or ہتھوں /hatth-õ/ 'from the hand of', as in example 7.71. The former is the grammaticalized locative of the noun for 'hand', and the latter its ablative form. The Layer II postposition سمیت /samet ~ smæt/ 'along with' is also illustrated in example 7.71.

(7.71) بالآخر اپنے شوہر سمیت ایہناں دے ہتھوں ای ماری گئی

bilāxar	*apṇ-e*	*šohar*	***samet***	*én-ã*
finally	self's-SG.M.OBL	husband.OBL	**along.with**	3PL-OBL.PL

d-e	***hath-õ***	*ī*	*mār-ī*	*ga-ī*
GEN-SG.M.OBL	**hand-ABL**	EMPH	kill.PP-SG.F	go.PP-SG.F

'Finally she, **along with** her husband, was killed **by** those very persons.' (Pj) (https://pnb.wikipedia.org/wiki/سلطنت, غوریہ)

7.2.6.3 Accompaniment, instrument, cause, manner – Saraiki

Accompaniment and instrumental relations are expressed with نال /nāl/ 'with', as shown in examples 7.72, 7.74, and 7.73, respectively. نال /nāl/ 'with' follows the genitive form of first and second person singular pronouns, e.g. میڈے نال /meḍe nāl/ 'with me', but an oblique form of nouns, as in 7.72 or third person or relative pronouns, as in 7.73. Example 7.74 shows both the instrumental and the manner senses, i.e. 'with ease'. The ablative case form of 'hand', ہتھوں /hathū̃/ 'by', is also used in Saraiki with instrumental or secondary agent meaning, as in 7.75. The causal meaning of نال /nāl/ 'with' is also illustrated in example 7.75.

(7.72) میں اوں بندے نال الیندا پیا ہامی جیکوں تیں نوکری کنو فارغ کیتے

mæ̃	*ũ̃*	*band-e*	***nāl***	*ale-nd-ā*	*p-yā*	*hā-mī*
1SG	3SG.OBL	man-OBL	**with**	talk-IP-SG.M	CONT.I-SG.M	be.PST-1SG

je-kũ̃	*tæ̃*	*nokarī*	*kanū*	*fāriy*	*kīt-æ*
whom-ACC	2SG.OBL	job	from	free	do.PP-SG.M+be.3SG.PRES

'I (M) was talking **with** the man you fired from his job.' (Sr) (UK)

(7.73) او کاتی کتھاں اے جت نال میں آلو کپیندا پیا ہامی

o	*kātī*	*kitthā̃*	*e*	*jit*	***nāl***	*mæ̃*	*ālū*
that	knife	where	be.PRES.3SG	which.OBL	**with**	1SG	potatoes

kape-nd-ā	*p-yā*	*hā-mī*
cut-IP-SG.M	CONT.I-SG.M	be.PST-1SG

'Where is the knife **with** which I (m.) was cutting potatoes?' (Sr) (UK)

(7.74) سرائیکی حروف نال اردو پنجابی کشمیری ھندکو آسانی نال لکھ سگیندے ھن

sarāikī	*harūf*	*nāl*	*urdū*	*panjābī*	*kašmīrī*	*hindko*	*asānī*	***nāl***
Saraiki	letters	with	Urdu	Panjabi	Kashmiri	Hindko	ease	**with**

likh	*saɠ-ī̃-d-e*	*han*
write	be.able-PASS-IP-PL.M	be.PRES.3PL

'Urdu, Panjabi, Kashmiri, and Hindko can **easily** be written with the Saraiki letters.' (Sr) (Adapted from http://saraiki.tumblr.com/page/29)

(7.75) امریکا وچ ݙو سال دے ٻال دے ہتھوں بندوق چلݨ نال ما ہلاک

amrīkā	*vic*	*ɗū*	*sāl*	*d-e*	*ɓāl*	***de***	***hath-ũ̃***
America	in	two	years	GEN-SG.M.OBL	child.OBL	**of**	**hand-ABL**

bandūk	*cala-ṇ*	***nāl***	*mā*	*halāk*
gun	fire-INF.OBL	**with**	mother	killed

'In America a mother is killed **when** a gun is fired **by** a two-year-old child (lit. goes off from the hands of).' (Sr) (http://saraiki.app.com.pk/saraiki/2016/04/)

7.2.7 Purpose, reason, and cause

7.2.7.1 Purpose, reason, and cause – Hindko

Hindko employs اسطے /āste/ ~ /vāste/ in the meaning of 'for', as in example 7.76. To indicate the reason for something, دی وجہ توں /dī vája tõ/ 'because of' is common, shown in example 7.77. Notice that in example 7.77, the complex postpositional expression دی وجہ توں /dī vája tõ/ 'because of''consists of four elements: oblique form of the feminine noun تکلیف /taklīf/, feminine genitive postposition دی /dī/, the feminine noun وجہ /vája/ 'reason', and the ablative postposition توں /tõ/. It can, therefore, be considered a Layer IV element.

(7.76) میں بہوں خوش آں کہ تیرے آسطے اچھا ہو گیا

mæ̃	*baũ̄*	*xuš*	*ã̄*	*ki*	*ter-e*	***āste***	*acchā*
1SG	very	happy	be.PRES.1SG	that	2SG.GEN-SG.M	**for**	good.SG.M

ho	*ga-yā*
be	go.PP-SG.M

'I am very happy that it turned out well **for** you.' (Hk) (AWT)

(7.77) تکلیف دی وجہ توں او ذرا وی ٹرنے جوگا نئیں رہیا

taklīf	***d-ī***	***vája***	***tõ***	*o*	*zarā*	*vī*
pain	**GEN-SG.F**	**reason.SG.F.OBL**	**from**	3SG	at.all	EMPH

ṭur-n-e	*jog-ā*	*naī̃*	*r-yā*
walk-INF-OBL	able.to-SG.M	NEG	remain-PP.SG.M

'**Because of** feeling pain, he wasn't able to walk at all.' (Hk) (AWT)

7.2.7.2 Purpose, reason, and cause – Panjabi

Punjabi employs لئی /laī/ 'for', as in example 7.78, and واسطے /vāste/ ~ آسطے /āste/ 'for', as in example 7.79. Both of these postpositions behave as Layer II elements with nouns, as in 7.78, and as Layer III elements with pronouns, as in 7.79.

(7.78) ماحول دی آلودگی ایس ویلے پوری دنیا لئی سبھ توں اہم مسئلہ بنیا ہویا اے

mahɔl	*d-ī*	*alūdagī*	*æs*	*veḷ-e*	*pūr-ī*
environment	GEN-SG.F	pollution.SG.F	this.OBL	time-OBL	entire-SG.F

duniyā	***laī***	*sáb*	*tõ*	*ǽm*	*maslā*	*baṇ-iyā*
world.SG.F.OBL	**for**	all	ABL	important	problem	become-PP.SG.M

ho-iyā	*e*
become-PP-SG.M	be.PRES.3SG

'These days environmental pollution is (lit. has become) the most important problem **for** the entire world.' (Pj) (Bashir and Kazmi 2012: 7)

(7.79) میں صرف تہاڈے واسطے اوہنوں جان دتا اے

mǣ	*siraf*	*tuȁ-ḍ-e*	***vāste***	*ó-nū̃*	*jāṇ*
1SG	only	2PL-GEN-SG.M.OBL	**for**	3SG.OBL-ACC	go.INF.OBL

dit-ā	*e*
give.PP-SG.M	be.PRES.3SG

'I have let him go only **for** your sake.' (Pj) (Bashir and Kazmi 2012: 598)

7.2.7.3 Purpose, reason, and cause – Saraiki

In the meaning 'for', Saraiki employs کیتے /kīte/, as in examples 7.80 and 7.81, and واسطے /vāste/, as in example 7.83. کیتے /kīte/ is employed in the sense of 'because of' in 7.82.

(7.80) میڈے کیتے گھر دی چاردواری کنوں نکلݨ مشکل تھی گے

mæɗ-e	***kīte***	*ghar*	*d-ī*	*cārdivārī*	*kanū̃*
1SG.GEN-SG.M.OBL	**for**	house	GEN-SG.F	four.walls.SG.F	from

nikl-aṇ	*muškal*	*thī*	*ɠ-æ*
emerge-INF.DIR	difficult	become	go.PP-SG.M+be.3SG.PRES

'It has become difficult **for** me to emerge from the confines of the house.'[18] (Sr)

18 Example from Shackle 1976: 137, cited from Rizwani 1971: 36.

(7.81) میکوں بہوں خشی ہے جو شیں تیڈے کیتے چنگیاں رہ گین

mæ-kū̃ *bahū̃* *xušī* *hæ* *jo* *šæ̃*
1SG-DAT much happiness be.PRES.3SG that things.PL.F

teḋ-e ***kīte*** *cãng-iyā̃* *rah* *ɠa-ī-n*
2SG.GEN-SG.M.OBL **for** good.PL.F remain go.PP-F-be.PRES.3PL

'I am very happy that things have turned out well **for** you.' (Sr) (UK)

(7.82) سئیں طارق رحمان دا اے حوالہ ایں کیتے اہم ہے جو اے ہک غیر سرائیکی (باہرلے) سکالر دا مشاہدہ ہے

saī̃ *tārik* *rahmān* *d-ā* *e* *hawāla* *ī̃*
Sain Tariq Rahman GEN-SG.M 3SG.DIR reference 3SG.OBL

kīte *aham* *hæ* *jo* *e* *hik* *yær* *sarāikī*
because.of important be.PRES.3SG that 3SG.DIR a non Saraiki

(ɓāharle) *skālar* *d-ā* *mušāhida* *hæ*
(outside) scholar GEN-SG.M observation be.PRES.3SG

'This reference to Sain Tariq Rahman is important **because** it is the observation of a non-Saraiki (outside) scholar.'[19] (Sr) (http://sunjjan.blogspot.com/2015/02/blog-post_10.html)

(7.83) ایہ دوا کیرھی بیماری واسطے ہے

e *davā* *kerh-ī* *bimārī* ***vāste*** *hæ*
this medicine which-SG.F illness.SG.F **for** be.PRES.3SG

'What illness is this medicine **for**?' (Sr) (Zahoor 2009: 38)

7.2.8 Similarity

In addition to the adjectival postposition ورگا /vargā/ 'like' discussed in Section 7.1.2.5 for Panjabi, similarity is expressed by several other postpositions:

19 We have left the word سئیں /saī̃/ untranslated since it is one of the culturally important terms that cannot be glossed with a single English word or phrase. It is a highly honorific term of reference or address which conveys heartfelt respect, reverence, and affection for elders and teachers. It is also used with God (Shackle 1976: 133).

7.2.8.1 وانگ ~ وانگوں /vāng ~ vāngū̃/ Pj / وانگوں /vāngõ/ Sr ونگڑ /vangaṛ/ Hk 'like'

This element is exemplified for Panjabi in 7.84 and 7.85, and for Saraiki in example 7.86. With first, second, and third person pronouns, it follows the genitive form. With nouns, it follows the oblique form. It is used in Hindko as well, as in 7.87.

(7.84) اوہناں سرکاری افسراں نوں ہدایت کیتی کہ اوہ اپنے آپ نوں حاکماں وانگ نہ سمجھن

ónā̃	*sarkārī*	*afsar-ā̃*	*nū̃*	*hidāyat*	*kīt-ī*
3PL.OBL	government	officer-OBL.PL	DAT	instruction.F	do.PP-SG.F

ki	*ó*	*āpṇe.āp*	*nū̃*	*hākm-ā̃*	***vāng***	*na*	*sámj-aṇ*
that	3PL	self	ACC	ruler-OBL.PL	**like**	NEG	consider-SBJV.3PL

'He advised the government officials that they should not consider themselves **like** rulers.' (Pj) (Bashir and Kazmi 2012: 602)

(7.85) پاکستان وچ جمہوریت وی بجلی وانگوں آوندی جاندی رہندی ہے

pākistān	*vic*	*jamȕriyat*	*vī*	*bijilī*	***vāngõ***	*ɔ-nd-ī*
Pakistan	in	democracy	also	electricity	**like**	come-IP-SG.F

jā-nd-ī	*ræ̃-nd-ī*	*e*
go-IP-SG.F	remain-IP-SG.F	be.PRES.3SG

'Democracy in Pakistan, **like** electricity, keeps on coming and going.' (Pj) (Bashir and Kazmi 2012: 602)

(7.86) روندی اکھ وِچ سُرمے وانگوں اسیں وی کدھرے ٹکے نئیں

ro-nd-ī	*akkh*	*vic*	*surm-e*	***vāngū̃***	*asī̃*	*vī*
weep-IP-SG.F	eye	in	kohl-SG.M.OBL	**like**	1PL.DIR	also

kidhare	*ṭik-e*	*naī*
anywhere	come.to.rest-PP.PL.M	NEG

'**Like** kohl in a weeping eye, we too have not come to rest.' (Sr) (http://saraikijhook.blogspot.com/2017/04/blog-post_56.html)

(7.87) دریا دے پاڑی ونگڑ صاف

daryā	*de*	*pāṛī*	***vangaṛ***	*sāf*
river	GEN.SG.M.OBL	water	**like**	clear

'**As** clear **as** river water.' (Hk) (Soz 2011: 21)

7.2.8.2 Genitive or oblique + طرح /tara/ 'like, similar to'

The feminine noun طرح /tara/ 'way, method, kind' follows the genitive form of the first and second person pronouns, and the oblique form of the third person pronouns and nouns, conveying the meaning of 'like, similar to'. This is illustrated for Hindko in example 7.88, for Panjabi in example 7.89, and for Saraiki in examples 7.90 and 7.91.

(7.88) ماؤ مانہہ اُس طرحاں دے کپڑے لانڑے توں ڈکیا

mā-ū	*mā̃*	*us*	***tarā̃***	*d-e*	*kapṛ-e*
mother.OBL	1SG.ACC	3SG.OBL	**kind**	GEN-PL.M	clothes-PL.M

lāṛ̃-e	*tõ*	*ḍak-iyā*
wear-INF.OBL	from	stop-PP.SG.M

'Mother stopped me from wearing clothes **like** that.' (Hk) (AWT)

(7.89) حکومت نوں چاہیدا اے کہ ایس طرح دی کارروائی توں گریز کرے

hakūmat	*nū̃*	*cā̃ī-d-ā*	*e*	*ki*	*æs*	***tarā***
government	DAT	be.needed-IP-SG.M	be.PRES.3SG	that	3SG.OBL	**kind**

d-ī	*kārravāī*	*tõ*	*gurez*	*kar-e*
GEN-SG.OBL	action	from	avoidance	do-SBJV.3SG

'The government should avoid this **kind** of action.' (Pj) (Bashir and Kazmi 2012: 74)

(7.90) اساں باہمت قوم ایں طرح دے واقعات توں گھبراونڑ آلے کائنی

assā̃	*bāhimmat*	*qɔm*	*ī̃*	***tarā***	*d-e*	*vākiyāt*	*tõ*
1.PL	courageous	nation	3SG.OBL	**kind**	GEN-PL.M	occurrences	from

ghabrāv-aṇ	*āle*	*kāinī*
fear-INF	NMLZ.PL.M	NEG

'We are a courageous people, not ones who fear this **kind** of occurrences.' (Sr) (http://saraiki.app.com.pk/saraiki/2017/02/)

(7.91) سائیں سارے بندے تساں دی طرح پڑھے لکھے نئی ہن

sāī̃	*sār-e*	*band-e*	*tussā̃*	*d-ī*	***tarā***
revered.sir	all-PL.M	person-PL.M	2PL.OBL	GEN-SG.F	**kind**

paṛh-e likh-e	*naī*	*han*
educated-PL.M	NEG	be.PRES.3PL

'Revered sir, not all people are educated **like** you.' (Sr) (https://sq-al.facebook.com/iqrarulhassanpage/)

8 Verbs

We begin our examination of verbs with a discussion of the types of events encoded by various verbal categories. The discussion in sections 8.1 and 8.2 applies to Hindko, Panjabi, and Saraiki. Following these general introductory sections, paradigms of the verb forms for each language are given. Preceding the presentation of individual tense-aspect forms, a brief summary table for each language is presented. Blank spaces in these tables indicate combinations of tense and mood/aspect which we have not encountered in the language concerned. The various tense-aspect forms are illustrated with the third person singular masculine form of the distal pronoun اوہ ~ او /o/ (Sr) ~ /ó/ (Hk Pj) . We have glossed this as 'he' for reasons of space, however 'she' and 'it' are also conveyed by this third person singular pronominal form. Verb forms used with the distal and proximal pronouns are the same. Since the verb 'to be' (Hk ہوڑا /hoṛ̃ā/; Pj ہونا /honạ̄/; Sr ہووݨ /hovaṇ/) is the only verb which has a simple present and a simple past tense, its forms, rather than those of a regular verb, appear in those cells in these overview tables.

8.1 Verbal categories and terminology

Verbal constructions encode various kinds of information about the event described. These constructions are referred to as tense-aspect forms since many are marked both for aspect and tense, for example the *past imperfect*. Tense refers only to grammatical marking which situates an event in time relative to the moment of speaking. Grammatical aspect concerns the temporal structure of events, which can be presented as completed (pointlike) or ongoing in some sense (having linear extent). Perfective tenses encode events that, if they occurred in the past, are completed, and if they are to occur in the future are presented as completed by a particular moment. By contrast, imperfective tenses encode events that, whether they begin in the past, present, or future, involve duration in some sense (continuity, iteration). For example, the English past progressive *was melting*, simple present *melts* , present progressive *is melting*, and future progressive *will be melting* can all be categorized as imperfective. Another grammatically encoded category is reality, which applies in this description to either realis or irrealis conditional sentences. Realis conditionals pertain to events which have occurred, may be occurring, or could possibly occur; while irrealis conditionals apply to events which have not occured, do not occur, or are presumed not to be going to occur.

In this description, we call the Hindko, Panjabi, and Saraiki imperfective tenses that emphasize durativity over a bounded time frame **continuous** tenses; for example *the ice is melting*. There are also specific tense-aspect forms that emphasize extended durativity, either of an activity or of a state. In imperfective tenses this is expressed by incorporating the imperfective participle of the verb 'be' ہوڑا /hoṛ̃ā/ (Hk),

https://doi.org/10.1515/9781614512257-008

ہوݨا /hoṇā/ (Pj), ہووݨ/hovaṇ/ (Sr). In this description these are called **habitual** tense-aspect forms. With perfective tenses there are specifically stative forms which emphasize an extended state resulting from a prior action. The contrast between non-stative and stative meanings can be illustrated by the contrast between present perfect *the ice has melted* (with focus on the event) and present perfect-stative *the ice is melted* (with focus on the resultant state). In Panjabi and Saraiki, these marked stative forms incorporate the perfective participle of 'to be': ہوݨا /hoṇā/ (Pj) or ہووݨ /hovaṇ/ (Sr); in Hindko, the agreeing adjectival particle دا /dā/ performs this function. These forms are called **perfect-stative** in this description.

Subjunctive is a centrally important term. In general, subjunctive forms encode actions or events which are not (yet) realized, but could be realized. Thus subjunctive and irrealis meanings are distinct from each other. Whereas subjunctive forms describe conditions that have not occurred but still might, irrealis forms describe conditions that might have occurred but did not, such as the English past irrealis conditional *if the ice had melted.* Subjunctive tenses encode potentiality (similar to the English modal auxiliary *may*) or desirability (similar to the English modal auxiliary *should*). Thus the subjunctive appears in the subordinate clause in some realis conditional constructions. In this grammar, the term *subjunctive* is used both for a particular basic form of the verb, as well as for a group of complex tense-aspect forms in which it appears.[1] Verbs that specifically encode commands are called **imperative**.

The future tense of 'to be' has the senses 'will be' (future time reference) and 'must be' (presumptive meaning). Thus future tenses in Panjabi, Hindko, and Saraiki, which include a future form of 'be' as auxiliary, encode not only events that will occur (as far as any future event can be asserted to be going to occur), but also events that the speaker presumes will occur, presumes to have happened, or presumes to be the case. For this reason, we gloss tenses formed from a participle plus the future form of 'be' with *will/must.* The gloss *must* in *will/must* should be read with the epistemic modal meaning of presumption in mind, rather than the deontic modal meaning of desirability or obligation.

The naming convention for verb forms adopted in this grammar combines the name of an aspect with the name of a tense or a mood. Names of tenses precede names of aspects (for example, "present imperfect"); names of aspects precede names of moods (for example, "imperfect subjunctive"). Additionally, terms for the extended duration category—"habitual" with imperfectives, and "stative" with perfectives—follow the term for aspect, e.g. "present continuous-habitual." Names for the simple forms consist only of the name of a tense or mood ("present," "subjunctive"). We follow established practice in calling the verb form that consists of the bare perfective participle "simple perfect."

1 The forms now called "subjunctive" are the historical reflexes of a former present-future form.

Verbs which carry information for tense, person, and number are called **finite**, while those which do not carry tense and person information are called **non-finite**.

8.2 The four basic non-finite verb forms

The various finite verb forms and verbal constructions shared by Hindko, Panjabi, and Saraiki are constructed on the following four basic forms of the verb: stem, infinitive, perfective participle, and imperfective participle. In addition, Saraiki has a gerundive form which is distinct from its infinitive.

8.3 Hindko verbs

8.3.1 Overview

An overview (Table 8.1), intended to give the reader a "bird's eye view" of the structure of the verbal system, precedes discussion of individual Hindko verb forms. In these paradigms, the Perso-Arabic spellings are as given by our consultant, AWT. These spellings reflect a strong preference for writing the morpheme اں /ã̄/ separately, regardless of whether it would be possible to join it to the preceding morpheme. This applies whether اں /ã̄/ represents the dative/accusative postposition, first person verbal ending, or the feminine plural ending. Another preference reflected here is to represent the nasalization of vowels unambiguously, again different from the usual Perso-Arabic joining conventions, by writing occurrences of morpheme-final *nūn gunna* separately, instead of joining it. This can be seen in the spelling of the imperfective participles of ہوڑا /hoṛ̃ā/ 'to be' as ہوں دا /hõdā/ instead of ہوندا /hondā/. Also, the spelling of the third person singular distal pronoun as او /o/ rather than اوہ /ó/ represents AWT's consistent usage, as opposed to the اوہ found in Sakoon (2002). AWT's spelling of the masculine singular simple past tense of 'be' /éyā/ varies between ایہیا (representing the y-glide) and ایہا (not representing the glide). Sakoon (2002: 26) gives اِیہا for this form. Because an orthographic standard for Hindko is still evolving, considerable variation will be found in the available sources, and the spellings presented here are not intended to be prescriptive. Rather, we hope that they will stimulate discussion within the Hindko-using community about how best to represent their language. Our roman representations attempt to represent how these forms sound to us. They are not intended to be either strictly phonemic or narrowly phonetic. Perhaps "broadly phonemic" is the most appropriate characterization of them at present.

Table 8.1: Overview of Hindko verb forms

	Tenses				Moods	
	Simple	**Present**	**Past**	**Future**	**Subjunctive**	**Irrealis**
(simple)		او اے o e 'he is'	اوایہا o éyā 'he was'	اوجُلسی o julsī 'he will go'	اوجُلے o jule 'he may/should go; if he goes'	اوجلدا o juldā 'if he had gone/were going'
Imperfect		اوجُلدے o juldæ 'he goes'	اوجُلدا ایہا o juldā éyā 'he used to go'	اوجُلدا ہوسی o juldā hosī 'he will/must go frequently'	اوجُلدا ہووے o juldā hove 'if he goes/went (regularly)' (he may)'	Imperfect Irrealis I اوجلدا ہووے آ o julda̅ hove ā 'if he went (habitually) (but he doesn't)' Imperfect Irrealis II اوجُلدا ہوں دا o juldā hõndā 'if he went frequently (but he doesn't)'
Imperfect-habitual		اوجُلدا ہوں دے o juldā hõdæ 'he goes usually'	اوجُلدا ہوں داایہا o juldā hõdā éyā 'he used to go usually'			

Table 8.1: (continued)

	Tenses				Moods	
	Simple	**Present**	**Past**	**Future**	**Subjunctive**	**Irrealis**
Continuous I		او پیا جُلدے o pyā juldæ (< o piyā juldā e) 'he is going'	او پیا جُلدا ایہا o pyā juldā éyā 'he was going'			
Continuous II		او جُل رہے o jul ryæ 'he is going'	او جُل رہیا ایہا o jul ryā éyā 'he was going'			
Perfect	اوگیا o gyā 'he went'	اوگے o gyæ 'he has gone, went'	اوگیا ایہا o gyā éyā 'he went/had gone'	اوگیا ہوسی o gyā hosī 'he will/must have gone'		Perfect Irrealis I اوگیا ہووے آ o gyā hove ā Perfect Irrealis II اوگیا ہوں دا o gyā hõdā 'if he had gone (but he did not go)'
Perfect-stative		اوگے دے o gyæ dæ 'he is gone (he is still away)'	اوگیا دا ایہا o gyā dā éyā 'he was gone'	اوگیا دا ہوسی o gyā dā hosī 'he will/must be gone '		

8.3.1.1 Stem formation

The processes of stem formation, described here in detail for Hindko, apply to Panjabi as well. In Saraiki, the situation is somewhat more complex.

8.3.1.1.1 Simple stem

The simple stem (sometimes called "root") is the base form of the verb, from which other derived stems are formed. Simple stems can be either intransitive or transitive.

8.3.1.1.2 First causative stem

The first causative formation from an intransitive verb is a transitive verb, increasing its valence by one, adding a direct object argument. A first causative (transitive) stem can be related to an intransitive stem through frequently occurring patterns, two of which are:

1. by vowel change; for example, ٹُر /ṭur-/ 'walk, go' (intransitive); ٹور /ṭor-/ 'cause to go, send off' (transitive);
2. by consonant change; for example, بھَج /pàj-/ 'break' (intransitive); بھن /pàn-/ 'break' (transitive);

A first causative stem can be derived from a simple transitive stem by adding stressed ا /-ˈā/ to the simple stem, for example, سُنڑ/suṛ̃-/ 'hear' (transitive) > سُنڑا /suṛ̃ˈā-/ ' tell (lit. 'cause [something] to be heard')' (first causative). First causatives derived from transitives can increase the valence of the verb by one, adding a third argument, typically an indirect object.

8.3.1.1.3 Double causative stem

A double causative stem adds وا /-vā-/ to the stem. For example, سُنڑ/suṛ̃-/ ' hear')' > سُنڑوا /suṛ̃ˈvā-/ ' cause someone to cause something to be heard'. Double causative forms can increase the valence of a verb, by two, adding an additional argument, which has the role of causee or secondary agent.

8.3.1.1.4 Passive stem

Hindko does not have a morphological passive stem, unlike Saraiki (for which see Section 8.5.1.5). It forms periphrastic passives consisting of the perfective participle plus a conjugated form of جُلنڑا /julṛ̃ā/ 'to go'. Panjabi and Saraiki also employ periphrastic 'go' passives.

8.3.1.2 Non-finite forms

8.3.1.2.1 Infinitive

Hindko infinitives consist of the stem + ڑا /-ṛā/ or نا /-nā/. Stems with final ڑ /ṛ/, ڑھ /ṛh/, ر /r/, and ڑ /ṝ/ have infinitives in dental /-nā/, while all others have infinitives in retroflex /-ṝā/; for example, کرنا /karnā/ 'to do'; but آخڑا /āxṝā/ 'to say'. As far as we know at this point, Hindko does not have a gerundive (verbal adjective) form distinct from the infinitive. However, the form consisting of stem + ڑا /ṝā/ or نا /nā/, which is referred to as the infinitive, does perform both the nominal infinitival and the adjectival gerundival functions. When it appears in adjectival gerundival function, i.e. in a form agreeing with the noun it modifies, it is usually described as an "agreeing infinitive". That the form has gerundival function is attested in example 8.1.

(8.1) ایہہ پیہرنی تھوڑی اے

é	*pérn-ī*	***tò-ṝ-ī***	*æ*
this	shirt-SG.F	**wash-INF/GRDV-SG.F**	be.PRES.3SG

'This shirt **needs to be washed.**' (Hk) (EB 1989, unpublished field notes, Abbottabad)

8.3.1.2.2 Conjunctive participle

The form most commonly called the conjunctive participle is also known as the "absolutive" (in older or European literature) or more recently "converb." The conjunctive participle consists of the stem + کے /ke/(from the stem of کرنا /kar-nā/ 'to do'). This formation is also found in Panjabi and Saraiki, as well as many other South Asian languages. Sometimes an older form consisting of the stem + -ī + ke is also encountered, e.g., جاڑی بجھی کے /jāṝī bújī ke/ 'intentionally '. Compare the Saraiki "connective participle" (Section 8.5.2.7). See also Masica (1991: 323) on the -ī form of the conjunctive participle.

8.3.1.2.3 Imperfective participle

The imperfective participle consists of the stem + دا /dā/, or نا /nā/ (in the first person singular and plural, and second person singular). This is a marked adjectival form, hence complex verb forms including this participle are marked for gender and number. For example, کردا /kar-dā/ 'doing-M.SG', کردے /kar-de/ 'doing-M.PL', کردی /kar-dī/ 'doing-F.SG', and کردیاں /kar-diyā̃/ 'doing-F.PL'.

8.3.1.2.4 Perfective participle

The perfective participle consists of the stem + the marked adjectival endings. The masculine singular form ends in ا /ā/, or یا /yā/with ā-final stems, e.g. آیا /ā-yā/ 'came.SG.M'. A few important verbs have irregular perfective participles, notably پیڑا /pæṛ̃ā/ 'to fall, lie' and جلڑا /julṛ̃ā/ 'to go', the perfective participles of which are shown in Table 8.2.

	پیڑا pæṛ̃ā ' to fall, lie'	جلڑا julṛ̃ā 'to go'
Masculine singular	پیا pyā	گیا gyā
Masculine plural	پئے pae	گئے gae
Feminine singular	پئی paī	گئی gaī
Feminine plural	پئیاں paiyā̃	گئیاں gaiyā̃

Table 8.2: Irregular perfective participles: پیڑا /pæṛ̃ā/ 'to fall' and جلڑا /julṛ̃ā/ 'to go'

These verbs are particularly important because پیڑا /pæṛ̃ā/ forms part of the continuous tenses I series, and جلڑا /julṛ̃ā/ is one of the most frequently used vectors in compound verbs and forms the periphrastic passive construction.

As with Panjabi, important classes of frequently used verbs have irregular perfective participles ending in تا /-tā/, for example, تھوتا /tòtā/ < /tò-/ 'wash', and in /-dā/ کھادا /khādā/ < کھا - /khā-/ 'eat'. Further research will likely reveal more such irregular perfective participles in Hindko.

8.3.1.2.5 Stative perfective participle

An adjectival form which describes a persistent state resulting from an action in past time is formed from the oblique perfective participle of the main verb + a form of the agreeing adjectival particle دا /dā/.[2] For example, موئے دا /moe dā/ '(in a state of being) dead (m.sg.)'. Both parts of this complex form are marked adjectival forms. This form is semantically parallel to the stative perfective forms in Panjabi and Saraiki, which

2 This use of the particle دا /dā/ is found in several other languages—some Western Pahari varieties, and to a certain extent in Dogri (see Bashir 2018). Its source poses interesting questions.

consist of the perfective participle of the main verb + the perfective participle of ہونا /hoṇā/ 'to be', as in Panjabi لکھی ہوئی /likhī huī/ 'written.SG.F'. The stative perfective participle can be used as an attributive adjective, as in examples 8.2 and 8.3 below, or predicatively as part of perfect-stative tense-aspect forms.

(8.2) سڑے دے آلوئے سالن خراب کیتا

saṛ-e	***d-e***	*ālū-e*	*sālan*
rot-PP.SG.M.OBL	**STAT-SG.M.OBL**	potato-SG.M.OBL	curry.SG.M.DIR

xarāb	*k-īt-ā*
spoiled	do-PP-SG.M

'The **rotten** potato spoiled the curry (dish).' (Hk) (AWT)

(8.3) اوناں مانہ موئے دا سپ دسے

unā̃	*mā̃*	***moe-d-ā***	*sapp*
3PL.OBL	1SG.DAT	**die.PP.SG.M.OBL-STAT-SG.M**	snake.SG.M

dass-æ
show-PP.SG.M+ be.3SG.PRES

'They showed me a **dead** snake.' (Hk) (EB 1989, unpublished field notes, Abbottabad)

8.3.1.3 Finite forms of ہوڑا /hoṛā/ 'to be'

We begin with the tenses of the verb ہوڑا /hoṛā/ 'to be', which functions both as a main verb and as an auxiliary in complex tenses.

8.3.1.3.1 Present forms of ہوڑا /hoṛā/ 'to be'

Present tense forms carry tense, person, and number marking; they are not marked for gender (Table 8.3).

Person	Singular	Plural
1st	میں آں mæ̃ ã̄ 'I am'	اسی آں assī ã̄ 'we are'
2nd	توں ایں tū̃ ẽ 'you are'	تسی او tussī o 'you are'
3rd	او اے o e 'he/she is'	او نیں o nẽ 'they are'

Table 8.3: Present tense forms of ہوݨا /hoṛ̃ā/ 'to be'

8.3.1.3.2 Negative present forms of ہوݨا /hoṛ̃ā/ 'to be'

Negation is indicated by the use of the negative particles نہ /na/, ناں /nā̃/, or نیھ /nīĩ/.[3] The negative particle ناں /nā̃/ 'not' appears to be favored with the first person. This may reflect fusion of نہ ~ ناں /na ~ nā̃/ + اں /ā̃/ (NEG + 'be' 1SG). With the third person singular and plural, the form نیھ /nī̃/ means 'is/are not'. In the second person singular and plural, however, the form نیھ /nī̃/ appears along with an overt form of the present of 'be'. See Table 8.4 for the forms.

3 This negative particle is found spelled in various ways: the spelling above is from Sakoon (2002: 247). Our consultant has spelled it نئیں, نیھ, نیٔں, and نیٔہ; and elsewhere it is sometimes seen as نئیں.

Person	Singular	Plural
1st	میں ناں mæ̃ nã̄ 'I am not'	اسّی ناں assī nã̄ 'we are not'
2nd	تُوں نِینْھ ایں tū nī̃ ẽ 'you are not'	تسّی نِینْھ ہو tussī nī̃ ho 'you are not'
3rd	او نِینْھ o nī̃ 'he/she is not'	او نِینْھ o nī̃ 'they are not'

Table 8.4: Negative present forms of ہونڑا /hoṟā/ 'to be'

8.3.1.3.3 Future forms of ہونڑا /hoṟā/ 'to be'

Hindko future forms are composed of the stem + س /-s-/ + a set of personal endings which are the same as the subjunctive endings, except for the third person singular, which has the unique future ending ی /-ī/. Future forms in /s/ are characteristic of both Hindko and Saraiki. Future forms are marked for person and number, but not for gender. The future form of ہونڑا /hoṟā/ 'to be' refers to states or actions that are predicted to occur or are presumed to be occurring or to have occurred. Complex verb forms including the future of ہونڑا /hoṟā/ also have these presumptive senses. These forms are displayed in Table 8.5.

	Singular	Plural
1st	میں ہوساں mæ̃ hosã̄ 'I will/must be'	اسّی ہوساں assī hosã̄ 'we will/must be'
2nd	تو ہوسیں tū hosẽ 'you will/must be'	تسّی ہوسو tussī hoso 'you will/must be'
3rd	او ہوسی o hosī 'he/she/it will/must be'	او ہوسن o hosan 'they will/must be'

Table 8.5: Future forms of ہونڑا /hoṟā/ 'to be'

8.3.1.3.4 Simple perfect forms of ہوڑا /hoṛā/ 'to be'

The simple perfect consists of the bare perfective participle. Perfective forms of ہوڑا /hoṛā/ 'to be' convey the meaning 'become' (change of state) rather than 'be' (stative). Since this is an adjectival form, it is marked for number and gender, but not for person. Table 8.6 shows these forms.

Person	Singular	Plural
Masculine	ہویا hoiyā '(any m.sg. subject) became'	ہوئے hoe '(any m.pl. subject) became'
Feminine	ہوئی hoī '(any f.sg. subject) became'	ہوئی آں hoī ā̃ '(any f.pl. subject) became'

Table 8.6: Simple perfect forms of ہوڑا /hoṛā/ 'to be'

8.3.1.3.5 Past forms of ہوڑا /hoṛā/ 'to be'

The suppletive Hindko past-tense forms of 'be', shown in Table 8.7, carry morphological marking for person, number, and gender in the first and second persons, and for number and gender in the third person. These past-tense forms of 'be' are written in Perso-Arabic script with ہ /-h/ following the initial vowel. This orthographic /-h/ represents high tone in the initial vowel rather than being pronounced as a consonant /h/; a /y/ glide then appears between the initial vowel /é/ and the personal ending. The Romanization in Table 8.7 shows these developments. The first and second person masculine singular forms reflect elision of the /ā/ of the masculine singular and the initial vowel of the person/number ending.

Person	Singular	Plural
1st	میں ایہاں mæ̃ éyã$_M$ میں ایہی آں mæ̃ éyī ã$_F$ 'I was'	اسی ایہے آں assī éye ã$_M$ اسی ایہی آں assī éyī ã$_F$ 'we were'
2nd	توں ایہیں tū̃ éyẽ$_M$ توں ایہی ایں tū̃ éyī ẽ$_F$ 'you were'	تُسی ایہے او tussī éye o$_M$ تُسی ایہی او tussī éyī o$_F$ 'you were'
3rd	او ایہا o éyā$_M$ 'he was' او ایہی o éyī$_F$ 'she was'	او ایہے o éye$_M$ او ایہی آں o éyī ã$_F$ 'they were'

Table 8.7: Past tense of ہوڑا /hoṛā/ 'to be'

8.3.1.3.6 Negative past forms of ہوڑا /hoṛā/ 'to be'

Negative past tense forms of ہوڑا /hoṛā/ 'to be' carry information for person, number, and gender in first and second person, and number and gender in the third person. The paradigm is as follows in Table 8.8.

Person	Singular	Plural
1st	میں ناں ایہاں mæ̃ nā̃ éyā̃$_{M}$ میں ناں ایہی آں mæ̃ nā̃ éyī ā̃$_{F}$ 'I was not'	اسی ناں ایہے آں assī nā̃ éye ā̃$_{M}$ اسی ناں ایہی آں assī nā̃ éyī ā̃$_{F}$ 'we were not'
2nd	توں نینہ ایہیں tū̃ nī̃ éyẽ$_{M}$ توں نینہ ایہی ایں tū̃ nī̃ éyī ẽ$_{F}$ 'you were not'	تُسی نینھ ایہے او tussī nī̃ éye o$_{M}$ تُسی نینھ ایہی او tussī nī̃ éyī o$_{F}$ 'you were not'
3rd	او نینہ ایہا o nī̃ éyā$_{M}$ 'he was not' او نینہ ایہی o nī̃ éyī$_{F}$ 'she was not'	او نینہ ایہے o nī̃ éye$_{M}$ او نینھ ایہی آں o nī̃ éyī ā̃$_{F}$ 'they were not'

Table 8.8: Negative past of ہوڑا /hoṛā/ 'to be'

8.3.1.3.7 Subjunctive forms of ہوڑا /hoṛā/ 'to be'

Subjunctive forms are marked for person and number, but not for gender, as shown in Table 8.9.

Person	Singular	Plural
1st	میں ہوواں mæ̃ hovā̃ 'I may/should be; if I am'	اسی ہوواں assī hovā̃ 'we may/should be; if we are'
2nd	توں ہوویں tū̃ hovẽ 'you may/should be; if you are'	تُسی ہووو tussī hovo 'you may/should be; if you are'
3rd	او ہووے o hove 'he/she/it may/should be; if he/she/it is'	او ہوون o hovan 'they may/should be; if they are'

Table 8.9: Subjunctive forms of ہوڑا /hoṛā/ 'to be'

8.3.1.4 The verb تھی /thī-/ 'become'

Saraiki has a distinct verb تھی /thī-/, with the change of state meaning 'become', as opposed to Panjabi, in which the single verb ہونا /hoṇā/ encodes both the stative meaning 'to be' and the change of state meaning 'to become'. To what extent this verb is used in Abbottabad Hindko is a question needing investigation.[4] Sakoon (2002: 90) gives the forms تھیّا /thiyyā/ 'is, is present' and تھئے /thie/ 'are, are present'. These appear to be, respectively, fossilized masculine singular and masculine plural perfective participles of تھی /thī-/ 'become'. The question of whether use of ہوڑا /hoṛā/ to express change of state meaning has entirely replaced تھی /thī-/ 'become' in Hazara Hindko deserves exploration.

8.3.1.5 Forms constructed on the stem

Forms constructed on the stem include: (1) imperative; (2) subjunctive; (3) future; (4) continuous II tense-aspect forms.

4 It does appear in the language spoken in Mianwali, which is closer to Saraiki and considered a Saraiki variety by many. Jukes (1900) includes words from Dera Ghazi Khan and the Salt Range, and gives the meaning 'to be done' for thī- (p. 95).

8.3.1.5.1 Imperatives

Shackle (1980: 493), discussing imperative forms in Peshawar and Kohat Hindko, found two imperative forms. He called these "simple" and "aorist," a term which is not much in use now. Shackle's "aorist" corresponds to what is elsewhere called a "distanced" or "polite" imperative. The simple singular form consists of the bare verb stem, and the simple plural form is the verb stem + و /o/. Simple and polite/"aorist" imperatives for کرنا /karnā/ 'to do' are given in Table 8.10. The plural distanced/polite form is from Shackle (1980: 493), who describes it as characterized by tonal shift, and compares it to a Saraiki form in -ahe; we mark this in the table. The singular form of the distanced/polite imperative with a hortative particle is illustrated in examples 8.4 and 8.5.

	2nd person singular	2nd person plural
Simple	کر kar 'do (now)!'	کرو karo 'do (now)!'
Distanced/polite/"aorist"	کریں karī̃ 'do (please)'	کرے karé 'do (please)'

Table 8.10: Imperatives of کرنا /karnā/ 'to do'

(8.4) توں ایہ کم کریں آں

tū̃ é kam ***kar-ī̃-ā̃***

you this work **do-POL.SG.IMP-HORT**

'(Please) **do** this work.' (Hk) (AWT)

(8.5) اُس دے کہروں پھیرا پا آویں آں

us de kàr-õ phīrā pā ***ā-vī̃-ā̃***

his of house-ABL trip put.CP **come-2SG.IMP-HORT**

'Just make a visit to his house.' (Hk) (Bismil 2011: 41)

8.3.1.5.2 Subjunctive

The subjunctive consists of the stem plus the person-number endings in Table 8.11. With consonant-final stems, these vowel-initial endings combine simply. With vowel-final stems, the consonant glide و /-v-/ appears between the stem and the personal ending.

Person	Singular	Plural
1st	اں -ā̃	اں -ā̃
2nd	ِیں -ẽ	و -o
3rd	ے -e	اں -an

Table 8.11: Personal endings of Hindko subjunctive

Since no tense or gender-marked auxiliary is involved, subjunctive forms agree with the subject of the sentence in person and number, but have no gender or tense. As in Panjabi and Saraiki, the subjunctive encodes modal meanings like potentiality, desirability, or contingency, and is thus often found in the subordinate ('if') clause of realis conditional constructions. The following paradigms illustrate the subjunctive forms of a vowel-final stem, آ /ā-/ 'come' (Table 8.12), and the consonant-final stem جُل /jul-/ 'go' (Table 8.13). In the paradigms that follow this section, the verb جُلنڑا /julṛ̃ā/ 'to go' and sometimes آنڑا /āṛ̃ā/ 'to come' will be used to exemplify the form discussed in the imperfective aspect. For perfective aspect, the transitive verb کرنا /karnā/ 'to do' and intransitive جُلنڑا /julṛ̃ā/ 'to go' will be used to exemplify the forms.

Person	Singular	Plural
1st	میں آواں mæ̃ āvā̃ 'I may/should come; if I come'	اسی آواں assī āvā̃ 'we may/should come; if we come'
2nd	توں آویں tū̃ āvẽ 'you may/should come; if you come'	تسی آئو tussī āo 'you may/should come; if you come'
3rd	او آوے o āve 'he/she/it may/should come; if he/she/it comes'	او آون o āvan 'they may/should come; if they come'

Table 8.12: Subjunctive of آنڑا /āṛā/ 'to come'

Person	Singular	Plural
1st	میں جلاں mæ̃ julā̃ 'I may/should go; if I go'	اسی جلاں assī julā̃ 'we may/should go; if we go'
2nd	توں جلیں tū̃ julẽ 'you may/should go; if you go'	تسی جلو tussī julo 'you may/should go; if you go'
3rd	او جلے o jule 'he/she/it may/should go; if he/she/it goes'	او جلن o julan 'they may/should go; if they go'

Table 8.13: Subjunctive of جلنڑا /julṛā/ 'to go'

8.3.1.5.3 Perfect irrealis I

The perfect irrealis I consists of the subjunctive plus the particle آں /ā̃/. For examples of this form in context, see examples 9.213, 9.214, and 9.215.

8.3.1.5.4 Future

Unlike the future in Panjabi, which is built on the subjunctive form, the future in Hindko and Saraiki consists of the stem + /s/ + personal endings.

For ease of reference, future forms of the vowel-stem آنڑا /āṛ̃ā/ 'to come' and consonant-stem جُلنڑا /julṛ̃ā/ 'to go' are given in Table 8.14 and Table 8.15.

Person	Singular	Plural
1st	میں آساں mæ̃ āsā̃ 'I will come'	اسی آساں assī āsā̃ 'we will come'
2nd	تُوں آسیں tū̃ āsẽ 'you will come'	تُسی آسو tussī āso 'you will come'
3rd	او آسی o āsī 'he/she will come'	او آسن o āsan 'they will come'

Table 8.14: Future of آنڑا /āṛ̃ā/ 'to come'

Person	Singular	Plural
1st	میں جُلساں mæ̃ julsā̃ 'I will go'	اسی جُلساں assī julsā̃ 'we will go'
2nd	تُوں جُلسیں tū̃ julsẽ 'you will go'	تُسی جُلسو tussī julso 'you will go'
3rd	او جُلسی o julsī 'he/she will go'	او جُلسن o julsan 'they will go'

Table 8.15: Future of جُلنڑا /julṛ̃ā/ 'to go'

8.3.1.5.5 Continuous tenses II

Continuous tenses II are formed from the stem + the grammaticalized perfective participle of رہݨا /ræhɽā/ 'to remain' + tensed auxiliary.[5]

This continuous II formation is found in Hindko, Panjabi, and Saraiki. When it occurs in Hazara Hindko, it is characteristic of speakers who are familiar with Panjabi and Urdu. Since these forms include a tensed auxiliary as well as a participial form, they are marked for person, number, and gender. More forms of this type can be found in the Panjabi section (Section 8.4.4.4.1). The Hindko present continuous II forms for کرنا /karnā/ 'to do' appear in Table 8.16.

Person	Singular	Plural
1st	میں کر رہیاں mæ̃ kar ryā̃$_M$ میں کر رہی آں mæ̃ kar raī ā̃$_F$ 'I am doing'	اسی کر رہے آں assī kar rye ā̃$_M$ اسی کر رہی آں assī kar raī ā̃$_F$ 'we are doing'
2nd	تُوں کر رہیا ایں tū̃ kar ryā ẽ$_M$ تُوں کر رہی ایں tū̃ kar raī ẽ$_F$ 'you are doing'	تُسی کر رہے او tussī kar rye o$_M$ تُسی کر رہی او tussī kar raī o$_F$ 'you are doing'
3rd	او کر رہیے o kar ryæ$_M$ 'he is doing' او کر رہی اے o kar raī e$_F$ 'she is doing'	او کر رہے ان o kar rye an$_M$ او کر رہی ان o kar raī an$_F$ 'they are doing'

Table 8.16: Present continuous II of کرنا /karnā/ 'to do'

The past continuous is constructed in the same way as the present continuous, except that instead of the present auxiliary, the past auxiliary appears. Past continuous II forms for the intransitive verb دوڑنا /dauṛnā/ 'to run' are given in Table 8.17. Note the elision of the final vowel of the past auxiliary preceding the initial vowel of the personal ending in the second person singular form: /éyā ẽ > éyẽ/. The first and second

---

5 Continuous tenses I are formed on the imperfective participle.

person plural forms have the feminine singular رہی /raī/in the present continuous II (Table 8.55), but the plural رہیاں /raiyā̃/in the past continuous II (Table 8.56). This may be because the form رہیاں آں /raiyā̃ ā̃/in the present continuous II would involve a repetition of /ā̃ ā̃/ (apparently resolved here to /ā̃/). In the past continuous II, on the other hand, the sequence رہیاں ایہی /raīā̃ éyī/does not present this problem.

Person	Singular	Plural
1st	میں دوڑ رہیا ایہاں mæ̃ dauṛ ryā éyā̃$_{M}$ میں دوڑ رہی ایہی آں mæ̃ dauṛ raī éyī ā̃$_{F}$ 'I was running'	اسی دوڑ رہے ایہے آں assī dauṛ rae éye ā̃$_{M}$ اسی دوڑ رہی آں ایہی آں assī dauṛ raī ā̃ éyī ā̃$_{F}$ 'we were running'
2nd	توں دوڑ رہیا ایہیں tū̃ dauṛ ryā éyẽ$_{M}$ توں دوڑ رہی ایہی ایں tū̃ dauṛ raī éyī ẽ$_{F}$ 'you were running'	تسی دوڑ رہے ایہے او tussī dauṛ rae éye o$_{M}$ تسی دوڑ رہی آں ایہی او tussī dauṛ raī ā̃ éyī o$_{F}$ 'you were running'
3rd	او دوڑ رہیا ایہا o dauṛ ryā éyā$_{M}$ 'he was running' او دوڑ رہی ایہی o dauṛ raī éyī$_{F}$ 'she was running'	او دوڑ رہے ایہے o dauṛ rae éye$_{M}$ او دوڑ رہی آں ایہی آں e dauṛ raī ā̃ éyī ā̃$_{F}$ 'they were running'

Table 8.17: Past continuous II of دوڑنا /dauṛnā/ 'to run'

8.3.1.6 Forms constructed on the imperfective participle

Forms constructed on the imperfective participle include the following: present imperfect, past imperfect, present imperfect-habitual, past imperfect-habitual, imperfect subjunctive, future imperfect, present continuous I, and past continuous I. The present imperfect and past imperfect consist of the imperfective participle + tensed auxiliary forms. The habitual forms consist of the imperfective participle + imperfective participle of ہوڑا /hoṛ̃ā/ 'to be' + tensed auxiliary forms. Importantly, the present continuous I and the past continuous I consist of the imperfective participle + the grammaticalized perfective participle of پیڑا /pæṛ̃ā/ 'to fall, lie' + tensed auxiliary forms.

8.3.1.6.1 Present imperfect

The present imperfect is constructed from the imperfective participle + the present tense of ہوڑا /hoṛā/ 'to be'. It usually conveys general or non-specific present tense meanings. Since it includes both the present tense of ہوڑا /hoṛā/ 'to be' and a participial form, it is marked for tense, person, number, and gender. This also means that it is subject to coalescence (elision, sandhi) of the final vowel sound of the imperfective participle and the initial vowel sound of the present auxiliary. In addition to the fact that various writers represent the results of this coalescence differently, this can make it difficult to recognize or analyze some verb forms. For this reason, we present this paradigm for the present imperfect of جلڑا /julṛā/ 'to go' in two ways. First, Table 8.18 shows the form as given by our consultant; the Perso-Arabic forms reflect the way the words are written by him, and the romanizations reflect the way they sound to us. Notice that in the first and second person singular the participial form appears with نا /-nā/, while in second person plural and third person forms the imperfective participle appears with دا /-dā/. This appearance of /n/ in the first and second person singular and first person plural probably results from nasal assimilation from the nasal vowel in the auxiliary component. This analysis is somewhat supported by the fact that this assimilation does not occur in the simple past imperfect, where the initial sound of the past auxiliary is an oral rather than a nasalized vowel. This appearance of /n/ instead of underlying /d/ in imperfective participles in syllables immediately followed by a nasal vowel is seen in the present imperfect-habitual, shown in Table 8.20, the present continuous I, shown in Table 8.25, and in the past continuous I, shown in Table 8.26.

Second, in Table 8.19, the forms are presented as analyzed by the authors for the benefit of the reader into their component parts in a process of "undoing sandhi". The forms in Table 8.19 represent our hypothesis about the structures underlying the surface pronunciations, which reflect nasal assimilation in first person singular and plural and second person singular, as well as vowel elision in the masculine forms.

Person	Singular	Plural
1st	میں جُلناں mæ̃ julnā̃$_{M}$ میں جُلنی آں mæ̃ julnī ā̃$_{F}$ 'I go'	اسی جُلنے آں assī julne ā̃$_{M}$ اسی جُلنی آں assī julnī ā̃$_{F}$ 'we go'
2nd	تُوں جُلنیں tū̃ julnæ̃$_{M}$ تُوں جُلنی ایں tū̃ julnī ẽ$_{F}$ 'you go'	تُسی جُلدے او tussī julde o$_{M}$ تسی جُلدی او tussī juldī o$_{F}$ 'you go'
3rd	او جُلدے o juldæ$_{M}$ 'he goes' او جُلدی اے o juldī e$_{F}$ 'she goes'	او جُلدین o julden$_{M}$ 'they go' جُلدی ان o juldī an$_{F}$ 'they go'

Table 8.18: Present imperfect of جلنڑا /julṛ̃ā/ 'to go' (actual forms)

Person	Singular	Plural
1st	میں جُلدا آں mæ̃ juldā ã$_{M}$ میں جُلدی آں mæ̃ juldī ã$_{F}$ 'I go'	اسّی جُلدے آں assī julde ã$_{M}$ اسّی جُلدی آں assī juldī ã$_{F}$ 'we go'
2nd	توُں جُلدا ایں tū̃ juldā ẽ$_{M}$ توُں جُلدی ایں tū̃ juldī ẽ$_{F}$ 'you go'	تُسّی جُلدے او tussī julde o$_{M}$ تُسّی جُلدی آں او tussī juldī ã o$_{F}$ 'you go'
3rd	او جُلدا اے o juldā e$_{M}$ 'he goes' او جُلدی اے o juldī e$_{F}$ 'she goes'	او جُلدے ان o julde an$_{M}$ او جُلدی ان o juldī an$_{F}$ 'they go'

Table 8.19: Present imperfect of جلنڑا /julṝā/ 'to go' (hypothesized underlying forms)

8.3.1.6.2 Present imperfect-habitual

The present imperfect-habitual consists of the imperfective participle + the imperfective participle of ہوڑا /hoṛ̃ā/ 'to be' + the present tense of ہوڑا /hoṛ̃ā/ 'to be'. This form is illustrated in Table 8.20 for the verb جلنڑا /julṛ̃ā/ 'to go'. The Perso-Arabic spellings in Table 8.20 reflect AWT's perception that the imperfective participle of ہوڑا /hoṛ̃ā/ 'to be' contains a nasalized /õ/, and not a consonant /n/ when the form contains /d/. He therefore prefers to write the word as shown here in the third person and second person plural forms, preferring to write the nasalized vowel unambiguously when it precedes /d/ rather than following the usual rules of joining Perso-Arabic letters which would join this medial nūn gunna (nasalization), causing it to appear identical in medial position with a consonant ن /n/. This is not the usual practice in writing these forms, but AWT argues for it. When the imperfective participle form has /n/ rather than /d/ (first person singular and plural, and second person singular), consonant /n/ appears. We hope that it will engender discussion among Hindko speakers.

Person	Singular	Plural
1st	میں جُلنا ہوناں mæ̃ julnā hõnã$_M$ میں جُلنی ہونی آں mæ̃ julnī hõnī ã$_F$ 'I usually go '	اسی جُلنے ہونے آں assī julne hõne ã$_M$ اسی جُلنیاں ہونی آں assī julnīã̄ hoñī ã$_F$ 'we usually go'
2nd	تُوجُلنا ہونیں tū̃ julnā hõnæ̃$_M$ تُوں جُلنی ہونی ایں tū̃ julnī hoñī ẽ$_F$ 'you usually go '	تُسی جُلدے ہوں دے او tussī julde hõde o$_M$ تُسی جُلدی آں ہوں دی او tussī juldī ã̄ hõdī o$_F$ 'you usually go '
3rd	او جُلدا ہوں دے o juldā hõdæ$_M$ 'he usually goes' او جُلدی ہو دی اے o juldī hõdī e$_F$ 'she usually goes'	او جُلدے ہوندین o julde hõden$_M$ او جُلدی آں ہوں دی ان o juldī ã hõdī an$_F$ 'they usually go '

Table 8.20: Present imperfect-habitual of جلنڑا /julṛ̃ā/ 'to go'

8.3.1.6.3 Past imperfect

The past imperfect consists of the imperfective participle + the past of ہوڑا /hoṛ̃ā/ 'to be'. This form is illustrated here for جُلنڑا /julṛ̃ā/ 'to go' in Table 8.21.

Person	Singular	Plural
1st	میں جُلدا ایہاں mæ̃ juldā éyā̃$_M$ میں جُلدی ایہی آں mæ̃ juldī éyī ā̃$_F$ 'I used to go'	اسی جُلدے ایہاں assī julde éyā̃$_M$ اسی جُلدی آں ایہی آں assī juldī ā̃ éyī ā̃$_F$ 'we used to go'
2nd	توں جُلدا ایہا ایں tū̃ juldā éyẽ$_M$ توں جُلدی ایہی ایں tū̃ juldī éyī ẽ$_F$ 'you used to go'	تُسی جُلدے ایہے او tussī julde éye o$_M$ تُسی جُلدی آں ایہی او tussī juldī ā̃ éyī o$_F$ 'you used to go'
3rd	او جُلدا ایہا o juldā éyā$_M$ 'he used to go' او جُلدی ایہی o juldī éyī 'she used to go'	او جُلدے ایہے o julde éye$_M$ او جُلدی آں ایہی آں o juldīā̃ éyī ā̃$_F$ 'they used to go'

Table 8.21: Past imperfect of جُلنڑا /julṛ̃ā/ 'to go'

8.3.1.6.4 Past imperfect-habitual

The past imperfect-habitual consists of the imperfective participle + the imperfective participle of ہونڑا /hoṛ̃ā/ 'to be' + the past of ہونڑا /hoṛ̃ā/ 'to be'. This form is illustrated for جُلنڑا /julṛ̃ā/ 'to go' in Table 8.22, below.

Person	Singular	Plural
1st	میں جُلدا ہوں دا ایہاں mæ̃ juldā hõdā éyā̃$_M$ میں جُلدی ہوں دی ایہی آں mæ̃ juldī hõdī éyī ā̃$_F$ 'I used to go usually'	اسی جُلدے ہوں دے ایہاں assī julde hõde éyā̃$_M$ اسی جُلدی آں ہوں دی آں ایہی آں assī juldī ā̃ hõdī ā̃ éyī ā̃$_F$ 'we used to go usually'
2nd	تُوں جلدا ہوں دا ایہا ایں tū̃ juldā hõdā éyẽ$_M$ تُوں جُلدی ہو ں دی ایہی ایں tū̃ juldī hõdī éyī ẽ$_F$ 'you used to go usually'	تُسی جُلدے ہوں دے ایہے او tussī julde hõde éye o$_M$ تُسی جُلدی آں ہوں دی آں ایہی او tussī juldī ā̃ hõdī ā̃ éyī o$_F$ 'you used to go usually'
3rd	اوجُلدا ہوں دا ایہیا o juldā hõdā éyā$_M$ 'he used to go usually' اوجُلدی ہوں دی ایہی o juldī hõdī éyī$_F$ 'she used to go usually'	اوجُلدے ہوں دے ایہے o julde hõde éye$_M$ اوجُلدی آں ہوں دی آں ایہی آں o juldī ā̃ hõdī ā̃ éyī ā̃$_F$ 'they used to go usually'

Table 8.22: Past imperfect-habitual of جُلنڑا /julṛ̃ā/ 'to go'

8.3.1.6.5 Imperfect subjunctive

The imperfect subjunctive consists of the imperfective participle + subjunctive of ہونڑا /hoṛ̃ā/ 'to be'. This form is illustrated for جُلنڑا /julṛ̃ā/ 'to go' in Table 8.23.

Person	Singular	Plural
1st	میں جُلدا ہوواں mæ̃ juldā hovā̃$_M$ میں جُلدی ہوواں mæ̃ juldī hovā̃$_F$ 'I may/should go frequently; if I go frequently'	اسی جُلدے ہوواں assī julde hovā̃$_M$ اسی جُلدی آں ہوواں assī juldī ā̃ hovā̃$_F$ 'we may/should go frequently; if we go frequently'
2nd	توں جُلدا ہوویں tū̃ juldā hovẽ$_M$ توں جُلدی ہوویں tū̃ juldī hovẽ$_F$ 'you may/should go frequently; if you go frequently'	تُسی جُلدے ہووو tussī julde hovo$_M$ تُسی جُلدی آں ہووو tussī juldī ā̃ hovo$_F$ 'you may/should go frequently; if you go frequently'
3rd	او جُلدا ہووے o juldā hove$_M$ 'he may/should go frequently; if he goes frequently' او جُلدی ہووے o juldī hove$_F$ 'she may/should go frequently; if she goes frequently'	او جُلدے ہوون o julde hovan$_M$ او جُلدی آں ہوون o juldī ā̃ hovan$_F$ 'they may/should go frequently; if they go frequently'

Table 8.23: Imperfect subjunctive of جلنڑا /julṛ̃ā/ 'to go'

8.3.1.6.6 Future imperfect

Future imperfect forms consist of the imperfective participle + future of ہونڑا /hoṛ̃ā/ 'to be'. This tense is illustrated here for جلنڑا /julṛ̃ā/ 'to go' in Table 8.24.

Person	Singular	Plural
1st	میں جلدا ہوساں mæ̃ juldā hosā̃$_M$ میں جلدی ہوساں mæ̃ juldī hosā̃$_F$ 'I will/must go frequently'	اسی جلدے ہوساں assī julde hosā̃$_M$ اسی جلدی آں ہوساں assī juldī ā̃ hosā̃$_F$ 'we will/must go frequently'
2nd	توں جلدا ہوسیں tū̃ juldā hosẽ$_M$ توں جلدی ہوسیں tū̃ juldī hosẽ$_F$ 'you will/must go frequently'	تسی جلدے ہوسو tussī julde hoso$_M$ تسی جلدی آں ہوسو tussī juldī ā̃ hoso$_F$ 'you will/must go frequently'
3rd	او جلدا ہوسی o juldā hosī$_M$ 'he will/must go frequently' او جلدی ہوسی o juldī hosī$_F$ 'she will/must go frequently'	او جلدے ہوسن o julde hosan$_M$ او جلدی آں ہوسن o juldī ā̃ hosan$_F$ 'they will/must go frequently'

Table 8.24: Future imperfect of جلنڑا /julṛ̃ā/ 'to go'

8.3.1.6.7 Present continuous I formation

This construction consists of the grammaticalized perfective participle of پیئڑا /pæṛ̃ā/ 'to fall, lie' + the imperfective participle + the present auxiliary. This is one of the most characteristic verb forms of Hindko, and is also frequent in Saraiki and Panjabi. This form conveys a strong sense of actuality and immediacy. The order of elements presented in the paradigms here is the preferred order. However, the order placing the imperfective participle of the main verb first, followed by the grammaticalized perfective participle of پیئڑا /pæṛ̃ā/ 'to lie, fall', also occurs. According to Sultan Sakoon (p.c. 1989), the perfective participle of پیئڑا /pæṛ̃ā/ can follow or precede any constituent of the sentence, and confers emphasis or focus on the element it follows or precedes. Present continuous I forms of جلنڑا /julṛ̃ā/ 'to go' are given in Table 8.25.

Table 8.25 gives the Perso-Arabic forms exactly as written by our consultant. Notice the ن /-n-/forms of the imperfective participle in first person (singular and plural) and the second person singular of the present continuous I. The past continuous I, however, shows only د /d/ forms of the imperfective participle. These forms also show the vowel elision (coalescence) previously discussed. Thus, a hypothetical decomposed "underlying form" for the first person singular masculine form might be as shown in example 8.6.

Person	Singular	Plural
1st	میں پیا جلناں mæ̃ pyā julnā̃$_{M}$ میں پئی جُلنی آں mæ̃ paī julnī ā̃$_{F}$ 'I am going'	اسی پۓ جُلنے آں assī pae julne ā̃$_{M}$ اسی پئی آں جُلنی آں assī paī ā̃ julnī ā̃$_{F}$ 'we are going'
2nd	تُوں پیا جُلنیں tū̃ pyā julnẽ$_{M}$ تُوں پئی جُلنی ایں tū̃ paī julnī ẽ$_{F}$ 'you are going'	تُسی پۓ جُلدے او tussī pae julde o$_{M}$ تُسی پئی آں جُلدی او tussī paī ā̃ juldī o$_{F}$ 'you are going'
3rd	او پیا جُلدے o pyā juldæ 'he is going' او پئی جُلدی اے o paī juldī e 'she is going'	او پۓ جُلدین o pae julden$_{M}$ او پئی آں جُلدی ان o paī ā̃ juldī an$_{F}$ 'they are going'

Table 8.25: Present continuous I of جلنڑا /julṛ̃ā/ 'to go (actual forms)'

(8.6) میں پیا کردا آں

mæ̃ *py-ā* *kar-d-ā* *ā̃*
I fall.PP-SG.M do-IP-SG.M be.PRES.1SG
'I (M) am doing.' (Hk) (EB, hypothetical 'underlying' form)

8.3.1.6.8 Past continuous I

Past continuous I tenses are constructed as follows: perfective participle of پینڑا /pæṛ̃ā/ 'to fall, lie' + imperfective participle + past auxiliary. This tense is illustrated for جلنڑا /julṛ̃ā/ 'to go' in Table 8.26.

Person	Singular	Plural
1st	میں پیا جُلدا ایہاں mæ̃ pyā juldā éyā̃$_{M}$ میں پئی جُلدی ایہی آں mæ̃ paī juldī éyī ā̃$_{F}$ 'I was going'	اسی پئے جلدے یہے آں assī pae julde éye ā̃$_{M}$ اسی پئی آں جُلدی آں ایہی آں assī paī ā̃ juldī ā̃ éyī ā̃$_{F}$ 'we were going'
2nd	تُوں پیا جُلدا ایہیں tū̃ pyā juldā éyẽ$_{M}$ تُوں پئی جُلدی ایہی ایں tū̃ paī juldi éyī ẽ$_{F}$ 'you were going'	تُسی پئے جُلدے ایہے او tussī pae julde éye o$_{M}$ تُسی پئی آں جُلدی آں ایہی او tussī paī ā̃ juldī ā̃ éyī o$_{F}$ 'you were going'
3rd	او پیا جُلدا ایہا o pyā juldā éyā$_{M}$ 'he was going' او پئی جُلدی ایہی o paī juldī éyī$_{F}$ 'she was going'	او پئے جُلدے ایہے o pae julde éye$_{M}$ او پئی آں جُلدی آں ایہی آں o paī ā̃ juldī ā̃ éyī ā̃$_{F}$ 'they were going'

Table 8.26: Past continuous I of جلنڑا /julr̃ā/ 'to go'

8.3.1.7 Verb forms constructed on the perfective participle

Tense-aspect forms built on the perfective participle include the simple perfect, present perfect, present perfect-stative, past perfect, past perfect-stative, perfect irrealis, and future perfect.

8.3.1.7.1 Simple perfect

Simple perfect forms are identical to the perfective participle. Since there is no element bearing person or tense information, simple perfect forms are marked only for number and gender. Simple perfect forms of intransitive verbs agree with the subject of the sentence. The simple perfect of جلنڑا /julr̃ā/ 'to go', the most frequently used intransitive verb aside from 'be', is given in Table 8.27. Since perfective participles of both transitive and intransitive verbs are marked only for the number and gender of the direct object or the subject, respectively, there are only four such forms: masculine singular, masculine plural, feminine singular, and feminine plural. Most occurrences of simple perfect forms of 'go' seem to be in passive forms or as the vector in compound verbs. With statements about specific subjects, however, the present perfect tends to occur for meanings most often rendered in English using the simple past.

Gender of subject	Singular	Plural
Masculine	گیا gyā '(any m.sg. subject) went'	گئے gae ~ gæ '(any m.pl. subject) went'
Feminine	گئی gaī '(any f.sg. subject) went'	گئی آں gaī ā̃ '(any f.pl. subject) went'

Table 8.27: Simple perfect of جلنڑا /julṛā/ 'to go'

Simple perfect forms of transitive verbs agree with the direct object of the sentence, provided that it is not marked with the accusative postposition آں /ā̃/, in which case the default masculine singular form of the perfective participle appears. The simple perfect of کرنا /karnā/ 'to do', the most frequently occurring transitive verb, is presented in Table 8.28.

Gender of direct object	Singular	Plural
Masculine	کیتا kītā '(any subject) did (m.sg. direct object)'	کیتے kīte '(any subject) did (m.pl. direct object)'
Feminine	کیتی kītī '(any subject) did (f.sg. direct object)'	کیتی آں kītī ā̃ '(any subject) did (f.pl. direct object)'

Table 8.28: Simple perfect of کرنا /karnā/ 'to do'

8.3.1.7.2 Present perfect

The present perfect consists of the perfective participle + the present tense of ہونڑا /hoṛā/ 'to be' as auxiliary. In some cases, the auxiliary is written separately, and in some cases, it is written together with the perfective participle (with elisions). Table 8.29 displays the present perfect of intransitive جلنڑا /julṛā/ 'to go', and Table 8.30 the present perfect of transitive /karnā/ کرنا ‘to do’. Since Hindko present perfect forms frequently correspond to English simple pasts, glosses are given with both English simple past and present perfect forms.[6]

Person	Singular	Plural
1st	میں گیاں mæ̃ gyā̃$_M$ میں گئی آں mæ̃ gaī ā̃$_F$ ‘I went/have gone’	اسی گئے آں assī gae ā̃$_M$ اسی گئی آں assī gaī ā̃$_F$ ‘we went/have gone’
2nd	تُوں گئے ایں tū̃ gyæ̃$_M$ تُوں گئی ایں tū̃ gaī ẽ$_F$ ‘you went/have gone’	تُسی گئے او tussī gae o$_M$ تُسی گئی او tussī gaī o$_F$ ‘you went/have gone’
3rd	او گئے اے o gyæ$_M$ ‘he went/has gone’ او گئی اے o gaī e$_F$ ‘she went/has gone’	او گیے ان o gæn$_M$ او گئی ان o gaī an$_F$ ‘they went/have gone’

Table 8.29: Present perfect of جلنڑا /julṛ̃ā/ ‘to go’

6 The Perso-Arabic forms are as spelled by AWT; the roman representations follow the Perso-Arabic.

Gender of direct object	Singular	Plural
Masculine	کیتے kītæ ‘(any subject) did/has done (m.sg. direct object)’	کیتے ان kītēn ‘(any subject) did/has done (m.pl. direct object)’
Feminine	کیتی اے kītī e ‘(any subject) did/has done (f.sg. direct object)’	کیتی ان kītī an ‘(any subject) did/has done (f.pl. direct object)’

Table 8.30: Present perfect of کرنا /karnā/ ‘to do’

8.3.1.7.3 Present perfect-stative

The present perfect-stative consists of the oblique perfective participle + a form of دا /dā/ agreeing in number and gender with the subject for intransitives, or the direct object for transitives + the present tense of ہوڑا /hoṛā/ ‘to be’. The perfective participle + agreeing form of دا /dā/ constitutes a distinct stative perfective participle, which can also be used adjectivally. This type of perfect-stative is unique to Hindko among the three languages discussed here. Its counterparts in Panjabi and Saraiki are constructed with the perfective participle of ہووݨ/ہونا /hovāṇ/ , /honā/ ‘to be’ instead of دا /dā/. In all three languages these forms focus on the persistent state resulting from an action or event, rather than on the action itself. Table 8.31 shows the present perfect-stative of the intransitive verb جُلڑا /julṛā/ ‘to go’. Parallel past perfect-stative forms can also be constructed in which the past tense of ہوڑا /hoṛā/ ‘to be’ appears as an auxiliary. These forms have the meaning that a resultant state existed at some time in the past, and may or may not still be the case. The present perfect-stative forms are felt to be the closest in sense to the English present perfect.

The use of a present perfect-stative form is shown in example 8.7, and a past perfect-stative is shown in 8.8.

(8.7) تُداں نیندر آئی دی اے

tud-ā̃	*nīndar*	***ā-ī-d-ī***	***e***
2SG.OBL-DAT	sleep.SG.F	**come-PP.SG.F-STAT-SG.F**	**be.PRES.3SG**

‘Are you (sg.) feeling sleepy? (lit. **Has** sleep **come** to you (and remained)?’ (Hk) (AWT)

Person	Singular	Plural
1st	میں گیے داں mæ̃ gyæ dā̃$_{M}$	اسی گیے دے آں assī gye de ā̃$_{M}$
	میں گئی دی آں mæ̃ gaī dī ā̃$_{F}$ 'I have gone (and am still away)'	اسی گئی دی آں assī gaī dī ā̃$_{F}$ 'we have gone (and are still away)'
2nd	توں گیے دیں tū̃ gyæ dæ̃$_{M}$	تسی گیے گیدے او tussī gye de o$_{M}$
	توں گئی دی ایں tū̃ gaī dī ẽ$_{F}$ 'you have gone (and are still away)'	تسی گئی دیو tussī gaī dī o$_{F}$ 'you have gone (and are still away)'
3rd	او گیے دے o gyæ dæ$_{M}$ 'he has gone (and is still away)'	او گیے دین o gyeden$_{M}$
	او گئی دی اے o gaī dī e$_{F}$ 'she has gone (and is still away)'	او گئی دی ان o gaī dī an$_{F}$ 'they have gone (and are still away)'

Table 8.31: Present perfect-stative of جلنڑا /julṛā/ 'to go'

(8.8) چاکو زمی تے پے دا ایہیا

cākū	*zamī*	*te*	***pæ-d-ā***	***éy-ā***
knife.SG.M	ground	on	**lie.PP.M.OBL-STAT-SG.M**	**be.PST-SG.M**

'The knife **was lying** on the ground.' (Hk) (AWT)

8.3.1.7.4 Past perfect

The past perfect is formed from the perfective participle + the past tense of ہونڑا /hoṛā/ 'to be'. It is used with two types of meanings. (1) Sometimes it functions like the English past perfect—that is, to refer to an event in the past which took place prior to another event, also in the past. (2) Usually, however, it refers to events which took place at a fixed time in the past, often a long time ago. In this function, it is best rendered by an English simple past tense. Table 8.32 shows the past perfect conjugation of the intransitive verb جلنڑا /julṛā/ 'to go' and Table 8.33 that of the transitive verb کرنا /karnā/ 'to do'.

In examining these paradigms, notice that the forms of intransitive جُلنڑا /julṛā/ 'to go' agree in person, number, and gender. This is because they agree with the subject, which can be any person, and include the past tense of 'be', which inflects for person. The forms of transitive کرنا /karnā/ 'to do', however, show only number and gender agreement. This is because any first or second person direct object would obligatorily be marked with the accusative postposition, thus forcing default masculine singular agreement. Thus the only possible direct objects with which the verb could agree are third person objects, either singular or plural.

Person	Singular	Plural
1st	میں گیا ایہاں mæ̃ gyā éyā̃$_{M}$ میں گئی ایہی آں mæ̃ gaī éyī ā̃$_{F}$ 'I went/had gone'	اسی گئے ایہے آں assī gae éye ā̃$_{M}$ اسی گئی آں ایہی آں assī gaī ā̃ éyī ā̃$_{F}$ 'we went/had gone'
2nd	توں گیا ایہا ایں tū̃ gyā éyẽ$_{M}$ توں گئی ایہی ایں tū̃ gaī éyī ẽ$_{F}$ 'you went/had gone'	تسی گئے ایہے او tussī gae éye o$_{M}$ تسی گئی آں ایہی او tussī gaī ā̃ éyī o$_{F}$ 'you went/had gone'
3rd	او گیا ایہا o gyā éyā$_{M}$ 'he went/had gone' او گئی ایہی o gaī éyī$_{F}$ 'she went/had gone'	او گئے ایہے o gae éye$_{M}$ او گئی آں ایہی آں o gaī ā̃ éī ā̃$_{F}$ 'they went/had gone'

Table 8.32: Past perfect of جُلنڑا /julṛā/ 'to go'

Gender of direct object	Singular	Plural
Masculine	کیتا ایہا kītā éyā '(any subject) did/had done (m.sg. direct object)'	کیتے ایہے kīte éye '(any subject) did/had done (m.pl. direct object)'
Feminine	کیتی ایہی kītī éyī '(any subject) did/had done (f.sg. direct object)'	کیتی آں ایہی آں kītī ā̃ éyī ā̃ '(any subject) did/had done (f.pl. direct object)'

Table 8.33: Past perfect of کرنا /karnā/ 'to do'

8.3.1.7.5 Perfect irrealis II

The perfect irrealis II consists of the perfective participle of the main verb + the imperfective participle of ہوڑا /hoṛ̃ā/ 'to be'; thus these forms are marked only for number and gender. They agree with the subject in the case of intransitive verbs, and a non-accusative marked direct object in the case of transitive verbs. Table 8.34 shows the perfect irrealis II conjugation and glosses for the intransitive verb جلنڑا /julṛ̃ā/ 'to go', and Table 8.35 that of the transitive verb کرنا /karnā/ 'to do'. The perfect irrealis I construction consists of a subjunctive form + the particle آ /ā/.

Gender of subject	Singular	Plural
Masculine	گیا ہوں دا gyā hõdā 'if (any m.sg. subject) had gone (but didn't)'	گئے ہوں دے gae hõde 'if (any m.pl. subject) had gone (but didn't)'
Feminine	گئی ہوں دی gaī hõdī 'if (any f.sg. subject) had gone (but didn't)'	گئی آں ہوں دی آں gaī ā̃ hõdī ā̃ 'if (any f.pl. subject) had gone (but didn't)'

Table 8.34: Perfect irrealis II of جلنڑا /julṛ̃ā/ 'to go'

Gender of direct object	Singular	Plural
Masculine	کیتا ہوں دا kītā hõdā 'if (any subject) had done (m.sg. direct object) (but didn't)'	کیتے ہوں دے kīte hõde 'if (any subject) had done (m.pl. direct object) (but didn't)'
Feminine	کیتی ہوں دی kītī hõdī 'if (any subject) had done (f.sg. direct object) (but didn't)'	کیتی آں ہوں دی آں kītī ā̃ hõdī ā̃ 'if (any subject) had done (f.pl. direct object) (but didn't)'

Table 8.35: Perfect irrealis II of کرنا /karnā/ 'to do'

8.3.1.7.6 Future perfect

The future perfect can refer to actions which will have happened by some time in the future, to actions which are presumed to be going to have happened by some time in the future, or to actions which are presumed to have happened. Table 8.36 shows these forms for the intransitive verb جُلنڑا /julṛ̃ā/ 'to go', and Table 8.37 forms for the transitive verb کرنا /karnā/ 'to do'.

Person	Singular	Plural
1st	میں گیا ہوساں mæ̃ gyā hosā̃$_{M}$ میں گئی ہوساں mæ̃ gaī hosā̃$_{F}$ 'I will/must have gone'	اسی گئے ہوساں assī gae hosā̃$_{M}$ اسی گئی آں ہوساں assī gaī ā̃ hosā̃$_{F}$ 'we will/must have gone'
2nd	تُوں گیا ہوسیں tū̃ gyā hosẽ$_{M}$ تُوں گئی ہوسیں tū̃ gaī hosẽ$_{F}$ 'you will/must have gone'	تُسی گئے ہوسو tussī gae hoso$_{M}$ تُسی گئی آں ہوسو tussī gaī ā̃ hoso$_{F}$ 'you will/must have gone'
3rd	او گیا ہوسی o gyā hosī$_{M}$ 'he will/must have gone' او گئی ہوسی o gaī hosī$_{F}$ 'she will/must have gone'	او گئے ہوسن o gae hosan$_{M}$ او گئی آں ہوسن o gaī ā̃ hosan$_{F}$ 'they will/must have gone'

Table 8.36: Future perfect of جُلنڑا /julṛā/ 'to go'

Gender of direct object	Singular	Plural
Masculine	کیتا ہوسی kītā hosī '(any subject) will/must have done (m.sg. direct object)'	کیتے ہوسن kīte hosan '(any subject) will/must have done (m.pl. direct object)'
Feminine	کیتی ہوسی kītī hosī '(any subject) will/must have done (f.sg. direct object)'	کیتی آں ہوسن kītī ā̃ hosan '(any subject) will/must have done (f.pl. direct object)'

Table 8.37: Future perfect of کرنا /karnā/ 'to do'

8.4 Panjabi verbs

8.4.1 Overview

The four basic non-finite forms—stem, infinitive, perfective participle, and imperfective participle—combine with the auxiliary verb ہونا /hoṇā/ 'to be;', the grammaticalized perfective participle of the verbs پینا/pæṇā/ 'to fall, lie', or رہنا /rǽṇā/ 'to remain'; or the subjunctive person-number endings and the number and gender-agreeing future suffix گا /gā/. The imperfective participle is the base of the imperfect tenses; perfect tenses are built on the perfective participle. The continuous tenses consist of the imperfective participle plus the grammaticalized perfective participle of پینا/pæṇā/ 'to fall, lie', or the verb stem plus the grammaticized perfective participle of رہنا /rǽṇā/ 'to remain', plus tensed auxiliaries. These forms encode durative events taking place during a bounded interval. They convey both durativity and a strong sense of actuality. Forms of the auxiliary verb ہونا /hoṇā/ encode tense (past, present, or future) and mood (actual, subjunctive, or presumptive). With regard to event structure, the imperfective participle encodes durative events, and the perfective participle encodes completed or pointlike events. The future is expressed by the subjunctive form of the main verb or an auxiliary verb plus a form of the marked adjectival particle گا /gā/, and is used for states or events that are predicted to happen in the future or presumed to be happening, or have happened. Both the present tense of the auxiliary verb ہونا /hoṇā/ 'to be' and its suppletive past tense inflect for person and number in all persons.[7] The future suffix گا /gā/ inflects only for gender and number. Verb forms may agree with one of the arguments in the clause, or may take default agreement identical to the third person singular masculine form.

The following discussion begins with a brief description of each of the four basic non-finite forms. After that, the full conjugation of the auxiliary verb ہونا /hoṇā/, forms of which enter into most complex verb forms, is provided. Finally, we discuss each tense-aspect form separately, organized by the basic verb form on which it is constructed.

Table 8.38 provides an overview of Panjabi verb forms.

7 Hindko, Panjabi, and Saraiki all have agreement for person and number in the past tense of 'be', which is different from the situation in Urdu.

Table 8.38: Overview of Panjabi verb forms

	Tenses				Moods	
	Simple	**Present**	**Past**	**Future**	**Subjunctive**	**Irrealis**
Simple		اوہ اے ó e 'he is'	اوہ سی ó sī 'he was'	اوہ جاوے گا ó jāve gā 'he will go'	اوہ جاوے ó jāve 'he may/should go; if he goes'	اوہ جاندا ó jāndā 'if he had gone/were going (but he did not go/is not going'
Imperfect	اوہ جاندا ó jāndā 'he would go'	اوہ جاندا اے ó jāndā e 'he goes'	اوہ جاندا سی ó jāndā sī 'he used to go'	اوہ جاندا ہووے گا ó jāndā hove gā 'he will/must go (frequently)'	اوہ جاندا ہووے ó jāndā hove 'he may/should go (frequently); if he goes (frequently)'	اہو جاندا ہوندا ó jāndā hondā 'if he went (frequently) (but he does not go)'
Imperfect-habitual		اوہ جاندا ہوندا اے ó jāndā hondā e 'he usually goes '	اوہ جاندا ہوندا سی ó jāndā hondā sī 'he usually used to go '			
Continuous-I		اوہ جاندا پیا اے ó jāndā pyā e 'he is going'	اوہ جاندا پیا سی ó jāndā pyā sī 'he was going'		اوہ جاندا پیا ہووے ó jāndā pyā hove 'if he is going'	

Table 8.38: (continued)

	Tenses				Moods	
	Simple	**Present**	**Past**	**Future**	**Subjunctive**	**Irrealis**
Continuous-II		اوہ جا رہیا اے ó jā ryā̃ e 'he is going'	اوہ جا رہیا سی ó jā ryā̃ sī 'he was going'	اوہ جا رہیا ہووے گا ó jā ryā̃ hove gā 'he will/must be going'	اوہ جا رہیا ہووے ó jā ryā̃ hove 'he may/should be going; if he is going'	اوہ جا رہیا ہوندا ó jā ryā̃ hondā 'if he were going (but he is not going)'
Perfect	اوہ گیا ó gayā 'he went'	اوہ گیا اے ó gayā e 'he has gone'	اوہ گیا سی ó gayā sī 'he went/had gone'	اوہ گیا ہووے گا ó gayā hove gā 'he will/must have gone'	اوہ گیا ہووے ó gayā hove 'he may have gone; if he has gone'	اوہ گیا ہوندا ó gayā hondā 'if he had gone (but he did not go)'
Perfect-stative		اوہ گیا ہویا اے ó gayā hoiyā e 'he is gone (i.e. went, and is still away)'	اوہ گیا ہویا سی ó gayā hoiyā sī 'he was gone (i.e. he went, and was still away) '			اوہ گیا ہویا ہوندا ó gayā hoiyā hondā 'if he had been ~ were gone (i.e. had gone, and were still away)'

8.4.2 Non-finite forms

Non-finite forms are not marked for person or tense. They include the stem, the infinitive, the conjunctive participle, the imperfective participle, and the perfective participle.

8.4.2.1 Stem

The stem (sometimes called "root") is the base form to which affixes are added. Generally speaking, the stem of a given verb can be inferred from the infinitive, which is the citation form of the verb, i.e. the form that appears in dictionaries. The stem is the form to which the infinitive affix ڻا /ṇā/or /nā/ is added.

Panjabi stems have three forms: (i) plain stem, (ii) first causative stem (plain stem + /-ā/), and (iii) double causative stem (plain stem + وا /-vā/). With a basic intransitive, first causative formation yields a derived transitive. With a basic transitive, first causative formation can add a secondary agent (causee) argument to the verb. Double causative formation adds yet a third argument, a secondary sub-agent. Panjabi no longer has a productive passive stem formation process, but older passives survive in a deontic modal construction (Section 19.4.2.1). Table 8.39 shows the plain, first causative, and second causative stems for a basic transitive stem کر /kar-/ 'do' and the basic intransitive بݨ /baṇ/- 'be made, become'.

Plain stem	کر kaṛ- 'do'	بݨ baṇ- 'be made, become'
Causative stem	کرا karā- 'cause to be done'	بݨا baṇā- 'make = cause [something] to be made'
Double causative stem	کروا karvā- 'have done = cause [someone] to cause [something] to be done'	بݨوا baṇvā- ' have made = cause [someone] to cause [something] to be made'

Table 8.39: Verb stems—transitivity sets

However, the matter of transitivity sets is more complicated than this introductory summary would suggest. Not all verbs have three stems. For example, آ /ā-/ 'come' and جا

/jā-/ 'go' have only one stem. Not all intransitive-transitive pairs differ by the presence or absence of the causative morpheme /-ā-/. For example, گواچ /gvāc-/ 'be lost' (intransitive), and گوا /gvā-/ 'lose' (transitive). Additionally, some verbs can be either transitive or intransitive, e.g. لبھ /ḷáb-/ 'be found, find'.

8.4.2.2 Infinitive

The infinitive is the citation form of the verb, which appears in most dictionaries. It is grammatically a verbal noun, occurring in the direct case or the singular oblique case like other nouns. It has no oblique plural form. When used in this way, it is inflected as a singular masculine marked noun: نا /-ṇā/ or /-nā/ in the direct case and ان /-aṇ/ or /-an/ in the oblique. See Chapter 9 for functions of the infinitive and constructions in which it appears.

The infinitival suffix is default نا /-ṇā/ (Panjabi) for stems ending in vowels and all consonants except ر /r/, ڑ /ṛ/, ڑھ /ṛh/,[8] ن /ṇ/, and ل /ḷ/, whose infinitives are formed with نا /-nā/. Writers of Panjabi rarely represent the contrast between /n/ and /ṇ/, writing both as ن /ṇ/.[9] Compare سننا /suṇna/ 'to listen to' and مننا /mannā/ 'to accept, agree to, obey'. The contrast between dental /l/ and retroflex /ḷ/ is not represented in the Perso-Arabic orthography, both sounds being written as ل /l/. Compare بولنا /bolṇā/ 'to speak' with ملنا /maḷnā/ 'to rub'. Despite being pronounced very differently, the sequences /ḷnā/ and /lṇā/ are written the same.[10]

In some varieties of Panjabi and some people's pronunciation, stems ending in ا /-ā/ are pronounced as و /ɔ ~ au/ before the infinitive ending, e.g. پڑھانا /paṛā̀ṇā/ 'to teach' is sometimes pronounced پڑھاونا /paṛɔ̀ṇā/ (Shackle 1972: 78–79). However in contemporary, urban Lahore Panjabi, the او /ɔ ~ au/ pronunciation is yielding to that with ا /ā/.

8.4.2.3 Conjunctive participle

The conjunctive participle consists of the stem + کے /ke/, e.g. for جانا /jāṇā/ 'to go': stem جا /jā/ + کے /ke/ → conjunctive participle جا کے /jā ke/ 'having gone'. Stems that end in a geminate consonant have only a single consonant in the conjunctive participle. For example: for پچھنا /pucchṇā/ 'to ask', stem: پچھ /pucch-/ + کے /ke/ → conjunctive participle پچھ کے /puch ke/ 'having asked'.

---

8 Stems ending in orthographic ڑھ /ṛh/ represent high tone on a preceding vowel, but behave like stems in plain ڑ /ṛ/ in having infinitives in dental ن /n/.

9 However the /n/ /ṇ/ contrast is regularly represented in Hindko and in Saraiki.

10 For these reasons, some Panjabi language experts recommend the introduction of distinct Perso-Arabic characters for retroflex /ṇ/ and /ḷ/.

The basic/original function of the conjunctive participle is to express two sequential actions or events. Rather than using two separate finite clauses joined with a coordinating conjunction like 'and', two verbs are usually conjoined by putting the first verb in the conjunctive participle form and the second in a finite conjugated form. The subject of both verbs is usually the same, and the verb that is reduced to a conjunctive participle is understood as having the same tense as the finite main verb. The marking of the agent depends on the transitivity and aspect (perfective or imperfective) of the finite main verb. See also Section 7.2.1, and Section 9.3.2.3. Conjunctive participial forms are frequently grammaticalized and acquire lexicalized adverbial, sometimes idiomatic, meanings. For example, رلنا /raḷnā/ 'to mix, mingle' → conjunctive particle: رل کے /raḷ ke/ 'having mingled', idiomatically 'together'. جاننا /jāṇnā/ 'to know' → conjunctive particle: جان کے /jāṇ ke/ 'having known', i.e. 'intentionally'. The conjunctive participle of کرنا /karnā/ 'to do', کر کے /kar ke/ 'having done', has been grammaticalized as a derivational morpheme and a postposition (see Section 7.2.1, Section 10.9.1, Section 10.10.1.5, and Section 10.10.3.2) . As a postposition, کر کے /kar ke/ means 'because of', as in ایس کر کے /æs kar ke/ 'because of this, therefore, so', as in مینہ کر کے /mĩ̄ kar ke/ 'because of the rain'. As a derivational morpheme, کر کے /kar ke /derives adverbs from adjectives, e.g. عام کر کے /ām kar ke/ 'generally, usually'.

8.4.2.4 Imperfective participle

The imperfective participle consists of the stem followed by a marked adjectival particle which inflects for number and gender. If the stem ends in a consonant, then the adjectival particle is دا- /-dā/. If the stem ends in a vowel, the suffix is ندا /-ndā/. This /n/ is usually realized as nasalization of the stem-final vowel. See Table 8.40 for the inflected forms of the imperfective participial suffix.

If the stem ends in ا /-ā/, except for the verbs جا- /jā-/ 'go' and کھا - /khā-/ 'eat', the final ا /-ā/ can change to و /-ɔ ~ au/ before the participial suffix in some dialects (Shackle 1972: 109). This pronunciation is increasingly less frequent in Lahore Panjabi, and is characteristic of more easterly varieties.

The imperfective participle of the verb ہونا /hoṇā/ 'to be' is regular, and its inflected forms are as follows: ہونا /hoṇā/ 'to be'→ ہوندا، ہوندی، ہوندے، ہوندیاں /hõdā, hõdī, hõde, hõdiyā̃/.

The imperfective participle is an adjectival form that, when forming part of a complex verb form, agrees in number and gender with the grammatical subject. When functioning adjectivally it can also agree with some other argument of the verb. Table 8.40 displays the suffixes of the imperfective participle.

	Singular	Plural
Masculine	دا -dā [C-final] ندا -ndā [V-final]	دے -de [C-final] ندے -nde [V-final]
Feminine	دی -dī [C-final] ندی -ndī [V-final]	دیاں -diyā̃ [C-final] ندیاں -ndiyā̃ [V-final]

Table 8.40: Suffixes of the imperfective participle

8.4.2.5 Perfective participle

The perfective participle consists of the verb stem + the marked adjectival endings. The masculine singular form appears as /-ā/ or /-iyā/ depending on whether the perfective stem is regular or irregular and whether it is consonant- or vowel-final. Regular C- and V-final masculine singular forms end in /-iyā/ ~ /yā/, while those of irregular C-final perfective stems end in /-ā/. These forms are displayed in Table 8.41. Masculine plural and feminine endings are displayed in Table 8.42.

	Regular perfective stem		Irregular perfective stem	
	Verb	Participle	Verb	Participle
C-final stem	مار mār- 'beat, kill '	ماریا mār-iyā	بنھ bánn- 'tie'	بدّھا bádd-ā
V-final stem	بنا baṇā- 'make' ہو ho- 'be, become'	بنایا baṇā-yā ہویا ho-iyā	دے de- 'give'	دتّا ditt-ā

Table 8.41: Masculine singular perfective participles from regular and irregular perfective stems

Like the imperfective participle, the perfective participle agrees in number and gender with an argument of the verb (see Section 9.1.5.3, Section 9.3.1.3.2, and Section 9.3.2).

Perso-Arabic script does not distinguish between the sequences /īā/, /iyā/: both are spelled یا /*choṭī ye-alif*/. When ی /ī/ and ے /e/ are suffixed to a vowel-final stem, however, the hiatus between the two vowels is represented by ء *hamza* (see Section 3.6.1.2).

	Singular	Plural
Masculine	-یا -iyā [ĕā] $_{\text{C-final}}$ -iyā $_{\text{V-final}}$ -ا -ā $_{\text{Irregular C-final}}$	-ے -ئے -e
Feminine	-ی -ī	-یاں -iyā̃$_{\text{C-final}}$ -yā̃$_{\text{V-final}}$

Table 8.42: Suffixes of the perfective participle

Many frequently used verbs have irregular perfective participles. A few of them are presented here. The following numbered classes of irregular verbs are organized by perfective subtypes; within each class, lettered subclasses indicate subtypes.

Ia. Perfective stem involves only vowel changes:

- لینا /læṇā/ 'to take, get, buy' → لیا، لئی، لئے، لیاں /lyā [lĕyā], laī, lae, lyā̃ [lĕyā̃]/
- پینا/pæṇā/ 'to lie' → پیا، پئی، پئے، پیاں /pyā [pĕya], paī, pae, paīā̃ [paiyā̃]/
- رہنا /rǽṇā/ 'to remain, stay, live' → رہیا، رہی، رہے، رہیاں /ryā́, raī́, raé, raíyā̃/; transliteration: <rahnā> <rahyā rahī rahe rahiyā̃>
- کہنا /kǽṇā/ 'to say' → کیا، کئی، کئے، کئیاں /kyā́, kaī́, kaé, kaíyā/; transliteration: <kahnā>, <kahyā, kahī, kahe, kahiyā̃>

Ib. Perfective stem involves vowel change and consonant loss

- مرنا /marnā/ 'to die' → مویا، موئی، موئے، مویاں /moyā, moyī, moye, moiyā̃/[11]

11 In addition to this original perfective participle, the regular formation مریا /mariyā/ is also found.

II. Perfective stem ends in /-t/, /-tt/:
IIa. Perfective stem vowel is unchanged:

- پینا/pīṇā/ 'to drink' → پیتا، پیتی، پیتے، پیتیاں/pītā, pītī, pīte, pītiyā̃/
- نہاؤنا ~ نہانا /nā̀ṇā ~ nɔ̀ṇā/ 'to bathe' → نہاتا، نہاتی، نہاتے، نہاتیاں /nā̀tā, nā̀tī, nā̀te, nā̀tiyā̃/
- کھلونا /khloṇā/ 'to stand' → کھلوتا، کھلوتی، کھلوتے، کھلوتیاں /khlotā, khlotī, khlote, khlotiyā̃/
- دھونا /tòṇā/ 'to wash' → دھوتا، دھوتی، دھوتے، دھوتیاں /tòtā, tòtī, tòte, tòtiyā̃/

IIb. Perfective stem has vowel changes:

- کرنا /karnā/ 'to do' کیتا، کیتی، کیتے، کیتیاں → /kītā, kītī, kīte, kītiyā̃/
- ویونا /syūṇā/ 'to sew' سیتا، سیتی، سیتے، سیتیاں → /sītā, sītī, sīte, sītiyā̃/
- دینا /deṇā/ 'to give' دتّا، دتّی، دتّے، دتّیاں → /dittā, dittī, ditte, dittiyā̃/
- سونا /soṇā/ 'to sleep' ستّا، ستّی، ستّے، ستّیاں → /suttā, suttī, sutte, suttiyā̃/
- لیہنا /lǽṇā/ 'to go down' لتّھا، لتّھی، لتّھے، لتّھیاں → /látthā, látthī, látthe, látthiyā̃/

III. Perfective stem ends in /-ṭh/ :

- بیہنا/bǽṇā/ 'to sit'→ بیٹھا، بیٹھی، بیٹھے، بیٹھیاں/bæṭhā, bæṭhī, bæṭhe, bæṭhiyā̃/
- ڈھینا /ṭæ̀ṇā/ 'to fall' → ڈھٹّا، ڈھٹّی، ڈھٹّے، ڈھٹّیاں /ṭàṭṭhā, ṭàṭṭhī, ṭàṭṭhe, ṭàṭṭhiyā̃/

IV. Perfective stem ends in /-dh, -ddh/:

- کھانا /khāṇā/ 'to eat' → کھادھا، کھادھی، کھادھے، کھادھیاں /khā́dā, khā́dī, khā́de, khā́diyā̃/
- بنّھنا /bánnṇā/ 'to tie' → بدّھا، بدّھی، بدّھے، بدّھیاں /báddā, báddī, bádde, báddiyā̃/[12]

V. Perfective stem vowel is unchanged but stem-final consonant is geminated:

- لبھنا /lábṇā/ 'to look for; get, find' → لبّھا، لبّھی، لبّھے، لبّھیان /lábbā, lábbī, lábbe, lábbiyā̃/

12 These irregular stems, with historical stem-final voiced aspirates, now have high tone on the stem vowel.

- لگنا /lagṇā/ 'to attach, adhere to' → لگّا، لگّی، لگّے، لگّیاں /laggā, laggī, lagge, laggiyā̃/
- ٹُٹنا /ṭuṭnā/ 'to break (intr.)' → ٹُٹّا، ٹُٹّی، ٹُٹّے، ٹُٹّیاں /ṭuṭṭā, ṭuṭṭī, ṭuṭṭe, ṭuṭṭiyā̃/

VI. Perfective stem is suppletive:

- جانا /jāṇā/ 'to go' → گیا، گئی، گئے، گئیاں /gayā, gaī, gae, gaiyā̃/

8.4.3 The verb ہونا /hoṇā/ 'to be'

The verb ہونا /hoṇā/ 'to be' functions both as a main verb and as an auxiliary. As a main verb it expresses either existence or identity. As an auxiliary, it encodes tense (past, present, future), mood (realis, irrealis, presumptive), and in some cases person (1st, 2nd, 3rd), in complex verb constructions in which it appears. Since ہونا /hoṇā/ is irregular, full paradigms are presented in the following subsections.

8.4.3.1 Present tense of ہونا /hoṇā/ 'to be'

In complex verb constructions, the present form of ہونا /hoṇā/ 'to be' contributes present tense meaning. Complex forms that include a participle plus the present of ہونا /hoṇā/ are marked for person, number, gender, and tense. Negatives are formed with نہیں /naī̃/. In present-tense negative sentences, the auxiliary itself is usually not present, leaving only نہیں /naī̃/, which itself can mean 'is/are not'.

Table 8.43 gives the present tense forms of ہونا /hoṇā/. The first and second person plural pronouns occur in two variants: اسیں and تسیں, showing nasalization of the final vowel (e.g. Shackle 2003 and Bhatia 1993), and اسی and تسی, with no nasalization indicated (e.g. Bashir and Kazmi 2012). We use the forms showing nasalization consistently in the Panjabi verbal paradigms in this chapter. The third person plural forms نیں /nẽ/ and نے /ne/ are found as alternate spellings of the same morpheme. In this grammar, we will use the most common spelling, نیں /nẽ/ , to illustrate verbal paradigms.

Person	Singular	Plural
1st	میں آں mæ̃ ā̃ 'I am'	اسیں آں asī̃ ā̃ 'we are'
2nd	توں ایں tū̃ æ̃ 'you are'	تسیں او tusī̃ o 'you are'
3rd	اوہ اے ó e 'he/she/it is'	اوہ نیں ó nẽ 'they are'

Table 8.43: Present tense of ہونا /hoṇā/ 'to be'

8.4.3.2 Past tense of ہونا /hoṇā/ 'to be'

The past tense forms for ہونا /hoṇā/ are suppletive—that is, formed from a different stem than the infinitive and the present tense. In complex verb constructions, the past form of ہونا /hoṇā/ contributes past tense meaning. Complex forms including a participle plus the past of ہونا /hoṇā/ are marked for person, number, gender, and tense. Negatives are formed either with نہیں /naī̃/ or with نہ /na/. Table 8.44 shows the past tense forms of ہونا /hoṇā/.

Person	Singular	Plural
1st	میں ساں mæ̃ sā̃ 'I was'	اسیں ساں asī̃ sā̃ 'we were'
2nd	توں سیں tū̃ sæ̃ 'you were'	تسیں سو tusī̃ so~sau 'you were'
3rd	اوہ سی ó sī 'he/she/it was'	اوہ سن ó san 'they were'

Table 8.44: Past tense of ہونا /hoṇā/ 'to be'

8.4.3.3 Subjunctive of ہونا /hoṇā/ 'to be'

In complex verb constructions, the subjunctive form of ہونا /hoṇā/ encodes meanings such as potentiality, desirability, or contingency; it frequently, therefore, appears in the subordinate "if" clause in realis conditional constructions. Subjunctive forms agree in person and number, but are not marked for gender or tense. Negatives are formed with the simple negative element نہ /na/'not'. Table 8.45 shows the subjunctive of ہونا /hoṇā/ 'to be'.

Person	Singular	Plural
1st	میں ہوواں mǣ hovā̃ 'I may/should be; if I am'	اسیں ہوئیے asī̃ hoiye 'we may/should be; if we are'
2nd	توں ہوویں tū̃ hovẽ 'you may/should be; if you are'	تسیں ہووو tusī̃ hovo 'you may/should be; if you are'
3rd	اوہ ہووے ó hove 'he/she/it may/should be; if he/she/it is'	اوہ ہون ó hoṇ '~' اوہ ہوون ó hovaṇ 'they may/should be; if they are'

Table 8.45: Subjunctive of ہونا/hoṇā/ 'to be'

8.4.3.4 Future of ہونا /hoṇā/ 'to be'

As described in Section 8.1, the future form of ہونا /hoṇā/ 'to be' is used in future tense-aspect constructions, which describe events predicted to occur or presumed to have occurred as well as those presented as presumed to be happening. The future form is formed by adding the suffix گا /gā/, which inflects for number and gender, to the subjunctive form, except in the first person plural. A productive way to think about the future form in Panjabi is as a strengthened[13] subjunctive.[14] Since the future particle agrees in number and gender, and the subjunctive is marked for person and number, the future form agrees in person, number, and gender, and is marked for tense. The future ending گا /gā/ can be written separately or together with the subjunctive base; in this case, a final ں *nūn yunna* appears as ن *nūn*, since it is no longer ligature-final. Negatives are usually formed with نہیں /naī̃/. Table 8.46 displays future forms of ہونا /hoṇā/.

Person	Singular	Plural
1st	میں ہوواں گا mæ̃ hovā̃ gā$_{M}$ میں ہوواں گی mæ̃ hovā̃ gī$_{F}$ 'I will be'	اسیں ہوواں گے asī̃ hovā̃ ge$_{M}$ اسیں ہوواں گیاں asī̃ hovā̃ gıyā̃$_{F}$ 'we will be'
2nd	توں ہوویں گا tū̃ hovẽ gā$_{M}$ توں ہوویں گی tū̃ hovẽ gī$_{F}$ 'you will be'	تسیں ہووو گے tusī̃ hovo ge$_{M}$ تسیں ہووو گیاں tusī̃ hovo giyā̃$_{F}$ 'you will be'
3rd	اوہ ہووے گا ó hove gā$_{M}$ 'he/it will be' اوہ ہووے گی ó hove gī$_{F}$ 'she will be'	اوہ ہون گے ó hoṇ ge$_{M}$ اوہ ہون گیاں ó hoṇ gıyā̃$_{F}$ 'they will be'

Table 8.46: Future of ہونا /hoṇā/ 'to be'

13 The strengthening effect of the particle گا /gā/ (< gataḥ, Old Indo-Aryan past particle of 'go'), is also seen in present and past tense formations. For example, ہیگا /hægā/ is a form with emphatic existential force, as in جہدے کول ویزا ہیگا /jíde kol vīzā hægā/ 'who(ever) (actually) has a visa'. One of the characters of the popular children's television show Kalian of the 1970s was named "Haiga" because of his habit of using this form frequently. The past tense form سیگا /sīgā/ 'he was' is found in some Panjabi varieties.

14 This analysis does not apply to the future forms in /s/ of Hindko and Saraiki, which retain the /s/ in future forms from Old and Middle Indo Aryan.

8.4.4 Verb forms constructed on the stem

8.4.4.1 Imperative

There are two specifically imperative forms in Panjabi, called here the "informal imperative" and the "formal" or "polite imperative".[15] The informal and formal imperatives each have a singular and plural form. The singular form is used in contexts when the second person singular pronoun تُوں /tũ̄/ is appropriate and the plural form in contexts calling for the second person plural pronoun تُسیں /tusī̃/. Imperatives are negated with نہ /na/, e.g. نہ کرو /na karo/ 'don't do it.' In addition to these specifically imperative forms, other forms like the infinitive and the subjunctive are also used in imperative-like functions (see Section 9.1.5, Section 9.3.1.3.1, Section 9.3.2.4).

8.4.4.1.1 Informal imperative

The singular form of the informal imperative is equivalent to the stem; the plural form consists of the stem + و /-o/. For example, from جانا /jāṇā/ 'to go', we have /jā́/ 'go! (to one person)', and جاؤ /jáō/ 'go! (to one or more than one person)'.

High tone appears regularly in the imperative and future tenses in some cases where the verbal stems themselves do not have tone (Shackle 2003: 593). For example, کھا - /khā-/ 'eat' and دے- /de-/ 'give' have informal imperative forms کھا /khā́/ (sg.) 'eat!', کھاؤ /khā́o/ 'eat!' (pl.) and دے /dé/ 'give!' (sg.), دیو /deó/ 'give!' (pl), and future کھاویگا /khā́vegā/ 'he will eat', and دیویگا /dévegā/ 'he will eat' for example. Since this high tone is not the reflex of historic aspiration, most writers do not represent it in the orthography. Some stems that end in a geminate consonant have a single consonant in the singular informal imperative but a geminate consonant in the plural informal imperative. Most writers do not represent this gemination in the orthography. For example, /rakkhṇā/ 'to put, keep' → singular: رکھ /rákh/ 'put! (to one person)'; and plural: رکھو /rakkhó/ 'put! (to one or more than one person)'

The honorific particle جی /jī/ following a plural informal imperative forms polite informal requests: آنا /āṇā/ [ɔṇa] 'to come', آؤ جی /āo jī/ 'please come'.

15 Various scholars have characterized imperative formations in different ways. Bashir and Kazmi (2012) and Gill and Gleason (1969) call them "informal" and "polite" imperatives; Shackle (2003), however, calls the two imperative forms "present" and "aorist," in view of the distancing function of the second imperative form, which softens its force and causes it to be interpreted as less immediate, hence more polite than the present or informal imperative.

8.4.4.1.2 Polite/formal imperative

The singular polite imperative consists of the stem + اـیں /ĩ/,[16] and the plural polite imperative is formed from the stem + اِیـو /iyo/. For example: رکھنا /rakhṇā/ 'to put' → singular polite imperative: رکّھیں /rakkhĩ/ 'please put (addressed to one person)', and plural polite imperative: رکھیو /rakkhiyo/ 'please put (addressed to one or more persons)'. The plural polite imperative is frequently used with the second person plural pronominal suffix ـجے /je/, e.g. اُٹھیئو ـجے /uṭṭhiyo je/ 'please get up' (Bailey 1904b: 43).

Table 8.47 summarizes Panjabi imperative forms.

	Singular	Plural
Informal	Ø (no ending)	و -o
Formal/Polite	ـیں ĩ ~ ویں vĩ	یو -iyo

Table 8.47: Panjabi imperative endings

8.4.4.2 Subjunctive

The subjunctive is formed from the stem + personal endings (see Table 8.48). Subjunctive forms are marked only for person and number. Vowel-final stems insert و /v/ between the stem and the ending obligatorily in the first person singular form, and optionally in the second person singular, third person singular, second person plural, and third person plural forms. The third-person singular subjunctive forms with epenthetic و /v/ are more common in spoken Panjabi, while forms without epenthetic و /v/ are sometimes encountered in writing. The third person plural ending varies for consonant-final and vowel-final stems. The third person plural ending is /-(v)aṇ/, except with stems ending in /n/, /ṇ/, /r/, /ṛ/, and /ḷ/, where the ending is /-(v)an/. The ending of the second person plural subjunctive is identical to that of the informal plural imperative. This follows from the fact that both subjunctives and imperatives point

16 This final اـیں /ĩ/could also be analyzed as a second-person singular pronominal suffix. See Section 6.8.2 on pronominal suffixes in Panjabi.

to unrealized actions or events. Table 8.48 shows the person-number suffixes of the subjunctive conjugation.

Person	Singular	Plural
1st	اں -ã$_{\text{C-final}}$ واں -vã$_{\text{V-final}}$	یے -iye
2nd	یں -ẽ$_{\text{C-final, V-final}}$ ویں -vẽ$_{\text{V-final}}$	و -o
3rd	ے -e$_{\text{C-final, V-final}}$ وے -ve$_{\text{V-final}}$	ن -aṇ$_{\text{C-final}}$ ون -vaṇ$_{\text{V-final}}$

Table 8.48: Personal endings of the subjunctive

Table 8.49 and Table 8.50 illustrate the regular subjunctive conjugation with the verbs بولنا /bolṇā/ 'to speak', a consonant-final stem, and جانا /jāṇā/ 'to go', a vowel-final stem.

Person	Singular	Plural
1st	میں بولاں mæ̃ bolā̃ 'I may/should speak; if I speak'	اسیں بولئے ~ بولیے asī̃ bolıye 'we may/should speak; let's speak; if we speak'
2nd	توں بولیں tū̃ bolẽ 'you may/should speak; if you speak'	تسیں بولو tusī̃ bolo 'you may/should speak; if you speak'
3rd	اوہ بولے ó bole 'he/she/it may/should speak; if he/she speaks'	اوہ بولن ó bolaṇ 'they may/should speak; if they speak'

Table 8.49: Subjunctive of بولنا /bolṇā/ 'to speak'

Verbs with stems that end in ے /æ/ or و /o/ are somewhat irregular. Table 8.51 shows the irregular subjunctive conjugation in the verb لینا /læṇā/ 'to take, get, buy'.

Person	Singular	Plural
1st	میں جاواں mæ̃ jāvā̃ ‘I may/should go; if I go’	اسیں جائیے asī̃ jāiye ‘we may/should go; let’s go; if we go’
2nd	توں جاویں tū̃ jāvẽ ~ توں جائیں tū̃ jāẽ ‘you may/should go; if you go’	تسیں جاؤ tusī̃ jāo ~ تسیں جاوو tusī̃ javo ‘you may/should go; if you go’
3rd	اوہ جاوے ó jāve ~ اوہ جائے ó jae ‘he/she/it may/should go; if he/she/it/goes’	اوہ جاون ó jāvaṇ ~ اوہ جان ó jāṇ ‘they may/should go; if they go’

Table 8.50: Subjunctive of جانا /jāṇā/ ‘to go’

Person	Singular	Plural
1st	میں لواں mæ̃ lavā̃ ‘I may/should take; if I take’	اسیں لئیے asī̃ laiye ‘we may/should take; let’s take; if we take’
2nd	توں لویں tū̃ lavẽ ~ توں لئیں tū̃ læ̃ ‘you may/should take; if you take’	تسیں لوو tusī̃ lavo ~ تسیں لو tusī̃ lo ‘you may/should take; if you take’
3rd	ایہ لوے é lave ~ ایہ لے é læ ‘he/she/it may/should take; if he/she/it takes’	اوہ لین ó læṇ ‘they may/should take; if they take’

Table 8.51: Subjunctive of لینا /læṇā/ ‘to take, get, buy’

8.4.4.3 Future

The future form is obtained by suffixing the appropriate inflected form of the future particle گا /gā/ to the subjunctive form, except in the first person plural, where the subjunctive base is the same as for the first person singular. The subjunctive base agrees in person and number; the future particle agrees in gender and number. Negatives are usually formed with نہیں /naĩ/ Table 8.52 shows the conjugation of the future tense of the verb بولنا /bolṇā/ 'to speak'. In this table, the future particle is written separately from the subjunctive base - for the sake of clarity. In actual practice, it is perhaps more frequently found written together. For example, we can find بولانگا as well as بولاں گا..

Person	Singular	Plural
1st	میں بولاں گا mæ̃ bolā̃gā$_M$ میں بولاں گی mæ̃ bolā̃gī$_F$ 'I will speak'	اسیں بولاں گے asī̃ bolā̃ge$_M$ اسیں بولاں گیاں asī̃ bolā̃gıyā̃$_F$ 'we will speak'
2nd	توں بولیں گا tū̃ bolẽgā$_M$ توں بولیں گی tū̃ bolẽgī$_F$ 'you will speak'	تسیں بولو گے tusī̃ bologe$_M$ تسیں بولو گیاں tusī̃ bologıyā̃$_F$ 'you will speak'.
3rd	اوہ بولے گا ó bolegā$_M$ 'he/it will speak' اوہ بولے گی ó bolegī$_F$ 'she/it will speak'	اوہ بولن گے ó bolaṇge$_M$ اوہ بولن گیاں ó bolaṇgıyā̃$_F$ 'they will speak'

Table 8.52: Future of بولنا /bolṇā/ 'to speak'

8.4.4.4 Continuous tenses

Continuous tenses encode durative activity over a bounded period of time. Often they have a marked nuance of actuality. There are several continuous tense formations in Panjabi. These are numbered to facilitate comparison with similar forms found in Hindko and Saraiki. Those constructed on the imperfective participle plus the perfective participle of پیٹا/pæṇā/ 'to fall, lie' are labeled present continuous I and past continuous I. Those constructed on the stem plus the perfective participle of تہنا /ræ̃ṇā/ 'to remain' are labeled present continuous II and past continuous II. Additionally, there is a third continuous form in Panjabi, which we will call present continuous III. This form is constructed on the oblique infinitive, and will be discussed later, in Section 8.4.7. In this section we present the present continuous II forms, since these are more characteristic of Lahore Panjabi than of either Hindko or Saraiki, and they are shared with more easterly varieties of Panjabi. Continuous I forms can be found in Section 8.3.1.6.7 for Hindko and Section 8.5.6.3.1 for Saraiki.

8.4.4.4.1 Present continuous II

Formation: Stem + رہنا /rǣṇā/ (perfective participle) + ہونا /hoṇā/ (present).

The grammaticalized perfective participle of رہنا /rǣṇā/ (ریا /ryā́/), which inflects for gender and number, contributes durative aspect. The auxiliary verb ہونا /hoṇā/ encodes tense (present, past, or future), mood (realis or irrealis), and person of the complex verb form. The present continuous both describes events which are in progress at the time of speaking and future actions which can be considered to have already begun, or to be imminent. Negatives are formed with نہیں ~ نئیں /naī̃́/; negative sentences in this tense usually omit the auxiliary.

Table 8.53 shows the conjugation of the verb کرنا /karnā/ 'to do' in the present continuous II. Note the epenthetic /v/ between the final ا /ā/ in ریا /ryā/ and the first person singular ending اں /ā̃/ in the phrase میں کر ریا واں /mǣ kar ryā vā̃/ 'I (m.) am doing.' These epenthetic consonants prevent a sequence of two identical vowels.

Person	Singular	Plural
1st	میں کر رہیا واں mæ̃ kar ryá̃ vā̃$_M$ میں کر رہی آں mæ̃ kar raí̃ ā̃$_F$ 'I am doing'	اسیں کر رہے آں asī̃ kar raé ā̃$_M$ اسیں کر رہیاں آں asī̃ kar raíyā̃ ā̃$_F$ 'we are doing'
2nd	توں کر رہیا ایں tū̃ kar ryá̃ ẽ$_M$ توں کر رہی ایں tū̃ kar raí̃ ẽ$_F$ 'you are doing'	تسیں کر رہے او tusī̃ kar raé o$_M$ تسیں کر رہیاں او tusī̃ kar raíyā̃ o$_F$ 'you are doing'
3rd	اوہ کر رہیا اے ó kar ryá̃ e$_M$ 'he/it is doing' اوہ کر رہی اے ó kar raí̃ e$_F$ 'she/it is doing'	اوہ کر رہے نیں ó kar raé nẽ$_M$ اوہ کر رہیاں نیں ó kar raíyā̃ nẽ$_F$ 'they are doing'

Table 8.53: Present continuous II of کرنا /karnā/ 'to do'

8.4.4.4.2 Past continuous II

Formation: stem + رہنا /rǽṇa/ (perfective participle) + ہونا /hoṇā/ (past).

The past continuous describes actions or events which were in progress or were imminent at a point prior to the moment of speaking. Negatives are formed with نہیں /naī̃/. Table 8.54 shows the conjugation of کرنا /karnā/ 'to do' in the past continuous II.

Person	Singular	Plural
1st	میں کر رہیا ساں mæ̃ kar ryā́ sā̃$_{M}$ میں کر رہی ساں mæ̃ kar raī́ sā̃$_{F}$ 'I was doing'	اسیں کر رہے ساں asī̃ kar raé sā̃$_{M}$ اسیں کر رہیاں ساں asī̃ kar raíyā̃ sā̃$_{F}$ 'we were doing'
2nd	توں کر رہیا سیں tū̃ kar ryā́ sæ̃$_{M}$ توں کر رہی سیں tū̃ kar raī́ sæ̃$_{F}$ 'you were doing'	تسیں کر رہے سو tusī̃ kar raé so$_{M}$ تسیں کر رہیاں سو tusī̃ kar raíyā̃ so$_{F}$ 'you were doing'
3rd	اوہ کر رہیا سی ó kar ryā́ sī$_{M}$ 'he/it was doing' اوہ کر رہی سی ó kar raī́ sī$_{F}$ 'she/it was doing'	اوہ کر رہے سن ó kar raé san$_{M}$ اوہ کر رہیاں سن ó kar raíyā̃ san$_{F}$ 'they were doing'

Table 8.54: Past continuous II of کرنا /karnā/ 'to do'

8.4.4.4.3 Past continuous II – habitual

Formation: stem + رہنا /rǽṇā/(perfective participle) + ہونا /hoṇā/(imperfective participle) + ہونا /hoṇā/ (past)

The imperfective participle of ہونا /hoṇā/adds a component of extended durativity. Bashir and Kazmi (2012: 651) gloss the meaning of this construction as (for example) 'I was habitually doing that at that time, but I don't follow this routine any longer.' Table 8.55 shows the conjugation of کرنا /karnā/ 'to do' in the past continuous II-habitual.

Person	Singular	Plural
1st	میں کر رہیا ہوندا ساں mæ̃ kar ryā́ hondā sã$_M$ میں کر رہی ہوندی ساں mæ̃ kar raī́ hondī sã$_F$ 'I was usually doing '	اسیں کر رہے ہوندے ساں asī̃ kar raé honde sã$_M$ اسیں کر رہیاں ہوندیاں ساں asī̃ kar raíyā̃ hondiyā̃ sã$_F$ 'we were usually doing '
2nd	توں کر رہیا ہوندا سیں tū̃ kar ryā́ hondā sæ̃$_M$ توں کر رہی ہوندی سیں tū̃ kar raī́ hondī sæ̃$_F$ 'you were usually doing '	تسیں کر رہے ہوندے سو tusī̃ kar raé honde so$_M$ تسیں کر رہیاں ہوندیاں سو tusī̃ kar raíyā̃ hondiyā̃ so$_F$ 'you were usually doing '
3rd	اوہ کر رہیا ہوندا سی ó kar ryā́ hondā sī$_M$ 'he/it was usually doing ' اوہ کر رہی ہوندی سی ó kar raī́ hondī sī$_F$ 'she/it was usually doing'	اوہ کر رہے ہوندے سن ó kar raé honde san$_M$ اوہ کر رہیاں ہوندیاں سن ó kar raíyā̃ hondiyā̃ san$_F$ 'they were usually doing '

Table 8.55: Past continuous II-habitual of کرنا /karnā/ 'to do'

8.4.4.4.4 Continuous II – subjunctive

Formation: Stem + رہنا /ræṇā/ (perfective participle) + ہونا /hoṇā/ (subjunctive)

The continuous subjunctive describes unrealized continuous actions or states which are potentially realizable. Thus it expresses meanings, such as potentiality, desirability, or contingency, which typically occur in the subordinate clause in a realis conditional construction. The negative is formed with نہ /na/. Table 8.56 shows the conjugation of کرنا /karnā/ 'to do' in the continuous II-subjunctive.

Person	Singular	Plural
1st	میں کر رہیا ہوواں mæ̃ kar ryā́ hovā̃$_{M}$ میں کر رہی ہوواں mæ̃ kar raī́ hovā̃$_{F}$ 'I may/should be doing; if I were to be doing'	اسیں کر رہے ہوئیے asī̃ kar raé hoiye$_{M}$ اسیں کر رہیاں ہوئیے asī̃ kar raíyā̃ hoiye$_{F}$ 'we may/should be doing; if we were to be doing'
2nd	توں کر رہیا ہوویں tū̃ kar ryā́ hovẽ$_{M}$ توں کر رہی ہوویں tū̃ kar raī́ hovẽ$_{F}$ 'you may/should be doing; if you were to be doing'	تسیں کر رہے ہووو tusī̃ kar raé hovo$_{M}$ تسیں کر رہیاں ہووو tusī̃ kar raíyā̃ hovo$_{F}$ 'you may/should be doing; if you were to be doing'
3rd	اوہ کر رہیا ہووے ó kar ryā́ hove$_{M}$ 'he/it may/should be doing; if he/it is doing' اوہ کر رہی ہووے ó kar raī́ hove$_{F}$ 'she/it may/should be doing; if she/it were to be doing'	اوہ کر رہے ہون ó kar raé hoṇ$_{M}$ اوہ کر رہیاں ہون ó kar raíyā̃ hoṇ$_{F}$ 'they may/should be doing; if they were to be doing'

Table 8.56: Continuous II-subjunctive of کرنا /karnā/ 'to do'

8.4.4.4.5 Future continuous II

Formation: stem + رہنا /ræ̃ṇā/ (perfective participle) + ہونا /hoṇā/ (future).

This form describes events which will be occurring in the future, or which the speaker presumes are occurring in the present. This presumptive meaning is often conveyed by 'must' in an English gloss, where *he must be doing* means 'I presume he is doing.' Table 8.57 shows the conjunction of کرنا /karnā/ 'to do' in the future continuous II.

Person	Singular	Plural
1st	میں کر رہیا ہوواں گا mǣ kar ryā́ hovā̃gā$_M$ میں کر رہی ہوواں گی mǣ kar raī́ hovā̃gī$_F$ 'I will/must be doing'	اسیں کر رہے ہوواں گے asī̃ kar raé hovā̃ge$_M$ اسیں کر رہیاں ہوواں گیاں asī̃ kar raíyā̃ hovā̃giyā̃$_F$ 'we will/must be doing'
2nd	توں کر رہیا ہوویں گا tū̃ kar ryā́ hovẽgā$_M$ توں کر رہی ہوویں گی tū̃ kar raī́ hovẽgī$_F$ 'you will/must be doing'	تسیں کر رہے ہووو گے tusī̃ kar raé hovoge$_M$ تسیں کر رہیاں ہووو گیاں tusī̃ kar raíyā̃ hovogiyā̃$_F$ 'you will/must be doing'
3rd	اوہ کر رہیا ہووے گا ó kar ryā́ hovegā$_M$ 'he will/must be doing' اوہ کر رہی ہووے گی ó kar raī́ hovegī$_F$ 'she will/must be doing'	اوہ کر رہے ہون گے ó kar raé hoṇge$_M$ اوہ کر رہیاں ہون گیاں ó kar raíyā̃ hoṇgiyā̃$_F$ 'they will/ must be doing'

Table 8.57: Future continuous II of کرنا /karnā/ 'to do'

8.4.4.4.6 Continuous II – irrealis

Formation: stem + رہنا /rǣṇā (perfective participle) + ہونا /hoṇā/ (imperfective participle).

This form is used to describe counterfactual actions or states, which would be in progress at the time of speaking, if they were true. Since this form consists entirely of non-finite forms, it agrees with the subject only in number and gender. Table 8.58 shows the conjugation of the verb کرنا /karnā/ 'to do' in the continuous II-irrealis.

Gender of Subject	Singular	Plural
Masculine	کر رہیا ہوندا kar ryā̃ hondā 'if (any m.sg. subject) were doing'	کر رہے ہوندے kar raé honde 'if (any m.pl. subject) were doing'
Feminine	کر رہی ہوندی kar raī̃ hondī 'if (any f.sg. subject) were doing'	کر رہیاں ہوندیاں kar raíyā̃ hondiyā̃ 'if (any f.pl. subject) were doing'

Table 8.58: Continuous II-irrealis of کرنا /karnā/ 'to do'

8.4.5 Verb forms constructed on the imperfective participle

As described in Section 8.4.2.4, the imperfective participle consists of the verb stem plus a form of the suffix (ن)دا- /-(n)dā/, which agrees in gender and number with the subject of the clause or other nominal. The imperfective participle encodes imperfectivity/durativity. It enters into complex verbal constructions with forms of the auxiliary verb ہونا /hoṇā/, 'to be', which contribute tense, mood and person. The bare participle, without a form of ہونا /hoṇā/, expresses irrealis mood.

8.4.5.1 Bare imperfective participle

8.4.5.1.1 Irrealis II

The imperfective participle may be used on its own, with no auxiliary, in one or both of the two clauses of a conditional sentence to describe an unfulfilled or unfulfillable condition. The negative is formed with نہ /na/. Table 8.59 shows the paradigm of /karnā/ 'to do' in the simple imperfect, functioning with irrealis meaning.

This meaning is illustrated in example 8.9.

(8.9) جے تُسیں اوہنوں معاف کردے تاں چنگا ہوندا

je	*tusī̃*	*ó-nū̃*	*māf*	***kar-d-e***	*tā̃*	*cā̃g-ā*	***ho-nd-ā***
if	2PL	3SG-DAT	forgiveness	**do-IP-PL.M**	then	good-SG.M	**be-IP-SG.M**

'If **you had** forgiven him, it **would have been** good.' (Pj) (Shackle 1972: 124)

Gender of Subject	Singular	Plural
Masculine	کردا kardā 'if (any m.sg. subject) had done, were doing, were going to do'	کردے karde 'if (any m.pl. subject) had done, were doing, were going to do'
Feminine	کردی kardī 'if (any f.sg. subject) had done, were doing, were going to do'	کردیاں kardiyā̃ 'if (any f.pl. subject) had done, were doing, were going to do'

Table 8.59: Simple irrealis II of کرنا /karnā/ 'to do'

8.4.5.1.2 Imperfective participle as attributive adjective

Imperfective participles also function as attributive adjectives,[17] as in English *flowing river*, or *rising water*. Frequently in this usage, the imperfective participle is followed by the perfective participle of ہونا /hoṇā/, which adds the meaning of extended duration/stativity. Both participles are Class I adjectives and agree with the noun they modify, as in 8.10.

(8.10) روندی ہوئی کُڑی ماں کول گئی

ro-nd-ī	***ho-ī***	*kuṛ-ī*	*mā̃*	*koḷ*	*ga-ī*
weep-IP-SG.F	**be.PP-SG.F**	girl-SG.F	mother	to	go.PP-SG.F

'The **weeping** girl went to [her] mother.' (Pj) (Shackle 1972: 106)

8.4.5.2 Imperfective tenses

8.4.5.2.1 Present imperfect

Formation: imperfective participle + ہونا /hoṇā/ 'to be' (present)

This form describes actions or states which occur generally or regularly, at or around the time of speaking. It can also be used to present an event as imminent. The negative is formed with نہیں /naī̃/, and the auxiliary verb is usually omitted in negative clauses; inclusion of the auxiliary conveys contrastive emphasis. Table 8.60 shows the conjugation of کرنا /karnā/ 'to do' in the present imperfect.

17 Analogously, the imperfective tenses could be analyzed as predicative adjectival uses of the participles.

Person	Singular	Plural
1st	میں کردا واں mæ̃ kardā vā̃$_{M}$ میں کردی آں mæ̃ kardī ā̃$_{F}$ 'I do'	اسیں کردے آں asī̃ karde ā̃$_{M}$ اسیں کردیاں آں asī̃ kardiyā̃ ā̃$_{F}$ 'we do'
2nd	توں کردا ایں tū̃ kardā ẽ$_{M}$ توں کردی ایں tū̃ kardī ẽ$_{F}$ 'you do'	تسیں کردے او tusī̃ karde o$_{M}$ تسیں کردیاں او tusī̃ kardiyā̃ o$_{F}$ 'you do'
3rd	اوہ کردا اے ó kardā e$_{M}$ 'he does' اوہ کردی اے ó kardī e$_{F}$ 'she does'	اوہ کردے نیں ó karde nẽ$_{M}$ اوہ کردیاں نیں ó kardiyā̃ nẽ$_{F}$ 'they do'

Table 8.60: Present imperfect of کرنا /karnā/ 'to do'

8.4.5.2.2 Present continuous I

Formation: imperfective participle + پینٹا/pæṇā/ 'to fall, lie' (perfective participle) + ہونا /hoṇā/ 'to be' (present)

This construction is used in all three languages. It originates in Hindko and Saraiki but is also frequent in the spoken Panjabi of Lahore. For paradigms see Section 8.3.1.6.7 on Hindko and Section 8.5.6.3.1 on Saraiki. On the other hand, the present continuous II, presented in Section 8.4.4.4.1, originates farther eastward, and is common to Urdu, eastern varieties of Panjabi, and Hindi.

8.4.5.2.3 Present imperfect – habitual

Formation: imperfective participle + ہونا /hoṇā/ (imperfective participle) + ہونا /hoṇā/ (present)

The present imperfective-habitual stresses the regularity and persistence of an action in the present.[18] Table 8.61 shows the conjugation of the verb کرنا /karnā/ 'to do' in the present imperfect-habitual.

Person	Singular	Plural
1st	میں کردا ہوندا واں mæ̃ kardā hondā vā̃$_M$ میں کردی ہوندی آں mæ̃ kardī hondī ā̃$_F$ 'I usually do'	اسیں کردے ہوندے آں asī̃ karde honde ā̃$_M$ اسیں کردیاں ہوندیاں آں asī̃ kardiyā̃ hondiyā̃ ā̃$_F$ 'we usually do'
2nd	توں کردا ہوندا ایں tū̃ kardā hondā ẽ$_M$ توں کردی ہوندی ایں tū̃ kardī hondī ẽ$_F$ 'you usually do'	تسیں کردے ہوندے او tusī̃ karde honde o$_M$ تسیں کردیاں ہوندیاں او tusī̃ kardiyā̃ hondiyā̃ o$_F$ 'you usually do'
3rd	اوہ کردا ہوندا اے ó kardā hondā e$_M$ 'he usually does' اوہ کردی ہوندی اے ó kardī hondī e$_F$ 'she usually does'	اوہ کردے ہوندے نیں ó karde honde nẽ$_M$ اوہ کردیاں ہوندیاں نیں ó kardiyā̃ hondiyā̃ nẽ$_F$ 'they usually do'

Table 8.61: Present imperfect-habitual of کرنا /karnā/ 'to do'

8.4.5.2.4 Past imperfect

Formation: imperfective participle + ہوݨا /hoṇā/(past)

The past imperfect describes events or states which occurred generally or regularly in the past. Depending on context and the specific verb involved, it may be translated in English with 'used to V', 'V-ed', or 'was/were V-ing'. The negative is formed with نہیں /naī̃/. Table 8.62 displays the past imperfect of کرنا /karnā/ 'to do'.

---

[18] Bashir and Kazmi (2012: 649) call this form an "Emphatic Habitual Present". Their "emphatic" refers to the characteristic which we call "persistence" here.

Person	Singular	Plural
1st	میں کردا ساں mæ̃ kardā sā̃$_M$ میں کردی ساں mæ̃ kardī sā̃$_F$ 'I used to do'	اسیں کردے ساں asī̃ karde sā̃$_M$ اسیں کردیاں ساں asī̃ kardiyā̃ sā̃$_F$ 'we used to do'
2nd	توں کردا سیں tū̃ kardā sæ̃$_M$ توں کردی سیں tū̃ kardī sæ̃$_F$ 'you used to do'	تسیں کردے سو tusī̃ karde so$_M$ تسیں کردیاں سو tusī̃ kardiyā̃ so$_F$ 'you used to do'
3rd	اوہ کردا سی ó kardā sī$_M$ 'he used to do' اوہ کردی سی ó kardī sī$_F$ 'she used to do'	اوہ کردے سن ó karde san$_M$ اوہ کردیاں سن ó kardiyā̃ san$_F$ 'they used to do'

Table 8.62: Past imperfect of کرنا /karnā/ 'to do'

8.4.5.2.5 Past imperfect – habitual

Formation: imperfective participle + ہونا /hoṇā/(imperfective participle) + ہونا /hoṇā/ (past)

The past imperfect-habitual stresses the persistent regularity of an action in the past. Table 8.63 shows the conjugation of کرنا /karnā/ 'to do' in the past imperfect-habitual.

Person	Singular	Plural
1st	میں کردا ہوندا ساں mæ̃ kardā hondā sā̃$_M$ میں کردی ہوندی ساں mæ̃ kardī hondī sā̃$_F$ 'I usually used to do '	اسیں کردے ہوندے ساں asī̃ karde honde sā̃$_M$ اسیں کردیاں ہوندیاں ساں asī̃ kardiyā̃ hondiyā̃ sā̃$_F$ 'we usually used to do '
2nd	توں کردا ہوندا سیں tū̃ kardā hondā sæ̃$_M$ توں کردی ہوندی سیں tū̃ kardī hondī sæ̃$_F$ 'you usually used to do '	تسیں کردے ہوندے سو tusī̃ karde honde so$_M$ تسیں کردیاں ہوندیاں سو tusī̃ kardiyā̃ hondiyā̃ so$_F$ 'you usually used to do '
3rd	اوہ کردا ہوندا سی ó kardā hondā sī$_M$ 'he used to do usually' اوہ کردی ہوندی سی ó kardī hondī sī$_F$ 'she usually used to do '	اوہ کردے ہوندے سن ó karde honde san$_M$ اوہ کردیاں ہوندیاں سن ó kardiyā̃ hondiyā̃ san$_F$ 'they usually used to do '

Table 8.63: Past imperfect-habitual of کرنا /karnā/ 'to do'

8.4.5.2.6 Imperfect subjunctive

Formation: imperfective participle + ہونا /hoṇā/(subjunctive)

The imperfective subjunctive presents durative actions or events as potential, desirable, or contingent, as in conditional constructions. The negative is formed with نہ /na/. Table 8.64 shows the conjugation of کرنا /karnā/ 'to do' in the imperfect subjunctive.

Person	Singular	Plural
1st	میں کردا ہوواں mǣ kardā hovā̃$_{M}$ میں کردی ہوواں mǣ kardī hovā̃$_{F}$ 'I may/should do frequently; if I were to do frequently'	اسیں کردے ہوئیے asī̃ karde hoiye$_{M}$ اسیں کردیاں ہوئیے asī̃ kardiyā̃ hoiye$_{F}$ 'we may/should do frequently; if we were to do frequently'
2nd	توں کردا ہوویں tū̃ kardā hovẽ$_{M}$ توں کردی ہوویں tū̃ kardī hovẽ$_{F}$ 'you may/should do frequently; if you were to do frequently'	تسیں کردے ہووو tusī̃ karde hovo$_{M}$ تسیں کردیاں ہووو tusī̃ kardiyā̃ hovo$_{F}$ 'you may/should do frequently; if you were to do frequently'
3rd	اوہ کردا ہووے ó kardā hove$_{M}$ 'he may/should do frequently; if he were to do frequently' اوہ کردی ہووے ó kardī hove$_{F}$ 'she may/should do frequently; if she were to do frequently'	اوہ کردے ہون ó karde hoṇ$_{M}$ اوہ کردیاں ہون ó kardiyā̃ hoṇ$_{F}$ 'they may/should do frequently; if they were to do frequently'

Table 8.64: Imperfect subjunctive of کرنا /karnā/ 'to do'

8.4.5.2.7 Future imperfect

Formation: imperfective participle + ہونا /hoṇā/(future)

The future imperfect describes actions or states which are presumed to occur regularly in the present, or are predicted to occur regularly in the future. The word *must* in the gloss conveys this presumptive meaning, where *he must be doing* is equivalent to *I presume he is doing*. Table 8.65 shows the conjugation of کرنا /karnā/ 'to do' in the future imperfect. These forms are shown with the گا /gā/ future suffix written both separately and joined with the subjunctive base.

Person	Singular	Plural
1st	میں کردا ہوواں گا / ہووانگا mæ̃ kardā hovā̃gā$_{M}$ میں کردی ہوواں گی / ہووانگی mæ̃ kardī hovā̃gī$_{F}$ 'I will/must do frequently'	سیں کردے ہوواں گے / ہووانگے asī̃ karde hovā̃ge$_{M}$ اسیں کردے ہوں گے / ہونگے asī̃ karde hõge$_{M}$ اسیں کردیاں ہوواں گیاں / ہووانگیاں asī̃ kardiyā̃ hovā̃giyā̃$_{F}$ اسیں کردیاں ہوں گیاں / ہونگیاں asī̃ kardiyā̃ hõgiyā̃$_{F}$ 'we will/must do frequently'
2nd	توں کردا ہوویں گا / ہووینگا tū̃ kardā hovẽgā$_{M}$ توں کردی ہوویں گی / ہووینگی tū̃ kardī hovẽgī$_{F}$ 'you will/must do frequently'	تسیں کردے ہووو گے tusī̃ karde hovoge$_{M}$ تسیں کردیاں ہووو گیاں tusī̃ kardiyā̃ hovogiyā̃$_{F}$ 'you will/must do frequently'
3rd	اوہ کردا ہووے گا / ہوویگا ó kardā hovegā$_{M}$ 'he/it will/must do frequently' اوہ کردی ہووے گی / ہوویگی ó kardī hovegī$_{F}$ 'she/it will/must do frequently'	اوہ کردے ہوون گے / ہوونگے ó karde hovaṇge$_{M}$ اوہ کردے ہون گے / ہونگے ó karde hoṇge$_{M}$ اوہ کردیاں ہوون گیاں / ہوونگیاں ó kardiyā̃ hovaṇgiyā̃$_{F}$ اوہ کردیاں ہون گیاں / ہونگیاں ó kardiyā̃ hoṇgiyā̃$_{F}$ 'they will/must do frequently'

Table 8.65: Future imperfect of کرنا /karnā/ 'to do'

8.4.5.2.8 Imperfect irrealis

Formation: imperfective participle + ہونا /hoṇā/(imperfective participle)

The imperfect irrealis describes counterfactual habitual actions or states—actions which could have occurred regularly, but are, in fact, unrealized or impossible. Since both parts of this form are participles, they are marked only for gender and number. Table 8.66 shows the conjugation of کرنا /karnā/ 'to do' in the imperfect irrealis.

Gender of Subject	Singular	Plural
Masculine	کردا ہوندا kardā hondā 'if (any m.sg. subject) were doing/ had done/were going to do'	کردے ہوندے karde honde 'if (any m.pl. subject) were doing/ had done/were going to do'
Feminine	کردی ہوندی kardī hondī 'if (any f.sg. subject) were doing/ had done/were going to do'	کردیاں ہوندیاں kardiyā̃ hondiyā̃ 'if (any f.pl. subject) were doing/ had done/were going to do'

Table 8.66: Imperfect irrealis of کرنا /karnā/ 'to do'

8.4.6 Verb forms constructed on the perfective participle

The perfective participle regularly consists of the stem plus the marked adjectival suffix آ /-ā/, which inflects for gender and number. The participle encodes completed or punctual events and enters into finite verb constructions with forms of ہونا /hoṇā/ 'to be', which contribute tense (past, present, future), or mood (subjunctive). The bare participle, without any auxiliary, functions as a simple perfect. The perfective participle also appears in the passive construction (see Section 9.1.2.2).

In transitive clauses, elements of perfective verb constructions (including the main verb, auxiliary verbs, and the future particle) do not agree with the subject/agent. Rather, they either agree with a direct object or take default masculine singular inflection. For this reason, we give most of the paradigms in this section using the intransitive verb جاݨا /jāṇā/ 'to go' instead of transitive کرنا /karnā/ 'to do'.

8.4.6.1 Bare perfective participle

8.4.6.1.1 Simple perfect

The simple perfect can refer to events in the past or the immediate future, or to unrealized events (in realis conditionals). The simple perfect of an intransitive verb agrees with its subject, while that of a transitive verb agrees with its direct object if the object is unmarked, and otherwise takes default masculine singular agreement. Table 8.67 and Table 8.68 show the simple perfect conjugation of the intransitive verb جاݨا /jāṇā/ 'to go' and the transitive verb کرنا /karnā/, respectively.

Gender of Subject	Singular	Plural
Masculine	گیا gayā '(any m.sg. subject) went'	گئے gae '(any m.pl. subject) went'
Feminine	گئی gaī '(any f.sg. subject) went''	گئیاں gaiyā̃ '(any f.pl. subject) went''

Table 8.67: Simple perfect of جاݨا /jāṇā/ 'to go'

Gender of Object	Singular	Plural
Masculine	کیتا kītā '(any subject) did (m.sg. object)'	کیتے kīte '(any subject) did (m.pl object)'
Feminine	کیتی kītī '(any subject) did (f.sg.object)'	کیتیاں kītiyā̃ '(any subject) did (f.pl object)'

Table 8.68: Simple perfect of کرنا /karnā/

8.4.6.1.2 Perfective participle used adjectivally

As with the imperfective participle, the perfective participle can also be used as an attributive adjective, as in 8.11, where the perfective participle of 'die', i.e. 'dead', appears.[19]

(8.11) سڑک تے مویا سپّ پیا سی

saṛak	*te*	***moiyā***	*sapp*	*p-yā*	*sī*
road	on	**die-PP.SG.M**	snake[M]	fall-PP.SG.M	be.PST.3SG

'A **dead** snake was lying on the road.' (Pj) (EB)

19 As with the imperfective participle, the present and past perfect tenses could be analyzed in terms of a predicative adjectival use of the perfective participle.

8.4.6.2 Present perfect

Formation: perfective participle + ہونا /hoṇā/(present)

The present perfect describes an event which is completed, and the effects of which persist into the present—that is, an action which has has resulted in a state which is (still) relevant to the present situation. Thus, it frequently refers to a recently completed event. Negatives are nowadays usually formed with نہیں /naĩ/. As with other complex forms including the present auxiliary, the auxiliary is usually omitted in negative sentences. The result of this is that negated simple perfect and present perfect sentences appear the same. For example, اوہ نہیں آیا /ó naĩ āyā/ could be the negation of either اوہ آیا /ó āyā/ 'he came', or اوہ آیا اے /ó āyā e/ 'he has come.' Whether such a sentence is to be understood as a negated simple perfect or a negated present perfect must be determined from context. However, if the simple negative particle نہ /na/ is used to negate a sentence in the simple perfect, as used to be more frequently done, then the distinction remains. Table 8.69 displays the present perfect conjugation of جاݨا /jāṇā/ 'to go'.

Person	Singular	Plural
1st	میں گیا واں mæ̃ gayā vā̃$_M$ میں گئی آں mæ̃ gaī ā̃$_F$ 'I have gone'	اسیں گئے آں asī̃ gae ā̃$_M$ اسیں گئیاں آں asī̃ gaiyā̃ ā̃$_F$ 'we have gone'
2nd	توں گیا ایں tū̃ gayā ẽ$_M$ توں گئی ایں tū̃ gaī ẽ$_F$ 'you have gone'	تسیں گئے او tusī̃ gae o$_M$ تسیں گئیاں او tusī̃ gaiyā̃ o$_F$ 'you have gone'
3rd	اوہ گیا اے ó gayā e$_M$ 'he/it has gone' اوہ گئی اے ó gaī e$_F$ 'she/it has gone'	اوہ گئے نیں ó gae nẽ$_M$ اوہ گئیاں نیں ó gaiyā̃ nẽ$_F$ 'they have gone'

Table 8.69: Present perfect of جاݨا /jāṇā/ 'to go'

8.4.6.3 Present perfect-stative

Formation: perfective participle + ہونا /hoṇā/(perfective participle) + ہونا /hoṇā/(present)

The present perfect-stative adds the perfective participle of ہونا /hoṇā/ to the present perfect. This form emphasizes the persistence of the state resulting from the perfective action: 'he went/has gone (and is still gone).' This meaning of persistent state is contributed by the perfective participle of ہونا /hoṇā/ 'to be'. Table 8.70 shows the conjugation of the verb جانا /jāṇā/ 'to go' in the present perfect-stative.

Person	Singular	Plural
1st	میں گیا ہویا واں mæ̃ gayā hoiyā vã$_{M}$ میں گئی ہوئی آں mæ̃ gaī hoī ã$_{F}$ 'I have gone (and am still away)'	اسیں گئے ہوئے آں asī̃ gae hoe ã$_{M}$ اسیں گئیاں ہوئیاں آں asī̃ gaiyā̃ hoiyā̃ ã$_{=F}$ 'we have gone (and are still away)'
2nd	توں گیا ہویا ایں tū̃ gayā hoiyā ẽ$_{M}$ توں گئی ہوئی ایں tū̃ gaī hoī ẽ$_{F}$ 'you have gone (and are still away)'	تسیں گئے ہوئے او tusī̃ gae hoe o$_{M}$ تسیں گئیاں ہوئیاں او tusī̃ gaiyā̃ hoiyā̃ o$_{F}$ 'you have gone (and are still away)'
3rd	اوہ گیا ہویا اے ó gayā hoiyā e$_{M}$ 'he/it has gone (and is still away)' اوہ گئی ہوئی اے ó gaī hoī e$_{F}$ 'she/it has gone (and is still away)'	اوہ گئے ہوئے نیں ó gae hoe nẽ$_{M}$ اوہ گئیاں ہوئیاں نیں ó gaiyā̃ hoiyā̃ nẽ$_{F}$ 'they have gone (and are still away)'

Table 8.70: Present perfect-stative of جانا /jāṇā/ 'to go'

Older stative perfectives are constructed with the perfective participle of the main verb plus the perfective participle of پینا/pæṇā/ 'to fall'. 8.12 shows a past perfect stative of this type.

(8.12) جتھے کئی صدیاں توں بہت بیش قیمتی دھن دولت اکٹھی کیتی پئی سی

jithe	*kaī*	*sadiyā̃*	*tõ*	*bɔ̃t*	*beš.kīmtī*	*tàn-dɔlat*
where[REL]	many	century-OBL.PL	from	much	priceless	treasure[F]

ikaṭṭhī	*kīt-ī*	*pa-ī*	*sī*
together	do.PP-SG.F	lie.PP-SG.F	be.PST.3SG

'Where much very priceless treasure had been collected.' (https://www.wikizero.com/pnb/%D9%BE%D9%86%D8%AC%D8%A7%D8%A8_%D8%AF%DB%8C_%D8%AA%D8%B1%DB%8C%D8%AE)

This type is also found in Saraiki.

8.4.6.4 Past perfect

Formation: perfective participle + ہوݨا /hoṇā/ (past)

The past perfect describes an event which was completed in the past and, often, the effects of which no longer persist—that is, an action which resulted in a state which no longer obtains. It frequently occurs describing actions (i) completed in the remote past, (ii) within a specific past time frame, or (iii) prior to another past action. Since it occurs more often in functions (i) and (ii), it frequently corresponds to an English simple past, as indicated in the paradigm below. Negatives are usually formed with نہیں /naĩ̃/. Table 8.71 shows the conjugation of the verb جاݨا /jāṇā/ 'to go' in the past perfect.

Person	Singular	Plural
1st	میں گیا ساں mæ̃ gayā sā̃$_M$ میں گئی ساں mæ̃ gaī sā̃$_F$ 'I went/had gone'	اسیں گئے ساں asī̃ gae sā̃$_M$ اسیں گئیاں ساں asī̃ gaiyā̃ sā̃$_F$ 'we went/had gone'
2nd	توں گیا سیں tū̃ gayā sæ̃$_M$ توں گئی سیں tū̃ gaī sæ̃$_F$ 'you went/had gone'	تسیں گئے سو tusī̃ gae so$_M$ تسیں گئیاں سو tusī̃ gaiyā̃ so$_F$ 'you went/had gone'
3rd	اوہ گیا سی ó gayā sī$_M$ 'he/it had gone' اوہ گئی سی ó gaī sī$_F$ 'she/it went/had gone'	اوہ گئے سن ó gae san$_M$ اوہ گئیاں سن ó gaiyā̃ san$_F$ 'they went/had gone'

Table 8.71: Past perfect of جاݨا /jāṇā/ 'to go'

8.4.6.5 Past perfect-stative

Formation: Perfective participle + ہونا /hoṇā/ (perfective participle) + ہونا /hoṇā/ (past)

The past perfect-stative stresses the persistence (in past time) of the state resulting from a perfective event or action, as in 'he was still gone.' Table 8.72 shows the conjugation of the verb جانا /jāṇā/ 'to go' in the past perfect-stative.

Person	Singular	Plural
1st	میں گیا ہویا ساں mæ̃ gayā hoiyā sā̃$_M$	اسِیں گئے ہوئے ساں asī̃ gae hoe sā̃$_M$
	میں گئی ہوئی ساں mæ̃ gaī hoī sā̃$_F$	اسِیں گئیاں ہوئیاں ساں asī̃ gaiyā̃ hoiyā̃ sā̃$_F$ 'we went and were still away'
	'I went and was still away'	
2nd	توں گیا ہویا سیں tū̃ gayā hoiyā sæ̃$_M$	تُسِیں گئے ہوئے سو tusī̃ gae hoe so$_M$
	توں گئی ہوئی سیں tū̃ gaī hoī sæ̃$_F$ 'you went and were still away'	تُسِیں گئیاں ہوئیاں سو tusī̃ gaiyā̃ hoiyā̃ so$_F$ 'you went and were still away'
3rd	اوہ گیا ہویا سی ó gayā hoiyā sī$_M$ 'he/it went and was still away'	اوہ گئے ہوئے سن ó gae hoe san$_M$
	اوہ گئی ہوئی سی ó gaī hoī sī$_F$ 'she/it went and was still away'	اوہ گئیاں ہوئیاں سن ó gaiyā̃ hoiyā̃ san$_F$ 'they went and were still away'

Table 8.72: Past perfect-stative of جانا /jāṇā/ 'to go'

8.4.6.6 Perfect subjunctive

Formation: perfective participle + ہونا /hoṇā/ (subjunctive)

The perfect subjunctive represents events or actions as potentially complete. It encodes modal meanings such as potentiality, desirability, or contingency; thus it often appears in the subordinate clause of a realis conditional sentence. The negative is formed with نہ /na/. Table 8.73 shows the perfect subjunctive conjugation of جانا /jāṇā/ 'to go'.

Person	Singular	Plural
1st	میں گیا ہوواں mæ̃ gayā hovā̃$_{M}$ میں گئی ہوواں mæ̃ gaī hovā̃$_{F}$ 'I may/should have gone; if I have gone'	اسیں گئے ہوئیے asī̃ gae hoiye$_{M}$ اسیں گئیاں ہوئیے asī̃ gaiyā̃ hoiye$_{F}$ 'we may/should have gone; if we have gone'
2nd	توں گیا ہوویں tū̃ gayā hovẽ$_{M}$ توں گئی ہوویں tū̃ gaī hovẽ$_{F}$ 'you may/should have gone; if you have gone'	تسیں گئے ہووو tusī̃ gae hovo$_{M}$ تسیں گئیاں ہووو tusī̃ gaiyā̃ hovo$_{F}$ 'you may/should have gone; if you have gone'
3rd	اوہ گیا ہووے ó gayā hove$_{M}$ 'he/it may/should have gone; if he/it has gone' اوہ گئی ہووے ó gaī hove$_{F}$ 'she/it may/should have gone; if she/it has gone'	اوہ گئے ہون ó gae hoṇ$_{M}$ اوہ گئیاں ہون ó gaiyā̃ hoṇ$_{F}$ 'they may/should have gone; if they have gone'

Table 8.73: Perfect subjunctive of جانا /jāṇā/ 'to go'

8.4.6.7 Future perfect

Formation: perfective participle + ہونا /hoṇā/(future)

The future perfect describes events which are presumed to have occurred, or are to be completed in the future. Table 8.74 shows the conjugation of the future perfect form of the verb جانا /jāṇā/ 'to go'

Person	Singular	Plural
1st	میں گیا ہوواں گا / ہووانگا mæ̃ gayā hovā̃gā$_M$ میں گئی ہوواں گی / ہووانگی mæ̃ gaī hovā̃gī$_F$ 'I will/must have gone'	اسیں گئے ہوواں گے / ہووانگے asī̃ gae hovā̃ge$_M$ اسیں گئیاں ہوواں گیاں / ہووانگیاں asī̃ gaīā̃ hovā̃giyā̃$_F$ 'we will/must have gone'
2nd	توں گیا ہوویں گا / ہووینگا tū̃ gayā hovẽgā$_M$ توں گئی ہوویں گی / ہووینگی tū̃ gaī hovẽgī$_F$ 'you will/must have gone'	تسیں گئے ہووو گے tusī̃ gae hovoge$_M$ تسیں گئیاں ہووو گیاں tusī̃ gaiyā̃ hovogiyā̃$_F$ 'you will/must have gone'
3rd	اوہ گیا ہووے گا / ہوویگا ó gayā hovegā$_M$ 'he will/must have gone' اوہ گئی ہووے گی / ہوویگی ó gaī hovegī$_F$ 'she will/must have gone'	اوہ گئے ہوون گے / ہوونگے ó gae hovaṇge$_M$ اوہ گئے ہون گے / ہونگے ó gae hoṇge$_M$ اوہ گئیاں ہوون گیاں / ہوونگیاں ó gaiyā̃ hovaṇ giyā̃$_F$ اوہ گئیاں ہون گیاں / ہونگیاں ó gaiyā̃ hoṇ giyā̃$_F$ 'they will/must have gone'

Table 8.74: Future perfect of جانا /jāṇā/ 'to go'

8.4.6.8 Perfect irrealis

Formation: perfective participle + ہونا /hoṇā/(imperfective participle)

The perfect irrealis mentions events which have not occurred, but which had they occurred, would have been completed in the past. Table 8.75 shows the conjugation of جانا /jāṇā/ 'to go' in the perfect irrealis.

Gender of Subject	Singular	Plural
Masculine	گیا ہوندا gayā hondā 'if (any m.sg. subject) had gone'	گئے ہوندے gae honde 'if (any m.pl. subject) had gone'
Feminine	گئی ہوندی gaī hondī 'if (any f.sg. subject) had gone'	گئیاں ہوندیاں gaiyā̃ hondiyā̃ 'if (any f.pl. subject) had gone'

Table 8.75: Perfect irrealis of جانا /jāṇā/ 'to go'

8.4.7 Form constructed on the oblique infinitive: Continuous III

Formation: oblique infinitive + ڈیہنا /ḍǽṇā/ 'to begin' (perfective participle) + ہونا /hoṇā/ (present or past)[20]

The perfective participial form of ڈیہنا /ḍǽṇā/ meaning 'having begun, to be engaged in' is ڈیہا /ḍéā/, which inflects for number and gender to agree with the subject.[21] This form is frequent in spoken, colloquial Panjabi; it conveys a strong feeling of actuality and emphasis, and perhaps because of this it is perceived by some people as "rough". Since the meanings of this form are quite specific, the wider range of forms that is found for continuous I and continuous II forms is not encountered. Table 8.76 shows present tense forms of the continuous III construction of کرنا /karnā/ 'to do'. Because of the forceful and immediate nuances of this form, the third person proximal forms are chosen to illustrate it. Notice the elision (ā + ā̃ > ā̃) in the first person singular, masculine. As far as the present authors know, this form is specific to Panjabi.

Examples 8.13, 8.14, and 8.15 illustrate the present continuous III, and 8.16 the past continuous III.

(8.13) میں آن ڈیہا آں

mæ̃ āṇ ḍé-ā ā̃
1SG come.INF.OBL CONT.III-SG.M be.PRES.1SG
'I am coming!' (Pj) (Bashir and Kazmi 2012: 663)

20 Bukhari (2000: 951) gives the gloss 'to begin' for ڈیہنا /ḍǽṇā/; Malik (1995: 270) glosses this verb as 'to be engaged in'.

21 The masculine singular perfective participle of the homophonous verb ڈیہنا /ḍǽṇā/ 'to be placed' is ڈٹھا /ḍaṭṭhā/, as in منجی ڈٹھی اے /manjī ḍaṭṭhī e/ 'the charpai is in place (laid down horizontally, ready for use)' (Bailey 1904b: 40).

Person	Singular	Plural
1st	میں کرن ڈیہا آں mæ̃ karan ḍéā̃$_M$ میں کرن ڈیہی آں mæ̃ karan ḍéī ā̃$_F$ 'I am doing'	اسیں کرن ڈیہے آں asī̃ karan ḍé(y)e ā̃$_M$ اسیں کرن ڈیہیاں آں asī̃ karan ḍéiyā̃ (ā̃) $_F$ 'we are doing''
2nd	توں کرن ڈیہا ایں tū̃ karan ḍéā ẽ$_M$ توں کرن ڈیہی ایں tū̃ karan ḍéī ẽ$_F$ 'you are doing.'	تسیں کرن ڈیہے او tusī̃ karan ḍé(y)e o$_M$ تسیں کرن ڈیہیاں او tusī̃ karan ḍéiyā̃ o$_F$ 'you are doing'
3rd	ایہہ کرن ڈیہا اے é karan ḍéā e$_M$ 'he is doing' ایہہ کرن ڈیہی اے é karan ḍéī e$_F$ 'she is doing'	ایہہ کرن ڈیہے نیں é karan ḍé(y)e nẽ$_M$ ایہہ کرن ڈیہیاں نیں é karan ḍéiyā nẽ$_F$ 'they are doing'

Table 8.76: Present continuous III کرنا /karnā/ 'to do'

(8.14) توں رون کیوں ڈیہی ایں

tū̃	***roṇ***	*kyõ*	***ḍê-ī***	***ẽ***
2SG	**cry.INF.OBL**	why	**CONT.III-SG.F**	**be.PRES.2SG**

'Why **are** you (f.sg) **crying**?' (Pj) (EB)

(8.15) کون ایہہ حادثہ دسن ڈیہیا تے کیہڑا چینل ایہہ رپورٹ دین ڈیہیا اے

kɔṇ	*é*	*hādsa*	***dasaṇ***	***ḍé-ā***	*te*	*kéṛ-ā*
who	this	incident	**tell.INF.OBL**	**CONT.III-SG.M**	and	which-SG.M

cænal	*é*	*riporṭ*	***deṇ***	***ḍé-ā***	***e***
channel	this	report	**give.INF.OBL**	**CONT.III-SG.M**	**be.PRES.3SG**

'Who **is telling** about this incident and which channel **is giving** this report?'[22] (Pj)

22 Notice that in this compound sentence, the tensed auxiliary appears only once, in the second clause. This example was taken from a link that is no longer active. (https://www.google.com/url?sa=t&rct=j&q=&esrc=s&source=web&cd=20&cad=rja&uact=8&ved=0ahUKEwiZiuv98-vNAhWGbj4KHQItA9g4ChAWCFcwCQ&url

(8.16) سورج صافے دے وچوں وی اوہدا مغز ابالے چاڑھن ڈیہا سی

sūraj	*sā̃fe*	*de.vicõ*	*vī*	*ó*	*dā*	*magaz*	***ubāle.cā̂ṛan***
sun	matting	through	even	3SG.OBL	of-SG.M	brain	**boil.INF.OBL**
ḍé-ā	***sī***						
CONT.III-SG.M	**be.PST.3SG**						

'Even through the matting the sun **was boiling** his brain.'[23] (Pj)

8.5 Saraiki verbs

Table 8.77 provides an overview of Saraiki verb forms. We exemplify most forms on the basis of the third person singular masculine of the verb وٙنجݨ /vãʄaṇ/ 'to go', perhaps the second most frequently used intransitive verb; however, since only the verb ہووݨ /hovaṇ/ 'to be' has forms for the simple present and the simple past, we use the third person singular of this verb to illustrate those forms. In Saraiki, /e/ vowels are inherently long. Some third-person plural forms are pronounced with what is phonetically a short /ĕ/, but is probably best understood as an allomorph of /i/. Thus we represent phonetic /ĕ/ with the short /i/ diacritic in our Perso-Arabic forms. All /o/ vowels, however, are treated as long, and are not marked for length. Forms involving the imperfective participle (formed on the present-future stem) appear with the stem vowel /e/, characteristic of the pronunciation of our consultant. However the stem vowel is often pronounced /æ/ in these forms, and this should be considered an alternate pronunciation in these cases. This alternation is indicated in a few of the cells of Table 8.77. Blank spaces in the table indicate combinations of tense and mood/aspect for which we do not have information. The forms in this table are intended to show the structure, and do not always reflect elisions normally heard in speech, especially with masculine singular forms. For example, for the perfect-stative form, instead of /o ʄiyā hoyā e/, /ʄiyā hoe/ is the actual pronunciation of this form.

=http%3A%2F%2Fgloss2.lingnet.org%2Fproducts%2Fgloss%2Fpjb_cul430%2Fpjb_cul430.xml&usg=AFQjCNHZcdqzmnWvb7TWrsRoN2L8r4Bd7A)

23 This example was taken from (http://www.wichaar.com/news/153/ARTICLE/31260/2014-09-23.html) . This URL is sometimes not available directly.

Table 8.77: Overview of Saraiki verb forms

		Tenses			Moods	
	Simple	Present	Past	Future	Subjunctive	Irrealis
(Simple)		او اے o e 'he is'	او ہا o hā 'he was'	او ویسی o vesī ~ o væsī 'he will go'	او وڄے o vāʄe 'he may/should go; if he goes'	Irrealis-I او وڄے ہا o vāʄe hā 'if he went/were going (but doesn't/ isn't)' Irrealis-II او ویندا o vēdā 'if he went (but he does not go)'
Imperfect		او ویندے o vēde (< o vēdā e) ~ væ̃de 'he goes'	او ویندا ہا o vēdā/væ̃dā hā 'he used to go'	او ویندا ہوسی o vēdā/væ̃dā hosī 'he will/must go frequently'	او ویندا ہووے o vēdā/væ̃dā hove 'he may/should go frequently; if he goes frequently'	او ویندا ہووے ہا o vēdā/væ̃dā hove hā 'if he went frequently (but doesn't)'

Table 8.77: (continued)

	Tenses				Moods	
	Simple	**Present**	**Past**	**Future**	**Subjunctive**	**Irrealis**
Imperfect-habitual		او ویندا ہوندے o vẽdā honde (< o vẽdā hondā e) 'he usually goes'	او ویندا ہوندا ہا o vẽdā hondā hā 'he usually used to go'			او ویندا ہوندا ہووے ہا o vẽdā hondā hove hā 'if he had usually been going (but wasn't)'
Continuous I (IP + PP of 'to fall/lie')		او ویندا پے o vẽdā pe (< o vẽdā piyā e) 'he is going'	او ویندا پیا ہا o vẽdā piyā hā 'he was going'	او ویندا پیا ہوسی o vẽdā piyā hosī 'he will/must be going'	او ویندا پیا ہووے o vẽdā piyā hove 'he may/should be going; if he is going'	
Perfect	او ڳیا o ɠiyā 'he went'	او ڳئے o ɠe (< o ɠiyā e) 'he has gone'	او ڳیا ہا o ɠiyā hā 'he had gone'	او ڳیا ہوسی o ɠiyā hosī 'he will/must have gone'	او ڳیا ہووے o ɠiyā hove 'he may/should have gone; if he has gone'	او ڳیا ہووے ہا o ɠiyā hove hā 'if he had gone (but he did not go)'
Perfect-stative		او ڳیا ہوئے o ɠiyā hoe (< o ɠiyā hoiyā e) 'he is gone (he is still away)'	او ڳیا ہویا ہا o ɠiyā hoyā hā 'he was gone (he was still away)'	او ڳیا ہویا ہوسی o ɠiyā hoyā hosī 'he will/must be gone'	او ڳیا ہویا ہووے o ɠiyā hoyā hove 'he may/should be gone; if he is gone'	او ڳیا ہویا ہووے ہا o ɠiyā hoyā hove hā 'if he had been gone (but he was not gone)'

Table 8.77: (continued)

	Tenses				Moods	
	Simple	**Present**	**Past**	**Future**	**Subjunctive**	**Irrealis**
Habitual perfect-stative		او ڳیا ہوندے o ɠīyā honde (< o ɠīyā hondā e) 'he is usually gone'	او ڳیا ہوندا ہا o ɠīyā hondā hā 'he was usually gone'			

8.5.1 Saraiki stem types

8.5.1.1 Simple stem

The simple stem (sometimes called "root") is the simplest, underived form of the verb. From it, other, derived stems are formed.

8.5.1.2 Basic intransitive and transitive pairs

A simple transitive stem is related to an intransitive stem in several ways: (i) by vowel alternation between a centralized vowel in the intransitive stem and a peripheral vowel in the transitive stem, e.g. ٹُر /ṭur-/ 'go, leave (intransitive)', ٹور /ṭor-/ 'send off (transitive)'; (ii) by consonant change, e.g. بھڄ /bhaʄ-/ 'break (intransitive)', بھن /bhan-/ 'break (transitive)'; (iii) by the presence of a final consonant in the intransitive and its absence in the transitive with additional vowel differences, e.g. سیپ /sīp-/ 'be sewn (intransitive)', سی /sī-/ 'sew', and (iv) both vowel and consonant changes, e.g. تپ /tap-/ 'be hot (intransitive)', تائیو /tāev-/ 'heat (transitive)'. See Shackle (1976: 73–77) for detailed discussion of these stem types and formations.

8.5.1.3 First causative/derived transitive stem

Some consonant-final stems, either intransitive or transitive, can be extended by adding stressed آ /ˈā/ to the simple stem, for example پڑھ /paṛh-/ 'read, study' > پڑھا /paṛhˈā-/ 'teach' (Shackle 1976: 74). Not all stems have both first and second causative formations; some have only second causatives.

8.5.1.4 Second/double causative stem

Double causatives can be formed from most stems. When formed on a single causative, the double causative stem adds و /-v-/ between the stem and the stressed ا /-ˈā/ of the first causative extension; for example, ڈِکھ /ɗikh-/ 'be seen' > ڈِکھا /ɗikhˈā-/ 'show, cause to be seen' > ڈِکھوا /ɗikhˈvā-/ 'have shown (by someone to someone)' (Shackle 1976: 79). Monosyllabic vowel stems have only the double causative, e.g. کھا /khā-/ 'eat' > کھوا /khvā-/ 'feed'. Double causatives related to non-basic transitives are formed on the intransitive stem, e.g. اُٻل /uɓɓil-/ 'boil (intransitive)', اُٻال /uɓāl-/ 'boil (transitive)', اُٻلوا /uɓlvā-/ 'have boiled'.

8.5.1.5 Passive stem[24]

A passive stem is formed from transitives by adding stressed /-ˈīj/ to the stem, with a change of a peripheral stem vowel to a centralized vowel; for example, آکھ /ākh-/ 'say, call' > اکھیج /akhˈīj/ 'be said, called' and ݙے /ɗe-/ 'give' > ݙویج /ɗivīj-/ 'be given'.[25]

8.5.1.6 Present-future stem

The existence of a distinct present-future stem is one of the unique features of Saraiki. Present-future (PF) stems are formed differently for passive, intransitive, and various classes of transitive stems. Passive stems form their PF stem by losing their final ج /j/; thus, مریج /marīj-/ (passive stem) > مری /marī-/ 'be killed' (PF passive stem). Intransitive (PF) stems are identical to the simple stem, e.g. مر /mar-/ 'die'. PF stems of basic underived transitives with vowel-final stems are identical to the simple stem, e.g. ݙے /ɗe-/ 'give' remains the same. PF stems of underived transitives with consonant-final stems, for example, /mār-/ 'kill' add stressed ے /-ˈe/ to the simple stem and shorten the stem vowel: مار /mār-/ 'kill' (stem) + ے /-ˈe/> مرے /marˈe-/ 'kill (PF stem)'. The PF stem of most disyllabic transitive roots is formed with stressed ے /-ˈe/, showing vowel shortenings, and deletions following the patterns of schwa deletion, e.g. پکڑ /pakaṛ-/ 'grasp' > PF stem پکڑے /pakṛe-/. Those ending in stressed /ˈā/ drop the /ˈā/ and add /-ˈæ/ or /-ˈe/, e.g. ݙوا /ɗīvā-/ 'cause to be given' > ݙوے /ɗīvæ-/.

Some monosyllabic transitive roots ending in /ā/, which are among the most frequently occurring verbs in the language, change /ā/ to /æ/ in the intransitive. They include چا /cā-/ 'raise, lift', ڈھا /ḍhā-/ 'throw down', لا /lā-/ 'apply', and پا /pā-/ 'put', e.g. ڈھا /ḍhā-/'knock down' > ڈھے /ḍhæ-/ 'be knocked down'. The centrally important intransitive verb ونج /vãj-/ 'go', in addition to using an abbreviated stem, behaves in this way, yielding وے /væ-/~ /ve-/ as the present-future stem. Forms of this verb constructed on the PF stem show the characteristic variation between the southern variant /e/ and central variant /æ/ (Shackle 1976: 16–17).

The present-future stem occurs in the imperfective participle and forms constructed on it, and in the future (Shackle 1976: 76–77).

24 In Jhangi Saraiki, speakers do not add 'j' in passive forms. Rather they add only a long high front vowel, yielding the passive forms e.g. akhī and khav, instead of akhīj and khavīj respectively from the stems akh- *say* and kha:- *eat*. (Nasir Abbas Syed, p.c.)

25 Ali Hussain Birahimani (p.c.) comments that the morphological passive is now infrequently used in "standard" urban Saraiki.

8.5.2 Other non-finite forms

8.5.2.1 Infinitive

Saraiki infinitives consist of verb stem + اݨ /-aṇ/, except for stems ending in the retroflex sonorants ݨ /ṇ/, ڑ /ṛ/, or ڑھ /ṛh/, whose infinitives are formed in dental ان /an/. Compare کرݨ /kar-aṇ/ 'to do' and چھوڑن /choṛ-an/ 'to leave'.

This is different from Panjabi, where /r/-final stems form the infinitive in dental /-nā/, as in کرنا /karnā/. The direct and oblique forms of the infinitive are identical, different from the situation in Hindko and Panjabi.

8.5.2.2 Gerundive

Saraiki has a gerundive form distinct from the infinitive. This consists of the stem + ݨا /-ṇā/~ نا /-nā/. The gerundive is a marked adjective. The distinction between the infinitive and gerundive form is, or was,[26] characteristic of Saraiki as opposed to Panjabi and (perhaps) Hindko.

Example 8.17, contains the oblique infinitive, and 8.18 contains the gerundive; these examples are both courtesy of Ali Hussain Birahimani.

(8.17) پڑھݨ کیتے کیا کروں

paṛh-aṇ	*kīte*	*kyā*	*karũ̄*
study-INF.OBL	for	what	do-SBJV.1PL

'What should we do in order to **study**?' (Sr)

(8.18) میں پڑھنا اے

mǣ	***paṛh-nā***	*e*
1SG.OBL	**study-GRDV**	be.PRES.3SG

'I have to **study**.' (Sr)

26 According to Shackle (1976: 82), the distinction between infinitive and gerundive is not always maintained, especially in the modern, educated colloquial language; hence our uncertainty about the degree to which the two forms are (still) distinct in 2018. Nasir Abbas Syed, however, thinks that the distinction remains robust (p.c.). See also 8.17 and 8.18.

8.5.2.3 Imperfective participle

The imperfective participle consists of the present-future stem + ند /-(n)d/ + the marked adjectival ending ا /-ā/. Vocalic and h-final stems nasalize the stem vowel (add orthographic ں /-n-/) preceding دا /-dā/ (Shackle 1976: 84). This is a marked adjectival form, hence complex verb forms including this participle are marked for gender and number. For example, آندا /ā̃-dā/ 'coming (m.sg.)', کریندے /karẽ-de/ 'doing (m.pl)', رہندی /rah-ndī/ 'living (f.sg.)', and ٹُردیاں /ṭur-diyā̃/ 'going (f.pl.)'.

8.5.2.4 Perfective participle

The perfective participle consists of the stem + the marked adjectival endings یا /-(y)ā ~ -iyā/ '(m.sg.)' ی /-ī/ '(f.sg.)', ے /-e/ '(m.pl.)', ایاں/-iyā̃/ '(f.pl.)'. For example, from سݨاوݨ /suṇāvaṇ/ 'to tell, cause to be heard', the regularly formed perfective participles are: سݨایا /suṇā-yā/ '(m.sg.)', سݨایے /suṇā-ye/ '(m.pl.)', سݨائی /suṇā-ī/ '(f.sg.)', سݨائیاں /suṇā-iyā̃/ '(f.pl.)'.

A few centrally important verbs have unique irregular perfective participles, notably پووݨ/povaṇ/ 'to lie', ونڄݨ /vā̃ʄaṇ/ 'to go', and تھیوݨ /thīvaṇ/ 'to become'—the perfective participles of which are پیا/piyā/ '(m.sg.)', پئی/p(a)ī/ '(f.sg.)', پئے /p(a)e/ '(m.pl.)', پئیاں /p(a)iyā̃/ '(f.pl)'; ڳیا /ɠiyā/ '(m.sg.)', ڳئی /ɠaī/ '(f.sg.)', ڳئے /ɠ(a)e/ '(m.pl.)', ڳئیاں /ɠ(a)iyā̃/ '(f.pl.)', and تھیا /theā/ (m.sg.), تھے /the/ (m.pl), تھی /thī/ (f.sg.), تھیاں /thiyā̃/ (f.pl.), respectively (Shackle 1976: 86).

In addition to these, other significant classes of verbs have inherited irregular perfective participles. Formation of perfective participles of these types is no longer productive, and according to Ali Hussain Birahimani (p.c), many of these irregular perfective participles have now shifted to regular formations, especially in urban speech. Important classes are those ending in the following sounds, of which class IV perfective participles in تا /-tā/ are the most numerous. Masculine singular forms of some of the most important of these are listed below.[27]

1. ٹھا /-ṭhā/, e.g. ڈِٹھا /ɗīṭhā/ (< ڈِس /ɗis-/ 'be seen, appear');
2. ݨا /-ṇā/, e.g. الاݨا /alāṇā/ (< الا /alā-/ 'speak');
3. ڑھا /-ṛhā/, e.g. وڑھا /vuṛhā/ (< وہ /vah-/ 'be plowed');
4. تا /-tā/, e.g. دھوتا /dhotā/ (< دھو /dho-/ 'wash');
5. تھا /-thā/, e.g. نکتّھا /nikatthā/ (< نکل /nikal-/ 'go out, exit');

27 See Shackle (1976: 87–91) for exhaustive lists of the verbs in each class.

6. دا /-dā/, e.g. کھادا /khādā ~ khādhā/ (< کھا /khā-/ 'eat');

7. دھا /-dhā/, e.g. ٻدھا /ɓadhā/ (< ٻنھ /ɓanh-/ 'tie'); and

8. نا /-nā/, e.g. بھُنا /bhunā/ (< بھُڄ /bhuʄ-/ 'be parched, roasted').

Shackle (1976: 76) states that perfective participles are not formed from passive stems; however, example 8.19 appears to involve the perfective participle of a passive stem. These forms may have developed since the time reflected in Shackle's 1976 book.

(8.19) اساں مریجے ہاں

assā̃ *mar-ij-e* *hā̃*

1PL beat-PASS-PL.M be.PRES.1PL

'We have been beaten.'[28] (Sr) (UK)

8.5.2.5 Stative perfective participle

The stative perfective participle, called "perfective participle" by Shackle (1976: 85), denotes a persistent state resulting from a completed action in past time. It is formed from the perfective participle + the perfective participle of ہووݨ /hovaṇ/ 'to be'; for example ٹُریا ہویا /ṭuryā hoyā/ '(m.sg.) went and is/was still gone'. Both parts of this complex form are marked adjectival forms. These formations participate in the perfect-stative tense-aspect forms.

8.5.2.6 Linking participles

Three different participial forms function to link verbs; the names used here follow Shackle (1976: 125–127), who states that the choice among the catenative, conjunctive, and connective participles depends on the closeness of the connection between the actions described by the two verbs, and gives detailed discussion and examples of these nuances. See Chapter 10 for some examples of these types.

28 This sentence could apply to either male or female speakers. Masculine plural forms are often used in both Panjabi and Saraiki to refer to multiple women and girls, especially in the first person plural.

8.5.2.6.1 Catenative participle

Shackle (1976: 82) identifies a "catenative participle," which for most verbs is identical to the stem. Disyllabic stems with stress on the initial syllable and /a/ in the second syllable which end in ر /r/, ڑ /ṛ/, and ل /l/ change the /a/ to /i/, e.g. نِکّل- /nik.kal/ 'go out, emerge' > /nik.kil/ 'having gone out, emerged' (Shackle 1976:82). A few important verbs, however, have irregular forms. The most important of these is پو/po-/ 'lie', the catenative participle of which is پے /pæ-/. In function, the catenative participle is often similar to the conjunctive participle, in stem + کر ~ کے /kar ~ ke/ 'having done' or تے /te/.

8.5.2.6.2 Conjunctive participle ("absolutive," "converb")

The conjunctive participle consists of the stem + کر /kar/, or کے /ke/ in the case of stems ending in ر /ar/, or تے /te/, especially in southern varieties. The conjunctive participle is also important in Hindko and Panjabi.

8.5.2.6.3 Connective participle

Additionally, a "connective participle," formally identical to the feminine singular of the perfective participle, is formed from transitive verbs, e.g. پیتی/pītī/ from پیوݨ/pīvaṇ/ 'to drink'.

8.5.3 Finite forms

Finite verbs, i.e. those which are marked for person and tense, fall into the following form classes: those formed on (i) the stem, (ii) the imperfective participle, and (iii) the perfective participle. Additionally, bare imperfective or perfective participles, which lack person and tense marking, can function as main verbs in irrealis or simple perfect clauses.

8.5.3.1 The verb ہووݨ /hovaṇ/ 'to be'

The verb ہووݨ /hovaṇ/ 'to be' functions as an existential, copular, and auxiliary verb.

8.5.3.1.1 Present tense of ہووݨ /hovaṇ/ 'to be'

The present tense of ہووݨ /hovaṇ/ 'to be' has both long and short forms (Shackle 1976: 94). The long forms, with initial ہ /h-/, in Table 8.78, are as given by our consultant; they are identical to those in Shackle; the short forms delete the initial ہ /h-/. The long forms are used as existential verbs or for emphasis; the short forms appear in most other contexts, including, importantly, as the present auxiliary in complex tense-aspect forms. There is no gender distinction in the present auxiliary. The third person plural forms are pronounced with short /ĕ/ by our consultant, but given by Shackle with short /i/. Hence, the best choice for indicating the short vowel in Perso-Arabic seems to be as done in Table 8.78, with the diacritic for short /i/, since the use of ی would imply a long vowel.[29] When the short forms occur in periphrastic tenses consisting of a participle plus the present auxiliary, they are subject to elision. That is, the initial vowel of the (short form) auxiliary coalesces with the final vowel of the participial form; such elisions are written together as one word, e.g. ٹردا اے /ṭurdā e/ > ٹردے /ṭurde ~ ṭurdæ/ 'he walks'. A long form here, i.e. ٹردا ہے /ṭurdā he ~ hæ/, would convey an emphatic sense like 'he *really does* walk'. In other contexts, the short forms are written separately. To observe the elision characteristic of such Saraiki forms, see the paradigms of the compound tenses involving the present tense auxiliary, such as the present imperfect, shown in Table 8.97 below.[30]

The present tense of ہووݨ /hovaṇ/ 'to be' is usually negated syntactically, as shown in Table 8.79.

Negative present forms of ہووݨ /hovaṇ/ 'to be' with personal endings that appear to incorporate direct form pronominal suffixes, are shown in Table 8.80:[31]

29 We have tried to represent this consistently in the paradigms in Chapter 8, but we have not attempted to normalize spelling in sentences provided by our consultant.

30 In order to distinguish the third person plural present /h{ĕ~i}n/ from the third person plural past /han/ it is necessary either to use the *zēr* diacritic to represent /ĕ~i/, or to use ی to represent this vowel sound. The second solution is not ideal, since ی normally represents a long vowel. However, the first is also not ideal, since diacritics are usually not printed, and the lack of any diacritic could cause confusion between the third person plural present /h{ĕ~i}n/ and the third person plural past /han/. We have chosen to use the zēr diacritic in our examples.

31 First and second person forms in Table 8.80 were provided by UK, and the third person forms are from Shackle (1976: 107).

Person	Singular		Plural	
	Long forms	Short forms	Long forms	Short forms
1st	میں ہاں mæ̃ hã̄ ‘I am’	اں ã̄ ‘I am’	اسّاں ہِسّے assã̄ hissē اساں ہیں assã̄ hæ̃ اساں ہوں assã̄ hū̃ ‘we are’	سے se ایں æ̃ اوں ū̃ ‘we are’
2nd	توں ہیں tū̃ hẽ ‘you are’	ایں ẽ ‘you are’	تسّاں ہِوّے tussã̄ hivve تساں ہو tussã̄ ho ‘you are’	وے ve اہ o ‘you are’
3rd	او ہے o he ∼ hæ ‘he/she/it is’	اے e ‘he/she/it is’	او ہِن o hĕn ‘they are’	اِن ĕn ‘they are’

Table 8.78: Present tense of ہووݨ /hovaṇ/ ‘to be’

Person	Singular	Plural
1st	میں نئیں mæ̃ naĩ ‘I am not’	اساں نئیں assã̄ naĩ ‘we are not’
2nd	توں نئیں tū̃ naĩ ‘you are not’	تساں نئیں tussã̄ naĩ ‘you are not’
3rd	او نئیں o naĩ ‘he/she/it is not’	او نئیں o naĩ ‘they are not’

Table 8.79: Syntactically negated present tense of ہووݨ /hovaṇ/ ‘to be’

Person	Singular	Plural
1st	میں نِمھی mǣ nimhī 'I am not'	اسّاں نِسے assā̃ nise 'we are not'
2nd	توں نِوھیں tū̃ nivhẽ 'you are not'	تسّاں نِوھے tussā̃ nivhe 'you are not'
3rd	نِسی nisī 'he/she/it is not'	نِنھے ninhe 'they are not'

Table 8.80: Morphological negative present of ہووݨ /hovaṇ/ 'to be'

8.5.3.1.2 Past tense of ہووݨ /hovaṇ/ 'to be'

Past tense forms of ہووݨ /hovaṇ/ 'to be' are given in Table 8.81. Importantly, gender is marked in the third person forms[32]; thus gender will also be marked in the third person of complex forms including the past tense of 'to be'.

32 Nasir Abbas Syed says that in his dialect these forms are not distinguished for gender, whereas another speaker (AHB) has maintained that the distinction does exist. It seems that marking of gender distinctions across dialects is another topic requiring further research.

Person	Singular	Plural
1st	میں ہامی mæ̃ hāmī 'I was'	اساں ہاسے assā̃ hāse 'we were'
2nd	توں ہاویں tū̃ hāvẽ 'you were'	تساں ہاوے tussā̃ hāve 'you were'
3rd	او ہا ō $hā_M$ 'he was' او ہئی o $haī_F$ 'she was'	او ہن o han_M او ہین o $hæn_F$ 'they were'

Table 8.81: Past tense of ہووݨ /hovaṇ/ 'to be'

8.5.3.1.3 Past negative tense of ہووݨ /hovaṇ/ 'to be'

Past tense forms of 'be' are usually negated with the separate negative particle نئیں /naī̃/ or نہ /na/, as shown in Table 8.82, which shows forms provided by our consultant. However, Shackle (1976: 96) also gives a set of forms in which the simple negative particle نہ /na/ is fused with the past forms of 'be'.[33] These are shown in Table 8.83.

The third person forms of both the long and the fused third person past negative forms show a gender difference.

33 Mughal (2010: 935) gives the spellings نہ and ناں for the simple negative particle.

Person	Singular	Plural
1st	میں نا ہامی mæ̃ nā hāmī 'I was not'	اساں نا ہاسے assā̃ nā hāse 'we were not'
2nd	توں نا ہاویں tū̃ nā hāvẽ 'you were not'	تساں نا ہاوے tussā̃ nā hāve 'you were not'
3rd	او نا ہا o nā hā$_{\text{M}}$ 'he was not' او نا ہئی o nā haī$_{\text{F}}$ 'she was not'	او نا ہن o nā han$_{\text{M}}$ او نا ہین o nā hæn$_{\text{F}}$ 'they were not'

Table 8.82: Long form of negative past tense of ہووݨ /hovaṇ/ 'to be'

Person	Singular	Plural
1st	نہم naham 'I wasn't'	نہاسے nhāse 'we weren't'
2nd	نہاویں ~ ناہویں nhāvẽ ~ nāhvẽ 'you weren't'	نہاوے ~ ناہوے nhāve ~ nāhve 'you weren't'
3rd	نہا nahā$_{\text{M}}$ 'he wasn't' نہئی ~ نہی nahaī ~ nahī$_{\text{F}}$ 'she wasn't'	نہن nahan$_{\text{M}}$ نہین nahæn$_{\text{F}}$ 'they weren't'

Table 8.83: Fused negative past forms of ہووݨ /hovaṇ/ 'to be'

8.5.3.1.4 Future forms of ہووݨ /hovaṇ/ 'to be'

Formation: stem of ہووݨ /hovaṇ/ 'to be' + س /s/ + personal endings.

The future forms of ہووݨ /hovaṇ/ 'to be' are shown in Table 8.84. The personal endings are the same as those used for the subjunctive (see Table 8.88), except for the third person singular, which is ی /-ī/, as in Hindko.

Person	Singular	Plural
1st	میں ہوساں mǣ hosā̃ 'I will/must be'	اساں ہوسوں assā̃ hosū̃ 'we will/must be'
2nd	توں ہوسیں tū̃ hosẽ 'you will/must be'	تساں ہوسو tussā̃ hoso 'you will/must be'
3rd	او ہوسی o hosī 'he/she/it will/must be'	او ہوسن o hosĕn 'they will/must be'

Table 8.84: Future forms of ہووݨ /hovaṇ/ 'to be'

8.5.3.1.5 Subjunctive forms of ہووݨ /hovaṇ/ 'to be'

The subjunctive of ہووݨ /hovaṇ/ 'to be' is formed regularly, employing the subjunctive endings given in Section 8.5.4.3. Its subjunctive forms are shown in Table 8.85.

Person	Singular	Plural
1st	میں ہوواں mæ̃ hovā̃ 'if I am'	اساں ہوووں assā̃ hovū̃ 'if we are'
2nd	توں ہووےں tū̃ hovẽ 'if you are'	تُساں ہووو tussā̃ hovo 'if you are'
3rd	او ہووے o hove 'if he/she/it is'	او ہووِن o hovĕ∼in 'if they are'

Table 8.85: Subjunctive forms of ہووݨ /hovaṇ/ 'to be'

8.5.3.2 The verb تھیوݨ /thīvaṇ/ 'to become'

Unlike Panjabi, Saraiki has a separate change-of-state verb تھیوݨ /thīvaṇ/ 'to become', distinct from stative ہووݨ /hovaṇ/ 'to be'. While ہووݨ /hovaṇ/ 'to be' functions as an auxiliary in complex verb forms, تھیوݨ /thīvaṇ/ 'to become' does not. It productively forms intransitive conjunct verbs, e.g. شُروع تھیوݨ /šurū thīvaṇ/ 'to begin (intransitive)', just as کرݨ /karaṇ/ 'to do' forms transitive conjunct verbs, e.g. شُروع کرݨ /šurū karaṇ/ 'to begin (transitive)'. Its perfective participle is formed somewhat irregularly; for example, تھیا /theā/ 'became (m.sg. perfective)' (Shackle 1976: 86). With the exception of its irregular perfective participle, it behaves as any other verb. It occurs frequently in compound verb formations with ونڄݨ /vãʄaṇ/ 'to go', as in example 8.20, and پووݨ /povaṇ/ 'to fall, lie', as in example 8.21. For more examples of such compound verb formations, see Chapter 9.[34]

(8.20) او بیمار تھی گیا

o	*bimār*	***thī***	***ʄy-ā***
3.SG.DIR	sick	**become**	**go.PP-SG.M**

'He **got** sick.' (Sr) (Shackle 1976: 142)

34 Ali Hussain Birahimani (p.c.) thinks that approximately 50% of urban speakers in Multan have lost this distinction and do not actively use this verb. However Zahoor (2009: 37) gives an ordinary conversational example employing this form: خیر ہے کیا تھئے / xær e! kyā thiæ/ 'Is anything wrong! What has happened?'.

(8.21) میں وی تیار تاں سویر دی تھیوݨ پئی آں

mæ̃	*vī*	*tiyār*	*tā̃*	*saver*	*d-ī*	***thīvaṇ***	***pa-ī***
1SG	also	ready	TOP	morning	GEN-SG.F	**become-INF**	**fall-PP.SG.F**
ā̃							
be.PRES.1SG							

'I also **started** to get ready early.'[35] (Sr)

8.5.4 Verb forms built on the stem

8.5.4.1 Imperative

Imperatives are found only for the second person singular and plural. There are two forms, a plain (or direct) and a polite (or distanced, "aorist") form. The singular plain imperative is usually identical with the stem; the plural plain imperative consists of stem + و /o/, and is identical to the second person plural subjunctive. The polite imperatives are formed as follows: the singular polite imperative consists of the stem + یں /-ī̃/; the plural polite imperative is formed by adding ابے /-āhe/ to the stem (Shackle 1976: 92). Imperatives for ٹُر /ṭur-/ 'walk, go' are shown in Table 8.86.[36] The use of these imperative forms in simple sentences is illustrated in examples 8.22, 8.23, 8.24, and 8.25. For the use of the infinitive (Panjabi, Hindko) and gerundive (Saraiki) in imperative function, see Section 10.5.6.

	2nd person singular	2nd person plural
Direct/plain	ٹُر ṭur 'go, walk (now)!'	ٹُرو ṭuro 'go, walk (now)!'
Polite/"aorist"	ٹُریں ṭurī̃ '(please) go, walk'	ٹُرے ~ ٹُرابے ṭuræ ~ ṭurāhe '(please) go, walk'

Table 8.86: Imperative forms of ٹُرݨ /ṭuraṇ/ 'to walk, go'

35 Shackle (1976: 169), cited from Lashari (1971: 23)

36 The form ٹُرابے /ṭurāhe/ was not accepted by our consultant, who gives the form ٹُرے. However /-āhe/ does occur on p. 26 of Zahoor (2009) (see example 8.20). Possibly our consultant's forms reflect more elisions than the written forms in Zahoor (2009).

(8.22) کوڑ نہ مارو

koṛ	*na*	***mār-o***
lie	NEG	**beat-IMP.2PL**

'Don't lie! (i.e. tell falsehoods)' (Sr) (Zahoor 2009: 26)

(8.23) گھر ونج

ghar	***vãj***
home	**go.IMP.2SG**

'Go home!' (Sr) (Zahoor 2009: 26)

(8.24) روویں نہ

rov-ĩ̄	*na*
cry-IMP.POL.2SG	NEG

'Don't **cry**!' (Sr) (Zahoor 2009: 27)

(8.25) ساکوں کنو کراہے

sā-kū̃	*kaū*	***kar-āhe***
1PL-DAT	listening	**do-IMP.POL.2PL**

'Please **tell/inform** us.' (Sr) (Zahoor 2009: 26)

8.5.4.2 Future

Formation: present-future stem + /s/ + personal endings

Future forms of two high-frequency verbs are given in Table 8.87. Future forms are marked for person and number, but not gender. Verb forms involving the future form of ہووݨ 'to be' ', as in Hindko and Panjabi, can denote either actions or states that are predicted to occur in the future or that are presumed to be happening.

---

37 UK comments that the forms in Table 8.87 represent her pronunciation. The presence of /æ/ instead of /e/ is, according to both our consultant and Ali Hussain Birahimani, due to Panjabi influence on central varieties of Saraiki.

Person	ونڄݨ vãʄaṇ 'to go'		کرݨ karaṇ 'to do'	
	Singular	**Plural**	**Singular**	**Plural**
1st	میں ویساں mæ̃ vesã 'I will go'	اسّاں ویسوں assã vesũ 'we will go'	میں کریساں mæ̃ karesã 'I will do'	اسّاں کریسوں assã karesũ 'we will do'
2nd	توں ویسیں tũ vesẽ 'you will go'	تسّاں ویسو tussã veso 'you will go'	توں کریسیں tũ karesẽ 'you will do'	تسّاں کریسو tussã kareso 'you will do'
3rd	او ویسی o vesī 'he/she will go'	او ویسِن o vesĕn 'they will go'	اوکریسی o karesī 'he/she will do'	اوکریسِن o karesĕn 'they will do'

Table 8.87: Future of the verbs ونڄݨ /vãʄaṇ/ 'to go' (intransitive) and کرݨ /karaṇ/ 'to do' (transitive)[37]

8.5.4.3 Subjunctive

The subjunctive consists of the simple stem + the personal endings shown in Table 8.88.

Person	Consonant-final stems		Vowel-final stems	
	Singular	**Plural**	**Singular**	**Plural**
1st	اں -ã	وں -ũ	واں -vã	وں -vũ
2nd	ایں -ẽ	و -o	ویں -vẽ	و -vo
3rd	ے -e	اِن -in ~ -ĕn	وے -ve-	وِن -vin ~ -vĕn

Table 8.88: Subjunctive personal endings

Table 8.89 gives subjunctive paradigms for three very high frequency verbs, 'to come', 'to go', and 'to do'.

Person	آوݨ āvaṇ ‘to come’		ونجݨ vā̃ʄaṇ ‘to go’		کرݨ karaṇ ‘to do’	
	Singular	Plural	Singular	Plural	Singular	Plural
1st	میں آواں mæ̃ āvā̃ ‘I may/should come; if I come’	اساں آووں assā̃ āvū̃ ‘we may/should come; if we come’	میں ونجاں mæ̃ vā̃ʄā̃ ‘I may/should go; if I go’	اساں ونجوں assā̃ vā̃ʄū̃ ‘we may/should go; if we go’	میں کراں mæ̃ karā̃ ‘I may/should do; if I do’	اساں کروں assā̃ karū̃ ‘we may/should do; if we do’
2nd	توں آویں tū̃ āvẽ ‘you may/should come; if you (sg.) come’	تُساں آوو tussā̃ āvo ‘you may/should come; if you (pl.) come’	توں ونجیں tū̃ vā̃ʄẽ ‘you may/should go; if you go’	تساں ونجو tussā̃ vā̃ʄo ‘you may/should go; if you go’	توں کریں tū̃ karẽ ‘you may/should do; if you do’	تساں کرو tussā̃ karo ‘you may/should do; if you do’
3rd	او آوے o āve ‘he/she may/should come; if he/she comes’	اوآوِن o āvĕn ‘they may/should come; if they come’	او ونجے o vā̃ʄe ‘he/she may/should go; if he/she goes’	او ونجِن o vā̃ʄĕn ‘they may/should go; if they go’	او کرے o kare ‘he/she may/should do; if he/she does’	اوکرِن o karĕn ‘they may/should do; if they do’

Table 8.89: Subjunctive of the verbs آوݨ /āvaṇ/ ‘to come’ (intransitive), ونجݨ /vā̃ʄaṇ/ ‘to go’ (intransitive), and کرݨ /karaṇ/ ‘to do’ (transitive)

8.5.4.4 Irrealis I

This distinctive irrealis form (= Shackle’s “Conditional I”) consists of the stem + a personal ending (= the subjunctive) + the invariant form ہا /hā/. This final invariant form is identical to the masculine singular past tense of ہووݨ /hovaṇ/ ‘to be’. Irrealis forms are not marked for gender. These forms are equivalent in meaning and function to the bare imperfective participle used in irrealis clauses, which we will call irrealis II. Irrealis I belongs to the older stratum of the language, while irrealis II is modeled on Panjabi and Urdu. Table 8.90 gives irrealis I forms of ونجݨ /vā̃ʄaṇ/ ‘to go’. Irrealis I forms are also found in Hindko.

One example of the irrealis I form in context is shown here in example 8.26.

Person	Singular	Plural
1st	میں ونڄاں ہا mæ̃ vãʄã hā 'if I had gone/were going (but didn't/am not)'	اسّاں ونڄوں ہا assã vãʄũ hā 'if we had gone/were going (but didn't/aren't)'
2nd	توں ونڄیں ہا tũ vãʄẽ hā 'if you had gone/were going (but didn't/aren't)'	تسّاں ونڄو ہا tussã vãʄo hā 'if you had gone/were going (but didn't/aren't)'
3rd	او ونڄے ہا o vãʄe hā 'if he/she had gone/were going (but didn't/isn't)'	او ونڄن ہا o vãʄẽn hā 'if they had gone/were going (but didn't/aren't)'

Table 8.90: Irrealis I of ونڄݨ /vãʄaṇ/ 'to go'

(8.26) جے او اندا پیا ہووے ہا تاں فون کرے ہا

je	*o*	*ān-d-ā*	*piy-ā*	***ho-ve***	***hā***	*tā̃*	***fon***
if	3SG	come-IP-SG.M	lie.PP-SG.M	**be-SBJV.3SG**	**IRR**	then	**phone**

kar-e	***hā***
do-SBJV.3SG	**IRR**

'If he were coming today, he **would have phoned.**' (Sr) (UK)

8.5.5 Morphological passive forms

Saraiki has two types of passive construction: (1) older, inherited morphological passives formed on the passive stem, the forms of which are presented in this section, and (2) newer periphrastic passives, treated in Section 10.4.3.2, consisting of the perfective participle of the main verb plus a conjugated form of ونڄݨ /vãʄaṇ/ 'to go'.

Passive stems in /-īj/ are formed from (most) transitive and a few causative stems, but not from intransitive stems (Shackle 1976: 76). Imperatives of any kind are not normally formed from passive stems (Shackle 1976: 92). However, the present subjunctive of passive stems usually has a desiderative sense; for example, the third person singular present passive subjunctive of کرݨ /karaṇ/ 'to do', کریجے /karīje/, has the sense 'should be done'.

Passive stems lose their final /-j/ in their present-future stem, from which the future and the imperfective participle are formed (see Table 8.91). In the imperfective participle, the ی /-ī/ of the present-future stem becomes nasalized beause of the underlying /-nd/ of the imperfective participle, e.g. مری /marī-/ < مار/kill, beat/ becomes مرِیں /marī̃-/ in the imperfect tenses, but remains as مری /marī-/ in the future. To observe this, compare the third person singular future forms constructed on the plain, transitive, and passive stems of the stem سُݨ /suṇ-/ 'hear' in Table 8.91.

Stem type	Stem	Future form	Imperfective participle	Gloss
Plain	سُݨ sunṇ-	سُݨسی suṇsī		he/she/it will hear
Derived transitive (first causative)	سُݨا suṇā-	سُݨیسی suṇesī		he/she/it will tell (lit. 'cause to be heard')
Passive	سُݨیج suṇīj-			
Passive-present/future (future tense)	سُݨی suṇī-	سُݨیسی suṇīsī		he/she/it will be heard
Passive-present/future (imperfect tenses)	سُݨیں suṇī̃-		سُݨیندا suṇī̃dā (m.sg.)	he/it is heard

Table 8.91: Comparison of simple, causative, and passive future forms of سُݨ /suṇ-/ 'hear'

Representative paradigms for passive tense-aspect forms of the prototypical transitive verb مار /mār-/ 'beat, kill' in the present imperfect, past imperfect, future, subjunctive, and irrealis I are presented below in Table 8.92 through Table 8.96. Paradigms for perfective passive tenses are not presented, since data on them available to us are not yet sufficient to allow this. For examples of the Saraiki morphological passive, see Section 10.4.3.1.

Future imperfect (shown in Table 8.94) and subjunctive forms (shown in Table 8.95) are marked for person and number, but not for gender.

Passive stems are quite frequently used in compound verb constructions consisting of the passive stem plus a finite form (often the perfective participle) of the verbs پووݨ/povaṇ/ 'to fall, lie' and وَنڄݨ /vãfaṇ/ 'to go' with perfective aspect and past tense reference. See the discussion and examples in Chapter 9.

Person	Singular	Plural
1st	میں مریندااں mæ̃ marĩdã$_{M}$ میں مریندی اں mæ̃ marĩdī ã$_{F}$ ‘I am killed/beaten’	اسّاں مرندے ایں~ ہیں assã marĩde (h)æ̃$_{M}$ اسّاں مریندیاں ایں~ ہیں assã marĩdiyã (h)æ̃$_{F}$ ‘we are killed/beaten’
2nd	توں مریندااں ایں tũ marĩdã ẽ$_{M}$ توں مریندی ایں tũ marĩdī ẽ$_{F}$ ‘you are killed/beaten’	تسّاں مریندے ہِوّے tussã marĩdē hivve$_{M}$ تساں مریندے آو tussã marĩde o$_{M}$ تسّاں مریندیاں ہِوّے tussã marĩdiyã hivve$_{F}$ تساں مریندیاں آو tussã marĩdīã o$_{F}$ ‘you are killed/beaten’
3rd	او مریندے o marĩde/marĩdæ$_{M}$ ‘he is killed/beaten’ او مریندی اے o marĩdī e$_{F}$ ‘she is killed/beaten’	او مریندِن o marĩdĕn$_{M}$ او مریندیَن ō marĩdiyĕn$_{F}$ ‘they are killed/beaten’

Table 8.92: Present imperfect of مریج /marīj-/ ‘be killed, beaten’

Person	Singular	Plural
1st	میں مریندا ہامی mæ̃ marī̃dā hāmī$_{M}$ میں مریندی ہامی mæ̃ marī̃dī hāmī$_{F}$ 'I used to be killed/beaten'	اساں مریندے ہاسے assā̃ marī̃de hāse$_{M}$ اساں مریندیاں ہاسے assā̃ marī̃diyā̃ hāse$_{F}$ 'we used to be killed/beaten'
2nd	توں مریندا ہاویں tū̃ marī̃dā hāvẽ$_{M}$ توں مریندی ہاویں tū̃ marī̃dī hāvẽ$_{F}$ 'you used to be killed/beaten'	تساں مریندے ہاوے tussā̃ marī̃de hāve$_{M}$ تساں مریندیاں ہاوے tussā̃ marī̃diyā̃ hāve$_{F}$ 'you used to be killed/beaten'
3rd	او مریندا ہا o marī̃dā hā$_{M}$ 'he used to be killed/beaten' او مریندی ہئی o marī̃dī haī$_{F}$ 'she used to be killed/beaten'	او مریندے ہن o marī̃dē han$_{M}$ 'they used to be killed/beaten' او مریندیاں ہین o marī̃diyā̃ hæn$_{F}$ 'they used to be killed/beaten'

Table 8.93: Past imperfect of مریج /marīj-/ 'be killed, beaten'

Person	Singular	Plural
1st	میں مریساں mæ̃ marīsā̃ 'I will be killed/beaten'	اساں مریسوں assā̃ marīsū̃ 'we will be killed/beaten'
2nd	توں مریسیں tū̃ marīsẽ 'you will be killed/beaten'	تساں مریسو tussā̃ marīso 'you will be killed/beaten'
3rd	او مریسی o marīsī 'he/she/it will be killed/beaten'	او مریسن o marīsĕn 'they will be killed/beaten'

Table 8.94: Future imperfect of مریج /marīj-/ 'be killed, beaten'

Person	Singular	Plural
1st	میں مریجاں mǣ marījā̃ 'I may/should be killed/ beaten; if I am killed/beaten '	اسّاں مریجوں assā̃ marījū̃ 'we may/should be killed/beaten; if we are killed/beaten'
2nd	توں مریجیں tū̃ marījẽ 'you may/should be killed/ beaten; if you are killed/beaten '	تسّاں مریجو tussā̃ marījo 'you may/should be killed/ beaten; if you are killed/beaten '
3rd	او مریجے o marīje 'he/she/it may/should be killed/ beaten; if he/she/it is killed/beaten'	او مریجن o marījĕn 'they may/should be killed/ beaten; if they are killed/beaten'

Table 8.95: Subjunctive of مریج /marīj-/ 'be killed, beaten'

Person	Singular	Plural
1st	میں مریجاں ہا mǣ marījā̃ hā 'if I were/had been killed/ beaten; would that I be killed/ beaten (but I am/ was not killed/beaten) '	اسّاں مریجوں ہا assā̃ marījū̃ hā 'if we were/had been killed/ beaten; would that we were killed/ beaten' (but we are/ were not killed/ beaten)'
2nd	توں مریجیں ہا tū̃ marījẽ hā 'if you were/had been killed/ beaten; would that you be killed/ beaten; (but you are/were not killed/ beaten)'	تسّاں مریجو ہا tussā̃ marījo hā 'if you were/had been killed/ beaten; would that you were killed/ beaten (but you are/were not killed/ beaten)'
3rd	او مریجے ہا o marīje hā 'if he/she/it were/had been killed/ beaten (but he/she/it is/ was not killed/ beaten)'	او مریجن ہا o marījĕn hā 'if they were/had been killed/ beaten (but they are/ were not killed/ beaten)'

Table 8.96: Irrealis I of مریج /marīj-/ 'be killed, beaten'

8.5.6 Verb forms built on the imperfective participle

The imperfective participle consists of the PF stem + (n)d + marked adjectival endings.

8.5.6.1 Bare participial forms: Irrealis II

As in Panjabi and Hindko, the imperfective participle may be used on its own, with no auxiliary, in one or both clauses of an irrealis conditional sentence, to describe an unfulfilled or unfulfillable condition. Since these forms consist of an adjectival participle alone, they distinguish gender and number, but not person. The meaning of this form is the same as that of the original irrealis I forms described in Section 8.5.4.4 above. For examples, see the discussion of irrealis conditionals in Chapter 10.

8.5.6.2 Imperfect tenses

Imperfect tenses consist of the imperfective participle (+ imperfective participle of ہووݨ /hovaṇ/ 'to be) + a conjugated form of ہووݨ /hovaṇ/ 'to be'.

8.5.6.2.1 Present imperfect

Formation: imperfective participle + ہووݨ /hovaṇ/ 'to be' (present)

Table 8.97 shows the present imperfect of ونڄݨ /vãʄaṇ/ 'to go'.

Person	Singular	Plural
1st	میں ویندا‌ں mæ̃ vēdā̃$_{M}$ میں ویندی اں mæ̃ vēdī ā̃$_{F}$ 'I go'	اسّاں ویندے ایں ~ ہیں assā̃ vēde (h)æ̃$_{M}$ اسّاں ویندیاں ایں ~ ہیں assā̃ vēdiyā̃ (h)æ̃$_{F}$ 'we go'
2nd	توں ویندیں tũ vēdẽ$_{M}$ توں ویندیں (< ویندی ایں) tũ vēdī̃$_{F}$ 'you go'	تسّاں ویندے ہِوّے tussā̃ vēde hivve$_{M}$ تساں ویندے او tussā̃ vēde o$_{M}$ تسّاں ویندیاں ہِوّے tussā̃ vēdiyā̃ hivve$_{F}$ تساں ویندیاں او tussā̃ vediyā̃ o$_{F}$ 'you go'
3rd	او ویندے o vēde$_{M}$ 'he goes' او ویندی اے o vēdī e$_{F}$ 'she goes'	او ویندِن o vēdĕn$_{M}$ او ویندیَن o vēdīĕn$_{F}$ 'they go'

Table 8.97: Present imperfect of ونڄݨ /vãʄaṇ/ 'to go'

8.5.6.2.2 Present imperfect-habitual

Imperfect-habitual tenses add the imperfective participle of the auxiliary ہووݨ /hovaṇ/ 'to be' to emphasize the persistence of the activity or state. Table 8.98 shows these forms for ونڄݨ /vãʄaṇ/ 'to go'.

Person	Singular	Plural
1st	میں ویندا ہونداں mæ̃ vēdā hondā̃$_{M}$ میں ویندی ہوندی اں mæ̃ vēdī hondī ā̃$_{F}$ 'I usually go'	اساں ویندے ہوندے ایں ~ ہیں assā̃ vēde honde (h)æ̃$_{M}$ اساں ویندیاں ہوندیاں ایں ~ ہیں assā̃ vēdiyā̃ hondiyā̃ (h)æ̃$_{F}$ 'we usually go'
2nd	توں ویندا ہوندیں tū̃ vēdā hondẽ$_{M}$ توں ویندی ہوندیں tū̃ vēdī hondī̃$_{F}$ 'you (sg.) usually go'	تساں ویندے ہوندے وے tussā̃ vēdẽ honde ve$_{M}$ تساں ویندیاں ہوندیاں وے tussā̃ vēdiyā̃ hondīyā̃ ve$_{F}$ 'you (pl.) usually go'
3rd	او ویندا ہوندے o vēdā honde$_{M}$ 'he usually goes' او ویندی ہوندی اے o vēdī hondī e$_{F}$ 'she usually goes'	او ویندے ہوندِن o vēde hondĕn$_{M}$ او ویندیاں ہوندیئن o vēdiyā̃ hondiyĕn$_{F}$ 'they usually go'

Table 8.98: Present imperfect-habitual of وینجݨ /vãʄaṇ/ 'to go'

8.5.6.2.3 Past imperfect

Formation: imperfective participle + ہووݨ /hovaṇ/ 'to be'(past)

Table 8.99 displays the past imperfect of وینجݨ /vãʄaṇ/ 'to go'.

Person	Singular	Plural
1st	میں ویندا ہامی mǣ vẽdā hāmī$_{M}$ میں ویندی ہامی mǣ vẽdī hāmī$_{F}$ 'I used to go'	اسّاں ویندے ہاسے assā̃ vẽde hāse$_{M}$ اسّاں ویندیاں ہاسے assā̃ vẽdiyā̃ hāse$_{F}$ 'we used to go'
2nd	توں ویندا ہاویں tū̃ vẽdā hāvẽ$_{M}$ توں ویندی ہاویں tū̃ vẽdī hāvẽ$_{F}$ 'you used to go'	تسّاں ویندے ہاوے tussā̃ vẽde hāve$_{M}$ تسّاں ویندیاں ہاوے tussā̃ vẽdiyā̃ hāve$_{F}$ 'you used to go'
3rd	او ویندا ہا o vẽdā hā$_{M}$ 'he used to go' او ویندی ہئی o vẽdī haī$_{F}$ 'she used to go'	او ویندے ہن o vẽde han$_{M}$ او ویندیاں ہین o vẽdiyā̃ hæn$_{F}$ 'they used to go'

Table 8.99: Past imperfect of ونڄݨ /vãʄaṇ/ 'to go'

8.5.6.2.4 Past imperfect-habitual

Formation: imperfective participle + ہووݨ /hovaṇ/ 'to be' (imperfective participle) + ہووݨ /hovaṇ/(past)

Table 8.100 shows past imperfect-habitual forms of ونڄ /vãʄaṇ/ 'to go'.

Person	Singular	Plural
1st	میں ویندا ہوندا ہامی mæ̃ vẽdā hondā hāmī$_M$ میں ویندی ہوندی ہامی mæ̃ vẽdī hondī hāmī$_F$ 'I usually used to go'	اسّاں ویندے ہوندے ہاسے assā̃ vẽde honde hāse$_M$ اسّاں ویندیاں ہوندیاں ہاسے assā̃ vẽdiyā̃ hondiyā̃ hāse$_F$ 'we usually used to go'
2nd	توں ویندا ہوندا ہاویں tū̃ vẽdā hondā hāvẽ$_M$ توں ویندی ہوندی ہاویں tū̃ vẽdī hondī hāvẽ$_F$ 'you usually used to go'	تسّاں ویندے ہوندے ہاوے tussā̃ vẽde honde hāve$_M$ تسّاں ویندیاں ہوندیاں ہاوے tussā̃ vẽdiyā̃ hondiyā̃ hāve$_F$ 'you usually used to go'
3rd	او ویندا ہوندا ہا o vẽdā hondā hā$_M$ 'he usually used to go' او ویندی ہوندی ہئی o vẽdī hondī haī$_F$ 'she usually used to go'	او ویندے ہوندے ہن o vẽde honde han$_M$ او ویندیاں ہوندیاں ہین o vẽdiyā̃ hondiyā̃ hæn$_F$ 'they usually used to go'

Table 8.100: Past imperfect-habitual of ونجݨ /vãʄaṇ/ 'to go'

8.5.6.2.5 Future imperfect

Formation: imperfective participle + ہووݨ /hovaṇ/ 'to be (future)'

Future imperfect forms of ونجݨ /vãʄaṇ/ 'to go' are given in Table 8.101.

Person	Singular	Plural
1st	میں ویندا ہوساں mæ̃ vẽdā hosā̃$_M$ میں ویندی ہوساں mæ̃ vẽdī hosā̃$_F$ 'I will/must go frequently'	اسّاں ویندے ہوسوں assā̃ vẽde hosū̃$_M$ اسّاں ویندیاں ہوسوں assā̃ vẽdiyā̃ hosū̃$_F$ 'we will/must go frequently'
2nd	توں ویندا ہوسیں tū̃ vẽdā hosẽ$_M$ توں ویندی ہوسیں tū̃ vẽdī hosẽ$_F$ 'you will/must go frequently '	تسّاں ویندے ہوسو tussā̃ vẽde hoso$_M$ تسّاں ویندیاں ہوسو tussā̃ vẽdiyā̃ hoso$_F$ 'you will/must go frequently'
3rd	او ویندا ہوسی o vẽdā hosī$_M$ 'he will/must go frequently' او ویندی ہوسی o vẽdī hosī$_F$ 'she will/must go frequently'	او ویندے ہوسن o vẽde hosĕn$_M$ او ویندیاں ہوسن ō vẽdiyā̃ hosĕn$_F$ 'they will/must go frequently'

Table 8.101: Future imperfect of ونڄݨ /vãʄaṇ/ 'to go'

8.5.6.2.6 Imperfect subjunctive

Formation: imperfective participle + ہووݨ /hovaṇ/ 'to be (subjunctive)'

Table 8.102 gives imperfect subjunctive forms of ونڄݨ /vãʄaṇ/ 'to go'.

Person	Singular	Plural
1st	میں ویندا ہوواں mæ̃ vẽdā hovā̃$_M$ میں ویندی ہوواں mæ̃ vẽdī hovā̃$_F$ 'I may/should go frequently; if I go frequently'	اسّاں ویندے ہووؤں assā̃ vẽde hovū̃$_M$ اسّاں ویندیاں ہووؤں assā̃ vẽdiyā̃ hovū̃$_F$ 'we may/should go frequently; if we go frequently'
2nd	توں ویندا ہوویں tū̃ vẽdā hovẽ$_M$ توں ویندی ہوویں tū̃ vẽdī hovẽ$_F$ 'you may/should go frequently; if you go frequently'	تسّاں ویندے ہووو tussā̃ vẽde hovo$_M$ تسّاں ویندیاں ہووو tussā̃ vẽdiyā̃ hovo$_F$ 'you may/should go frequently; if you go frequently'
3rd	او ویندا ہووے o vẽdā hove$_M$ 'he may/should go frequently; if he goes frequently' او ویندی ہووے o vẽdī hove$_F$ 'she may/should go frequently; if she goes frequently'	او ویندے ہووِن o vẽde hovĕn$_M$ او ویندیاں ہووِن o vẽdiyā̃ hovĕn$_F$ 'they may/should go frequently; if they go frequently'

Table 8.102: Imperfect subjunctive of ونجݨ /vãʄaṇ/ 'to go'

8.5.6.2.7 Imperfect irrealis I

Formation: imperfective participle + ہووݨ/hovaṇ/ 'to be (subjunctive)' + the invariant form ہا /hā/

The paradigm for the imperfect irrealis I of ونجݨ /vãʄaṇ/ 'to go' is given in Table 8.103.

Person	Singular	Plural
1st	میں ویندا ہوواں ہا mæ̃ vēdā hovā̃ hā$_M$ میں ویندی ہوواں ہا mæ̃ vēdī hovā̃ hā$_F$ 'if I went frequently (but I do not go)'	اسّاں ویندے ہووُوں ہا assā̃ vēde hovū̃ hā$_M$ اسّاں ویندیاں ہووُوں ہا assā̃ vēdiyā̃ hovū̃ hā$_F$ 'if we went frequently (but we do not go)'
2nd	توں ویندا ہوویں ہا tū̃ vēdā hovē hā$_M$ توں ویندی ہوویں ہا tū̃ vēdī hovē hā$_F$ 'if you went frequently (but you do not go)'	تسّاں ویندے ہووو ہا tussā̃ vēde hovo hā$_M$ تسّاں ویندیاں ہووو ہا tussā̃ vēdiyā̃ hovo hā$_F$ 'if you went frequently (but you do not go)'
3rd	او ویندا ہووے ہا o vēdā hove hā$_M$ 'if he went frequently (but he does not go)' او ویندی ہووے ہا o vēdī hove hā$_F$ 'if she went frequently (but she does not go)'	او ویندے ہووِن ہا o vēde hovĕn hā$_M$ او ویندیاں ہووِن ہا o vēdiyā̃ hovĕn hā$_F$ 'if they went frequently (but they do not go)'

Table 8.103: Imperfect irrealis I of ونڄݨ /vãʄaṇ/ 'to go'

8.5.6.3 Continuous tenses

The most common type of continuous form in Saraiki consists of the imperfective participle + the grammaticalized perfective participle of پووݨ/povaṇ/ 'to fall, lie' (پیا، پئی، پئے، پئیاں /piyā/, /paī/, /pae/, /paiyā̃/) + auxiliary (present, past, subjunctive, or future). We call these continuous I. These forms convey a sense of concreteness, of an action actually in progress.

Continuous II forms employing the grammaticalized perfective participle of رہنا /rahṇā/ 'to remain' (ریا، رئی، رے، رئیاں /ryā/, /raī/, /rae/, and /raiyā̃/) are also found for present, past, and future continuous; but they are less frequent in Saraiki and are characteristic of Urdu-influenced urban speech. These forms can be found in Section 8.4.4.4.1 on Panjabi verbs, listed as present continuous II, etc.

8.5.6.3.1 Present continuous I

Formation: imperfective participle + پووݨ /povaṇ/ 'to fall, lie'(perfective participle) + ہووݨ /hovaṇ/ 'to be' (present)[38]

Table 8.104 gives the present continuous I conjugation of ونجݨ /vãǰaṇ/ 'to go'. The forms given here (and their Perso-Arabic spellings) reflect coalescence of the initial vowel of the short forms of the present auxiliary with preceding final vowels of the participle ("elision," or "sandhi"). For example, the first person singular masculine form میں ویندا پیاں /mæ̃ vẽdā piyā̃/ 'I (m.) am going' reflects elision of the underlying form: ویندا پیا اں /vẽdā piyā ā̃/ (imperfective participle ویندا /vẽdā/ (m.sg.) + پیا /piyā/ (m.sg.) + اں /ā̃/ (first person singular present auxiliary). All forms given here should be understood as reflecting elision and be analyzed in a similar way. As Shackle (1976: 94) notes, the orthography of native speaker writers is inconsistent in how such elisions are written. Such inconsistency will be seen in the forms given here as well.

38 Notice that the default order of elements presented here is different from that of Hindko, but similar to that shown for Panjabi.

Person	Singular	Plural
1st	میںویندا پیاں mæ̃ vēdā piyã$_{M}$ میں ویندی پئی آں mæ̃ vēdī paī ã$_{F}$ 'I am going'	اسّاں ویندے پے ایں~ہیں assã vēde pe (h)æ̃$_{M}$ اسّاں ویندیاں پیاں ایں~ہیں assã vēdiyã piyã (h)æ̃$_{F}$ 'we are going'
2nd	توں ویندا پیں tū̃ vēdā pẽ$_{M}$ توں ویندی پئیں tū̃ vēdī paī̃$_{F}$ 'you are going'	تسّاں ویندے پے ہِوّے tussã vēde pe (hi)vve$_{M}$ تساں ویندے پے tussã vēde pe o$_{M}$ تسّاں ویندیاں پیاں ہِوّے tussã vēdiyã piyã (hi)vve$_{F}$ تساں ویندیاں پیاں ہو tussã vēdiyã paiyã o$_{F}$ 'you are going'
3rd	او ویندا پے o vēdā pæ$_{M}$ 'he is going' او ویندی پئی اے o vēdī paī e$_{F}$ 'she is going'	او ویندے پین o vēde pen$_{M}$ او ویندیاں پین o vēdiyã pæ̃n (< o vēdiyã paiyān$_{F}$) 'they are going'

Table 8.104: Present continuous I of ونجݨ /vãɉaṇ/ 'to go'

8.5.6.3.2 Past continuous I

Formation: imperfective participle + پووݨ/povaṇ/ 'fall/lie'(perfective participle) + ہووݨ /hovaṇ/ 'to be'(past)

See Table 8.105 for the past continuous-I forms of ونجݨ /vãɉaṇ/ 'to go'.

Person	Singular	Plural
1st	میں ویندا پیا ہامی mæ̃ vẽdā piyā hāmī$_{M}$ میں ویندی پئی ہامی mæ̃ vẽdī paī hāmī$_{F}$ 'I was going'	اساں ویندے پے ہاسے assā̃ vẽde pe hāse$_{M}$ اساں ویندیاں پیاں ہاسے assā̃ vẽdiyā̃ piyā̃ hāse$_{F}$ 'we were going'
2nd	توں ویندا پیا ہاویں tū̃ vẽdā piyā hāvẽ$_{M}$ توں ویندی پئی ہاویں tū̃ vẽdī paī hāvẽ$_{F}$ 'you were going'	تساں ویندے پے ہاوے tussā̃ vẽde pe hāve$_{M}$ تساں ویندیاں پیاں ہاوے tussā̃ vẽdiyā̃ piyā̃ hāve$_{F}$ 'you were going'
3rd	او ویندا پیا ہا o vẽdā piyā hā$_{M}$ 'he was going' او ویندی پئی ہئی o vẽdī paī haī$_{F}$ 'she was going'	او ویندے پے ہن o vẽde pe han$_{M}$ او ویندیاں پیاں ہین o vẽdiyā̃ piyā̃ hæn$_{F}$ 'they were going'

Table 8.105: Past continuous I of ونجݨ /vãɟaṇ/ 'to go'

8.5.6.3.3 Future continuous I

Formation: imperfective participle + پووݨ/povaṇ/ 'fall/lie' (perfective participle) + ہووݨ /hovaṇ/ 'to be' (future)

Table 8.106 presents the future continuous I forms of ونجݨ /vãɟaṇ/ 'to go'.

Person	Singular	Plural
1st	میں ویندا پیا ہوساں mæ̃ vẽdā piyā hosã$_{M}$ میں ویندی پئی ہوساں mæ̃ vẽdī paī hosã$_{F}$ 'I will/must be going'	اساں ویندے پے ہوسوں assã vẽde pe hosũ$_{M}$ اساں ویندیاں پیاں ہوسوں assã vẽdiyã piyã hosũ$_{F}$ 'we will/must be going'
2nd	توں ویندا پیا ہوسیں tũ vẽdā piyā hosẽ$_{M}$ توں ویندی پئی ہوسیں tũ vẽdī paī hosẽ$_{F}$ 'you will/must be going'	تساں ویندے پے ہوسو tussã vẽde pe hoso$_{M}$ تساں ویندیاں پیاں ہوسو tussã vẽdiyã piyã hoso$_{F}$ 'you will/must be going'
3rd	او ویندا پیا ہوسی o vẽdā piyā hosī$_{M}$ 'he will/must be going' او ویندی پئی ہوسی o vẽdī paī hosī$_{F}$ 'she will/must be going'	او ویندے پے ہوسن o vẽde pe hosĕn$_{M}$ او ویندیاں پیاں ہوسن o vẽdiyã piyã hosĕn$_{F}$ 'they will/must be going'

Table 8.106: Future continuous I of ونجݨ /vãʄaṇ/ 'to go'

8.5.6.3.4 Continuous I subjunctive

Formation: imperfective participle + پووݨ/povaṇ/ 'to fall, lie'(perfective participle) + ہووݨ /hovaṇ/ 'to be' (subjunctive)

Table 8.107 shows the continuous I subjunctive forms of ونجݨ /vãʄaṇ/ 'to go'.

Person	Singular	Plural
1st	میں ویندا پیا ہوواں mæ̃ vẽdā piyā hovā̃$_{M}$ میں ویندی پئی ہوواں mæ̃ vẽdī paī hovā̃$_{F}$ 'I may/should be going; if I am going'	اساں ویندے پے ہووُں assā̃ vẽde pe hovū̃$_{M}$ اسّاں ویندیاں پیاں ہووُں assā̃ vẽdiyā̃ piyā̃ hovū̃$_{F}$ 'we may/should be going; if we are going'
2nd	توں ویندا پیا ہوویں tū̃ vẽdā piyā hovẽ$_{M}$ توں ویندی پئی ہوویں tū̃ vẽdī paī hovẽ$_{F}$ 'you may/should be going; if you are going'	تسّاں ویندے پے ہووو tussā̃ vẽdẽ pe hovo$_{M}$ تسّاں ویندیاں پیاں ہووو tussā̃ vẽdiyā̃ piyā̃ hovo$_{F}$ 'you may/should be going; if you are going'
3rd	او ویندا پیا ہووے o vẽdā piyā hove$_{M}$ 'he may/should be going; if he is going' او ویندی پئی ہووے o vẽdī paī hove$_{F}$ 'she may/should be going; if she is going'	او ویندے پے ہووِن o vẽde pe hovĕn$_{M}$ او ویندیاں پیاں ہووِن o vẽdiyā̃ piyā̃ hovĕn$_{F}$ 'they may/should be going; if they are going'

Table 8.107: Continuous I subjunctive of ونجݨ /vãʄaṇ/ 'to go'

8.5.7 Verb forms built on the perfective participle

8.5.7.1 Simple perfect

The simple perfect form is equivalent to the bare perfective participle. It is often translatable as the English simple past; however it is not morphologically marked for tense, and can also refer to events in future or hypothetical time. For intransitive verbs, the perfective participle agrees in gender and number with the subject; for transitives, it agrees in gender and number with an unmarked direct object. This is reflected in the structure of Table 8.108 for the intransitive verb ونجݨ /vãʄaṇ/ 'to go' and Table 8.109, for the transitive verb کرݨ /karaṇ/ 'to do. The perfective participles of both these centrally important verbs are irregular, as they are in Hindko and Panjabi.

Gender of subject	Singular	Plural
Masculine	گیا ɠiyā '(any m.sg. subject) went'	گئے ɠae گۓ ɠæ '(any m.pl. subject) went'
Feminine	گئی ɠaī '(any f.sg. subject) went'	گئیاں ɠaiyā̃ '(any f.pl. subject) went'

Table 8.108: Simple perfect of ونڄݨ /vãʄaṇ/ 'to go'

Gender of direct object	Singular	Plural
Masculine	کیتا kītā '(any subject) did (m.sg. direct object)'	کیتے kīte '(any subject) did (m.pl. direct object)'
Feminine	کیتی kītī '(any subject) did (f.sg. direct object)'	کیتیاں kītiyā̃ '(any subject) did (f.pl. direct object)'

Table 8.109: Simple perfect of کرݨ /karaṇ/ 'to do'

8.5.7.2 Present perfect

Formation: perfective participle + ہووݨ /hovaṇ/ 'to be'(present)

See Table 8.110 and Table 8.111 for the present perfect forms of ونڄݨ /vãʄaṇ/ 'to go' and کرݨ /karaṇ/ 'to do', respectively. As with the present imperfect, these forms are subject to elision, the final vowel of the participle coalescing with the initial vowel of the auxiliary. For example, the following present perfect forms show elision of the short forms of the present auxiliary: کیتا اے /kītā e/ > کیتے /kīte ~kītæ/ (see Shackle 1976: 94). These forms are present perfect in terms of their morphological composition; however, they usually carry the sense of an English simple past tense. Therefore their glosses are given as both English simple pasts and present perfects.

Person	Singular	Plural
1st	میں ڳیاں mæ̃ ɠiyā̃$_M$ میں ڳئی اں mæ̃ ɠaī ā̃$_F$ 'I went/have gone'	اساں ڳئے ایں~ ہیں assā̃ ɠae (h)æ̃$_M$ ~ اسّاں ڳئے ہِسّے assā̃ ɠae hisse$_M$ اساں ڳئیاں ایں~ ہیں assā̃ ɠaiyā̃ (h)æ̃$_F$ ~ اسّاں ڳیاں ہِسّے assā̃ ɠaiyā̃ hisse$_F$ 'we went/have gone'
2nd	توں ڳئیں tū̃ ɠaẽ$_M$ توں ڳئیِں tū̃ ɠaī̃$_F$ ~ ڳئی ایں gaī ẽ$_F$ 'you went/have gone'	تُساں ڳئے او tussā̃ ɠae o$_M$ ~ تسّاں ڳئے ہِوّے tussā̃ ɠae hivve$_M$ تپساں ڳئیاں او tussā̃ ɠaiyā̃ o$_F$ ~ تسّاں ڳیاں ہِوّے tussā̃ ɠaiyā̃ hivve$_F$ 'you went/have gone'
3rd	او ڳئے o ɠae$_M$ 'he went/has gone' او ڳئی اے o ɠaī e$_F$ 'she went/has gone'	او ڳُئین o ɠaen$_M$ او ڳیاں اِن o ɠaiyā̃ ĕn$_F$ 'they went/have gone'

Table 8.110: Present perfect of ونڄڻ /vãʄaṇ/ 'to go'

Table 8.112 presents a set of negative forms for the present perfect of the transitive verb کرڻ /karaṇ/ 'to do' with a masculine singular direct object. These consist of oblique forms of the pronominal suffixes (see Section 6.8.1) added to a negative element originating in NEG + 'be' (present).

39 We are grateful to Ali Hussain Birahimani for this valuable information.

Gender of direct object	Singular	Plural
Masculine	کیتے kīte ~ æ '(any subject) did/has done (m.sg. direct object)'	کیتین kīten '(any subject) did/has done (m.pl. direct object)'
Feminine	کیتی اے kītī e '(any subject) did/has done (f.sg. direct object)'	کیتیں ~ کیتیَں kītiyěn '(any subject) did/has done (f.pl. direct object)'

Table 8.111: Present perfect of کرݨ /karaṇ/ 'to do'

Person	Singular	Plural
1st	نِمّھی کیتا nimmhī kītā 'I have not done (m.sg. object)'	نِسّے کیتا nisse kītā 'We have not done (m.sg. object)'
2nd	نِوھی کیتا nivhī kītā 'you have not done (m.sg. object)'	نِوھے کیتا nivhe kītā 'you (pl.) have not done (m.sg. object)'
3rd	نِسّی کیتا nissī kītā 'she/he has not done (m.sg. object)'	نِنّھے کیتا ninnhe kītā 'they have not done (m.sg. object)''

Table 8.112: Negative forms of present perfect of کرݨ /karaṇ/ 'to do' with oblique pronominal suffixes[39]

Table 8.113 is a paradigm for the present perfect of the transitive verb کرݨ /karaṇ/ 'to do' employing the oblique pronominal suffixes indexing the agent; the object in all the sentences in this paradigm is masculine singular. The use of such forms enables the verb both to be marked for its subject/agent and agree in number and gender with its direct object.[40]

---

40 The second person singular form is obtained as a result of elision from the original kītā heī.

Person	Singular	Plural
1st	کیتیمی ~ کیتم kīte-mī ~ kīte-m 'I did/have done (m.sg. object)'	کیتسے kīte-se 'we did/have done/ (m.sg. object)'
2nd	کیتئی kītĕī 'you (sg.) did/have done (m.sg. object''	کیتیوے kīte-ve 'you (pl.) did/have done (m.sg. object)'
3rd	کیتیسی ~ کیتیس kīte-sī ~ kīte-s 'she/he has done (m.sg. object)'	کیتن kītĕn 'they have done (m.sg. object)'

Table 8.113: Present perfect of کرݨ /karaṇ/ 'to do' with oblique pronominal suffixes

8.5.7.3 Present perfect-stative

Formation: perfective participle + ہووݨ /hovaṇ/ 'to be'(perfective participle), which contributes the stative meaning + ہووݨ /hovaṇ/ 'to be'(present)

Table 8.114 and Table 8.115 give present perfect-stative forms for ونجݨ /vãʄaṇ/ 'to go' and کرݨ /karaṇ/ 'to do', respectively. Notice that the English glosses reflect the meaning of these forms as very close to that of the English present perfect.[41]

If the perfect-stative forms of the transitive verb کرݨ /karaṇ/ 'to do' occur without a subject/agent, they can have a passive-like interpretation, since both forms are perfective participles focusing on a resultant state rather than activity. If a subject/agent appears, it is in its oblique form, and the meaning is close to that of an English present perfect, as in example 8.27.

(8.27) اوں کیتا ہویا اے

ũ̃	*kīt-ā*	*ho-yā*	*e*
3SG.OBL	do.PP-SGM	be-PP.SG.M	be.PRES.3SG

'S/he has done (m.sg. object)' (Sr) (AHB)

Sentences like 8.27, apparently similar to contemporary Panjabi models, occur in urban registers and written Saraiki (Ali Hussain Birahimani, p.c.).[42]

41 Ali Hussain Birahimani (p.c.) thinks that these present-perfect stative forms are a result of Panjabi influence and are characteristic of urban speech.

42 See Section 8.4.6.3 on older forms of perfective statives in Panjabi.

Person	Singular	Plural
1st	میں ڳیا ہویا آں ~ میں ڳیا ہویا ہاں mæ̃ ɠiyā hoyā (h)ā̃$_{M}$~ میں ڳیا ہویاں mæ̃ ɠiyā hoiyā̃$_{M}$ میں ڳئی ہوئی آں mæ̃ ɠaī hoī ā̃$_{F}$ 'I have gone (and remain gone)'	اساں ڳئے ہوئے ایں assā̃ ɠae hoe (h)æ̃$_{M}$ ~ اسّاں ڳئے ہوئے ہِسّے assā̃ ɠae hoe hisse$_{M}$ اساں ڳئے ہویاں ایں assā̃ ɠaiyā̃ hoiyā̃ (h)æ̃$_{F}$ ~ اسّاں ڳیاں ہویاں ہِسّے assā̃ ɠaiyā̃ hoiyā̃ hisse$_{F}$ 'we have gone (and remain gone)'
2nd	توں ڳیا ہویا ایں tū̃ ɠiyā hoyā ẽ$_{M}$ توں ڳئی ہوئی ایں tū̃ ɠaī hoī ẽ$_{F}$ 'you have gone (and remain gone)'	تُساں ڳئے ہوئے او tussā̃ ɠae hoe o$_{M}$ ~ تسّاں ڳئے ہوئے ہِوّے tussā̃ ɠae hoe hivve$_{M}$ تُساں ڳئیاں ہویاں او tussā̃ ɠaiyā̃ hoiyā̃ o$_{F}$ ~ تسّاں ڳیاں ہویاں ہِوّے tussā̃ ɠaiyā̃ hoiyā̃ hivve$_{F}$ 'you have gone (and remain gone)'
3rd	او ڳیا ہویا اے o ɠiyā hoyā e$_{M}$ 'he/it has gone (and remains gone)' او ڳئی ہوئی اے o ɠaī hoī e$_{F}$ 'she/it has gone (and remains gone)'	او ڳئے ہوئے ہِن o ɠae hoe hĕn$_{M}$ او ڳیاں ہویاں ہِن o ɠaiyā̃ hoiyā̃ hĕn$_{F}$ 'they have gone (and remain gone)'

Table 8.114: Present perfect-stative of وَنجݨ /vā̃ʄaṇ/ 'to go'

Gender of direct object	Singular	Plural
Masculine	کیتا ہویا اے kītā hoyā e '(any subject) has done (m.sg. object) (and result remains relevant)'	کیتے ہوئے اِن kīte hoe ĕn '(any subject) has done (m.pl. object) (and result remains relevant)'
Feminine	کیتی ہوئی اے kītī hoī e '(any subject) has done (f.sg. object) (and result remains relevant)'	کیتیاں ہویاں اِن kītiyā̃ hoiyā̃ ĕn '(any subject) has done (f.pl. object) (and result remains relevant)'

Table 8.115: Present perfect-stative of کرݨ /karaṇ/ 'to do'

8.5.7.4 Present perfect-habitual

Formation: perfective participle + ہووݨ /hovaṇ/ 'to be (imperfective participle)' + ہووݨ /hovaṇ/ 'to be'(present)

Table 8.116 and Table 8.117 present the forms and meanings of the present perfect-habitual for ونڄݨ /vãʄaṇ/ 'to go' and کرݨ /karaṇ/ 'to do', respectively.

Person	Singular	Plural
1st	میں ڳیا ہونداں mæ̃ ʄiyā hondā̃$_M$ میں ڳئی ہوندی اں mæ̃ ʄaī hondī ā̃$_F$ 'I am usually gone '	اسّاں ڳئے ہوندے ہئیں assā̃ ʄae honde (h)æ̃$_M$ اسّاں ڳیاں ہوندیاں ہئیں assā̃ ʄaiyā̃ hondiyā̃ æ̃$_F$ 'we are usually gone '
2nd	توں ڳیا ہوندیں tū̃ ʄiyā hondẽ$_M$ توں ڳئی ہوندی ایں tū̃ ʄaī hondī ẽ$_F$ 'you are usually gone '	تسّاں ڳئے ہوندے او tussā̃ ʄae honde o$_M$ تسّاں ڳیاں ہوندیو tussā̃ ʄaiyā̃ hondiyo$_F$ 'you are usually gone '
3rd	او ڳیا ہوندے o ʄiyā honde$_M$ 'he is usually gone ' او ڳئی ہوندی اے o ʄaī hondī e$_F$ 'she is usually gone '	او ڳئے ہوندِن o ʄae hondĕn$_M$ او ڳیاں ہوندی اِن o ʄaiyā̃ hondiyĕn$_F$ 'they are usually gone '

Table 8.116: Present perfect-habitual of ونڄݨ /vãʄaṇ/ 'to go'

Gender of direct object	Singular	Plural
Masculine	کیتا ہوندے kītā honde '(any subject) has usually done (m.sg. object)'	کیتے ہوندِن kīte honděn '(any subject) has usually done (m.pl. object)'
Feminine	کیتی ہوندی اے kītī hondī e '(any subject) has usually done (f.sg. object)'	کیتیاں ہوندی اِن kītiyā̃ hondī ěn '(any subject) has usually done (f.pl. object)'

Table 8.117: Present perfect-habitual of کرݨ /karaṇ/ 'to do'

8.5.7.5 Past perfect

Formation: perfective participle + ہووݨ /hovaṇ/ 'to be'(past)

The past perfect is sometimes elsewhere referred to as the "pluperfect" or the "distant past." It usually corresponds to an English simple past (either distant past, or a past action disconnected in some way from the present), and less frequently to an English past perfect proper. Past perfect forms of ونجݨ /vãȷ̃aṇ/ 'to go' and کرݨ /karaṇ/ 'to do' are given in Table 8.118 and Table 8.119, respectively.

Person	Singular	Plural
1st	میں گیا ہامی mæ̃ ɗīyā hāmī$_{M}$ میں گئی ہامی mæ̃ ɗaī hāmī$_{F}$ 'I went/had gone'	اساں گئے ہاسے assā̃ ɗae hāse$_{M}$ اساں گیاں ہاسے assā̃ ɗaiyā̃ hāse$_{F}$ 'we went/had gone'
2nd	توں گیا ہاویں tū̃ ɗīyā hāvẽ$_{M}$ توں گئی ہاویں tū̃ ɗaī hāvẽ$_{F}$ 'you went/had gone'	تساں گئے ہاوے tussā̃ ɗae hāve$_{M}$ تساں گیاں ہاوے tussā̃ ɗaiyā̃ hāve$_{F}$ 'you went/had gone'
3rd	او گیا ہا o ɗīyā hā$_{M}$ 'he went/had gone' او گئی ہئی o ɗaī haī$_{F}$ 'she went/had gone'	او گئے ہن o ɗae han$_{M}$ او گیاں ہین o ɗaiyā̃ hæn$_{F}$ 'they went/had gone'

Table 8.118: Past perfect of ونجݨ /vãʄaṇ/ 'to go'

Gender of direct object	Singular	Plural
Masculine	کیتا ہا kītā hā '(any subject) did/had done (m.sg. direct object)'	کیتے ہن kīte han '(any subject) did/had done (m.pl. direct object)'
Feminine	کیتی ہئی kītī haī '(any subject) did/had done (f.sg. direct object)'	کیتیاں ہین kītiyā̃ hæn '(any subject) did/had done (f.pl. direct object)'

Table 8.119: Past perfect of کرݨ /karaṇ/ 'to do'

8.5.7.6 Past perfect-stative

Formation: perfective participle + ہووݨ /hovaṇ/ ‘to be ’(perfective participle) + ہووݨ /hovaṇ/ ‘to be’(past)

Past perfect-stative forms of ونجݨ /vãʄaṇ/ ‘to go’ and کرݨ /karaṇ/ ‘to do’ are given in Table 8.120 and Table 8.121, respectively.

Person	Singular	Plural
1st	میں گیا ہویا ہامی mæ̃ ɠiyā hoyā hāmī$_{M}$ میں گئی ہوئی ہامی mæ̃ ɠaī hoī hāmī$_{F}$ ‘I went/had gone (and remained gone); I was gone’	اسّاں گئے ہوئے ہاسے assã̄ ɠae hoe hāse$_{M}$ اسّاں گیاں ہویاں ہاسے assã̄ ɠaiyã̄ hoiyã̄ hāse$_{F}$ ‘we went/had gone (and remained gone); we were gone’
2nd	توں گیا ہویا ہاویں tũ̄ ɠiyā hoyā hāvẽ$_{M}$ توں گئی ہوئی ہاویں tũ̄ ɠaī hoī hāvẽ$_{F}$ ‘you went/had gone (and remained gone); you were gone’	تسّاں گئے ہوئے ہاوے tussã̄ ɠae hoe hāve$_{M}$ تسّاں گیاں ہویاں ہاوے tussã̄ ɠaiyã̄ hoiyã̄ hāve$_{F}$ ‘you went/had gone (and remained gone); you were gone’
3rd	او گیا ہویا ہا o ɠiyā hoyā hā$_{M}$ ‘he went/had gone (and remained gone); he was gone’ او گئی ہوئی ہئی o ɠaī hoī haī$_{F}$ ‘she went/had gone (and remained gone); she was gone’	او گئے ہوئے ہن o ɠae hoe han$_{M}$ او گیاں ہویاں ہین o ɠaiyã̄ hoiyã̄ hæn$_{F}$ ‘they went/had gone (and remained gone); they were gone’

Table 8.120: Past perfect-stative of ونجݨ /vãʄaṇ/ ‘to go’

Gender of direct object	Singular	Plural
Masculine	کیتا ہویا ہا kītā hoyā hā ‘(any subject) did/had done (m.sg. object)’	کیتے ہوئے ہَن kīte hoe han ‘(any subject) did/had done (m.pl. object)’
Feminine	کیتی ہوئی ہئی kītī hoī haī ‘(any subject) did/had done (f.sg. object)’	کیتیاں ہویاں ہین kītiyā̃ hoiyā̃ hæn ‘(any subject) did/had done (f.pl. object)’

Table 8.121: Past perfect-stative of کرݨ /karaṇ/ ‘to do’

8.5.7.7 Past perfect-habitual

Formation: perfective participle + ہووݨ /hovaṇ/ ‘to be’(imperfective participle) + ہووݨ /hovaṇ/ ‘to be’(past)

See Table 8.122 and Table 8.123 for past perfect-habitual forms of ونڄݨ /vãʄaṇ/ ‘to go’ and کرݨ /karaṇ/ ‘to do’, respectively.

Person	Singular	Plural
1st	میں گیا ہوندا ہامی mǣ ɠīyā hondā hāmī$_{M}$ میں گئی ہوندی ہامی mǣ ɠaī hondī hāmī$_{F}$ 'I was usually gone'	اساں گئے ہوندے ہاسے assā̃ ɠae honde hāse$_{M}$ اساں گیاں ہوندیاں ہاسے assā̃ ɠaiyā̃ hondiyā̃ hāse$_{F}$ 'we were usually gone'
2nd	توں گیا ہوندا ہاویں tū̃ ɠīyā hondā hāvẽ$_{M}$ توں گئی ہوندی ہاویں tū̃ ɠaī hondī hāvẽ$_{F}$ 'you were usually gone'	تساں گئے ہوندے ہاوے tussā̃ ɠae honde hāve$_{M}$ تساں گیاں ہوندیاں ہاوے tussā̃ ɠaiyā̃ hondiyā̃ hāve$_{F}$ 'you were usually gone'
3rd	او گیا ہوندا ہا o ɠīyā hondā hā$_{M}$ 'he was usually gone' او گئی ہوندی ہئی o ɠaī hondī haī$_{F}$ 'she was usually gone'	او گئے ہوندے ہن o ɠae honde han$_{M}$ او گیاں ہوندیاں ہین o ɠaiyā̃ hondiyā̃ hæn$_{F}$ 'they were usually gone'

Table 8.122: Past perfect-habitual of ونڄݨ /vāʄaṇ/ 'to go'

Gender of direct object	Singular	Plural
Masculine	کیتا ہوندا ہا kītā hondā hā '(any subject) usually did/had done (m.sg. object)'	کیتے ہوندے ہن kīte honde han '(any subject) usually did/had done (m.pl. object)'
Feminine	کیتی ہوندی ہئی kītī hondī haī '(any subject) usually did/had done (f.sg. object)'	کیتیاں ہوندیاں ہین kītiyā̃ hondiyā̃ hæn '(any subject) usually did/had done (f.pl. object)'

Table 8.123: Past perfect-habitual of کرݨ /karaṇ/ 'to do'

8.5.7.8 Future perfect

Formation: perfective participle + ہووݨ /hovaṇ/ 'to be'(future)

Table 8.124 and Table 8.125 give these forms for وَنجݨ /vāfaṇ/ 'to go' and کرݨ /karaṇ/ 'to do', respectively.

Person	Singular	Plural
1st	میں گیا ہوساں mæ̃ ɠiyā hosā̃$_M$ میں گئی ہوساں mæ̃ ɠaī hosā̃$_F$ 'I will/must have gone'	اساں گئے ہوسوں assā̃ ɠae hosū̃$_M$ اساں گیاں ہوسوں assā̃ ɠaiyā̃ hosū̃$_F$ 'we will/must have gone'
2nd	توں گیا ہوسیں tū̃ ɠiyā hosē̃$_M$ توں گئی ہوسیں tū̃ ɠaī hosē̃$_F$ 'you will/must have gone'	تساں گئے ہوسو tussā̃ ɠae hoso$_M$ تساں گیاں ہوسو tussā̃ ɠaiyā̃ hoso$_F$ 'you will/must have gone'
3rd	او گیا ہوسی o ɠiyā hosī$_M$ 'he will/must have gone' او گئی ہوسی o ɠaī hosī$_F$ 'she will/must have gone'	او گئے ہوسن o ɠae hosĕn$_M$ او گیاں ہوسن o ɠaiyā̃ hosĕn$_F$ 'they will/must have gone'

Table 8.124: Future perfect of وَنجݨ /vāfaṇ/ 'to go'

Gender of direct object	Singular	Plural
Masculine	کیتا ہوسی kītā hosī '(any subject) will/must have done (m.sg. direct object)'	کیتے ہوسن kīte hosĕn '(any subject) will/must have done (m.pl. direct object)'
Feminine	کیتی ہوسی kītī hosī '(any subject) will/must have done (f.sg. direct object)'	کیتیاں ہوسن kītiyā̃ hosĕn '(any subject) will/must have done (f.pl. direct object)'

Table 8.125: Future perfect of کرݨ /karaṇ/ 'to do'

8.5.7.9 Future perfect-stative

Formation: perfective participle + ہووݨ /hovaṇ/ 'to be'(perfective participle) +ہووݨ /hovaṇ/ 'to be '(future)

Paradigms of future perfect-stative forms of ونڄݨ /vãʄaṇ/ 'to go' and کرݨ /karaṇ/ 'to do' appear in Table 8.126 and Table 8.127, respectively.

Person	Singular	Plural
1st	میں ڳیا ہویا ہوساں mæ̃ ɠiyā hoyā hosā̃$_M$ میں ڳئی ہوئی ہوساں mæ̃ ɠaī hoī hosā̃$_F$ 'I will/must have gone (and still be gone)'	اساں ڳئے ہوئے ہوسوں assā̃ ɠae hoe hosū̃$_M$ اساں ڳیاں ہویاں ہوسوں assā̃ ɠaiyā̃ hoiyā̃ hosū̃$_F$ 'we will/must have gone (and still be gone)'
2nd	توں ڳیا ہویا ہوسیں tū̃ ɠiyā hoyā hosẽ$_M$ توں ڳئی ہوئی ہوسیں tū̃ ɠaī hoī hosẽ$_F$ 'you will/must have gone (and still be gone)'	تساں ڳئے ہوئے ہوسو tussā̃ ɠae hoe hoso$_M$ تساں ڳیاں ہویاں ہوسو tussā̃ ɠaiyā̃ hoiyā̃ hoso$_F$ 'you will/must have gone (and still be gone)'
3rd	او ڳیا ہویا ہوسی o ɠiyā hoyā hosī$_M$ 'he will/must have gone (and still be gone)' او ڳئی ہوئی ہوسی o ɠaī hoī hosī$_F$ 'she will/must have gone (and still be gone)'	او ڳئے ہوئے ہوسن o ɠae hoe hosĕn$_M$ او ڳیاں ہویاں ہوسن o ɠaiyā̃ hoiyā̃ hosĕn$_F$ 'they will/must have gone (and still be gone)'

Table 8.126: Future perfect-stative of ونڄݨ /vā̃ʄaṇ/ 'to go'

Gender of direct object	Singular	Plural
Masculine	کیتا ہویا ہوسی kītā hoyā hosī '(any subject) will/must have done (m.sg. object)'	کیتے ہوئے ہوسن kītē hoē hosĕn '(any subject) will/must have done (m.pl. object)'
Feminine	کیتی ہوئی ہوسی kītī hoī hosī '(any subject) will/must have done (f.sg. object)'	کیتیاں ہویاں ہوسن kītiyā̃ hoiyā̃ hosĕn '(any subject) will/must have done (f.pl. object)'

Table 8.127: Future perfect-stative of کرݨ /karaṇ/ 'to do'

8.5.7.10 Perfect subjunctive

Formation: perfective participle + ہووݨ /hovaṇ/ 'to be' (subjunctive)

See Table 8.128 and Table 8.129 for perfect subjunctive forms of ونڄݨ /vãʄaṇ/ 'to go' and کرݨ /karaṇ/ 'to do', respectively.

Person	Singular	Plural
1st	میں گیا ہوواں mæ̃ ɠiyā hovā̃$_{M}$ میں گئی ہوواں mæ̃ ɠaī hovā̃$_{F}$ 'I may have gone; if I have gone'	اساں گئے ہووؤں assā̃ ɠae hovū̃$_{M}$ اساں گیاں ہووؤں assā̃ ɠaiyā̃ hovū̃$_{F}$ 'we may have gone; if we have gone'
2nd	توں گیا ہوویں tū̃ ɠiyā hovẽ$_{M}$ توں گئی ہوویں tū̃ ɠaī hovẽ$_{F}$ 'you may have gone; if you have gone'	تساں گئے ہووو tussā̃ ɠae hovo$_{M}$ تساں گیاں ہووو tussā̃ ɠaiyā̃ hovo$_{F}$ 'you may have gone; if you have gone'
3rd	او گیا ہووے o ɠiyā hove$_{M}$ 'he/it may have gone; if he has gone' او گئی ہووے o ɠaī hove$_{F}$ 'she/it may have gone; if she has gone'	او گئے ہووِن o ɠae hovĕn$_{M}$ او گیاں ہووِن o ɠaiyā̃ hovĕn$_{F}$ 'they may have gone; if they have gone'

Table 8.128: Perfect subjunctive of ونڄݨ /vãʄaṇ/ 'to go'

Gender of direct object	Singular	Plural
Masculine	کیتا ہووے kītā hove '(any subject) may have done; if (any subject) has done (m.sg. direct object)'	کیتے ہوون kīte hověn '(any subject) may have done; if (any subject) has done (m.pl. direct object)'
Feminine	کیتی ہووے kītī hove '(any subject) may have done; if (any subject) has done (f.sg. direct object)'	کیتیاں ہوون kītiyā̃ hověn '(any subject) may have done; if (any subject) has done (f.pl. direct object)'

Table 8.129: Perfect subjunctive of کرݨ /karaṇ/ 'to do'

8.5.7.11 Perfect-stative subjunctive

Formation: perfective participle + ہووݨ /hovaṇ/ 'to be'(perfective participle) + ہووݨ /hovaṇ/ 'to be '(subjunctive)

Perfect-stative subjunctive forms and their glosses are given for ونجݨ /vãɟaṇ/ 'to go' and کرݨ /karaṇ/ 'to do' in Table 8.130 and Table 8.131, respectively.

Person	Singular	Plural
1st	میں ڳیا ہویا ہوواں mæ̃ ɠiyā hoiyā hovā̃$_M$ میں ڳئی ہوئی ہوواں mæ̃ ɠaī hoī hovā̃$_F$ 'I may have gone; if I have gone (and am still gone)'	اسّاں ڳئے ہوئے ہووؤں assā̃ ɠae hoe hovū̃$_M$ اسّاں ڳئیاں ہویاں ہووؤں assā̃ ɠaiyā̃ hoiyā̃ hovū̃$_F$ 'we may have gone; if we are gone (and are still gone)'
2nd	توں ڳیا ہویا ہوویں tū̃ ɠiyā hoiyā hovẽ$_M$ توں ڳئی ہوئی ہوویں tū̃ ɠaī hoī hovẽ$_F$ 'you may have gone; if you have gone (and are still gone)'	تسّاں ڳئے ہوئے ہووو tussā̃ ɠae hoe hovo$_M$ تسّاں ڳئیاں ہویاں ہووو tussā̃ ɠaiyā̃ hoiyā̃ hovo$_F$ 'you may have gone; if you have gone (and are still gone)'
3rd	او ڳیا ہویا ہووے o ɠiyā hoiyā hove$_M$ 'he may have gone; if he has gone (and is still gone)' او ڳئی ہوئی ہووے o ɠaī hoī hove$_F$ 'she may have gone; if she has gone (and is still gone)'	او ڳئے ہوئے ہوون o ɠae hoe hovĕn$_M$ او ڳئیاں ہویاں ہوون o ɠaiyā̃ hoiyā̃ hovĕn$_F$ 'they may have gone; if they have gone (and are still gone)'

Table 8.130: Perfect-stative subjunctive of وڄݨ /vãʄaṇ/ 'to go'

Gender of direct object	Singular	Plural
Masculine	کیتا ہویا ہووے kītā hoiyā hove ‘(any subject) may have done (m.sg. object); if (any subject) has done (m.sg. object)’	کیتے ہوئے ہووِن kīte hoe hovĕn ‘(any subject) may have done (m.pl. object); if (any subject) has done (m.pl. object)’
Feminine	کیتی ہوئی ہووے kītī hoī hove ‘(any subject) may have done (f.sg. object); if (any subject) has done (f.sg. object)’	کیتیاں ہویاں ہووِن kītiyā̃ hoiyā̃ hovĕn ‘(any subject) may have done (f.pl. object); if (any subject) has done (f.pl. object)’

Table 8.131: Perfect-stative subjunctive of کرݨ /karaṇ/ ‘to do’

8.5.7.12 Perfect irrealis I

Formation: perfective participle + ہووݨ /hovaṇ/ 'to be'(subjunctive) + the invariant form ہا /hā/

Table 8.132 and Table 8.133 give these forms for ونڄݨ /vãʄaṇ/ 'to go' and کرݨ /karaṇ/ 'to do', respectively.

Person	Singular	Plural
1st	میں ڳیا ہوواں ہا mæ̃ ʄiyā hovā̃ hā$_{M}$ میں ڳئی ہوواں ہا mæ̃ ʄaī hovā̃ hā$_{F}$ 'if I had gone'	اساں ڳئے ہووُں ہا assā̃ ʄae hovū̃ hā$_{M}$ اساں ڳیاں ہووُں ہا assā̃ ʄaiyā̃ hovū̃ hā$_{F}$ 'if we had gone'
2nd	توں ڳیا ہوویں ہا tū̃ ʄiyā hovẽ hā$_{M}$ توں ڳئی ہوویں ہا tū̃ ʄaī hovẽ hā$_{F}$ 'if you had gone'	تساں ڳئے ہووو ہا tussā̃ ʄae hovo hā$_{M}$ تساں ڳیاں ہووو ہا tussā̃ ʄaiyā̃ hovo hā$_{F}$ 'if you had gone'
3rd	او ڳیا ہووے ہا o ʄiyā hove hā$_{M}$ 'if he/it had gone' او ڳئی ہووے ہا o ʄaī hove hā$_{F}$ 'if she/it had gone'	او ڳئے ہووِن ہا o ʄae hovĕn hā$_{M}$ او ڳیاں ہووِن ہا o ʄaiyā̃ hovĕn hā$_{F}$ 'if they had gone'

Table 8.132: Perfect irrealis I of ونڄݨ /vãʄaṇ/ 'to go'

Gender of direct object	Singular	Plural
Masculine	کیتا ہووے ہا kītā hove hā 'if (any subject) had done (m.sg. direct object)'	کیتے ہوون ہا kīte hovĕn hā 'if (any subject) had done (m.pl. direct object)'
Feminine	کیتی ہووے ہا kītī hove hā 'if (any subject) had done (f.sg. direct object)'	کیتیاں ہوون ہا kītiyā̃ hovĕn hā 'if (any subject) had done (f.pl. direct object)'

Table 8.133: Perfect irrealis I of کرݨ /karaṇ/ 'to do'

8.5.7.13 Perfect-stative irrealis I

Formation: perfective participle + ہووݨ /hovaṇ/ 'to be' (perfective participle) + ہووݨ /hovaṇ/ 'to be' (subjunctive) + invariant ہا /hā/

These forms for ونڄݨ /vãʄaṇ/ 'to go' and کرݨ /karaṇ/ 'to do' are given in Table 8.134 and Table 8.135, respectively.

Person	Singular	Plural
1st	میں گیا ہویا ہوواں ہا mæ̃ ɠiyā hoiyā hovā̃ hā$_M$ میں گئی ہوئی ہوواں ہا mæ̃ ɠaī hoī hovā̃ hā$_F$ 'if I had been gone'	اساں گئے ہوئے ہووؤں ہا assā̃ ɠae hoe hovū̃ hā$_M$ اساں گیاں ہویاں ہووؤں ہا assā̃ ɠaiyā̃ hoiyā̃ hovū̃ hā$_F$ 'if we had been gone'
2nd	توں گیا ہویا ہوویں ہا tū̃ ɠiyā hoiyā hovẽ hā$_M$ توں گئی ہوئی ہوویں ہا tū̃ ɠaī hoī hovẽ hā$_F$ 'if you had been gone'	تساں گئے ہوئے ہووو ہا tussā̃ ɠae hoe hovo hā$_M$ تساں گیاں ہویاں ہووو ہا tussā̃ ɠaiyā̃ hoiyā̃ hovo hā$_F$ 'if you had been gone'
3rd	او گیا ہویا ہووے ہا o ɠiyā hoiyā hove hā$_M$ 'if he had been gone' او گئی ہوئی ہووے ہا o ɠaī hoī hove hā$_F$ 'if she had been gone'	او گئے ہوئے ہوون ہا o ɠae hoe hovĕn hā$_M$ او گیاں ہویاں ہوون ہا o ɠaiyā̃ hoiyā̃ hovĕn hā$_F$ 'if they had been gone'

Table 8.134: Perfect-stative irrealis I of ونجݨ /vãɟaṇ/ 'to go'

Gender of direct object	Singular	Plural
Masculine	کیتا ہویا ہووے ہا kītā hoyā hove hā 'if (any subject) had done (m.sg. object)'	کیتے ہوئے ہوون ہا kīte hoe hovĕn hā 'if (any subject) had done (m.pl. object)'
Feminine	کیتی ہوئی ہووے ہا kītī hoī hove hā 'if (any subject) had done (f.sg. object)'	کیتیاں ہویاں ہوون ہا kītiyā̃ hoiyā̃ hovĕn hā 'if (any subject) had done (f.pl. object)'

Table 8.135: Perfect-stative irrealis I of کرݨ /karaṇ/ 'to do'

9 Sentential syntax

9.1 Simple sentences

This chapter deals first with basic patterns of syntax in the simple sentence: word order, agreement patterns, subject/agent marking and the matter of grammatical and semantic subjects, object marking, the split ergative alignment pattern, negation, and questions. Then it considers compound sentences consisting of conjoined simple sentences, and finally various types of complex sentences consisting of a matrix clause and embedded clauses of various types. Unless otherwise stated, the patterns discussed here apply to all three languages. As far as has been possible, examples from all three languages are given. For Hindko and Saraiki elided present tense verb forms, we gloss elided verb forms as [Participle+be.PRES.3SG], as in 9.3.

For examples cited from works which do not use Perso-Arabic script representations, e.g. Shackle (1976) Shackle (1970), Bhatia (1993), and Bailey (1904b), the Perso-Arabic representations are due to the present authors. For sources which include Perso-Arabic representations, e.g. websites, Bashir and Kazmi (2012), and our Hindko and Saraiki colleagues, the Perso-Arabic spellings are mostly as given in those sources. For sources which do not give English translations, the translations are due to the present authors. If we have abridged or modified an example from its source, this is indicated by "adapted from (author date: page number)".

9.1.1 Word order

9.1.1.1 Default word order in simple sentences

The default word order is S(ubject) O(bject) V(erb). Typologically consistent with this are default Adjective-Noun and Noun-Postposition order. Word order is, however, quite free, and topicalization and focus-marking are usually achieved by manipulation of word order, with sentence-initial position occupied by the TOPIC (old information) and pre-verbal position by FOCUSED (new) information.

There are three types of simple declarative sentences: intransitive, transitive, and ditransitive. In intransitive sentences, with only one nominal argument (the subject), the neutral order of constituents is SV, as shown in examples 9.1, 9.2, and 9.3. Pronominal arguments are indicated by inflectional endings, as in examples 9.4 and 9.5.

(9.1) کُئی پھیڈ نئیں مری

kuī pèḍ nī̃ mar-ī
any sheep[F] NEG die-PP.SG.F
'No sheep died.' (Hk) (AWT)

https://doi.org/10.1515/9781614512257-009

(9.2) اوہ جاویگا

ó	*jā-ve-g-ā*
3SG.DIST	go-SBJV.3SG-FUT-SG.M

'He will go.' (Pj) (EB)

(9.3) دریا دا پانڑی لہہ گے

daryā	*d-ā*	*pāṇī*	*lah*	*ɠ-e*
river	GEN-SG.M	water.SG.M	come.down	go.PP-SG.M.+be.PRES.3SG

'The river has subsided.' (Sr) (Zahoor 2009: 70)

(9.4) میرے نال چلوگے

mer-e	*nāḷ*	*cal-o-g-e*
1SG.GEN-SG.M.OBL	with	come/go-2PL-FUT-PL.M

'Will you come/go with me?' (Pj) (EB)

(9.5) آہو چلانگا

āho	*cal-ā̃-g-ā*
yes	come/go-1SG-FUT-SG.M

'Yes, I (M) will (go with you).' (Pj) (EB)

Transitive sentences, such as in 9.6, 9.7, and 9.8, have both a subject and an object, and display canonical SOV word order. In example 9.8, the pronominal subject is indicated by the third person plural inflectional ending.

(9.6) مسعود سوٹی تروڑی

masūd	*soṭī*	*troṛ-ī*
Masud	stick[F]	break-PP.SG.F

'Masud broke the stick.' (Hk) (AWT)

(9.7) میں کپڑے دھوتے

mæ̃	*kapṛe*	*tò-t-e*
1SG.DIR/OBL	clothes.PL.M.DIR	wash-PP-PL.M

'I washed (the) clothes.' (Pj) (EB)

(9.8) کیا او تہاکوں تنگ کریندن

kyā	*o*	*tuhā-kũ*	*tang*	*karẽd-ĕn*
Q	3PL.DIR	2PL.OBL-ACC	teasing	do.IP-PRES.3PL

'Do they tease you?' (Sr) (Zahoor 2009: 70)

A ditransitive sentence has a subject, a direct object, and an indirect object, as in 9.9, where 'we' is the subject, 'money' is the direct object, and 'some poor people' is the indirect object. In ditransitive sentences, the neutral word order is SIOV, where I represents the indirect object, as shown in examples 9.9, 9.10, and 9.11. Notice that while the sentence in 9.9 is structurally a past perfect, its natural English translation is as a simple past. The Saraiki sentence in 9.11 exemplifies the use of the third person singular pronominal suffix سی /sī/ to indicate the agent, 'she, he'.

(9.9) اساں کجھ غریب لوکاں آں پیسے دتے ایہے

assã̄	*kuj*	*yarīb*	*lok-ã̄*	*ã̄*	*pæse*	*di-tt-e*
1PL.OBL	some	poor	people-OBL	DAT	money.PL.M	give-PP-PL.M

éy-e
be.PST-PL.M

'We gave money to some poor people.' (Hk) (AWT)

(9.10) اوہ نے سانوں دو کتاباں دتیاں

ó	*ne*	*sa-nũ*	*do*	*katāb-ã̄*	*di-tt-iyã̄*
3SG	ERG	1PL.OBL-DAT	two	book-PL.F	give-PP-PL.F

'She/he gave us two books.' (Pj) (EB)

(9.11) میکوں نواں چولا ڈتیسی

mæ-kũ	*nav-ã̄*	*colā*	*ɗi-te-sī*
1SG.OBL-DAT	new-SG.M	shirt.SG.M	give-PP.SG.M+be.PRES-PS3SG

'He/she has given/gave me a new shirt.'[1] (Sr) (UK)

Auxiliaries, modals, and light verbs follow the main verb, which provides the core semantic content. When the verbal complex includes multiple elements, the order is:

1 According to Shackle (1976: 101), the third person singular oblique pronominal suffix is /-s/. The /-ī/ in /-sī/ here may be euphonic, or it may be a dialectal variant.

main verb - light verb - modal/aspectual marker - tensed auxiliary. Example 9.12 illustrates both the general order of constituents and patterns of agreement in a Panjabi clause. In this example, the subject 'their two daughters' precedes the object 'the family meal', which in turn precedes the verbal complex 'were preparing', demonstrating SOV order. It further demonstrates head nouns such as 'daughters' preceded by adjectives like 'both', genitive elements like اوہناں /ónã̄/ 'their' followed by the postpositions like دیاں /diyã̄/ 'of', the pattern of modifier agreement, and verbal agreement, where the verbal complex agrees with the feminine plural subject دھیاں /tìyã̄/ 'daughters'.

(9.12) ہیٹھاں رسوئی وچ اوہناں دیاں دوویں دھیاں گھر دی روٹی خوشی خوشی تیار کر رہیاں سن

heṭhã̄	*rasoī*	*vic*	*ón-ã̄*	*d-iyã̄*	*dovẽ*	*tìy-ã̄*	*kàr*
below	kitchen	in	3PL-OBL	GEN-PL.F	both	daughter-PL.F	house

d-ī	*roṭī*	*xušī*	*xušī*	*tyār*	*kar*	*ra-íyã̄*
GEN-SG.F	bread[F]	happiness	happiness	ready	do	CONT.II-PL.F

san
be.PST.3PL

'Downstairs in the kitchen, their two daughters were happily preparing the family meal.' (Pj) (Shackle 2003: 611)

9.1.1.1.1 Scrambling

The preceding discussion deals with the basic neutral, or unmarked, word order of constituents within a clause. As noted, however, elements within a clause can appear in other positions. Manipulation of a relatively free word order is sometimes referred to as scrambling. For example, it is possible for the subject of a clause to appear at the end, rather than at the beginning, of a sentence, as in example 9.13. This functions to highlight different aspects of discourse-relevant information, such as emphasizing old or new information, or to background or foreground certain information.

(9.13) سارا کم خراب کیتا اے - اوس الو دے پٹھے نے

sār-ā	*kamm*	*xarāb*	*kī-t-ā*	*e*	***os***
all-SG.M	work.SG.M	spoiled	do-PP-SG.M	be.PRES.3SG	**3SG.DIST.OBL**

ullū	***d-e***	***paṭṭh-e***	***ne***
owl	**GEN-SG.M.OBL**	**disciple-SG.M.OBL**	**ERG**

'He has ruined everything – **that idiot!**' (Pj) (EB)

9.1.1.1.2 Cleft constructions

Clefts are another construction involving non-canonical word order that are used to highlight or focus information. In English, cleft constructions are generally translated with an equivalent of, 'It is X that/who V'. In Panjabi, a cleft construction is formed by placing the focused element of the clause in initial position, optionally followed by the emphatic particle ای /ī/, and then by a relative clause. The clefted element can vary; in example 9.14 it is the subject, and in example 9.15 it is the object.

(9.14) تارا سنگھ ای سی جھنے پنجابی صوبہ منگیا

tārā	***síŋ***	***ī***	*sī*	*jí-ne*	*panjābī*	*sūbā*
Tara	**Singh**	**EMPH**	be.PST.3SG	REL.OBL-ERG	Panjabi	province[M]

maŋ-iyā
demand-PP.SG.M

'It was **Tara Singh** who advocated for a Panjabi Province.' (Pj) (Adapted from Bhatia (1993: 155))

(9.15) پنجابی صوبہ ای سی جو تارا سنگ نے منگیا

panjābī	***sūbā***	*ī*	*sī*	*jo*	*tārā*	*síŋ*	*ne*
Panjabi	**province**[M]	EMPH	be.PST.3SG	REL.DIR	Tara	Singh	ERG

maŋ-iyā
demand-PP.SG.M

'It was a **Panjabi Province** that Tara Singh demanded.' (Pj) (Adapted from Bhatia (1993: 155))

9.1.1.2 Word order in the noun phrase

A noun phrase consists of a head noun and its modifiers: adjectives (including participial relative clauses) , possessives, quantifiers, and determiners. Minimally, a noun phrase consists of a bare noun or pronoun. The basic word order in a noun phrase is: possessive adjective > genitive phrase > determiner > quantifier > attributive adjective(s) > head noun, as in example 9.16. Like other adjectival modifiers, participial relative clauses precede the noun they modify. These statements hold for all three languages. The noun phrases in examples 9.16, 9.17, and 9.18 are bracketed.

(9.16) میریاں ایہہ دو نویاں کتاباں

[mer-iyā̃	*é*	*do*	*nav-iyā̃*	*kitab-ā̃]*
1SG.GEN-PL.F	these	two	new-PL.F	book-PL.F

'[these two new books of mine]' (Pj) (EB)

(9.17) پشتو صوبہ سرحد دی ہک بڈی تے اہم زبان اے

pašto *[sūbā* *sarhad* *d-ī* *hik* *baḍ-ī* *te* *ǽm*
Pashto province frontier GEN-SG.F one big-F and important

zabān] *e*
language[F] be.PRES.3SG

'Pashto is [a big and important language of the Frontier Province].'[2] (Hk) (Soz 2009: 6)

(9.18) میکوں ہر قسم دے کڈھائی آلے کپڑے بہوں پسند آندن

mæ-kũ *[har* *kisam* *d-e* *kaḍhaī* *āl-e*
1SG.OBL-DAT each kind GEN-PL.M embroidery NMLZ-PL.M

kapṛe] *baũ̄* *pasand* *ā-nd-ĕn*
clothes.PL.M very pleasing come-IP-PRES.3PL

'I like [all kinds of embroidered clothes].' (Sr) (Zahoor 2009: 49)

There are no definite or indefinite articles in Hindko, Panjabi, or Saraiki, but the numeral اک /ikk/ (Pj) or ہک /hik(k)/ (Hk Sr) 'one' indicates specific indefinites, as shown in example 9.17, while the indefinite pronoun کوئی /koī/ 'some' indicates non-specific indefinites, as in example 9.19. These elements fall in the quantifier slot. Some quantifiers, such as سبھ /sáb/ 'all', optionally follow the head noun, especially when the head is a pronoun. Discourse particles such as ای /ī/ 'only' and وی /vī/ 'also' obligatorily follow the element they emphasize.

(9.19) کوئی بندہ آیا اے

koī *bandā* *ā-yā* *e*
a/some man come-PP.SG.M be.PRES.3SG

'**A/some** (unknown) man has come.' (Pj) (EB)

2 The former North West Frontier Province is now named Khyber Pakhtunkhwa.

9.1.1.3 Status of the existential verb and copula

In affirmative equational sentences of the form x = y, and in present tense existential sentences, the copula is obligatory in these languages. For example, 9.20 is a good sentence, but 9.21, lacking the copula, is not.

(9.20) میرا بھرا ڈاکٹر اے

mer-ā	*prā̀*	*ḍākṭar*	***e***
1SG.GEN-SG.M	brother.M	doctor	**be.PRES.3SG**

'My brother **is** a doctor.' (Pj) (EB)

(9.21) *میرا بھرا ڈاکٹر

**mer-ā*	*prā̀*	*ḍākṭar*
1SG.GEN-SG.M	brother.M	doctor

'*My brother **is** a doctor.' (Pj) (EB)

Similarly, 9.22 affirming the existence of 'my brother' in a specific location in example is good, but not example 9.23, which lacks the verb 'be'.

(9.22) میرا بھرا گھر اے

mer-ā	*prā̀*	*kàr*	***e***
1SG.GEN-SG.M	brother[M]	home.OBL	**be.PRES.3SG**

'My brother **is** at home.' (Pj) (EB)

(9.23) *میرا بھرا گھر

**mer-ā*	*prā̀*	*kàr*
1SG.GEN-SG.M	brother[M]	home.OBL

'*My brother **is** at home.' (Pj) (EB)

In negative present-tense sentences involving the verb 'be', however, the present tense form of 'be' is normally not present, as in example 9.24. This is because the negative form نئیں /naī̃/ 'is not' already etymologically includes a present-tense form of 'be'.

(9.24) میرا بھرا ڈاکٹر نہیں

mer-ā	*prā̀*	*ḍākṭar*	***naī̃***
1SG.GEN-SG.M	brother[M]	doctor	**NEG**

'My brother **is not** a doctor.' (Pj) (EB)

However, in negative sentences including the past tense of ہونا /hoṇā/ 'be' the form of 'be' cannot be omitted, since to do so would lose tense marking. In such cases, one must use a sentence such as that in 9.25.

(9.25) میرا بھرا ڈاکٹر نہیں سی

mer-ā	*prā̀*	*ḍākṭar*	***naī̃***	***sī***
1SG.GEN-SG.M	brother[M]	doctor	**NEG**	**be.PST.3SG**

'My brother **was not** a doctor.' (Pj) (EB)

9.1.1.4 Omission of subject and object pronouns

9.1.1.4.1 Subject marked on verb

All three of these languages are what are sometimes called "pro-drop languages". This means that either object or subject pronouns can be omitted when they are indicated by inflectional endings, or, given the right context, even when they are not indicated by inflectional endings. Since the subject of a sentence is often clear by virtue of verbal agreement on a tense-aspect form, when the subject is a pronoun it is not usually represented by an independent, full pronoun. For example, in all three languages the subject is marked on the verb in the future/presumptive form, and an independent subject pronoun is thus often omitted. This is shown in examples 9.26, 9.27, and 9.28.[3]

(9.26) جلساں

jul-s-ā̃
go-FUT-1SG
'I will go.' (Hk) (AWT)

(9.27) جاواں گا

jā-vā̃-g-ā
go-1SG-FUT-SG.M
'I (M) will go.' (Pj) (EB)

3 In 9.28, the pronunciation with /e/ is characteristic of UK's speech; that with /æ/ is more characteristic of the "big city" language of Multan.

(9.28) ویساں

ve-s-ã̄	~	*væ-s-ã̄*
go-FUT-1SG	~	go-FUT-1SG

'I will go.' (Sr) (UK)

In perfective tenses of transitive verbs in Hindko and Panjabi, however, the subject is not marked on the verb, so unless it is unambiguously recoverable from context, it is usually indicated by an independent pronoun, as in examples 9.29 and 9.30.

(9.29) اُنھاں روٹی کھادی

ún-ã̄	*roṭī*	*khā́-d-ī*
3PL.DIST-OBL	bread[F]	eat-PP-SG.F

'They (M or F) ate bread/food.' (Hk) (AWT)

(9.30) میں امب کھادھا

mæ̃	*amb*	*khā́-d-ā*
1SG	mango[M]	eat-PP-SG.M

'I (M or F) ate a mango.' (Pj) (EB)

The case in Saraiki, however, is different for perfective transitive sentences. Saraiki often makes use of pronominal suffixes to mark the subject on the verb of such sentences, as in example 9.31. In 9.31 the verb indexes the first person singular subject 'I'. Notice that in this sentence an independent subject pronoun is absent.

(9.31) ٹکر کھادے می

ṭukur	*khā-d-e-mī*
bread[M]	eat-PP-SG.M+be.PRES.3SG-PS.1SG

'I ate/have eaten bread/food.' (Sr) (UK)

9.1.1.4.2 Omission of repeated identical subjects, objects, or verbs

When the subject continues in two or more successive clauses and is clear from discourse, it is usually not repeated. Consider the question in example 9.32, to which the sentence in 9.33 provides a natural response. Since both the subject and the object are unambiguously recoverable from the immediate context, full pronouns are not needed for either subject or object, and are therefore omitted.

(9.32) توں بچیاں نوں روٹی دتی اے

tū̃	*bacĕ-ā̃*	*nū̃*	*roṭī*	*di-tt-ī*	*e*
2SG	children-OBL	DAT	bread/food.F	give-PP-SG.F	be.PRES.3SG

'Have you given the children food?' (Pj) (EB)

(9.33) آہو دتی اے

āho	*di-tt-ī*	*e*
yes	give-PP-SG.F	be.PRES.3SG

'Yes (I) have given (it).' (Pj) (EB)

If the subject and verb of two coordinated clauses are identical, either the first or the second occurrence of either the verb or the subject, or even both, may be omitted. This is shown in example 9.34, where both grammatical and semantic subject (i.e. the grammatical subject 'life' and the semantic subject 'I'), as well as the verb 'like' are the same in both clauses. Neither the grammatical subject nor the verb are repeated in the second conjunct.

(9.34) مینوں پنڈ دی زندگی پسند اے پر میرے بھرا نوں شہر دی

mæ-nū̃	*pinḍ*	*d-ī*	*zindagī*	*pasand*	*e*	*par*
1SG.OBL-DAT	village	GEN-SG.F	life[F]	pleasing	be.PRES.3SG	but

mer-e	*prā̀*	*nū̃*	*šǽr*	*d-ī*
1SG.GEN-M.SG.OBL	brother.M.OBL	DAT	city	GEN-SG.F

'I like village life, but my brother [likes] city [life].' (Pj) (EB, modeled on Bhatia (1993: 115).)

However, if both formal and semantic identity are not present, this does not happen. Thus a sentence like that in 9.35, in which the first conjunct is a dative subject construction but the second is not, is not well formed.

(9.35) * مینوں پنڈ دی زندگی پسند اے پر میرا بھرا شہر دی

mæ-nũ̃	*pinḍ*	*d-ī*	*zindagī*	*pasand*	*e*	*par*
1SG-DAT	village	GEN-SG.F	life.SG.F	pleasing	be.PRES.3SG	but

mer-ā	*prà̃*	*šǽr*	*d-ī*
1SG.GEN-M.SG.DIR	brother.M.SG.DIR	city	GEN-SG.F

'*I like village life, but my brother [likes] city [life].' (Pj) (EB, modeled on Bhatia (1993: 115).)

9.1.2 Agreement

9.1.2.1 Adjective agreement

Adjectival modifiers, whether single word or phrasal, agree with the nouns they modify in number, gender, and case. This agreement is not always evident, because many nouns and adjectives in all three languages belong to the unmarked, invariant classes. (See Section 4.3 and Section 5.1.1.6.)

9.1.2.2 Verb agreement: split ergativity

All three languages have a split ergative alignment system. In such a system, intransitive verbs and imperfective tenses of transitive verbs pattern together, while perfective tenses of transitive verbs are treated differently. There are two aspects of this split ergativity: verb agreement, and subject/agent marking.

The verb maximally agrees with the grammatical subject in person, number, and gender with all intransitive verbs, as shown in 9.36 and 9.37, and with transitive verbs in imperfective tenses, as shown in 9.38.

(9.36) ایہہ میری تہیو دی کتاب اے

é	*mer-ī*	*tì̃-ū*	*d-ī*	*kitāb*
3SG.PROX	1SG.GEN-SG.F	daughter-OBL	GEN-SG.F	book[F]

e
be.PRES.3SG

'**This is** my daughter's book.' (Hk) (AWT)

(9.37) اسی سبھ فیکٹری وچ کم کردے آں

asī	*sâb*	*fækṭrī*	*vic*	*kamm*	***kar-d-e***	***ã̄***
1PL	all	factory	in	work	**do-IP-PL.M**	**be.PRES.1PL**

'**We (m)** all **work** in a/the factory.' (Pj) (EB)

(9.38) تُہاڈے والد صاحب کیا کریندِن

tuāḍe	*vālid.sāhib*	*kyā*	***kar-e-nd-e-n***
your.PL.M	father	what	**do-PF-IP-PL.M-PRES.3PL**

'What does your father do?' (Sr) (Zahoor 2009: 40)

Perfective forms of transitive verbs agree with a direct object that is not marked with the accusative postposition. The following sections show perfective transitive verb agreement in Hindko, Panjabi, and Saraiki.

Verb agreement in simple perfect forms of the transitive verb 'eat' is provided in examples 9.39 through 9.42. The verb agrees in number and gender with unmarked feminine singular in 9.39, feminine plural in 9.40, masculine singular in 9.41, and masculine plural direct objects in 9.42. Notice that the subjects/agents of these perfective forms of transitive verbs appear in their oblique form.

(9.39) میں روٹی کھادی

mæ̃	*roṭī*	*khā́-d-**ī***
1SG.OBL	bread.**SG.F**	eat-PP-**SG.F**

'I ate bread/a meal.' (Hk) (AWT)

(9.40) میں دو روٹیاں کھادیاں

mæ̃	*do*	*roṭi-ã̄*	*khā́-d-**iyã̄***
1SG.OBL	two	bread-**PL.F**	eat-PP-**PL.F**

'I ate two breads.' (Hk) (AWT)

(9.41) تُد ہِک ام کھادا

tud	*hik*	*am*	*khā́-d-**ā***
2SG.OBL	one	mango.**SG.M**	eat-PP-**SG.M**

'You ate one mango.' (Hk) (AWT)

(9.42) تُد دو ام کھادے

tud	*do*	*am*	*khā́-d-**e***
2SG.OBL	two	mango.**PL.M**	eat-PP-**PL.M**

'You ate two mangoes.' (Hk) (AWT)

Verb agreement in Panjabi behaves in the same way as it does in Hindko, as shown in examples 9.43 and 9.44.

(9.43) میں دو امب کھادے

mæ̃	*do*	*amb*	*khā́-d-**e***
1SG.OBL	two	mango-**PL.M**	eat-PP-**PL.M**

'I ate two mangoes.' (Pj) (EB)

(9.44) اوہ نے میرا کم کر دتا

ó	*ne*	*mer-ā*	*kamm*	*kar*	*di-tt-**ā***
3SG.OBL	ERG	1SG.GEN-SG.M	work.**SG.M**	do	give-PP-**SG.M**

'S/he did my work/task [i.e. did a task for me].' (Pj) (EB)

Saraiki's verbal agreement pattern is like that of Hindko and Panjabi. This is shown in examples 9.45, 9.46, and 9.47.

(9.45) اگلی رات میں عجیب خاب ڈِٹھے

aɠalī	*rāt*	*mæ̃*	*ajīb*	*xāb*
preceding	night	1SG.DIR/OBL	strange	dream**[M]**

ɗī-ṭh-e
see-PP-**SG.M**+be.PRES.**3SG**

'Last night I had a strange dream.'[4] (Sr) (UK)

(9.46) اوں میکوں چٹھی ڈِتی

ũ̄	*mæ-kũ̄*	*ciṭṭhī*	*ɗī-tt-**ī***
3SG.OBL	1SG.DIR/OBL-DAT	letter**[F]**	give-PP-**SG.F**

'He gave me a letter.' (Sr) (UK)

4 This sentence can also be expressed with the first person singular pronominal suffix expressing the agent, as: /aɠalī rāt ajīb xāb ɗī-ṭh-e-mi/.

(9.47) چوکیدار کوں چور کھوپیا ہا

cokidār-kū̃ *cor* *khop-iy**ā*** ***hā***
watchman-ACC thief stab-PP.**SG.M** be.PST.**SG.M**
'A thief stabbed the watchman.' (Sr) (UK)

In example 9.47 the verb shows default masculine singular agreement because of the accusative marked direct object 'watchman'. Contrastive stress on چور /cor/ 'thief', as the new information, produces an emphasis similar to that of a cleft construction (see Section 9.1.1.1.2), but without the extra syntactic mechanism.

In Saraiki, an additional pattern is available, which uses pronominal suffixes to index the agent on the verb, as in example 9.48. If there is also an unmarked direct object, the verb agrees with the direct object in number and gender, and the agent is indexed on the verb. Compare examples 9.48 and 9.49; in 9.48, the verb agrees with the feminine singular direct object 'bread', and in 9.49, the verb agrees with the masculine singular direct object 'egg'. In both sentences, though, a third person singular agent is indexed on the verb with the third person singular pronominal suffix /-s/.

(9.48) روٹی کھادیئس

roṭī *khā-d-**ī**-e-**s***
bread**[F]** eat-PP-**SG.F**-be.PRES.3SG-**PS3SG**
'He/she has eaten bread/a meal.' (Sr) (UK)

(9.49) انڈا کھادیئس

anḍā *khā-d-e-**s***
egg**[M]** eat-PP-**SG.M**+be.PRES.3SG-**PS3SG**
'He/she ate an egg.'[5] (Sr) (UK)

If the direct object is marked by the accusative postposition—آں /ā̃/ (Hk), نوں /nū̃/ (Pj), کوں /kū̃/ (Sr)– the verb appears in the default masculine singular form. In example 9.50 the direct object (little boys) is masculine plural; in 9.51, the direct objects are feminine singular (daughter-in-law) and plural (little girls); and in 9.52, the direct object (that matter) is feminine singular; however, the verb is default masculine singular in all these sentences.

5 UK's sentence has انڈا /anḍā/, the Urdu word for 'egg'. Zahoor (2009: 28) has آنہا /ānhā/, while NAS has آنا /ānā/.

(9.50) لمیاں جاتکاں ساریاں نکیاں جاتکاں آں ہرایا

lamm-e-ã̄ *jātk-ã̄* *sār-e-ã̄* *nikk-e-ã̄*
tall-PL.M-OBL.PL boy-OBL.PL all-PL.M-OBL.PL little-PL.M-OBL.PL

jātk-ã̄ ***ã̄*** *harā-**yā***
boy-OBL.PL **ACC** defeat-**PP.SG.M**

'The tall boys defeated all the little boys.' (Hk) (AWT)

(9.51) ڈاکوواں نے اوہدی بہو تے تن بالڑیاں نوں فائرنگ کر کے مار دتا

ḍākū-vã̄ *ne* *ó-d-ī* ***báū*** *te* *tin*
robber-OBL.PL ERG 3SG.OBL-GEN-SG.F **daughter.in.law** and three

bālaṛi-yã̄ ***nū̃*** *fāiring* *kar* *ke* *mār* *di-tt-**ā***
little.girl-OBL.PL **ACC** firing do CP kill give-PP-**SG.M**

'The robbers fired and killed his daughter-in-law and three young girls.' (Pj) (Bashir and Kazmi 2012: 520)

(9.52) اوں دیاں اکھیں اوں ڳالھ کوں کھول تے بیان کر ڈِتا

ū̃ *d-iyã̄* *akh-ī̃* *ū̃* ***ɠālh*** ***kū̃*** *khol* *te*
3SG.OBL GEN-PL.F eye[F]-OBL.PL 3SG.OBL **matter[F]** **ACC** open CP

biyān *kar* *ɗi-tt-**ā***
explanation do give-PP-**SG.M**

'Her eyes openly explained that (matter).' (Sr) (Shackle 1976: 141, cited from Lashari 1971:161)

9.1.2.3 Verb agreement with coordinated nouns

Verb agreement in number and gender with coordinated nouns arises (1) with compound subjects in the direct case, and (2) with unmarked compound direct objects.

9.1.2.3.1 Verb agreement with compound subjects

Some aspects of this situation are straightforward: when two feminine nouns are conjoined, the phrase takes feminine plural agreement, as shown in 9.53. When two masculine nouns are conjoined, the agreement is masculine plural, as in 9.54.

(9.53) میری امی تے نجمہ دی بھین بازار جا رہیاں سن

mer-ī	*ammī*	*te*	*najmā*	*d-ī*	*pæ̃ṇ*	*bazār*	*jā*
1SG.GEN-SG.F	mother	and	Najma	GEN-SG.F	sister	bazaar	go

ra-íyā̃	***san***
CONT.II-PL.F	**be.PST.3PL**

'My mother and Najma's sister were going to the bazaar.' (Pj) (EB)

(9.54) سلیم تے بلو آ گئے نیں

salīm	*te*	*billū*	*ā*	***g-ae***	***nẽ***
Salim[M]	and	Billu[M]	come	**go-PP.PL.M**	**be.PRES.3PL**

'Salim and Billu have come/arrived.' (Pj) (EB)

However, when the elements of the compound subject differ in gender, or in number, the generalizations about agreement depend on several variables: (i) word order—position relative to the verb, (ii) properties of the nouns involved—whether they refer to animate beings, especially humans and whether they are singular or plural, and (iii) the verb itself. Not all authors agree about which variables take priority, and different patterns are attested. The following generalizations are based on Panjabi data.

When a singular masculine and a singular feminine noun are conjoined and the verb is something other than ہونا /hoṇā/ 'be', the agreement is usually masculine plural, as in example 9.55.

(9.55) پچھلے دناں وچ ساڈے اک بیلی دی گھر والی تے سوہرا امریکہ اپڑے

pichle	*din-ā̃*	*vic*	*saḍe*	*ikk*	*belī*	*d-ī*
previous	day-OBL.PL	in	our	one	friend[M]	GEN-SG.F

kàr	*vāl-ī*	*te*	*sɔ́rā*	*amrīkā*
house.SG.M.OBL	NMLZ-SG.F	and	father.in.law[M]	America

apṛ-e
reach-PP.PL.M

'A few days ago, my friend's wife and father-in-law arrived in America.' (Pj) (Bashir and Kazmi 2012: 383)

However, with simple sentences involving existential 'be', if a singular noun is closer to the verb, agreement is singular, as in 9.56 and 9.57. Since ہونا /hoṇā/ 'be' is not marked for gender in either the present or past tense in Panjabi, gender agreement is not present.

(9.56) میرے دوست دے دو بال تے اک بالڑی اے

mer-e *dost* *d-e* *do* *bāl* *te* *ikk*
1SG.GEN-SG.M.OBL friend.OBl GEN-PL.M two child.PL.M and one

bāḷrī ***e***
girl.child.SG.F **be.PRES.3SG**

'My friend has two boys and a girl.' (Pj) (Bashir and Kazmi 2012: 87)

(9.57) میری بھین دیاں دو بیٹیاں تے اک بیٹا اے

mer-ī *pæ̀ṇ* *d-iyā̃* *do* *beṭiy-ā̃* *te* *ikk* *beṭā*
1SG.GEN-SG.F sister GEN-PL.F two daughter-PL.F and one son.SG.M

e
be.PRES.SG.M

'My sister has two daughters and a son.' (Pj) (Bashir and Kazmi 2012: 127)

When plural masculine and feminine nouns are conjoined, the result can be masculine plural, whether the masculine noun is closer to the verb, as in 9.59 or the feminine noun, as in 9.58.

(9.58) پیدل ٹُر پئے مُنڈے تے کُڑیاں جوان

juvān *mũḍ-e* *te* *kuṛi-yā̃* *pædal* *ṭur* ***pa-e***
young boy-PL.M and girl-PL.F on.foot set.out **fall-PP.PL.M**

'The young boys and girls set off on foot.' (Pj) (http://quarterlyneelkanth.blogspot.com/2017/05/blog-post.html)

(9.59) اے اک مخلوط تلیمی ادارہ اے جتھے کُڑیاں تے منڈے کٹھے پڑھدے نیں

é *ikk* *maxlūt* *talīmī* *idarā* *e* *jithe* *kuṛi-yā̃*
this a mixed educational institution be.PRES.3SG where girl-PL.F

te *mũḍ-e* *kaṭṭhe* ***pá̃ṛ-d-e*** ***nẽ***
and boy-pl.m together **study-IP-PL.M** **be.PRES.3PL**

'This is a co-educational institution, where girls and boys study together.' (Pj) (https://commons.wikimedia.org/wiki/Category:Government_College_University,_Lahore)

However, for some people word order takes precedence. For example, Gill and Gleason (1969: 52) give priority to the word order criterion, saying that when the nouns are plural, the verb phrase usually agrees with the last noun, and give example 9.60. Example 9.61, showing the same pattern, is from a recent Internet source.

(9.60) چار آدمی تے دو عورتاں آیاں

cār	*ādmi*	*te*	*do*	*ɔrt-ā̃*	***ā-iyā̃***
four	man.PL.M	and	two	woman-PL	**come-PP.PL.F**

'Four men and two women came.' (Pj) (Gill and Gleason 1969: 52)

(9.61) رنبیاں لے کے بندے تے زنانیاں گوڈی کر دیاں

rā̃bi-yā̃	læ	ke	bande	te	zanāni-yā̃	***goḍī***	***kar-d-iyā̃***
trowel-PL.F	take	CP	men	and	woman-PL.F	**cultivation**	**do-IP-PL.F**

'Taking their trowels, men and women would cultivate ...' (Pj) (http://www.urduweb.org/mehfil/threads/32763)

With conjoined singular inanimate entities, verb agreement in gender and number (singular) is consistently with the noun closest to the verb. See examples 9.62, 9.63, and 9.64, below.

(9.62) ایہدے لئی تہانوں سرکہ لیموں دا رس لون تے کالی مرچ چاہیدی اے

é-de	*laī*	*tuā̀-nū̃*	*sirkā*	*limū̃*	*d-ā*	*ras*
this.OBL-GEN	for	2PL.OBL-DAT	vinegar	lime	GEN-SG.M	juice[M]

lūṇ	*te*	*kāḷ-ī*	*marc*	***cā̂ī-d-ī***	***e***
salt[M]	and	black-F	pepper.**SG.F**	**be.needed-IP-SG.F**	**be.PRES.3SG**

'For this you need vinegar, lemon juice, salt, and black pepper.' (Pj) (Bashir and Kazmi 2012: 532)

(9.63) اوہ بندوقاں تے اسلحہ کشمیریاں نوں شوقیہ طور تے نہیں چاہیدا

ó	*bandūk-ā̃*	*te*	*aslā*	*kašmīrī-ā̃*	*nū̃*	*šokiyā*
3PL	gun-PL.F	and	weaponry.**SG.M**	Kashmiri-OBL.PL	DAT	enthusiast

tor	*te*	***naī̂***	***cā̂i-d-ā***
way	on	**NEG**	**be.needed-IP-SG.M**

'Kashmiris don't need those guns and weapons for fun.' (Pj) (Bashir and Kazmi 2012: 67)

(9.64) عدالتاں توں انصاف نہیں ملے گا تے معاشرے وچ بدامنی تے انتشار پھیلے گا

adālt-ā̃ *tõ* *insāf* *naī̃* *mil-e-g-ā* *te*
court-OBL.PL from justice NEG be.obtained-3SG-FUT-SG.M then

māšr-e *vic* *badamnī* *te* *intašār* ***phæl-e-g-ā***
society-OBL in unrest[F] and anxiety**[M]** **spread-SBJV.3SG-FUT-SG.M**

'If justice is not obtained through the courts, then unrest and anxiety will spread in society.' (Pj) (Bashir and Kazmi 2012: 163)

9.1.2.3.2 Verb agreement with compound objects

Since human direct objects are usually marked with the accusative postposition, verb agreement is default masculine singular even with conjoined objects. With non-human animates and inanimates, if the second noun is plural, the verb usually agrees with it in number and gender, as in examples 9.65, 9.66, and 9.67.

(9.65) میں سویٹر دا پچھا تے باہنواں بنا لئیاں نیں

mæ̃ *sveṭar* *d-ā* *pichā* *te* *bā̃v-ā̃* *banā* ***la-iyā̃***
1SG sweater GEN-SG.M back.SG.M and arm-**PL.F** make **take-PP.PL.F**

nẽ
be.PRES.3PL

'I have made the back and sleeves of the sweater …' (Pj) (Adapted from Bashir and Kazmi 2012: 163)

(9.66) سانوں اپنے کھانیاں وچ سبزیاں تے پھل چوکھے ورتنے چاہیدے نیں

sa-nū̃ *apṇe* *khāṇ-ĕā̃* *vic* *sabziy-ā̃* *te* *phal*
PL.OBL-DAT self's meal-OBL.PL in vegetable-PL.F and fruit.**PL.M**

cokh-e *vart-ṇe* ***cā̃ī-d-e*** ***nẽ***
plenty.of-PL.M use-INF.PL.M **be.needed-IP-PL.M** **be.PRES.3PL**

'We should use more vegetables and fruits in our meals.' (Pj) (Bashir and Kazmi 2012: 472)

(9.67) اوہناں گھر وچ موجود نقدی تے دو موبائل فون اڈا لئے

ón-ā̃	*kàr*	*vic*	*mojūd*	*nakadī*	*te*	*do*	*mobāil*	*fon*
3PL-OBL	house	in	present	cash[F]	and	two	mobile	phone.**PL.M**

uḍā	***li-ye***
steal	**take-PP.PL.M**

'They stole cash and two mobile phones that were in the house.' (Pj) (Bashir and Kazmi 2012: 30)

If the second member of the conjunct is singular, the verb agrees with it in gender, and is singular, as in 9.68, 9.69, 9.70, and 9.71.

(9.68) میں لسی تے پانی پیتا

mæ̃	*lassī*	*te*	*pāṇī*	***p-īt-ā***
1SG.DIR	buttermilk[F]	and	water**[M]**	**drink-PP-SG.M**

'I drank buttermilk and water.' (Pj) (EB)

(9.69) میں پانی تے لسی پیتی

mæ̃	*pāṇī*	*te*	*lassī*	***p-īt-ī***
1SG.DIR	water[M]	and	buttermilk**[F]**	**drink-PP-SG.F**

'I drank water and buttermilk.' (Pj) (EB)

(9.70) اوہناں نے موسیقی وچ بوہت جدت تے سرور پیدا کیتا اے

ónā̃	*ne*	*mosikī*	*vic*	*bɔ́t*	*jiddat*	*te*	*sarūr*
3PL.OBL	ERG	music	in	much	innovation[F]	and	exhilaration**[M]**

pædā	***k-it-ā***	***e***
created	**do-PP-SG.M**	**be.PRES.3SG**

'He has introduced great innovation and exhilaration in music.' (Pj) (Bashir and Kazmi 2012: 104)

(9.71) میری سہیلی نے گھر اچ اک بلا تے اک کتا رکھیا ہویا اے

mer-ī	*sèlī*	*ne*	*kàr*	*ic*	*ikk*	*billā*	*te*	*ikk*
1SG.GEN-SG.F	girlfriend	ERG	house	in	a	male.cat.SG.M	and	a

kuttā	***rakh-iyā***	***ho-yā***	***e***
dog.**SG.M**	**keep-PP.SG.M**	**be.PP.SG.M**	**be.PRES.3SG**

'My friend has a cat and a dog in her house.' (Pj) (Bashir and Kazmi 2012: 104)

While these generalizations are based on Panjabi data, it is likely that they apply to Hindko and Saraiki as well. In the following Saraiki example, 9.72, a singular feminine noun and a singular masculine noun give masculine plural agreement.

(9.72) جھنگ الے علاقے اچ کرنٹ لگڑ نال بھینڑ تے بھرا جانبحق تھی گئیں

jhang	*āle*	*alāk-e*	*ic*	*karanṭ*	*laɠaṛ̃*	*nāl*	*bheṇ*	*te*
Jhang	of	region-OBL	in	current	attach.INF.OBL	with	sister	and

bhirā	*jā̃.bahak*	*thī*	***ɠæn***
brother	dead	become	**go.PP.PL.M+be.PRES.3PL**

'In the Jhang area a brother and sister have died by electrocution.' (Sr) (adapted from https://www.pakistanpoint.com/skr/national/news/story-16080.html)

9.1.3 Subject and agent marking

9.1.3.1 The split-ergative system

All three languages show a split ergative pattern of subject marking, in which subjects of transitive verbs in perfective tenses are treated differently from other subjects. Subjects of all intransitive verbs and of non-perfective (imperfective, continuous, subjunctive, and future/presumptive) tenses of transitive verbs are in the direct case, as in examples 9.73, 9.74, and 9.75.

(9.73) سلیم کراچی بچ ہی کم کردا ہوندا ایہا

salīm	*karācī*	*bic*	*hī*	*kamm*	*kar-d-ā*	*hõ-d-ā*
Salim[M]DIR	Karachi	in	EMPH	work	do-IP-SG.M	be-IP-SG.M

éy-ā
be.PST-SG.M

'Salim used to work (only) in Karachi.' (Hk) (AWT)

(9.74) حکومت بساں دی درآمد لئی پنج ارب روپئے سبسڈی دے گی

hakūmat	*bas-ā̃*	*d-ī*	*darāmad*	*laī*	*panj*	*arab*
government[F]DIR	bus-OBL.Pl	GEN-SG.F	import[F]	for	five	billion

rupae	*sabsiḍī*	*de-g-ī*
rupee.PL.M	subsidy	give-FUT-SG.F

'The government will give a subsidy of five billion rupees for the import of buses.' (Pj) (Bashir and Kazmi 2012: 32)

(9.75) اے اوں تریمت دا پتر ہے جس کنو میں کپڑے دھویندا ں

e	*ū*	*trīmat*	*d-ā*	*putr*	*he*
3SG.PROX.DIR	3SG.DIST	woman	GEN-SG.M	son	be.PRES.3Sg

jis	*kanū*	***mæ̃***	*kapṛe*	*dho-vẽ-d-ā̃*
REL.OBL.SG	by	**1SG.DIR**	clothes	wash-CS-IP-SG.M+be.PRES.1SG

'He is the son of the woman by whom I (m.) get clothes washed.'[6] (Sr) (UK)

In all three languages the subject of perfective tenses of transitive verbs appears in a non-direct case form. In Hindko it appears in the oblique case, as in example 9.76, or in the oblique case followed by the ergative postposition سنڑ /suṛ̃/, as in example 9.77.

(9.76) تُد سائن.بورڈ ٹھایا ایہا

tud	*sāinborḍ*	*ṭā̀-yā*	*é-yā*
2SG.OBL	signboard.SG.M	knock.down-PP-SG.M	be.PST-SG.M

'You knocked down the signboard.' (Hk) (AWT)

(9.77) دربار بچوں ہک درباری سنڑ اُٹھ کے بہوں ادب نال عرض کیتی

darbār	*bicõ*	*hik*	***darbārī-suṛ̃***	*uṭh-ke*	*báũ*	*adab*	*nāl*
court	from	one	**courtier-ERG**	get.up-CP	much	courtesy	with

arz	*kī-t-ī*
request[F]	do-PP-SG.F

'A courtier rose from the court gathering and made a very courteous request…' (Hk) (Soz 2011: 1)

6 The ablative ending is consistently given by Shackle (1976) as /-ũ/. However UK consistently spells it as /-ū/. Nasir Abbas Syed has previously noted that there is some dialectal difference with regard to this.

In Panjabi the subject is in the direct form with first and second person subjects, as shown in examples 9.78 and 9.79; with third person subjects, it is in either the oblique case, or the oblique case followed by the ergative marker نے /ne/, as shown in example 9.80. The main difference among these languages is that Panjabi employs نے /ne/ with third person agents of transitive perfectives much more than does either Hindko or Saraiki.

(9.78) میں دو امب کھادے

mæ̃	*do*	*amb*	*khā́-d-e*
1SG.DIR	two	mango-PL.M	eat-PP-PL.M

'I ate two mangoes.' (Pj) (EB)

(9.79) توں کیہہ کیتا اے

tū̃	*kí*	*kī-t-ā*	*e*
2SG.DIR	what	do-PP-SG.M	be.PRES.3SG

'What have you done?' (Pj) (EB)

(9.80) حکام نے تحقیق دا حکم دے دتا اے

hukām	***ne***	*tækīk*	*d-ā*	*hukam*	*de*	*di-tt-ā*
official.PL	**ERG**	investigation	GEN-SG.M	order[M]	give	give-PP-SG.M

e
be.PRES.3SG

'The officials have ordered an investigation.' (Pj) (Bashir and Kazmi 2012: 263)

In Panjabi, a few frequently used intransitive verbs have transitive translation equivalents in English, which can sometimes cause confusion. Frequently encountered ones are بولنا /bolṇā/ 'to speak', and لیاونا /lyāuṇā/ 'to bring'.[7] The verb in clauses involving these verbs will agree with the subject, as in 9.81, where the verb agrees with the masculine singular subject 'brother', not the feminine plural object 'books'.

7 This verb is intransitive because of its origin in the fusion of a participle of transitive 'take' and a finite form of intransitive 'come'.

(9.81) میرا بھرا میرے لئی دو کتاباں لیایا

mer-ā	***prā̀***	*mere*	*laī*	*do*	*katāb-ā̃*
1SG.GEN-SG.M	**brother.SG.M.DIR**	me	for	two	book-PL.F

*lyā-**yā***
bring-**PP.SG.M**
'My brother brought two books for me.' (Pj) (EB)

There is also a small class of intransitive verbs in Panjabi and Saraiki (probably Hindko as well), mostly involving bodily functions, whose third person subjects are sometimes in Panjabi marked with the ergative marker. Panjabi verbs include تھکنا /thukkṇā/ 'to spit', as in example 9.82 and نچھنا /nicchṇā/ 'to sneeze' (Bhatia 1993: 86). Saraiki verbs of this type include ہنگ /hãg-/ 'defecate' and متر /mutr-/ 'urinate' (Shackle 1976: 148).[8]

(9.82) دادے نے تھکیا

dād-e	***ne***	*thukk-iyā*
grandfather-SG.M.OBL	**ERG**	spit-PP.SG.M

'Grandfather spat.' (Pj) (EB)

In Saraiki, third person subjects of perfective transitives appear in the oblique case; no ergative postposition is normally employed, as in example 9.83.

(9.83) اوں سلیم کوں کتل کیتے

ū̃	*salīm-kū̃*	*katal*	*kī-t-æ*
3SG.OBL	Salim-ACC	murder	do-PP-SG.M+be.PRES.3SG

'She/he murdered Salim.' (Sr) (UK)

8 These verbs have been discussed by various authors, including Barker (1967); Tuite, Agha, and Graczyk (1985); Butt and King (1991); and Bashir (1999) in the context of ne-marking in Hindi and Urdu.

9.1.3.2 Grammatical and semantic subjects: "dative subjects"

The distinction between a "grammatical subject" and a "semantic subject" is central in all these languages. The grammatical subject is that nominal argument with which the verb in all intransitive and in non-perfective transitive sentences agrees. The semantic subject refers to semantic role, and includes agents, actors, and experiencers; in some cases the verb agrees with it and in others it does not. In an ergative construction, a noun marked with نے /ne/ is both the grammatical and the semantic subject. However, in such constructions, the verb agrees with the direct object, unless it is marked with the accusative postposition (see Section 9.1.3.1 above). In the dative subject construction, the semantic subject is marked with the dative/accusative postposition اں /ã/ (Hk), نوں /nũ/ (Pj), or کوں /kũ/ (Sr), and the grammatical subject is in the direct case.[9] If a reflexive element is present in a sentence, it will refer back to the subject—which can be either a grammatical subject, as in examples 9.84 and 9.85, or a semantic subject in a dative subject construction, as in example 9.86.[10]

(9.84) میں اپنے سرائیکی رواج دے کپڑے آپ بݨیندی ہاں

mæ̃	***apṇ-e***	*sarāikī*	*ravāj*	*d-e*	*kapṛ-e*	*āp*
1SG.DIR	**REFL-PL.M**	Saraiki	style	GEN-PL.M	clothes-PL.M	EMPH

baṇēn-d-ī	*h-ā̃*
make-IP-SG.F	be.PRES-1SG

'**I** (F) make **my** traditional Saraiki-style clothes myself.'[11] (Sr) (Zahoor 2009: 49)

(9.85) اوں آپݨے پراݨے سنگتیں کوں چٹھی لکھی اے

ũ̃	***āpṇ-e***	*purāṇ-e*	*sangatī̃*	*kū̃*	*ciṭṭhī*
3SG.OBL	**REFL-SG.M.OBL**	old-SG.M.OBL	friend.OBL	DAT	letter[F]

likh-ī-e
write-PP.SG.F-be.PRES.3SG

'**He** wrote a letter to **his** old friend.' (Sr) (UK)

9 These constructions are sometimes also referred to as "indirect constructions."

10 There may be some differences among the ways the reflexive adjective is used in the three languages; this topic requires further detailed study.

11 Notice the Urdu form of the reflexive here; this is evidence of the language contact effects operating in Multan.

(9.86) میٔنوں آپنا گھر چنگا لگدا اے

mæ-nũ	*āpṇ-ā*	*kàr*	*cãgā lag-d-ā*	*e*
1SG-DAT	**REFL.ADJ-SG.M**	house[M]	good seem-IP-SG.M	be.PRES.3SG

'**I** like **my (own)** house.' (Pj) (EB)

The dative subject construction, in which the logical and the grammatical subject are different, is centrally important. In these and many other languages of South Asia, expressions of mental and physical states and modal concepts are expressed with this construction. In this construction, the experiencer of the physical, psychological, or modal state (the semantic subject) appears in its oblique or dative case form, and the experience or state (the grammatical subject) appears in the direct case and triggers agreement on the verb. This reflects the fact that such states are conceptualized as originating from the external environment and affecting an experiencer. The use of the dative case, which expresses a generalized notion of GOAL, for such roles reflects this conceptualization. Examples of dative subject usages are given below for each language.

9.1.3.2.1 Dative subject – Hindko

In example 9.87, مانہہ /mā̃/ 'I' is the semantic subject (an experiencer), and فلم /filam/ 'film, movie' is the grammatical subject, with which the verb agrees. In example 9.88, the semantic subject is اساں /assā̃/ 'we', and the grammatical subject is the infinitive اٹھنڑا /uṭh-ṝā/ 'to get up'. Similar examples are provided below for both Hindko and Panjabi.

(9.87) مانہہ اس طرحاں دی فلم اچھی نئیں لگدی

mā̃	*us*	*tarhā̃*	*d-ī*	***filam***	*acch-ī*	*nī̃*
1SG.OBL	3SG.OBL	kind	GEN-SG.F	**film.SG.F**	good-SG.F	NEG

*lag-d-**ī***
affect-IP-**SG.F**

'I don't like that kind of film.' (Hk) (AWT)

(9.88) اَساں کل فزری سویرے اُٹھنڑا پیسی

assā̃	*kal*	*fazrī*	*saver-e*	***uṭh-ṝā***	*pæ-s-**ī***
1PL.OBL	tomorrow	early	morning-OBL	**get.up-INF**	fall-FUT-**3SG**

'We will have to get up very early tomorrow morning.' (Hk) (AWT)

(9.89) اُس آں بہوں پھکھ لگدی ایہی

us-ã̄ *baũ̄* ***pùkh*** *lag-d-ī* *éy-**ī***

3SG.OBL-DAT much **hunger[F]** attach-IP-SG.F be-PST.**SG.F**

'She/he was (often) very hungry. (lit. Much hunger used to afflict him/her.)' (Hk) (AWT)

(9.90) اُس آں تاپ چڑھ گیا

us-ã̄ ***tāp*** *cáṛ* *ga-**yā***

3SG.OBL-DAT **fever[M]** climb go-**PP.SG.M**

'He/she got a fever.' (Hk) (AWT)

(9.91) اُس بہوں پڑھیا اور اُس آں اچھا نتیجہ تھیایا

us *báũ̄* *páṛ-iyā* *ɔr* ***us-ã̄*** *acchā*

3SG.OBL much study-PP.SG.M and **3SG.OBL-DAT** good.SG.M

natījā *thā́-**yā***

result.SG.M be.obtained-**PP.SG.M**

'He/she studied a lot and got a good result.' (Hk) (AWT)

9.1.3.2.2 Dative subject – Panjabi

(9.92) مینوں اوہ منڈا چنگا لگدا اے

mæ-nũ̄ *ó* ***mũḍā*** *cãg-ā* *lag-d-ā* ***e***

1SG.OBL-DAT 3SG.DIST **boy[M]** good-SG.M seem-IP-SG.M be.PRES.3SG

'I like that boy. (lit. That boy seems good to me.)' (Pj) (EB)

(9.93) مینوں پتا نہیں کہ کتھے جاواں

mæ-nũ̄ ***patā*** *nĩ́* *ki* *kithe* *jā-vã̄*

1SG.OBL-DAT **information** NEG that where go-SBJV.1SG

'I don't know where to go. (lit. I don't have information where I should/can go.)' (Pj) (EB)

(9.94) میری کڑی نوں بخار چڑھیا اے

mer-ī	***kuṛī-nū̃***	***buxār***	*cáṛ-**iyā***	***e***
1SG.GEN-SG.F	**girl-DAT**	**fever[M]**	climb-**PP.SG.M**	be.PRES.**3SG**

'My daughter has (gotten) a fever.' (Pj) (EB)

Stative and inchoative experiences are represented differently. The verb ہونا /hoṇā/ 'to be' appears with stative constructions, shown in examples 9.95 and 9.96, and آونا ~ آنا /auṇā ~ āṇā/ 'to come', with inchoative constructions, shown in examples 9.97 and 9.98.

(9.95) مینوں بڑا غصہ سی

mæ̃-nū̃	*baṛ-ā*	*gussā*	*sī*
1SG.OBL-DAT	great-SG.M	anger[M]	be.PST.3SG

'I was very angry. (lit. 'to me great anger was.')' (Pj) (EB)

(9.96) مینوں چینی کھانا بہت پسند اے

mæ-nū̃	*cīnī*	*khāṇā*	*bɔ́t*	*pasand*	*e*
1SG-DAT	Chinese	food	very	liked	be-PRES.3SG

'I like Chinese food a lot.' (Pj) (EB)

The light verb آونا / آنا /āuṇā ~ āṇā/ 'to come' imparts the nuance of some new mental or conceptual content coming from the outside to the experiencer, as in examples 9.97 and 9.98.

(9.97) سانوں غصہ آیا

sā-nū̃	*gussā*	*ā-yā*
1PL.OBL-DAT	anger[M]	come-PP.SG.M

'We became angry.' (Pj) (EB)

(9.98) سانوں کلھ دا نواں کھانا پسند آیا

sā-nū̃	*kál*	*d-ā*	*nav-ā̃*	*khāṇā*	*pasand*
1PL.OBL-DAT	yesterday	GEN-SG.M	new-SG.M	dish[M]	liked

ā-yā
come-PP.SG.M

'We liked yesterday's new dish.' (Pj) (EB)

A dative subject construction with a noun or an infinitive denoting some learned skill or behavior plus اونا /ɔṇā/ 'to come' means 'to know (how to)', as in example 9.99.

(9.99) اوہ نوں پنجابی نہیں اوندی

ó-nū̃	*panjābī*	*nā́ĩ*	*ɔ-nd-ī*
3.DIST.OBL-DAT	Panjabi[F]	NEG	come-IP-SG.F

'She/he doesn't know Panjabi.' (Pj) (Shackle 1972: 79)

The construction سمجھ اونا /sámaj ɔnā/ plus dative subject means for something (new) to be understood, as in example 9.100.

(9.100) سانوں کوئی گل نہیں سی سمجھ اوندی

sā-nū̃	*koī*	*gall*	*nā́ĩ*	*sī*	*sámaj*
1PL.OBL-DAT	any	matter[F]	NEG	be.PST.3SG	understanding

ɔ-nd-ī
come-IP-SG.F

'We didn't understand anything.' (Pj) (Shackle 1972: 79)

9.1.3.2.3 Dative subject – Saraiki

Examples of the dative subject in Saraiki are given here in the following four examples.

(9.101) میکوں بہوں تریہ لگیے

mæ-kū̃	*bahū̃*	*treh*	*lag-ī-e*
1SG.OBL-DAT	much	thirst[F]	attach-PP.SG.F-be.PRES.3SG

'I am very thirsty. (lit. Much thirst has affected me.)' (Sr) (UK)

(9.102) جمبیل کوں پتا کینھا ہا جو کتھاں ونجݨے

jambīl	*kū̃*	*patā*	*kænhā*	*hā*	*jo*	*kithā̃*
Jamil	DAT	knowledge[M]	NEG	be.PST.SG.M	that	where

vãf-ṇ-æ
go-GRDV-SG.M+be.PRES.3SG

'Jamil didn't know where to go.' (Sr) (UK)

(9.103) میکوں پریں پہاڑ ڈِسدے پین

mæ-kũ	*par-ẽ*	*pahāṛ*	*ɗis-d-e*
1SG.OBL-DAT	afar-LOC	mountains	be.seen-IP-PL.M

pæ-n
CONT.I.PL.M-be.PRES.3PL

'I see mountains in the distance.' (Sr) (UK)

(9.104) میکوں کہیں شے کنوں ڈر نہیں لگدا

mæ-kũ	*kahĩ*	*šæ*	*kanū*	*ɗar*	*nĩ*	*laɠ-d-ā*
1SG.OBL-DAT	any	thing	from	fear[M]	NEG	attach-IP-SG.M

'I am not afraid of anything.' (Sr) (UK)

9.1.4 Object marking

Variables influencing direct object marking operate independently of the split ergative system and of perfectivity or imperfectivity. Semantic roles of the object including recipient, beneficiary, affected entity, direction; referential status; and the intensity of volitionality of the agent are indicated on the direct object with the dative/accusative postposition—نوں /nũ/ in Panjabi, آں /ã/ in Hindko, and کوں /kũ/ in Saraiki. All uses of these postpositions can be generalized as marking some sort of GOAL—physical, abstract, or metaphorical.

All indirect objects/recipients are marked with the dative-accusative postposition, as shown in examples 9.105, 9.106, and 9.107. Note that the agent in 9.107 is expressed by the third-person plural pronominal suffix.

(9.105) میں اپڑی کتاب سلیم آں دتی اے

mæ̃	*apṛ-ī*	*kitāb*	***salīm***	***ã̄***	*di-tt-ī*	*e*
1SG.DIR	REFL-SG.F	book[F]	**Salim**	**DAT**	give-PP-SG.F	be.PRES.3SG

'I have given my book to Salim.' (Hk) (AWT)

(9.106) میں تہانوں کل کہہ رہیا ساں

mæ̃	***tuā̀-nũ***	*kál*	*kǽ*	*r-yā*	*sã̄*
1SG.DIR	**2PL.OBL-DAT**	yesterday	say	CONT.II-SG.M	be.PST.1SG

'I was saying to you yesterday.' (Pj) (EB)

(9.107) میکوں موا نانگ ڈکھالینے

mæ-kū̃ *mū-ā* *nāng*
1SG.OBL-DAT dead-SG.M snake.DIR.SG.M

d̤ikhāl-e-ne
show-PP.SG.M+be.PRES.3SG-PS.3PL
'They showed me a dead snake.' (Sr) (UK)

Direct objects can appear in either the direct case or the oblique case followed by the dative-accusative postposition— اں /ã/ in Hindko, نوں /nū̃/ in Panjabi, and کوں /kū̃/ in Saraiki. The variables that determine whether an object appears in the direct case or is marked with the postposition are complex and often interact with one another. They include referential status and animacy of the object, and volitionality of the agent. In this paradigm, an object is considered epistemically specific if the speaker has a particular referent in mind for the entity denoted by the object noun phrase and definite if the listener also knows what is being referred to. This is illustrated in examples 9.108 and 9.109 from Panjabi. Sentences like that in 9.108 involving a specific indefinite, mean that the speaker knows which book he means, but assumes that the hearer does not. Sentences like this are often followed by the speaker offering further information about the object, in this case 'a book'. The speaker of a sentence like that in 9.109, on the other hand, assumes that the hearer knows which book is being referred to, i.e. the book is part of the prior discourse. In general, these same variables also affect direct object marking in Hindko and Saraiki.

(9.108) میں اک کتاب ویکھی

mæ̃ *ikk* ***katāb*** *vekh-ī*
I.OBL a **book[F]** see-PP.SG.F
'I saw a (specific) book.' (Pj) (EB)

(9.109) میں کتاب نوں ویکھیا اے

mæ̃ ***katāb*** ***nū̃*** *vekh-iyā* *e*
I.OBL **book[F]** **ACC** see-PP.SG.M be.PRES.3SG
'I have seen the (definite) book.' (Pj) (EB)

In contrast to inanimate direct objects, where the postposition is optional, definite animate direct objects, particularly human referents, are almost always marked with the dative-accusative postposition آں /ã/ in Hindko, shown in example 9.110, نوں /nū̃/ in Panjabi, shown in example 9.111, or کوں /kū̃/ in Saraiki, shown in example 9.112. Human objects referred to by a proper name always take the postposition.

(9.110) اُس بلو آں چاکو ماریا

us	***billū***	***ā̃***	*cākū*	*mār-iyā*
3SG.OBL	**Billu**	**ACC**	knife	strike-PP.SG.M

'S/he stabbed Billu.' (Hk) (AWT)

(9.111) میں منڈے نوں ویکھیا

mæ̃	***mũḍe***	***nũ***	*vekh-iyā*
I.OBL	**boy.SG.M.OBL**	**ACC**	see.PP-SG.M

'I saw the boy.' (Pj) (EB)

(9.112) اوں سلیم کوں کتل کیتے

ũ	***salīm***	***kũ***	*katal*	*kīt-e*
3SG.OBL	**Salim**	**ACC**	murder	do.PP-SG.M+be.PRES.3SG

'S/he murdered Salim.' (Sr) (UK)

With specific indefinite animate objects, including humans, the accusative postposition usually does not appear, as in example 9.113, and with non-specific indefinites it never does, as in 9.114.

(9.113) میں اک منڈا ویکھیا

mæ̃	*ikk*	***mũḍā***	*vekh-iyā*
I.OBL	a	**boy.SG.M.DIR**	see.PP-SG.M

'I saw a (specific) boy.' (Pj) (EB)

(9.114) میری پہنڑو چوہا ماریا

mer-ī	*pæ̀ṛ-ū*	***cū̃-ā***	*mār-iyā*
1SG.GEN-SG.F	sister-OBL	**rat-SG.M**	kill-PP.SG.M

'My sister killed a rat.' (Hk) (AWT)

When, according to semantic criteria, both the direct object and the indirect object would be marked by the dative-accusative postposition, marking of the indirect object takes precedence over the direct object. In such clauses, if the direct object is a noun (rather than a pronoun), it may appear in the direct case, since the indirect object must be marked with the postposition, and with perfective tenses of transitives, the verb will agree with the direct object, as in example 9.115. In example 9.115, marking both the direct object (daughter) and the indirect object (my son) with نوں /nũ/ would result in an infelicitous sentence. However, if the direct object in such a sentence is a personal pronoun, both the direct and the indirect object take the accusative postposition, as in example 9.116.

(9.115) اوہ نے آپنی کڑی میرے سانوں دتی

ó	*ne*	*āpṇ-ī*	***kuṛī***	***sā-nū̃***	*di-tt-ī*
3SG.OBL	ERG	REFL-SG.F	**daughter.SG.F**	**2PL.OBL-DAT**	give-PP-SG.F

'S/he gave her/his daughter to us (i.e. our whole family) (in marriage).' (Pj) (EB)

(9.116) اوہدے پیو نے اوہنوں آپنے دوست دے پترنوں دتا

ó-de	*pyo*	*ne*	***ó-nū̃***	*āpṇ-e*
3SG.OBL-GEN.SG.M.OBL	father	ERG	**3SG.OBL-ACC**	REFL-SG.M.OBL

dost	*d-e*	***puttar***	***nū̃***	*di-tt-ā*
friend.SG.M.OBL	GEN-SG.M.OBL	**son**	**DAT**	give-PP-SG.M

'Her father gave her to his friend's son (in marriage).' (Pj) (EB)

9.1.5 Negation

Sentential negation is indicated with two distinct negative markers, which usually appear in different clause types. The basic negative particle is نہ ~ نا /ná ~ na/; the extended negative particle نہیں /naĩ́/ نئیں ~ /naĩ/ نی ~ /nī/ historically consists of نہ plus an emphatic component and/or the present tense of the verb 'be' (Bashir 2006). The simple negative particle نہ /na/ is used consistently in all three languages for imperatives, for subjunctives, with irrealis meanings, to negate non-finite verbal forms, and often with simple perfect sentences. When it is used in negative imperatives in Hindko and Panjabi, a high tone is usually heard, i.e. /ná/ ~ /nā́/. The extended particle نہیں /nahī̃/, etc. is more likely to occur with other tense-aspect forms.

In all three languages, with tenses whose affirmative forms include the present tense of 'be', as auxiliary, light verb, or copula, this form is usually omitted in negative sentences, as in examples 9.117, 9.118, 9.119, and 9.120, leaving the negative particle نہیں /naĩ́/ in final position. This is because the form نہیں /naĩ́/ already includes a (covert) present tense form of 'be'.

(9.117) اس کول کوئی اہجی جا نیھ جتھے جلے

us	*kol*	*koī*	*ehjī*	*jā*	***ní***	*jithe*	*jul-e*
3SG.OBL	near	any	such	place	**NEG**	where.REL	go-SUBJV.3SG

'S/he doesn't have any place to go. (lit. 'where s/he could go)' (Hk) (AWT)

(9.118) اوہ کوئی کم نہیں کردا

ó	*koī*	*kamm*	***naī̃***	*kar-d-ā*
3SG.DIST.DIR	any	work	**NEG**	do-IP-SG.M

'He doesn't do any work.' (Pj) (EB)

(9.119) ایہہ میرا گھر نہیں

é	*mer-ā*	*kàr*	***naī̃***
3SG.PROX.DIR	1SG.GEN-SG.M	house	**NEG**

'This is not my house.' (Pj) (EB)

(9.120) میں ھݨے ڈاکٹر کنے ویندا پیاں۔ پشاور نہیں ونج سگدا

mæ̃	*huṇe*	*ḍākṭar*	*kane*	*vẽ-d-ā*	*p-iyā̃*
1SG	now	doctor	to	go-IP-SG.M	CONT.I-SG.M+be.PRES.1SG

pišāvar	***nahī̃***	*vā̃f*	*saɠ-d-ā*
Peshawar	**NEG**	go	be.able-IP-SG.M

'I'm going to the doctor now; I can't go to Peshawar.' (Sr) (UK)

Compare the negative forms in examples 9.118 and 9.119 with the affirmative counterparts 9.121 and 9.122.

(9.121) اوہ بہت کم کردا اے

ó	*bɔ̃t*	*kamm*	*kar-d-ā*	***e***
3SG.DIST.DIR	much	work	do-IP-SG.M	**be.PRES.3SG**

'He does a lot of work.' (Pj) (EB)

(9.122) ایہہ میرا گھر اے

ê	*mer-ā*	*kàr*	***e***
3SG.PROX.DIR	1SG.GEN-SG.M	house	**be.PRES.3SG**

'This is my house.' (Pj) (EB)

If in such negative sentences the auxiliary or copula is included, an emphatic sense is conveyed, as in example 9.123.

(9.123) ایہہ سلیم دا گھر نہیں اے

é	*salīm*	*d-ā*	*kàr*	***naī̃***	***e***
this	Salim	GEN-SG.M	house[M]	**NEG**	**be.PRES.3SG**

'This is not Salim's house (despite what you may think or say).' (Pj) (EB)

9.1.5.1 Hindko negation

In Hindko, in addition to appearing in the contexts common to all three languages (imperatives, subjunctives, and with irrealis meanings), نہ /ná/ appears more frequently with tense-aspect forms where نہیں /naĩ/ usually appears in Panjabi. In examples 9.124, 9.125, and 9.126, نہ /ná/ occurs in the present imperfect, future, and simple perfect, respectively.

(9.124) میں کسی چیزاں کولوں نہ ڈردا

mæ̃	*kisī*	*cīz-ā̃*	*kol-õ*	***ná***	*ḍar-d-ā*
1SG.DIR	any.OBL.PL	thing-OBL.PL	from	**NEG**	fear-IP-SG.M

'I am not afraid of anything.' (Hk) (AWT)

(9.125) مسعود سوٹی نہ پہن ہکسی

masūd	*soṭī*	***na***	*pàn*	*hak-s-ī*
Masud	stick	**NEG**	break	be.able-FUT-3SG

'Masud will not be able to break the stick.' (Hk) (AWT)

(9.126) اس اسطے میں تداں ملنے آں نہ آ ہکیاں

is	*aste*	*mæ̃*	*tud-ā̃*	*mil-n-e-ā̃*	***ná***	*ā*
3SG.OBL	for	1SG.DIR	2SG.OBL-ACC	meet-INF-OBL-DAT	**NEG**	come

hak-iyā̃
be.able-PP.SG.M

'This is why I was not able to come to see you.' (Hk) (AWT)

The following sentences, with نئیں /naĩ/ in the present imperfect in example 9.127, and simple perfect in 9.128, carry emphatic senses—of annoyance in 9.127 and surprise or disappointment in 9.128.

(9.127) رضیہ چپ نئیں رہ سکدی

raziyā	*cup*	***naĩ***	*ræ̃*	*sak-d-ī*
Razia	quiet	**NEG**	remain	be.able-IP-SG.F

'Razia can**not** keep quiet.' (Hk) (AWT)

(9.128) تیرا پہرا کیوں نئیں آیا

ter-ā	*prà*	*kyố*	***naī̃***	*ā-yā*
2SG.GEN-SG.M	brother	why	**NEG**	come-PP-SG.M

'Why didn't your brother come?' (Hk) (AWT)

In our corpus of Hindko sentences, the negative existential meaning 'is/are not' is consistently rendered with نہیں /naī̃/ in its various spellings, as in example 9.129.

(9.129) اس کول کوئی ایہجی جا نیہ جتھے جلے

us	*kol*	*koī*	*éi-j-ī*	*jā*	***nī́***	*jithe*
3SG.DIST.OBL	with	any	PROX-such-SG.F	place[F]	**NEG**	where.REL

jul-e
go-SBJV.3SG

'He has no place to go.' (Hk) (AWT)

9.1.5.2 Panjabi negation

In Panjabi, the basic negative particle نہ is used consistently for imperative, as in example 9.130; subjunctive, as in example 9.131; irrealis conditionals; *neither... nor* constructions; non-finite verbal forms (infinitives and infinitive phrases/clauses, and participles); and sometimes for the simple perfect, as in example 9.132. Other tense-aspect forms are more often negated with نہیں /naī̃/. The default placement of the negative particle is immediately preceding the verb; placing it after the verb adds emphatic force, as in example 9.133.

(9.130) توں نہ جا

tū̃	***ná***	*jā*
2SG.DIR	**NEG**	go.IMP.2SG

'(You) don't go!' (Pj) (Bhatia 1993: 117)

(9.131) اوہ چنوندی اے کہ سلیم نہ جاوے

ó	*cɔ́n-d-ī*	*e*	*ki*	*salīm*	***ná***	*jā-ve*
3SG.DIR	want-IP-SG.F	be.PRES.3SG	that	Salim	**NEG**	go-SBJV.3SG

'She does not want Salim to go.' (Pj) (EB)

(9.132) میں کئی واری چابی مروڑی پر تالا نہ کھلیا

mæ̃	*kaī*	*vārī*	*cābī*	*mroṛ-ī*	*par*	*tālā*	***nâ***
1SG.DIR/OBL	many	times	key[F]	turn-PP.SG.F	but	lock.SG.M	**NEG**

khul-iyā
open-PP.SG.M

'I turned the key many times, but the lock did not open.' (Pj) (Bashir and Kazmi 2012: 534)

(9.133) بےنظیر مری نئیں، اوہنوں ماریا گیا اے

benazīr	*mar-ī*	***naĩ̂***	*ó-nū̃*	*mār-iyā*	*g-yā*
Benazir	die-PP.SG.F	**NEG**	3SG.OBL-ACC	kill-PP.SG.M	go-PP.SG.M

e
be.PRES.3SG

'Benazir did not die. She has been killed.' (Pj) (Bashir and Kazmi 2012: 533)

In negative Panjabi sentences involving a past tense form of ہونا /hoṇā/ 'to be' as auxiliary or as light verb in a conjunct verb formation, the past tense of 'be' immediately follows the negative element and precedes the participial or nominal component of the verbal form, causing the participial or nominal component to be clause final. This happens in the past imperfect, as in example 9.134; past perfect, as in example 9.135; past continuous, as in example 9.136; or dative subject construction, making the nominal subject clause final, as in example 9.137.

(9.134) ایہہ کم اینج نہیں سی ہونا چاہیدا

é	*kamm*	*æ̃j*	***nĩ̂***	***sī***	*ho-ṇā*
3SG.PROX	work	like.this	**NEG**	**be.PST.3SG**	be-INF

cā̃i-d-ā
be.wanted-IP-SG.M

'This work should not have been done this way.' (Pj) (Bashir and Kazmi 2012: 76)

(9.135) میں اج صبح بنک گیا تے اوہ حالے نئیں سی کھلیا

mæ̃	*ajj*	*suba*	*bæ̃k*	*g-yā*	*te*	*ó*	*hāle*	***naĩ̂***
1SG	today	morning	bank	go-PP.SG.M	and	3SG.DIST	yet	**NEG**

sī	*khul-iyā*
be.PST.3SG	open-PP.SG.M

'I went to the bank this morning but it had not opened yet.' (Pj) (Bashir and Kazmi 2012: 210)

(9.136) اوہنوں اکا چیتا نئیں سی آ رہیا کہ اوہ پیسے کتھے رکھ بیٹھی سی

ó-nũ̃	*ukkā*	*cetā*	***naī̃***	***sī***	*ā-ryā*
3SG.OBL-NŨ̃	at.all	memory[M]	**NEG**	**be.PST.3SG**	come-CONT.II.SG.M

ki	*ó*	*pæse*	*kithe*	*rakh*	*bæṭh-ī*	*sī*
that	3SG.DIR	money	where	put	sit-PP.SG.F	be.PST.3SG

'She just could not remember where she had put the money.' (Pj) (Bashir and Kazmi 2012: 254)

(9.137) مینوں نئیں سی پتہ کہ اوہ پچھلے دو سالاں توں ایس نوکری تے لگا ہویا سی

mæ-nũ̃	***nī̃***	***sī***	*patā*	*ki*	*ó*	*pichle*	*do*
1SG-DAT	**NEG**	**be.PST.3SG**	knowledge	that	3SG.DIST	previous	two

sāl-ā̃	*tõ*	*æs*	*nokrī*	*te*	*lag-ā*	*ho-iyā*
year-OBL.PL	from	this.OBL	job	at	attach-PP.SG.M	be-PP.SG.M

sī
be.PST.3SG

'I did not know that he had been employed at this job for the last two years.' (Pj) (Bashir and Kazmi 2012: 512)

However, this generalization may be weakening, as exceptions are also found, in the past imperfect, as in example 9.138; past perfect, as in example 9.139; and past continuous, as in example 9.140. Whether these exceptions are the result of recent contact effects, or whether they carry some semantic nuance remains a subject for investigation.

(9.138) اسی مرکزی کابینہ وچ شامل نہیں ہونا چاہندے ساں

assī	*markazī*	*kābīnā*	*vic*	*šāmal*	***nī̃***	*ho-ṇā*	*cā̃-nd-e*
1PL	central	cabinet	in	included	**NEG**	be-INF	want-IP-PL.M

s-ā̃
be.PST-1PL

'We did not want to join the Federal Cabinet.' (Pj) (Bashir and Kazmi 2012: 36)

(9.139) میں شکایت لے کے عدلیا دے کول نہیں گیا سی کیونکہ مینوں ایس تے اعتماد نہیں

mæ̃ šikæt læ-ke adliyā de kol ***naī̃́*** *g-yā*
1SG complaint take-CP judiciary GEN near **NEG** go-PP.SG.M

sī *kyõki mæ-nũ̄ æs te ætmād nī̃́*
be.PST.3SG because 1SG.OBL-DAT 3SG.PROX on confidence NEG

'I did not go to the judiciary with a complaint because I didn't trust it.' (Pj) (Bashir and Kazmi 2012: 469)

(9.140) اوہ میری گل نیئیں سن رہی سی تے اپنے ای خیالاں اچ کدرے گم سی

ó mer-ī gall ***nī̃́*** *suṇ ra-ī́*
3SG.DIST my-SG.F utterance.SG.F **NEG** listen CONT.II-SG.F

sī *te āpṇ-e ī xyāl-ā̃-c kídare*
be.PST.3SG and REFL-PL.M EMPH thought-PL.OBL-in somewhere

gum sī
lost be.PST.3SG

'She was not listening to me and was lost somewhere in her own thoughts.' (Pj) (Bashir and Kazmi 2012: 494)

9.1.5.3 Saraiki negation

In Saraiki, in addition to the two negative particles نہ /na/ and نہیں /nhĩ/ ~ نیں/nĩ/ there are emphatic negative elements کینھا ~ کینھی ~ کینھیں ~ کوئینی /kænhā ~ kænhī ~ kaenhĩ̄ ~ koīnī/, which include the /k/ 'any' element present in کوئی /koī/ 'any', as in examples 9.141 and 9.142. The simple negative نہ /na/ ~ نا /nā/ or its emphatic counterpart کینھا /kænhā/ is regularly used to negate the subjunctive, imperfective participle functioning as irrealis, imperative forms, and future, and also sometimes with other tense forms, e.g. simple perfect, as in example 9.141, or past imperfect, as in example 9.142. نہیں /nhĩ̄/ ~ نیں/nĩ̄/ often occurs with tenses formed with imperfective or perfective participles, as in example 9.143. Notice that in 9.141, the first person singular pronominal suffix indexing the agent 'I' is attached to the negative element.[12]

12 NAS prefers kæ-nhā-m instead of kæ-nhā-mā in example 9.141.

(9.141) تیکوں اوں کنے کینھاما پٹھیا

tæ-kū̃	*ū̃*	*kane*	***kæ-nhā-mā***	*paṭh-iyā*
2SG.OBL-ACC	3SG.OBL	to	**EMPH-NEG-PS1SG**	send-PP.SG.M

'I did not send you to him.' (Sr) (UK)

(9.142) توں دہان کینھا رکھیندا پیا ھاویں؟ ٹکر سڑ گئے

tū̃	*dihān*	***kæ-nhā***	*rakhē-nd-ā*	*p-iyā*	*hā-vē̃*
2SG.DIR	attention	**NEG**	put-IP.SG.M	CONT.I-SG.M	be.PST-2SG

ṭukur	*saṛ*	*ɠ-e*
bread[M]	burn	go.PP-SG.M.+be.PRES.3SG

'Weren't you paying attention!? The bread has burned.' (Sr) (UK)

(9.143) ڳائوں دا گوشت میکوں موافق نی آندا

ɠāū̃	*d-ā*	*gošt*	*mæ-kū̃*	*moafik*	***nī***
cow.OBL	GEN-SG.M	meat[M]	1SG.OBL-DAT	suitable	**NEG**

ān-d-ā
come-IP-SG.M

'Beef does not agree with me.' (Sr) (Zahoor 2009: 68)

9.1.6 Questions

9.1.6.1 Yes-no questions

Yes-no questions are of two types: neutral, which do not presuppose either an affirmative or a negative answer; and tag or confirmatory, which do anticipate an affirmative or a negative answer. Neutral yes-no questions can be formed simply by using a rising intonation and maintaining a normal declarative word order, as in examples 9.144 and 9.145. Intonation rises to the stressed syllable of the main element in the verbal phrase. Alternatively, a question word 'what' کیہ /kī́/ (Pj), کے /ke/ (Hk), کیا /kyā/ (Sr) may optionally be placed at the beginning of a sentence, as in example 9.146. Indicating yes-no questions by intonation is far more common in speaking, while the use of an initial 'what' occurs more often in writing.

(9.144) تُداں اپڑا بچپن یاد اے

tud-ã̄	*apṛ-ā*	*bacpan*	*yād*	*e*
2SG.OBL-DAT	REFL-SG.M	childhood[M]	memory	be.PRES.3SG

'Do you remember your childhood?' (Hk) (AWT)

(9.145) تیڈے کنے ڈاہ رپے ہن

tēɗ-e	*kane*	*ɗāh*	*rupē*	*hĕn*
2SG.GEN-OBL	with	ten	rupee.PL.M	be.PRES.3PL

'Do you have ten rupees (with you)?' (Sr) (UK)

(9.146) کیہہ تسیں اج کہانی سناووگے

kī́	*tussī̃*	*ajj*	*kā̀ṇī*	*suṇā-vo-ge*
Q	2PL.DIR	today	story.SG.F	tell-2PL-FUT.PL.M

'Will you tell a story today?' (Pj) (Bhatia 1993: 5)

The second type of yes-no question anticipates either a "yes" or a "no" answer and is called a confirmatory, or tag question. To illustrate these kinds of questions in English: a negative declarative statement is followed by a simple affirmative phrase requesting confirmation, e.g. "He wasn't here, was he?", with the expected reply, "No, he wasn't." An affirmative statement is followed by a negative tag, e.g., "He is coming, isn't he?", with the expected confirmatory reply, "Yes, he is coming."

In Panjabi and Saraiki, the negative particle نا /nā/ is added at the end of both affirmative assertions, as in examples 9.147 and 9.149, and negative assertions, as in example 9.148, to indicate that a confirmatory answer is expected.[13]

(9.147) اج مینہ پویگا نا

ajj	*mī̃́*	*pa-ve-g-ā*	***nā***
today	rain.SG.M.DIR	fall-SBJV.3SG-FUT-SG.M	**TAG**

'It will rain today, **won't it**?' (Pj) (Adapted from Bhatia (1993: 7).)

(9.148) اج مینہ نہیں پویگا نا

ajj	*mī̃́*	*naī̃́*	*pa-ve-g-ā*	***nā***
today	rain.SG.M.DIR	NEG	fall-SBJV.3SG-FUT-SG.M	**TAG**

'It won't rain today, **will it**?' (Pj) (Adapted from Bhatia (1993: 7).)

13 Bhatia (1993: 4–8) includes a detailed discussion of question answering systems in Panjabi.

(9.149) محبت تاں شے وی ایجھی ہے نا

muhabbat	*tā̃*	*šæ*	*vī*	*ējhī*	*he*	*nā*
love	TOP	thing[F]	INCL	such.SG.F	be.PRES.3SG	TAG

'(Well), love is just like this, **isn't it**?' (Sr) (Shackle (1976: 159) citing Lashari (1971: 154).)

In Panjabi and Saraiki the uninflected interjection بھلا /bhalā/ Sr , بھلا /pàlā/ 'well!' Pj often appears in rhetorical questions implying that a negative answer is expected, as in examples 9.150 and 9.151.

(9.150) اوہ بھلا ایتھے آندا اے

ó	***pàlā***	*ethe*	*ān-d-ā*	*e*
3SG.DIST	**NEG.EMPH**	here	come-IP-SG.M	be.PRES.3SG

'Does he (ever) come here?' (Pj) (Bhatia 1993: 7)

(9.151) ساکوں بھلا کوئی اعتراض اے

sa-kũ	***bhalā***	*kuī*	*itrāz*	*e*
1PL.OBL-DAT	**NEG.EMPH**	any	objection	be.PRES.3SG

'Should we have any objection?' (Sr) (Shackle (1976: 160) citing Lashari (1971: 67).)

Frequently, yes-no questions equivalent to an English question '... or not?' are preferred, especially when pressing for an answer. To form such questions, یا /yā/ or کہ /ki/, both meaning 'or' plus the negative element , is added to the end of a positive declarative statement, as in example 9.152.

(9.152) تسیں کم کروگے کہ نہیں

tussī̃	*kamm*	*kar-o-g-e*	***ki***	***naī̃́***
2PL.DIR	work	do-2PL-FUT-PL.M	**or**	**NEG**

'Will you do the work/task **or not**?' (Pj) (EB)

In these 'or not' questions, the intonation contour also rises, but the peak is on the verb. The sentence-initial interrogative marker کیہ /kī́/ (Pj) does not occur in such questions.

9.1.6.2 Constituent questions: Wh-phrases

A full range of open-ended questions are expressed in all three languages by question words that begin with /k/. The basic interrogative adjectives and adverbs in Hindko, Panjabi, and Saraiki are given in Chapter 5, in Table 5.15, Table 5.16, Table 5.18, Table 5.32, and Table 5.33. The relationship of the interrogative phrase(s) to other pronominal adjectives and adverbs is discussed in Section 5.1.5.

The forms for both the personal interrogative pronoun کَوݨ /kauṇ/ 'who' and impersonal interrogative pronoun کیہہ /kī/ 'what' for Panjabi were presented in Table 6.8.

A few examples from Hindko follow in 9.153 through 9.155.

(9.153) اس دی کے قیمت اے

us	*d-ī*	***ke***	*kīmat*	*e*
3SG.OBL	GEN-SG.F	**what**	price[F]	be.PRES.3SG

'What does it cost?' (Hk) (AWT)

(9.154) تُسی کتنے پہنڑ پھرا ہو

tussī	***kitn-e***	*pæ̀ř-prā̀*	*ho*
2PL.DIR	**how.many-PL.M**	sister-brother	be.PRES.2PL

'How many brothers and sisters are you?'[14] (Hk) (AWT)

(9.155) تیرے کپڑیاں دا رنگ کیھوجے

ter-e	*kapṛ-eā̃*	*d-ā*	*rang*
2SG.GEN-SG.M.OBL	clothes-PL.M.OBL	GEN-SG.M	color[M]

kéoj-æ
what.kind.of-SG.M+be.PRES.3SG

'What color are your clothes? (lit. what is the color of your clothes?)' (Hk) (AWT)

A few simple examples from Panjabi, adapted from Bhatia (1993: 9–10), follow in 9.156 through 9.161.

14 پہنڑ پھرا /pæ̀ř-prā̀/ 'sister-brother' is a compound. Notice that in these languages 'sister' is the first element of the compound, whereas in English 'brother' usually comes first, as in 'brothers and sisters'.

(9.156) تہاڈا ناں کیہہ اے

tuȁḍ-ā	*nā̃*	***kī̂***	*e*
2PL.GEN-SG.M	name.SG.M.DIR	**what**	be.PRES.3SG

'What is your name?' (Pj)

(9.157) حمزہ کتھے اے

Hamzā	***kítthe***	*e*
hamza.SG.M	**where**	be.PRES.3SG

'Where is Hamza?' (Pj)

(9.158) اوہ کون اے

ó	***kauṇ***	*e*
3SG.DIST	**who**	be.PRES.3SG

'Who is that?' (Pj)

(9.159) تسیں ایہہ کم کیویں کیتا

tusī̃	*é*	*kamm*	***kīvẽ***	*kī-t-ā*
2PL.DIR	3SG.PROX	work[M]	**how**	do-PP-SG.M

'How did you do this work?' (Pj)

(9.160) ایہدا کنّا مل اے

é-dā	***kinnā***	*mull*	*e*
3SG.PROX.OBL-GEN.SG.M	**how.much**	price.SG.M.DIR	be.PRES.3SG

'What is the cost of this?' (Pj)

(9.161) توں اوتھے کیوں گیا

tū̃	*otthe*	***kyõ***	*gyā*
2SG.DIR	there	why	go.PP.SG.M

'Why did you go there?' (Pj)

The following are similar sentences from Saraiki.

(9.162) اتھوں کنو لہور کہوتلا پریں ہے

ith-ū̃	*kan-ū*	*lahɔr*	***kihotalā***	*parẽ*	*he*
here-ABL	vicinity-ABL	Lahore	**how.much**	distant	be.PRES.3SG

'How far is it from here to Lahore?' (Sr) (UK)

(9.163) اما ڈسیا ہا جو کپڑا کیویں رنگیندے

ammā	*ɗas-iyā*	*h-ā*	*jo*	*kapṛā*	***kīvẽ***
Mother	tell-PP.SG.M	be.PST-SG.M	that	cloth[M]	**how**

rangī̃-d-e
dye.PASS-IP-SG.M+be.PRES.3SG

'Mother told (me) how to dye cloth. (lit. how cloth is dyed)' (Sr) (UK)

(9.164) میکوں اوں کنے کیوں پٹھیئی

mæ-kū̃	*ū̃*	*kan-e*	***kyū̃***	*pa-ṭhe-ī*
1SG.OBL-ACC	3SG.OBL	vicinity-LOC	**why**	send-PP-PS2SG

'Why did you send me to him/her?' (Sr) (UK)

(9.165) میکوں ڈس جو کیرھلے آونے

mæ-kū̃	*ɗass*	*jo*	***kerhele***	*āu-ṇ-e*
1SG.OBL-DAT	tell	that	**when**	come-GRDV-SG.M+be.PRES.3SG

'Tell me when to come.' (Sr) (UK)

Intonation rises in questions, with the question word itself usually receiving primary sentence stress. As in other Indo-Aryan languages, a reduplicated k-word indicates that a plural or list answer is expected, as in example 9.166. See Section 10.10 on reduplication.

(9.166) ایہ شعر اساں کنھاں کنھاں کتاباں اچوں ڳولوں

e	*šer*	*assā̃*	***kinh-ā̃***	***kinh-ā̃***	*kitab-ā̃*	*ic-ū̃*
3SG.PROX	verse	1PL	**which.PL-OBL**	**REDUP**	book-PL.OBL	in-ABL

ɠol-ū̃
search-SBJV.1PL

'In which books are we to search for this verse?' (Sr) (Shackle 1976: 113)

9.2 Compound (coordinate) sentences

Compound sentences consist of two independent clauses joined by a coordinating conjunction, like English 'and', 'or', and 'but'. These structures are similar in all three languages.

9.2.1 Compound (coordinate) sentences – Hindko

The most frequently occurring Hindko coordinating conjunctions are تے /te/ 'and', اور /aur/ 'and', یا /yā/ 'or', and پر/par/ 'but'. The use of پر/par/ 'but' is illustrated in example 9.167.

(9.167) میں اس دا ناں پھل گیاں پر تیرا نا پھلیا

mæ̃	*us*	*d-ā*	*nā̃*	*pùl*	*g-yā̃*
1SG.DIR	3SG.OBL	GEN-SG.M	name[M]	forget	go-PP.SG.M+be.PRES.1SG

par	*ter-ā*	*nā*	*pùl-iyā*
but	2SG.GEN-SG.M	NEG	forget.PP-SG.M

'I (m) have forgotten his/her name **but** I haven't forgotten yours.' (Hk) (AWT)

9.2.2 Compound (coordinate) sentences – Panjabi

The use of the conjunctions پر /par/ 'but' and یا /yā/ 'or' in Panjabi are illustrated in examples 9.168 and 9.169, respectively.

(9.168) سبزی والا بڑی دیر تیکر گلی وچ واجاں لاندا رہیا پر کسے وی کجھ نہ خریدیا

sabzī	*vāl-ā*	*baṛī*	*der*	*tikar*	*gaḷī*	*vic*
vegetable	NMLZ-SG.M	great-SG.F	time.SG.F	until	street	in

vāj-ā̃	*lā-nd-ā*	*r-yā́*	***par***	*kise*	*vī*	*kúj*
voice-PL.F	put-IP-SG.M	remain-SG.M	**but**	anyone	even	anything

na	*xarīd-iyā*
NEG	buy-PP.SG.M

'The vegetable seller kept calling in the street for a long time, **but** no one bought anything.' (Pj) (Bashir and Kazmi 2012: 10)

(9.169) تسی کلے او یا فیملی دا کوئی ہور وی فرد ایتھے کوئی جاب کردا اے

tussī	*kalle*	*o*	***yā***	*fæmlī*	*d-ā*	*koī*	*hor*	*vī*
2PL.DIR	alone	be.PRES.2PL	**or**	family	GEN-SG.M	any	other	INCL

fard	*ethe*	*koī*	*jāb*	*kar-d-ā*	*e*
person	here	some	job	do-IP-SG.M	be.PRES.3SG

'Are you here by yourself **or** does some other family member have a job here, too?' (Pj) (Bashir and Kazmi 2012: 61)

9.2.3 Compound (coordinate) sentences – Saraiki

Saraiki coordinating conjunctions include اتے /ate/ ~ تے /te/ 'and', پر /par/ 'but', and یا /yā/ 'or'. Coordinating conjunctions can link clauses, phrases, or single words, e.g. بھینڑو تے بھراوو /bheṇ-o te bhirā-vo/ '(o) sisters and brothers!'. Pairs of coordinating conjunctions are: یا - - - یا /yā ... yā/ 'either ... or' ہکے ... ہکے /hike... hike/ 'either ... or'; نا ... نا /nā ... nā/ 'neither ... nor'; کیا ... کیا /kyā ... kyā/ 'whether ... or' (Shackle 1976: 69).

The conjunction اتے /ate/ 'and' appears in examples 9.170 and 9.171.

(9.170) ٻال کوں بکھ لگیے اتے رونے

ɓāl	*kū̃*	*bukh*	*laɠī-e*	***ate***
baby.SG.M	DAT	hunger[F]	attach.PP.SG.F-be.PRES.3SG	**and**

rū-n-e
cry-PP-SG.M+be.PRES.3SG

'The baby (m.) got hungry **and** (he) cried.' (Sr) (UK)

(9.171) اوکوں نانگ ڈنگھ ماریے اتے او موے

ū	*kū̃*	*nāng*	*ɗangh*	*mār-iye*	***ate***
3SG	ACC	snake.SG.M	sting[M]	beat-PP.SG.M+be.PRES.3SG	**and**

o	*mo-e*
3SG.DIR	die.PP-SG.M+be.PRES.3SG

'A snake stung him **and** he has died.' (Sr) (UK)

The Saraiki conjunction مڑی /maṛī/ 'but' is illustrated in example 9.172.

(9.172) میں کلھ سرٹیفکیٹ ڳولیے مڑی میکوں لدھا نھیں

mæ̃	*kalh*	*sarṭifkeṭ*	*ɠol-iye*	***maṛī***
1SG	yesterday	certificate[M]	search.for-PP.SG.M+be.PRES.3SG	**but**

mæ-kū̃	*la-dhā*	*nhī̃*
1SG-DAT	be.found-PP.SG.M	NEG

'I looked for the certificate yesterday, **but** I didn't find it.' (Sr) (UK)

The paired conjunction ہکے... ہکے /hike ... hike/ 'either... or' is illustrated in example 9.173.

(9.173) ہکے سگرٹ پی ہکے چاہ

hike	*sigreṭ*	*pī*	***hike***	*cāh*
either	cigarette	drink.2SG.IMP	**or**	tea

'**Either** have a cigarette, **or** some tea.'[15] (Sr) (Shackle 1976: 161)

9.3 Complex sentences

Complex sentences consist of a main (matrix) clause and an embedded subordinate clause. Subordinate clauses may function as nouns, adjectives, or adverbs. Relative clauses are often adjectival, but can also function adverbially, expressing temporal, spatial, causal, or manner relations. Two types of subordinate clauses are found in these languages: finite and non-finite. Finite subordinate clauses contain a fully conjugated verb, while non-finite clauses have a form not marked for person or tense, like an infinitive or participle.

9.3.1 Finite subordinate clauses

9.3.1.1 Nominal clauses

In addition to local indigenous forms, the ubiquitous subordinating conjunction کہ /ki/ 'that' is employed in all three languages, especially by people living in urban environments or having more formal education.

15 Inhaling (vapors) and drinking (liquids) are expressed with the same verb in all three languages: پیڑا /pīṛ̃a/ Hk , پیݨا /pīṇā/ Pj , and پیوݨ /pīvaṇ/ Sr 'to drink'.

9.3.1.1.1 Finite nominal clauses – Hindko

The complementizer introducing most nominal subordinate clauses in Hindko is جے /je/, which fulfills the same function as کہ /ki/ in Urdu and Panjabi. جے /je/ also is part of complex conjunctions like تاں جے /tã̄ je/ 'so that/in order that' and کیہں جے /kyõ je/ 'because'. A typical sentence of this type is shown in example 9.174.

(9.174) ایہ بالکل ٹھیک اے جے ہندکو ہک بوہنہ پرانڑیں زبان اے

é	*bilkul*	*ṭhik*	*e*	***je***	*hindko*	*hik*	*báũ̄*	*purāṝĩ*
this	completely	right	be.PRES.3SG	**that**	Hindko	one	very	old

zaban	*e*
language	be.PRES.3SG

'It is entirely correct **that** Hindko is a very old language.' (Hk) (Soz 2009: 6)

However, کہ /ki/ is also used, especially by urban dwellers, as in example 9.175.

(9.175) میں کسے آں آخساں کہ تداں یاد کراوے

mæ̃	*kise-ã̄*	*āx-s-ã̄*	***ki***	*tud-ã̄*
1SG.DIR/OBL	someone.OBL-DAT	say-FUT-1SG	**that**	2SG.OBL-DAT

yād	*kar-ā-ve*
memory	do-CS-SBJV.3SG

'I will have someone remind you. (lit. I will tell someone that he should remind you.)' (Hk) (AWT)

9.3.1.1.2 Finite nominal clauses – Panjabi

In contemporary urban Panjabi, nominal clauses are usually introduced by the subordinating conjunction (complementizer) کہ /ki/, both in written texts, as in example 9.176, and in everyday speech, as in example 9.177.

(9.176) میں ایہہ سن کے بڑی حیران ہوئی کہ اوہ ایس مکان اچ اکلی رہندی سی

mæ̃	*é*	*suṇ-ke*	*baṛ-ī*	*hærān*	*ho-ī*	***ki***
1SG.DIR	this	hear-CP	very-SG.F	surprised	become-PP-SG.F	**that**

ó	*æs*	*makān*	*ic*	*akall-ī*	*ræ̃n-d-ī*
3SG.DIST.DIR	3SG.PROX.OBL	house	in	alone-SG.F	live-IP-SG.F

sī
be.PST.3SG

'I (f) was really surprised to hear **that** she was living alone in this house.'[16] (Pj) (Bashir and Kazmi 2012: 46)

(9.177) میرا خیال اے کہ اوہ جاویگا

mer-ā *xyāl* *e* *ki* *ó*
1SG.GEN-SG.M thought[M] be.PRES.3SG **that** 3SG

jā-ve-g-ā
go-3SG.SUBJ-FUT-SG.M

'I think **that** he will go.' (Pj) (Bhatia 1993: 42–43)

Older forms like جو /jo/, as in example 9.178 or جے /je/, as in example 9.179, are also found.

(9.178) چیف جسٹس آف پاکستان جسٹس انورظہیر جمالی نے آکھیا ہے جو ستھاں نوں نویں سوچ اتے ٹیکنالوجی دی لوڑ ہے

cīf *jasṭis* *āf* *pākistān* *jasṭis* *anwar* *zahīr* *jamālī* *ne*
chief justice of Pakistan justice Anwar Zahir Jamali ERG

ākh-iyā *he* ***jo*** *sathā̃-nū̃* *nav-ī̃* *soc*
say-PP.SG.M. be.PRES.3SG **that** groups-DAT new-SG.F thought[F]

ate *ṭĕknāloji* *d-ī* *loṛ* *e*
and technology[F] GEN-SG.F need[F] be.PRES.3SG

'The Chief Justice of Pakistan has said **that** groups need new thinking and technology.' (Pj) (http://vehari.sujag.org/khulasa/45356)

(9.179) ایہی وڈی وجہ اے جے ساڈے دیس دا تعلیمی رتبہ دن بدن گھٹدا جا رہیا اے

é-ī *vaḍḍī* *vajā* *e* ***je*** *sāḍ-e*
this-EMPH big.SG.F reason[F] be.PRES.3SG **that** our-SG.M.OBL

des *d-ā* *tālīmī* *rutbā* *din-ba-din*
country.SG.M.OBL GEN-SG.M educational standard.SG.M day-by-day

kàṭ-d-ā *jā-ry-ā́* *e*
decrease-IP-SG.M go-CONT.II-SG.M be.PRES.3SG

'This the main reason **that** the educational standard of our country is declining day by day.' (Pj) (Rafiq 2000)

16 Agreeing adverbs like بڑا /baṛā/ are an interesting feature of Panjabi. Feminine gender appears in this sentence because the subject is feminine.

9.3.1.1.3 Finite nominal clauses – Saraiki

The subordinating conjunction mostly used in Saraiki is جو /jo/ 'that', as in examples 9.180 and 9.181.

(9.180) میکوں ڈس جو کیرھلے آوݨے

mæ-kū̃	*ɗas*	***jo***	*kerh-l-e*	*āv-ṇ-e*
1SG.OBL-DAT	tell	**that**	which-time-OBL	come-GRDV-SG.M+be.PRES.3SG

'Tell me **when** to come.' (Sr) (UK)

(9.181) فروک سچیندا ہا جو نوکری مل ویسی

farūk	*sac-ẽd-ā*	*h-ā*	***jo***	*nokarī*	*mil*	*ve-s-ī*
Farooq	think-IP-SG.M	be.PST-SG.M	**that**	job	be.gotten	go-FUT-3SG

'Farooq thought he would get the job.'[17] (Sr) (UK)

9.3.1.2 Relative clauses

Both finite and non-finite relative clauses are freely used in all three languages. Finite (as opposed to participial) relative clauses consist of a relative (subordinate) clause and a correlative (main) clause, both of which contain conjugated verb forms. The relative clause contains a j-initial relative element (pronoun, adjective, or adverb), and the correlative (main) clause contains a distal pronominal, adjectival, or adverbial element. These constructions are thus typically called relative-correlative constructions. The forms of the various relative pronouns and adjectives are given in Section 6.7 and Section 5.1.3.3.2 respectively. The paradigm for جو /jo/ is given in Table 6.13. Non-finite relative clauses are formed in two principal ways: (1) with perfective or imperfective participles, (2) with the adjective-forming element والا ~ آلا /vālā ~ ālā/.

17 The proper name Farooq is usually spelled فاروق, but here it is spelled in P-A as it sounds.

9.3.1.2.1 Adjectival relative clauses

Adjectival relative clauses modify a noun or noun phrase. In these constructions, the case of the nominal (phrase) in the relative clause is determined by its grammatical role in the relative clause; and in the same way, the case of the nominal (phrase) in the correlative (main) clause is determined by its role in the correlative clause.

In the Hindko example 9.182, the relative element in the adjectival relative clause is جس /jis/, and the correlative element is اُس /us/ '3SG.OBL'. These elements both appear in their oblique forms in the example since they encode the subject/agent of a perfective transitive clause in both the relative and correlative clauses.

(9.182) جس جنڑیں اساں دی منجھ چھپائی ، اُس دوے گرائیں بچ کھوڑا چھپایا

jis	*jaṛ̃-ẽ*	*assā̃*	*d-ī*	*mā̃j*	*chupā-ī*
which.REL.OBL	man-OBL	1PL.OBL	GEN-SG.F	buffalo[F]	steal-PP.SG.F

us	*du-e*	*grā̃-ẽ*	*bic*	*kòṛā*
3SG.DIST.OBL	other-SG.M.OBL	village-OBL	in	horse[M]

chupā-yā
steal-PP.SG.M

'The man who stole our buffalo stole a horse in another village.' (Hk) (AWT)

In example 9.183, the relative element جیھڑا /jéṛā/ is in its direct case form, since it is the unmarked direct object in the relative clause; in the correlative clause, the element اُس کہرے /us kàr-e/ 'in that house' is oblique, since it is the object of the postposition بچ /bic/ 'in'.

(9.183) میں اُس آں اُس کہرے بچ دیکھیا جیھڑا تُد بعد بچ کہدا ایہیا

mæ̃	*us-ā̃*	***us***	***kàr-e***	*bic*
1SG.DIR	3SG.DIST.OBL-ACC	**3SG.DIST.OBL**	**house-OBL**	in

dex-iyā	***jéṛ-ā***	*tud*	*bād*	*bic*	*kìd-ā*
see-PP.SG.M	**REL-SG.M.DIR**	2SG.OBL	afterwards	in	take.PP-SG.M

éy-ā
be.PST-SG.M

'I saw her/him in the house which you later bought.' (Hk) (AWT)

In example 9.184, the correlative element اس /us/ is oblique because it modifies the indirect object 'boy' in the correlative (matrix) clause; the relative element جس /jis/ is oblique because it precedes the dative postposition اں /ā̃/ in the relative clause.

(9.184) میں اپڑی کتاب اُس جاتکے آں دتی اے جس آں تُد فوٹو دسیا

mæ̃	*apṛ-ī*	*kitāb*	***us***	***jātk-e-ā̃***
1SG.OBL	REFL-SG.F	book[F]	**3SG.DIST.OBL**	**boy-OBL-DAT**

di-tt-ī	*e*	***jis-ā̃***	*tud*	*foṭo*
give-PP-SG.F	be.PRES.3SG	**REL.OBL-DAT**	2SG.OBL	photo[M]

dass-iyā
show.PP-SG.M

'I have given my book to the boy to whom you showed the photograph.' (Hk) (AWT)

In Panjabi, جیڑھا /jéṛā/ 'who/which.REL ' is the relative element which appears the most frequently. In examples 9.185 and 9.186, the two main word order possibilities for relative clauses are illustrated. In example 9.185, the relative clause is sentence final, and in example 9.186, it is sentence initial. Sentence-final placement of a relative clause adds (new) information to that of the main clause, and often is employed to express an afterthought, thus often being comparable to a non-restrictive relative clause. Sentence-initial placement of a relative clause topicalizes it and produces a restrictive relative clause, as in example 9.186.[18]

(9.185) اوہ منڈا کون اے جیڑھا اوتھے بیٹھا اے

ó	***mū̃ḍā***	*kɔṇ*	*e*	***jéṛ-ā***	*othe*
3SG.DIST.DIR	**boy**	who	be.PRES.3SG	**REL.DIR-SG.M**	there

bæṭh-ā	*e*
sit-PP.SG.M	be.PRES.3SG

'Who is that boy, who is sitting there?' (Pj) (EB)

(9.186) جیڑھا منڈا اوتھے بیٹھا اے اوہ کون اے

jéṛ-ā	*mū̃ḍā*	*othe*	*bæṭh-ā*	*e*	***ó***
REL.DIR.-SG.M	**boy**	there	sit-PP-SG.M	be.PRES.3SG	**3SG.DIST.DIR**

kɔṇ	*e*
who	be.PRES.3SG

'The boy who is sitting there – who is he?' (Pj) (EB)

18 Occasionally, one may find a sentence-medial relative clause immediately following the noun it modifies in written texts, as in the Panjabi sentence اوہ منڈا جیڑھا اوتھے بیٹھا اے کون اے /ó muṇḍā jéṛā othe bæṭhā e kɔṇ e / "Who is the boy who is sitting there", but this order is difficult to process, and is dispreferred. It is thought by many to be an influence of English.

In Saraiki, the most common relative elements are جو /jo/ 'which/who.REL' and جیرھا /jerhā/ 'which/who.REL'. In the adjectival relative clause in example 9.187, the correlative element, او کاتی /ū kātī/ 'that knife', is in the direct case since it is the subject of the intransitive main clause; and the relative element is جیں /jæ̃/ 'which/who.OBL' since it is the object of the postposition نال /nāl/ 'with'.

(9.187) او کاتی کتھاں اے جیں نال میں آلو کپیندا پیا ہامی

ū	***kātī***	*kithā̃*	*e*	***jæ̃***	*nāl*	*mæ̃*
3SG.DIST.DIR	**knife.DIR**	where	be.PRES.3SG	**REL.OBL**	with	1SG

ālū	*kap-ẽd-ā*	*p-yā*	*hā-mī*
potatoes	cut-IP-SG.M	CONT.I-SG.M	be.PST-1SG

'Where is the knife with which I (m.) was cutting potatoes?' (Sr) (UK)

In example 9.188, in the main clause ہک کاتی /hikk kātī/ 'a knife' is oblique since it is the object of the postposition نال /nāl/ 'with'. It corresponds with the relative element جیرھی /jerhī/ 'which', which is in the direct case since it is the subject of the intransitive relative clause.

(9.188) اوں چورکوں ھک کاتی نال ماریے جیرھی بھوے تے پی ہی

ū̃	*cor-kū̃*	*hikk*	***kātī***	*nāl*	*mār-iye*
3SG.OBL	thief-ACC	a	**knife[F]**	with	kill.PP-SG.M+be.PRES.3SG

jerh-ī	*bhū-e*	*te*	*p-ī*	*h-ī*
which-F	ground-OBL	on	lie.PP-SG.F	be.PST-SG.F

'He/she killed the thief with a knife that was lying on the ground.' (Sr) (UK)

In example 9.189, the relative element is جیرھا بندا /jerhā bandā/ 'the man who', and the correlative element is represented by the third person singular pronominal suffix سی /sī/, which indexes the agent in the main clause.

(9.189) جیرھا بندا اساڈی منجھ چوری کیتی ھئی اوں کھوہ تے گھوڑا چوری کیتیسی

jerh-ā	***bandā***	*asāḍ-ī*	*mā̃jh*	*corī*	*k-īt-ī*	*h-aī*
REL-SG.M	man	our-F	buffalo[F]	theft[F]	do-PP-SG.F	be.PST-SG.F

ū̃	*khoh*	*te*	*ghoṛā*	*corī*	*kī-t-ī-**sī***
3SG.DIST.OBL	village	in	horse[M]	theft[F]	do-PP-SG.F-**PS3SG**

'The man who stole our buffalo stole a horse in that village.' (Sr) (UK)

The proverb in example 9.190 shows a relative correlative clause comparing quantity. Notice that the invariant element جتی /jittī/ 'as much as' does not change to match the masculine gender of گڑ /guṛ/ 'brown sugar'.

(9.190) جِتّی گُڑ اُتّی مِٹّھا

jittī	*guṛ*	***uttī***	*miṭṭh-ā*
as.much.as	brown.sugar.SG.M	**that.much**	sweet-SG.M

'The more brown sugar (you put in it), the sweeter it will be.' (Sr) (Mughal 2010: 336)

9.3.1.2.2 Adverbial relative clauses

Adverbial relations of time, space, reason, and manner can be expressed with finite relative clauses in all these languages.

The Hindko sentences in examples 9.191, 9.192, and 9.193 contain adverbial relative clauses that express various temporal relations.

(9.191) میں اُس ویلے تک نہ کھاندا جد تک توں نہ آسیں

mæ̃	***us***	***vel-e***	***tak***	*ná*	*khā̃-d-ā*	***jad***
1SG.DIR	**3SG.DIST.OBL**	**time-OBL**	**until**	NEG	eat-IP-SG.M	**when[REL]**

tak	*tū̃*	***ná***	*ā-s-ẽ*
until	2SG	**NEG**	come-FUT-2SG

'I (m) won't eat until you come.' (Hk) (AWT)

In example 9.191, a negative element نہ /na/ appears in the relative clause meaning 'until', pointing to the end point of the interval during which you have *not* come, as it also does in Panjabi and Urdu. However, with the meaning 'so long as', i.e. pointing to the interval during which 'it *is* raining', as in example 9.192, a negative element does not appear.

(9.192) جد تک بارش ہو رہی اے اسی باہر نہ جلدے

jad	***tak***	*bāriš*	*ho*	*ra-ī́*	*e*	*assī*
when[REL]	**until**	rain[F]	be	CONT.II-SG.F	be.PRES.3SG	1PL

bā́r	*ná*	*jul-d-e*
outside	NEG	go-IP-PL.M

'As long as it's raining we won't go out.' (Hk) (AWT)

Although an overt correlative temporal element is absent in the main clause in examples 9.192 and 9.193, they are nevertheless relative constructions. 9.193 also illustrates the periphrastic passive in Hindko.

(9.193) مفرور جوں ہی سٹیشن تے پہنچیا او سیانیا گیا

mafrūr	***jū̃***	***hī***	*sṭešan*	*te*	*pɔ̃́c-iyā*	*o*
fugitive	**as.soon.as**	**EMPH**	station	to	reach.PP-SG.M	3SG.DIST.DIR

syān-iyā	*g-yā*
recognize.PP-SG.M	go.PP-SG.M

'As soon as the fugitive got to the station, he was recognized.' (Hk) (AWT)

In example 9.194, a spatial relation is expressed by the correlative element اس گرائیں /us grā̃ẽ/ 'in that village'. This sentence also exhibits another fairly recent development, the reinforcing of the j-initial relative element جتھے /jithe/ 'where.REL' with the complementizer کہ /ki/ 'that'.

(9.194) او اس گرائیں بچ نیں رہنڑا چاہندا کہ جتھے بجلی ای نئیں

o	*us*	*grā̃-ẽ*	*bic*	*nī̃*	*rǽṛā*	*cā́-nd-ā*	***ki***
3SG.DIR	3SG.OBL	village-OBL	in	NEG	live.INF	want-IP-SG.M	**that**

jithe	*bijilī*	*ī*	*naī̃*
where.REL	electricity	EMPH	NEG

'He doesn't want to live in that village, where there is no electricity.' (Hk) (AWT)

In Panjabi, example 9.195 expresses a spatial relation in a simple, prototypical relative-correlative construction through the topicalized, sentence-initial relative clause.

(9.195) جتھے میرا بھرا رہندا اے اوتھے ہر چیز مہنگی اے

jithe	*mer-ā*	*prà*	*rǽn-d-ā*	*e*	***othe***
where.REL	1SG.GEN-SG.M	brother	live-IP-SG.M	be.PRES.3SG	**there**

har	*cīz*	*méng-ī*	*e*
every	thing[F]	expensive-F	be.PRES.3SG

'Where my brother lives everything is expensive.' (Pj) (EB)

The relative element جتھے /jithe/ 'where.REL' could also, very felicitously, follow the subject of the relative clause, as in example 9.196. This observation about word-order alternatives holds true for all types of relative clauses, in all three languages.

(9.196) میرا بھرا جتھے رہندا اے اوتھے ہر چیز مہنگی اے

mer-ā	*prā̀*	***jithe***	*rǽn-d-ā*	*e*	***othe***
1SG.GEN-SG.M	brother	**where.REL**	live-IP-SG.M	be.PRES.3SG	**there**

har	*cīz*	*méng-ī*	*e*
every	thing[F]	expensive-F	be.PRES.3SG

'Where my brother lives everything is expensive.' (Pj) (EB)

A temporal relative clause is illustrated in example 9.197. Note that in this example there is no overt correlative element (اوہدوں دی /ódõ dī/ 'since then') corresponding to the relative element جدوں دی /jadõ dī/ 'since when' expressed. This sentence type, in which an overt correlative element is absent, is increasingly frequent in the contemporary language. This sentence also illustrates the compound verb گھٹ جانا /kàṭ jāṇā/ 'to decrease' (see Section 10.1 for a discussion of compound verbs.)

(9.197) جدوں دی ایہہ کندھ اسری اے گڈیاں دا شور گھٹ گیا اے

jadõ	***dī***	*é*	*kánd*	*ussar-ī*	*e*	*gaḍḍi-yā̃*
when.REL	**of**	this	wall[F]	raised-PP.SG.F	be.PRES.3SG	vehicle-PL.F

d-ā	*šor*	*kàṭ*	*ga-yā*	*e*
of-SG.M	noise[M]	lessen	go-PP.SG.M	be.PRES.3SG

'Ever since this wall was built, the traffic noise has decreased.' (Pj) (Bashir and Kazmi 2012: 35)

In example 9.198, a relative clause compares conditions of manner. The relative element is جیویں /jīvẽ/ 'in which way', and the correlative element is ایس طرحاں /æs tarhā̃/ 'in this way'.

(9.198) اوہ میریاں گلاں تے ایس طرحاں ہس رہیا سی جیویں میں پاگل آں

ó	*mer-iyā̃*	*gall-ā̃*	*te*	***æs***	***tarā̃***	*has*	*r-yā*
3SG.DIR	my-PL.F	word-PL.F	on	**this**	**way**	laugh	CONT.II-SG.M

sī	***jīvẽ***	*mǣ*	*pāgal*	*ā̃*
be.PST.3SG	**as.if**	1SG.DIR	crazy	be.PRES.1SG

'He was laughing at my remarks as if I were insane.' (Pj) (Bashir and Kazmi 2012: 135)

Saraiki temporal relations are illustrated in the relative-correlative examples 9.199 and 9.200, and a spatial relation in 9.202. According to Nasir Abbas Syed (p.c.), Saraiki prefers relative-correlative 'until, as long as' structures in which either both clauses are negative or both are positive, as in 9.199 and 9.200.

(9.199) جے تاݨی توں اوسیں میں اے کم کر گھنساں

je.taṇī	*tū̃*	*ɔ-s-ẽ*	*mæ̃*	*e*	*kam*	*kar*	*ghin-s-ā̃*
by.the.time	2SG	come-FUT-2SG	1SG	this	work	do	take-FUT-1SG

'I will complete this task by the time you come.' (Sr) (NAS, p.c.)

(9.200) جے تاݨی توں نا اوسیں میں اے کم نا کریساں

je.tāṇī	*tū̃*	*nā*	*ɔ-s-ẽ*	*mæ̃*	*e*	*kam*	*nā*
by.the.time	2SG	NEG	come-FUT-2SG	I	this	work	NEG

kare-s-ā̃
do-FUT-1SG

'I will not do this task until you come.' (Sr) (NAS, p.c.)

(9.201) جیرھے ݙیھیں بیمار ھامی پتر گھر دا سبک کینا کریندا ھا

jerh-e	***ɗīh-ī̃***	*bimār*	*hā-mī*	*putr*	*ghar*	*d-ā*
REL-PL.M	**day-LOC.PL**	ill	be.PST-1SG	son	home	GEN-SG.M

sabak	*kænā*	*kar-ẽd-ā*	*h-ā*
lesson[M]	NEG.EMPH	do-IP-SG.M	be.PST-SG.M

'While I was sick my son wasn't doing his homework. (lit. in the days when I was sick.)'[19] (Sr) (UK)

(9.202) او اینجھی جاہ تے نا رہندا ہا جتھاں بجلی ہی کینھی

ū	***ĩjh-ī***	***jāh***	*te*	*nā*	*rahn-d-ā*	*h-ā*
3SG.DIR	**such.a-F.SG**	**place[F]**	at	NEG	live-IP-M.SG	be.PST-SG.M

jithā̃	*bijlī*	*hī*	*kænhī*
where.REL	electricity	even	NEG.EMPH

'He wasn't willing to live in a place where there isn't even electricity.' (Sr) (UK)

19 Note that the spelling of بیمار 'sick' would suggest the pronunciation /bīmār/. However, it is actually pronounced /bimār/. This non-correspondence between spelling and pronunciation is a result of the incorporation of many Urdu words into these languages, along with their Urdu spellings. Many such words, however, are pronounced according to the phonological patterns of the recipient languages.

9.3.1.3 Conditional clauses

Conditional clauses involve hypothetical relationships between events: 'if X happens, then Y'. Two basic types of conditionals—realis and irrealis—are treated here separately. Realis conditionals are those which refer to events which are as yet unrealized but are presented as possible. Irrealis conditionals refer to a situation or event that is known (or assumed) not to have happened or not to be going to happen.

9.3.1.3.1 Realis conditionals

In our Hindko corpus, the subordinating conjunction introducing conditional clauses is usually کدے /kade/ 'if' when the 'if'-clause (subordinate) begins the sentence, as in examples 9.203 and 9.204, and جے /je/ 'if' when the 'if'-clause follows the matrix clause, as in example 9.205. Many realis conditionals in Hindko have a future (as in examples 9.203 and 9.204) or a simple perfect verb (as in example 9.205) in the 'if'-clause and a future form in the 'then'-clause. The correlative conjunction تے /te/ 'then' (usually) appears when the 'if'-clause begins the sentence, as in examples 9.203 and 9.204.

(9.203) کدے ادھوانڑا کھانڑے توں بعد توں ٹھنڈا پانڑی پیسیں تے تداں ہیضہ ہو جلسی

kade	*adwā̀ṛā*	*khāṛ-e*	*tõ*	*bād*	*tū̃*	*ṭhanḍā*	*pāṛī*
if	watermelon	eat-INF.OBL	from	after	you	cold	water

pī-s-ẽ	***te***	*tud-ā̃*	*hæzā*	*ho*	*jul-s-ī*
drink-FUT-2SG	**then**	2SG.OBL-DAT	diarrhea	be	go-FUT-3SG

'**If** you drink cold water after eating watermelon you will get diarrhea.' (Hk) (AWT)

(9.204) کدے توں اے دوائی کہنسیں تے تیرے سرے دا درد کہٹ جُلسی

kade	*tū̃*	*é*	*davāī*	*kȉn-s-ẽ*	***te***	*ter-e*
if	2SG	this	medicine	take-FUT-2SG	**then**	2SG.GEN-OBL.SG.M

sir-e	*d-ā*	*dard*	*kȁṭ*	*jul-s-ī*
head-OBL	GEN-SG.M	pain[M]	lessen	go-FUT-3SG

'**If** you drink this medicine your headache will lessen.' (Hk) (AWT)

(9.205) تُوں کے کرسیں جے تیرا جہاز لیٹ ہو گیا

tũ ke kar-s-ẽ ***je*** *ter-ā jȁz leṭ ho*
2SG what do-FUT-2SG **if** 2SG.GEN-SG.M plane[M] late be

ga-yā
go.PP-SG.M

'What will you do **if** your flight is late?' (Hk) (AWT)

In Panjabi, the 'if'-clause (protasis) of realis conditionals is formed with both the indigenous conjunction جے /je/ 'if' and Urdu اگر /agar/ 'if'. Frequently occurring tenses in the protasis are the simple perfect, as in examples 9.206 and 9.207, subjunctive, as in 9.208, and present, as in 9.209. The future may appear in the 'if'-clause, as in the Hindko example 9.204 above. An overt 'if' element like اگر /agar/ 'if' or جے /je/ 'if' is frequently omitted, however, especially in conversation. The 'then'-clause (apodosis) can employ various tense-aspect forms, including the infinitive in its distanced imperative function, in examples 9.206 and 9.207, future, as in 9.208, subjunctive, as in 9.209, and present imperfect, as in 9.210.

(9.206) جے تسی اودھر گئے تے میرا خط وی پا دینا

je *tussī udhar ga-e* ***te*** *mer-ā xat vī pā*
if 2PL there go.PP-M.PL **then** 1SG.GEN-SG.M letter[M] also put

de-ṇā
give-INF

'**If** you go that way please mail my letter as well.' (Pj) (Bashir and Kazmi 2012: 63)

(9.207) جے ساڈے پچھوں کسے دا فون آیا تے اوہدا ناں تے نمبر لکھ لینا

je *sāḍe pich-õ kise d-ā fon ā-yā*
if our after-ABL anyone.OBL GEN-SG.M phone[M] come-PP.SG.M

te *ó d-ā nā̃ te nambar likh læ-ṇā*
then 3SG.DIST GEN-SG.M name and number write take-INF

'**If** someone calls in our absence, take down his name and number.' (Pj) (Bashir and Kazmi 2012: 142)

(9.208) جے تسی اج کمپیوٹر خریدو تے تہانوں سو ڈالر دی بچت ہووے گی

je	*tussī*	*ajj*	*kampyūṭar*	*xarīd-o*	***te***	*tuā̀-nū̃*
if	2PL	today	computer	buy-SBJV.2PL	**then**	2PL.OBL-DAT

sɔ	*ḍālar*	*d-ī*	*bacat*	*hove-g-ī*
hundred	dollars	GEN-SG.F	saving[F]	be.SBJV.3SG-FUT-SG.F

'**If** you purchase a computer today, you will save a hundred dollars.' (Pj) (Bashir and Kazmi 2012: 91)

(9.209) اگر ایہناں نوں ایس فیصلے تے اعتراض اے تے سپریم کورٹ نال رجوع کرن

agar	*én-ā̃-nū̃*	*æs*	*fæsl-e*	*te*	*itrāz*
if	3PL.PROX-OBL-DAT	this.OBL	decision-OBL	on	objection

e	***te***	*saprīm*	*korṭ*	*nāḷ*	*rujū*	*kar-aṇ*
be.PRES.3SG	**then**	supreme	court	with	contact	do-SBJV.3PL

'**If** they have an objection to this decision, **then** they should contact the Supreme Court.' (Pj) (Bashir and Kazmi 2012: 91)

The conjunctions meaning 'if' need not appear in clause initial position, as in 9.210, where جے /je/ 'if' appears in pre-verbal position. In the apodosis (then-clause) both تے /te/ 'then', as in examples 9.206, 9.207, 9.208, and 9.209, and تاں /tā̃/ 'then', as in 9.210, are found. تاں /tā̃/ is somewhat more emphatic.

(9.210) بھارت اتے پاکستان دے لبرل لوک جے اکٹھے ہو جان تاں اوہ اپنے ملکاں وچوں مذہبی نفرت مکا سکدے ہن

pàrat	*ate*	*pākistān*	*de*	*libral*	*lok*	***je***	*ikaṭṭhe*	*ho*
India	and	Pakistan	GEN	liberal	people	**if**	together	be

jā-ṇ	***tā̃***	*ó*	*āpṇ-e*	*mulk-ā̃*	*vic-õ*
go-SBJV.3PL	**then**	3PL.DIST	REFL-PL.M.OBL	country-OBL.PL	in-ABL

mázabī	*nafrat*	*mukā*	*sak-d-e*	*han*
religious	hatred	finish.off	be.able-IP-PL.M	be.PRES.3PL

'**If** the liberal people in India and Pakistan unite, they can end religious hatred in their countries.' (Pj) (Bashir and Kazmi 2012: 45)

In Saraiki realis conditional clauses, the protasis is usually introduced by the conjunction جے /je/ or جےکر /jekar/ 'if', and may either precede the apodosis, as in example 9.211, or follow it, as in example 9.212. The apodosis begins with تاں /tā̃/ 'then', or often no correlative conjunction at all. In both examples 9.211 and 9.212, the verb of the 'if'-clause is a present subjunctive, and that of the 'then'-clause is in the future form.

(9.211) جے توں اے دوا پیویں تیڈے سر دا سول گھٹسی

je	*tũ̄*	*e*	*dawā*	*pī-vẽ*	*teḍ-e*
if	2SG	this	medicine	drink-SBJV.2SG	2SG.GEN-SG.M.OBL

sir	*d-ā*	*sūl*	*ghaṭ-s-ī*
head.SG.M.OBL	GEN-SG.M	pain[M]	lessen-FUT-3SG

‘**If** you drink this medicine your headache will lessen.’ (Sr) (UK)

(9.212) توں کیا کریسیں جے تیڈی فلایٹ چرکیں ہووے

tũ̄	*kyā*	*kare-s-ẽ*	***je***	*teḍ-ī*	*flāiṭ*	*cirkẽ*	*ho-ve*
2SG	what	do-FUT-2SG	**if**	2SG.GEN-SG.F	flight[F]	late	be-SBJV.3SG

‘What will you do **if** your flight is late?’ (Sr) (UK)

9.3.1.3.2 Irrealis conditionals

Irrealis conditionals refer to actions or events which are known not to have happened or assumed not to be going to happen, or to states of affairs known not to be the case. A closely related meaning, that of things wished to have happened or to be the case (wishful thinking), is also expressed by irrealis conditional forms.

The original Hindko irrealis construction (irrealis-I) consists of a subjunctive verb form plus an irrealis particle آ /ā/ in both the ‘if’ and ‘then’ clauses. This construction is not found in contemporary Panjabi, but it is similar to the Saraiki irrealis-I construction consisting of the subjunctive plus ہا /hā/, an irrealis particle homophonous with the masculine singular past tense of ‘be’. This is a common heritage of both Hindko and Saraiki.[20] Irrealis-I appears in examples 9.213, 9.214, and 9.215. Sentence 9.215, however, shows a present perfect form in the ‘then’-clause followed by the irrealis particle.

(9.213) کدے او اج آوے آ تے او ضرور ٹیلیفون کرے آ

kade	*o*	*ajj*	*ā-ve-**ā***	***te***	*o*	*zarūr*	*ṭelifon*
if	3SG	today	come-SBJV3SG-**IRR**	**then**	3SG	definitely	telephone

*kar-e-**ā***
do.SBJV.3SG-**IRR**

‘If he were coming today he would definitely have telephoned.’ (Hk) (AWT)

20 Grierson (1919: 267), discussing “Lahndā”, says about this form: “Past Conditional is formed by adding hā to the Old Present. Thus, mārā̃hā, I should have struck, (if) I had struck...” Grierson also mentions the occurrence of the imperfective participle (his “present participle”) (our irrealis-II) in this meaning.

(9.214) او جلے آ تے کم ہووے آ

o	*jul-e*	***ā***	***te***	*kamm*	*ho-ve*	***ā***
3SG.DIR	go-SBJV.3SG	**IRR**	**then**	work	become-SBJV.3SG	**IRR**

'If he had gone, the work would have been done.' (Hk) (AWT)

(9.215) مانہ دسیں آ میں بندا پیہج چھوڑے آ

mā̃́	*das-ẽ*	***ā***	*mæ̃*	*bandā*	*pèj*
1SG.DAT	tell-2SG.SBJV	**IRR**	1SG.DIR	person	send

choṛ-e	***ā***
leave-PP.SG.M+be.PRES.3SG	**IRR**

'If you had told me I would have sent someone.' (Hk) (AWT)

Irrealis conditional sentences also appear in two other construction types, which are common to these languages. (i) Both the protasis and the apodosis employ a bare imperfective participle, as in example 9.216 (our irrealis-II); (ii) the protasis verb is a perfective participle plus the imperfective participle of ہونا /honā/ 'be', as in example 9.217 (a variant of irrealis-II). Notice that the 'then'-clause also includes a past tense form of 'be'. This also happens in Panjabi.

(9.216) اگر اُس اج آنڑاں ہوندا تے اوہ فون کردا

agar	*us*	*ajj*	*ā-ṛā̃*	***hõ-d-ā***	***te***	*o*	*fon*
if	3SG.OBL	today	come-INF	**be-IP-SG.M**	then	3SG.DIR	phone

kar-d-ā
do-IP-SG.M

'If he was to come today, he would have phoned.' (Hk) (AWT)

(9.217) اگر میں ایبٹ آباد نہ آیا ہوندا تے مانہ اے کتاب نیں مل ہکدی ایہی

agar	*mæ̃*	*æbṭabād*	*na*	*ā-yā*	***hõ-d-ā***	***te***
if	1SG.DIR	Abbottabad	NEG	come-PP.SG.M	**be-IP-SG.M**	**then**

mā̃́	*é*	*kitāb*	*nī̃́*	*mil*	*hak-d-ī*	***éy-ī***
1SG.DAT	this	book[F]	not	be.found	be.able-IP-SG.F	**be.PST-SG.F**

'If I hadn't come to Abbottabad, I wouldn't have been able to get this book.' (Hk) (AWT)

Panjabi employs four structures for irrealis conditionals. In structure (i), the verb in both the protasis and the apodosis of irrealis conditionals appears as the bare imperfective participle, agreeing with the grammatical subject of the clause, as in examples 9.218 and 9.219.

(9.218) میٹوں پتا ہوندا تاں دوجی واری نہ جاندا

mæ-nũ̄ patā ***ho-nd-ā*** *tā̃ dūj-ī vār-ī*
1SG.OBL-DAT knowledge **be-IP-SG.M** then second-SG.F time-SG.F

na ***jān-d-ā***
NEG **go-IP.SG.M**

'If I had known, I would not have gone a second time.' (Pj) (Shackle 1972: 124)

(9.219) اوہناں کہیا جے تسی کسے وزیر دی چھٹی لے آندے تے تہانوں پرمٹ مل جاندا

ón-ā̃ k-yā́ ***je*** *tussī kis-e vazir d-ī ciṭṭhī*
3PL-OBL say-PP.SG.M **if** 2SG some-OBL minister GEN-SG.F note[F]

læ ***ān-d-e te*** *tuā̀-nũ̄ parmiṭ mil*
take **come-IP-PL.M then** 2PL.OBL-DAT permit[M] be.received

jā-n-d-ā
go-IP-SG.M

'He said that if I had brought a note from a minister then I would have gotten the permit.'[21] (Pj) (Bashir and Kazmi 2012: 237)

In structure (ii), the protasis contains a perfective participle plus the imperfective participle of ہونا /hoṇā/ 'to be', and the apodosis contains a bare imperfective participle, as in example 9.220.

(9.220) جے کجھ کیتا ہوندا تے اج پنجاب نوں ایہ دن نہ دیکھنا پیندا

je *kúj kī-t-ā* ***ho-nd-ā te*** *ajj panjāb nũ̄*
if something do-PP-SG.M **be-IP-SG.M then** today Punjab DAT

ǽ din na dekh-ṇā ***pæ-nd-ā***
this day NEG see-INF **befall-IP-SG.M**

'If (someone) had done something, then today Punjab would not have had to see this day.' (Pj) (http://www.punjabics.com/Punjab_day_totay_nateeja.html)

In structure (iii), another variant of irrealis-II, both the protasis and the apodosis contain a perfective participle plus the imperfective participle of ہونا /hoṇā/ 'to be', as in example 9.221.

21 n these languages, the original pattern of representing reported speech is with direct speech, which reproduces the exact words of the speaker. Thus, English 'He said he would come' is expressed in Panjabi, for example as 'He said, "I will come"' as in 9.219.

(9.221) پترتوں سارا دن ویلیاں کھان دی بجائے کوئی کم تندہ کیتا ہوندا دبئی جا کے دو چار کروڑ اکٹھے کیتے ہوندے

puttar tũ sārā din veḷeã̄ khā-ṇ dī.bajāe koī kamm
son 2SG all day idly eat-OBL.INF instead.of any work

tandā kī-t-ā ***ho-nd-ā*** *dubai jā ke do cār*
attentively do-PP-SG.M **be-IP-SG.M** Dubai go CP two four

kroṛ ikaṭṭhe kī-t-e ***ho-nd-e***
ten.million together do-PP-PL.M **be-IP-PL.M**

'Son, if instead of eating idly (i.e. without doing any work) all day you had done any work attentively, you could have gone to Dubai and amassed several crores (of rupees).' (Pj) (http://www.siasat.pk/forum/showthread)

In structure (iv), yet another variant of irrealis-II, illustrated in examples 9.222 and 9.223, the protasis contains a bare imperfective participle and the apodosis a past imperfective form or simple past of 'be'. This structure, which includes a past-tense marked form in the apodosis, appears to be characteristic of Panjabi, and appears quite frequently.

(9.222) جے حکومت ذرا وی عقل نال کم لیندی تے مظاہرہ بالکل پرامن طریقے نال ختم ہو سکدا سی

je *hukūmat zarā vī aqal nāḷ kamm* ***læn-d-ī te***
if government a.bit even sense with work **take-IP-SG.F then**

muzā́irā bilkul puraman tarīq-e nāḷ xatam ho
demonstration[M] completely peaceful way-OBL with finished be

sak-d-ā ***sī***
be.able-IP-SG.M **be.PST.3SG**

'If the government had shown even a little prudence, then the demonstration could have ended peacefully.' (Pj) (Bashir and Kazmi 2012: 542)

(9.223) کوئی اگر انقلاب لیانا چاہ رہیا ہوندا پاکستان دے وچ تے ایہہ اک بہترین وقت سی

koī ***agar*** *inkalāb lyā(u)-ṇā cā́ r-yā* ***ho-nd-ā***
anyone **if** revolution bring-INF want CONT.II-SG.M **be-IP-SG.M**

pākistān de.vic ***te*** *ǽ ikk bétarīn vakat* ***sī***
pākistān in **then** 3SG.PROX an excellent time **be.PST**.3SG

'If someone had wanted to bring revolution to Pakistan, this would've been an excellent time for it.' (Pj) (Bashir and Kazmi 2012: 60)

The imperfective participle may also occur by itself (irrealis-II) when expressing wishful thinking or unrealized alternatives, as in example 9.224.

(9.224) تسی مینوں اوتھے بلا لیندے

tusī	*mæ-nū̃*	*othe*	*bulā*	***læ-nd-e***
2PL	1SG.OBL-ACC	there	call	**take-IP-PL.M**

'You could/should have called me there. (i.e. Why didn't you call me there; I wish you had.)' (Pj) (Bashir and Kazmi 2012: 185)

In the Panjabi of Wazirabad as documented in Bailey (1904b), the irrealis-I type, with a subjunctive followed by an irrealis particle/ā/ in both clauses was also found, as in example 9.225 (the Perso-Arabic representation is ours). This type occurs today in Hindko and Saraiki.

(9.225) جے تسی بھجو آ تاں مار نہ کھاؤو آ

je	*tussī̃*	*pàjj-**o***	***ā***	***tā̃***	*mār*	*na*	*khā-**ō***
if	you(pl.)	run-**SBJV.2PL**	**IRR**	**then**	beating	NEG	eat-**SBJV.2PL**

ā
IRR

'If you had run you would not have been beaten.' (Pj) (Bailey 1904b: 47)

In Saraiki, there are two irrealis conditional constructions: irrealis I and irrealis II. Irrealis I constructions are different from those now common in Panjabi, but are similar to the irrealis I of Hindko. In example 9.226, with present tense reference, the 'if'-clause contains the continuous subjunctive plus the irrealis particle (homophonous with the masculine singular past of 'be'); and the 'then'-clause contains the subjunctive plus the irrealis particle. In example 9.227, with hypothetical past time reference, both the 'if'-clause and the 'then'-clause use a perfective participle, plus subjunctive plus the irrealis particle.

(9.226) جے او اندا پیا ہووے ہا تاں فون کرے ہا

je	*o*	*a-nd-ā*	*p-yā*	*ho-**ve***	***hā***	***tā̃***	*fon*
if	3SG	come-IP-SG.M	CONT.I-SG.M	be-**SBJV.3SG**	**IRR**	**then**	phone

*kar-**e***	***hā***
do-**SBJV.3SG**	**IRR**

'If he were coming today, he would have phoned.' (Sr) (UK)

(9.227) جے میں ملتان نا آیا ہوواں ہا اے کتاب کݙہیں نا لدھا ہووے ہا

je *mæ̃* *multān* *nā* *ā-yā* *ho-**vā̃*** ***hā*** *e*
if 1SG.DIR Multan NEG come-PP.SG.M be-**SBJV.1SG** **IRR** this

kitāb *kaɗhī̃* *nā* *ladh-ā* *ho-**ve*** ***hā***
book[M] ever NEG find-PP.SG.M be-**SBJV.3SG** **IRR**

'If I hadn't come to Multan, I wouldn't ever have found this book.'[22] (Sr) (UK)

As in Panjabi, wishful thinking is expressed with an irrealis construction, shown in examples 9.228 and 9.229.

(9.228) توں وی شراب پیویں ہا

tū̃ *vī* *šarāb* *pī-**vẽ*** ***hā***
you.SG too wine drink-**SBJV.2SG** **IRR**

'If only you too drank alcohol.' (Sr) (Shackle 1976: 157)

(9.229) توں ناوہیں آندا تاں پہلے ݙسائیں ہا چا

tū̃ *nāvhẽ* *ā̃-**dā*** ***tā̃*** *pæhle* *ɗasā-**ẽ*** ***hā*** *cā*
2SG NEG.2SG come-**IP-SG.M** **then** before tell-**SBJV.2SG** **IRR** HORT

'If you weren't coming, (then) you should have told us first.' (Sr) (Shackle 1976: 165)

The element چا /cā/in 9.229 is glossed here as a hortative particle. Our consultant (UK) describes it as a sort of "softening" element.[23] Note that in this Saraiki example چا /cā/ follows rather than precedes the verb. It appears that post-verbal چا /cā/ has a softening or hortative meaning, while pre-verbal چا /cā/ is the vector in a compound verb formation. It thus appears that post-verbal cā may have a different origin than the preverbal /cā/ of Hindko (see Section 10.1.3).

Irrealis II usages, employing the bare imperfective participle, which are shared with Hindko and Panjabi, appear to be a later development due to convergence effects with Urdu and Panjabi. This is illustrated in example 9.230.

---

22 In UK's speech, کتاب /kitāb/ 'book' is masculine, whereas in most other varieties it is feminine.

23 This post-verbal چا /cā/ in Saraiki is very similar to the post-verbal cæ found in Dogri. Shankar (1931: 119) describes it as being added to a verbal form in two meanings: (1) a conditional, and (2) an imperative sense with a permissive force. Shankar finds that it is used in the 1st person plural only. For example, /ho cæ/ 'if we be' and /kha cæ/ 'Let us eat'.

(9.230) میں آپ نہ آندی

mæ̃	*āp*	*na*	***ā-nd-ī***
1SG.DIR	REFL	NEG	**come-IP-SG.F**

'Had I (F) not come myself.' (Sr) (Shackle 1976: 151)

9.3.2 Non-finite subordinate clauses

Three very common types of non-finite subordinate clauses are found in all three languages. These involve the infinitive, the conjunctive participle, and the imperfective or perfective participles. Infinitive clauses can function as subject, direct object, or objects of postpositions.[24] The word order within a non-finite subordinate clause is less flexible than in a finite clause, and the order of the non-finite subordinate clause within the main clause is also more fixed. For the use of the bare infinitive as a verbal noun, see Section 10.5.1.2, Section 10.5.2.2, Section 10.5.3, and others.

9.3.2.1 Infinitive clauses

Infinitive clauses, that is, an infinitive with a subject and/or direct object, can function as the subject or the direct object of a sentence.

9.3.2.1.1 Infinitive clause as subject

The infinitive clause in each of examples9.231, 9.232, 9.233, and 9.234, includes a direct object. Where an agent of the infinitive verb is also mentioned, as in example 9.231 and 9.234, it appears with the genitive postposition دا /dā/ 'of'.

(9.231) اُس دا اس معاملے آں جانڑا ضروری نئیں

us	***d-ā***	***is***	***māml-e***	***ā̃***
3SG.DIST.OBL	**GEN-SG.M**	**3SG.PROX.OBL**	**matter-OBL**	**ACC**

jān-ṛā	*zarūrī*	*nĩ*
know-INF.DIR	necessary	NEG

'His knowing about this matter isn't necessary.' (Hk) (AWT)

24 Such constructions are also sometimes analyzed as infinitive phrases, that is as noun phrases.

(9.232) ایہو جیہا کم کرنا بڑا اوکھا اے

éo	***jíyā***	***kamm***	***kar-nā***	*baṛ-ā*	*aukh-ā*	*e*
this	**like**	**deed**	**do-INF.DIR**	very-SG.M	hard-SG.M	be.PRES.3SG

'To do something like this is very difficult.' (Pj) (EB)

(9.233) کیا تہاکوں کمپیوٹر چلاوݨ آندے

kya	*tuhā-kū̃*	***kampyūṭar***	***calāv-aṇ***	*ā-nd-e*
Q	2PL.OBL-DAT	**computer**	**run-INF.DIR**	come-IP-SG.M+be.PRES.3SG

'Can you operate a computer?' (Sr) (Zahoor 2009: 41)

(9.234) اوندا اے کسا جاݨݨ دی لوڑ نہیں

ū̃	***d-ā***	***æ***	***kissā***	***jāṇ-aṇ***	*d-ī*
3SG.OBL	**GEN-SG.M**	**3SG.PROX.DIR**	**story**	**know-INF.OBL**	GEN-F.SG

loṛ	*nahī̃*
need[F]	NEG

'His knowing about this matter isn't necessary.' (Sr) (UK)

9.3.2.1.2 Infinitive clause as (direct) object

The complements of certain verbs involve what is structurally an infinitive clause functioning as direct object. Others involve such a clause appearing as the object of a postposition. Examples are presented for each language, beginning with Hindko.

Hindko examples 9.235, 9.236, and 9.237 illustrate complements of 'want', 'tell/show', and 'teach', respectively; and the infinitive clause functions as direct object of the matrix sentence. The infinitive in these complement structures is in the direct case.

(9.235) میں سگریٹ گھنڑا چاہناں

mæ̃	***sigreṭ***	***kìn-ṛā***	*cā́-nn-ā̃*
1SG.DIR	**cigarettes**	**take-INF.DIR**	want-IP-SG.M+1SG

'I want to get some cigarettes.' (Hk) (AWT)

(9.236) مائو مانہہ کپڑے رنگنڑا دسیا

māū	*mā̃ ̃*	***kapṛ-e***	***rang-ṛ̃ā***	*dass-iyā*
mother.OBL	1SG.DAT	**cloth-PL.M**	**dye-INF.DIR**	tell-PP.SG.M

'Mother told/showed me how to dye clothes.' (Hk) (AWT)

(9.237) نکے جاتکے آں ٹرنا سکھا

nikk-e	*jātk-e-ā̃ ̃*	***ṭur-nā***	*sikh-ā*
little-OBL.SG.M	boy-OBL-DAT	**walk-INF.DIR**	learn-CS.IMP.SG

'Teach the little boy to walk!' (Hk) (AWT)

The complement of دیڑا /deṛ̃ā/ 'to give > to allow', as in example 9.238, involves an oblique infinitive, while those of انکار کرنا /inkār karnā/ 'to refuse', as in example 9.239, and آخڑا /āxṛ̃ā/ 'to tell/instruct to', as in examples 9.240 and 9.241, involve an oblique infinitive plus a postposition.

(9.238) کیوں جے اساں اِس زبان آں اگے بدھڑیں ہی نینھ دِتا

kyū̃ ̃.je	*as-ā̃ ̃*	*is*	*zaban-ā̃ ̃*	*age*	***bâdṛ-ẽ***
because	we-OBL	this.OBL	language.OBL-DAT	ahead	**advance-INF.OBL**

hī	*nī̃ ̃*	***di-tt-ā***
EMPH	NEG	**give-PP-SG.M**

'Because we didn't let this language advance at all.' (Hk) (Soz 2009: 6)

(9.239) ہندکو آں قبول کرنے توں انکار ہی کیتا اے

hindko-ā̃ ̃	***kabūl***	***kar-n-e***	***tõ***	*inkār*	*hī*
Hindko-ACC	**accepted**	**do-INF-OBL**	**from**	refusal[M]	EMPH

kī-t-ā	*e*
do-PP-SG.M	be.PRES.3SG

'…have completely refused to accept Hindko.' (Hk) (Soz 2009: 6)

The oblique infinitive with the verb 'say' and the postposition دا /dā/ 'of' frequently expresses the idea 'tell (someone) to do something'. All three languages do this similarly; they use the postposition دا /dā/ 'of' with an oblique infinitive as the complement of 'to say'—آخھڑا /āxṛ̃ā/ for Hindko, shown in 9.240 and 9.241; آکھنا /ākhṇā/ for Panjabi, shown in 9.242; and آکھڻ /ākhaṇ/for Saraiki, shown in examples 9.254 and 9.255 below.

(9.240) میں اُس آں کپڑے تھوانڑے دا آخیا

mæ̃	*us-ã̄*	*kapṛe*	***tuā̀-ṛ̃-e***	***d-ā***
I.OBL	3SG.DIST.OBL-DAT	clothes	**wash.CS-INF-OBL**	**GEN-SG.M**

āx-iyā	
say-PP.SG.M	

'I told him/her to get the clothes washed.' (Hk) (AWT)

(9.241) والد صاحب ماہنہ کتیاں دے نسانڑیں دا آخیا

vālid	*sā́b*	*mā̃́*	*kutt-eā̃*	*d-e*	***nas-ā-ṛ̃-ẽ***
father	HON	1SG.DAT	dog-M.PL.DAT	GEN-SG.M.OBL	**run-CS-INF-OBL**

d-ā	*āx-iyā*
GEN-SG.M	say-PP.SG.M

'Father had me chase the dogs away. (lit. 'told me to make the dogs run away')' (Hk) (AWT)

(9.242) میں سلیم نوں شامل کرن دا آکھیا

mæ̃	*salīm*	*nū̃*	*šāmal*	***kar-an***	***d-ā***	*ākh-iyā*
1SG.OBL	Salim	DAT	included	**do-INF.OBL**	**GEN-SG.M**	say-PP.SG.M

'I said to include Salim.' (Pj) (EB)

In Panjabi, the direct-case infinitive appears with the verbs چاہنا /cɔ̃́ṇā ~ cā̃́ṇā/ 'to want', as in 9.243, and شروع کرنا /šurū karnā/ 'to begin', as in 9.244.

(9.243) اوہ کلھ اونا چاؤندے نیں

ó	*kál*	***ɔ-ṇā***	*cɔ̃́-nd-e*	*nẽ*
3PL.DIST.DIR	tomorrow	**come-INF.DIR**	want-IP-PL.M	be.PRES.3PL

'They want to come tomorrow.' (Pj) (Shackle 1972: 78)

In transitive complement clauses, as in 9.244, if the direct object is unmarked, the infinitive may (or may not) be inflected like an adjective to agree with this argument. In Panjabi (and Urdu), this behavior is often described as an "agreeing infinitive." One reason for speaker variation and vacillation is the structural similarity between the infinitive (a verbal noun) and the gerundive (a verbal adjective). In Panjabi (and Urdu), this distinction has been weakened, whereas it (mostly) remains in Saraiki (Shackle 1976: 71). For some speakers of Panjabi, agreement or non-agreement in these constructions depends on the referential status of the object. Example 9.244 shows a case of agreement, while 9.245 shows a non-agreeing case.

(9.244) اوہ چٹھی لکھنی کدوں شروع کریگا

ó	*ciṭṭh-ī*	***likh-ṇ-ī***	*kadõ*	*šurū*
3.SG.DIST	letter-SG.F	**write-INF-SG.F**	when	beginning

kar-e-g-ā
do-SBJV.3SG-FUT-SG.M

'When will he begin to write the letter [definite]?' (Pj) (Shackle 1972: 78)

(9.245) اوہ چٹھی لکھنا کدوں شروع کریگا

ó	*ciṭṭh-ī*	***likh-ṇ-ā***	*kadõ*	*šurū*
3.SG.DIST	letter-SG.F	**write-INF-SG.M**	when	beginning

kar-e-g-ā
do-SBJV.3SG-FUT-SG.M

'When will he begin to write letters (i.e. to do letter-writing) [non-specific indefinite, generic]?' (Pj) (EB)

Oblique infinitive complements occur with لگنا /lagṇā/ 'to be attached, applied' and دینا /deṇā/ 'to give > allow/let', and آکھنا /ākhṇā/ 'to say'. The oblique infinitive + دینا /deṇā/ 'to give' expresses permission for the action of the infinitive. If the infinitive complement is intransitive, as in 9.246, the form of دینا /deṇā/ 'to give' is default masculine singular. If the infinitive complement is transitive and has a direct object, in perfective tenses the form of دینا /deṇā/ agrees in number and gender with an unmarked direct object, as in 9.247. But if the direct object is marked with the accusative postposition نوں /nū̃/, the form of دینا /deṇā/ 'to give' is default masculine singular, as in 9.248.

(9.246) اوہناں نے سانوں جان دتا

ón-ā̃	*ne*	*sa-nū̃*	***jā-ṇ***	*di-tt-ā*
3PL.DIST-OBL	ERG	1PL.OBL-DAT	**go-INF.OBL**	give-PP-**SG.M**

'They allowed us to go.' (Pj) (Shackle 1972: 88)

(9.247) میں اوہناں نوں دو کتاباں خریدن دتیاں

mæ̃	*ón-ā̃*	*nū̃*	*do*	*kitāb-ā̃*	***xarīd-aṇ***
1SG.OBL	3PL.DIST-OBL	DAT	two	book-F.PL	**buy-INF.OBL**

di-tt-iyā̃
give-PP-**F.PL**

'I let them buy two books.' (Pj) (EB)

(9.248) ابو مینوں سلیم نوں شامل کرن دتا

abbū mæ-nũ salīm nũ ***šāmal kar-an*** *di-tt-ā*
Father 1SG.OBL-DAT Salim ACC **included do-INF.OBL** give-PP-**SG.M**
'Father let me include Salim.' (Pj) (EB)

Panjabi also employs the postposition لئی /laī/ 'for' in the "tell to/instruct" construction 9.249.

(9.249) اساں اوہناں نوں اون لئی آکھیا

asā̃ ón-ā̃ nũ ***ɔ-ṇ*** *laī ākh-iyā*
1PL.OBL 3PL.DIST-OBL DAT **come-INF.OBL** for say-PP-SG.M
'We told them to come.' (Pj) (Shackle 1972: 89)

The oblique infinitive + لگنا /lagṇā/ 'to be attached to' indicates the (imminent) inception of an action 9.250.

(9.250) اوہ کم کرن لگے

ó ***kamm kar-an*** *lag-e*
3PL.DIST.DIR **work do-INF.OBL** begin-PP.PL.M
'They began to work.' or 'They are about to begin work.' (Pj) (EB)

In Saraiki, the direct and the oblique form of the infinitive are homophonous. Consequently, the case of the infinitive is ambiguous unless it is followed by a postposition, allowing it to be identified as oblique. Judging by form alone, the infinitives سکھاوݨ /sikhāvaṇ/ 'to teach', as in example 9.251, چاہوݨ /cāhvaṇ/ 'to want', as in example 9.252, and ڈیوݨ /ɗevaṇ/ 'to allow/let', as in example 9.253, could be either in the direct or oblique case.

(9.251) میں آپݨی بھیݨ کوں پچ سیوݨ سکھالیا

mæ̃ āpṇ-ī bheṇ-kũ puc ***sīv-aṇ*** *sikhā.li-yā*
1SG REFL-SG.F sister-DAT clothes **stitch-INF** teach.take-PP.SG.M
'I taught my sister how to stitch clothes.' (Sr) (UK)

(9.252) توں کتھاں ونجݨ چہیندیں

tũ kithā̃ ***vãj-aṇ*** *cah-ẽd-ẽ*
2SG where **go-INF** want-IP-2SG
'Where do you (sg.) want to go?' (Sr) (UK)

(9.253) اساڈے پیو اساں او کتاب نہیں گھنݨ ڈِتے

asād-ē *pyū* *assā̃* *ū* *kitāb* *nhī̃* ***ghin-aṇ***
our-PL.M father 1PL.OBL that book[M] NEG **take-INF**

dĩ-t-ē
give-PP-SG.M+be.PRES.3SG

'Our father didn't let us buy that book.' (Sr) (UK)

Several Saraiki complement structures involve an oblique infinitive plus the genitive postposition دا /dā/ 'of'. With the simple verbs 'tell/instruct to', as in examples 9.254 and 9.255, and 'agree', in 9.256, دا /dā/ immediately follows the oblique infinitive and has default masculine singular agreement, whereas with the conjunct verb کوشش کرنا /košiš karnā/ 'to try/attempt', as in example 9.257, دا /dā/ precedes and agrees in gender with the nominal element کوشش /košiš/ 'attempt[F]'.

(9.254) میڈی اماں میکوں کتاب تیکوں ڈیوݨ دا آکھیا

med-ī *ammā̃* *mæ-kū̃* *kitāb* *tæ-kū̃* ***de-vaṇ***
1SG.GEN-SG.F mother.SG.F 1SG.OBL-DAT book 2SG-DAT **give-INF.OBL**

d-ā *ākh-iyā*
GEN-SG.M say-PP.SG.M

'My mother told me to give the book to you.' (Sr) (UK)

(9.255) استاد شاگردیں کوں وردیاں پا کرے آوݨ دا آکھیے

ustād *šāgird-ẽ* *kū̃* *wardiy-ā̃* *pā* *kar-e*
teacher pupil-OBL.PL DAT uniform-PL.F put.on do-CONN?

āv-aṇ ***dā*** *ākh-iye*
come-INF.OBL **GEN-SG.M** say-PP.SG.M+be.PRES.3SG

'The teacher told the students to put on their uniforms and come.'[25] (Sr) (UK)

25 The oblique plural in /-ẽ/ on 'pupils' is a feature of the Southern variety (Shackle 1976: 45–46).

(9.256) اساں سبھیں سویل دے ڈاہ وجے ملݨ دا مکایا

assā̃	*sabhī̃*	*savel*	*de*	*ɗah*	*vaʄe*	***mil-aṇ***	***d-ā***
1PL	all	morning	GEN	ten	o'clock	**meet-INF.OBL**	**GEN-SG.M**

mukā-yā
agree-PP.SG.M

'We all agreed to meet at 10 o'clock tomorrow morning.' (Sr) (UK)

(9.257) اوں اتھاں وکتی پہنچݨ دی کوشش کیتی مڑی پڄ نا سگیا

ū̃	*ithā̃*	*vakt-ī*	***pɔ̃c-aṇ***	***d-ī***	*košiš*
3SG.DIST.OBL	here	time-LOC	**arrive-INF.OBL**	**GEN-SG.F**	attempt[F]

kī-t-ī	*maṛī*	*paʄ*	*nā*	*saɠ-iyā*
do-PP-SG.F	but	reach	NEG	be.able-PP.SG.M

'He tried to reach here on time, but couldn't.' (Sr) (UK)

Several meanings involving prevention or cessation of an action are expressed with either an infinitive in the ablative case or the oblique infinitive plus the ablative postposition کنوں /kanũ/ 'from'. These include 'stop/cease', shown in example 9.258, 'refuse/decline', in example 9.259, 'forbid', in example 9.260, and 'prevent', in example 9.261.

(9.258) میݨھ وسݨوں کھڑ گیا

mī̃h	***vas-ṇ-ū̃***	*khaṛ*	*ɠy-ā*
rain[M]	**rain-INF.OBL-ABL**	stand	go.PP-SG.M

'It stopped raining.' (Sr) (Shackle (1976: 134) , cited from Lashari (1971: 200).)

(9.259) تیں میڈے نال آوݨ کنو کیوں الیا چا

tæ̃	*meɗ-e*	*nāl*	***āw-aṇ***	***kanū***	*kyõ*	*aliyā*
2SG.OBL	1SG.OBL	with	**come-INF.OBL**	**from**	why	say.PP.SG.M

cā
HORT

'Why did you refuse to come with me?' (Sr) (UK)

(9.260) اماں میکوں اونجھے کپڑے گھنݨ کنوں ہٹکیے

ammā̃	*mæ-kū̃*	*ū̃jhe*	*kapṛe*	***ghin-aṇ***	***kanū̃***
mother	1SG-ACC	that.kind.of	clothes	**take-INF.OBL**	**from**

haṭk-ie
forbid-PP.SG.M+be.PRES.3SG

'Mother forbade me to wear (lit. from taking) that kind of clothes.' (Sr) (UK)

(9.261) تیں میکوں او کرݨ کنوں جھلیا ہا

tæ̃	*mæ-kū̃*	*ū*	***kar-aṇ***	***kanū̃***	*jhal-iy-ā*	*hā*
2SG.OBL	1SG-ACC	that	**do-INF.OBL**	**from**	stop-PP-SG.M	be.PST.SG.M

'You stopped me from doing that.' (Sr) (UK)

9.3.2.2 Oblique infinitive + والا، آلا /vāḷā, āḷā/

In all three languages, an oblique infinitive may be followed by the suffix والا ~ آلا /vāḷā ~ āḷā ~ vālā ~ ālā/ yielding a marked adjectival form.[26] These adjectives function both adjectivally—attributively or predicatively—and frequently, like other adjectives, as nouns. والا، آلا /vāḷā ~ āḷā ~ vālā ~ ālā/ occurs with nouns, adjectives, postpositions, postpositional phrases, and verbs.

When these forms are used as predicate adjectives, they often carry a gerundival (desiderative) sense, as in example 9.262.

(9.262) ایہہ فلم ویکھݨ والی اے

é	*filam*	***vekh-aṇ***	***vāl-ī***	*e*
3SG.PROX.DIR	movie[F]	**see-INF.OBL**	**NMLZ-SG.F**	be.PRES.3SG

'This movie is worth seeing (should be seen).' (Pj) (EB)

If the action of a verb is anticipated but has not yet occurred, this construction can denote imminence, and is often translated with the phrase 'about to', as in examples 9.263, 9.264, 9.265, and 9.266.

26 Forms of والا /vāla/ are glossed as NMLZ, even though the primary function of this suffix is to form adjectives.

(9.263) میں کنڑک کہدی ، جیہڑی سڑنے آلی ایہی

mæ̃	*kaṛ̃ak*	*kì-d-ī*	*jéṛ-ī*	***saṛ-n-e***
1SG.DIR/OBL	wheat[F]	buy-PP-SG.F	REL-SG.F	**rot-INF-OBL**

āl-ī	*éy-ī*
NMLZ-SG.F	be.PST-SG.F

'I bought the wheat - which was about to rot.' (Hk) (AWT)

(9.264) گڈی ٹرن والی اے

gaḍḍ-ī	***ṭur-aṇ***	***vāḷ-ī***	*e*
train-SG.F	**leave-INF.OBL**	**NMLZ-SG.F**	be.PRES.3SG

'The train is about to leave.' (Pj) (Shackle 1972: 95)

(9.265) اجکل میڈا امتحان تھیوݨ والا ہے

afkal	*meḋ-ā*	*imtihān*	***thī-vaṇ***	***vāl-ā***
these.days	1SG.GEN-SG.M	exam[M]	**become-INF.OBL**	**NMLZ-SG.M**

he
be.PRES.3SG

'My exam is about to take place now.' (Sr) (Shackle (1976: 138), cited from Lashari (1971: 112).)

(9.266) جنگ چھڑݨ آلی اے

jang	***chiṛ-aṇ***	***āl-ī***	*e*
war[F]	**break.out-INF.OBL**	**NMLZ-SG.F**	be.PRES.3SG

'War is about to break out.' (Sr) (Zahoor 2009: 68)

When an infinitive clause with آلا~والا precedes a noun, in attributive position, it functions like a participial relative clause, as in examples 9.267 (Hindko), 9.268 (Panjabi), and 9.270 (Saraiki).

(9.267) شہر بچ ملازمت کرنے والے لوک صبح سویرے گرائیں بچوں سوزوکی اتے شہر جلدِن

šǽr	*bic*	*mulāzmat*	***kar-n-e***	***vāl-e***	*lok*
city	in	employment	**do-INF-OBL**	**NMLZ-PL.M**	people.PL.M

subo	*savere*	*grā̃-ẽ*	*bic-õ*	*suzūkī*	*ute*	*šǽr*
morning	early	village-OBL	in-ABL	Suzuki	on	city

jul-d-en
go-IP-PL.M+be.PRES.3PL

'People who work in the city go to the city early in the morning by Suzuki.'[27] (Hk)

(9.268) کم کرن والیاں کڑیاں نے سانوں ویکھیا

kamm	***kar-an***	***vāḷ-iyā̃***	*kuṛ-iyā̃*	*ne*	*sā-nū̃*
work	**do-INF.OBL**	**NMLZ-PL.F**	girl-PL.F	ERG	1PL.OBL-ACC

vekh-iyā
see-PP.SG.M

'The girls who were working saw us.' (Pj) (Shackle 1972: 95)

When آلا ~ والا follows a postposition, as in example 9.269 (Hindko), or a noun, as in example 9.270 (Saraiki), it conveys various adjectival or adverbial relations.

(9.269) ماہنہ نال آلے کمرے بچ چوہے دی آواز آندی اے

mā̃	***nāl-āle***	*kamr-e*	*bic*	*cū̃-e*
1SG.DAT	**adjacent-NMLZ.SG.M.OBL**	room.SG.M-OBL	in	rat-SG.M.OBL

d-ī	*avāz*	*ā-nd-ī*	*e*
GEN-SG.F	sound[F]	come-IP-SG.F	be.PRES.3SG

'I hear a rat in the next room.' (Hk) (AWT)

(9.270) اے امب ٹوکری آلیاں کنو ڈھیر مٹھا ہے

e	*amb*	***ṭokrī***	***āl-eā̃***	*kanū*	*ḍher*	*miṭṭh-ā*
this	mango.SG.M	**basket**	**NMLZ-PL.M.OBL**	than	very	sweet-SG.M

he
be.PRES.3SG

27 This is from the Year 2, term 4 set of children's stories appearing on the website of the Hindko Language and Cultural Society, based in Mansehra. http://www.hindko.org

‘This mango is sweeter than the ones in the basket.’[28] (Sr) (UK)

As with other adjectives, these forms are freely employed as nouns. They can indicate agents, or indicate other relations between a noun and another noun or the action of the infinitive verb. The resulting construction—including any arguments, complements, or modifying adverbs the infinitive may have—is a noun phrase, as in examples 9.271, 9.272, and 9.273. In examples 9.271 and 9.272, the nominalization creates an agent of the verbs ‘beg’ and ‘watch’, respectively, i.e. ‘one who begs’ or ‘those who watch’, while in example 9.273, the nominalized phrase ھٹی آلا /haṭṭī ālā/ indicates a relationship of “possession” to the noun ‘shop’, and means ‘one who owns a shop’.

(9.271) ایہہ روٹی اُس منگنڑے والے آں چا دے

é *roṭī* *us* ***mang-ṛ-e*** ***vāl-e-ā̃***
3SG.PROX bread 3SG.DIST.OBL **beg-INF-OBL** **NMLZ-SG.M.OBL-DAT**

cā *de*
lift give

‘Give this bread to that beggar.’ (Hk) (AWT)

(9.272) فلم ویکھن والیاں نے ہور پیسے نہیں سن دتے

filam ***vekh-aṇ-vāḷ-eā̃*** *ne* *hor* *pæs-e* *naĩ̄*
film **see-INF.OBL-NMLZ-PL.M.OBL** ERG more money-PL.M NEG

san *di-tt-e*
be.PST.3PL give-PP-PL.M

‘Those who were watching the film (lit. the film-watchers) didn’t pay any more money.’ (Pj) (Shackle (1972: 95); translation modified slightly.)

(9.273) میں اے ھک ھٹی آلے کنوں گھدے

mæ̃ *e* *hikk* ***haṭṭī-āl-e*** *kanū̃*
1SG.DIR 3SG.PROX.DIR a **shop-NMLZ-SG.M-OBL** from

ghi-d-e
take-PP-SG.M+be.PRES.3SG

‘I bought this from a shopkeeper.’ (Sr) (UK)

28 This example also illustrates the comparative construction of adjectives.

9.3.2.3 Conjunctive participial clauses in Hindko and Panjabi

Conjunctive participial clauses in all three languages can express relations of temporal sequence, as in examples 9.274, 9.277, and 9.278; causality, as in 9.275 and 9.276; or manner, as in 9.279 and 9.281, below. As is seen in examples 9.279 and 9.281, these conjunctive participial clauses sometimes function as simple adverbial expressions.

(9.274) سلیم دے کہر خط دیخ کے مانہہ پتا چلیا

salīm	*d-e*	*kàr*	*xat*	*dex*	*ke*	*mā̃*	*patā*
Salim	GEN-SG.M.OBL	house[M]	letter	see	CP	1SG.DAT	knowledge

cal-iyā
move-PP-SG.M

'I found out when I saw the letter in Salim's house.' (Hk) (AWT)

(9.275) تداں مل کے میں بہوں خوش آں

tud-ā̃	*mil*	*ke*	*mæ̃*	*baū̃*	*xuš*	*ā̃*
2SG.OBL-ACC	meet	CP	1SG.DIR	very	happy	be.PRES.1SG

'I am very happy to have met you.' (Hk) (AWT)

(9.276) تُوں ہر روز ٹہاکے چڑھ چڑھ کے تھک جلدا ہوسیں

tū̃	*har*	*roz*	*ṭā̀k-e*	*cáṛ*	*cáṛ*	*ke*	*thak*	*jul-d-ā*
2SG	every	day	mountain-OBL	climb	climb	CP	tire	go-IP-SG.M

ho-s-ẽ
be-FUT-2SG

'You must get tired of climbing mountains every day.' (Hk) (AWT)

In Panjabi, where some third-person ergative subjects (of perfective tenses of transitive verbs) are marked differently from non-ergative subjects, if the transitivity of the matrix clause and the participial clauses differs, subject marking depends on the transitivity and tense-aspect of the finite matrix verb, not that of the participial form. In example 9.277, the matrix verb لکھنا /likhṇā/ 'to write', is transitive; therefore its subject is marked with the ergative postposition نے /ne/. Contrast this with example 9.278, where the transitivity of the matrix and the participial clause is reversed. In example 9.278, the subject appears in the direct case since the matrix verb 'go' is intransitive.

(9.277) اوہ نے خط آ کے لکھیا

ô	***ne***	*xat*	*ā*	*ke*	***likh-iyā***
3SG.OBL	**ERG**	letter[M]	come	CP	**write-PP.SG.M**

'S/he wrote the letter after coming. (lit. having come, she/he wrote the letter.)' (Pj) (Adapted from Bhatia 1993: 69)

(9.278) اوہ خط لیکھ کے گیا

ô	*xat*	*likh*	*ke*	***ga-yā***
3SG.DIR	letter	write	CP	**go-PP-SG.M**

'He left after writing the letter (lit. having written the letter, he left.)' (Pj) (EB)

(9.279) کس کے بنھ

kass	*ke*	*bân*
tighten	CP	tie.2SG.IMP

'Tie it tightly.' (Pj) (EB)

Since Saraiki has three distinct types of these joining participles, these are treated separately in the following section.

9.3.2.4 Saraiki catenative, conjunctive, and connective participles

Shackle (1976: 82–83) identifies three types of participles which serve to connect verbs or clauses. In addition to the conjunctive participle common to all three languages (Section 9.3.2.3), it has two other forms: the catenative and connective participle.

The marker of the conjunctive participle in Saraiki is either کے /ke/ (more characteristic of the innovative Central variety), illustrated in example 9.280, or تے /te/ (characteristic of the Southern or more conservative varieties), illustrated in example 9.281, which is homophonous with /te/ 'and'. In some cases with the appearance of تے /te/ it is difficult for the analyst to determine whether a given construction consists of a stem imperative plus تے /te/ 'and', yielding a conjoined construction, or a stem imperative plus the conjunctive participle تے, yielding a subordinate clause. This is an interesting question for further research.

(9.280) کیمتاں گھٹا کے حکومت ڈھیر چاول وکویندی پئی اے

kīmt-ā̃ *ghaṭā* ***ke*** *hukūmat* *ḍher* *cāval* *vik-vẽd-ī*
price-PL.F reduce **CP** government much rice sell-CS.IP-SG.F

pa-ī *e*
CONT.I-SG.F be.PRES.3SG

'Having reduced the price, the government is causing much rice to be sold.' (Sr) (UK)

(9.281) ڳنڈھڑی گھٹ تے بنھ رکھو

ɗanḍhṛī *ghaṭ* ***tē*** *banh* *rakh-o*
bundle pull **CP** tie keep-2PL.IMP

'Tie up the bundle tightly.' (Sr) (UK)

The catenative participle (Shackle 1976: 82–83) is now identical to the stem, for example stem /kar-/, catenative participle /kar/ 'having done'. Its older form ended in /-i/, which has caused disyllabic stems ending in /r/, /ṛ/, and /l/ to change a second, unstressed /a/ to /i/ by retrogressive vowel harmony, for example stem /ˈni.kal-/ > catenative participle /ˈni.kil/. Two important exceptional forms add /ī/ to the stem: stem اُٹھ /uṭh-/ 'rise' > catenative participle اُٹھی /uṭhī/ 'having risen'; and stem وٹھ /vaṭh-/ 'seize' > catenative participle وٹھی /vaṭhī/ 'having seized. Two important intransitive verbs with vowel-final stems have exceptional catenative participles: stem آ /ā-/ 'come' > catenative participle آن /ān/ 'having come', and stem پو/po-/ 'lie' > catenative participle پے /pæ/ 'having fallen/lain'.

The connective participle (Shackle 1976: 85) is formally identical to the feminine singular of the perfective participle, and is usually formed only from transitive verbs, e.g. سݨائی /suṇāī/ 'having caused to be heard', from سݨاوݨ /suṇāvaṇ/ 'to cause to be heard'. It links verbal sequences with the closest temporal connection between the actions. This form is not found in most varieties of Panjabi.[29]

Actions can be linked with the catenative, connective, or conjunctive participles, depending upon the closeness of the connection between the actions of the two verbs. The closest connection is expressed with the connective participle. In linkages with the catenative participle, the action of the first verb precedes that of the second, and is

29 It appears that the frozen Urdu (and Hindi) collocations سنائی دینا /sunāī denā/ 'to be heard' and دکھائی دینا /dikhāī denā/ 'to be visible' are fossilized remnants of a formerly more widespread usage.

"subordinate to it" (Shackle 1976: 125). With the conjunctive participle, the two actions are still less closely connected than with the catenative participle. These distinctions are quite subtle, and are illustrated in examples 9.282, 9.283, and 9.284, all selected by Shackle, arranged in descending order of closeness.[30]

- Connective participle – closest temporal connection

(9.282) اے آٹا تے گھیؤ گھر چائی ونجو

e	*āṭā*	*te*	*ghiū*	*ghar*	*cā-**ī***	*vãf-o*
3SG.PROX	flour	and	ghee	home	pick.up-**CONN**	go-2PL.IMP

'Take this flour and ghee home. (lit. 'Pick up this flour and ghee and go home.')' (Sr) (Shackle (1976: 126), cited from Alvi (1972: 30))

- Catenative participle – slightly less close connection

(9.283) کتاباں وی گھن ݙتونیس

kitāb-ā̃	*vī*	***ghin***	*dī-t-on-is*
book-PL	also	**buy.CAT.P**	give-PP-PS3PL-PS3SG

'He bought books too, and gave them to him.' (Sr) (Shackle (1976: 125), cited from Alvi (1972: 8))

- Conjunctive participle – least close connection

(9.284) میں ونج تے کارڈ بھجویندی آں

mæ̃	*vãf*	***te***	*kārḍ*	*bhij-vẽd-ī*	*ā̃*
1SG	go	**CP**	card	send-CS.IP-SG.F	be.PRES.1SG

'I (F) am going and getting the card sent.' (Sr) (Shackle (1976: 127), cited from Lashari (1971: 163))

30 The present authors do not know the extent to which these distinctions remain in the language of 2019.

9.3.2.5 Imperfective participial phrases

Imperfective participial phrases can employ either an agreeing direct case, or the masculine singular oblique form of the participle, as in examples 9.285 and 9.286, respectively. These constructions are found in all three languages. Oblique imperfective participial phrases can refer either to the direct object, as in examples 9.287 and 9.288, or to the subject of a sentence, as in examples 9.286, 9.289, 9.290 and 9.291. In example 9.285, the direct form of the adjectival participle modifies the masculine singular direct object of the sentence, 'him'. In example 9.286, a masculine singular oblique imperfective participle (adverbial) highlights the temporal relationship between the two actions of the agent 'they'. In this sentence, نیں /nẽ/ is a third person plural pronominal suffix indexing the agent ('they'). In example 9.287, the masculine singular oblique participle indicates the temporal relationship between the object's act of writing and the agent's act of seeing him/her writing. Note that the endings for the masculine singular oblique form of the imperfective participle are ایوں /eū̃/ in Hindko (9.286, 9.287); ایاں /eā̃/ in Panjabi (9.288, 9.289); and ائیں /iẽ/ in Saraiki (9.290, 9.291).

(9.285) میں اُس آں اے بڑھاندا دیکھیا

mæ̃	*us-ā̃*	*e*	***baṛhā-nd-ā***	*dex-iyā*
1SG.DIR	3SG.OBL-ACC	3SG.PROX	**build-IP-SG.M.DIR**	see-PP.SG.M

'I saw him building it.' (Hk) (AWT)

(9.286) اُس آں پکڑدیوں ہی جیل بچ پایا نیں

us-ā̃	***pakaṛ-d-eū̃***	*hī*	*jel*	*bic*	*pā-yā*	*nẽ*
3SG.OBL-ACC	**catch-IP-SG.M.OBL**	EMPH	jail	in	put-PP.SG.M	PS3PL

'Having been arrested, he was put in prison. (lit. as soon as they caught him they put him in jail.)' (Hk) (AWT)

(9.287) میں اُس آں لکھدیوں دیکھیا

mæ̃	*us-ā̃*	***likh-d-eū̃***	*dex-iyā*
1SG.DIR	3SG.OBL-ACC	**write-IP-SG.M.OBL**	see-PP.SG.M

'I saw him/her writing.' (Hk) (AWT)

(9.288) میں اوس منڈے نوں کڑی دے گھر جاندیاں ویکھیا سی

mæ̃	*os*	*mū̃ḍ-e*	*nū̃*	*kuṛī*	*d-e*	*kàr*
1SG.OBL	3SG.DIST.OBL	boy-OBL	ACC	girl	GEN-SG.M.OBL	house.OBL

jā-nd-eā̃	*vekh-iyā*	*sī*
go-IP-SG.M.OBL	see-PP.SG.M	be.PST.3SG

'I saw that boy going to the girl's house.' (Pj) (EB)

(9.289) منڈے نوں کڑی دے گھر جاندیاں ویکھیا گیا سی

mũḍ-e	*nũ*	*kuṛī*	*de*	*kàr*	***jā-nd-eā̃***
boy-OBL	ACC	girl	GEN-SG.M.OBL	house[M]	**go-IP-SG.M.OBL**

vekh-iyā	*ga-yā*	*sī*
see-PP.SG.M	go-PP.SG.M	be.PST.3SG

'The boy was seen going to the girl's house.' (Pj) (http://www.wichaar.com/news/122/ARTICLE/13421/2009-04-03.html)

A reduplicated masculine singular oblique imperfective participle carries the sense of 'right in the middle of V-ing, ...[something else happened]', as in the Saraiki examples 9.290 and 9.291. In 9.291, the person to whom sleep came is indicated by the third person singular pronominal suffix /-us/.

(9.290) کھاندیئیں کھاندیئیں اوہ بیمار تھی گیا

khān-d-iẽ	***khān-d-iẽ***	*o*	*bīmar*	*thī*	*ɠa-yā*
eat-IP-SG.M.OBL	**REDUP**	3SG.DIST	ill	become	go-PP.SG.M

'While eating he fell ill.' (Sr) (Shackle 1976: 142)

(9.291) پتہ نہیں کیا بکدیئیں بکدیئیں نندر آ ڳیئس

patā	*naī̃*	*kyā*	***bak-d-iẽ***	***bak-d-iẽ***	*nindr*
knowledge	NEG	what	**talk.nonsense-IP-SG.M.OBL**	**REDUP**	sleep[F]

ā-ɠa-ī-us
come-go.PP-SG.F-PS3SG

'He was overcome by sleep, talking heaven knows what nonsense.' (Sr) (Shackle (1976: 142) , cited from Alvi (1972: 66))

9.3.2.6 Perfective participial phrases

Perfective participial phrases also appear in all of these languages, either in the direct case form, as in examples 9.292 and 9.293, or in the masculine singular oblique, as in examples 9.294 and 9.295.

(9.292) اوہ نے منڈے نوں درخت تھلے بیٹھا ہویا ویکھیا

ó *ne* *mũḍ-e* *nũ̄* *draxat* *thalle* ***bæṭh-ā*** ***ho-yā***
3SG.OBL ERG boy-OBL ACC tree under **sit-PP.SG.M** **be-PP.SG.M**

vekh-iyā
see-PP.SG.M

'She/he saw the boy seated under the tree.' (Pj) (adapted from Bhatia (1993: 71))

(9.293) ایہہ اَم پچھی بچ پہے دے امے کولوں زیادہ مٹھا اے

é *am* *pachī* *bic* ***p-é*** ***d-e***
3SG.PROX mango sack in **lie-PP.SG.M.OBL** **STAT-SG.M.OBL**

am-e *kolõ* *zyādā* *miṭṭh-ā* *e*
mango.SG.M-OBL from more sweet-SG.M be.PRES.3SG

'This mango is sweeter than the one (lying) in the sack.' (Hk) (AWT)

(9.294) مانہہ اس گرائیں بچ آئے دیوں دو سال ہو گئے ان

mā̃́ *is* *grā̃-ẽ* *bic* ***ā-e-d-eũ̄***
1SG.OBL 3SG.OBL village-OBL in **come-PP.SG.M.OBL-STAT-SG.M.OBL**

do *sāl* *ho* *ga-e* *an*
two year.PL.M become go-PP-PL.M be.PRES.3PL

'Two years have passed since I came to this village.' (Hk) (AWT)

(9.295) اوکوں اتھاں آیاں ہویاں اج پندروھاں ڈینہ ہا

ū-kũ̄ *ithā̃* ***ā-y-ā̃*** ***ho-y-ā̃*** *aj*
3SG.DIST.OBL-DAT here **come-PP-SG.M.OBL** **be-PP-SG.M.OBL** today

pandrvhā̃ *dĩh* *hā*
fifteenth day be.PST.SG.M

'Today it was a fortnight since he'd come.' (Sr) (Shackle (1976: 142), cited from Lashari (1971: 50))

10 Morphosemantics

This chapter treats a variety of topics dealing with relationships between form (morphology) and meaning (semantics). Some of these questions have been touched on in the preceding chapters as well, but a more thorough treatment is given here.

10.1 Complex predicates

All three languages have complex predicates of two types: (1) Noun or adjective + verbalizing light verb (conjunct verbs), and (2) main verb + vector verb (compound verbs). Both conjunct and compound verbs consist of a combination of elements that form a semantic unit taking a single subject and expressing a single event. Small, closed classes of items serve as the light verb element in both types of complex predicates.

10.1.1 Conjunct verbs, or N/ADJ - V, light verb constructions

Conjunct verbs, that is, verbs consisting of a noun or adjective plus a verbalizer, or light verb, are increasingly numerous in all three languages, largely because of increasing numbers of borrowings. The most commonly used light verbs in all three languages are those meaning 'do', 'be/become', 'give', 'take', and 'beat'. Pairs constructed with 'be/become' and 'do' form predictable intransitive-transitive pairs.

As with many other South Asian languages, conjunct verb formation is the main mechanism by which new verbs enter these languages today. They typically involve a borrowed nominal element (previously mostly from Arabic or Persian, now increasingly from English) plus an indigenous light verb. Predictably, such items are often shared by multiple languages. Illustrative examples are given in this section. These formations vary in the degree to which they can be considered transparent verbal notions, or idiomatic collocations. For example, several verbal concepts involving negative experiences are expressed with the verbalizer کھا /khā-/ 'eat'. These constructions with 'eat' are all grammatically transitive, but can have either intransitive semantics, as in دھوکا کھا /tòkā khā-/ 'be deceived' (lit. 'eat a deception'), or transitive semantics, as in سر کھا /sir khā-/ 'pester' (lit. 'eat [someone's] head').[1]

Table 10.1 and Table 10.2 show conjunct verbs constructed with the adjective صاف /sāf/ 'clean' and transitive and intransitive verbalizers, and conjunct verbs consisting of noun + verbalizer, respectively.

---

1 For comparative and diachronic discussion of 'eat' expressions, see Hook and Pardeshi 2009.

2 Although English uses intransitives to express the concepts 'to be deceived' and 'to jump', they are grammatically transitive in these languages.

https://doi.org/10.1515/9781614512257-010

ADJ - V
صاف ہونا /sāf hoṇā/ 'to be clean; to become clean' Pj (intransitive)
صاف ہونڑا /sāf hoṛ̃ā/ 'to be clean; to become clean' Hk (intransitive)
صاف ہووݨ /sāf hovaṇ/ 'to be clean' Sr (stative) (intransitive)
صاف تھیوݨ /sāf thīvaṇ/ 'to become clean' Sr (change-of-state) (intransitive)
صاف کرنا /sāf karnā/ 'to clean ' Hk, Pj (transitive)
صاف کرݨ /sāf karaṇ/ 'to clean' Sr (transitive)

Table 10.1: ADJ - V conjunct verbs

N - V
کم ہونا /kamm hoṇā/ 'work to be done/take place' Pj (intransitive)
کم ہونڑا /kamm hoṛ̃ā/ 'work to be done/take place' Hk (intransitive)
کم تھیوݨ /kamm thīvaṇ/ 'work to be done/take place' Sr (intransitive)
کم کرنا /kamm karnā/ 'to work' Hk, Pj (transitive)
کم کرݨ /kamm karaṇ/ 'to work ' Sr (transitive)
چھال مارنا /chāl mārnā/ 'to jump' Hk, Pj (transitive)
دکھ دینا /dukh deṇā/ 'to cause grief' Pj (transitive)
دھوکا کھانا /tòkā khāṇā/ 'to be deceived' Pj (transitive)[2]
سر کھانا /sir khāṇā/ 'to pester, bother' Pj (transitive)

Table 10.2: N - V conjunct verbs

10.1.2 Compound verbs, or V-V light verb constructions

All three languages make important use of compound verb formations, as do most other South Asian languages (Masica 1976). By "compound verbs"[3] we mean complex predicates consisting of the stem of a main verb which bears the main lexical meaning, plus a conjugated form of a vector verb (light verb), which contributes additional meanings. Our preferred term, "vector verb," recognizes the fact that these light verbs include either a concrete or abstract motional component. They form a small closed class, including intransitive verbs meaning 'go', 'come', 'fall', 'sit', 'get up/rise'; and transitives meaning 'give', 'take', 'leave', 'keep'. The transitivity of the vector verb determines the transitivity of the clause.

These light verbs are homophonous with verbs having full lexical meaning. However, when used as vector verbs, they are semantically bleached, losing their normal lexical meaning, and instead contributing an extra semantic component to the main verb in the V_{main} - V_{vector} sequence. The vector verb can add a range of meanings to an utterance, including other-benefactive, self-benefactive, mirative, completive, volitional, and intensive. Vector verbs often come in pairs that reflect complementary or opposing meanings. For example, when used as a vector verb, جل /jul-/ (Hk), جا /jā-/ (Pj), ونڄ /vãʄ-/ (Sr) 'go' conveys action away from a deictic center; whereas آ /ā-/ (Pj, Hk, Sr), او /ɔ-/ (Pj) 'come' conveys action toward a deictic center. Similarly, when used as a vector verb, دے /de-/ (Pj, Hk), ݙے /ɗe-/ (Sr) 'give' often indicates an action performed for the benefit of someone other than the agent; whereas لے /læ-/ (Pj), کہن /kìn-/ (Hk), گھن /ghin-/ (Sr) 'take' indicates a self-benefactive or directed action. The precise nature of the additional elements of meaning depends on the individual main verb, the vector, and the context.

Compound verb usages are exemplified here for Hindko, Panjabi, and Saraiki.

10.1.2.1 Compound verbs – Hindko

10.1.2.1.1 Vector جل /jul-/ 'go'

The most frequently occurring vector in Hindko is جل /jul-/ 'go'. The meanings it usually conveys are of change of state, or completion. It frequently indicates events that are in some way anticipated, as in examples 10.1 - 10.4.

3 We continue to use the traditional South Asianist term "compound verbs", rather than the more recently introduced "converbs", to maintain continuity in discussion of these constructions for the non-specialist reader.

(10.1) فاروق سوچیا ایہا کہ اس آں نوکری تھہا جلسی

farūk	*soc-iyā*	*éy-ā*	*ki*	*us-ā̃*	*nokrī*
Farooq[M]	think-PP.SG.M	be.PST-SG.M	that	3SG.OBL-DAT	job

thā́	***jul-s-ī***
be.obtained	**go-FUT-3SG**

'Farooq thought that he would get a/the job.' (Hk) (AWT)

(10.2) میرا پہرا آخر آہی گیا

mer-ā	*prā̀*	*āxir*	*ā-hī*	***ga-yā***
my-SG.M	brother	finally	come-EMPH	**go-PP.SG.M**

'My brother finally arrived.' (Hk) (AWT)

(10.3) تیرا تہیان کہڑے پاسے وے؟ روٹی سڑ گئی اے

ter-ā	*tyā̀n*	*kíṛ-e*	*pās-e*
2SG.GEN-SG.M	attention[M]	which-SG.M.OBL	side-SG.M.OBL

ve	*roṭī*	*saṛ*	***ga-ī***	***e***
be.PRES.3SG	bread[F]	burn	**go-PP.SG.F**	**be.PRES.3SG**

'Why aren't you paying attention? The bread has burned.' (Hk) (AWT)

(10.4) اُس آں سپ لڑیا تے او مر گیا

us-ā̃	*sapp*	*laṛ-iyā*	*te*	*o*	*mar*	***ga-yā***
3SG.OBL-ACC	snake	sting-PP.SG.M	and	3SG.DIR	die	**go-PP.SG.M**

'A snake stung him and he died.' (Hk) (AWT)

10.1.2.1.2 Vector پے /pæ-/ 'fall, lie'

(10.5) بلی ددھ پینڑیاں لگ پئی

billī	*dúdd*	*pīr̃-e-ā̃*	*lagg*	***pa-ī***
cat[F]	milk	drink-OBL.INF-DAT	attach	**fall-PP.SG.F**

'The cat began to drink milk.' (Hk) (EB 1989, unpublished field notes, Abbottabad)

10.1.2.1.3 Vector چھوڑ /choṛ-/ 'leave, let go'

The vector چھوڑ /choṛ-/ 'leave, let go' frequently appears in contexts where the vector دے /de-/ 'give' is seen in other languages, as shown in examples 10.6 - 10.11. It conveys nuances of finality.

(10.6) جس ویلے توں اتھے آئیاں اس مانہہ خط دے چھوڑیا ایہا

jis	*vel-e*	*tū̃*	*ithe*	*ā-yā̃*	*us*
which.OBL	time-OBL	2SG.DIR	here	come-PP.SG.M+2SG	3SG.OBL

mā̃́	*xat*	*de*	***choṛ-iyā***	***éy-ā***
1SG.DAT	letter[M]	give	**leave-PP.SG.M**	**be.PST-SG.M**

'By the time you came here he had given me the letter.' (Hk) (AWT)

(10.7) تد ضرور کسے آں کتاب دے چھوڑی ہوسی

tud	*zarūr*	*kise-ā̃*	*kitāb*	*de*	***choṛ-ī***
2SG.OBL	definitely	someone.OBL-DAT	book[F]	give	**leave-PP.SG.F**

ho-s-ī
be-FUT-3SG

'You must have given the book to someone.' (Hk) (AWT)

(10.8) دریا کتھے وے ؟ہک کلومیٹر سدھا جل اور کسے کولوں پچھ کہن۔ کئی دس چھوڑ سی آ

daryā	*kithe*	*ve?*	*hikk*	*kilomīṭar*	*síddā*	*jul*
river	where	be.PRES.3SG	one	kilometer	straight	go

ɔr	*kise*	*kolõ*	*puch*	*kìn*	*kuī*	*das*
and	someone.OBL	from	ask	take.2SG.IMP	anyone	tell

choṛ-s-ī-ā
leave-FUT-3SG-PS2SG

'Where is the river? Go straight ahead one kilometer and ask someone. Anyone will tell you!'[4] (Hk) (AWT)

---

4 The sentence-final particle آ / ā / in this sentence is unclear to us at this time, but we think it may be a second person singular pronominal suffix functioning as a dative (see Cummings and Bailey 1912: 109).

(10.9) اَساں سارے ام کھا چھوڑے ان

asā̃	*sāre*	*am*	*khā*	***choṛ-e***	***an***
1PL.OBL	all.PL.M	mango-PL.M	eat	**leave-PP.PL.M**	**be.PRES.3PL**

'We have eaten up all the mangoes.'[5] (Hk) (AWT)

(10.10) اے خط لکھنڑے توں بعد میں اس آں پوسٹ کرچھوڑساں

e	*xat*	*likh-ṝ-e*	*tõ*	*bād*	*mæ̃*	*us-ā̃*	*posṭ*
this	letter	write-INF-OBL	from	after	1SG.DIR	3SG.OBL-ACC	post

kar	***choṛ-s-ā̃***
do	**leave-FUT-1SG**

'After writing this letter I will post it.' (Hk) (AWT)

(10.11) اکثر لوک آپنڑیں کہاراں دا کوڑا کرکٹ باہر سٹ چھوڑدن

aksar	*lok*	*ãpṝ-ĕā̃*	*kā̰r-ā̃*	*d-ā*	*kūṛā*	*kirkaṭ*
most	people	REFL-OBL.PL	house-OBL.PL	GEN-SG.M	garbage	trash

bā̰r	*saṭ*	***choṛ-d-e-n***
outside	throw	**leave-IP-PL.M-be.PRES.3PL**

'Most people throw the garbage and trash of their houses outside.' (Hk) (Ayub (2015), Term 4, Story 7, آلودگی [Pollution])

10.1.2.1.4 Vector کہن /kìn-/ 'take'

(10.12) کل آخر میں سرٹیفکیٹ ٹھونڈ ہی کہدے

kal	*āxir*	*mæ̃*	*sarṭifkeṭ*	*tʉ̀nd-hī*
yesterday	finally	1SG.DIR	certificate	find-EMPH

kì-d-æ
take-PP-SG.M+be.PRES.3SG

'Yesterday I finally found the certificate.' (Hk) (AWT)

5 The form ان /an/ appears to be a variant third person plural, present tense form of 'be'.

(10.13) رضیہ جلدی کپڑے سیڑ کہنسی

raziyā	*jaldī*	*kapṛe*	*sīṛ*	***kìn-s-ī***
Razia	quickly	clothes	stitch	**take-FUT-3SG**

'Razia will sew the clothes quickly.' (Hk) (AWT)

10.1.2.1.5 Vector رکھ /rakh-/ 'put/keep'

In perfective tenses, this vector imparts a nuance of volitional action with the intent that the result be permanent. Example 10.14, with its Urdu-influenced journalistic style, could be considered Hindko, Panjabi, or Saraiki.

(10.14) پاکستان کشمیری عوام دی اخلاقی، سیاسی اتے سفارتی حمایت دا عزم کر رکھیا ہے

pākistān	*kašmīrī*	*avām*	*d-ī*	*ixlāqī*	*syāsī*	*ate*
Pakistan	Kashmiri	people	of-SG.F	moral	political	and

safārtī	*himāyat*	*d-ā*	*azam*	*kar*	***rakh-iyā***
diplomatic	support[F]	of-SG.M	determination[M]	do	**keep-PP.SG.M**

hæ
be.PRES.3SG

'Pakistan has resolved to maintain moral, political, and diplomatic support for the Kashmiri people.' (Hk, Pj, Sr) (http://www.pakistanpoint.com/skr/national/news/story-24836.html)

10.1.2.1.6 Vector سٹ /saṭ-/ 'throw'

(10.15) اُنھاں مکان بڑھا نڑا شروع کر سٹیا

ún-ā̃	*makān*	*baṛà-ṛā*	*šurū*	*kar*	***saṭ-iyā***
3PL.DIST-OBL	house	make-INF.DIR	beginning	do	**throw-PP.SG.M**

'They started to build a house.' (Hk) (AWT)

(10.16) مال مویشی سارے بیچ سٹے پر فر بھی تسلی نہ ہوئی

māl.movešī sāre bec ***saṭ-e*** *par fir bī*
cattle[PL.M] all sell **throw-PP.PL.M** but again even

tasallī na ho-ī
satisfaction[F] NEG become.PP.SG.F

'She sold all her cattle, but she still wasn't satisfied.' (Hk) (Soz 2011: 12)

(10.17) اس سارے معاملے اتے گوگل تے ایپل کسی وی قسم دا تبصرہ کرن توں انکار کرسٹیا وے

is sār-e māml-e ute gūgal te
3SG.PROX.OBL entire-SG.M.OBL matter-SG.M.OBL on google and

æpal kisī vī kisam d-ā tabsarā kar-aṇ tõ
apple any EMPH kind GEN-SG.M comment do-INF.OBL from

inkār kar ***saṭ-iyā ve***
refusal[M] do **throw-PP.SG.M be.PRES.3SG**

'Google and Apple have refused to make any comment on this entire matter.' (Hk) (http://www.hindkonews.com/گوگل سرچ انجن آن ایپل)

10.1.2.2 Compound verbs – Panjabi

10.1.2.2.1 Vector جا /jā-/ 'go'

Examples 10.18 and 10.19 provide a simple illustration of the difference between the use of a simple verb and of a compound verb with جانا /jāṇā/ 'to go'. In 10.19, the vector verb adds the sense of completion of an anticipated event.

(10.18) اک خط آیا

ikk xat ā-yā
one/a letter[M] come-PP.SG.M

'A letter came (unexpectedly).' (Pj) (EB)

(10.19) خط آ گیا اے

xat ā ***ga-yā e***
letter come **go-PP.SG.M be.PRES.3SG**

'The (awaited) letter has come.' (Pj) (EB)

In example 10.20, the vector 'go' adds a directional component, away from the deictic center 'home'.

(10.20) کسے چھوٹی - موٹی گلّ توں گھروں نکل گیا

kise	*choṭ-ī*	*moṭ-ī*	*gall*	*tõ*	...	*kàr-õ*	*nikal*
some.OBL	small-SG.F	big-SG.F	matter[F]	from	...	home-ABL	exit

ga-yā
go-SG.M

‘Because of some insignificant matter he left home.’ (Pj)

10.1.2.2.2 Vector آ ~ او /au- ~ ā-/ ‘come’

Notice how in example 10.21 the vector ‘come’ is associated with an unexpected event affecting the observer, in contrast to 10.19 above, in which the vector ‘go’ is associated with an anticipated event.

(10.21) غسل خانے وچوں اک چھ فٹا سپ نکل آیا

gusal	*xān-e*	*vic-õ*	*ikk*	*che*	*fuṭ-ā*	*sapp*	*nikal*
bath	room-OBL	in-ABL	a	six	foot-SG.M	snake[M]	emerge

ā-yā
come-PP.SG.M

‘A six-foot snake (suddenly) came out of the bathroom.’ (Pj) (http://www.wichaar.com/news/123/ARTICLE/6313/2008–06–22.html)

In 10.22, auto-benefactive and completive nuances are imparted by the vector ‘come’.

(10.22) بس دعا کرو کہ ہن کوئی حل نکل آئے

bas	*duā*	*kar-o*	*ki*	*huṇ*	*koī*	*hal*	*nikal*
just	prayer	do-IMP.2PL	that	now	some	solution	emerge

ā-e
come-3SG.SBJV

‘Just pray that some solution may emerge now.’ (Pj) (Bashir and Kazmi 2012: 296)

In example 10.23, the force of the vector is directional. Here, the motional component is oriented toward the deictic center ‘I’, and the discourse continues describing the next actions of this person (‘I’). Compare 10.23 with 10.20 above, in which the motion is away from the deictic center ‘home’.

(10.23) میں اوہنا دے کمرے وچوں نکل آیا

mæ̃	*ónā̃*	*d-e*	*kamr-e*	*vic-õ*	*nikal*
1SG	3PL.OBL	GEN-SG.M.OBL	room.SG.M-OBL	in-ABL	emerge

āy-ā
come-PP.SG.M

'I came out of his/her/their room.' (Pj) (http://www.wichaar.com/news/123/ARTICLE/6313/2008-06-22.html)

10.1.2.2.3 Vector بہہ /bǽ-/ 'sit'

The following pair of examples—10.24 with a simple verb and 10.25 with a compound verb—illustrate the kind of meaning contributed by the vector بہہ /bǽ-/ 'sit'. In example 10.24, the verb 'told' is a neutral statement, without any particular emotional affect. In 10.25, however, the sense is of dismay about an action that could have unexpected negative consequences.

(10.24) اوہناں میٔنوں اک نویں گل دسی

ón-ā̃	*mæ-nū̃*	*ikk*	*navī̃*	*gall*	*dass-ī*
they-OBL	1SG.OBL-DAT	a	new-SG.F	matter[F]	tell-PP.SG.F

'They told me something new.' (Pj) (EB)

(10.25) سمجھ نہیں آندی کیوں توں ساری گل اوہنوں دس بیٹھی ایں

sámaj	*naī̃*	*ā-nd-ī*	*kyõ*	*tū̃*	*sārī*
understanding[F]	NEG	come-IP-SG.F	why	2SG.DIR	all.SG.F

gall	*ó-nū̃*	*dass*	***bǽ-ṭh-ī***	***ẽ***
matter.SG.F	3SG.OBL-DAT	tell	**sit-PP-SG.F**	**be.PRES**.2SG

'I just don't understand why you've told her everything! (Now she will really exaggerate it and tell the whole city!)' (Pj) (Kanwal Bashir, p.c. to T. Conners.)

Since بہنا/bǽṇā/ 'to sit' is intransitive, the entire compound verb is intransitive. Consequently, the verb agrees with the subject. Therefore, since the verb in 10.25 is feminine, it implies a female agent, the addressee 'you'. The interpretation of the gender of the person to whom 'everything' was told as feminine (told 'her') depends on (cultural) context, and is not determined by the form of the sentence.

10.1.2.2.4 Vector پے /pæ-/ 'fall, lie'

This vector can add meanings of inception as in 10.26, chance, suddenness as in 10.27, or finality, as in example 10.27.

(10.26) گڈی ٹر پئی

gaḍḍī	*ṭur*	***pa-ī***
train[F]	move	**fall-PP.SG.F**

'The train **began** to move.' (Pj) (Malik 1995: 315)

(10.27) پہاڑی راہ تے گڈی ڈرائیور توں بے قابو ہو کے کھائی وچ ڈگ پئی

pā̀ṛī	*rā́*	*te*	*gaḍḍī*	*ḍrævar*	*tõ*	*be-kābū*	*ho-ke*
hilly	road	on	car.SG.F	driver	from	without-control	become-CP

khāī	*vic*	*ḍigg*	***pa-ī***
ravine	in	fall	**fall-PP.SG.F**

'On the hilly road, the car went out of control [lit. from the driver] and fell in a ravine.' (Pj) (Bashir and Kazmi 2012: 487)

10.1.2.2.5 Vector دے /de-/ 'give'

The vector دے /de-/ 'give' adds completive or allo-benefactive meanings. Compare examples 10.28 and 10.29.

(10.28) اوہ نے اک خط لکھیا اے

ó	*ne*	*ikk*	*xat*	*likh-iyā*	*e*
3SG	ERG	one/a	letter[M]	write-PP.SG.M	be.PRES.3SG

'S/he has written a (specific) letter.' (Pj) (EB)

(10.29) اوہ نے بابے واسطے خط لکھ دتا

ó	*ne*	*bāb-e*	*vāste*	*xat*	*likh*	***di-tt-ā***
3SG	ERG	old.man-OBL	for	letter[M]	write	**give-PP-SG.M**

'S/he wrote a/the letter for the old man.' (Pj) (EB)

Example 10.30 shows the vector, in this case دے /de-/ 'give', preceding the main verb, a non-default word order making the statement more forceful.

(10.30) اوہ پیالہ بڑے زور نال فرش تے دے ماریا

ó	*pyālā*	*baṛ-e*	*zor*	*nāḷ*	*faraš*	*te*
3SG.DIST.DIR	bowl[M]	great-SG.M.OBL	force.OBL	with	floor	on

***de**-mār-iyā*
give-beat-PP.SG.M

'S/he threw the bowl on the floor forcefully.' (Pj) (http://www.wichaar.com/news/119/ARTICLE/1411/2007–12–05.html)

10.1.2.2.6 Vector لے /læ-/ 'take'

The vector 'take', on the other hand generally imparts auto-benefactive senses.

(10.31) بچیاں نے آپنا سارا ہوم ورک کر لیا اے

bacc-ĕā̃	*ne*	*āpṇ-ā*	*sār-ā*	*homvark*	*kar*
child-OBL.PL	ERG	REFL-SG.M	all-SG.M	homework[M]	do

li-yā	***e***
take-PP.SG.M	**be.PRES.3SG**

'The children have done all their homework.' (Pj) (EB)

10.1.2.2.7 Vector سٹ /suṭṭ- ~ saṭṭ/ 'throw'

The vector سٹ /suṭṭ-/ 'throw' can add a sense of recklessness or carelessness, as in example 10.32, or of a vehement deliberate action, as in example 10.17.

(10.32) جنے میرا دل لٹیا جنے مینوں مار سٹیا

ji-ne	*mer-ā*	*dil*	*luṭ-iyā*
who.REL.OBL-ERG	1SG.GEN-SG.M	heart[M]	loot-PP.SG.M

ji-ne	*mæ-nū̃*	*mār*	***saṭ-iyā***
who.REL.OBL-ERG	1SG-ACC	kill	**throw-PP.SG.M**

'...who stole my heart,... who killed me (carelessly/mercilessly)' (Pj) (http://waptubes.co/video/superhit-songs-720p)

10.1.2.2.8 Vector رکھ /rakh-/ 'keep, put'

(10.33) اس نے اپنیاں مچھاں نوں کمال صفائی نال تاؤ دے رکھیا سی

us	*ne*	*apn-iyā̃*	*much-ā̃*	*nū̃*	*kamāl*	*safāī*
3SG.OBL	ERG	REFL-PL.F	mustaches-PL.F	ACC	perfect	neatness

nāl	*tāo*	*de*	***rakh-iyā***	***sī***
with	curl[M]	give	**keep-PP.SG.M**	**be.PST.3SG**

'He had kept his mustaches perfectly curled.' (Pj) (http://www.punjabikahani.punjabi-kavita.com/ChhabbiAadmiAteIkKuriMaximGorkyShahmukhi.php)

10.1.2.2.9 Vector مار /mār-/ 'beat, kill'

The light verb مارنا /mārnā/ 'to beat' conveys vehemence of a deliberate action, as in 10.34.

(10.34) اوہناں دے خلاف کالم لکھ ماریا

ón-ā̃	*d-e*	*xilāf*	*kālam*	*likh*	***mār-iyā***
3PL.DIST-OBL	GEN-SG.M.OBL	against	column[M]	write	**beat-PP.SG.M**

'(someone) (forcefully) wrote a column against them/him/her.' (Pj) (http://wichaar.com/news/127/ARTICLE/12057/2009–02–08.html)

10.1.2.2.10 Vector چھڈ /chaḍḍ-/ 'leave, let go'

In 10.35, the sense of finality, with a negative sense of indifference, is conveyed.

(10.35) اس بے پرواہ دی اس عادت نے ساڈا حال تباہ کر چھڈیا اے

us	*beparvā*	*d-ī*	*is*	*ādat*	*ne*
3SG.DIST.OBL	careless	GEN-SG.F	3SG.PROX.OBL	habit[F]	ERG

sā́ḍ-ā	*hāl*	*tabā́*	*kar*	***chaḍ-iyā***	***æ***
our-SG.M	condition[M]	ruined	do	**leave-PP.SG.M**	**be.PRES.3SG**

'This habit of that careless person has ruined our life (lit. condition.)' (Pj) (lovely124.blogspot.com)

10.1.2.3 Compound verbs – Saraiki

The most frequently occurring vector verbs in Saraiki are وڃ /vãʄ-/ 'go', گھن /ghin-/ 'take', ݙے /ɗe-/ 'give', چھوڑ /choṛ-/ 'leave', سٹ /saṭ-/ 'throw', and پو /po-/ 'fall/lie'.[6] Some examples follow.

10.1.2.3.1 Vector وڃ /vãʄ-/ 'go'

The vector وڃ /vãʄ-/ 'go' often adds the meaning of (anticipated) change of state, as in 10.36, or of completion, as in 10.37.

(10.36) زیاتیاں ڈھیر منگپھلیاں نا کھا۔ تیکوں کھنگ تھی ویسی

zyāt-iyā̃	*ḍher*	*mungphaliy-ā̃*	*nā*	*khā*	*tæ-kū̃*
too.many-PL.F	many	peanut-PL.F	NEG	eat.IMP.2SG	you-DAT

khang	*thī*	***væ-s-ī***
cough.SG.F	become	**go-FUT-3SG**

'Don't eat too many peanuts. You will get a cough.' (Sr) (UK)

(10.37) جیھ تاݨی تیں میکوں چٹھی ݙتی ھی او آ ڳیا ھا

jih	*tāṇī*	*tæ̃*	*mæ-kū̃*	*ciṭṭh-ī*	*ɗī-t-ī*	*h-ī*
when	by	2SG.OBL	1SG-DAT	letter-SG.F	give-PP-SG.F	be.PST-3SG.F

o	*ā*	***ɠ-iyā***	***h-ā***
3SG.DIST.DIR	come	**go-PP.SG.M**	**be.PST-3SG.M**

'By the time you gave me the letter he had (already) come (here).' (Sr) (UK)

10.1.2.3.2 Vector آ /ā-/ 'come'

6 These formations are called "intensive catenative compounds" in Shackle (1976: 123).

(10.38) کھیر کوں اوں ویلے تئیں ولڑیندے رہو جے تئیں مکھݨ نہ نکل آوے

khīr	*kū̃*	*ū̃*	*vel-e*	*taī̃*	*valaṛe-nd-e*
milk	ACC	3SG.DIST.OBL	time-OBL	until	churn-IP-PL.M

rah-o	*je*	*taī̃*	*makkhaṇ*	*na*	*nikal*
remain-2PL.IMP	when.REL	until	butter	NEG	emerge

āv-e
come-3SG.SBJV

'Churn the milk until butter is formed. (lit. keep on churning)' (Sr) (Zahoor 2009: 34)

10.1.2.3.3 Vector پو/po-/ 'fall, lie'

This vector occurs with intransitive verbs, often referring to sudden actions or to events in past time, as in 10.39. Passive stems can also be employed in compound verb formations, as in example 10.40. In 10.41, the vector signifies inception.

(10.39) دال دی پلیٹ ڈیڈھ سو روپے دی تھی پئی ہے

dāl	*dī*	*pleṭ*	*ḍeḍh_sau*	*rupe*	*dī*	*thī*
lentils	of.SG.F	plate[F]	150	rupees	of.SG.F	become

pa-ī	*he*
fall-PP.SG.F	be.PRES.3SG

'A plate of lentils now costs 150 rupees.' (lit. 'A plate of lentils has become of 150 rupees).' (Sr) (adapted from https://groups.yahoo.com/neo/groups/siraiki/conversations/topics/20#)

(10.40) کھیر وٹیج پیا

khīr	*viṭ-īj*	***pi-yā***
milk[M]	spill-PASS	**fall-PP.SG.M**

'The milk was spilt.' (Sr) (Shackle 1976: 124)

(10.41) توں روز پہاڑ چڑھݨ کنو تھک پوسیں

tū̃	*roz*	*pahāṛ*	*caṛh-aṇ*	*kanū*	*thak*	***po-s-ẽ***
2SG	daily	mountains	climb-INF.OBL	from	tire	**fall-FUT-2SG**

'You will get tired of climbing mountains every day.' (Sr) (UK)

10.1.2.3.4 Vector بہہ /bah-/ 'sit'

The verb 'sit' functions as a vector in Saraiki following the stem (= "catenative participle") (see Section 9.3.2.4 above), usually in perfective tenses, as in 10.42. According to Shackle (1976: 122), the meaning contributed is 'have finished doing, have already done'. It is not clear to us yet whether it has the nuance of (negative) unintended consequences that it does in Panjabi.

(10.42) او آکھ بیٹھی ہئی

o	*ākh*	***bæ-ṭh-ī***	***ha-ī***
3SG.DIST.DIR	say	**sit-PP-SG.F**	**be.PST-SG.F**

'She had already spoken.' (Sr) (Shackle (1976: 122), cited from Lashari (1971: 141))

10.1.2.3.5 Vector گھن /ghin-/ 'take'

The vector گھن /ghin-/ 'take' expresses agent-directed, or self-beneficial action, as in examples 10.43 and 10.44.

(10.43) کیا تساں سکول دا کم کر گھدے

kyā	*tussā̃*	*skūl*	*d-ā*	*kamm*	*kar*
Q	2PL.OBL	school	GEN-SG.M	work[M]	do

ghi-d-æ
take-PP-SG.M+be.PRES.3SG

'Have you done your schoolwork?' (Sr) (Zahoor 2009: 24)

(10.44) ہتھ دھو گھنو

hath	*dho*	***ghin-o***
hands	wash	**take-IMP.2PL**

'Wash your hands!' (Sr) (Zahoor 2009: 28)

10.1.2.3.6 Vector ڈٻے /ɗe-/ 'give'

The vector ڈٻے /ɗe-/ 'give', on the other hand, contributes a meaning of other-directed action, as in example 10.45.

(10.45) پکھا بند کر ڈٻیوو

pakhā	*band*	*kar-**ɗe-vo***
fan	closed	do-**give-IMP.2PL**

'Turn off the fan (for my benefit/at my request).' (Sr) (Zahoor 2009: 27)

10.1.2.3.7 Vector رکھ /rakh-/ 'put, keep'

In Saraiki, this vector appears in construction with the connective participle (stem + /ī/), as in examples 10.46 and 10.47, or the catenative participle (= stem) 10.48. The sense imparted is of emphatic continuity, or with simple perfective forms, permanence.

(10.46) پڑھی رکھ

paṛh-ī	***rakh***
read-CONN	**keep.2SG.IMP**

'**Go on** reading (don't stop now).' (Sr) (Shackle 1976: 131)

(10.47) جیویں انہاں ہتھاں ٻہوں عرصہ اوکوں سنبھالی رکھیا ہووے

jīvẽ	*in-hā̃*	*hath-ā̃*	*ɓahū̃*	*arsā*	*ū-kū̃*
as.if	these-OBL.PL	hand-OBL.PL	much	time	3SG.OBL-ACC

sā̃bhāl-ī	***rakh-iyā***	*ho-ve*
look.after-CONN	**keep-PP.SG.M**	be-SBJV.3SG

'As if these hands had long been looking after her.' (Sr) (Shackle (1976: 128), cited from Lashari (1971: 288).)

(10.48) ہک ڈٻاند او بولڈ سٹ رکھیے

hikk	*ɗānd*	*ū*	*boḷḍ*	*saṭ*	***rakh-iy-æ***
a	bull	3SG.DIST.DIR	board[M]	throw	**keep-PP-SG.M+PRES.3SG**

'A bull knocked down that signboard.' (Sr) (UK)

10.1.2.3.8 Vector چھوڑ /choṛ-/ ‘leave’

The vector چھوڑ /choṛ-/ ‘leave’ contributes a meaning of other-directed action similar to that of ݙے /ɗe-/ ‘give’, as in example 10.49.

(10.49) پیو میڈے کنو کتیاں کوں درکوا چھوڑیے

pyū	*meɗe*	*kanū*	*kutt-ĕā̃*	*kū̃*	*druk-vā*
father	1SG.GEN-OBL	from	dog-PL.M.OBL	ACC	be.chased.away-CS

choṛ-ie
leave-PP.SG.M + be.PRES.3SG

‘(My) father had me chase the dogs away.’ (Sr) (UK)

10.1.2.3.9 Vector گھت /ghat-/ ‘throw, cast’

This vector, seen in 10.50, imparts senses similar to but more forceful than ݙے /ɗe-/ ‘give’ and چھوڑ /choṛ-/ ‘leave’.

(10.50) اختر حسین خان کوں رضامند کر گھتیوس

akhtar	*husæn*	*xān*	*kū̃*	*razāmand*	*kar*	***ghat-iu-s***
Akhtar	Husain	Khan	ACC	agreeable	do	**cast-PP.SG.M-PS3SG**

‘He/she forced Aktar Husain Khan to agree.’ (Sr) (Shackle (1976: 125), cited from Lashari (1971: 72))

10.1.2.3.10 Vector سٹ /saṭ-/ ‘throw’

(10.51) نازو اپݨے ہنجو پونجھ سٹیے

nāzū	*apṇ-e*	*hā̃jū̃*	*pū̃jh*	***saṭ-iye***
Nazu	REFL-PL.M	tears.PL.M	wipe	**throw-PP.PL.M**

‘Nazu wiped away her tears.’[7] (Sr) (Shackle (1976: 125), cited from Lashari (1971: 259))

7 Here, ‘tears’ is treated as an unmarked masculine (see Shackle 1976: 49)

10.1.3 The invariant form چا /cā/ 'lift, raise'

The invariant element چا /cā/ occurs in Hindko, Saraiki, and some varieties of western Panjabi. Although it imparts nuances similar to those of the vector verbs in compound verb collocations, the grammatical behavior of چا /cā/ is different. It can be analyzed as either the stem (for Hk) or catenative participle (Sr, Shackle's term) of the verb for 'lift, raise'. This element occurs before the main verb, where it has semantic effects similar to those of vector verbs, which usually come after the main verb.. A homophonous form occurs clause finally, where it seems to function more like a discourse particle.

10.1.3.1 Hindko چا /cā-/ 'lift, raise'

In Hindko, invariant چا /cā/, the stem of چا /cā-/ 'lift' , patterns differently from vector verbs: (i) it precedes the main verb, rather than following it; and (ii) it is invariant. Varma (1936: 54–55) commented on this form, noting that it can be used with any verb and in any tense or mood in the active voice. Varma compares the effect of pre-verbal چا /cā/ to the use of the vectors لے /le-/ 'take' and دے /de-/ 'give' in Hindi, Urdu, or Panjabi with their full lexical verbs, as in لے لینا le lenā/ and دے دینا /de denā/, as in example 10.52. Examples 10.52, 10.53, and 10.54 are from 1936, but the form is still robustly in use today; see examples 10.55, 10.56 and 10.57.[8]

(10.52) وت چا کہن

vat **cā** *kĩn*
again **lift** take
'Take it again.' (Hk) (Varma 1936: 84)

(10.53) میں اساں چا دتا

mæ̃ *us-ā̃* **cā** *d-itt-ā*
1SG 3SG.DIST.OBL-ACC **lift** give-PP-SG.M
'I gave it away.' (Hk) (Varma 1936: 54)

8 Smirnov (1975: 118–119) also discusses چا /cā/, giving several examples but without specific provenance for them. He comments that "on rare occasions the component /cā/ may be inversed" and gives the example آوے چا /āve cā/ 'let him come', with post-verbal /cā/. This post-verbal /cā/ also seems to have the hortative sense found in 10.58 and in Saraiki.

(10.54) میں اساں اتھے چا رکھساں

mæ̃	*us-ā̃*	*utthe*	***cā***	*rakh-s-ā̃*
1SG.DIR	3SG.OBL-ACC	there	**lift**	put-FUT-1SG

'I will put it down there.' (Hk) (Varma 1936: 54)

(10.55) کدے سلیم آوے اے کتاب اس کو چا دو

kade	*salīm*	*āv-e*	*e*	*katab*	*us-ko*	***cā***
if	Salim	come-SBJV.3SG	3SG.PROX	book	3SG.OBL-DAT	**lift**

do
give.IMP.2SG

'If Salim comes, give him this book.' (Hk) (EB field notes, Mansehra usage, 1989)

(10.56) او پیسے اُس کولوں چا کہن

o	*pæse*	*us*	*kolõ*	***cā***	*kìn*
3PL.DIST	money	3SG.OBL	from	**lift**	take.IMP

'Take that money from him!' (Hk) (AWT)

(10.57) ایہہ روٹی اُس منگنے والے آں چا دے چھوڑ جس آں جاتک چھیڑدے نیں

é	*roṭī*	*us*	*mang-n-e*	*vāl-e-ā̃*	***cā***	*de*
this	bread	3SG.OBL	beg-INF-OBL	NMLZ-OBL-DAT	**lift**	give

choṛ	*jis-ā̃*	*jātak*	*cheṛ-d-e*	*nẽ*
leave.2SG.IMP	who.OBL-ACC	boy.PL.M	tease-IP-PL.M	be.PRES.3PL

'Give this bread to that beggar whom the boys are teasing.' (Hk) (AWT)

Importantly, 10.57 contains both invariant چا /cā/ 'lift' and the vector چھوڑ /choṛ/ 'leave', indicating that invariant چا /cā/ 'lift' does not occupy exactly the same slot as vector verbs like چھوڑ /choṛ/ 'leave'. Rather, it appears to be a stem functioning as does a catenative participle (Shackle's definition) in Saraiki.

Our contemporary Hindko attestations of چا /cā/ show it in pre-verbal position, but post-verbal چا /cā/ also appeared in the Hindko of 1936, as in example 10.58. In this example, it seems to have the hortative force found in Saraiki and pointed to in footnote 11.

(10.58) لکھ/لخ چا

likh~x **cā**
write **just**
'Just write!' (Hk) (Varma 1936: 77)

10.1.3.2 Saraiki چا /cā-/ 'lift, raise'

Invariant چا /cā/ 'lift, pick up' patterns differently in Saraiki than do its vector verbs, and possibly also differently from the way it does in Hindko. In Saraiki, چا /cā/ can freely either precede or follow, the verb. Shackle (1976: 158) finds a pronunciation difference between pre- and post-verbal چا /cā/, such that when چا /cā/ precedes the main verb the word preceding /cā/ is stressed, as in 10.59, in which sentence stress falls on پکا /pakkā/ 'firm'.

(10.59) مونھ ول پکا چا کیتس

mũh *val* *pakkā* ***cā*** *kī-t-us*
face again firm **lift** do-PP-PS3SG
'She (quickly) composed her features.' (Sr) (Shackle (1976: 158), cited from Lashari (1971: 62).)

However, the majority of the contemporary attestations we have found show چا /cā/ following the finite main verb. Some of these are (10.61)–(10.66). The element چا /cā/ is left unglossed here, since its contribution seems so varied, and we have not yet been able to find a satisfactory general gloss for it. In some cases it seems to function as a hortative particle, as in (10.61), (10.62), (10.63). Our consultant (UK) describes it as a sort of "softening" element. It might appear to originate in the verb چا /cā/ 'lift' as does invariant pre-verbal چا /cā/; but in post-verbal position it seems to convey different meaning(s). While pre-verbal چا /cā/ contributes meanings similar to those of the vectors in compound verb constructions, post-verbal چا /cā/, conveys hortative, softening, or perhaps even evidential meanings. Thus it seems possible that post-verbal چا /cā/ has a different etymology.[9]

9 Some possibilities are suggested in T486 and T4533 with the meaning of 'and', T4775 with the meanings 'see, look for, desire', or T11759 with the meaning 'attach to, apply'.

(10.60) او ٹکر اوں فکیر کوں ڈے چا جیکوں چھوہر چھڈیندے پین

ū *ṭukur* *ū̃* *fakīr-kū̃* *ɗe-**cā*** *je-kū̃* *chūhar*
3SG.DIR bread 3SG.OBL beggar-DAT give-**cā** who.REL-ACC boys

chiḍend-e *p-e-n*
tease.IP-PL.M CONT.I-PL.M-be.PRES.3PL

'Give that bread to that beggar whom the boys are teasing.' (Sr) (UK)

(10.61) توں ناوھیں آندا تاں پہلے ڈسائیں ہا چا

tū̃ *nāvhe* *ā̃-d-ā,* *tā̃* *pæhle* *ɗasā-ẽ* *hā* ***cā***
2SG.DIR NEG-2SG come-IP-SG.M then first tell-SBJV.2SG IRR **cā**

'If you weren't coming, than you should have told us first.' (Sr) (Shackle 1976: 165)

(10.62) سدھی طرح ڈسا چا اوں مشین دا

siddhī *tarā̃* *nā̃* *ɗasā* ***cā*** *ū̃* *mašīn* *d-ā*
straight way name tell.2SG.IMP **cā** 3SG.DIST.OBL machine of-SG.M

'Tell me its name properly - that machine's!' (Sr) (Shackle (1976: 158), translation slightly modified, cited from Lashari (1971: 62).)

(10.63) ساکوں وی اپنا اتہ پتہ ڈسّو چا

sa-kū̃ *vī* *apnā* *atā.patā* *ɗasso* ***cā***
1PL-DAT also REFL.SG.M whereabouts[M] tell-IMP.PL **cā**

'(Please) also tell us your whereabouts.' (Adapted from https://www.facebook.com/kohe.sulaiman.baloch/posts/947684331973777)

(10.64) میں کتاب سلیم کوں ڈتے چا

mæ̃ *kitāb* *salīm-kū̃* *ɗit-æ* ***cā***
1SG.DIR book Salim-DAT give-PP-SG.M+be.PRES.3SG **cā**

'I gave the/my book to Salim. (unintentionally, by mistake, in a confused state of mind).' (Sr) (UK)

Interestingly, 10.64 contrasts with 10.65, which includes the vector چھوڑ /choṛ-/ 'leave'.[10] This points to (i) the nuance of volitionality contributed by چھوڑ /choṛ/ 'leave' and (ii)

10 The morphological gloss on example 10.64 reflects the authors' analysis of the verb form as including an elided form of the short form of the present tense of 'be'.

the possible involvement of post-verbal چا /cā/ in the evidentiality or mirativity-marking system of Saraiki.[11]

(10.65) میں کتاب سلیم کوں ڈے چھوڑیے

mǣ *kitāb* *salīm-kū̃* *ḍe* ***choṛ-iy-e***
1SG.DIR book Salim-DAT give **leave-PP.SG.M + be.PRES.3SG**
'I gave the/my book to Salim. (intentionally)' (Sr) (UK)

10.2 Complex durative verbal constructions

Several complex durative/continuative/iterative verbal constructions are found in these languages. They are variously built on the imperfective participle, perfective participle, or verb stem, including constructions consisting of a main verb in several possible forms plus کرنا /karnā/ 'to do' or ونجݨ، جلنڑا، جانا /vã̄ʄaṇ, julṛā, jāṇā/ 'to go', رہنا /rǣṇā/ 'to remain' Pj or رکھݨ /rakhaṇ/ 'to put, place' Sr . A few of the most common are illustrated in the following subsections.

10.2.1 Forms using the imperfective participle

10.2.1.1 Imperfective participle + 'remain'

All three languages have complex durative constructions consisting of the imperfective participle plus a conjugated form of 'remain', as shown in 10.66 - 10.68.

(10.66) ایہہ کہار اُس کولوں سوہنڑا جس بچ اَسی رہندے رہے آں

é *kàr* *us* *kolõ* *sóṛā* *jis* *bic* *asī*
this house 3SG.OBL than nice REL.3SG.OBL in 1PL.DIR

rǣ-nd-e ***ra-é*** ***ā̃***
live-IP-1PL.M **remain-PP.PL.M** **be.PRES.1PL**

'This house is better than the one in which we have been living.' (Hk) (AWT)

11 Shackle (1976: 158) observes that: "With tenses other than the imperative /cā/ often implies sudden action, sometimes casual action." Though apparently incompatible, the meanings of sudden, and casual action can both be considered as actions cut off from their origin in volitionality or planning, as in 10.64. This is is consistent with it being analyzed as a mirativity marker in some contexts.

(10.67) اہو مال چاردا رہیا

ó	*māl*	*cār-d-ā*	***ry-ā***
3SG.DIR	cattle	graze-IP-SG.M	**remain.PP-SG.M**

'He continued to graze cattle.' (Pj) (Cummings and Bailey 1912: 95)

(10.68) پڑھدا رہ

paṛh-d-ā	***rah***
read-IP-SG.M	**remain.2SG.IMP**

'Keep reading/studying (over a period of time)' (Sr) (Shackle 1976: 131)

10.2.1.2 Imperfective participle + 'go' or 'come'

Constructions consisting of the imperfective participle plus the verbs for 'go' and 'come' are also found in all three languages. This is shown for Hindko in 10.69 and 10.70, for Panjabi in 10.71 and 10.72, and for Saraiki in 10.73 and 10.74. The constructions with 'go' express actions moving forward from a deictic viewpoint, often toward some implied culmination; those with 'come' express actions begun in the past and continuing up to the (present) deictic center.

(10.69) محبت بدھدی گئی

muhabbat	***bád-d-ī***	***ga-ī***
love[F]	**increase-IP-SG.F**	**go.PP-SG.F**

'(Their) love kept on increasing.' (Hk) (Soz 2011: 6)

(10.70) مریم دے داج دکھنڑ دی تیاری بوہنہ سالاں تو کردی آئی ایہی

mariam	*de*	*dāj*	*dikh-aṝ*	*d-ī*	*tayārī*	*bṍ*
Mariam	of	dowry	be.seen-INF.OBL	GEN-SG.F	preparation	many

sāl-ā̃	*to*	***kar-d-ī***	***ā-ī***	***éy-ī***
year-OBL.PL	from	**do-IP-SG.F**	**come-PP.SG.F**	**be.PST-SG.F**

'She had been preparing for many years for Mariam's dowry to be seen.' (Hk) (Soz 2011: 18)

(10.71) سیاستداناں نوں کوئی پرواہ نئیں کہ ملک دی حالت وگڑدی جاندی اے

syāsatdān-ā̃ *nū̃* *koī* *parvā́* *naī̃́* *ki* *mulk* *d-ī*
politician-OBL.PL DAT any care NEG that country GEN-SG.F

hālat ***vigaṛ-d-ī*** ***jā-nd-ī*** ***e***
condition[F] **deteriorate-IP-SG.F** **go-IP-SG.F** **be.PRES.3SG**

'Politicians don't care that the country's situation keeps deteriorating.' (Pj) (Bashir and Kazmi 2012: 212)

(10.72) ہن اوہو کجھ پیا ہوندا اے جیہڑا پاکستان بنن توں ہوندا آرہیا اے

huṇ *óho* *kúc* *p-yā* *ho-nd-ā* *e* *jéṛā*
now the.same something CONT.I-SG.M be-IP-SG.M be.PRES.3S which

pākistān *baṇ-an* *tõ* ***ho-nd-ā*** ***ā*** ***r-yā́***
Pakistan be.made-INF.OBL from **be-IP-SG.M** **come** **CONT.II-SG.M**

e
be.PRES.3S

'The very same thing is happening now which has been happening since Pakistan's creation.' (Pj) (Bashir and Kazmi 2012: 230)

(10.73) وقت تیزی نال بھجدا ویندا ہا

vakt *tezī* *nāl* ***bhaf-d-ā*** ***vẽ-d-ā*** ***hā***
time[M] speed with **run-IP-SG.M** **go-IP.SG.M** **be.PST.SG.M**

'Time was swiftly racing past.' (Sr) (Shackle (1976: 130), cited from Lashari (1971: 78))

(10.74) سندھ وادی وچ ہزاراں سالیں توں شاعری تھیندی آئی اے

sindh *vādī* *vic* *hazār-ā̃* *sāl-ẽ* *tū̃* *šāirī*
Sindh valley in thousand-OBL.PL year-OBL.PL from poetry[F]

thī-nd-ī ***ā-ī*** ***e***
become-IP-SG.F **come-PP.SG.F** **be.PRES.3SG**

'Poetry has been created for thousands of years in the Indus Valley.' (Sr) (http://www.wichaar.com/news/153/ARTICLE/30414/2013–12–28.html)

10.2.1.3 Imperfective participle + both 'remain' and 'go'

Example 10.75 from Saraiki shows the imperfective participle of the main verb with both the stem of 'remain' and a conjugated form of 'go'.

(10.75) اونکوں ہر مہینے ڈاکٹر کوں ݙکھیندے رہ ونڄائے

ū-kũ̄	*har*	*mahīn-e*	*ḍākṭar*	*kũ̄*	***ɗikhẽ-d-e***	***rah***
3SG.OBL-ACC	every	month-OBL	doctor	DAT	**show-IP-PL.M**	**remain**

vãf-āe
go-POL.IMP.PL

'Please bring him for a monthly checkup.' (Sr) (Zahoor 2009: 40)

10.2.2 Forms using the perfective participle: Perfective participle + کرنا /karnā/ 'to do'

In Panjabi,[12] these perfective participles are invariant masculine singular, and in this construction they are the regular formations کھلویا /khloĕā/, as in 10.76, /nā̀-yā/ in 10.77, and /kar-ĕā/ in 10.78, instead of the irregular forms used in finite conjugations (کھلوتا /khlotā/, نھاتا /nā̀tā/, and کیتا /kītā/, respectively) (see Section 8.4.2.5).[13]

(10.76) ایتھے کھلویا کر

ethe	***khlo-ĕā***	***kar***
here	**stand-PP.SG.M**	**do.2SG.IMP**

'Stand here (regularly).' (Pj) (Adapted from Cummings and Bailey (1912: 96).)

(10.77) روز نھایا کر ۔ سردیاں وچ وی

roz	***nā̀-yā***	***kar***	*sardiyā̃*	*vic*	*vī*
daily	**bathe-PP.SG.M**	**do.2SG.IMP**	winter	in	also

'Bathe every day, even in winter.' (Pj) (EB)

12 It is likely that these forms occur in Hindko, but we do not have any attestations.
13 The regularly formed جایا /jāyā/ < جانا 'to go' is used in this construction in Panjabi.

(10.78) غصہ نہ کریا کرو

gussā	*na*	***kar-ĕā***	***kar-o***
anger	NEG	**do-PP.SG.M**	**do-2PL.IMP**

'Don't get angry (repeatedly)!' (Pj) (EB)

Saraiki's construction differs in at least two ways from that of Panjabi. Notice that in 10.79, the irregular perfective participle ڳیا /ɗayā/ of ونڄݨ /vãɟaṇ/ 'to go' appears, not the regular form جایا /jāyā/ which would appear in the Panjabi equivalent. Also, in Saraiki the perfective participial form is not invariant masculine singular; rather, it agrees with the subject of an intransitive verb or the unmarked direct object of a transitive. In 10.79, the subject is masculine singular, but in 10.80, the subject is masculine plural. In the transitive sentence 10.81, the participle agrees with the unmarked feminine plural direct object 'words'.

(10.79) گھر آ ڳیا کر

ghar	*ā*	***ɗa-yā***	***kar***
home	come	**go-PP.SG.M**	**do.2SG.IMP**

'Keep coming home.' (Sr) (Shackle 1976: 132)

(10.80) تساں رُنے نہ کرو

tussā̃	***rune***	*na*	***kar-o***
2PL	**cry.PP.PL.M**	NEG	**do-2PL.IMP**

'Don't keep crying!' (Sr) (Shackle 1976: 132)

(10.81) بھولیاں ڳالھیں نہ کیتیاں کر

bhol-iyā̃	*ɗālh-ĩ*	*na*	***kīt-iyā̃***	***kar***
silly-PL.F	words-PL.F	NEG	**do-PP.PL.F**	**do.2SG.IMP**

'Don't keep saying such silly things!' (Sr) (Shackle 1976: 132)

10.2.3 Stem + /-ī/ + 'go', 'remain', or 'keep'

A construction consisting of verb stem + /-ī/ + 'go' is widely attested in Panjabi and Saraiki.[14] This construction is analyzed in different ways by several scholars. Cummings and Bailey (1912: 95), who do not comment as to the origin of this /-ī/, say, when discussing Panjabi: "Continuance is expressed also by prefixing the root (with -ī added) to the various parts of /jāṇā/ and /calṇā/," and give example 10.82. Examples 10.83 - 10.85 are from contemporary Panjabi. We are analyzing these as "CONNECTIVE PARTICIPLES" (CONN) on the model of Shackle's analysis of Saraiki (see Section 9.3.2.4).

(10.82) سنائی چل

sun-ā-ī	***cal***
hear-CS-CONN	**move.**2SG.**IMP**

'Keep on telling.' (Pj) (Cummings and Bailey 1912: 25)

(10.83) کم کری جا

kamm	***kar-ī***	***jā***
work	**do-CONN**	**go.2SG.IMP**

'Keep on working.' (Pj) (EB)

(10.84) اوہ بندہ چپ نہیں سی کردا ، بولی جا رہیا سی

ó	*bandā*	*cupp*	*naī̃*	*sī*	*kar-d-ā*	***bol-ī***
3SG.DIR	man	quiet[F]	NEG	be.PST.3SG	do-IP-SG.M	**speak-CONN**

jā	*r-yā*	*sī*
go	CONT.II-SG.M	be.PST.3SG

'That man wouldn't keep quiet, he kept on talking.' (Pj) (EB)

(10.85) ایہہ کتھوں دی شرافت اے جناب! تسیں میری سیٹ ہلائی جا رہے او

é	*kith-õ*	*dī*	*šarāfat*	*e*	*janāb!*	*tusī̃*
this	where-ABL	of.SG.F	good.behavior[F]	be.PRES.3SG	sir!	2PL

merī	*sīṭ*	***hilā-ī***	***ja-ré***	*o*
my.F	seat	**move-CONN**	**go-CONT.II**	be.PRES.2PL

'What kind of (good) behavior is this, sir! (Implied: this is not good behavior) You keep on moving my seat.' (Pj) (Bashir and Kazmi 2012: 448)

---

14 Probably in Ḥindko as well, but we do not have attestations.

Shackle (1976: 85) calls the form consisting of stem + ی /-ī/ in Saraiki the "connective participle", describing it as "formally identical to the f.sg. of the past p[ar]ti[c]iple" , in other words, as ending in /-ī/, but not commenting on the origin of the form. Discussing Saraiki connective compounds consisting of stem + /-ī/ + رہ /rah-/ 'remain', رکھ /rakkh-/ 'keep', or ونڄ /vãʄ-/ 'go', Shackle (1976: 128) says that constructions of this type have a strongly continuative sense, as in 10.86.

(10.86) غلام نبی موٹر بھجائی ویندا ہا

yulām	*nabī*	*moṭar*	***bhaf-ā-ī***	***vẽ-dā***	*hā*
Ghulam	Nabi	car	**run-CS-CONN**	**go-IP.SG.M**	be.PST.SG.M

'Ghulam Nabi kept the car racing along.' (Sr) (Shackle 1976: 128)

Because the connective participle ending ی /-ī/ and the emphatic particle ی /-ī/ are homophonous, this construction has been analyzed for Panjabi by Bhardwaj (2016: 280) as stem + /-ī/ 'emphatic'; he gives the examples in 10.87.

(10.87) بچا روئی جاندا اے

baccā	***ro-ī***	***jā-nd-ā***	*e*
child	**cry-EMPH**	**go-IP-SG.M**	be.PRES.3SG

'The child goes on crying.' (Pj) (Bhardwaj 2016: 280)

10.2.4 Main verb + 'do' in the same TAM form

Panjabi has a class of complex iterative constructions consisting of a main verb + a form of کرنا /karnā/ 'to do', in which both the main verb and 'do' appear in the same tense-aspect form. For example:

- Imperative + imperative

(10.88) ایتھے نا ہسیں کریں

ethe	*nā*	***hass-ĩ***	***kar-ĩ***
here	NEG	**laugh-SG.POL.IMP**	**do-SG.POL.IMP**

'Don't make a habit of laughing here.' (Pj) (Cummings and Bailey 1912: 96)

- Infinitive/gerundive + infinitive/gerundive

(10.89) بار بار اتھے نہیں اونا کرنا چاہیدا

bār	*bār*	*ethe*	*naī̃*	***au-ṇā***	***kar-nā***	*cā̃i-dā*
time	time	here	NEG	**come-INF**	**do-INF**	be.wanted-IP.SG.M

'One shouldn't come here repeatedly.' (Pj) (Adapted from Cummings and Bailey (1912: 96).)

- Subjunctive + future

Regarding this construction, Cummings and Bailey (1912: 96) say, "In the future the terminations -gā, etc., of the first verb are omitted." This yields an analysis like: [subjunctive of the main verb, subjunctive of 'do'] + /-gā/, in which the main verb and 'do' form a structural as well as semantic unit. Cummings & Bailey's statement also suggests that the construction is to be found in all persons and numbers. However, the only example they provide (10.90) is in the first person singular. It seems that in contemporary Panjabi too, first person singular usages are most frequent, as in 10.91.

(10.90) میں گھلاں کرانگا

mæ̃	*kàll-ā̃*	*kar-ā̃-g-ā*
1SG	send-SBJV.1SG	do-SBJV.1SG-FUT-SG.M

'I (M) shall make a habit of sending.' (Pj) (Cummings and Bailey 1912: 96)

(10.91) میں آواں کراں گی

mæ̃	*ā-vā̃*	*kar-ā̃-g-ī*
1SG[F]	come-SBJV.1SG	do-SBJV.1SG-FUT-SG.F

'I (F) will come (repeatedly).' (Pj) (EB)

10.3 Causativization and intransitivization: transitivity sets

Causative morphology was introduced in Chapter 8, in Section 8.3.1.1, Section 8.4.2.1, and Section 8.5.1. The three-way stem alternation described there allows for the construction of three distinct clause types: intransitive, shown in example 10.92, derived transitive (= first causative), shown in 10.93, and double causative, in 10.94. These examples are from Panjabi, but the same transitivity relations hold in Hindko and Saraiki.

(10.92) اے کار تیز چلدی اے

é	*kār*	*tez*	***cal-d-ī***	*e*
this	car[F]	fast	**move-IP-SG.F**	be.PRES.3SG

'This car moves fast.' (Pj) (Bhardwaj 1995: 142)

(10.93) میں کار تیز چلاؤندا آں

mæ̃	*kār*	*tez*	***cal-ɔ-nd-ā***	*ā̃*
1SG.DIR	car	fast	**move-CS-IP-SG.M**	be.PRES.1SG

'I (M) drive the car fast.' (Pj) (Bhardwaj 1995: 142)

(10.94) میں آپنے پتر کولوں کار چلوائی

mæ̃	*āpṇ-e*	*puttar*	*koḷ-õ*	*kār*
1SG.OBL	REFL-SG.M.OBL	son	near-ABL	car[F]

cal-v-ā-ī
move-CS2-CS1-PP.SG.F

'I made my son drive the car' (Pj) (Bhardwaj 1995: 142)

Non-volitional actions are usually expressed with intransitive verbs, illustrated in examples 10.95 and 10.96, where the Hindko and Panjabi intransitive verb /pàjṇā/ 'to break' is employed rather than its transitive counterpart بھننا /pànṇā/. In such cases, the involuntary agent, as in 10.95 , is often marked with کولوں /koḷõ/ 'from', the same postposition used for the causee or secondary actor as in 10.94. Compare this with the transitive sentences in 10.97, 10.98, and 10.99 which express volitional acts.

(10.95) پلیٹ میرے کولوں بھجی

pileṭ	*mere*	***koḷõ***	*pàjj-ī*
plate-SG.F.DIR	my-SG.M.OBL	**from**	break(INTRANS)-PP.SG.F

'I broke the plate (accidentally).' (Pj) (EB)

(10.96) کاٹھی ترٹی

kāṭhī	***truṭ-ī***
stick[F]	**break(INTRANS)**-PP.SG.F

'The stick broke (by itself).' (Sr) (UK)

(10.97) اُس کڑی میری پلیٹ پھنی

us *kuṛī* *mer-ī* *pileṭ* ***pàn-ī***
3SG.OBL girl my-SG.F plate[F] **break(TRANS)-PP.SG.F**
'That girl broke my plate (intentionally).' (Hk) (AWT)

(10.98) اوہ نے غصے وچ پلیٹ بھنی

ó *ne* *guss-e* *vic* *pileṭ* ***pàn-ī***
3SG.OBL ERG anger-OBL in plate[F] **break(TRANS)-PP.SG.F**
'S/he broke the/a plate in anger.' (Pj) (EB)

(10.99) مسعود کاٹھی تروڑی

masūd *kāṭhī* ***troṛ-ī***
Masud stick[F] **break(TRANS)-PP.SG.F**
'Masud broke the stick (intentionally).' (Sr) (UK)

The discussion of transitivization and causativization in Chapter 8 presented the intransitive verb as the basic form, from which transitives and causatives are derived. However, with some verbs, the basic form is the transitive, from which the intransitive and the causative are derived. A few Panjabi examples follow here.

Basic transitive	Derived intransitive	Derived Causative(s)
دھونا tòṇā 'to wash'	دھپنا tùpṇā 'to be washed'	دھوانا tuā̀ṇā 'to have / get washed'
پیہنا pī́ṇā 'to grind'	پسنا pisṇā 'to be ground'	پسانا ~ پیہانا pisāṇā ~ pyā́ṇā 'to have / get ground'
ٹھوکنا ṭhokṇā 'to hammer in'	ٹھکنا ṭhukṇā 'to be hammered'	ٹھکانا ~ ٹھکوانا ṭhukāṇā ~ ṭhukvāṇā 'to have / get hammered'

Table 10.3: Derived intransitives

Two points should be noted about these verbs. (1) In the derived intransitive forms the stem vowel is shortened. (2) The causative forms are constructed on the derived intransitive stem, not the basic transitive stem. This has the semantic consequence that the causative forms mean 'to have/get an action done (by someone), rather than to have someone do an action. The secondary agent in such causative constructions is thus more instrumental than agentive. Shackle (1976: 75) notes the same point for Saraiki, "The simple causative . . . of a transitive represents its conversion to the causal of its passive."

Not all verbs participate in the same derivational relationships. For example, the basic transitive verb meaning 'to catch, grasp', Hindko and Saraiki پکڑ/pakaṛ-/, Panjabi پھڑ/phaṛ-/ has no derived intransitive form and has only the derived first and second causatives پکڑا /pakṛā-/ 'hand to someone' پکڑوا /pakaṛvā-/ (Hk, Sr) 'have handed to someone', and پھڑا /phaṛā-/ 'hand to someone' پھڑوا /phaṛvā-/(Pj) 'have handed to someone'.

10.4 Passive constructions

Hindko, Panjabi, and Saraiki all distinguish active and passive voice. When the agent of an action is the grammatical subject, the sentence is in the active voice (e.g. *The police caught the thief.*), while if the patient is the grammatical subject, the sentence is in the passive voice, (e.g. *The thief was caught by the police.*). The relationship between active and passive voice in these languages, however, is not a simple transformational one, as it sometimes would appear from English-language examples. For instance, the English example *The thief was caught by the police* does not translate felicitously to a passive sentence in any of these three languages. Rather, an active construction, 'the police caught the thief', is used.

All three languages have a periphrastic passive construction consisting of the perfective participle of the main verb plus a conjugated form of that language's verb for 'to go'— جلڑا /julṝā/ Hk , جاݨا /jāṇā/ Pj , and ونڄݨ /vãɟaṇ/ Sr .[15] The perfective participle agrees in number and gender with the grammatical subject of the sentence, and the conjugated form of 'go' agrees with it potentially in number, gender, and person, except that if the subject (patient) of the passive sentence is marked with the accusative postposition—آں /ã/ Hk , نوں /nũ/ Pj , and کوں /kũ/ Sr —both the perfective participle and the form of 'go' default to the masculine singular form.

In addition, Saraiki retains a morphological passive inherited from Middle Indic. Vestigial traces of this morphological passive are also found in Panjabi.[16]

15 See Schokker (1969) and Bubenik (1998) for discussion of the origins of the periphrastic 'go' passive in NIA languages.

16 We do not have enough data yet to know whether or not Hindko retains vestiges of the morphological passive discussed for Panjabi and Saraiki.

10.4.1 Passive construction – Hindko

Hindko's periphrastic passive construction is typical of the general pattern for the three languages. In example 10.100, for instance, the subject of the sentence is کپڑے /kapṛe/ 'clothes (PL.M)'. The perfective participle سیتے /sīte/ 'stitched' is masculine plural, and جلسن /julsan/ 'will go' is third person plural. Thus the full verb form in this sentence agrees with the subject in person, number, and gender. In 10.101, where the subject is marked with the accusative آں /ā̃/, both the perfective participle of 'do' and the conjugated form of 'go' are default masculine singular, even though the grammatical subject (the patient) 'language' is feminine.

(10.100) کپڑے جلدی سیتے جُلسن

kapṛ-e	*jaldī*	***sī-t-e***	***jul-s-an***
clothes-PL.M	quickly	**stitch-PP-PL.M**	**go-FUT-3PL**

'The clothes will be stitched soon.' (Hk) (AWT)

(10.101) اس زبان آں نظرانداز کیتا گیا اے

is	*zubān*	*ā̃*	*nazar.andāz*	***kī-t-ā***
3SG.PROX.OBL	language[F]	ACC	ignored	**do-PP-SG.M**

ga-yā	***e***
go-PP.SG.M	**be.PRES.3SG**

'This language has been ignored.' (Hk) (Soz 2009: 6)

In spoken Hindko, however, the passive is infrequently used. For example, 10.102, which appears naturally with a passive in English, is spontaneously rendered in Hindko with a third person plural, impersonal subject in an active construction.

(10.102) کدے توں اتھے گیاں تے تداں قتل کر چھوڑسن

kade	*tū̃*	*uthe*	*ga-yā̃*	*te*	*tud-ā̃*	***katal***
if	2SG.DIR	there	go-PP.SG.M+2SG	then	2SG.OBL-ACC	**murder**

kar	***choṛ-s-an***
do	**leave-FUT-3PL**

'If you (sg.) go there, you will be murdered. (lit. They will murder you.)' (Hk) (AWT)

10.4.2 Passive constructions – Panjabi

Three passive constructions are found in Panjabi: (1) periphrastic جانا /jāṇā/ 'go' passive,[17] (2) vestigial morphological passive, and (3) infinitive plus ہونا /honā/ 'be' passive. For discussion of types (2) and (3), see Section 10.5.1 below on the expression of ability.

The periphrastic passive is almost never used to passivize transitive constructions mentioning both patient and agent; rather, an active construction is preferred. The passive typically appears in written texts, particularly news reports, as in 10.103, but still without naming the agent.

(10.103) پولیس کاروائی وچ اٹھ شرپسند مارے گئے جدکہ باقی فرار ہو گئے

polīs	*kārvāī*	*vic*	*aṭh*	*šarpasand*	***mār-e***	***ga-e***
police	action	in	eight	miscreant.PL.M	**kill-PP.PL.M**	**go-PP.PL.M**

jadki	*bākī*	*farār*	*ho*	*ga-e*
while	rest	escaped	become	go.PP-PL.M

'Eight miscreants were killed in the police action, while the rest escaped.' (Pj) (Bashir and Kazmi 2012: 87)

The subject of a passivized transitive verb can either appear in the direct case or be marked with the accusative postposition نوں /nū̃/. Compare 10.104 and 10.105. In 10.104, with the direct case subject, the sentence is unmarked for volitionality, whereas in 10.105, with the accusative marked subject, it is clear that the thief's being caught is the result of a directed, volitional action.

(10.104) راتیں ساڈی گلی وچ اک چور پھڑیا گیا

rāt-ĩ	*sāḍ-ī*	*gal-ī*	*vic*	*ikk*	*cor*	***phaṛ-iyā***
night-LOC	1PL.GEN-SG.F	street[F]	in	a	thief	**catch-PP.SG.M**

ga-yā
go.PP-SG.M

'Last night a thief was caught in our street.' (Pj) (EB)

17 A second type of periphrastic passive, constructed with the verb stem plus a conjugated form of the transitive verb گھتنا /kàttṇā/ 'to throw, cast' was described by Cummings and Bailey (1912: 84, 90), e.g. مارگھتیا /mār kàttiyā/ 'he was killed', but this type is no longer heard in urban Panjabi.

(10.105) آخر چور نوں پھڑیا گیا

āxar	*cor*	*nū̃*	***phaṛ-iyā***	***ga-yā***
finally	thief	ACC	**catch-PP.SG.M**	**go.PP-SG.M**

'The thief was finally caught.' (Pj) (EB)

When an agent is mentioned, as in 10.106, passivized transitives yield an abilitative reading, usually in negative contexts.

(10.106) میرے کولوں ایہہ کتاب نئیں پڑھی جاندی

mer-e	*koḷõ*	*é*	*katāb*	***naı̃́***	***pắṛ-ī***
1SG.GEN-SG.M.OBL	from	3SG.PROX	book[F]	**NEG**	**read-PP.SG.F**
jā-nd-ī					
go-IP-SG.F					

'I can't read this book.' (Pj) (EB)

Intransitive verbs can also be passivized. Passivized intransitives express ability (usually negative), as in 10.107. With passivized intransitives, both the perfective participle and the finite form of 'go' are in the default masculine singular.

(10.107) میرے کولوں ٹریا نہیں جائیگا

mer-e	*koḷõ*	*ṭur-iyā*	*naı̃́*	*jā-e-g-ā*
1SG.GEN-SG.M.OBL	from	walk-PP.SG.M	NEG	go-3SG.SBJV-FUT-SG.M

'I won't be able to walk.' (Pj) (Bhatia 1993: 177)

10.4.3 Passive constructions – Saraiki

Saraiki has two types of passive construction: (1) morphological passives, formed on the passive stem in /-īj/ (see Section 8.8.5 for the paradigms), and (2) periphrastic passives like those of Hindko and Panjabi.

10.4.3.1 Saraiki morphological passive

The Saraiki passive stem in ایج /-īj/ is inherited from the Middle Indic passive in /-ijja-/, which itself came from the Old Indo-Aryan passive in /-ya-/ (Bubenik 1998: 118). Compound verbs are readily formed from passive stems, as in examples 10.108–10.111.

(10.108) سٹیشݨ تے پوہچݨ سیت مفرور سنڄݨیج ڳے

sṭešaṇ	*te*	*pɔhc-aṇ*	*set*	*mafrūr*	***sãfaṇ-īj***
station	to	reach-INF.OBL	with	fugitive	**recognize-PASS**

ɠ-æ
go-PP.SG.M+be.PRES.3SG

'As soon as the fugitive got to the station, he was recognized.' (Sr) (UK)

(10.109) کھیر وٹیج پیا

khīr	***viṭ-īj***	***p-iyā***
milk.SG.M	**spill-PASS**	**fall-PP.SG.M**

'The milk was spilt.' (Sr) (Shackle 1976: 124)

(10.110) صندوق دا کونڈا مرڑیج ڳیا ہا

sandūk	*d-ā*	*kū̃ḍā*	***murṛ-īj***	***ɠy-ā***	***h-ā***
box	GEN-SG.M	lock.SG.M	**twist-PASS**	**go.PP-SG.M**	**be.PST-SG.M**

'The lock of the box had been twisted (open).' (Sr) (Shackle 1976: 124)

(10.111) اپڑیجݨ دے باد او ڈھکیج ڳے

apṛ-īj-aṇ	*de*	*bād*	*ō*
apprehend-PASS-INF.OBL	GEN-SG.M.OBL	after	3SG.DIST.DIR

ḍhak-īj	***ɠ-æ***
imprison-PASS	**go-PP.SG.M+be.PRES.3SG**

'After being arrested, he was imprisoned.' (Sr) (UK)

The morphological passive also conveys capabilitative meanings in Saraiki, as in 10.112.

(10.112) میڈے کنوں اے وݨ نا کپیسی

meɗ-e	*kanū*	*e*	*vaṇ*	***nā***	***kap-ī-s-ī***
1SG.GEN-SG.M.OBL	by	3SG.PROX.DIR	tree	**NEG**	**cut-PASS-FUT-3SG**

'I will not be able to cut this tree.' (Sr) (UK)

10.4.3.2 Saraiki periphrastic passive

The periphrastic passive is also employed in Saraiki (example 10.113). It is often found in formal or written registers, and is increasing in frequency under the influence of Panjabi and Urdu. Example 10.114 is from a Saraiki text written in what Shackle considers the formal style, in the central variety of Saraiki (Shackle 1976: 167). In Shackle's time, however, the morphological passive was the preferred form, at least in speech.

(10.113) اے پارسل تیکوں نہیں ݙتا ونڄ سڳدا

e	*pārsal*	*tæ-kũ̃*	***nhĩ̃***	***ɗi-tā***	***vãʄ***
this	parcel.SG.M	2SG.OBL-DAT	**NEG**	**give.PP-SG.M**	**go**

saɠ-d-ā
be.able-IP-SG.M

'This parcel cannot be given to you.' (Sr) (Shackle 1976: 77)

(10.114) دھیاں کوں گھر دے کم کار اچ مصروف رکھیا ویندا ہا

dhiy-ã̃	*kũ̃*	*ghar*	*d-e*	*kamm.kār*	*ic*	*masrūf*
daughter-PL.F.OBL	ACC	home	GEN-PL.M	work	in	busy

rakh-iyā	***væ̃-d-ā***	***h-ā***
keep-PP.SG.M	**go-IP-SG.M**	**be.PST-SG.M**

'Daughters were kept busy in household tasks.' (Sr) (Shackle (1976: 167), cited from Haq (1974: 44–45))

There is no significant difference in meaning between the morphological /-īj/ passive and the periphrastic 'go' passive. Passive meanings can be expressed with the passive stem plus pronominal suffixes (10.114 and 10.115). Both of these sentences mean 'If I am killed/beaten'. Importantly, both of them involve the first person singular pronominal suffix م /-um/, which indexes a first-person singular patient.

(10.115) جے مریج ڳیم

je	*mar-īj*	*ɠe-um*
if	kill-PASS	go.PP.SG.M-PS1SG

'if I am killed' (Sr) (Shackle 1976: 132)

(10.116) جے ماریا ڳیم

je	*mār-iyā*	*ɠe-um*
if	kill-PP.SG.M	go.PP.SG.M-PS1SG

'if I am killed' (Sr) (Shackle 1976: 132)

10.5 Deontic and epistemic modality

Deontic modality refers to ideas of ability, desirability, or necessity with respect to acts by an agent having conscious choice. Epistemic modality includes concepts of possibility, probability, speaker confidence in the truth of an assertion, and inferentiality. Even in Late Middle Indo-Aryan, gerundives were used to express both deontic and epistemic modality (Bubenik 1998: 190), as continues to be the case today. It is often difficult to determine (without access to rich context) which type of modality is conveyed by a particular utterance. For this reason, a range of specific modal meanings are discussed in this section.

10.5.1 Ability

Several different construction types are employed to express ability. (1) The most transparent of these involves the stem of the main verb plus a conjugated form of the verb meaning ‘be able’. (2) Formally passive, but semantically abilitative, constructions are employed. (3) The verb ‘come’ is employed to express ability to perform learned skills.

10.5.1.1 The verb ‘to be able’

Expression of ability involves the closely related verbs ہکڑا /hakṛ̃ā/ Hk , سکنا /sakṇā/ Pj , and سگݨ /saɠaṇ/ Sr , meaning ‘to be able’ or ‘to be possible’. In all three languages, the simplest expression of ability consists of the stem of the main verb plus a conjugated form of the verb ‘to be able’. Most attested instances of this verb are negative sentences, since if a person is able to do something, that usually results in a statement expressing the performance of the action, rather than the ability to do it. Examples follow.

(10.117) میں تیرے نال پشاور نہ جُل ہکدا

mæ̃	*ter-e*	*nāl*	*pišɔr*	***na***	***jul***	***hak-d-ā***
1SG.DIR	2SG.GEN-SG.M.OBL	with	Peshawar	**NEG**	**go**	**be.able-IP-SG.M**

‘I (M) cannot go with you to Peshawar.’ (Hk) (AWT)

(10.118) اسیں اپنا وعدہ نہیں توڑ سکدے

assī̃	*āpṇ-ā*	*vādā*	***naī̃***	***toṛ***	***sak-d-e***
1PL.DIR	REFL-SG.M	promise[M]	**NEG**	**break**	**be.able-IP-PL.M**

‘We cannot break our promise.’ (Pj) (Bashir and Kazmi 2012: 14)

(10.119) ای بھلا تھی سگدے

e	*bhalā*	***thī***	***saǥ-d-e***
this	really	**become**	**be.able-IP-SG.M+be.PRES.3SG**

'Can this possibly happen?' (Sr) (Shackle (1976: 160), cited from Lashari (1971: 58))

(10.120) میں پشاور نہیں ونج سگدا

mæ̃	*pišāwar*	***naī̃***	***vãǰ***	***saǥ-d-ā***
1SG.DIR	Peshawar	**NEG**	**go**	**be.able-IP-SG.M**

'I (M) can't go to Peshawar.' (Sr) (UK)

(10.121) او ٹر نا سگدا ہا

o	*ṭur*	*nā*	*saǥ-d-ā*	*h-ā*
3SG	walk	NEG	be.able-IP-SG.M	be.PST-SG.M

'He wasn't able to walk.' (Sr) (UK)

10.5.1.2 Other intransitive abilitative constructions

As seen in Section 10.3.2.1 above, periphrastic passivization of both transitive and intransitive verbs yields abilitative meanings; see examples 10.106 and 10.107 above, and 10.122 below.

(10.122) ہن میرے کولوں تے نہیں جایا جانا

huṇ	*mer-e*	*kolõ*	*te*	*naī̃*	*jā-yā*	*jā-ṇā*
now	1SG.GEN-SG.M.OBL	by	TOP	NEG	go-PP.SG.M	go-INF

'I won't be able to go now!' (Pj) (Bashir and Kazmi 2012: 470)

In addition, another class of intransitive abilitative constructions consisting of a nominal plus a conjugated form of ہونا /hoṇā/ 'to be' are employed in Panjabi. In these constructions, the agent can either be indicated by the postposition کولوں /kolõ/ 'by', as in example 10.122, or appear in its genitive form, as in 10.123. These construction types are as follows:

- Oblique infinitive + conjugated form of 'be', as in examples 10.123 through 10.129. Bhatia (1993: 235) and Malik (1995: 299) discuss this construction. Bashir and Kazmi (2012) provide more recent attestations. In 10.123 the oblique infinitive of کھلونا /khloṇā/ 'to stand' is followed by the negated present imperfect of ہونا /hoṇā/ 'to be'. The other examples are similarly constructed.

(10.123) اج میرا کھلون وی نئیں ہوندا

ajj	*mer-ā*	*khlo-ṇ*	*vī*	*naĩ́*	*ho-nd-ā*
today	1SG.GEN-SG.M	stand-OBL.INF	even	NEG	be-IP-SG.M

'Now I cannot even stand.' (Pj) (Cummings and Bailey 1912: 93)

(10.124) تیرے کولوں بکسا چک (چکن) نئیں ہوئیگا

ter-e	*kol-õ*	*baksā*	*cukk*	*(cukk-aṇ)*	***naĩ́***
2SG.GEN-SG.M.OBL	vicinity-ABL	box[M]	lift	(lift-INF.OBL)	**NEG**

ho-e-g-ā
be-SBJV.3SG-FUT-SG.M

'You will not be able to lift the box.' (Pj) (Malik 1995: 299)

(10.125) او دے کولوں کتاب نئیں پڑھن ہوندا

o	*d-e*	*kol-õ*	*katāb*	***naĩ́***
3SG.DIST.OBL	GEN-SG.M.OBL	vicinity-ABL	book[F]	**NEG**

pá̖ṛ-aṇ	***ho-nd-ā***
read-INF.OBL	**be-IP-SG.M**

'Books/the book cannot be read by him. (i.e. He is not able to read books/the book.)' (Pj) (Bhatia 1993: 235)

(10.126) اوہ کہندا اے میرے کولوں نئیں اینی دور تک ٹرن ہوندا

ó	*kǽ-nd-ā*	*e*	*mer-e*	*kolõ*
3SG.DIST.DIR	say-IP-SG.M	be.PRES.3SG	1SG.GEN-SG.M.OBL	by

naĩ́	*enn-ī*	*dūr*	*tak*	***ṭur-aṇ***	***hon-d-ā***
NEG	this.much-SG.F	distance[F]	up.to	**walk-INF.OBL**	**be-IP-SG.M**

'He says that he cannot walk that far.' (Pj) (Bashir and Kazmi 2012: 635)

(10.127) میں کہیا اینی بلدی گرمی اچ میرے کولوں نئیں جان ہویا

mæ̃	*k-yā́*	*enn-ī*	*bal-d-ī*	*garmī*	*ic*
1SG.OBL	say-PP.SG.M	this.much-SG.F	burn-IP-SG.F	heat[F]	in

mer-e	*kolõ*	***naĩ́***	***jā-ṇ***	***ho-yā***
1SG.GEN-SG.M.OBL	by	**NEG**	**go-INF.OBL**	**become-PP.SG.M**

'I said I could not go out in that scorching heat.' (Pj) (Bashir and Kazmi 2012: 636)

(10.128) اچھا ویکھو جے آن ہویا تے آجاواں گے

acchā	*vekh-o*	*je*	***ā-ṇ***	***ho-yā***	*te*	*ā*
okay	see-2PL.IMP	if	**come-INF.OBL**	**become-PP.SG.M**	then	come

jā-vā̃-g-e
go-SBJV.1PL-FUT-PL.M

'All right, let's see. If we can come, we will.' (Pj) (Bashir and Kazmi 2012: 636)

(10.129) ہر اک دے جہڑا پچھے ٹر پئے اوہ دے پچھے جان نہیں ہوندا

har	*ikk*	*de*	*jéṛa*	*piche*	*ṭur*	*pa-e*	*ó*	*de*
every	one	of	who	behind	walk	fall-SBJV.3SG	3SG.OBL	GEN

piche	***jā-ṇ***	***naĩ́***	***ho-nd-ā***
behind	**go-OBL.INF**	**NEG**	**be-IP-SG.M**

'(One) cannot follow (a person) who follows behind everyone.' (Pj) (http://www.aruuz.com/mypoetry/poetry/111)

- Verb stem (+ NEG) + conjugated form of 'be', as in 10.130 and shown as an option in example 10.124.

(10.130) میتھوں کجھ کہہ نہیں ہوندا ، بس

mæ-thõ	*kúc*	***kǽ***	***naĩ́***	***ho-nd-ā***	–	*bas*
1SG.OBL-ABL	something	**say**	**NEG**	**be-IP-SG.M**	–	enough

'I cannot say anything – that's all.' (Pj) (http://www.wichaar.com/news/125/ARTICLE/21393/2010–08–10.html)

- A common noun referring to some sort of activity, like کم /kamm/ 'work, task' + a conjugated form of 'be', as in 10.131.

(10.131) ایہہ پڑھن پڑھان والا کم ساڈے کولوں نئیں ہوندا

ǽ	*páṛ-aṇ*	*paṛà-ṇ*	*vāl-ā*	***kamm***
3SG.PROX	study-INF.OBL	teach-INF.OBL	NMLZ-SG.M	**work[M]**

sāḍ-e	*kolõ*	***naĩ́***	***ho-nd-ā***
1PL.GEN-SG.M.OBL	by	**NEG**	**become-IP-SG.M**

'We can't do this work of studying and book learning.' (Pj) (www.siasat.pk > Forum > Lounge > Non-Siasi)

10.5.1.3 Ability to perform learned skills: the verb 'to come'

With learned behaviors, like learning foreign languages or driving a car, ability is expressed in all three languages with a construction involving a dative subject construction and the verb 'to come' (Section 9.1.3.2 above.)

(10.132) تداں چینی آندی اے

tud-ā̃	*cīnī*	***ā-nd-ī***	***e***
2SG.OBL-DAT	Chinese[F]	**come-IP-SG.F**	**be.PRES.**3SG

'Do you (sg. informal) know Chinese?' (Hk) (AWT)

(10.133) مینوں سندھی نہیں آؤندی

mæ-nū̃	*síndī*	*nā́ī̃*	***au-nd-ī***
1.SG.OBL-DAT	Sindhi[F]	NEG	**come-IP-SG.F**

'I don't know Sindhi.' (Pj) (EB)

(10.134) انھاکوں سرائکی نھی آندی

unhā-kū̃	*sarāikī*	*nhī*	***ā-nd-ī***
3PL.DIST.OBL-DAT	Saraiki[F]	NEG	**come-IP-SG.F**

'They do not know Siraiki.' (Sr) (Shackle 1976: 146)

10.5.2 Desirability or advisability

10.5.2.1 Vestigial morphological passive

A vestige of the morphological passive (still common in Saraiki) is used in Panjabi, with a deontic modal sense, as in examples 10.135 - 10.137. This is a frequently used construction, appearing now only with the imperfective participle, and usually found in negative contexts with a prohibitive sense.[18]

18 This construction has received different analyses by various authors. For example, Malik (1995: 268–269) calls this form the "optative" and considers it different from the passive, while Cummings and Bailey (1912: xiv, 85) consider it an "organic passive" and give an infinitive for an organic passive stem. Bhardwaj (2016: 168) calls this construction a "subtractive phase" of the verb, since an agent is not named.

(10.135) گھر دیاں گلاں باہر نہیں کریدیاں

kàr *d-iyā̃* *gall-ā̃* *bā́r* *naī̃* *kar-ī-d-iyā̃*
home GEN-PL.F matter-PL.F outside NEG do-PASS-IP-PL.F
'One should not discuss domestic matters outside the home.' (Pj) (EB)

(10.136) اینج نہیں کریدا

æ̃j *naī̃* *kar-ī-d-ā*
like.this NEG do-PASS-IP-SG.M
'One shouldn't do like this. (lit. It isn't done like this.)' (Pj) (EB)

(10.137) بہوتا ہسیدا نئی

bɔ̃́tā *hass-ī-d-ā* *naī̃*
too.much laugh-PASS-IP-SG.M NEG
'One should not laugh too much. (i.e. Don't laugh too much.)' (Pj) (Bhardwaj 2016: 169)

The older attestation in 10.138 shows the construction in an affirmative sentence, apparently without the modal sense.

(10.138) آکھیدا ہوندا سی

ākh-ī-d-ā *hu-nd-ā* *sī*
say-PASS-IP-SG.M be-IP-SG.M be.PST.3SG
'It used to be said.' (Pj) (Cummings and Bailey 1912: 85)

10.5.2.2 The verb 'to be wanted'

In Hindko and Panjabi, an infinitive or gerundive followed by a form of چاہیدا /cā̃īdā/ 'is wanted/needed' indicates desirability; it is usually translated in English with 'should' or 'ought to'. This form is the imperfective participle (marked adjective) of the vestigial passive of the verb چاہ /cā̃-/ 'want' (Section 10.5.2.1). The agent appears with the dative postposition. Examples follow for Hindko in 10.139, and Panjabi in 10.140 and 10.141. With intransitive complements like those in 10.139 and 10.140, the infinitive form is default masculine singular. With transitive complements like that in 10.141, the infinitive/gerundive agrees in number and gender with an unmarked direct object.[19]

19 In example 10.139, the verb form چاہی دے /cāhi dæ/ is as given by AWT. It probably reflects an ellipsis: ā + e > æ.

(10.139) تداں ٹیم تے اتھے ہوڑا چاہی دے

tud-ā̃	*ṭæm*	*te*	*uthe*	*ho-r̥ā*	***cā̂i-d-æ***
2SG.OBL-DAT	time	on	there	be-INF	**be.needed-IP-SG.M+be.PRES.3SG**

'You should be there on time.' (Hk) (AWT)

(10.140) مینوں کل جانا چاہیدا سی

mæ-nū̃	*kál*	*jā-ṇā*	***cā̂ī-d-ā***	***sī***
1SG.OBL-DAT	yesterday	go-INF	**be.wanted-IP-SG.M**	**be.PST.3SG**

'I ought to have gone yesterday.' (Pj) (Shackle 1972: 83)

(10.141) اوہ نوں انگریزی سکھنی چاہیدی اے

ó-nū̃	*ā̃grezī*	*sikh-ṇ-ī*	***cā̂ī-d-ī***
3.DIST.OBL-DAT	English[F]	learn-INF-SG.F	**be.wanted-IP-SG.F**

e
be.PRES.3SG

'He should learn English.' (Pj) (Shackle 1972: 83)

In Saraiki, the regular passive form of چہݨ /cahaṇ/ 'to want' plus the gerundive of ہووݨ /hovaṇ/ 'to be' expresses the meaning 'should, ought to', as in 10.142.

(10.142) سرائیکی ٹیچر فورم ہووݨا چاہیندا ہے

saraikī	*ṭīcar*	*foram*	*hov-aṇ-ā*	***cāh-ī̃-d-ā***
Saraiki	teacher	forum.SG.M	be-GRDV-SG.M	**want-PASS-IP-SG.M**

hæ
be.PRES.3SG

'There should be a Saraiki teacher's forum.' (Sr) (http://sunjjan.blogspot.com/2015/01/blog-post.html)

10.5.3 Prospective meanings: Weak obligation, need, desire, intended or expected activity

This category is fuzzy, including a variety of meanings expressed by the infinitive/gerundive, and has been so for a long time. In late Middle Indo Aryan (MIA), the gerundive was reanalyzed as an infinitive (Bubenik 1998: 120), and today in these languages, the infinitive (nominal) and gerundive (adjectival) forms are often homophonous, and often overlap in use.[20] Sometimes it is not clear whether a given form is an instance of the infinitive or of the gerundive. In such cases we will refer to the infinitive/gerundive. Cases in which the infinitive functions nominally, as subject of the sentence 10.143, or when its oblique form is used in a verbal construction, as in 10.144, are clear instances of the infinitive.

(10.143) جھوٹھ بولنا بھیڑا اے

cũṭh	***bol-ṇā***	*pæ̃ṛ-ā*	*e*
lie	**speak-INF.DIR**	bad-SG.M	be.PRES.3SG

'It is wrong to lie. (lit. lying is bad)' (Pj) (Shackle 1972: 78)

(10.144) کڑی رون لگی

kuṛī	***ro-ṇ***	*lag-ī*
girl[F]	**cry-INF.OBL**	begin-PP.SG.F

'The girl began to cry.' (Pj) (EB)

Since the gerundive occurs in predicative adjectival position, we can conclude that a sentence like 10.145, with the subject 'books', involves the (historical) gerundive. The adjectival form in والا /vālā/ performs a similar function in both predicative and attributive adjectival position, as in 10.146.

(10.145) ایہہ کتاباں پڑھنیاں نیں

é	*katāb-ā̃*	***páṛ-n-iyā̃***	*nẽ*
3PL.PROX	book-PL.F	**read-GRDV-PL.F**	be.PRES.3PL

'These books should be/are to be read.' (Pj) (EB)

20 Bhardwaj (2016: 223) calls the gerundive a "potential participle", and the infinitive a "gerund". The term "gerundive" employed by Shackle, Bubenik, and by us here, comes from the Indological tradition. Other terms encountered for this form are "future passive participle" and "participle of obligation" (Masica 1991: 288).

(10.146) اے پڑھن والیاں کتاباں نیں

é	***pá̇r-an***	***vāl-iyā̃***	*katāb-ā̃*	*nẽ*
3PL.PROX	**read-OBL.INF**	**NMLZ-PL.F**	book-PL.F	be.PRES.3PL

'These are books worth reading [lit. worth-reading books].' (Pj) (EB)

Regarding the semantic interpretation of sentences with gerundives, we find ambiguity even at earlier stages of the language. Discussing Late MIA Apabhraṃśa, Bubenik (1998: 193) says, "we cannot be quite sure whether we are dealing with the modal category or the future tense. These are the cases involving the 1st Pers[on] where one hesitates between the volitional 'I want to V' and the future 'I will V' interpretation." This cluster of meanings can be subsumed under a more general category of prospectivity. These meanings are realized in similar but somewhat varying ways in Hindko, Panjabi, and Saraiki.

10.5.3.1 Weak obligation, need, desire, intention, expectation – Hindko

A construction consisting of the oblique or dative form of the actor/experiencer with the direct form of the infinitive or gerundive carries meanings of (a) (weak) obligation, (b) intention, (c) desire, or (d) expectation. Examples involving necessary/intended activity are given as 10.147, 10.148, and 10.149.

(10.147) ماہنہ ڈاکٹر کول جلنڑا ایہا

mā̃́	*ḍākṭar*	*kol*	***jul-ṛ̃ā***	***éy-ā***
1SG.DAT	doctor	to	**go-INF.SG.M**	**be.PST-SG.M**

'I had to go to the doctor.' (Hk) (AWT)

(10.148) جمیل آں ایہہ نئیں پتا ایہا کہ اس کدر جلنڑا

jamīl-ā̃	*é*	*naī̃́*	*patā*	*éy-ā*	*ki*	*us*
Jamil-DAT	3SG.PROX	NEG	known	be.PST-SG.M	that	3SG.DIST.OBL

kídar	***jul-ṛ̃ā***
where	**go-INF.SG.M**

'Jamil didn't know where to go.' (Hk) (EB 1989, unpublished field notes, Abbottabad)

(10.149) ایہہ کپڑے تہونڑے نیں

é	*kapṛ-e*	***tò-ṛ̃-e***	***nẽ***
3PL.PROX	garment-PL.M	**wash-GRDV-PL.M**	**be.PRES.3PL**

'These clothes need to be washed.' (Hk) (EB 1989, unpublished field notes, Abbottabad)

10.5.3.2 Weak obligation, need, intention, expectation, future – Panjabi

An infinitive followed by a conjugated form of ہونا /hoṇā/ 'to be' can indicate desire, intention, futurity, or necessity; the construction is usually translated by English expressions like 'wants to', 'is going to', or 'has to'. When the subject is a human, having agentivity and conscious choice, it appears in the oblique case, as in examples 10.150 and 10.151; or, with some third-person subjects, followed by the postposition نے /ne/, as in 10.152. Although we continue to label the postposition نے as ERG(ative) for the sake of consistency, its meaning is clearly different in this type of Panjabi construction from the usual understanding of "ergative" as marking the subjects of perfective transitive verbs.[21] In the constructions discussed in this section, it marks agentivity. If the subject, typically denoting an inanimate entity, does not possess agentivity, however, it appears in the direct case, as in 10.153. In transitive sentences of this type, e.g. 10.150, the form لکھنی /likh-ṇ-ī/ agrees in number and gender with its direct object. In Saraiki, this would be a clearly gerundive construction. We are labelling usages with desiderative nuances GRDV for Panjabi as well. This convergence of the categories, forms, and meanings of the infinitive and gerundive in Panjabi continues a process begun in Middle Indo-Aryan (Bubenik 1998: 190–193).

(10.150) میں چٹھی لکھنی اے

mæ̃	*ciṭṭh-ī*	***likh-ṇ-ī***	***e***
1SG.OBL	letter-F	**write-GRDV-SG.F**	**be.PRES.3SG**

'I want to/am going to write a letter.' (Pj) (Shackle 1972: 84)

(10.151) میں نہیں کھانی

mæ̃	*naĩ*	***khā-ṇ-ī***
1SG.OBL	NEG	**eat-GRDV-SG.F**

'I don't want to/won't eat (it) (SG.F object, usually روٹی /roṭī/ bread, food)' (Pj) (EB)

(10.152) کڑی نے جانا اے

kuṛ-ī	*ne*	***jā-ṇā***	***e***
girl-SG.F.OBL	ERG	**go-GRDV**	**be.PRES.3SG**

'The girl has to/wants to/is going to go.' (Pj) (Shackle 1972: 84)

21 See Bashir (1999) on the evolving role of the postposition نے /ne/ in Urdu.

(10.153) کل دن سویرے پنج وجے چڑھنا اے

kál	*din*	*saver-e*	*panj*	*vaje*
tomorrow	day.SG.M.DIR	morning-OBL	five	o'clock

cáṛ-n-ā	***e***
climb-GRDV-SG.M	**be.PRES.3SG**

'Tomorrow dawn will be at five o'clock in the morning.' (Pj) (EB)

In the Panjabi examples 10.154 and 10.155, the infinitive refers to an anticipated or predicted action or state.

(10.154) حال چال پچھیا تے آکھیا تسیں کتھوں آئے او تے ہن کتھے جانا ہے

hāl.cāl	*puch-iyā*	*te*	*ākh-iyā*	*tussī̃*	*kith-õ*
condition	ask-PP.SG.M	and	say-PP.SG.M	2PL.DIR	where-ABL

ā-e	*o*	*te*	*huṇ*	*kithe*	***jā-ṇā***	***hæ***
come-PP.PL.M	be.PRES.2PL	and	now	where	**go-INF**	**be.PRES.3SG**

'(Someone) asked about (someone's) condition and said, "Where have you come from and now where are you going?"' (Pj) (www.hin.islamic-sources.com ... قصہ-چار-درویشاں-دا)

This anticipated/predicted action can be situated at any time vis-à-vis the moment of speech. For example in 10.155 it is in past time, and in 10.156 and 10.157 it is situated in future time.

(10.155) میرے پتر نے اج دس وجے آنا سی پر اجے نہیں آیا

mer-e	*puttar*	*ne*	*ajj*	*das*	*vaje*	***ā-ṇā***
my-SG.M.OBL	son	ERG	today	ten	o'clock	**come-INF**

sī	*par*	*aje*	*nī̃*	*ā-yā*
be.PST.3SG	but	still	NEG	come-PP.SG.M

'My son was (supposed/going) to come at ten o'clock today, but he still hasn't come.' (Pj) (EB)

(10.156) میرے پتر نے کل دس وجے آنا اے

mer-e	*puttar*	*ne*	*kal*	*das*	*vaje*	***ā-ṇā***
my-SG.M.OBL	son	ERG	tomorrow	ten	o'clock	**come-INF**

e
be.PRES.3SG

'My son is (going/supposed) to come at ten o'clock tomorrow.' (Pj) (EB)

(10.157) ہن میرے کولوں تے نہیں جایا جانا

huṇ	*mer-e*	*kolõ*	*te*	***naĩ***	***jāyā***	***jā-ṇā***
now	my-SG.M.OBL	by	TOP	**NEG**	**go.PP.SG.M**	**go-INF**

'I won't be able to go now!' (Pj) (Bashir and Kazmi 2012: 470)

In the example above, the form جایا /jāyā/ is the regularly formed perfective participle of جانا /jāṇā/ 'to go'. It appears here in the periphrastic passive construction indicating (in)ability. Compare 10.157 with 10.107 above.

10.5.3.3 Weak obligation, need, desirability, intention, expectation – Saraiki

In Saraiki too, the categories of weak obligation, need, desirability, and expectation overlap. The meanings 'need to, be supposed to, have to (in the weak sense)' were expressed in Shackle's time (1976) with the oblique (or direct) case of the person who is to do something (the non-volitional experiencer/agent) plus the gerundive of the verb expressing the action that needs/is desired to be done. In 10.158, with the verb ملݨ /milaṇ/ 'to meet', you (PL. OBL) is the person who needs to do the action, and the verb ملݨ /milaṇ/ 'to meet' appears in its masculine singular gerundive form. The analysis of this example reflects elision of the masculine singular ending ا /ā/ and اے /e/, the third person singular present of 'be'. In example 10.159, with the transitive verb لکھݨ /likhaṇ/ 'to write', the gerundive agrees in number and gender with its direct object کتاب /kitāb/ 'book (F)'.[22] Sentences (10.160–10.164) give further examples. The agreement patterns appearing in 10.162 and 10.163 need to be explored. In 10.162 the third singular pronoun ایں /ī̃/ 'it' is clearly oblique, whereas in 10.163 the feminine noun گݙی /ɠaḍḍī/ 'train' could be either direct or oblique.

(10.158) تساں ڈاکٹر صاحب کوں ملݨے

tussã̄	*ḍākṭar*	*sæhib*	*kũ*	***mil-ṇ-æ***
2PL.OBL	doctor	HONORIFIC	ACC	**meet-GRDV-SG.M+be.PRES.3SG**

'You must meet the doctor.' (Sr) (Shackle 1976: 139)

22 Shackle (1976), along with most others, treats کتاب /kitāb/ 'book' as feminine, but our consultant (UK) treats it as masculine.

(10.159) اوں کتاب لکھݨی ہئی

ũ̃	*kitāb*	***likh-ṇ-ī***	***ha-ī***
3SG.OBL	book.SG.F	**write-GRDV-SG.F**	**be.PST-SG.F**

'S/he was (supposed) to write a book.' (Sr) (Shackle 1976: 148)

(10.160) تے ونڄݨا ہا

tæ	*vãf-ṇā*	*hā*
2SG.OBL	go-GRDV.SG.M	be.PST.SG.M

'You should have gone.' (Sr) (Shackle 1976: 147)

It appears that this construction may have changed somewhat since Shackle's time. Compare 10.161, in which the experiencer takes the dative case, with 10.158, in which the experiencer is in its oblique form.

(10.161) تیکوں ڈاکٹر کنے ونڄݨے

tæ-kũ̃	*ḍākṭar*	*kane*	*vãf-ṇ-æ*
2SG.OBL-DAT	doctor	near	go-GRDV-SG.M+be.PRES.3SG

'You have to go to the doctor.' (Sr) (UK)

(10.162) ایں ݙاہ وڄے روانہ تھیوݨاں ہئی

ĩ̃	*ɗah*	*vafe*	*ravānā*	*thī-vuṇã̄*
3SG.PROX.OBL	ten	o'clock	departed	become-GRDV.SG.M

ha-ī
be.PST-SG.F

'It was supposed to depart at ten o'clock.' (Sr) (Zahoor 2009: 47)

(10.163) ڳڈی رات دے اڈھائی وڄے راولپنڈی پڄݨا ہا

ɠaḍḍī	*rāt*	*de*	*aḍhāī*	*vafe*	*rāvalpinḍī*	*puf-ṇ-ā*
train.F.OBL	night	GEN	2½	o'clock	Rawalpindi	reach-GRDV-SG.M

h-ā
be.PST-SG.M

'The train was to reach Rawalpindi at 2:30 a.m.' (Sr) (Shackle (1976: 139), cited from Lashari (1971: 120))

In 10.164 a volitional agent 'the child' appears in the oblique case; compare 10.164 with 10.161 above.

(10.164) پر ٻال نہ ٻاہر آوݨا ہا تے نہ آیا

par	***ɓāl***	*na*	*ɓæhir*	*āv-ṇ-ā*	*hā*	*te*
but	**child.M.OBL**	NEG	out	come-GRDV-SG.M	be.PST.SG.M	and

na	*ā-yā*
NEG	come-PP.SG.M

'But the child was not going to come out, and didn't.' (Sr) (Shackle (1976: 139) cited from Lashari (1971: 99).)

Desirable but unrealized acts or states are expressed with irrealis constructions. In 10.165 we see irrealis I, and in 10.166 irrealis II.

(10.165) توں اوہ کتاب گھنیں ہا

tū̃	*ō*	*kitāb*	***ghin-ẽ***	***h-ā***
2SG.DIR	that	book[M]	**take-SBJV.2SG**	**be.PST-SG.M**

'You (SG) should have bought that book.' (Sr) (UK)

(10.166) او ہو! جے میں دولت وند ہوندا

o-ho!	*je*	*mæ̃*	*dɔlatvand*	***ho-nd-ā***
oh	if	1SG.DIR	rich	**be-IP-SG.M**

'Oh! Would that I (M) were rich.' (Sr) (Zahoor 2009: 70)

10.5.4 Presumption (epistemic modality)

A presumptive statement is one that speakers make based on their best knowledge of a likely state of affairs. It overlaps in some cases with the meaning we have called "expectation" in Section Section 10.5.3.2, but in some cases is distinctively presumptive. The infinitive/gerundive is frequently used with this meaning similarly to the way in which presumptive meaning is conveyed by a future/presumptive form. For example, in 10.167, the infinitive/gerundive phrase ویکھی ہوݨی /vekhī hoṇī/ conveys the meaning of 'must have seen'. It is feminine singular, agreeing with its direct object 'video'.

(10.167) سوات دے تحصیل کبل دی کڑی نوں کوڑے مارن دی ویڈیو تسیں وی ویکھی ہونی آ

swāt	*de*	*tæsīl*	*kabal*	*d-ī*	*kuṛ-ī*	*nū̃*	*koṛe*
Swat	GEN	sub-district	Kabal	GEN-SG.F	girl-SG.F	ACC	lashes

mār-aṇ	*d-ī*	*viḍiyo*	*tussī̃*	*vī*	***vekh-ī***
beat-INF.OBL	GEN-SG.F	video[F]	2PL.DIR	also	**see.PP-SG.F**

ho-ṇ-ī	*ā*
be-GRNDV-SG.F	HORT

'You too must have seen the video of the girl from Tehsil Kabal in Swat being lashed.' (Pj) (http://www.wichaar.com/news/122/ARTICLE/13422/2009–04–03.html)

(10.168) تسی خبر ای نئی کیتی ہونی ورنہ ضرور ہو جانی سی

tussī	*xabar*	*ī*	*naī̃*	***k-īt-ī***	***ho-ṇ-ī***
2PL	information[F]	EMPH	NEG	**do-PP-SG.F**	**be-GRDV-SG.F**

varnā	*zarūr*	*ho*	*jā-ṇ-ī*	*sī*
otherwise	definitely	become	go-GRDV-SG.F	be.PST.3SG

'You must not even have informed (anyone), otherwise it (F) would have happened.' (Pj) (http://www.hamariweb.com/poetries/poetry.aspx?id=16940)

10.5.5 Strong obligation or compulsion

In all three languages an infinitive or gerundive followed by a conjugated form of the verb پئیڑا /pæṛā/ Hk , پینا/pæṇā/ Pj , پووݨ/povuṇ/ Sr 'to fall' indicates strong obligation or lack of choice; this construction is usually translated as 'must', 'be obliged to', or 'have to' (in the strong sense). This is another instance of the dative or oblique subject construction, in which the person compelled to do something appears in the oblique or dative case, and the compelled action is an infinitive (or gerundive) which is the grammatical subject of the sentence. If that infinitive/gerundive is of a transitive verb, it agrees in number and gender with an unmarked direct object, as in 10.169; if it is intransitive, the infinitive/gerundive is default masculine singular, as in 10.170 and 10.171.

10.5.5.1 Strong obligation or compulsion – Hindko

In Hindko, a form of the verb پیڑا /pæṛ̃ā/ 'to fall' is used.

(10.169) اساں جلدی کرنی پیسی

assā̃	*jaldī*	***kar-n-ī***	***pæ-s-i***
1PL.OBL	hurry.SG.F	**do-GNDV-SG.F**	**fall-FUT-3SG**

'We will have to hurry.' (Hk) (AWT)

(10.170) اَساں کل فزری سویرے اُٹھنڑا پیسی

assā̃	*kal*	*fazrī*	*saver-e*	***uth-ṛ̃ā***	***pæ-s-ī***
1PL.OBL	tomorrow	dawn	morning-OBL	**rise-INF.DIR**	**fall-FUT-3SG**

'We will have to get up very early tomorrow morning.' (Hk) (AWT)

10.5.5.2 Strong obligation or compulsion – Panjabi

In Panjabi, a form of the verb پینا /pæṇā/ 'to fall' is used.

(10.171) کل سانوں جانا پویگا

kál	*sā-nū̃*	***jā-ṇā***	***pa-ve-g-ā***
tomorrow	1PL.OBL-DAT	**go-INF.DIR**	**fall-SBJV.3SG-FUT-SG.M**

'We will have to go tomorrow.' (Pj) (Shackle 1972: 84)

(10.172) اوہناں نوں مڑنا پیا

ón-ā̃	*nū̃*	***muṛ-nā***	***p-yā***
3PL.DIST-OBL	DAT	**turn-INF**	**fall-PP.SG.M**

'They had to turn back.' (Pj) (Shackle 1972: 84)

10.5.5.3 Strong obligation or compulsion – Saraiki

In Saraiki, the compelled action is in the gerundive form. In the case of transitive verbs, both the gerundive and the form of پووڻ/povuṇ/ 'to fall' agree with an unmarked direct object (examples 10.173 to 10.175). As with the other languages, when a direct object bears the accusative marker, as in 10.176, or when the infinitive is of an intransitive verb, as in 10.177, both the gerundive and the form of پووڻ/povuṇ/ 'to fall' are default masculine singular.

(10.173) اوکوں ٻہوں سارے خط لکھڻے پوسن

ū-kũ̄	*ɓahũ̄*	*sāre*	*xat*	***likh-ṇ-e***	***po-s-in***
3SG.OBL-DAT	very	all	letter.PL.M	**write-GRDV-PL.M**	**fall-FUT-3PL**

'S/he will have to write lots of letters.' (Sr) (Shackle 1976: 148)

(10.174) ہڻیں نال پنجھ وڄ ڳین اساکوں جلتی کرڻی پوسی

huṇẽ	*nāl*	*panjh*	*vaʄ*	*ɠa-e-n*	*assā-kũ̄*
now	with	five	strike	go.PP-PL.M-be.PRES.3PL	1PL.OBL-DAT

jaltī	***kar-ṇ-ī***	***po-s-ī***
hurry[F]	**do-GRDV-SG.F**	**fall-FUT-3SG**

'Its already five o'clock; we will have to hurry.' (Sr) (UK)

(10.175) میکوں کتنے پیسے جمع کراوڻے پوسن

mæ-kũ̄	*kitn-e*	*pæse*	*jamā*
1SG.OBL-DAT	how.much-PL.M	money.PL.M	deposited

kar-ɔ-ṇ-e	***po-s-in***
do-CS-GRDV-PL.M	**fall-FUT-3PL**

'How much money will I have to pay.' (Sr) (Zahoor 2009: 57)

(10.176) ایں نکی کوں تیکوں پالڻا پوسی

ĩ̄	*nikk-ī*	*kũ̄*	*tæ-kũ̄*
3SG.PROX.OBL	little.one-SG.F	ACC	2SG.OBL-DAT

pāl-ṇā	***po-s-ī***
bring.up-GRDV-SG.M	**fall-FUT-3SG**

'You will have to bring up this little girl.' (Sr) (Shackle (1976: 149), cited from Lashari (1971: 12).)

(10.177) تہاکوں سنگاپور رکنا پوسی

tuhā-kũ̄	*sĩgāpor*	***ruk-ṇ-ā***	***po-s-ī***
2PL.OBL-DAT	Singapore	**stop-GRDV-SG.M**	**fall-FUT.3SG**

'You will have to stop in Singapore.' (Sr) (Zahoor 2009: 48)

10.5.6 Infinitive/gerundive as distanced (softened) imperative

In all three languages, the infinitive or gerundive may be used as a distanced imperative, where distance may be spatial, temporal, and/or social.[23] For instance, it can be used to tell someone to do something at some (hypothetical or unspecified) time in the future; thus it is appropriate for public notices, announcements, and instructions. It is unmarked with regard to social status and formality or politeness distinctions. In gerundive constructions like those illustrated in the preceding sections, the gerundive is followed by a finite verb (conjugated form of 'be' or 'befall'). When the infinitive/gerundive is used as a distanced imperative, it appears without a finite auxiliary, as a bare gerundive/infinitive.

10.5.6.1 Hindko and Panjabi infinitive/gerundive as distanced (softened) imperative

(10.178) اِس دی جگہ تسی کل میرے نال چلے جاڑا

is	*d-ī*	*jagā*	*tussī*	*kal*	*mer-e*
3SG.OBL	GEN-SG.F	place[F]	2PL.DIR	tomorrow	1SG.GEN-SG.M.OBL

nāl	*cal-e*	***jā-ṛā***
with	move-PP.PL.M	**go-INF/GRDV.SG.M**

'You go with me tomorrow instead of him.' (Hk) (Peshawar Hindko, Toker (2014: 113), cited from Malik 2003: 141)

In Panjabi and Hindko, negatives are formed with نہ /na/, as shown in examples 10.179 - 10.181. See also Section 8.5.1.

(10.179) ایتھے سامان نہ رکھنا

éthe	*samān*	*na*	***rakh-ṇā***
here	luggage.M	NEG	**put-INF/GRDV.SG.M**

'Don't put luggage here!' (Pj) (Shackle 1972: 78)

23 Bashir and Kazmi (2012: 653) call this usage the "urbanized future imperative."

(10.180) پاکستان جا کے میرے واسطے پنجابی دیاں کجھ کتاباں لینیاں

pākistān	*jā-ke*	*mer-e*	*vāste*	*panjābī*	*d-iyā̃*	*kúc*
Pakistan	go-CP	1SG.GEN-SG.M.OBL	for	Panjabi	GEN-PL.F	some

katāb-ā̃	***læ-ṇ-iyā̃***
book-PL.F	**buy-INF/GRDV-PL.F**

'When you go to Pakistan, buy some Panjabi books for me.' (Pj) (EB)

(10.181) صرف سکول دیاں کتاباں ہی پڑھنیاں

siraf	*skūl*	*d-iyā̃*	*katāb-ā̃*	*ī*	***pár̥-n-iyā̃***
only	school	GEN-PL.F	book-PL.F	EXCL	**read-INF/GRDV-PL.F**

'Only read (your) schoolbooks.' (Pj) (http://www.sanjhapunjab.net/ajit-kaur/)

10.5.6.2 Saraiki gerundive as imperative

In Saraiki, the comparable construction involves the gerundive, as in 10.182. Especially in negative contexts, it functions as a forceful command, e.g. 10.183. Notice that with this emphatic prohibition, the negative element is نہیں /naī̃/, whereas with most negative imperatives or subjunctives the simple negative particle نہ /na/ appears, as in 10.184.[24]

(10.182) رحمت کوں آکھ جو ڈو سیر آلوں آݨے

rahmat	*kū̃*	*ākh*	*jo*	*dū*	*ser*	*ālū̃*
Rahmat	DAT	say.2SG.IMP	that	two	seer.PL.M	potato.PL.M

ā-ṇ-e
bring-GRDV-PL.M

'Tell Rahmat to bring two seers of potatoes.' (Sr) (UK)

24 Homophony between the gerundive and the infinitive, and the use of نہیں /naī̃/ 'is not, NEG.EMPH' with the gerundive as a negative imperative in Saraiki example 10.183 may have influenced the recent appearance of نہیں /naī̃/ 'not, do not' with ordinary imperatives in Panjabi (and also Urdu), e.g. نہیں کرو /nahī̃ karo/ 'don't do it', which is not accepted by many speakers.

(10.183) نہیں ونجݨا

naĩ̄	***vãf-ṇā***
NEG	**go-GRDV.SG.M**

'Don't go!' (Sr) (Shackle 1976: 139)

(10.184) اینکوں بھل نہ ونجیں

ĩ̄-kũ̄	*bhul*	*na*	*vãf-ẽ*
3SG.PROX.OBL-ACC	forget	NEG	go-SBJV.2SG

'Don't forget this.' (Sr) (Zahoor 2009: 26)

10.6 Referentiality: Definiteness, indefiniteness, genericity

Neither Hindko, Panjabi, nor Saraiki has either a definite article like English 'the' or a single indefinite article like English 'a'. Definiteness (i.e. unique referential status of a given noun phrase) is marked in different ways, distributed through the grammar. One means of marking definiteness is by positioning a nominal in sentence-initial (topic) position, signifying that it is old information, hence definite, e.g. 10.185 and 10.186. Marking an animate direct object with the accusative postposition can also indicate definiteness, as in 10.187. Demonstrative adjectives also indicate definiteness, as in 10.188. Inanimate direct objects, even when definite, often appear in the direct case, as in 10.188.

(10.185) راجہ آپے توں باہر ہو گیا

rājā	*āp-e*	*tõ*	*bā́r*	*ho*	*ga-yā*
king	self-OBL	from	outside	become	go-PP.SG.M

'**The** king was beside himself (with rage).' (Hk) (Soz 2011: 7)

(10.186) کتاباں میز دے تھلّے نیں

katāb-ā̃	*mez*	*de*	*thalle*	*nẽ*
book-PL.F	table	GEN	below	be.PRES.3PL

'**The** books are underneath the table.' (Pj) (EB)

(10.187) اوں چور کوں ھک کاتی نال ماریے

ũ	***cor-kũ***	*hikk*	*kātī*	*nāl*
3SG.DIST.OBL	**thief.OBL-ACC**	a	knife	with

mār-iye
kill-PP.SG.M+ be.PRES.3SG
'S/he killed **the** thief with a knife.' (Sr) (UK)

(10.188) اے گھر میں بݨاے

e	***ghar***	*mæ̃*	*baṇā-ye*
3SG.PROX.DIR	**house**	1SG.DIR	make-PP.SG.M+ be.PRES.3SG

'I built **this** house.' (Sr) (UK)

Definite noun phrases tend to occur with certain tense-aspect forms (Sections 8.6.2.2 and 8.9.3.4.7), like the continuous-I and II forms, because of the strong sense of actuality they convey, as in 10.189. In contrast, non-specific indefinite nominals tend to occur with imperfective habitual tense-aspect forms, as in 10.190.

(10.189) کڑیاں بھانڈے دھوندیاں پیاں نیں

kuṛiy-ā̃	*pā̀ṇḍe*	*tòn-d-iyā̃*	*p-iyā̃*	*nẽ*
girl-PL.F	vessels	wash-IP-PL.F	CONT.I-PL.F	be.PRES.3PL

'The girls are washing dishes.' (Pj) (EB)

(10.190) کڑیاں گھر دا کم کردیاں ہوندیاں نیں

kuṛiy-ā̃	*kàr*	*d-ā*	*kamm*	*kar-d-iyā̃*	*ho-nd-iyā̃*
girl-PL.F	house	GEN-SG.M	work[M]	do-IP-PL.F	be-IP-PL.F

nẽ
be.PRES.3PL
'Girls (usually) do housework.' (Pj) (EB)

Non-specific indefinite noun phrases can either be unmarked, as in 10.190, or marked with the word کوئی /koī/ 'some, any', as in 10.191. Specific indefinites are usually marked with the word also meaning 'one', ہک /hikk/ Hk, Sr , اک /ikk/ Pj , as in 10.187.

(10.191) اوہ نوں کوئی چنگی چیز دینی چاہیدی اے

o-nũ̄	***koī***	***cãgī***	*cīz*	*de-ṇ-ī*
3SG.DIST.OBL-DAT	**some/any**	**good.SG.F**	thing[F]	give-INF/GNDV-SG.F

cā̃ī-d-ī	*e*
be.wanted-IP-SG.F	be.PRES.3SG

'She/he should be given something good (or) Someone should give him/her something good.' (Pj) (EB)

Generic referents are usually expressed with a singular noun phrase, as in 10.192.

(10.192) پرندے دیاں دو لاتھاں ہوندیاں نیں

parind-e	*d-iyā̃*	*do*	*lath-ā̃*	*ho-nd-iyā̃*	*nẽ*
bird-SG.M.OBL	of-PL.F	two	leg-PL.F	be-IP-PL.F	be.PRES.3PL

'**Birds** have two legs.' (Pj) (EB)

10.7 Evidentiality and mirativity

Evidentiality and mirativity distinctions are not morphologically marked in these languages. Rather, they are indicated syntactically or lexically. Compare the following set of Hindko sentences. In each case, the basic sentence is the same, regardless of whether the reported event was witnessed by the speaker or hearsay, or whether it is old or newly acquired information. Thus the Hindko sentence in 10.193 could be followed by any of the continuations in 10.194, 10.195, and 10.196.

(10.193) سلیم دے پیو اے کہار بڑھایا ایہا

salīm	*d-e*	*pyo*	*é*	*kàr*	*baṛā̀-yā*
Salim	GEN-SG.M.OBL	father	3SG.PROX	house[M]	make-PP.SG.M

éy-ā
be.PST-SG.M

'Salim's father made this house.' (Hk) (AWT)

(10.194) . . . میں اپڑیاں اکھیاں نال اُس آں اے بڑھاندا دیکھیا

mǣ̃	*apṛ-iyā̃*	*akh-iyā̃*	*nāl*	*us-ā̃*	*é*
1SG	REFL-PL.F	eye-PL.F.OBL	with	3SG.OBL-ACC	3SG.PROX

baṛā̀-nd-ā	*dex-iyā*
make-IP-SG.M	see-PP.SG.M

'. . . I saw him building it with my own eyes.' (Hk) (AWT)

(10.195) . . . جس طرحاں میں سنڑیا اے

jis	*tarhā̃*	*mǣ̃*	*suṛ̃-iyā*	*e*
which.REL.OBL	matter	1SG	hear-PP.SG.M	be.PRES.3SG

'. . .as I have heard' (Hk) (AWT)

(10.196) . . . میرے علم بچ ہونڑ آیا اے

mer-e	*ilam*	*bic*	*huṛ̃*	*ā-yā*
1SG.GEN-SG.M.OBL	knowledge.OBL	in	now	come-PP.SG.M

e
be.PRES.3SG

'. . . I have just learned this.' (Hk) (AWT)

However, like the indication of referentiality status, mechanisms indicating evidentiality and mirative semantics are distributed throughout the grammar in these languages. Mirative semantics are associated with the compound verb vs. simple verb distinction; see examples 10.18 and 10.19 above. Although this has not been investigated specifically for the languages discussed here, it is also likely that the choice between a tense-marked perfective and a simple perfective functions the same way in them as it does in Hindi and Urdu. That is, simple perfectives tend to occur with unexpected or new information,[25] while tense-marked perfectives express already established information. Also, recall that the use of the vector بہہ /bǣ-/ 'sit', at least in Panjabi, is often associated with unanticipated (negative) consequences, as illustrated in 10.25 above. See also footnote 18 in Section 10.1.3.2 on post-verbal چا /cā/ in Saraiki.

25 For discussion of this effect in Hindi and Urdu, see Montaut (2001) and Bashir (2006).

10.8 Expression of "possession"

In all three languages discussed here, different types of "possession"—inalienable, alienable, and intangible/abstract—which in English are generally expressed with the transitive verb 'to have', are conceptualized as intransitive, locative relations and are expressed with the verb 'to be' and various postpositions.[26] The specific construction depends on whether the "possession" is permanent (inalienable) or temporary (alienable), and whether the entity "possessed" is concrete or abstract.

In all three languages, the genitive postposition دا ~ دے ~ دی ~ دیاں /dā ~ de ~ dī ~ diyā̃/ 'of' or دے وچ /de vic/ 'in' for third person "possessor" entities, and the genitive forms (marked adjectives) of the first and second person pronouns are used to express inalienable possession—a permanent relation between things that are usually, customarily, or intrinsically connected, such as relatives, body parts, a home, a quality, a permanent part or quality of some entity. Alienable, or temporary, possession or control of tangible things is expressed in all three languages with a postposition meaning 'near, with' دے کول /de kol/ Hk دے کول /de koḷ/ Pj , کنے /kane/ Sr . "Possession" of abstract entities or states is often expressed with a dative subject construction.

10.8.1 Inalienable possession

(10.197) تیرے کتنے پہنڑ پہرا نیں

ter-e	*kitn-e*	*pæ̀ṛ̃*	*prā̀*	*nẽ*
2SG.GEN-PL.M	how.many-PL.M	sister	brother	be.PRES.3PL

'How many brothers and sisters do you have?' (Hk) (AWT)

(10.198) اوس بندے وچ / دی بڑی ہمت اے

os	***band-e***	***vic/d-ī***	*baṛ-ī*	*himmat*	*e*
that.OBL	**man-OBL**	**in/of-SG.F**	great-SG.F	courage[F]	be.PRES.3SG

'That man has great courage.' (Pj) (EB)

Notice that the Saraiki expression in 10.199, corresponding to 10.197 in Hindko, shows a dative subject construction.

26 These languages thus fall into the 'B-language' type in the widely discussed 'be' vs. 'have' typology (e.g. Isacenko 1974).

(10.199) تیکوں چوکھے بھیݨ بھرا ہن

tæ-kū̃	*cokhe*	*bheṇ*	*bhirā*	*hĕn*
2SG.OBL-DAT	how.many	sister	brother	be.PRES.3PL

'How many brothers and sisters do you have?' (Sr) (UK)

(10.200) اوندے راولپنڈی اچ ڈو گھر ہن

ū̃	***d-e***	*rāvalpiṇḍī*	*ic*	*ɗū*	*ghar*
3SG.DIST.OBL	**GEN-PL.M**	Rawalpindi	in	two	house.PL.M

hen
be.PRES.3PL

'He/she has two houses in Rawalpindi.' (Sr) (UK)

For inanimate "possessors", only inalienable possession is possible, as shown in 10.201.

(10.201) ایس کمرے دے / وچ چار دروازے نیں

æs	***kamr-e***	***d-e***	***/vic***	*cār*	*darvāz-e*	*nẽ*
this	**room-OBL**	**GEN-SG.M.OBL**	**/in**	four	door-PL.M	be.PRES.3PL

'This room has four doors.' (Pj) (EB)

10.8.2 Alienable possession

(10.202) تیرے کول دہ روپے ہین

ter-e	***kol***	*dah*	*rupe*	*hæn*
2SG.GEN-SG.M.OBL	**with**	ten	rupees.PL.M	be.PRES.3PL

'Do you have ten rupees (with you now)?' (Hk) (AWT)

(10.203) اوہ دے کول پنجابی دیاں چار کتاباں نیں

ó	***d-e***	***koḷ***	*panjābī*	*d-iyā̃*	*cār*	*kitāb-ā̃*
3SG.OBL	**GEN-SG.M.OBL**	**with**	Panjabi	GEN-PL[F]	four	book-PL[F]

nẽ
be.PRES.3PL

'S/he has four Panjabi books (with her/him now).' (Pj) (EB)

(10.204) تیڈے کنے ڈاہ رپے ہن

ted-e	***kane***	*dāh*	*rupe*	*hĕn*
2SG.GEN-SG.M.OBL	**with**	ten	rupees	be.PRES.3PL

'Do you have ten rupees (with you now)?' (Sr) (UK)

10.8.3 Abstract "possession"

In all three languages a non-direct case form is used to express the temporary "possession" of (i.e. being affected by) intangible or abstract things such as environmental, bodily, or emotional states; like feeling heat or cold, illnesses, and emotions. In Hindko it is the oblique case, and in Panjabi and Saraiki the dative.

(10.205) مانہہ بخار اے

mā̃	*buxār*	*e*
1SG.OBL	fever	be.PRES.3SG

'I have a fever.' (Hk) (AWT)

(10.206) مینوں بڑی خوشی ہوئی کہ تیرا پتر پاس ہوگیا

mæ-nū̃	*baṛ-ī*	*xušī*	*ho-ī*	*ki*
1SG.OBL-DAT	much-SG.F	happiness[F]	become-PP.SG.F	that

ter-ā	*puttar*	*pās*	*ho*	*ga-yā*
2SG.GEN-SG.M	son	pass	become	go-PP.SG.M

'I am very happy that your son passed (the examination).' (Pj) (EB)

(10.207) میکوں بخار ہے

mæ-kū̃	*buxār*	*he*
1SG-DAT	fever	be.PRES.3SG

'I have a fever.' (Sr) (UK)

10.9 Causal relations

10.9.1 Expressions of reason/cause (SOURCE)

Reasons are expressed with several constructions. Subordinate clause structures are frequently used, as illustrated in examples 10.208, 10.209, and 10.210. In 10.208, the subordinating conjunctions کیونجو /kyõjo/ 'because' and ایس لئی /æs laī/ 'for this (reason)' appear. Urdu کیونکہ /kyõki/ is also frequent in Panjabi, as in 10.209. These same conjunctions are also used in Saraiki, as in example 10.210 from Shackle (1976: 70).

(10.208) سبھ سوالاں دے جواب کیونجو اِک دُوجے توں وکھرے سن ایس لئی بادشاہ کسے نال وی سہمت نہ ہویا

sáb	*svāl-ā̃*	*d-e*	*javāb*	***kyõjo***	*ikk*	*dūje*
all	question-OBL.PL	GEN-PL.M	reply.PL.M	**because**	one	other

tõ	*vakhr-e*	*san*	*æs*	*laī*	*bādšā*	*kise*
from	separate-PL.M	be.PST.3PL	3SG.PROX.OBL	for	king	any.OBL

nāḷ	*vī*	*sǽmat*	*na*	*ho-yā*
with	EMPH	agreeable	NEG	become-PP.SG.M

'Because their replies to all the questions differed from each other, the king did not agree with anyone.' (Pj) (http://monthlyanhad.blogspot.com/2016/06/blog-post.html)

(10.209) میرا خیال اے تسی اپنا کوٹ پا لوو کیونکہ باہر کافی ٹھنڈ اے

mer-ā	*xyāl*	*e*	*tussī*	*āpṇ-ā*	*koṭ*
1SG.GEN-SG.M	opinion	be.PRES.3SG	2PL.DIR	REFL-SG.M	coat.SG.M

pā	*la-vo*	***kyõki***	*bā́r*	*kāfī*	*ṭhanḍ*	*e*
put.on	take-IMP.2PL	because	outside	much	cold	be.PRES.3SG

'I think you should put your coat on because its very cold outside.' (Pj) (Bashir and Kazmi 2012: 135)

(10.210) کیوں جو مینہ اے اساں ٻاہر نا ویسوں

kyũ̄.jo	*mĩ̄h*	*e*	*assā̃*	*ɓāhir*	*nā*	*ve-s-ũ̄*
because	rain	be.PRES.3SG	1PL.DIR	outside	NEG	go-FUT-1PL

'Since it's raining we won't go out.' (Sr) (UK)

Postpositional expressions with a noun or oblique infinitive expressing the reason for something are a second major construction type, illustrated in 10.211 - 10.213. Ablative postpositions like توں /tõ/ in 10.211 or پاروں /pārõ/ in 10.213 clearly show reason conceptualized as an abstract SOURCE.

(10.211) تکلیف دی وجہ توں او ذرا وی ٹرنے جوگا نئیں رہیا

taklif	*d-i*	***vájā***	***tõ***	*o*	*zarā*	*vī*
pain	GEN-SG.F	**reason[F]**	**from**	3SG.DIST	bit	EMPH

ṭur-n-e	*jog-ā*	*naı̃*	*r-yā́*
walk-INF-OBL	fit.to-SG.M	NEG	remain-PP.SG.M

'Because of feeling such pain, he wasn't able to walk at all.' (Hk) (AWT)

(10.212) قاسم نے سوچیا، شاید اوہ ڈر دے مارے اندر لک گئی ہے

kāsim	*ne*	*soc-iyā*	*šæd*	*o*	*ḍar*
Qasim	ERG	think-PP.SG.M	perhaps	3SG.DIST.DIR	fear

d-e	***māre***	*andar*	*luk*	*ga-ī*	*e*
GEN-SG.M.OBL	**because.of**	inside	hide	go-PP.SG.F	be.PRES.3SG

'Qasim thought, maybe she has hidden inside because of fear.' (Pj) (http://www.punjabikahani.punjabi-kavita.com/SharifanSaadatHasanMantoShahmukhi.php)

(10.213) بند سیوریج پاروں گلی وچ گندہ پانی پھیلیا ہویا سی

band	*sīvarej*	***pārõ***	*gaḷī*	*vic*	*gandā*	*pāṇī*	*phæl-iyā*
blocked	sewers	**because.of**	street	in	dirty	water	spread-PP.SG.M

ho-iyā	*sī*
become-PP.SG.M	be.PST.3SG

'There was dirty water in the street because of blocked sewers.' (Pj) (Bashir and Kazmi 2012: 108)

All three languages have postpositions derived from grammaticized forms of کر /kar-/ 'do'. Hindko's کیتے /kīte/ is an oblique masculine singular perfective participle, as in 10.214; Panjabi has a grammaticized conjunctive participle کر کے /karke/ 'having done', as in 10.215; and Saraiki has the form دے کاݨ /de kāṇ/ 'because of', as in 10.216.

(10.214) اس کیتے ہر کسی آستے ہوائی جہاز دا سفر کرنا ممکن نی ہوندا

is	***kīte***	*har*	*kise*	*āste*	*havāī*	*jā̀z*
3SG.PROX	**because.of**	each	someone.OBL	for	air	ship

d-ā	*safar*	*kar-nā*	*mumkin*	*nī*	*ho-nd-ā*
GEN-SG.M	travel[M]	do-INF	possible	NEG	be-IP-SG.M

'For this reason, it isn't possible for everyone to travel by air.' (Hk) (Ayub (2015)ذرائع آمدورفت (ہوائی جہاز) Year 2, term 4 Story #1.)

(10.215) بیمار ہون کرکے اوہ نہیں آیا

bimār	*ho-ṇ*	***karke***	*ó*	*nái͂*	*ā-yā*
ill	be-INF.OBL	**because.of**	3SG.DIST	NEG	come-PP.SG.M

'Because he was ill he didn't come.' (Pj) (Shackle 1972: 89)

(10.216) میکوں مینہ اچ ٹرݨ دے کاݨ زکام تھی ڳئے

mæ-kū̃	*mī̃h*	*ic*	*ṭur-aṇ*	***de***	***kāṇ***	*zukām*	*thī*
1SG.OBL-DAT	rain	in	walk-INF.OBL	**GEN**	**reason**	cold[M]	become

ɠ-e
go-PP.SG.M+be.PRES.3SG

'I got a cold from walking in the rain yesterday.' (Sr) (UK)

A repeated participle, as in 10.217, often has a causal interpretation.

(10.217) توُں ہر روز ٹھاکے چڑھ چڑھ کے تھک جلدا ہوسیں

tū̃	*har*	*roz*	*ṭhāk-e*	***cár̥***	***cár̥-ke***	*thak*	*jul-d-ā*
2SG	every	day	mountain-OBL	**climb**	**climb-CP**	tire	go-IP-SG.M

ho-s-ẽ
be-FUT-2SG

'You must get tired of climbing mountains every day.' (Hk) (AWT)

10.9.2 Expressions of purpose (GOAL)

Purpose is often expressed as an abstract GOAL, with the same morphological devices used for concrete goals. A concrete goal of motion receives oblique case marking, as in 10.218. Purpose clauses with simple verbs of motion (e.g., 'come', 'go', 'sit') are constructed with the oblique infinitive, shown in examples 10.219–10.224. In Hindko and Panjabi (examples 10.224 and 10.225, respectively), the oblique infinitive can be additionally marked with the dative postposition.

(10.218) میں اوہ دے گھر گیا

mæ̃	*ó*	*de*	***kàr***	*ga-yā*
1SG.DIR	3SG.DIST.OBL	GEN-SG.M.OBL	**home.OBL**	go-PP.SG.M
sā̃				
be.PST.1SG				

'I (M) went to his/her house.' (Pj) (EB)

(10.219) نجمہ کپڑے دھون گئی اے

najma	*kapṛe*	***tò-ṇ***	***ga-ī***	*e*
Najma	clothes	**wash-INF.OBL**	**go.PP-SG.F**	be.PRES.3SG

'Najma has gone to wash clothes.' (Pj) (EB)

(10.220) اوہ پانی پین گیا

ó	*pāṇī*	***pī-ṇ***	***ga-yā***
3SG.DIST.DIR	water.SG.M	**drink-INF.OBL**	**go.PP-SG.M**

'He went to drink (some) water.' (Pj) (Shackle 1972: 88)

(10.221) تساں میکوں ملݨ آسو

tussā̃	*mæ-kū̃*	***mil-aṇ***	***ā-s-o***
2PL.DIR	1SG.OBL-ACC	**meet-INF.OBL**	**come-FUT-2PL**

'Will you come to meet me?' (Sr) (Zahoor 2009: 23)

(10.222) او سیر بݨواوݨ گے

ū	*sir*	***baṇ-vā-uṇ***	***ʄæ***
3SG.DIR	head	**be.made-CS-INF.OBL**	**go.PP.SG.M+be.PRES.3SG**

'He has gone to get a haircut.' (Sr) (Zahoor 2009: 75)

(10.223) اوکوں تھپݨ بیہ گئی

ū-kū̃	***thap-aṇ***	*ɓæh*	*ʄa-ī*
3SG.DIST.OBL-ACC	**stroke-INF.OBL**	sit	go.PP-SG.F

'She sat down to stroke her.' (Sr) (Shackle (1976), cited from Lashari (1971: 57))

(10.224) جُدوں تُسی بیمار ایہیو تُساں دیکھنڑے آں کُئی نئیں آیا

jadõ	*tusī*	*bimār*	*éy-o*	*tusā̃*	***dex-ṝ-e-ā̃***
when	2PL.DIR	sick	be.PST-2PL	2PL.OBL	**see-INF-OBL-DAT**

kuī	*nī̃*	*ā-yā*
anyone	NEG	come-PP.SG.M

'When you (plural) were ill, no one came to visit you.' (Hk) (AWT)

(10.225) اوہ باڑی مارن نوں اٹھیا

ó	*bāṛ-ī*	***mār-aṇ***	***nū̃***	*uṭṭh-iyā*
3.SG.DIST.DIR	window[F]	**close-INF.OBL**	**DAT**	get.up-PP.SG.M

'He got up to close the window.' (Pj) (Shackle 1972: 88)

The postpositions واسطے ~ واستے /vāste/ ~ آستے /āste/ 'for', as in examples 10.226 and 10.227, or لئی /laī/ 'for' , as in 10.228, can supplement the oblique infinitive to expresses the purpose of performing an action.

(10.226) جس ویلے توں سینڑے آسطے گیاں

jis	*vel-e*	*tū̃*	***sẽ-ṝ-e***	***āste***	*ga-yā̃*
which.REL	time-OBL	2SG.DIR	**sleep-INF-OBL**	**for**	go-PP.SG.M+2SG

'when you went (in order) to sleep.' (Hk) (AWT)

(10.227) اوہ پیسے کمون لئی / واسطے کم کر رہیا سی

ó	*pæse*	***kamau-ṇ***	***laī/vāste***	*kamm*	*kar*
3.DIST	money-PL.M	**earn-INF.OBL**	**for**	work	do

r-yā́	*sī*
CONT.II-SG.M	be.PST.3SG

'He was working to earn money.' (Pj) (Shackle 1972: 89)

(10.228) ہر ورھے ہزاراں سیاح ایتھے ایس مسیت نوں ویکھن لئی آندے نیں

har	*vár-e*	*hazār-ā̃*	*sayā́*	*ethe*	*æs*
each	year-OBL	thousand-PL.OBL	tourist.PL.M	here	3SG.PROX.OBL

masīt	*nū̃*	***vekh-aṇ***	***laī***	*ā-nd-e*	*nẽ*
mosque	ACC	**see-INF.OBL**	**for**	come-IP-PL.M	be.PRES.3PL

'Every year, thousands of tourists come here to see this mosque.' (Pj) (Bashir and Kazmi 2012: 8)

When the purpose of an action is expressed in a full clause, the conjunctions تاں جے /tā̃ je/ Pj , as in 10.229, تا کہ /tā ki/ Hk, Pj , as in 10.230, and تاں جو /tā̃ jo/'so that' Sr , as in 10.231, appear in a کہ clause with a subjunctive verb.

(10.229) زرعی شعبے نوں مضبوط بنان دا فیصلہ کیتا گیا اے تاں جے زرعی پیداوار وچ وادھا ہووے

zarī	*šob-e*	*nū̃*	*mazbūt*	*banā-ṇ*
agricultural	department-OBL	ACC	strong	make-INF.OBL

dā	*fæsalā*	*k-ītā*	*ga-yā*	*e*	***tā̃.je***
of	decision[M]	do-PP.SG.M	go-PP.SG.M	be.PRES.3SG	**so.that**

zarī	*pædāvār*	*vic*	*vā́dā*	*ho-ve*
agricultural	production	in	increase	be-SBJV.3SG

'A decision has been made to strengthen the Department of Agriculture so that agricultural production may increase.' (Pj) (Bashir and Kazmi 2012: 174)

(10.230) اکانومی کلاس دے کرایاں وچ گھٹو گھٹ اضافا کیتا گیا اے تا کہ عام پبلک تے گھٹ بوجھ پئے

ikānomī	*klās*	*d-e*	*karāy-ā̃*	*vic*	*kā̀ṭo*	*kā̀ṭ*
economy	class	GEN-SG.M.OBL	fare-PL.OBL	in	less	REDUP

izāfā	*k-īt-ā*	*ga-yā*	*e*	***tā.ki***	*ām*
increase	do-PP-SG.M	go-PP.SG.M	be.PRES.3SG	**so.that**	ordinary

pablik	*te*	*kā̀ṭ*	*bój*	*p-æ*
public	on	less	burden	fall-SBJV.3SG

'The least possible increase has been made in economy class fares so that the general public is less burdened.' (Pj) (Bashir and Kazmi 2012: 112)

(10.231) پہلے میں کہیں چنگے ادارے نال کم کرن چاہنداں تاں جو کجھ تجربہ حاصل کر سگاں

pahle	*mæ̃*	*kahī̃*	*cãg-e*	*idār-e*	*nāl*
first	1SG.DIR	some.OBL	good-SG.M.OBL	institution-SG.M.OBL	with

kam	*kar-aṇ*	*cāh-nd-ã̄*	***tã̄.jo***	*kujh*	*tajarbā*
work	do-INF.DIR	want-IP-SG.M+be.PRES.1SG	**so.that**	some	obtain

hāsal kar	*saɗ-ã̄*
obtain	be.able-SBJV.1SG

'First, I hope to find a job with a good company so that I can gain some experience.' (Sr) (Zahoor 2009: 62)

10.10 Reduplicative processes

All three languages make extensive use of both full and partial reduplicative processes.[27] Nominal elements, adjectives, adverbs, postpositions, and verbal forms can be freely reduplicated. Numerous senses are conveyed by full reduplication, including distributivity, emphasis, duration, repetition, multiplicity, and make-believe. Partial reduplication is most often seen in the constructions usually referred to as "echo compounds," but also appears in other distinctive construction types.

10.10.1 Full reduplication

10.10.1.1 Reduplication of nouns

Reduplication of nouns performs a number of functions, a few of which are illustrated here. In 10.232 and 10.233, multiplicity and distributivity are conveyed.

(10.232) کشمیر توں کہن کے سندھ تک جائی جائی ہندو راجے حکمران ایہے

kašmīr	*tõ.kìn.ke*	*sínd*	*tak*	***jā-ī***	***jāī***	*hindū*
Kashmir	from	Sindh	up.to	**place-LOC**	**REDUP**	Hindu

rāj-e	*hukmarān*	*éye*
king-PL.M	ruler.PL.M	be.PST.PL.M

'From Kashmir to Sindh Hindu kings were rulers in many places.' (Hk) (Soz 2011: 1)

27 See Abbi (1992) for detailed treatment of reduplication in South Asian languages.

(10.233) قطرے قطرے

katr-e	*katre*
drop-OBL	REDUP

'drop by drop' (Hk) (Sakoon 2002)

Reduplication of a singular nominal can convey exhaustive meaning, as in examples 10.234 and 10.235.

(10.234) بچا بچا ایہہ خبر جاندا اے

baccā	***baccā***	*é*	*xabar*	*jān-d-ā*	*e*
child	**REDUP**	3SG.PROX	news	know-IP-SG.M	be.PRES.3SG

'Every child knows this news.' (Pj) (Bhatia 1993: 277)

(10.235) اے کون کون ان

e	***kɔn***	***kɔn***	*in*
3PL.PROX.DIR	**who**	**REDUP**	be.PRES.3PL

'Who are all these people?' (Sr) (Shackle (1976: 113), cited from Lashari (1971: 358))

In 10.236, plurality, exhaustivity, and emphasis are all conveyed, making this expression idiomatic and more forceful than the equivalent expression گوڈیاں تکر پانی سی /goḍeā̃ takar pāṇī sī/ 'water was up to the knees'.

(10.236) ساڈی گلی وچ گوڈے گوڈے پانی سی

sāḍ-ī	*gaḷī*	*vic*	***goḍ-e***	***goḍ-e***	*pāṇī*	*sī*
our-SG.F	street[F]	in	**knee-OBL**	**REDUP**	water	be.PST.3SG

'There was water (all the way) up to the knee in our street.' (Pj) (EB)

Reduplication of a plural noun can can convey exclusivity, as in 10.237, as well as multiplicity, as in 10.238.

(10.237) منڈے منڈے آئے کڑیاں وچوں کوئی نہیں آئی

mũḍ-e	***mũḍe***	*ā-e*	*kuṛiy-ā̃*	*vic-õ*	*koī*
boy-PL.M	**REDUP**	come-PP.PL.M	girl[F]-OBL.PL	among-ABL	any

naī̃	*ā-ī*
NEG	come-PP.SG.F

'Only the boys came; none of the girls came.' (Pj) (EB)

(10.238) گالھیں گالھیں وچ سارا وقت ضائع ہوندا ویندے

ɠālh-ĩ	***ɠālhĩ***	*vic*	*sārā*	*vakt*	*zāya*	*ho-nd-ā*
talk[F]-LOC.PL	**REDUP**	in	all	time	wasted	become-IP-SG.M

væ-nd-æ
go-IP-SG.M+be.PRES.3SG

'All (our) time is being wasted in this talking.' (Sr) (Shackle 1976: 113)

Reduplication of a noun referring to a role or an institution, as in 10.239, generates a class of expressions referring to imaginative play of children, e.g. 'to play house', 'to play doctor', 'to play school'.

(10.239) کڑیاں گھر گھر کھیڈدیاں سن

kuṛiy-ā̃	***kàr***	***kàr***	*kheḍ-d-iyā̃*	*san*
girl-PL.F	**house**	**REDUP**	play-IP-PL.F	be.PST.3PL

'The girls were playing "house".' (Pj) (EB)

Some meaning relations of reduplication are iconic. Example 10.240 is a Hindko idiom, apparently having an iconic relation to the agitated motion of a restless person. Reduplication is extremely common with transparently onomatopoetic forms, as in 10.241 and 10.242.

(10.240) اتسو اتسو کرنا

utsū	*utsū*	*karnā*
ONOM	REDUP	do.INF

'to be upset, anxious, restless' (Hk) (Sakoon 2002: 8)

(10.241) بڑ بڑ کرنا

buṛ	*buṛ*	*karnā*
ONOM	REDUP	do.INF

'to mumble, grumble (lit. to make the sound of bubbling liquid, e.g. boiling water or smoking a hookah)' (Hk) (Sakoon 2002: 40)

(10.242) پھسر پھسر

phusar	*phusar*
whispering	REDUP

'(secretive) whispering' (Pj) (EB)

10.10.1.2 Reduplication of adjectives

Reduplication of plural adjectives emphasizes the multiplicity of the modified noun, as in 10.243 and 10.244.

(10.243) انہاں دیاں آپڑیاں نکیاں نکیاں راجدھانیاں ہوندیاں ایہیاں

únã	*d-iyã*	*apṛ-iyã*	***nikk-iyã***	***nikkiyã***	*rājdān-iyã*
3PL.OBL	GEN-PL.F	REFL-PL.F	**little-PL.F**	**REDUP**	capital-PL.F

ho-nd-iyã	*éy-iyã*
be-IP-PL.F	be.PST-PL.F

'They (each) had their own small capitals.' (Hk) (Soz 2011: 1)

(10.244) بڈھے بڈھے بابے دھپے بیٹھے سن

búḍḍ-e	***búḍḍe***	*bāb-e*	*tùp-e*	*bæ-ṭh-e*
old-PL.M	**REDUP**	old.man-PL.M	sunshine-LOC	sit-PP-PL.M

san
be.PST.3PL

'Several old men were sitting in the sun.' (Pj) (EB)

A reduplicated reflexive adjective gives a distributive meaning. The reduplication of اپنے /āpṇe/ in (10.217) allows the pronoun to refer back to each group separately—feudal lords, landlords, and religious leaders.

(10.245) جاگیردار زمیندار تے پیراں دا اپنے اپنے علاقیاں وچ بہت اسر تے کنٹرول سی

jāgīrdār	*zamīndār*	*te*	*pīr-ã*	*d-ā*
feudal.lord	landlord	and	religious.leader-PL	GEN-SG.M

āpṇ-e	***āpṇe***	*alāq-iyã*	*vic*	*bɔ̃t*	*asar*
REFL.GEN-PL.M.OBL	**REDUP**	area-PL.OBL	in	much	influence

te	*kanṭrol*	*sī*
and	control	be.PST.3SG

'Feudal lords, landlords, and religious leaders had great influence and control over their respective areas.' (Pj) (Madgavkar 2012)

Reduplicated adjectives referring to quantity, as in 10.246, and numerals, as in 10.247, usually convey distributivity and iterativity. Also, expressions like دو دو سو /do do sɔ/ 'two hundred each', دو سو تیہہ تیہہ /do sɔ tī̃ tī̃/ 'two hundred thirty each', and so on, are common.

(10.246) دوا دا چمچا تھوڑی تھوڑی دیر دے بعد ڈیندی راہیں

davā *d-ā* *camcā* ***thoṛī*** ***thoṛī*** *der*
medicine[F] GEN-SG.M spoon[M] **little** **REDUP** time[F]

d-e *bād* *ḍe-nd-ī* *rah-ẽ*
GEN-SG.M.OBL after give-IP-SG.F remain-SBJV.2SG

'Keep giving him a dose of medicine at short intervals.' (Sr) (Shackle (1976: 114), cited from Lashari (1971: 249))

(10.247) بچیاں نوں دو دو کتاباں دینیاں نیں

bacc-ĕã̄ *nū̃* ***do*** ***do*** *kitāb-ã̄* *de-ṇ-iyã̄*
child-PL.M.OBL DAT **two** **REDUP** book-PL.F give-GRDV-PL.F

nẽ
be.PRES.3PL

'The children are to be given two books each.' (Pj) (EB)

Repetition of question words conveys plurality and asks for a reply in the form of a list, as in 10.248.

(10.248) کیڑھیاں کیڑھیاں چیزاں دی لوڑ اے

kéṛ-iyã̄ ***kéṛiyã̄*** *cīz-ã̄* *d-ī* *loṛ* *e*
which-PL.F **REDUP** thing-PL.F GEN-SG.F need[F] be.PRES.3SG

'Which things do (you) need? / Which things are needed?' (Pj) (EB)

Sometimes reduplication can emphasize a positive perception of something, as in examples 10.249 and 10.250, or a negative one, as in 10.251, depending on its default desirable state.

(10.249) گرم گرم چاہ

garam ***garam*** *cā́*
hot **REDUP** tea

'nice hot tea.' (Pj) (EB)

(10.250) ٹھنڈا ٹھنڈا پانی

ṭhanḍā ***ṭhanḍā*** *pāṇī*
cold.SG.M **REDUP** water[M]

'nice cold water' (Pj) (EB)

(10.251) اوہ دے پیلے پیلے دانت بڑے بھیڑے لگدے نے

ó	*d-e*	***pil-e***	***pile***	*dant*	*baṛ-e*
3SG.OBL	GEN-PL.M	**yellow-PL.M**	**REDUP**	teeth[M]	very-PL.M

pæ̀ṛ-e	*lag-d-e*	*san*
bad-PL.M	seem-IP-PL.M	be.PST.3PL

'His/her yellowish teeth looked very bad.' (Pj) (EB)

10.10.1.3 Reduplication of adverbs and postpositions

Reduplicated adverbs of space or time suggest (intermittent) iteration. When a negative element نہ /na/ intervenes between the first and second elements, the meaning becomes indefinite. Some examples of the common reduplicated adverbs کدی /kadī/ 'sometime' and کتے /kite/ 'somewhere' with and without the negative element are contrasted in the list below.

- کدی کدی /kadī kadī/ 'from time to time'
- کتے کتے /kite kite/ 'here and there'
- کدی نہ کدی /kadī na kadī/ 'sometime or other'
- کتے نہ کتے /kite na kite/ 'somewhere or other'

Iterative actions expressed via reduplicated adverbs are exemplified in examples 10.252 and 10.253 below.

(10.252) کدے کدے تے انجو لگدئیے جنجو کسی جن یا دیو سنڑ ایہہ بٹہ کسی ہور جائی توں آنڑ کے اتھے رکھ چھوڑئیے

kade	***kade***	*te*	*ĩjo*	*lag-d-æ*
sometimes	**REDUP**	TOP	like.this	seem-IP-SG.M+be.PRES.3SG

jĩjo	*kis-ī*	*jin*	*yā*	*dev*	*suṛ̃*	*é*	*baṭā*
like.REL	some-OBL	jinn	or	demon	ERG	3SG.PROX	stone[M]

kis-ī	*hor*	*jā-ī*	*tõ*	*āṛ̃-ke*	*ethe*	*rax*
some-OBL	other	place-OBL	from	bring-CP	here	put

choṛ-iæ
leave.PP.SG.M+be.PRES.3SG

'Sometimes it seems like some jinn or demon has brought this stone from some other place and put it here.' (Hk) (Soz 2011: 9)

(10.253) اوہ روز روز تنگ کردا اے

ó **roz** **roz** *tang* *kar-d-ā* *e*
3SG.DIST **daily** **REDUP** tight do-IP-SG.M be.PRES.3SG
'He pesters/annoys (me) every single day.' (Pj) (EB)

In 10.254, the reduplicated question adverb asks for a list of places.

(10.254) تساں سیل واسطے کتھاں کتھاں ویسو

tussā̃ *sæl* *vāste* ***kithā̃*** ***kithā̃*** *væ-s-o*
2PL.DIR outing for **where** **REDUP** go-FUT-2PL
'Which places are you going to visit?' (Sr) (Zahoor 2009: 64)

Reduplication of qualitative adverbs conveys intensification of the basic meaning, as in 10.255 and 10.256. Where the basic meaning is of slowness, reduplication adds the sense of gradualness; where the basic meaning is of speed, reduplication conveys increased speed.

(10.255) اسیں ہولی ہولی وچھڑ گیے

assī̃ *hɔḷī* *hɔḷī* *vichaṛ* *g-ae*
1PL slowly REDUP separate go-PP.PL.M
'We gradually became separated.' (Pj) (https://www.youtube.com/watch?v=hCT48PLcITE)

(10.256) میں چھیتی چھیتی اپنا کم مکایا

mæ̃ *chetī* *chetī* *āpṇ-ā* *kamm* *muk-ā-yā*
1SG.DIR quickly REDUP REFL-SG.M work be.finished-CS-PP.SG.M
'I quickly finished my chore…' (Pj) (Bashir and Kazmi 2012: 73)

The postposition نال /nāl/ Hk, Sr , /nāḷ/ Pj 'with, next to' is frequently repeated.

(10.257) تے کئی ویلے دے نال نال ختم ہو کے رہ گئیں

te *kaī* *vel-e* *d-e* ***nāl*** ***nāl*** *xatam*
and many time-OBL GEN-SG.M.OBL **with** **REDUP** finished

ho-ke *ræ̃* *ga-ī̃*
become-CP remain go-PP.PL.F
'and many have gradually died out with the passage of time.' (Hk) (Soz 2011: 16)

(10.258) نال نال بہو

nāḷ ***nāḷ*** *b-ó*
with **REDUP** sit-IMP.2PL
'Sit right next (to each other).' (Pj) (EB)

10.10.1.4 -o- reiteration

A noun or adjective followed by و /o/ and a reduplicated copy of the word conveys emphatic, totalizing, or distributive meanings. This morphological device is used in all three languages.

(10.259) ساہو ساہ

sā̃-o-sā̃
breath-o-REDUP
'out of breath, panting' (Hk) (Soz 2011: 19)

(10.260) وٹو وٹ

vaṭṭ-o-vaṭṭ
wrinkle-o-REDUP
'all wrinkled' (Pj) (EB)

(10.261) گھٹو گھٹ

kàṭṭ-o-kàṭṭ
less-o-REDUP
'at least' (Pj)

(10.262) انج او انج

anj-o-anj
separate-o-REDUP
'quite separate' (Sr) (Shackle 1976: 119)

(10.263) ڈینھ او ڈینھ

dĩh-o-dĩh
day-o-REDUP
'from day to day' (Sr)

10.10.1.5 Reduplication of participial forms

Reduplication of a conjunctive participle can signify continuity, as in 10.264 and 10.265, or iteration of an action, as in 10.266. When the conjunctive participle is repeated like this, the marker کے /ke/ (Hk Pj) or تے (Sr) appears only after the second iteration of the participle.

(10.264) بے چاری مینا تڑپ تڑپ کے مر گئی

becār-ī	*mænā*	***taṛap***	***taṛap-ke***	*mar*	*ga-ī*
helpless-SG.F	myna[F]	**writhe**	**REDUP-CP**	die	go-PP.SG.F

'The poor myna flopped around and died.' (Hk) (Soz 2011: 7)

(10.265) توں کتھے گئی سیں؟ میں تینوں لبھ لبھ کے پاگل ہو گیا واں

tū̃	*kithe*	*ga-ī*	*sæ̃*	*mæ̃*	*tæ-nū̃*	***lâbb***
2SG	where	go.PP-SG.F	be.PST.2SG	1SG.DIR	2SG.OBL-ACC	**search**

lâbb-ke	*pāgal*	*ho*	*ga-yā*	*vā̃*
REDUP-CP	crazy	become	go-PP.SG.M	be.PRES.1SG

'Where did you go? I've gone crazy searching continuously for you.' (Pj) (EB)

(10.266) ڈاکٹر اوزار چا چاتے ٻہر ویندیاں ہویا آکھیا

ḍākṭar	*aozār*	***cā***	***cā-te***	*ɓahar*	*væ̃-d-iā̃*
doctor	instruments	**lift**	**lift-CP**	out	go-IP-SG.M.OBL

ho-iyā̃	*ākh-iyā*
be-PP.SG.M.OBL	say-PP.SG.M

'The doctor picked up (each of) his instruments (in turn) and said as he went out.' (Sr) (Shackle (1976: 127), cited from Lashari (1971: 228))

Repetition of a direct case form of the imperfective participle tends to focus attention on the actor, in 10.267 'the boy' and in 10.268 'he'.

(10.267) منڈا نسدا نسدا آیا

mũḍā	***nas-d-ā***	***nas-d-ā***	*ā-yā*
boy	**run-IP-SG.M**	**REDUP**	come-PP.SG.M

'The boy came running (very fast).' (Pj) (Bhatia 1993: 69)

(10.268) کھاندا کھاندا اوہ ڈھے پیا

khā-nd-ā	***khā-nd-ā***	*o*	*ḍhæ*	*p-yā*
eat-IP-SG.M	**REDUP**	3SG.DIST	fall	fall-PP.SG.M

'While eating he fell down.' (Sr) (Shackle 1976: 141)

Repetition of a masculine singular oblique imperfective participle focuses on the temporal relationship between two events or actions. In 10.269 and 10.270, it indicates the occurrence of an event happening during or interrupting an ongoing activity or state.

(10.269) اک دن کم کردیاں کردیاں میرے ہتھوں قلم ڈگّ پئی

ikk	*din*	*kamm*	***kar-d-ĕā̃***	***kardĕā̃***	*mer-e*
one	day	work	**do-IP-SG.M.OBL**	**REDUP**	1SG.GEN-SG.M.OBL

hath-õ	*kalam*	*digg*	*pa-ī*
hand-ABL	pen[F]	fall	fall-PP.SG.F

'One day as I was working I dropped my pen. (lit. ...my pen fell from my hand)' (Pj) (http://www.punjabikahani.punjabi-kavita.com/TeraKamraMeraKamraDalipKaurTiwanaShahmukhi.php)

(10.270) بریڑی سنڑ شرماندے شرماندے آخیا

bareṛī	*suṛ̃*	***šarmā-nd-e***	***šarmānde***	*āx-iyā*
Bareri	ERG	**feel.bashful-IP-SG.M.OBL**	**REDUP**	say-PP.SG.M

'Overcoming her embarrassment, Bareri said ...' (Hk) (Soz 2011: 11)

The perfective participle of change of position verbs is frequently reduplicated, sometimes suggesting a causal relation between two events, as in 10.271.

(10.271) بیٹھے بیٹھے تنگ پے گیا

bæ-ṭhe	***bæṭhe***	*tang*	*pæ*	*ga-yā*
sit-PP.SG.M.OBL	**REDUP**	annoyed	fall	go-PP.SG.M

'He got tired of sitting (for a long time).' (Pj) (EB)

10.10.2 Partial reduplication

10.10.2.1 Echo formations

Echo words involve partial reduplication of a lexical item by replacing its initial consonant in the echoing form. These are the most productive type of partial reduplicative structures in these languages. The echo elements are in themselves meaningless, but taken together the complete echo formations extend and blur the boundaries of meaning, as in the following commonly occurring formations.

In Panjabi and Saraiki, the copy usually begins with ش /š/, as in examples 10.272 and 10.273. Some words, themselves beginning with ش /š/, form an m-initial echo copy, as in 10.273.

(10.272) چا شا، کم شم، روٹی شوٹی، گپ شپ

cā	*šā*	*kamm*	*šamm*	*roṭī*	*šoṭī*	*gapp*	*šapp*
tea	ECHO	work	ECHO	bread	ECHO	chat/gossip	ECHO

'tea and what goes with it'; 'work and what goes with it'; 'food and the rest of the meal'; 'chat, light conversation' (Pj) (EB)

(10.273) گھیو شیو، انڈے شنڈے، شیشے میشے

ghiū	*šiū*	*aṇḍe*	*šaṇḍe*	*šīše*	*mīše*
ghee	ECHO	eggs	ECHO	mirrors	ECHO

'ghee (or something like it)'; 'eggs (familiar or jocular)'; 'mirrors (and associated items)' (Sr) (Shackle 1976: 118)

In several words referring to spatial concepts, an echo component in which the initial consonant of the base word is dropped precedes the base word.

(10.274) آنڈھ گوانڈھ

ā̃ḍ	*gvā̃ḍ*
ECHO	neighborhood

'all around, nearby' (Hk) (Sakoon 2002: 7)

(10.275) آلے دوآلے

āḷe	*duāḷe*
ECHO	surrounding

'on all sides of' (Pj) (Cummings and Bailey 1912: 61)

(10.276) آمھݨے سامھݨے

āmhṇe sāmhṇe
ECHO facing
'right in front' (Sr) (Shackle 1976: 119)

10.10.2.2 Stem-vowel alternation

In addition to alternation of a initial consonant, stem-vowel alternation while maintaining the same syllable structure is common in Panjabi, as in 10.277 and 10.278.

(10.277) چپ چاں ٹھیک ٹھاک پا پو کے

cup	*cāp*	*ṭhīk*	*ṭhāk*	*pā*	*pū-ke*
quiet	V.ALT.ECHO	good	V.ALT.ECHO	put.on	V.ALT.ECHO-CP

'very quietly'; 'okay, fine'; 'having put on (e.g. clothes)' (Pj) (EB)

(10.278) شوں شاں

šũ šā̃
'pomp and show, vanity' (Pj)

10.10.2.3 Alliterative partial reduplicates

In items of this type, the initial consonant remains constant, but the alliterative element differs in syllable structure from the first.

(10.279) چپ چپیتا

cup capītā
quiet ALLIT.ECHO
'deceptively silent' (Hk) (Sakoon 2002: 115)

(10.280) ماڑا مڑنگ

māṛā maṛang
weak ALLIT.ECHO
'extremely weak' (Hk) (Sakoon 2002: 225)

(10.281) شور شرابہ

šor *šarābā*
noise ALLIT.ECHO
'noisy uproar, clamor, disturbance' (Pj) (EB)

(10.282) چوری چکاری

corī *cikārī*
theft ALLIT.ECHO
'theft (and what is generally understood to accompany it)' (Sr) (Shackle 1976: 118)

(10.283) سوݨھا سوڈّھا

soṇhā *savaḍḍhā*
beautiful ALLIT.ECHO
'very beautiful.' (Sr) (Shackle 1976: 118)

10.10.2.4 Rhyming partial reduplicates

In items of this type, the initial consonant differs, but the final syllable rhymes.

(10.284) لٹر پٹر

laṭṭar paṭṭar
'miscellaneous household items' (Hk, Pj) (Sakoon 2002: 216)

(10.285) لگڑ بگڑ

laggaṛ baggaṛ
'a fearsome creature/monster' (Hk) (Sakoon 2002: 219)

(10.286) بن ٹھن کے

baṇ *ṭhaṇ-ke*
be.made RHYM.REDUP-CP
'all dressed up'[28] (Pj) (EB)

---

28 The ٹھن element might possibly come from the verb ٹھنکنا /ṭhanakṇā/ 'to jingle, tinkle (as of women's bangles)'.

(10.287) وٹا سٹا

vaṭā *saṭā*
exchange RHYM.REDUP
'mutual exchange of daughters and sons in marriage'[29] (Pj) (EB)

(10.288) نواں سواں

navā̃ *savā̃*
new fresh
'quite new' (Sr) (Shackle 1976: 119)

There are a few fixed reduplicated phrases in which the reduplicated element begins with /m-/.[30] In some cases there appears to be a semantic connection between the first and second elements; for instance in 10.289, the second element مڑی /muṛī/ is likely a participial form of مڑنا /muṛnā/ 'to turn back'. In the collocation حال چال /hāl cāl/ 'condition, how one is doing', there is such a semantic relation, conveying both state and activity. In other cases, though, no semantic connection is apparent.

(10.289) گھڑی مڑی

kàṛī *muṛī*
moment PART.REDUP
'repeatedly' (Pj) (Cummings and Bailey 1912: 58)

(10.290) سچی مچی

sacī *mucī*
true PART.REDUP
'really and truly' (Pj) (EB)

(10.291) جھوٹھی موٹھی

cū̃ṭhī *mūṭhī*
false PART.REDUP
'false(ly)' (Pj) (EB)

29 For example, family A and family B each have a son and a daughter. An exchange relationship is established in which daughter A is married to son B, and son A is married to daughter B.
30 In several languages in the northwest of Pakistan, as well as in Persian, echo-formations in /m/ are common.

10.10.3 Semantic reduplication

10.10.3.1 Same or similar meanings

A common process involves semantic reduplication; that is, two words having the same or very similar meaning are joined in a quasi-compounding process. Often the two words involved come from different lexical stocks, as in 10.292, where فزری /fazrī/ comes from the Perso-Arabic side (< Ar. فجر /fajar/ 'dawn') and سویرے /savere/ 'in the morning/ from the Indo-Aryan side (سویرا /saverā/ 'dawn').

(10.292) اَساں کل فزری سویرے اُٹھڑا پئیسی

assā̃ *kal* ***fazr-ī*** ***saver-e*** *uṭh-ṛā* *pæ-s-i*
1PL.OBL tomorrow **dawn-OBL** **dawn-OBL** get.up-INF befall-FUT-3SG
'We will have to get up very early tomorrow morning.' (Hk) (AWT)

In the Saraiki semantic doublets in 10.293 and 10.294, the first elements کڑ /kuṛ/ 'lies' and کنّی /kannī/ 'edge' are of Indo-Aryan origin, while the second elements فریب /fareb/ 'deceit' and کنارہ /kinārā/ 'edge' are of Perso-Arabic origin.

(10.293) کڑ فاریب

kuṛ *fareb*
lies deceit
'lies' (Sr) (Shackle 1976: 119)

(10.294) کنّی کنارہ

kannī *kinārā*
edge edge
'edge' (Sr) (Shackle 1976: 119)

The doublets in 10.295 and 10.296 involve a redundant semantic copy of the base word, while 10.297 combines different words having very similar meaning. In these examples, both elements are Indo-Aryan in origin.

(10.295) چار چفیری

cār *cufer-ī*
four four.sides-LOC
'on all sides' (Hk) (Sakoon 2002: 119)

(10.296) چار چفیرے

cār *cufer-e*
four four.sides-LOC
'on all sides' (Pj) (Cummings and Bailey 1912: 61)

(10.297) چنگی بھلی

cā̃g-ī *pàl-ī*
good-SG.F good-SG.F
'perfectly fine' (Pj) (EB)

Color terms are salient in this category. For example 'red' in 10.298 and 'black' in 10.299. Other examples include چٹّا سفید /ciṭṭā safed/ 'lit. white (IA) white (< Prs.)' meaning 'snow white, pure white' and پیلا زرد /pīlā zard/ 'yellowish'. Interestingly, کالا سیاہ /kāḷā syā̃/ is usually glossed literally as 'jet black' or 'pitch black', but it its actual sense is usually 'very dark', as in 10.299.

(10.298) ملکہ دا منہ غصے نال لال سوہا ہویا اے

malikā	*d-ā*	*mũ̄*	*guss-e*	*nāl*	***lāl***	***sũ̄ā***
queen	GEN-SG.M	face[M]	anger-OBL	with	**red(<Ar.)**	**red(IA)**

ho-yā	*e*
become-PP.SG.M	be.PRES.3SG

'The queen's face is flushed (lit. bright red) with anger.' (Pj) (Example from http://www.hin.islamic-sources.com/book/6-قصہ-چار-درویشاں)

(10.299) دھپے پھر پھر کے تیرا رنگ کالا سیاہ ہوگیا اے

tùp-e	*phir*	*phir-ke*	*ter-ā*	*rang*	***kāḷā***
sunshine-LOC	roam	REDUP-CP	2SG.GEN-SG.M	color[M]	**black (IA)**

syā̃	*ho*	*ga-yā*	*e*
black(< Prs.)	become	go-PP.SG.M	be.PRES.3SG

'Your complexion has become very dark from roaming around in the sun.' (Pj) (EB)

10.10.3.2 Intransitive-causative participial doublets

Another common type of reduplicative structure consists of a form of an intransitive verb coupled with the same form of its transitive/causative counterpart. Example 10.300 involves the conjunctive participle, and 10.301 - 10.303 involve the perfective participle.

(10.300) چھپ چھپا کے

chup	*chup-ā-ke*
to.be.hidden(INTR)	to.be.hidden-CS-CP

'stealthily' (Hk) (Soz 2011: 3)

(10.301) بنے بنائے کپڑے

baṇ-e	*baṇ-ā-e*	*kapṛ-e*
be.made-PP.PL.M	be.made-CS-PP.PL.M	garment-PL.M

'ready-made clothes' (Pj) (EB)

(10.302) پکی پکائی روٹی

pakk-ī	*pak-ā-ī*	*roṭī*
be.cooked-PP.SG.F	be.cooked-CS-PP.SG.F	bread[F]

'ready-cooked bread' (Pj) (EB)

(10.303) سنی سنائی گل

sun-ī	*sun-ā-ī*	*gall*
hear-PP.SG.F	hear-CS-PP.SG.F	utterance[F]

'hearsay' (Pj) (EB)

10.10.3.3 Different or opposite meanings

When words of different or even opposite meanings are combined, the effect is to extend the meaning and make it less specific. Three such items involve the concept of size, as in examples 10.304–10.306.

(10.304) جنوبی پنجاب وچ بھچال دے جھٹکے، عمارتاں نوں ماڑا موٹا نقصان

janūbī	*panjāb*	*vic*	*pacǎl*	*d-e*	*cǎṭke*
southern	Punjab	in	earthquake	GEN-PL.M	shock.PL.M

imārt-ā̃	*nū̃*	***māṛā***	***moṭā***	*nuksān*
building-OBL.PL	DAT	**weak**	**fat**	damage

'Earthquake shocks in southern Punjab, **slight** damage to buildings' (Pj) (faisalabad.sujag.org/khulasa/27378)

(10.305) قرضیاں دے نویں پروگرام شروع کیتے جان گے تاں جے بے زمین لوگاں نوں اپنے چھوٹے موٹے
کاروبار شروع کرن اچ مدد مل سکے

karz-eā̃	*d-e*	*nav-ẽ*	*progrām*	*šuru*
loan-PL.M.OBL	GEN-PL.M	new-PL.M	program.PL.M	beginning

k-īt-e	*jān-g-e*	*tā̃.je*	*be-zamīn*
do-PP-PL.M	go.SBJV.3PL-FUT-PL.M	so.that	without-land

log-ā̃	*nū̃*	*apṇ-e*	***choṭ-e***	***moṭ-e***
people-PL.M.OBL	DAT	REFL-SG.M.OBL	**small-PL.M**	**fat-PL.M**

kārobār	*šurū*	*kar-an*	*ic*	*madad*	*mil*	*sak-e*
business[M]	beginning	do-INF.OBL	in	help	get	be.able-SBJV.3SG

'New loan programs will be launched so that landless persons can get help to start their own **small** businesses.' (Pj) (Bashir and Kazmi 2012: 252)

(10.306) نکّا موٹا کم

nikk-ā	*moṭ-ā*	*kamm*
small-SG.M	fat-SG.M	work[M]

'any type of work' (Pj) (Bhardwaj 2016: 404)

Other such items generalize meaning from other types of subordinate to superordinate classes, as in 10.307. The Panjabi slang term ماجا ساجا /mājā sājā/, which compounds two common nicknames for males, means something like English 'Tom, Dick and Harry' or 'hoi polloi'.

(10.307) مکھی مچھر

makkhī *macchar*
fly[F] mosquito[M]
'winged insects' (Pj) (Bhardwaj 2016: 403)

10.11 Discourse particles

In all three languages the three discourse particles—exclusive or emphatic ای /ī/; inclusive وی /vī/ (Pj Sr), ٻی /bī/ (Hk); and topic marker تاں /tā̃/ ~ تے /te/ immediately follow the element to which they apply.

10.11.1 Emphatic or exclusive particle

The emphatic or exclusive particle can follow nouns, as in 10.308; pronouns, in 10.309; or adjectives, adverbs, and verbal forms, as in 10.310. Although this particle is an enclitic, it is usually written separately from the word it follows (except in Saraiki).[31] Examples 10.308 and 10.309 show the exclusive meaning, and 10.310 the emphatic sense.

(10.308) لاہور والے ای آئے

lɔ̀r *vāle* ***ī*** *ā-e*
Lahore NMLZ-PL.M **EXCL** come-PP.PL.M
'Only the people from Lahore came.' (Pj) (EB)

(10.309) میں ای ویکھیا

mæ̃ ***ī*** *vekh-iyā*
1SG **EXCL** see-PP.SG.M
'Only I saw (it).' (Pj) (EB)

31 Although some writers spell the emphatic particle with an initial ہ /h/ as in Urdu, in these three languages, the particle is always pronounced and usually spelled ای /ī/.

(10.310) میں جاواںگا ای

mæ̃ *jā-vā̃-g-ā* *ī*
1SG go-1SG-FUT-SG.M **EMPH**
'I (m) *will* go (and nothing will stop me).' (Pj) (EB)

In Saraiki, some emphatic forms of direct and oblique pronominal forms involve contractions with the emphatic particle ای /ī/ forming single words; for example, direct first singular مئیں /maī̃/ 'only I', second person singular توئیں /tūī̃/ 'only you', first plural اسئیں /asaī̃/ 'we indeed', تسئیں second plural /tusaī̃/ 'you.pl indeed' (Shackle 1976: 58). The only distinctive oblique form is second person singular تئیں /taī̃/ 'only you'.[32]

10.11.2 Inclusive particle

All three languages have the inclusive particle وی /vī/ Pj, Sr , ٻی /bī/ Hk . In affirmative contexts this means 'also', 'too', as in 10.311. In negative contexts it usually means 'even', 'despite, in spite of', as in 10.312, or can add an exhaustive meaning, as in 10.313.

(10.311) سیر تے وی ٻلسوں

sær *te* ***vī*** *ʃul-s-ū̃*
walk on/for **INCL** go-FUT-1PL
'We shall be going for a walk/outing too.' (Sr) (Adapted from Shackle (1976: 133))

(10.312) سبھ کجھ ہوندیاں وی اوہ خوش نہیں سی

sə́b *kúj* *hon-d-ĕyā̃* ***vī*** *ó* *xuš* *nī̃*
all something be-IP-SG.M.OBL **INCL** 3SG.DIST happy NEG

sī
be.PST.3SG
'In spite of having everything, s/he wasn't happy.' (Pj) (EB)

32 There are also unique emphatic forms of سبھ /sabh/ 'all', ہک /hik/ 'one', and the proximal and distal demonstrative pronouns. In the singular direct form, masculine and feminine forms are distinguished. The forms for سبھ /sabh/ 'all' are shown here: M.SG.DIR سبھو /sabho/, F.SG.DIR سبھا /sabhā/, SG.OBL/PL.DIR سبھے /sabhe/ (Shackle 1976: 611).

(10.313) اُنھاں کدے بی ہندکو نئیں بولی

unh-ā̃	***kade***	***bī***	*hindko*	*nī̃*	*bol-ī*
3PL.DIST-OBL	**ever**	**INCL**	Hindko[F]	NEG	speak-PP.SG.F

'They have never spoken Hindko.' (Hk) (AWT)

10.11.3 Topic marker

In all three languages a topic marker, appearing in two forms—تاں (pronounced /tã/ with a short vowel),[33] and تے /te/—both topicalizes the element it follows marking it as old information, and implies a contrast. Its use is illustrated in 10.314, 10.315, and 10.316.

(10.314) پر ایہہ بی تے ہک حقیقت اے

par	*é*	*bī*	***te***	*hikk*	*hakīkat*	*e*
but	this	INCL	**TOP**	a	reality	be.PRES.3SG

'But this too is a reality...' (Hk) (Soz 2009: 6)

(10.315) میں تاں جاوانگا اوہ دا پتا نہیں

mæ̃	***tã***	*jā-vā̃-g-ā*	*ó-d-ā*	*patā*	*nī̃*
I	**TOP**	go-1SG.SBJV-FUT-SG.M	3SG.DIST.OBL-GEN-SG.M	information[M]	NEG

'(as for me) I (M) will go; I don't know about him/her.' (Pj) (EB)

(10.316) اوندا ناں تاں میکوں وسر گیا ھا مڑی تیڈا کینھا وساریا ھامی

ū̃-d-ā	*nā̃*	***tã***	*mæ-kū̃*	*visar*	*ɠ-iyā*	*hā*	*muṛī*	*teɗ-ā*	*kænhā*	*visār-iyā*	*hā-mī*
3SG.DIST.OBL-GEN-SG.M	name[M]	**TOP**	1SG.OBL-DAT	be.forgotten	go-PP.SG.M	be.PST.SG.M	but	2SG.GEN-SG.M	NEG	forget(TRANS)-PP.SG.M	be.PST-PS1SG

'I forgot his name but I didn't forget yours.' (Sr) (UK)

33 The spelling of this word in Hindko and Panjabi is the same as that of the word meaning 'then' /tã/, 'then', frequently encountered in the then-clause of conditional clauses. In Saraiki the word for 'then' is different.

References Cited or Consulted

Abbi, Anvita. 1992. *Reduplication in South Asian languages: An areal, typological and historical study*. New Delhi: Allied Publishers.

Addleton, Jonathan S. 1986. The importance of regional languages in Pakistan. *Al-Mushir* XXVIII.2: 55–80.

Advanced Centre for Technical Development of Punjabi Language Literature & Culture, Punjabi University. 2012. *Punjabi-English dictionary, online version*. Patiala, India.

Ahmad, Mumtaz. 1992. *Punjabi reader in the Arabic script*. Kensington, MD: Dunwoody Press.

Akhtar, Raja Nasim. 1997. Affix-s(uu) constructions in Punjabi. *Essex Graduate Student Papers in Language and Linguistics* 1: 1–18.

— 1999. Aspectual Complex Predicates in Punjabi. Doctoral dissertation.

Alvi, M.A. 1972. اپڻی رات جو پاڻی تھئی *Apṇī rat jo pāṇī thaī* [A short novel]. Bahawalpur.

Awan, Muhammad Safir, Abdul Baseer, and Muhammad Sheeraz. 2012. Outlining Saraiki phonetics: A comparative study of Saraiki and English sound system. *Language in India* 12 (7 July 2012).

Ayres, Alyssa. 2009. *Speaking like a state: Language and nationalism in Pakistan*. Cambridge, U.K.; New York: Cambridge University Press.

Ayub, Nayab. 2015. سنڑنے والیاں کہانڑیاں [Stories to listen to, Year 2, Term 4]. Mansehra: Hindko Language Academy. URL: http://www.hindko.org/en/listening-stories.

Baart, Joan L.G. 2014. Tone and stress in North-West Indo-Aryan. In: *Above and beyond the segments: Experimental linguistics and phonetics, 1-13*. Ed. by Johanneke Caspers et al. Amsterdam/Philadelphia: Benjamins.

Bahawalpuri, M. and Ahmad Zami Bashir. 1981. *The Seraiki language*. Bahawalpur: Markaz Seraiki Zaban-te-Adab.

Bahl, Kali Charan. 1969. Panjabi. In: *Linguistics in South Asia*. Ed. by Thomas A. Sebeok. Current Trends in Linguistics 5. The Hague: Mouton: 153–200.

— 1970. *A grammatical sketch of Panjabi*. Chicago: South Asian Language and Area Center, The University of Chicago.

Bahri, Hardev. 1962. *Lahndi phonology, with special reference to Awắṇkári*. Allahabad: Bharati Press.

— 1963. *Lahndi phonetics, with special reference to Awắṇkárī*. Allahabad: Bharati Press.

Bailey, T. Grahame. 1904a. *Grammar and dictionary of western Punjabi*. Lahore: Punjab Government Press.

— 1904b. *Panjabi Grammar: A brief grammar of Panjabi as spoken in the Wazirabad District*. Lahore: Punjab Government Press.

— 1920. Linguistic studies from the Himalayas: Being studies in the grammar of fifteen Himalayan dialects.

Barker, Muhammad Abd-al Rahman. 1967. *A course in Urdu*. Montreal: Institute of Islamic Studies, McGill University.

Bashir, Elena. 1999. The Urdu and Hindi ergative postposition *ne*: Its changing role in the grammar. In: *The yearbook of South Asian languages and linguistics*. Ed. by Rajendra Singh. New Delhi/Thousand Oaks/London: Sage Publications.

— 2003. Dardic. In: : *The Indo-Aryan languages*. Ed. by George Cardona and Dhanesh Jain. London: Routledge. Chap. 22: 818–894.

— 2006. Evidentiality in South Asian languages. In: *Proceedings of the LFG06 conference*. Ed. by Miriam Butt and Tracy Holloway King. Stanford, CA: CSLI.

Bashir, Elena. 2018. Stative resultative participles in Hazara Hindko. In: *Paper presented at the 34th South Asian Analysis Roundtabla (SALA-34)*. University of Konstanz.

Bashir, Kanwal and Abbas Kazmi. 2012. *Punjabi-English dictionary*. Hyattsville, MD: Dunwoody Press.

Bhardwaj, Mangat Rai. 1995. *Colloquial Panjabi: A complete language course*. London/ New York: Routledge.

— 2016. *Panjabi: A comprehensive grammar*. London/ New York: Routledge.

Bhatia, Tej K. 1993. *Punjabi: A cognitive-descriptive grammar*. New York: Routledge.

Bismil, Abdul Waheed. 2011. *Kheḍā̃ (Plays, Hindko dramas)*. Faisalabad: Misaal Publishers.

Bubenik, Vit. 1998. *A historical syntax of late Middle Indo-Aryan (Apabhraṃśa)*. Amsterdam/Philadelphia: Benjamins.

Bukhari, Tanvir. 2000. *Panjabi Urdu Lughat.* [Panjabi-Urdu dictionary]. Urdu Science Board.

Butt, Miriam. 2007. The role of pronominal suffixes in Punjabi. In: *Architectures, rules and preferences: A festschrift for Joan Bresnan*. Ed. by J. Grimshaw, J. Maling, C. Manning, J. Simpson, and A. Zaenen. Stanford, CA: CSLI Publications.

Butt, Miriam and Tracy Holloway King. 1991. Semantic case in Urdu. In: *Papers from the General Session at the Chicago Linguistic Society Regional Meeting*. Vol. 27. 1: 31–45.

Catford, J. C. 1982. *Fundamental problems in phonetics*. Bloomington, Indiana: Indiana University Press.

Chaudhry, Muhammad Ashraf. 1999. Computers. *Tamahi Punjabi* 2 (1).

Cummings, Thomas F. and T. Grahame Bailey. 1912. *Panjabi manual and grammar: A guide to the colloquial Panjabi of the Northern Panjabi.* Sialkot: United Presbyterian Church of North America Mission.

Dhillon, Rajdip. 2007. Stress in Punjabi. In: *Proceedings of the Berkeley Linguistic Society (BLS)*. Vol. 33: 84–95.

Emeneau, Murray B. 1980. The Indian linguistic area revisited. In: *Language and linguistic area: essays by Murray B. Emeneau*. Ed. by Anwar S. Dil. Stanford: Stanford University Press: 197–249.

Gill, Harjeet Singh and Henry A. Gleason. 1969. *A reference grammar of Punjabi*. 2nd ed. Patiala (India): Department of Linguistics, Punjabi University.

Grierson, George Abraham. 1915. The north-western group of the Indo-Aryan vernaculars. *Indian Antiquity* October 1915: 226–228.

— 1968[1916]. Pañjabi. In: *Linguistic survey of India*. Vol. 9, Part 1. Western Hindi and Panjabi. Originally published Calcutta: Office of the Superintendent of Government Printing, reprinted 1968, Delhi: Delhi, Varanasi & Patna: Motilal Banarsidass.

— 1919. *Linguistic survey of India, Part 1.* Vol. 8, Part 1. Calcutta: Superintendent of Government Printing.

Hallberg, Calinda E. and Claire F. O'Leary. 1992. Dialect variation and multilingualism among Gujars in Pakistan. In: *Hindko and Gujari*. Ed. by Calvin R. Rensch, Calinda E. Hallberg, and Clare F. O'Leary. Sociolinguistic survey of Northern Pakistan 3. Islamabad: National Institute of Pakistan Studies, Quaid-i-Azam University/Summer Institute of Linguistics.

Haq, Abdul M. 1974. *Nūr-e Jamāl*. The text cited is the introduction and prose commentary in central Saraiki on an early 19th century poem. Multan: publisher unknown.

Hook, Peter and Prashant Pardeshi. 2009. The semantic evolution of 'eat'-expressions: Ways and byways. In: *The linguistics of eating and drinking*. Ed. by John Newman. Amsterdam/Philadelphia: Benjamins.

Isacenko, Alexander. 1974. On 'have' and 'be' languages: A typological sketch. In: *Slavic Forum: Essays in linguistics and literature*. Ed. by Michael S. Flier. Slavic Printings and Reprintings 277. The Hague-Paris: Mouton: 43–77.

Javaid, Umbreen. 2004. Saraiki political movement: Its impact in south Punjab. *Journal of Research (Humanities)* 40(2): 45–55.

Joseph, John Earl. 1982. Dialect, language, and 'synecdoche'. *Linguistics* 20.7-8: 473–492.

Jukes, A. 1900. *Dictionary of the Jatki or western Panjabi language*. London: Kegan Paul, Trench, Trübner & Co.

Kalanchvi, Dilshad. 1979/1981. *Saraiki lughāt*. 2 vols. Bahawalpur: Seraiki Library.

Kalra, Ashok Kumar. 1982. Some topics in Punjabi phonology. PhD thesis. University of Delhi.

Kalra, Surjit Singh, Navtej Kaur Purewal, and Susan Tyson-Ward. 2004 [1999]. *Teach yourself Panjabi*. Lincolnwood,Illinois, USA: NTC/Contemporary Publishing.

Khan, Sardar Muhammad. 2009. *Punjabi Urdu dictionary*. Lahore: Sachal Studios, Pakistan Panjabi Adabi Board.

Lashari, Z. 1971. *Nāzū (a novel)*. Bahawalpur: Publisher not known.

Latif, Amna. 2003. *Phonemic inventory of Siraiki language and acoustic analyis of voiced implosives*. URL: http://www.cle.org.pk/Publication/Crulp_report/CR03_16E.pdf (visited on 02/26/2016).

Leopold, Werner F. 1968. The decline of German dialects. In: *Readings in the sociology of language*. Ed. by Joshua A. Fishman. The Hague: Mouton: 340–364.

Lewis, M. Paul, Gary F. Simons, and Charles D. Fennig. 2015. *Ethnologue: Languages of the world*. 18th ed. Dallas, Texas: SIL International.

Lothers, Michael and Laura Lothers. 2010. *Pahari and Pothwari: A sociolinguistic survey*.

Malik, Amar Nath. 1995. *The phonology and morphology of Panjabi*. New Dehli: Munshiram Manoharlal Publishers.

Malik, Khalid Suhail. 2003. *Apṛā Veṛā Apṛī Kahāṛī* [One's own courtyard, one's own story]. (Hindko Drama). Peshawar: Pakistan Markazi Hindki-Adabi Board.

Markey, Thomas L. 1985. Absolute vs. relative comparison: Typology and development. In: *Papers From the 6th International Conference on Historical Linguistics*. Ed. by Jacek Fisiak. Current Issues in linguistic Theory, 34. Amsterdam: Benjamins.

Masica, Colin P. 1976. *Defining a linguistic area: South Asia*. Chicago: The University of Chicago Press.

— 1991. *The Indo-Aryan languages*. Cambridge: Cambridge University Press.

Mir, Farina. 2010. *The social space of language: Vernacular culture in British colonial Punjab*. Berkeley: University of of California Press.

Montaut, Annie. 2001. On the aoristic behaviour of the Hindi/Urdu simple past: From aorist to evidenciality. In: *Tohfa-e-Dil: Festschrift Helmut Nespital*. Ed. by D. Lönne. Reinbek: Wezler: 345–364.

Mughal, Shaukat. 2002. *Sarāikī dīā̃ xās āwāzā̃ dī kahāṇī* [The story of unique sounds of Saraiki]. Multan: Jhok Publishers.

— 2004. *Āo, Sarāikī paṛhū̃ te Sarāikī likhū̃* [Come, let us read and write Saraiki]. Multan: Jhok Publishers.

— 2010. *Shaukat ullughāt* [Urdu-Saraiki dictionary]. Multan: Saraiki Adabi Board.

Pakistan, Government of. 2001. *Pakistan statistical year book 2011*. URL: http://www.pbs.gov.pk/sites/default/files/other/yearbook2011/Population/16-20.pdf.

Parvez, Sajjad Haider. 1992. *Saraiki Muallam* [Saraiki teacher]. Muzaffargarh (Pakistan): Majlis e Saraiki Musannifin.

Polomé, Edgar C. 1994. Can graphemic change cause phonemic change? In: *Language Change: Lexical Diffusion and Literacy*. Ed. by Goparaju Sambasiva Rao. Academic Foundation: 37.

Rafiq, Mian Muhammad. 2000. Problems of Pakistan's education policy. *Tamahi Punjabi*.

Rahman, Tariq. 1995. The Siraiki movement in Pakistan. *Language Problems and Language Planning* 19 (1): 1–25.

Rahman, Tariq. 2007. Punjabi language during British rule. *Journal of Punjab Studies* 14.1 (Spring 2007): 27–40.
Randhava, Afzal Ahsan. 2007. *Munnā koha Lahaura*. Singh Brothers.
Rashid, Haroon-ur and Raja Nasim Akhtar. 2012. Hindko vowel system. *Kashmir Journal of Language Research* 15 (2): 55–76.
Raza, Ghulam. 2016. Etymology of the Saraiki language name. *Journal of Linguistics and Literature* 1.1: 61–81.
Rensch, Calvin R., Calinda E. Hallberg, and Clare F. O'Leary. 1992. Hindko and Gujari. In: *Sociolinguistic survey of northern Pakistan*. Vol. 3: Islamabad. National Institute of Pakistani Studies, Quaid-i-Azam University, and Summer Institute of Linguistics.
Rizwani, Khan. 1971. وسدیاں جھوکاں [Vasdiā̃ jhokā̃]. Multan.
Sakoon, Sultan. 2002. *Hindko Urdu Lughat* [Hindko-Urdu dictionary]. Peshawar, Pakistan: Gandhara Hindko Board.
— 2009. *A river in a clay pot*. Faisalabad , Pakistan: Gandhara Hindko Board.
Schokker, G. H. 1969. The jānā-passive in the NIA languages. *Indo-Iranian Journal* 12: 1–23.
Shackle, Christopher. 1970. Punjabi in Lahore. *Modern Asian Studies* 4.3: 239–267.
— 1972. *Punjabi*. Teach Yourself Books. London: St. Paul's House.
— 1976. *The Siraiki language of central Pakistan*. London: School of Oriental and African Studies.
— 1977. 'Southwestern elements' in the language of the Ādi Granth. *Bulletin of the School of African Studies* 40.1: 36–50.
— 1978. Approaches to the Persian loans in the Ādi Granth. *Bulletin of the School of Oriental and African Studies* 41.1: 73–96.
— 1979. Problems of classification in Pakistan Punjab. *Transactions of the Philological Society* 77: 191–210.
— 1980. Hindko in Kohat and Peshawar. *Bulletin of the School of Oriental and African Studies* 43.3.
— 1983. *An introduction to the sacred language of the Sikhs*. London: SOAS.
— 2001. Siraiki. In: *Facts about the world's languages*. Ed. by J. Garry and C. Rubino. New York: H.W. Wilson.
— 2003. Panjabi. In: *The Indo-Aryan languages*. Ed. by George Cardona and Dhanesh Jain. London & New York: Routledge.
Shankar, G. 1931. A Short Account of Dogri Dialect. *Indian Linguistics* 1.2: 1–83.
Sharma, D.D. 1971. *Syllabic structure of Hindi and Panjabi*. Chandigarh: Publication Bureau, Panjab University.
Smirnov, Yuriy Andreyevich. 1975. *The Lahndi language* [Jazyk lendi]. Languages of Asia and Africa. Moscow: Nauka.
Soz, Bashir Ahmed. 2009. سوچ مینارے [Thought in the tower]. Abbottabad: Adabiāt e Hazara.
— 2011. ہک ایہا راجہ ہک ایہی رانی [There was a king, there was a queen]. Peshawar: Gandhara Hindko Board.
Syed, Nasir Abbas and Sultan Melfi Aldaihani. 2014. The Emergence of the unmarked in loanword phonology: Harmonic serialism account. In: *Crossing phonetics-phonology lines*. Ed. by Eugeniusz Cyran and Julanta Szypra-Kozlowska: 219–232.
Toker, Halil. 2014. *A practical guide to Hindko grammar*. Bloomington, IN: Trafford Publishing.
Tuite, Kevin J., Asif Agha, and Randolph Graczyk. 1985. Agentivity, transitivity and the question of active typology. *Papers from the Parasession on Agentivity and Causatives* 2 (21): 252–270.
Turner, H. L. 1962–1966. *A comparative dictionary of the Indo-Aryan languages*. Oxford University Press. Reprint 2008, Motilal Banarsidass.

Varma, Siddeshwar. 1936. The phonetics of Lahnda. *Journal of the Royal Asiatic Society of Bengal* Letters, Vol. II, Article No. 6: 47–118.

Wagha, Muhammad Ahsan. 1998. The development of Siraiki language in Pakistan. PhD thesis. School of Oriental and African Studies (University of London).

Wang, William S-Y. 1979. Language change–A lexical perspective. *Annual Review of Anthropology*: 353–371.

Wilson, James. 1899. *Grammar and dictionary of western Panjabi, as spoken in the Shahpur district with proverbs, sayings, and verses.* Lahore: Punjab Government Press.

Zahid, Saira and Sarmad Hussain. 2012. An acoustic study of vowel nasalization in punjabi. *Language & Technology*: 61.

Zahoor, Asma. 2009. *Sarāikī, Urdū, Angrezī bol cāl* [Saraiki, Urdu, English conversation]. Multan: Jhok Publishers.

Index

Absolutive *see* Participles conjunctive
Adi Granth 17, 18, 80
Adjectives
- adjectival postpositions 248
- agreement of 431
- attributive
  - infinitive clauses as 497
  - Persian 135
  - stative perfective participle as 287
- comparative 142
  - relative clause of comparison 474
- demonstrative *see* Demonstrative adjectives
- derivation of 80
- gender of 136
- indefinite 156
- interrogative 149, 463
  - as pronouns 211
  - in four-term set 151
  - reduplication of 465, 581
- marked 135, 136
  - imperfective participle 285
  - in genitives 190, 196
  - infinitives as 496
  - Layer II postpositions as 248
  - perfective participle 286
  - possessive 137
  - table of inflections 140
- order of 425
- reduplication of 580
  - color terms 592
- reflexive 160
  - reduplication of 580
- relative 148, 217
  - in four-term set 151
  - relative clauses 472
- stem vowel alternation in 139
- unmarked 135, 138
- "black" *see* Adjectives marked
- "red" *see* Adjectives unmarked
- "unfast" 135, 139

Adverbs 178
- as postpositional elements 256
- conjunctive participial clauses as 500
- in complex postpositions 258, 266
- in four-term set 183, 187
- indefinite 180, 183, 187
- interrogative 180, 183
  - reduplication of 583
- oblique noun phrases as 180
- reduplication of 582
- relative
  - relative clauses 475

Affixes
- adjective-forming 129, 131
  - as grammatical postposition 249
  - with infinitives 496
- approximating 176
- assigning feminine gender 81
- causative
  - double 284
  - first 284
- diminutive 86
- infinitival 83, 285
- izāfat 89
- locative 104
- negative 133, 134, 225
- noun-forming 81–89
  - abstract 82–86
  - agentive 81–82, 87
  - locational 87–88
- ordinal 174
- Persian 86–88
- Perso-Arabic 85–86, 88–89, 91, 131, 134
- plural 91
- pronominal suffixes *see* Pronouns
- totalizing 176
- vocative 98–101

Agency
- and deontic modality 545
- derivation of agent nouns 81–82
- in prospective expressions 554

Akbar the Great 15

Animacy
- and definiteness 564
- and gender assignment 93, 94
- and pronominal suffixes 219
- and vocative 97
- determining postposition in goal constructions 262

– in compound subjects 436, 438
– in direct objects 451
Arabic 79, 80
– broken plurals 92
– definite article 80
– dual 92
Aspect 279
Auxiliaries
– copula
  – in affirmational and existential sentences 427
  – in negative sentences 427, 428, 453
  – in stative constructions 448
  – with compound subjects 437
– in inchoative constructions 448
– order of 423
– with pronominal suffixes 236
– 'to become' 293
– 'to be' 279, 287
  – in sense 'to become' 290
  – negation of 288
  – past tense forms 290, 328
  – present tense forms 287, 328
  – simple perfect tense forms 290
  – subjunctive forms 292
  – subjunctive mood forms 329
  – *see also* Auxiliaries; copula

Balochi 12, 79
Brahmi 18

Case 96–128
– ablative 103, 259, 263
  – adverbial use 180
  – of comparison 143
  – of infinitives 495
  – of personal pronouns 193
  – of postpositions 258, 263, 267
– accusative 97, 244–246, 259, 434, 450
– dative 219, 259, 450
  – dative subjects 230, 232, 239, 243, 245, 430, 446, 549, 559, 568
  – marked by postposition 198, 244–246
  – marking experiencers 557
– direct 97
  – direct objects in 451, 452
  – indicated by pronominal suffixes 219
  – of first- and second-person pronouns 196
  – of gerundives 553
  – of infinitives 491, 553
– ergative 196
  – and person of subject 442
  – ergative subjects 229
  – marked by postposition 196, 244
  – of interrogatives 209
– genitive
  – assigned by postposition 248
  – of pronouns 190, 196
  – with reflexive pronouns 201
– in relative clauses 472
– locative 104–105
  – adverbial use 122, 180, 181
  – as instrumental 108
  – locative forms as postpositions 257
– oblique 97, 442, 443
  – adverbial use 180
  – marking experiencers 557
  – of agents in perfective tenses 432
  – of infinitives 490
– role of postpositions in 243
– vocative 97
Conjunctions
– coordinating 466
– correlative 479
– subordinating 468
  – expressing causation 571
  – introducing purpose clauses 576
Converb *see* Participles conjunctive

Deference 189
Demonstrative
– adjectives 147
– in four-term set 151
– pronouns
  – as third-person pronouns 189
  – distal 195, 279
  – proximal 195
Dialects
– Abbottabad 1, 44, 47, 48, 53, 56
– Awankari 60
– big city 10, 16
– dialectal variation
  – in Hindko 12
  – in Panjabi 14, 16, 226
– Gujrat 226
– Hazara 9, 10, 13, 26, 33, 39, 49, 76
– Lahore 1, 9, 16, 24, 46, 59, 195, 196, 219, 226
– Majhi 9, 16, 226

– Multan 1, 9, 10, 16, 60
– Peshawar 9, 10, 26
– vs languages 9
Diphthongs *see* Phonology diphthongs
Distance 151, 189, 195
Dogri 15

English 12, 17, 79, 443
Evidentiality 566

Gender 92–96
– affixes assigning 81
– agreement in compounds 436
– of addressee 516
Gerundives 562
– as distanced imperative 563
– expressing modality 545
  – presumption 558
  – prospective meanings 552, 556
– *see also* Verbs; infinitive
Glossing 4–7
Gujarati 12

Hindi 12, 16
Hindko
– name 10, 12
– promotion of 14
– speakers 14
– where spoken 12, 13
Hindko-Panjabi-Saraiki language area 12, 16

Infinitive *see* Verbs infinitive

Kinship terms *see* Nouns Class VI

Lahnda 10, 16, 33
Loanwords 79
– Arabic 53, 60, 66, 75, 79, 80, 92
– English 79, 81, 92, 104
– gender of 93
– in conjunct verb constructions 507
– orthography *see* Orthography of loanwords
– Persian 53, 60, 69, 70, 74, 79, 80, 92
  – semantic reduplication with 591
– sounds unique to 21
– Urdu 57, 79

Marathi 12

Modality 545
– ability 545
– deontic 545
– desirability 549
  – expressed with subjunctive 295
– epistemic 545, 558
– prospective 289, 552
Modals *see* Auxiliaries
Mutual intelligibility 16

Negation
– copula deletion with 453
– emphatic 459
– negative particles 453
  – as question tag 461
– of imperatives
  – distanced (softened) 562, 563
– of indefinite pronouns 214
– of pronominal suffixes 225, 233
– of reduplicated elements 582
– of statements of ability 545
– of statements of desirability 549
– of 'to be' 288
– sentential 453
– taking place of copula in present tense 427
– with affixes *see* Affixes; negative
Nouns 79–128
– abstract 82–86
– animacy *see* Animacy
– broken plurals 92
– case *see* Case
– Class I 108, 113, 115, 124
  – endings as adjectival inflections 136
– Class II 109, 114, 116, 119, 124
– Class III 111, 115, 117, 125, 126
  – endings as adjectival inflections 136
– Class IV 108, 110, 115, 117, 126
– Class V 108, 111
– Class VI 108, 112
– Class VII 108, 127
  – endings as adjectival inflections 139
– Class VIII 123, 125, 128
– compound 86, 435
– declension classes 106–108, 113, 121
– derivation of 80–89
– diminutive 86
– feminine 110, 120, 126
  – semantic classes of 94
– gender assignment in *see* Gender

- masculine 108, 123
  - semantic classes of 94
  - *see also* Nouns Class II
  - *see also* Nouns Class I
- noun phrases 425
  - infinitive clauses as 499
- possessive 90
- postpositions derived from 254, 257
- proper 68, 80, 89
- reduplication of 577

Number
- broken plurals 92
- dual 92
- in adjectives 136
- in nouns 90–92
  - ablative 103
  - locative 105
  - oblique 97
- in pronouns 189

Numbers 162
- cardinal 166
- fractional 164
- greater than one thousand 163
- indefinite 176
- one (as specific indefinite) 426, 565
- ordinal 172
- orthography 163
- reduplication of 580
- vigesimal 164

Orthography 19, 60–77
- baṛī he 66, 73
- baṛī ye 70
- choṭī he 66, 69, 73, 75, 76
- choṭī ye 70, 75
- do cašmī he 66, 72, 76
- Gurmukhi 18, 61
- hamza 70, 75
- Hindko 18, 48, 76, 281
- izāfat 69, 74
- names and forms of letters 62, 67
- Naskh 61, 67, 75
- Nastaʿlīq 18, 61
- negative particle 76
- of aspirates 66, 72, 77
- of consonants 64–67
- of geminates 71
- of implosives 77
- of loanwords 66, 68–70, 74
- of nasalization 71, 76, 197, 281
- of numerals 163
- of postpositions 246
- of pronominal suffixes 227
- of retroflexes 28, 66, 76, 77
- of third-person pronouns 76
- of tone 66, 72–73
- of vowels 67–70
- of 'to be' 290
- representations of /h/ 73
- Saraiki 18, 28, 29, 77
- Shahmukhi 18
- standardization 18, 69, 76, 77
- tashdīd 71
- transcription vs transliteration 19, 20

Panjabi
- literature 16, 17
- name 10
- speakers 1, 14
- status of 17
- where spoken 12, 14

Participles
- catenative 501, 522, 523, 525
- conjunctive 285, 501
  - clauses 500
  - expressing causation 572
  - reduplication of 585
- connective 501, 523, 535
- imperfective 285, 324
  - clauses 504
  - expressing desirability 549
  - in complex durative contructions 529
  - in irrealis conditionals 484
  - reduplication of 585
- perfective 286
  - agreement of 533
  - as simple perfect 290
  - clauses 505
  - in complex durative constructions 532
  - in irrealis conditionals 484
  - in passive periphrastic 539, 540
  - irregular 286
  - reduplication of 586
  - regular vs irregular forms 532
- Persian 135
- reduplication of 585
- stative perfective 286

Particles
- emphatic 535, 595
  - in contracted pronominal forms 596

- hortative 294, 487, 527
- inclusive 596
- topic marker 597
Partition of India 16
Pashto 12, 61, 79
Persian 12, 17, 79, 80, 86–88, 135, 200
Phonology 19–60
- allophones 24, 35
- assimilations 24
- consonants 21–33
  - aspirated 28, 47, 48
  - geminate 50, 52–56, 71
  - implosive 28, 60
  - retroflex 24, 26, 28, 57
- diphthongs 38–43
- epenthesis 58–60
- Hindko 21–27, 33–34, 39, 44–45, 47–49, 53, 56
- nasalization 44, 121, 137, 197, 217
- of loanwords 21, 56, 58–60
- Panjabi 21–24, 35–36, 39–40, 45, 48–59
- phonotactics 55–60
- Saraiki 28–33, 36–38, 41–43, 46, 49, 52, 55, 59–60
- segment inventory of Hindko 26, 33–35, 44
- segment inventory of Panjabi 35, 45
- segment inventory of Saraiki 30, 37, 46
- sound correspondences 26, 27, 47, 57
- stem vowel alternation
  - as reduplicative process 588
- stress 46, 49–53, 55, 58
- syllables 50, 52, 56–57, 59
- tone 46–49, 72
- transcription 19, 20, 25, 36
- vowels 33–43
  - centralized 33, 35, 36, 39, 42–44, 46, 55, 57, 58
  - elision of 34, 37, 58
  - harmony 502
  - length 35, 36, 50
  - nasalized 33, 43–46, 57, 71
  - peripheral 33, 35, 36, 39–41, 43–46, 57, 58
  - stem vowel alternation 120, 123, 128, 137, 139, 538
Plurals *see* Number
Possession
- of abstract entities 568
- possessive adjectives 137
- possessive pronouns 190
- types of 568
- with genitive postpositional phrase 90
  - *see also* Nouns; possessive
Postpositions 243–277
- ablative 103, 143, 193, 258, 263, 495
  - expressing casuation 571
- agentive *see* Postpositions ergative
- and animacy of goal 262
- assigning oblique case 97
- comparative 144, 146, 147
- dative-accusative 198, 244–246, 259, 539–541
  - in purpose clauses 573
  - marking definiteness 564
  - marking direct and indirect objects 450
  - obviates verbal agreement 434
  - with animate referents 451
  - with dative subjects 445
- derived from nouns 254, 257
- derived from verbs 254
- ergative 196, 244–246, 442, 443
  - intransitive verbs taking 444, 452
  - marking agentivity 554
- genitive 89, 90, 248
  - expressing inalienable possession 568
  - in infinitive clauses 488, 494
- in purpose clauses 575
- instrumental 271
- Layer I 243
- Layer II 243–253
- Layer III 253, 266, 267, 273
- Layer IV 258, 267, 273
- locative 254
  - adverbs as 256
- of accompaniment 269
- of purpose 273
- of similarity 275
- reduplication of 582
- temporal 258
- with infinitive complements 493
Pothwari 15
Prefixes *see* Affixes
Pronouns
- demonstrative *see* Demonstrative pronouns
- emphatic 596
- indefinite 212
  - adjectival use of 214

– compound forms of 216
– specific vs non-specific 426, 452
– with inclusive meaning 214
– with partitive meaning 214
– interrogative 207, 211, 463
– case marking with 207, 209, 212
– pronominal suffixes as 234
– reduplication of 465
– omission of (pro-drop) 428, 430
– personal 55, 191, 198
– as direct objects 453
– genitive 190, 193, 196, 568
– with negative particle 288
– pronominal suffixes 218–240
– and transitivity 221
– and word order 434
– as imperatives 233
– as interrogatives 234
– enabling pro-drop 429
– in negative sentences 233
– summary of functions 240
– with auxiliaries 236
– reciprocal 203
– reflexive 199
– as emphatic 200, 201
– spelling of 76
– with dative subjects 445
– relative 217
– relative clauses 471

Quantifiers 155
– order of 426

Reduplication 577
– -o- reiteration 584
– echo formations 587
– in indefinite and relative adverbials 183
– intransitive-causative doublets 593
– of adjectives 580
– of adverbs 183, 582
– of interrogatives 465
– of nouns 577
– of oblique imperfective participle 505
– of participles 573, 585
– of postpositions 582
– of verb forms in complex iterative constructions 535
– semantic 591
Referentiality 564

Sandhi *see* Phonology vowels elision of
Sanskrit 16
Saraiki
– literature 16, 17
– name 10
– promotion of 14
– speakers 14
– where spoken 12, 14
Sindhi 12, 16, 61, 79, 221
Split ergativity *see* Case ergative, 431, 441
Suffixes *see* Affixes
Syntax
– complex durative constructions 529
– conditional clauses 479
– irrealis 482
– realis 479
– conjunctive participal clauses 500
– coordination 466
– direct objects 450
– in direct case 451
– infinitives as 489
– marked by postposition 450
– indirect objects 450
– in ergative case 229
– marked by postposition 450
– preferential marking of 452
– infinitive clauses 488
– pro-drop 428
– questions
– rhetorical 462
– with interrogative words 463
– yes-no 460
– relative clauses 471
– infinitival clauses as 497
– of comparison 474
– omission of correlative in 477
– subjects
– agreement of 441
– dative 549
– *see also* Case dative dative subjects
– ergative 229
– experiencer 446
– impersonal 540
– stative vs inchoative 448
– types of 445
– subordination 468
– non-finite clauses 488
– word order 421, 434
– cleft constructions 425
– in noun phrases 425

- in realis conditionals 481
- in relative clauses 473, 476
- indicating definiteness 564
- of discourse particles 426
- of negatives 456
- of non-finite subordinate clauses 488
- scrambling 424
- with compound subjects 436
- with pronominal suffixes 434

Tense 279
- continuous 279
  - continuous future 397
  - continuous II forms 298
  - continuous irrealis 342
  - continuous past 309, 338, 396
  - continuous present 308, 337, 395
  - habitual continuous past 339
  - indicating definiteness 565
  - past continuous II forms 298
  - present continuous II 298
  - subjunctive 340, 398
- future 280, 296, 297, 335, 379
  - hypothetical, with infinitive 562
  - of 'to be' 289
  - pro-drop in 428
  - pronominal suffixes in 226
- habitual 280
  - indicating indefiniteness 565
- imperfect
  - agreement in 431
  - future imperfect 307, 349, 391
  - future imperfect passive 384
  - imperfective participle 285
  - past imperfect 304, 346, 389
  - past imperfect passive 384
  - past imperfect-habitual 305, 347, 390
  - present imperfect 301, 302, 344, 387
  - present imperfect passive 383
  - present imperfect-habitual 303, 345, 388
  - subjunctive imperfect 306, 348, 392
- imperfective
  - imperfective participial clauses 504
  - in complex durative constructions 529
  - in irrealis conditionals 483
- irrealis
  - imperfect irrealis 350, 393
  - in conditional clauses 482
  - in prospective expressions 558
  - irrealis I 381
  - passive 385
  - simple irrealis 343
- past
  - negation in 428
  - of 'to be' 290, 328
- perfect
  - agreement in 432
  - future perfect 317, 357, 411, 412
  - future perfect-stative 413
  - irrealis perfect 315, 316, 358, 418, 419
  - irrealis perfect-stative 420
  - of 'to be' 290
  - past perfect 314, 315, 354, 407
  - past perfect-stative 355, 408, 409
  - past stative habitual perfect 410
  - perfective participle 286
  - present perfect 311, 352, 400–402
  - present perfect-stative 313, 353, 403, 404
  - present stative habitual perfect 405, 406
  - pro-drop in 429
  - simple perfect 219, 351
  - stative perfective participle 286
  - subjunctive perfect 356, 414, 415
  - subjunctive perfect-stative 416, 417
- perfect-stative 280
- perfective
  - expressive mirativity 567
  - in complex durative constructions 532
  - in irrealis conditionals 483
  - perfective participial clauses 505
- present
  - negation in 427
  - of /hoṇā/ 328
  - of 'to be' 287
  - present perfect 312
- realis
  - in conditional clauses 479

Transitivity 382
- and pro-drop 429
- and volition 537
- and word order 421
- derived intransitives 538
- in conjunctive participial clauses 500
- in light verb constructions 507
- intransitive-causative doublets 593
- of vector verbs 509
- split ergativity 431, 441

– verbs of body functions (unergative verbs) 444

Urdu 12, 79
– influence of 12, 16, 58, 73, 79, 80, 88, 90, 196, 244, 487, 513, 544
– orthography 18, 19, 61, 71, 76, 77
– phonology 21, 26, 51, 53
– sound correspondences 47, 57, 58
– status of 17

Verbs 280
– agreement of 435
 – split ergativity 431
 – with addressee 516
 – with dative subjects 446
 – with direct objects 434
– causative 284, 382
 – intransitive-causative doublets 593
 – transitivity sets 536
– compound 509
 – expressive mirativity 567
 – on passive stems 543
 – passive stems in 521
– conjunct 507
– derivation of
 – intransitive 538
– finite 281
– imperative 280, 294
 – distanced (softened) 294, 562, 563
 – pronominal suffix reanalyzed as 233
 – with conjunctive participles 501
– infinitive 285
 – ablative 103, 495
 – as distanced imperative 562
 – as marked adjective 496
 – direct 491
 – expressing ability 546
 – expressing presumption 558
 – expressing prospective meanings 552, 554
 – in inceptive constructions 493
 – in nominalized phrases 499
 – in purpose clauses 573
 – infinitive clauses 488
 – inflection of 97
 – oblique 490, 492
 – verbal noun 83
 – with adjectival inflection (agreeing infinitive) 491
 – with gerundival function 285
– light verb
 – 'beat/kill' 519
– light verbs
 – in compound verb constructions 509
 – in conjunct verb constructions 507
 – in experiencer constructions 448
 – order of 424
 – vector verbs 509
 – 'come' 515, 521, 545, 549
 – 'fall, lie' 307, 369, 396, 510, 517, 521
 – 'give' 517, 523
 – 'go' 284, 509, 514, 520
 – 'leave, let go' 511, 519, 524
 – 'lift, raise' (invariant) 525
 – 'put/keep' 513, 519, 523
 – 'sit' 516, 522
 – 'take' 512, 518, 522
 – 'throw, cast' 524
 – 'throw' 513, 518, 524
 – 'to be able' 545
 – 'to be wanted' 550
– passive 539, 541
 – in compound verbs 521
 – morphological 381, 541, 543, 544, 549
 – periphrastic 284, 286, 475, 539–542, 544, 546
 – with infinitive + 'to be' 541
– postpositions derived from 254
– principal parts 281
– roots *see* Verbs stems
– stems 284, 321
 – passive 521, 543
– subjunctive 280, 295, 380
 – of 'to be' 292
 – passive 385
– table of forms 319, 361, 371
 – Hindko 282
– this grammar's naming conventions for 280
– transitivity
 – derived with causative affixes 284
– *see also* Participles
– *see also* Tense
– 'to be' *see* Auxiliaries; 'to be'
 – future tense forms 289
Vowels *see* Phonology vowels

Writing systems *see* Orthography

www.ingramcontent.com/pod-product-compliance
Lightning Source LLC
Chambersburg PA
CBHW080932300426
44115CB00017B/2785
9781501526602